Figure 3.14 DNA migration pattern map created from compiled research on DNA populations around the world. The first humans originated in Africa more than 100,000 years ago. Group L3 populated the rest of the planet during early human migrations. Northern Europeans (Groups H, T, U, V, W, and X) and Southern Europeans (Groups I, J, and K) migrated out of Africa some 45,000 years ago. Asian populations migrated out of Africa about 70,000 years ago and populated the Americas by crossing the Bering Strait in three different migrations. The first migration into the Americas was 10,000–20,000 years ago, the second was about 12,000–15,000 years ago, and the third was about 7,000–9,000 years ago. The data also demonstrate a possible fourth migration that took place about 15,000 years ago when Scandinavian Vikings crossed the Atlantic and mixed with Native Americans who crossed the Bering Strait (haplogroup X).

EVOLUTIONARY PSYCHOLOGY

To Jude as she begins new patterns in her life

ॐ

Psychology will be based on a new foundation, that of the necessary
acquirement of each mental power and capacity by gradation.
Light will be thrown on the origin of man and his history.

Charles Darwin

EVOLUTIONARY PSYCHOLOGY

Neuroscience Perspectives Concerning
Human Behavior and Experience

William J. Ray

Pennsylvania State University

Los Angeles | London | New Delhi
Singapore | Washington DC

Los Angeles | London | New Delhi
Singapore | Washington DC

FOR INFORMATION:

SAGE Publications, Inc.
2455 Teller Road
Thousand Oaks, California 91320
E-mail: order@sagepub.com

SAGE Publications Ltd.
1 Oliver's Yard
55 City Road
London EC1Y 1SP
United Kingdom

SAGE Publications India Pvt. Ltd.
B 1/I 1 Mohan Cooperative Industrial Area
Mathura Road, New Delhi 110 044
India

SAGE Publications Asia-Pacific Pte. Ltd.
33 Pekin Street #02-01
Far East Square
Singapore 048763

Acquisitions Editor: Vicki Knight
Associate Editor: Lauren Habib
Editorial Assistant: Kalie Koscielak
Copy Editor: Diana Breti
Typesetter: C&M Digitals (P) Ltd.
Proofreader: Susan Schon
Indexer: Judy Hunt
Cover Designer: Gail Buschman
Marketing Manager: Liz Thornton
Permissions Editor: Adele Hutchinson

Printed in the United States of America

Library of Congress Cataloging-in-Publication Data

Ray, William J., 1945-

Evolutionary psychology : neuroscience perspectives concerning human behavior and experience / William J. Ray.

p. cm.
Includes bibliographical references and index.

ISBN 978-1-4129-9589-4 (cloth)

1. Evolutionary psychology. I. Title.

BF698.95.R39 2013
155.7—dc23   2011045612

SFI label applies to text stock

This book is printed on acid-free paper.

12 13 14 15 16 10 9 8 7 6 5 4 3 2 1

Brief Contents

Detailed Contents

Preface

Many of us became involved in the science of psychology because we found the material exciting. To discover that humans function in ways we never expected offered a variety of surprises. However, more surprises were to come. As psychology began to incorporate additional perspectives from the neurosciences and evolution, the human species seemed even more amazing. This has taken us from asking how psychological processes work to why did these particular behaviors and experiences develop.

At times it is humbling to realize that we solve certain problems of life as many species have done for eons. Other times, we get a glimpse of human abilities not seen in other species. We use language. We purposely teach our children. We build large cities that survive long after a single generation. We create cultures that through their writings and art can influence other humans thousands of years later.

Darwin developed his insights concerning evolution on his trips of exploration throughout the world. He largely focused on physical characteristics of a variety of species. However, he also took notes that connected his ideas with humans. In *On the Origin of Species*, Darwin (1859) wrote, "Psychology will be based on a new foundation, that of the necessary acquirement of each mental power and capacity by gradation. Light will be thrown on the origin of man and his history" (p. 488).

Evolution results from the close interaction of organisms with their environment. In this close connection, the organism seeks ways to solve the fundamental problems or challenges of its existence. The environment for humans includes culture as well as nature. Humans throughout their evolutionary history have always lived in groups with other people. The evolution of our psychology is thus related to social and cultural factors.

In this book you can, like Darwin, think of yourself on a journey trying to understand yourself and the world you see around you. Part of our discussions will be framed by the traditional questions of life seen in a variety of species. These are the larger questions related to self-preservation, sexuality, and social relationships. We will also think about the factors involved in how you answer these questions. These factors range from cultural considerations to genetic ones. You can also think about what types of decisions your parents, and all of their parents before them, made that resulted in your being here today.

On this journey you will discover that you make an instant decision about people you meet in social situations. You will also discover that humans solve many moral problems quickly without much deliberation. You will also get a glimpse of the rich variety of life on earth. You will learn about a lizard species in New Mexico that is made up entirely of females. Still other species change genders depending on environmental conditions. You will see how the environment can influence genetics as well as how genetics can influence our culture. You will also discover that what your grandparents ate may actually determine aspects of your health.

The purpose of this text is to bring together current perspectives concerning the manner in which the human mind, behavior, and experience evolved. In addition to the traditional psychological literature, information from the cognitive and affective neurosciences, ethology, and genetics will be discussed. The focus is on a unification and integration of evolutionary understandings within a broader consideration.

Acknowledgments

I appreciated the many individuals who reviewed this book:

Shawn R. Charlton, University of Central Arkansas

Peter K. Jonason, University of South Alabama

Lawrence Josephs, Adelphi University

William H. Knapp, Istanbul Şehir University

Cory R. Scherer, Penn State Schuylkill

Jason Lyons, Tarleton State University

I also appreciate the staff at SAGE. Vicki Knight is an excellent editor who is not only well informed but also understands how to ask reviewers questions to make an author's book better. Lauren Habib worked hard to obtain permissions for illustrations and suggest better alternatives.

I would like to invite both students and faculty to make comments or offer suggestions that would contribute to this book. You may send these to me at wjr@psu.edu.

About the Author

William J. Ray is a Professor of Psychology at Penn State University. He received his PhD from Vanderbilt University and was a Fellow in Medical Psychology at the University of California Medical Center in San Francisco. He has also served as a visiting professor and researcher at the University of Hawaii, Münster University, University of Rome, Tübingen University and Konstanz University. At Penn State, he is currently the Director of the SCAN (Specialization in Cognitive and Affective Neuroscience) program and was previously the Director of the Clinical Psychology Program. His research has focused on approaching clinical questions from a neuroscience perspective. He has used psychophysiological and brain imaging techniques such as EEG, MEG, and fMRI to study emotionality, psychopathology and individual differences. These studies can be found in over 100 articles, book chapters, and books. This work has been funded by both national and international agencies including NIH, NIMH, NASA, NATO, and the DAAD. In addition to research, teaching has been an important part of his career. His other textbooks include *Methods Toward a Psychology of Behavior and Experience* (10th ed., 2012, Wadsworth Publishing) and *Psychophysiological Methods* (with Robert Stern & Karen Quigley, 2nd ed., 2000, Oxford University Press).

Introduction
and Background

PART I

Introduction to an Evolutionary Perspective

1

I f a being from another universe appeared on earth, what would be its impression of the life forms it would observe? It might note the great similarity between animals such as mammals: food is important; sex is important; caring for young is important; being with others is important. It might also note ways in which humans appear to be different from other **species**. We walk upright and have little hair on our bodies. We don't have natural predators as do other species. We build large cities and create qualitatively different types of technology as compared to other mammals. We use written and spoken language in ways that no other organism does. We produce art, not only to represent our experiences, but also to produce them. We use abstract and symbolic forms such as mathematics to describe the universe. We create theories and consider alternatives. We ask questions of ultimate concerns and display a spirituality not seen in other animals. Although the alien could describe our behaviors well, what the alien could not do is to understand why we do the things we do.

Why we do what we do is a question that can be answered in a number of ways. We may be tired, for example, because our blood sugar is low. We may be tired because we did not get enough sleep. We may feel tired because things are not going our way. Each one of these descriptions could be studied scientifically. Traditionally, many of the topics we study in psychology reflect research on a particular level. We study the physiological level, the individual level, the social level, and the cultural level. In general, each of these levels seeks to describe mechanisms that help us understand human behavior and experience. What is often missing is the larger question of how things came to be the way they are. In this book, I will suggest that the **evolutionary perspective** as seen from a variety of fields, including the neurosciences, not only helps us to understand critical mechanisms involved in behavior and experience, but also gives us valuable perspectives on how these processes came about. Because we are asking these two different types of questions at the same time, we will find ourselves going from very broad perspectives to very specific events. At one moment I will ask you to consider what your life would have been like if you had lived 10,000 or even 50,000 years ago. What would you need to survive and how would you spend your time? At other times, I will ask you to consider a particular person and ask whether you find that person attractive. Sometimes this seems to be strange research. What if you were given t-shirts that a variety of males or females had worn for the last two days? Would you find the smell of some of these shirts more pleasing and others more repulsive? Why? The answer is you would find some t-shirts more pleasing than others and, as you will see later, the reason is related to genetics. Actually, it is the relationship between your genetics and those of the other person that determines your preferences. However, your preference for one smell over another is actually a sophisticated calculus that can result in greater genetic variation and health in your offspring. Overall, you will come to see that as humans, we need to solve a variety of tasks. The evolutionary perspective helps us to determine which of these tasks have been and are currently critical. I will emphasize the evolutionary perspective as we consider human behavior and experience.

The Beginnings of an Evolutionary Neuroscience of Behavior and Experience

If you look at the history of science, it is clear that different questions were asked during different historical periods. With a few exceptions, in ancient Greece, more than 2,000 years ago, the earth and life on it was seen as stable and unchanging. In 1830, with the publication of Sir Charles Lyell's book *Principle of Geology,* scientists began to realize the age of the earth and the manner in which it had changed throughout history. Darwin and some others at the time came to realize that not only the physical earth but organic life on earth was going through an evolutionary process.

If we begin with Darwin's theory of evolution during the late 1800s and examine the history of intellectual thought in psychology until the present, we find a variety of perspectives on understanding life on earth in general and human behavior and experience in particular. As you will see, some have focused solely on the environment as a determining factor, whereas others have focused on the internal processes of the individual or group. In fact, many have conceptualized the history of psychology as an intellectual struggle between those who stress the importance of nurture and its impact on the environment and those who stress nature and its impact on biological determinants. As you will see, given limited exemplars, either side can make a case for its position.

However, the richness of a scientific psychology requires considerations of both in terms of their interaction.

Consistent with Darwin's description of a close and complex relationship between an organism and its environment, current theories have focused more on the interactive nature of the two rather than either separately. Although Darwin presented a theory that united life on earth and its connection with the environment, he did not emphasize psychological processes. This was left for others to develop. However, in terms of many processes important to psychologists, such as the recognition and expression of emotion, Darwin did point the way. I describe the study of emotional expression in Chapter 6.

Psychology during the 20th century can be characterized as beginning a rich laboratory research tradition. Initially, a variety of important questions were studied in this manner. However, near the end of the 20th century and the beginning of the 21st, it became apparent that one of the unintended consequences of this approach was to emphasize short-term changes in behavior. Much of this research examined environmental factors in the laboratory and ignored larger questions concerning human behavior and experience over time. Some of these larger questions relate to how we have interacted with each other and the variety of human processes that facilitate these interactions. Human interactions have developed over our evolutionary history. One critical aspect for humans is that we have always lived in groups. Thus, much of early history related not only to self-preservation and sexuality, but also to how to live in a group and understand other people. From an evolutionary standpoint, it is critical to consider the impact of such a lifestyle and the way in which behavior and experiences can be seen in a larger family and social context. In our 20th-century laboratory studies, questions related to the role of art, music, and spiritual experiences in human life were largely ignored. These experiences have also been a part of human history. Cave art, for example, can be dated to at least 30,000 years ago. Questions about human concerns such as sexuality, feeling accepted or left out of groups, or emotional feelings including love and aggression can be studied in the laboratory. However, taking a broader perspective gives a more complete picture of the process. For example, when studying aggression, a more complete picture is seen when we realize that there appears to have been almost no time in our human history when there was not a war taking place somewhere on earth. Additionally, there is data from around the world to indicate that when a murder is committed, it is 10 times more likely to have been committed by a man than by a woman. It might also come as a surprise to realize that there is less murder today than there was in the Middle Ages. In most of 20th century psychology research, there was little consideration of why humans kill other humans. The larger questions concerning the origins of human nature were often ignored and left in the background by traditional laboratory research.

Pathways Toward an Evolutionary Psychology

Darwin's theory of **natural selection** emphasized physiological adaptations and pointed the way to understanding psychological processes such as memory, perception, thoughts, and emotion. Considering psychology from an evolutionary perspective helps us to understand the tight coupling suggested by Darwin between organisms and their environment. The human visual system, for example, is most sensitive to the frequencies found in natural sunlight. Of course, we do not need to take an evolutionary perspective to determine the frequencies of light that the eye is most sensitive to. We can know this by using the methods of psychophysics and other experimental procedures. The evolutionary perspective adds the question, Why are we most sensitive to the frequencies found in natural sunlight? We could make up many reasons why this might be so. However, a better approach would be to consider all of the human perceptual systems and ask, If they had evolved over our evolutionary history, how might they look? In utilizing such an approach, we might be surprised to discover that the frequencies of light that humans are most sensitive to are also the frequencies that are able to travel through water. Why might this be? One possible answer is that the human eye evolved from basic structures seen in earlier organisms that lived in the water. Throughout the ages, adaptations to environmental conditions have given us the eyes that we have today. A broader evolutionary perspective also helps us to consider not only the adaptations over time, but also how these adaptations may have structured the mechanisms involved. Let's take vision again, as an example. It is initially surprising that, on first glance, the receptor system of the eye appears to be backward. That is, as you observe your retina, you notice that the rods and cones are located behind the neural mechanisms that transfer information from rods and cones to the brain. You also notice that there are no receptors at the place in the eye where information from the eye goes to the brain. This results in a blind spot. It is similar to placing the headlights on your car behind the electrical wiring that connects them to the controls. However, it makes sense once one asks, What if the visual system evolved from much simpler single receptors located directly beneath the skin? This is just one example that helps us understand the evolution of sensory processes. As you will see throughout this book, the evolutionary perspective offers additional insights into many human processes.

In order to fully understand human processes, we must draw from a variety of areas, including physics, chemistry, and biology, as well as psychology. Currently, the neurosciences exemplify the collaboration of a variety of scientific areas that focus on explaining the structure and function of human activity. These approaches should be viewed as supplemental levels of understanding. Each adds a different perspective. Understanding the chemistry of sadness or joy or the locations in the brain where these changes take place does not enable us to explain the experience itself or the environmental factors that might bring about these changes. Thus, one level of understanding cannot simply be reduced to another; rather, additional levels make for more integrated conceptualizations. Likewise, the theoretical perspectives of evolutionary psychology have been drawn from a variety of sources and intellectual traditions. Unfortunately, during the 20th century, these scientific traditions remained somewhat isolated and continued along parallel tracks with little interconnectedness. Because the evidence and perspectives have not been integrated and synthesized to offer a single theoretical perspective, what I must present in this book is the beginning of an evolutionary theory of behavior and experience, rather than a single comprehensive final articulation. The purpose of this current chapter is to consider some of the approaches that have contributed to the study of evolutionary psychology up to the present.

ETHOLOGY

Ethology is the study of animals and what they do. The word is derived from the Greek and means *manner, trait,* or *character.* At the heart of ethology is the naturalistic observation of behavior in an organism's natural environment. For example, an ethologist could describe the interaction of birds as they feed on common food, noting the manner in which feeding birds might react to newly arrived birds. He or she could also note the manner in which human infants will imitate the facial expressions of adults. In this field, it is assumed that behavioral processes have been shaped through evolution to be sensitive to environmental conditions. Thus, behavior can be understood only within the context of a particular environment. Environment, in this context, includes not only the physical characteristics of a particular setting but also the social and cultural milieu in which the organism lives. Given the complexity of behavior within an environment, the field of ethology has largely focused on particular patterns of behavior that have evolutionary significance and the possible mechanisms that produce these behaviors. The question for us, of course, is, Do humans have mechanisms similar to those studied by ethologists?

One of the pioneers in the field of ethology was Konrad Lorenz (1903–1989). From his early childhood on the outskirts of Vienna, Lorenz was interested in observing animals. After receiving a medical degree and continuing studies in zoology, Lorenz more formally studied behavioral patterns. He focused on the patterns he considered characteristic of a species. Most psychology students know Lorenz for his imprinting studies. **Imprinting** is a built-in pattern in which birds, such as ducks and geese, follow an object, usually their mother, that moves in front of them during the first 18 to 36 hours after birth. In a series of now-classic studies, Lorenz showed that orphaned baby birds would follow any moving organism, including Lorenz, as if it were their mother. Not only would they follow Lorenz, but they would also ignore members of their own species and, still later in life, attempt to court humans rather than other geese (see Figure 1.1). If the baby birds did not encounter a suitable object during this critical first 18 to 36 hours of their lives, the birds would not imprint and would even show terror.

How did Lorenz understand imprinting? He suggested that imprinting and other similar phenomena worked like a lock and key. The key in this case would be the characteristics of the mother, including the manner in which the mother moved in front of the babies. The lock would be an innate brain pattern or template, in which knowledge concerning the key would be encoded. Further, the lock and key would only work together for a critical period, in this case the first two days of life. More intriguing is the fact that once the imprinting has taken place, it is almost irreversible and cannot be changed. In more technical language, the key is referred to as a **social releaser**. More recent research with imprinting has shown the social releaser to be somewhat specific, in that newly hatched birds prefer to follow females of their own species, as compared to other objects. Studies with newly hatched chickens suggest that characteristics of the object's head serve as the social releaser (Johnson & Horn, 1988). The technical term for the lock is **innate schema** or **innate template**. The limited temporal period during which the lock and key work is referred to as the **critical period** or **sensitive period**.

| Figure 1.1 | Konrad Lorenz Being Followed by His Geese |

One feature of imprinting was that it was learned quickly and did not require a number of occurrences as with various types of skilled learning. This is referred to as *one-trial learning*. In addition to one-trial learning processes such as imprinting, there are also other patterns of species-specific behavior. In 1938, Lorenz, along with Niko Tinbergen, experimented with the egg-rolling movement of the Greylag goose. If the goose sees an egg outside its nest, it will reach past the egg with its bill and roll the egg back with the underside of its bill, balancing it carefully into the nest (see Figure 1.2).

| **Figure 1.2** | Greylag Goose Retrieving an Egg |

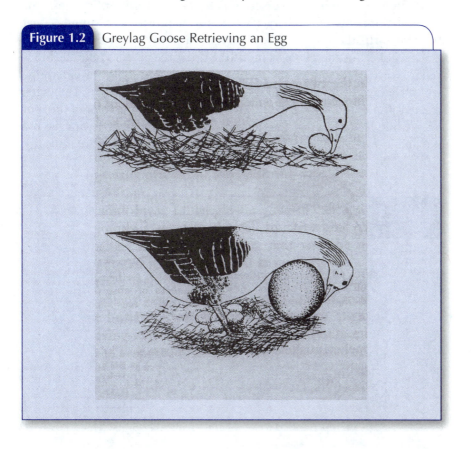

Lorenz observed that if he removed the egg once the rolling behavior had started, the behavior continued as if the egg were still there. However, the balancing movement was not seen. This suggests that the balancing movement is sensitive to ongoing stimulation and ceases in its absence, whereas the egg-rolling movement, once begun, does not require sensory stimulation to continue. Lorenz referred to the egg-rolling movement as a **fixed action pattern**.

A fixed action pattern has the following characteristics:

1. It is released by a stimulus,

2. It uses the same physiological mechanisms (e.g., muscles) to achieve the same sequence of actions,

3. It requires no learning,

4. It is characteristic of a species, and

5. It cannot be unlearned.

A fixed action pattern, once released, will continue in the absence of the releasing or triggering stimulus.

Tinbergen (1974) was particularly interested in understanding such **instinctual processes** as fixed action patterns in a variety of species. One particular interest of Tinbergen's was the nature of the stimulus that brought forth the response. For example, a newly hatched herring gull chick will beg for food by pecking at the tip of the parent's bill. The bill is yellow with a red spot at the end of the lower mandible. To determine which characteristics of the bill resulted in the pecking behavior, Tinbergen created a series of cardboard dummy birds and varied the color of the spot on the bill. He found that frequency of pecking was highest with the red dot and lowest when there was no dot at all (see Figure 1.3).

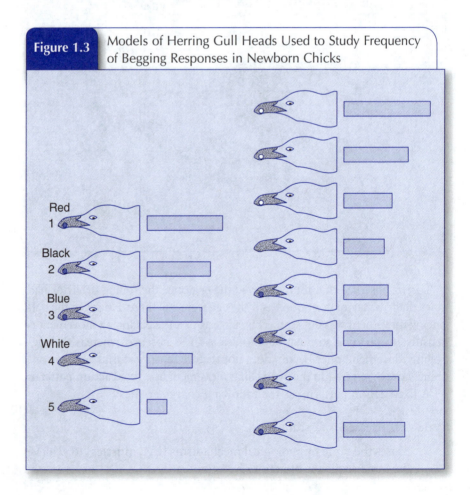

Figure 1.3   Models of Herring Gull Heads Used to Study Frequency of Begging Responses in Newborn Chicks

He also varied the color of the head and found that head color made no difference at all to the frequency of pecking. Another example of instinctual processes in birds was an alarm reaction to a predator flying overhead. The same bird of prey silhouette could produce a different reaction depending on its direction, suggesting some complexity in the reaction (see Figure 1.4).

In order to determine the exact stimulus required, Tinbergen varied the shape of the bird of prey. Using cardboard silhouettes of various birds, he discovered that short-necked silhouettes produced alarm reactions in ducks and geese (see Figure 1.5). Why would this be so? The answer is that short necks are characteristic of predatory birds, such as hawks or falcons, that prey on ducks and geese.

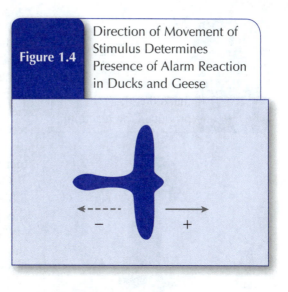

Figure 1.4 Direction of Movement of Stimulus Determines Presence of Alarm Reaction in Ducks and Geese

From an ethological perspective, Tinbergen (1963) suggested that there were four "whys" to be considered when studying behavior:

1. causation

2. development

3. evolution

4. function

First, what are the mechanisms that cause the behavior? *Cause,* in this case, refers to physiological mechanisms that are activated by environmental cues. Second, how does the behavior develop in the individual? Third, how has the behavior evolved? And fourth, what is the function or survival value of the behavior?

In the 1960s, Irenäus Eibl-Eibesfeldt extended the ethological perspective to include humans. He summarized this work in his book *Human Ethology,* published in 1989. Like ethological studies with animals, human ethology sought to understand how and why specific behavioral patterns in humans evolved, including the physiological processes involved. The initial criterion for this investigation was **fitness**. This criterion asks how a behavioral pattern contributes to the survival of the offspring. In discussing behavioral patterns, Eibl-Eibesfeldt points out that human ethology is more than just extending animal processes to humans. It also takes into account cultural behavioral patterns, which can include, for example, how we design uniforms or organize sports matches, as well as traditional cultural processes. Further, in the study of humans, speech plays an

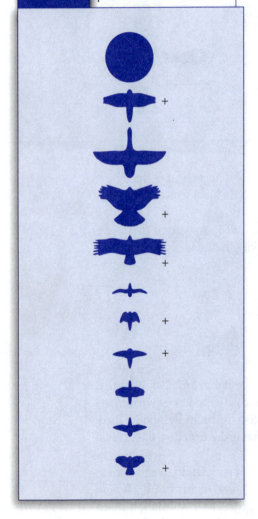

Figure 1.5 Bird Models Used by Lorenz and Tinbergen to Determine Alarm Reactions. Those marked with a "+" produced the reaction.

important role. The research methods of such an approach can be broad, ranging from data sampling, to non-participant observation using current technologies, to approaches that examine behavioral patterns across species. There is, however, an emphasis on initial research involving the behavior displayed in its natural context. After this, more experimental studies are possible.

One of the broader questions asked by Eibl-Eibesfeldt is the manner in which life should be considered. Borrowing from Hass (1970), Eibl-Eibesfeldt emphasizes that life should be considered an energetic process. From this perspective, one task of all organisms is to extract energy from their environment in forms such as food, sunlight, and so on, in order to live and perform other functions. Thus, the overall goal is to acquire more energy than one must expend in its acquisition. As we will see throughout this book, the idea of maximizing energy input and limiting energy expenditure will have profound implications for understanding human functioning. Accomplishing this task in ever-changing environments requires **adaptations.**

Adaptations reflect features of the environment relevant to survival, according to Eibl-Eibesfeldt. For example, characteristics of light transmission through water are represented in the construction of a fish's eye. However, the human visual system reflects the transmission of light through air. Some insects literally mimic the environment in which they live (e.g., a leaf). However, the characteristics reflected in the structure and function of an organism are mainly those related to fitness. Lorenz suggested that the thought processes of humans also reflect environmental fitness adaptations. That is to say, our cognitive processes reflect characteristics that maximize fitness. In this manner, our cognitive processes do not depict the external world as would a video recording; we process and store information according to basic instinctual processes. This is easy to demonstrate by asking a variety of people what they read in the morning newspaper. What one discovers in such an exercise is that most individuals remember very little in an organized or rational manner; instead, they retain only that which is directly relevant or interesting to them in some way. Even moving to a higher level of analysis, it is apparent that most of our human creations (e.g., computers) result from situational adaptations to the environment, rather than rational planning.

Adaptation over time becomes a key to understanding human behavioral processes. One of the first tasks in human ethology is to identify innate behavioral processes. As we will see throughout this book, and especially in the chapters involving developmental processes, humans display a variety of innate behavioral patterns. Examples of these are clearly seen in newborn babies, such as the grasping movements of the feet and hands when touched, or the rooting reflex when the lips and cheeks are touched. Here we have two very different behaviors in terms of functional significance. Human infants at birth can close their fingers and toes around an object such as a rope tightly enough to enable them to hold their own weight (see Figure 1.6).

| Figure 1.6 | Grasping Response of Human Newborn |

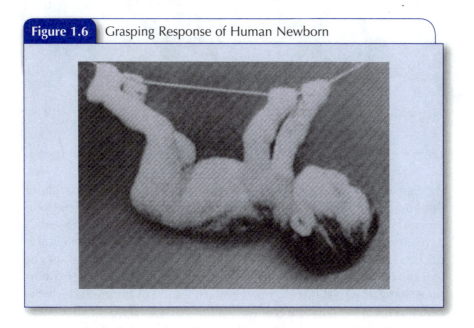

Clearly, this is not a task that human infants are required to do in their environment. However, given that one of the best stimuli for eliciting the response is a clump of hair, it may be that the response is related to the non-human primate infant grasping his mother as she moves through the trees, which does have great survival value. Thus, what has functional significance for non-human primates may have less functional significance for human infants. However, the rooting reflex, in which the infant moves toward a mother's nipple, clearly has significance for both human and non-human primates. Research has also supported the idea that an infant's facial features, including large eyes and forehead, may serve as releasing mechanisms that bring forth positively valenced affectionate responses from adults. Cartoon characters or toys that have similar characteristics are rated as "cute" across a variety of cultures. In fact, Eibl-Eibesfeldt (1989) illustrates the changes in the characteristics of Walt Disney's Mickey Mouse over 50 years (see Figure 1.7). What this suggests is that each new set of artists who drew Mickey Mouse over the years changed his features, emphasizing larger eyes and head, to make him more appealing to humans. This most likely happened without the artists being consciously aware of the slight changes they were making.

Figure 1.7 Changes in the Depiction of Mickey Mouse Over 50 years, Emphasizing Larger Eyes and Head

Many of the insights of the ethologists will be described throughout this book as they relate to specific topic areas. In studying the behavioral processes of animals and our own species, the ethologists have helped us develop a more sophisticated way of moving beyond the simple nature/nurture dichotomy. For example, a process such as imprinting shows us that innate components are important. However, there are other conditions that play a role. Imprinting is also a question of timing and what is taking place in the environment during this critical period. In later chapters of this book, we will see that human processes such as language development and mother-infant attachment can be understood as also reflecting a rich interaction between environmental and innate factors. In considering these processes, we will see that both innate and environmental factors place constraints on human behavior and experience that are not easy to describe in simplistic ways. You will also see that many of the approaches used in human ethology have also been important in psychology, as illustrated by Paul Ekman's study of human facial expressions in Chapter 6.

GENETIC TRADITIONS

R. A. Fisher

In the 1930s, statistician R. A. Fisher (1930/1999) published *The Genetical Theory of Natural Selection.* Fisher was interested in putting natural selection on a more scientific footing by developing an underlying mathematical formulation. This book is often described as the first major work to provide a synthesis of Darwin's theory of natural selection with Gregor Mendel's genetic research. As you will see in Chapter 3, Mendel worked with the pea plant and was able to show how traits such as flower color or height were passed on from generation to generation. Darwin described the process of evolution but lacked knowledge of the mechanisms by which it could take place. Darwin could not explain the specific causes of variation that drove evolutionary theory. What Fisher, along with others, began to do was to articulate the concept of variation as developed in genetics and integrate this with evolutionary theory using statistical concepts. In accomplishing this task, Fisher worked with Darwin's son, Leonard Darwin, to gain perspective. One of Fisher's important mathematical demonstrations was the understanding that natural selection progresses by the accumulation of many small changes in genes, rather than a few large changes. As you have learned in your statistics courses, many characteristics of organisms, such as height or bone or tooth size or wing length, fall on a normal distribution or bell-shaped curve.

How are we to understand the meaning of these distributions? Fisher related these to *fitness.* He suggested that there must be an optimal value that relates to the physical characteristics of the organism as well as the environment. Take, for example, the length of a bird's wing. If it is too short, it will not be able to lift the bird off the ground. If it is too long, the bird's muscles may not be strong enough to move the wings appropriately. Thus, there is an optimal length. For Fisher, the optimal measurement was the same as the mean, or average value, exhibited by the species. He also concluded that a small advantageous change in gene structure can occur only a small number of times before it changes the entire population. Let's look at a specific example of this. Assume that a variation in gene structure caused some individuals to become more intelligent than the rest of the population. If this higher intelligence were an advantage, then slowly over time, higher intelligence would become a characteristic of the entire population. Then, of course, what was previously high intelligence would now be average intelligence because it would be a characteristic of the entire population. Fisher's work helped to set the stage for an integration of the study of genetics with the study of evolution through natural selection.

INTEGRATION OF GENETICS AND EVOLUTION

Theodosius Dobzhansky

A step toward the modern synthesis of evolution and genetics took place in 1937 with the publication of *Genetics and the Origin of Species* by Theodosius Dobzhansky. Dobzhansky had been interested in studying insects in the wild since his early years as a child. After coming to America from Russia, he began studying fruit flies with Thomas Hunt Morgan at Columbia University and later at the California Institute of Technology. Morgan and his group had shown spontaneous variation in genes in the laboratory fly. Dobzhansky was able to integrate this work on genetic variation with the work of those who studied species in the wild. One of his original questions had to do with the genetic variability that determines the differences in populations of a species. While studying organisms both in the lab and in the wild, it became clear that members of the same species can have different genetic variations. It was not the case, as some thought at the time, that each member of a species had an identical set of genes. What, then, helped to define a *species?* Dobzhansky suggested it was sex. That is, a species is a group of animals or plants that mate among themselves. His book, *Genetics and the Origin of Species,* pointed to some ways in which species could come into existence. He began with the idea that genetic mutation leads to variation. However, this in itself would not lead to the changes necessary to produce a new species. What was necessary was for conditions to change in some manner that could lead to what Dobzhansky called **isolating mechanisms**. A variety of factors could help to produce these isolating mechanisms, ranging from changes in geography to changes in physiology. As a result of these changes, a part of a species could become isolated and begin to breed with each other, as would be expected. In the process, these organisms would become genetically different from the larger population. As additional variations developed in the isolated population, the mechanisms of natural selection would come into play, such that these traits would become part of the isolated population and thus they would be more dissimilar from the original population of animals. As shown in lab work, these isolated populations could carry genes that would interact negatively with those of the original population, such that no offspring would be produced or they would die prematurely. It is in this manner that species can develop and live side by side. Although beyond the scope of our present discussion, others such as Ernst Mayr, George Gaylord Simpson, Bernhard Rensch, and G. Ledyard Stebbins helped to complete the modern synthesis of genetics and evolution, which highlighted the similarity of understanding in such apparently unrelated fields as genetics, zoology, botany, and paleontology (Price, 1996; Zimmer, 2001).

The modern synthesis combining the study of evolution with the study of genetics was begun over 70 years ago. Presently, there is a call for a new synthesis that takes into account the complex ways in which organisms change over time (see Pennisi, 2008). As you will see in Chapter 3, since that original synthesis, a variety of important discoveries have been made. These include the discovery of the structure of DNA, the sequence of the human genome, and the additional ways, such as epigenetic mechanisms, for information to be transmitted from one generation to the next. Another important theme that you will be reading about throughout this book is the critical importance of the environment and its ability to turn genes on and off. Further, as you will read throughout this book, psychological factors play a crucial role in our understanding.

KIN SELECTION AND ALTRUISM

William Hamilton

William Hamilton (1936–2000) published two papers in 1964 that were to become a major part of what has been called the "second Darwinian revolution." Darwin's description of natural selection led scientists to ask how particular characteristics or behaviors would favor the survival and reproduction of the individual. Hamilton enlarged Darwin's view of reproductive success. As scientists after Darwin examined social systems, particularly those found in animal populations, a number of questions arose. What Darwin had not addressed was the question of social relations in general and **altruism** in particular. For example, why would individuals engage in behaviors that did not benefit them in terms of survival or passing on their genes? We know, for example, there are a number of social behaviors among insects that appear not to benefit the individual. Take the honeybee hive, with a queen, some males, and 20,000 to 40,000 females. These sterile females not only put effort into gathering food for others, but they will also defend the hive against attackers and die in the process. Before we understand why this happens, we need to know something about their genetics. Most vertebrates, including humans, have two copies of each chromosome in their cells; one comes from the mother and the other from the father. Bees, ants, and wasps may or may not have two copies, depending on their sex. Honeybee eggs, which are laid by the queen, do not have to be fertilized for the insect to hatch. Unfertilized eggs result in a male honeybee. Thus, males will have only one copy of each chromosome from the queen because they began as unfertilized eggs. Female worker bees come from fertilized eggs and will have two copies of the chromosomes. However, because all the sperm produced by the males is genetically identical, worker females have more genetic material in common with each other than is usually the case. In fact, sister bees are genetically more similar to one another than they are to their mother. That is, sister bees share approximately 75% of their genes. It is this relationship that helped Hamilton to explain altruism. By acting altruistically, Hamilton suggests, the organism ensures that genetic material more similar to its own is passed on. That is to say, if a behavior helps to ensure the passing on of genes similar to one's own, then this behavior would be favored.

Hamilton's answer to the question of altruism came to be called **kin selection** or **inclusive fitness**. Inclusive fitness as a property can be measured by considering the reproductive success of the individual plus the effects of an individual's actions on the reproductive success of its relatives. Given that we share different amounts of genetic material with our relatives, the relationship must be corrected by the degree of relatedness. For example, parents and their children or siblings share more genetic material than do first cousins: 50% vs. 12.5%, to be exact. One implication of this perspective is that we could test the idea that altruistic behavior will be greatest among those individuals who share the most similar genetic material. For example, a number of species produce vocalizations to raise an alarm if there is danger. We could test the kin selection hypothesis by seeing whether a particular species (e.g., ground squirrels) would give more alarm calls when those facing the danger are related to them than when they are not. Indeed, this is the case for female ground squirrels. They produce more alarm reactions to danger when their sisters are nearby than when unrelated squirrels are nearby. Other research suggests that in those insect colonies in which there is a single father, such as bees or ants, the workers take better care of the female larvae than the male larvae, which results in a 3-to-1 female-to-male ratio. In those colonies in which there are multiple fathers, the female-to-male ratio dropped to 1-to-1. The implication is that in single-father colonies, the genetic material of the female larvae is more similar to that of the female workers, whereas in the multiple-father colonies, the genetic material would be similar for both females and males. Although a number of studies have demonstrated kin recognition mechanisms in animals, current research shows that humans have also evolved mechanisms for assessing genetic relatedness (see Lieberman, Tooby, & Cosmides, 2007).

Hamilton's suggestion is often presented in the form of a mathematical relationship or rule, which states that a behavior will evolve if the cost to the individual is outweighed by the gain to another multiplied by the degree of genetic relationship. Mathematically, this is stated as "cost to the individual is less than the degree of relationship times the benefit" or ($C < R \times B$).

If you think about the implications of this rule, you realize that Hamilton has turned the question of evolution upside down. It is not the individual or even the group who is benefiting, but the gene. Hamilton suggested this in a 1963 paper in which he wrote that the ultimate criterion that determines whether a particular gene will spread is not whether the behavior will benefit the individual, but whether it will benefit the gene. This led to the concept of the "selfish gene," which was articulated in a book of the same name by Richard Dawkins in 1976. According to this view, even though the behavior of an individual may be altruistic, it is really performed in the service of the gene.

George Williams

Two years after Hamilton's introduction of the concept of inclusive fitness, George Williams (1966) published *Adaptation and Natural Selection*. This book helped to shift thinking in the field of evolutionary biology by clarifying a number of concepts. Williams begins his book by saying that its purpose is to purge biology of "unnecessary distractions that impede the progress of evolutionary theory and the development of a disciplined science for analyzing adaptation" (p. 4). Adaptation, according to Williams, is a concept that is often used in a loose manner and thus lacks any scientific power. Williams suggested that the concept of adaptation should be used only when it is really necessary. Consider one of Williams' examples: A fox heading to a hen house after a snowfall makes a path with its feet. It then uses this path on other trips to the hen house. We would not, however, want to say that the fox's paws evolved to make paths in the snow, although doing so would save considerable time and food energy for the fox, which, in turn, would be crucial for survival. Thus, there may be benefits of snow packing, but this should not be explained in terms of adaptation. However, it would be appropriate to view the legs and feet of the fox as designed for running and walking. In clarifying the logic of adaptation, Williams not only made an important contribution to biology, he also helped set the stage for evolutionary psychology. In his clearly written descriptions, Williams articulates Hamilton's formal description of inclusive fitness. He emphasized that natural selection should be understood in terms of the individual and the manner in which the genes of the individual are passed on. This was in contrast to some alternative views of his day that emphasized group selection and suggested that natural selection benefited the group. The group selection approach suggested that organisms displayed altruism as a means of benefiting the group. Within less than a decade following the publication of the books and articles of Hamilton and Williams, the group selection view had all but disappeared.

Robert Trivers

Robert Trivers originally went to Harvard to study mathematics, but after changing directions a number of times and never actually receiving his undergraduate degree, he did graduate work with the well-known biologist Ernst Mayr. He received his PhD in the early 1970s and stayed to become part of the Harvard faculty until 1978. During this period, Trivers wrote three important papers. The first paper (1971) described his theory of reciprocal altruism, or altruism among non-kin. The basic idea of reciprocal altruism is that our own fitness, in an evolutionary sense, can be increased if we can expect others to help us some time in the future. Trivers saw this tendency growing out of an evolutionary past in which humans lived in small groups. In a small group, it is possible to note who helped whom or who did not help. Those who helped were helped in return and thus had a greater chance of surviving and passing on the genes related to these processes. The second paper (1972) was directed at the question of parental investment. Actually, the idea of parental investment brought together questions related to investment of parents in their children, sexual selection, and mating behaviors. The basic idea is that the sex that invests the most in its offspring will have evolved to be the most discriminating in selecting its mating partner. *Investments*, in this case, are factors such as time, energy, and effort that increase the offspring's chances of survival. It should also be noted that when an organism is investing in an offspring, this in turn reduces its ability to produce additional offspring. Thus, there is a tradeoff between investment in offspring and mating success. The concept of parental investment further suggests that the sex that invests the least will be less discriminating in mate choices. Trivers' third paper (1974) addressed the question of parent and offspring conflict. At its heart, this paper considers the situation in which a parent and its offspring, who shares 50% of its genes, are both seeking to optimize their resources. One clear example is weaning, in which the mother may wish to wean the child before the child wants to be weaned. The mother may wish to use her resources for her other children. These three papers have brought forth important research in a large variety of areas.

SOCIOBIOLOGY

Edward O. Wilson

Edward O. Wilson is a biologist who throughout his career has brought together a number of disciplines. His early work took place at the interface between evolution and ecology, with an emphasis on ant colonies. In studying ants, he focused on a variety of problems, including the manner in which ants invade new territories as well as respond to different environments and limitations. Wilson's domain was insect societies and the pressures that influence them. The large-scale question Wilson next asked concerned the nature of all animal societies, ranging from termites to chimpanzees to humans. The answer he gave was contained in a 700-page book, *Sociobiology: The New Synthesis*, published in 1975. The synthesis was a grand one, ranging from cellular biology through physiology to psychology and ecology. The book even begins with quotations from the Hindu god Krishna and the French philosopher Camus. Wilson's basic theme focuses on social behavior and recapitulates Hamilton's idea of inclusive fitness and kin selection, with an emphasis on genetic reproduction as the ultimate goal. He states this as follows:

> In the process of natural selection, then, any device that can insert a higher proportion of certain genes into subsequent generations will come to characterize the species. One class of such devices promotes prolonged individual survival. Another promotes superior mating performance and care of the resulting offspring. As more complex social behavior by the organism is added to the genes' techniques for replicating themselves, altruism becomes increasingly prevalent and eventually appears in exaggerated forms. (Wilson, 2005, p. 3)

It is somewhat of a paradox that one of the shortest chapters in Wilson's book has caused the most controversy. This was the last chapter, which focused on humans. The idea of the chapter was to point out the evolutionary origins of humans on this planet. Wilson begins by describing how ecologically unique we are. There is basically only one species of humans, which is found throughout the planet but forms high-density communities. Humans are also different from other animals in terms of our erect posture and bipedal locomotion. Compared to other primates, humans have no hair but more sweat glands (2 to 5 million). Humans also have continuous sexual activity, as opposed to periods of "heat." Further, language and culture are extremely predominant aspects of human life. Although what Wilson said about humans was not new information and had been acknowledged by a variety of scientific disciplines, he became a straw man for those on the nurture side of the nature/nurture argument. In terms of psychological theory, the 1970s was a period in the social sciences in which many of the theories assumed that humans came into the world as a blank slate and that experience determined almost all of the psychological and societal characteristics they displayed.

Wilson himself saw his critics' objections as composed of two large issues. The first was biological determinism. Although Wilson emphasized synthesis and holism as well as reduction to basic principles, his critics saw his work as trying to reduce everything to the level of biology. However, it did not help that Wilson suggested that sociobiology would replace a number of disciplines, including psychology. The second objection to sociobiology, according to Wilson, was that of genetic determinism. This is the idea that all aspects of human behavior can be explained by the presence of genes. As you will see, both of these ideas result from a misunderstanding of science and the manner in which genes influence behavior.

In a new introduction to the 25th-anniversary edition of *Sociobiology*, Wilson (2000) states the task as follows:

> Where cognitive neuroscience aims to explain *how* the brains of animals and humans work, and genetics how heredity works, evolutionary biology aims to explain *why* brains work, or more precisely, in light of natural selection theory, what adaptations if any led to the assembly of their respective parts and processes. (p. vii)

Overall, Wilson approached humans from the viewpoint of zoology, with an emphasis on description and behavior. One important aspect of sociobiology was to help psychologists consider new questions to ask. What it did not do was to articulate a psychological perspective for understanding behavior and experience in light of evolutionary theory. Current evolutionary psychologists consider psychological mechanisms to be an important level of analysis that cannot be reduced to biological levels (e.g., Hass et al., 2000). The current evolutionary perspective emphasizes the manner in which biology and experience play intertwined roles in the development and operation of psychological mechanisms, which manifest in behavior and experience. What happened next in the development of evolutionary psychology was that psychologists considered humans from the standpoint of mind.

Bringing Evolution to Psychology

If you were entering college in the 1950s, there would be no computers in the classroom, no cell phones, few televisions in the country, and foreign travel would take considerable time. Going back another 50 years to the beginning of the 1900s, you would find radios or airplanes were yet to be invented, electric lights and telephones were few, and the mode of transportation was largely by horse and buggy, trains, or ships. Farming occupied far more people at that time than it does today. One way of thinking about these changes in the last 100 years is that they have given us a greater variety of environments in which to live. Sometimes, a seemingly simple invention such as the elevator can change our environments drastically. Before the elevator, buildings were usually no more than six floors high. After the elevator came skyscrapers. Another way to consider the changes of the last 100 years is to realize that humans live in culture as well as nature, and changes in culture and nature may move at different rates. That is to say, through learning, imitation, and other forms of adaptation, humans are able to copy each other and to make changes. Using language and other forms of communication, we can transmit new ideas quickly. This is especially true in the realm of technology. For example, in only about 10 years, computers and cell phones transformed how we communicate with one another. However, 10 years or even 100 years is just a flash in time when we consider the 100,000 years of evolutionary history during which humans developed their social, emotional, cognitive, and sexual patterns of behavior and experience. Even 100,000 years is just a flash if we consider the even broader history that led to the evolution of the human body and its physiology. Bowlby (1969), the British psychiatrist who studied the relationship between infants and their mothers, reminds us how different the environments that we live in today are from those of our ancestors. Unlike other species, humans today live in environments that are different in many respects from those that shaped our early evolutionary history. In fact, when considering more instinctual processes, Bowlby and others suggest that we need to look back a few million years and also consider these processes in primates other than humans. Bowlby referred to the historical environment in which humans experienced difficulties, found food, mated and raised children, and formed and lived with others in social groups as the **environment of evolutionary adaptedness** (EEA). We use the EEA to inform our considerations of our present-day behaviors and experiences, especially in terms of survival value.

Although Bowlby used the EEA as a way of understanding relationship patterns between mothers and their infants, his ideas of attachment were often studied in the 20th century without direct reference to an evolutionary perspective. One exception was an introductory psychology textbook based largely on evolutionary themes. It was written by Harry Harlow, James McGaugh, and Richard Thompson in 1971 and included Harry Harlow's work on attachment in primates and other evolutionary perspectives. However, it was not until the 1980s that the term *evolutionary psychology* began to appear in psychological discussions. This perspective for psychology was discussed by Leda Cosmides and John Tooby at the Center for Evolutionary Psychology at the University of California, Santa Barbara. They describe their views in a number of papers (e.g., Cosmides & Tooby, 1992) as well as on the Center's website (http://www.psych.ucsb.edu/research/cep/primer.html). They begin with a discussion of their goals for an evolutionary psychology that emphasizes research and the human mind.

> The goal of research in evolutionary psychology is to discover and understand the design of the human mind. Evolutionary psychology is an *approach* to psychology, in which knowledge and principles from evolutionary biology are put to use in research on the structure of the human mind. It is not an area of study, like vision, reasoning, or social behavior. It is a *way of thinking* about psychology that can be applied to any topic within it.

Cosmides and Tooby (1997) view their work within the historical context of Charles Darwin and William James. At the end of the 19th century,

William James (1890) suggested that humans had more instincts than other animals and that our brain gave us the ability to manipulate these instincts. Cosmides and Tooby (1997) reconceptualize instincts in terms of an information processing paradigm, to reflect specialized neural circuits developed through evolution for specific processes. These neural circuits, for Cosmides and Tooby, define human nature. In fact, they state, "In this view, the mind is a set of information-processing machines that were designed by natural selection to solve adaptive problems faced by our hunter-gatherer ancestors." In more recent work, they discuss these processes as computational (Tooby & Cosmides, 2005). *Computational* refers to the manner in which such processes as cognitive, emotional, and motor functions are regulated by neural networks in response to internal and external behavioral processes. The basic idea is that neural processes have evolved in response to the types of problems that humans needed to solve: How do you recognize another's face? How do you decode emotional experiences? How should you respond when you see a snake? Thus, one would expect to find the human brain to be packed with programs for solving a variety of domain-specific problems.

This view of human nature as an evolved set of predispositions based on the types of problems our ancestors needed to solve is contrasted with what Cosmides and Tooby (1997) call the **Standard Social Science Model** (SSSM). As noted previously, the metaphor for this model is the mind as a blank slate. That is to say, it is assumed that experience plays the major role in determining our behavior, and experience thus reflects the nurture side of the nature/nurture debate. Cosmides and Tooby describe the SSSM as follows:

> Over the years, the technological metaphor used to describe the structure of the human mind has been consistently updated, from blank slate to switchboard to general purpose computer, but the central tenet of these Empiricist views has remained the same. Indeed, it has become the reigning orthodoxy in mainstream anthropology, sociology, and most areas of psychology. According to this orthodoxy, all of the specific content of the human mind originally derives from the "outside"—from the environment and the social world— and the evolved architecture of the mind consists solely or predominantly of a small number of general purpose mechanisms that are content-independent, and which sail under names such as "learning," "induction," "intelligence," "imitation," "rationality," "the capacity for culture," or simply "culture."

According to this view, the same mechanisms are thought to govern how one acquires a language, how one learns to recognize emotional expressions, how one thinks about incest, or how one acquires ideas and attitudes about friends and reciprocity—everything but perception. This is because the mechanisms that govern reasoning, learning, and memory are assumed to operate uniformly, according to unchanging principles, regardless of the content they are operating on or the larger category or domain involved. (For this reason, they are described as content-independent or domain-general.) Such mechanisms, by definition, have no pre-existing content built in to their procedures, they are not designed to construct certain contents more readily than others, and they have no features specialized for processing particular kinds of content (Tooby & Cosmides, 1992).

The evolutionary psychology that Cosmides and Tooby (1997) offer as an alternative to the blank slate view has five guiding principles:

Principle 1. The brain is a physical system. It functions as a computer. Its circuits are designed to generate behavior that is appropriate to your environmental circumstances.

Principle 2. Our neural circuits were designed by natural selection to solve problems that our ancestors faced during our species' evolutionary history.

Principle 3. Consciousness is just the tip of the iceberg; most of what goes on in your mind is hidden from you. As a result, your conscious experience can mislead you into thinking that our circuitry is simpler that it really is. Most problems that you experience as easy to solve are very difficult to solve—they require very complicated neural circuitry.

Principle 4. Different neural circuits are specialized for solving different adaptive problems.

Principle 5. Our modern skulls house a Stone Age mind.

You need to consider these principles from a broader perspective. The broader perspective is not only our history throughout time as an organism but also what functions we are designed to perform in the world. This can best be seen by comparing humans with other organisms. Cosmides and Tooby (1997) give what seems like a simplistic example, that of a human and a dung fly. A female dung fly seeks out piles of dung as a place to lay her eggs. Humans, of course, avoid dung at all costs. The smell is repulsive. However, each organism was solving different problems. The dung fly was making sure her young would be taken care of. Humans, of course, did not evolve in a way that uses dung as food. As you think about this comparison, a number of specific questions may come to mind. We can also think of broader questions, such as, What are humans designed to do in their environment? One answer Cosmides and Tooby gives is that the design of the human brain and body allows it to solve adaptive problems.

Adaptive problems have two characteristics, according to Cosmides and Tooby (1997). First, adaptive problems are the problems that have been with us throughout our history as a species. Second, adaptive problems are the problems whose solution affects the reproduction of individual organisms. "What to do when one sees a bear" is not only a longstanding problem but also one that, if not solved, will prevent one from having children. Most adaptive problems have to do with the basics of life: how to provide food and shelter, how to communicate with others, how to have pair relationships and produce children, how to take care of children. From this perspective, knowing how to surf the waves off the Hawaiian coast is directly related to solving the problem of how to walk upright on two legs without losing one's balance. You can thank a complicated mechanism in your inner ear for that, by the way. Likewise, the majority of the use of modern technology can be seen as an extension of how we solve the problem of communicating with others. Of course, you can always use the brain circuitry designed for one solution for other purposes, as we do when we go on rides at amusement parks. However, you must solve the basic problems first. The overriding assumption is that those individuals who were not able to solve these problems are no longer with us. Although Cosmides and Tooby use the term *adaptive problems,* technically natural selection results in the passing on of adaptive solutions.

The third and fourth principles relate evolutionary psychology to our current knowledge of brain structure. I will discuss the cognitive and affective neurosciences in great detail throughout this book. We know that we are not always aware of the information we use for making a decision. In fact, we may even make up information to keep our stories consistent. We also know that different areas of the brain, or neural networks, are involved in different processes. We know, for example, that different brain processes answer the questions "What is the object?" and "Where is the object?" We also know that the brain answers questions related to emotional or social processing differently than it answers strict logic propositions, even though both questions may use the same underlying logic. As we think about social and economic issues, we will see we are generally not logical at all, at least in the traditional Aristotelian sense. We also know that when engineers try to design robots to perform what appears to be a simple human perceptual process, they often run into great difficulty, suggesting that what appears to be a simple human activity may not be that simple after all.

The final principle states that our modern skull houses a Stone Age mind. Current estimates suggest that the species *Homo sapiens* can be dated to about 170,000 years ago in Africa. It is suggested that most of this time was spent as hunters and gatherers. Only about 10,000 years ago does agriculture first appear. As noted, agriculture requires a different lifestyle. With agriculture, individuals must remain in one place while seeds are planted, taken care of, and harvested. By about 5,000 years ago, about half of all humans were engaged in agriculture. It was also 5,000 years ago that written documents began to appear. If you do the math, you realize that humans lived as hunter-gatherers at least 1,000 times longer than as anything else. If you jump to the present day, you realize many of the things you consider part of your everyday life, such as electric lights and high speed transportation, are a little more than 100 years old. Computers and the Internet have existed for less than one human lifetime. Given the manner in which natural selection works, it becomes clear that the adaptive problems our brains evolved to solve were those of hunters and gatherers. Of course, we use this circuitry to live in a very modern world, but its original design came from a time long ago.

According to Cosmides and Tooby (1997),

> The Five Principles are tools for thinking about psychology, which can be applied to any topic: sex and sexuality, how and why people cooperate, whether people are rational, how babies see the world, conformity, aggression, hearing, vision, sleeping, eating, hypnosis, schizophrenia and on and on.

Let's now turn to one example of evolutionary psychology research related to reasoning. In this research (Cosmides, 1989; Cosmides & Tooby, 1989), a logic problem known as the *Wason selection task* is presented. The task is as follows:

> Part of your new job for the City of Cambridge is to study the demographics of transportation. You read a report on the habits of Cambridge residents that says, **"If a person goes into Boston, then that person takes the subway."**
>
> The cards below have information about four Cambridge residents. Each card represents one person. One side of a card tells where a person went, and the other side of the card tells how that person got there. Indicate only those card(s) you definitely need to turn over **to see whether any of these people violated the subway rule.**

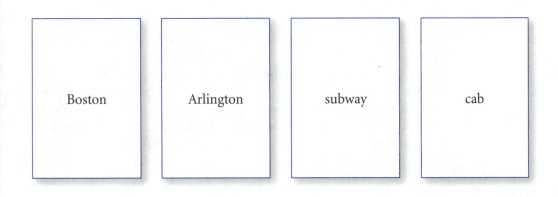

| Boston | Arlington | subway | cab |

From a logical point of view, the rule has been violated whenever some-one goes to Boston without taking the subway. Hence the logically correct answer is to turn over the *Boston* card (to see whether this person took the subway) and the *cab* card (to see whether the person taking the cab went to Boston). More generally, for a rule of the form *If P then Q*, one should turn over the cards that represent the values *P* and *not Q*.

What did you answer? If you are like most of the college students who took this logic test, three out of four of you gave the wrong answer. Other research has shown that even training in formal logic does not help to improve one's ability to solve Wason problems. However, if the problem is stated not as a logical problem but one of social exchange, then the number of people who correctly solve the problem increases drastically: from 25% to as high as 80%. The social exchange problem would be presented as follows:

If you are to eat those cookies, then you must first fix your bed.
Each card below represents one person. One side of the card tells whether the person ate the cookies, and the other side of the card tells whether that person fixed his bed. Indicate only those card(s) you definitely need to turn over **to see whether any of these people violated the cookie rule.**

| Ate Cookies | No Cookies | Fixed Bed | Didn't Fix Bed |

Why would the number getting the social exchange problem correct be three times higher than the number getting the logic problem correct? The answer is that our brains were not designed to generalize every problem into a single logical system. Rather, our cognitive processes have evolved in relation to *domains* of problems to solve. As a social group living together over the past 150,000 years, humans needed to be more sensitive to prob-lems relating to social relations, in this case cheating. These domains are living questions that our organism monitors. For example, we are quick to notice how we are treated by our friends and especially whether there is some change in our relationships. We are likewise sensitive when we are in a new group of people. We will return to these types of living questions later in this book. Overall, one important aspect of evolutionary psychology is an identification of specific domains and the manner in which humans process those domains.

ADAPTATION

In 1992, a book was published which sought to bring evolutionary psychology to a broader audience by asking a variety of scientists to discuss their area of expertise from the standpoint of evolutionary psychology. This book was *The Adapted Mind* edited by Jerome Barkow, Leda Cosmides, and John Tooby. To many, the book is a milestone in the emergence of evolutionary psychology. The authors of this book sought to articulate the manner in which evolutionary principles could be used to understand the development of cognitive processes such as the development of language, spatial abilities, and aesthetics, as well as characteristics of mate selection, sexuality, and the nature of caregiving. The central theme of the book suggests that there is a universal human nature. That is to say, there is a tendency of individuals to display similar predispositions in similar environmental situations throughout the world. The assumptions associated with this theme were (1) universal human nature results from evolved psychological mechanisms; (2) these evolved psychological mechanisms are adaptations, constructed by natural selection over evolutionary times; and (3) the structure of the human mind is adapted to the way of life of Pleistocene hunter-gatherers and not necessarily to that of the current era. This third point refers to what John Bowlby (1982) called the EEA. As you remember, the basic idea of EEA is that many of the processes of interest to psychologists, such as language, tool use, and culture, arose during the period that our human ancestors spent as hunter-gatherers on the African savanna prior to the development of agriculture some 10,000 years ago. A current challenge in terms of adaptation is to distinguish the behaviors that have resulted from an evolved adaptive process from those that have not.

Considering the evolutionary perspective has helped psychologists answer questions not easily answered from other perspectives. For example, it has even been suggested that evolutionary psychology is the only coherent theory that helps to explain such aspects of human existence as kinship, morality, cooperation, beauty, motherhood, sexuality, and violence (Pinker, 2002). Clearly, as we shall see in other chapters of this book, questions of human motivation in terms of sexuality, commitment, and family relationships have benefited greatly from the evolutionary perspective. As Darwin pointed out, organisms are in a dynamic and close connection with their environment. For humans, part of that environment is culture. We live in culture much more than we live in nature, although there is, of course, a dynamic interaction between these processes. What is important is that you not see culture and evolution as opposing explanations. As I have begun to point out, evolutionary perspectives ask a "why" question related to time. Culture offers a different level of analysis.

At this time in the study of evolutionary psychology, there is a rich discussion taking place concerning the theoretical underpinning of the field. For example, Bjorklund (Bjorklund, 2003; Bjorklund & Blasi, 2005; Bjorklund & Pellegrini, 2002; Geary & Bjorklund, 2000) has emphasized the importance of incorporating the developmental system perspective into evolutionary considerations, and I will discuss these ideas in Chapter 5. As you will see in Chapter 4, important insights from the neurosciences are informing the field. At this point, many scientists are searching for the appropriate ways to discuss the richness and complexity of human behavior and experience. For example, the manner in which an evolutionary understanding can inform the study of cognition, emotion, economics, art, and religion is beginning to be seen in major scientific journals. In the 20th century, we learned that as important as learning theory is, it presented a limited view of how humans acquire the understanding that we have of ourselves and the world. It is now totally clear that humans do not come into the world as blank slates. The emerging view is that we come into the world ready to ask certain types of questions at established times. Further, humans have a variety of behavioral decision rules. For example, we treat others who are related to us differently than those who are not. Evolutionary psychologists have been developing the scientific protocols with which to articulate these and other such processes, although the complexity of human behavior and experience leave this endeavor as a work in progress (as is all of science). The acquisition of language is one prime example. It is clear that we come into the world ready and wanting to express and acquire a language. This is so prevalent across humans that some researchers have referred to this as the "language instinct" (Pinker, 1994).

Some evolutionary psychologists have replaced the word "instinct" with "modules in the brain." In particular, they see the brain as composed of a number of modules or microcomputers. The metaphor is that of a Swiss army knife that contains a variety of independent tools. Each of these tools, or modules, evolved to solve a specific problem related to human functioning, such as survival or reproduction. One characteristic of such a module is that it is able to function somewhat independently of other brain processes. However, just because it is useful to view a process as self-contained does not, in turn, mean that there is a particular area of the brain that only does that process. Although a module is a useful metaphor, as we will see in Chapter 4, the actual structure of the brain is more complicated than that. In particular, some areas of the brain do function as if they were modules for solving particular problems. However, other cortical areas, such as those associated with higher forms of processing, appear more as a general purpose device able to solve a variety of problems. We will also see that over the course of evolutionary time, areas of the brain that begin to solve one type of problem become involved in a variety of other living questions we seek to answer. As evolutionary psychologists, we can speak of specific problems, but we also need to be aware that the developing brain shows an amazing degree of plasticity. Even on a short-term basis, learning a skill well will modify cortical areas involved in the task. How these changes relate to individual differences will be an important question for the next generation of evolutionary psychologists to understand. As important as the idea of localization of function in the brain is, we also know of extensive networks that enable us to live life successfully. Thus, a crucial question for future research is what modularity might mean, beginning at the level of the gene, especially in terms of its mapping to actual cortical processes (see Callebaut & Rasskin-Gutman, 2005, for an overview).

In summary, it may be useful to think about traditional instincts such as self-preservation, sexuality, and social processes as important domains that could be considered somewhat modular across species. Overall, in terms of brain processes, although it is true that certain processes can be localized, it is also important to understand the intensive dynamic networks that comprise our neural circuitry. In this light, some of the views of brain structure that have become popular in the field of evolutionary psychology should be seen in more metaphoric ways, rather than as descriptions of the actual neural network. The crucial question is the extent to which humans organize their functioning as a finite set of domains, and what these are.

Traditionally, the field of evolutionary psychology has emphasized human universals. For example, Tooby and Cosmides (1992), in their emphasis on universals, suggested that individual differences were really "noise" without adaptive significance. However, I will suggest in this book that some individual differences, such as the development of personality, may function in many ways like the development of language. As such, the development of specific personalities fits consistently with an evolutionary perspective and can be described in terms of genetic and human/environment interactions. As with any field, new discoveries inform and modify current speculation. This is a very challenging task because these new discoveries can come from a variety of sources, including genetics, ethology, ecology, paleontology, and the biological sciences as well as psychology itself.

Fictions About the Evolutionary Approach to Psychology

There are many misconceptions concerning evolutionary psychology. Some of these have recently been discussed by Dennis Krebs (2003). He describes six misconceptions concerning the focus and nature of evolutionary psychology.

1. Evolutionary approaches adopt a theoretically reductionistic "gene-centered" level of analysis.

2. Evolutionary theorists attempt to explain ontogenetic processes or outcomes by appealing to the creative or designing role of natural selection.

3. Evolutionary theorists believe genes are the sole source of transgenerational inheritance.

4. Evolutionary theorists believe that genes are self-contained and impervious to extragenetic influences.

5. Evolutionary approaches are genetically deterministic.

6. Evolutionary theorists pay lip service to environment.

In general, these misconceptions stem from a misunderstanding of genetics. As will be described in Chapter 3, genes turn on and off in relation to environmental conditions. For example, there is a butterfly that will be brightly colored if born in the rainy season but gray if born in the dry season. Except for blood type in humans, there are few traits that are not influenced by environmental interactions. Further, there are other ways that information is transmitted from one generation to another in humans. One of these is epigenetic transmission, in which the gene itself is not changed but the way in which it is turned on and off is. In this way, what a mouse, for example, eats can influence the hair color of her grandchildren. Additional means of generational transmission in humans include imitation, learning, and culture. Each of these means of information transmission requires a large environmental component.

SUMMARY

Building on a variety of perspectives, the field of evolutionary psychology has emerged as an important theoretical perspective. It has begun to reshape the questions asked in psychology as well as to offer answers to "how" and "why" questions concerning human behavior and experience. This chapter examined some of the major perspectives that shaped this view. The first was ethology, which is the study of organisms and their relationship to their natural environment, as seen in the research of Lorenz, Tinbergen, and Eibl-Eibesfeldt. One emphasis of ethology was the study of innate mechanisms and the environmental factors that evoked their expression. A second perspective examined was genetics and statistics and the work of Fisher. Fisher offered a statistical way to understand fitness over evolutionary time. A third perspective was that of Dobzhansky, who brought forth the synthesis of evolution and genetics, which is referred to as the modern synthesis. A fourth perspective drew from theoretical biology. Hamilton described a way to understand kin selection and altruism based on the degree of genetic relationship that one organism has with another. Williams helped to clarify the concept of inclusive fitness. Trivers better clarified altruism and the concept of parental investment. Finally, Wilson helped to establish the field of sociobiology, which emphasized "why" questions as applied to humans in terms of evolutionary theory. These perspectives offered a backdrop to considering psychological processes in the context of evolution. Bowlby focused on the relationship between mothers and their infants and the role of this relationship to anxiety. Cosmides and Tooby began to articulate a foundation for evolutionary psychology. As the 20th century ended, evolutionary psychology emphasized human processes that were universal to all individuals throughout the world. These universals, such as mate selection or emotional expression, were seen to reflect ways in which humans adapted to their environmental conditions during the broad historical period humans have inhabited the earth.

STUDY RESOURCES

Review Questions

1. What is the focus of the science of ethology, and how is it normally studied?

2. Define the following concepts discovered by Lorenz: imprinting, lock and key, social releaser, innate schema or template, critical period or sensitive period, fixed action pattern. How are they related?

3. What are the four "whys" that Tinbergen suggested should be considered in studying behavior?

4. Eibl-Eibesfeldt extended the ethological perspective to humans. What were the primary concepts he developed in thinking about the interaction between humans and their environment?

5. How did Fisher's work help to set the stage for an integration of the study of genetics with the study of evolution through natural selection?

6. What were two of Dobzhansky's important contributions to the modern synthesis of evolution and genetics?

7. Why would individuals engage in behaviors that did not benefit them in terms of survival or passing on their genes? What were the contributions of Hamilton, Williams, and Trivers that were significant enough to become a major part of what has been called "the second Darwinian revolution"?

8. Define Bowlby's concept of environment of evolutionary adaptedness (EEA). What does it mean for us today in studying evolutionary psychology?

9. What do Cosmides and Tooby mean by the "Standard Social Science Model" (SSSM)? What are the five principles of the evolutionary psychology perspective they offer to counter that model?

10. The central theme of *The Adapted Mind,* published in 1992, was that there is a universal human nature. What are the assumptions behind this model? Do you agree with their premise that all individual differences are really "noise" without adaptive significance? Can you think of any counterexamples?

For Further Reading

Dawkins, R. (1989). *The selfish gene.* New York: Oxford University Press.
Eibl-Eibesfeldt, I. (1989). *Human ethology.* New York: Aldine de Gruyter.
Lorenz, K. (1981). *The foundations of ethology.* New York: Springer-Verlag.
Pinker, S. (2002). *The blank slate.* New York: Viking.
Tinbergen, N. (1974). *The study of instinct.* New York: Oxford University Press.
Wilson, E. O. (2000). *Sociobiology: The new synthesis, twenty-fifth anniversary edition.* Cambridge, MA: Harvard University Press.

Key Terms and Concepts

- Introduction to an evolutionary perspective
- The beginnings of an evolutionary neuroscience of behavior and experience
- Pathways toward an evolutionary psychology
  - Ethology
  - Genetic traditions
    - R. A. Fisher
  - Integration of genetics and evolution
    - Theodosius Dobzhansky
  - Kin selection and altruism
    - William Hamilton
    - George Williams
    - Robert Trivers
  - Sociobiology
    - Edward O. Wilson
- Bringing evolution to psychology
  - Adaptation

SAGE Study Site

Visit the study site at **www.sagepub.com/ray** for chapter-specific study resources.

Glossary Terms

- Adaptation
- Adaptations
- Adaptive problems
- Altruism
- Critical period
- Environment of evolutionary adaptedness (EEA)
- Ethology
- Evolutionary perspective
- Fitness
- Fixed action pattern
- Imprinting
- Inclusive fitness
- Innate schema
- Innate template
- Instinctual processes
- Isolating mechanisms
- Kin selection
- Natural selection
- Sensitive period
- Social releaser
- Species
- Standard Social Science Model (SSSM)

What Is Evolution? 2

Evolution is a process that results in heritable changes in a population over many generations. As we shall see, evolution results from the close interaction of organisms with their environment. In this close connection, the organism seeks ways to solve the fundamental problems or challenges of its existence. At times, this leads to a new development or modification of the species that creates new possibilities. At other times, as with the dinosaurs, this leads to extinction. As you will see, the study of evolution is about change or, more precisely, how change came about. In particular, I will introduce you to one critical method of producing changes, also referred to as adaptation, which is the process of natural selection. Additionally, we will consider the role of conflict and competition. Conflict takes place on a variety of levels in the natural world. When you get sick, there is a conflict between parasites or pathogens in your body and your immune system. As everyone who has brothers and sisters knows, there is also conflict between siblings. Even before you were born, there was conflict between your needs in the womb and the needs of your mother. In thinking about conflict, we can also consider the larger question of resources and the fact that there is only a limited amount of energy available at any one time. This requires that we begin to understand how energy is conserved, transformed, and used in the process of life. To understand these processes, we must consider a variety of levels, including genetics. At its very fundamental level, evolution is about genetic changes over time. Thus, we need to have some understanding of how genes work. The factors that influence those genetic changes can come from a variety of environmental influences, so we also need to consider what these influences are over time. Thus, we need to think about history.

We all have a history that influences the way in which we interact with and react to the world. Some of these influences may be related to where we grew up. The languages we speak and the accents we use when we speak those languages are two examples. Having many brothers and sisters, or none, may likewise influence how we interact socially. Growing up in hard times or difficult neighborhoods may also influence what we expect from the world and how we experience it. We can all think of numerous examples of how our environment has influenced our perceptions and actions in the world. Psychology, as a science, has traditionally been interested in how our external environment influences our behavior. Yet, as we shall see, there is also an internal environment within our bodies that plays an important role in our behavior and experience and influences our developmental processes.

When we consider our development, we usually think about what has happened during our lifetime. We think of the people we have known, our parents, and the places we have lived. We create a history of ourselves that weaves these events into a logical narrative. For humans, having a sense of identity becomes an important variable in the equation. However, sometimes an apparently accidental event, such as sitting next to someone on a plane who later becomes our employer or spouse, reminds us of how single chance events can have tremendous impact on our lives. You can also think about the history of your own family and the types of decisions your parents, and their parents, and so on made in terms of whom to have sex with. Who you are today is related to those choices of mate selection. Thus, an important aspect of an evolutionary psychology examines who you are attracted to and why. Many of the characteristics you have today are the result of the decisions of your parents and their parents, and so on back through human history. Moving to a larger time scale, we can also think about what happened to our ancestors during the course of all human history. In doing this, we ask how our world and the earth upon which we live has influenced who we are as human beings. We know there have been major changes on earth. We know of climatic changes resulting in significant periods of ice and cold. We know that oceans once flooded significant parts of the United States. We even know that what we now consider to be magnetic north and south were once the other way around. Some changes happened gradually and others more quickly. Some changes completely changed life on earth in a dramatic manner. Other changes influenced life in a more gradual manner.

Given the large time frame of millions of years, how can we study these changes? Some of these changes to life on earth we know from examining the fossil records. In these records, we can see the shapes of bones and skulls and bodies changing. As we look from this broader perspective, we can trace the development of humans and consider the nature of our ancestors and their lives. Prior to 10,000 years ago, it appears that most humans lived in groups and hunted animals and gathered other food sources. However, some 5,000 years later, about half of all humans were involved in some type of agriculture. What produced this change has been a question of research and debate. As psychologists, we can think about the different skill sets required to be a hunter-gatherer versus being a farmer. As we do this, we can also think about how these different environmental situations created different types of problems to solve. Clearly, people who hunt and follow food sources need the ability to recognize the changes in plants as fruits ripen as well as the ability to note signs of wildlife that can be killed and eaten. They also need spatial skills to throw weapons and know where they are in the environment. Hunting requires a different set of skills from agriculture, with its requirements of remaining in one place and waiting for crops to grow. A critical question of evolutionary psychology is how this leads to the development of cognitive abilities and language.

How and Why Questions

What about the types of problems we have to solve today? How are these similar to and different from those of our ancestors? It is from this broader perspective that evolutionary psychology is beginning to consider the manner in which we think, feel, and act as reflective of our evolutionary history. Sometimes it requires looking at the obvious. Watch from a distance as two people interact. Without much difficulty, you can usually determine whether these two people are friends, lovers, or even people who have never met each other before. Watching their faces, you can guess whether they are happy or sad or angry. How you are able to accomplish this task so easily is one good place to begin. As we will see later in this book, people from all over the world perceive such interactions, especially facial expressions, in a similar manner. It does not matter whether you are part of a tribal group in Southeast Asia or live in Ames, Iowa; you tend to see similar facial expressions as reflecting similar emotions. However, the ability to recognize facial expressions involves more than just the features presented. Look at the two faces in Figure 2.1. At first, you don't notice much difference. Rotate the faces 180 degrees. Now what do you see? We can't help but see the facial expressions. They just pop out at us.

Figure 2.1 Photo of Former British Prime Minister Margaret Thatcher. Most people see the facial expressions as similar. Rotate the pictures 180° and then notice the expression.

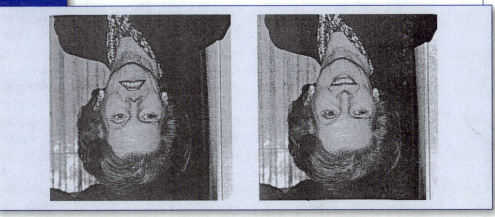

As we think about how we see these faces, we realize that when they are upside down we still know they are faces. However, we don't perceive the expression. How do we understand this? We can understand our perception on a number of levels. On one level, we can ask "how" questions. We can think about how the brain processes faces and emotions perceptually. We can discuss the various cortical pathways going from our eyes to our visual cortex. In such a discussion, we would consider the variety of brain structures, such as the right hemisphere and limbic regions involved in facial perception and emotion. We might even discover facial perception is not as simple as we originally thought. When we ask such questions, we ask, How does this process work? "How" questions are also called **proximate questions**. On another level, we can ask **ultimate questions,** or "why" questions. For example, we could ask why our brains developed to be sensitive to faces that are presented in one orientation rather than another. When asking this question, we might also note that our face has some 52 muscles that are intimately related to creating facial expressions. Why does the face enable us to make such a variety of expressions, and why are we so sensitive when we see changes in these expressions? One way in which evolutionary psychologists ask such "why" questions is to ask what type of advantage a particular behavior or method of processing gave our ancestors as well as ourselves. By doing this, we can think of many reasons why quickly noting facial expressions in others would help us adapt and survive.

Understanding Behavior From an Evolutionary Perspective

For humans, the ability to communicate emotionality with others serves a variety of purposes, from signaling danger to signaling caring to signaling the beginning of a sexual encounter. As you think about facial expressions a little more, you may realize that we rarely confuse facial expressions that suggest caring with those that suggest danger. This may seem obvious, but to an evolutionary psychologist, this suggests there is an advantage to making such discriminations. That is, it serves an important function for human existence. The value of comprehending facial expressions, of course, is that it helps one to better survive by not confusing when we need to avoid a situation with when we would want to approach the situation. Given that we can make these discriminations, as scientists we would expect to find a complex set of brain structures for making, recognizing, and discriminating between facial expressions. This is indeed the case, and they are referred to as the fusiform face area (FFA), located in the temporal lobe. We might also guess that the more important the discrimination, the faster we would make it. We would not want to waste time logically determining whether we were in danger when it would be better to leave the situation quickly and reason later. We might also assume that those individuals who could not discriminate between facial expressions would be at a disadvantage. They might even be killed. If they were killed, then of course they would not be able to reproduce, whereas those who were not killed could. This suggests one pathway or mechanism by which evolution can work. Characteristics that help one to survive are more likely to be passed on to the next generation. I will expand on this idea in more detail throughout this book.

Studying the types of tasks humans do well, as well as the physiological and cortical resources devoted to those tasks, helps us to gauge their importance in human evolution. We infer that processes given high priority by our nervous system are reflective of tasks that played important roles in the life of our ancestors and reflect the types of problems they needed to solve. To further expand these considerations, we can also look to other species to see the manner in which they solve the problems presented to them. If you were a frog, for example, you would pay less attention to faces and emotions and more to moving things, such as bugs. Otherwise, you would not eat. Although it may seem silly to say that humans value different things on this planet than frogs do, it is only by comparison that we come to see what is critical for us as humans as well as the variety of ways of obtaining the fundamentals of life. How humans come to value certain behaviors, thoughts, and feelings will be a large focus of this book.

Science as a Way of Knowing

In order to answer both "how" and "why" questions, we turn to science with its methodology for developing and testing theories. Good theories help us explain large amounts of information with a few simple principles. Sometimes these principles are mathematical, as with Einstein's $E = MC^2$. Such theories can be tested in a variety of ways in both the lab and the world. In your experimental design courses, you have learned a variety of methods for developing hypotheses, performing experiments, and analyzing the results. However, there are times when we wish to examine theories that are more conceptual in nature. Then, we must emphasize logic and hypothesize patterns of behavior than can be tested in non-laboratory settings. In astronomy, for example, we cannot perform lab experiments and move planets around to see their effect on one another. Thus, research in these fields must be more conceptually based, using observation as data. The same is true when we consider our evolutionary history. Suppose you want to know when humans first began to wear clothes. How might you go about answering this question? Three scientists, Ralf Kittler, Manfred Kayser, and Mark Stoneking (2003) answered this question by looking at the history of the human head louse, which we all know too well from elementary school, and the human body louse. It turns out that the body louse only infests clothes. So by dating through genetic methods the evolution of human head and body lice, one can also determine how long humans have been wearing clothes. The answer is at least for the last 42,000 to 72,000 years. This is supported by archaeological findings of clothing fibers from 36,000 years ago (Kvavadze et al., 2009). The range of 42,000 to 72,000 years may seem like a large range of years, but when you are dealing with hundreds of thousands of years, 30,000 is not that many. We can also use predictions based on our evolutionary history to create controlled experiments. One example is the Wason logic task I showed you in the last chapter. I will tell you about other types of studies throughout this book. As you will see, one challenge for evolutionary psychology is to integrate scientific knowledge drawn from a variety of areas. These include genetic factors, biological factors, cultural factors, paleontology, and the neurosciences, to name a few. Thus, it is necessary to use a broad integrative perspective in order to answer both "how" and "why" questions.

Whatever the field of study we draw from, we look for fundamental scientific principles to help guide our search for knowledge and understanding. One scientific principle is parsimony. Newton, for example, suggested that the same forces that cause rocks to fall to the earth in North America will also cause rocks to fall in Africa or Asia or wherever you are on earth. In evolutionary psychology, we start by assuming a similarity in processes across organisms. We know from biology that all life is related. All life shares similar basic mechanisms in terms of cells, genes, and basic physiological processes. The way these basic mechanisms function enables us to consider different pathways that different species took over evolutionary time. For example, we can look at such human processes as vision. One way to begin this approach is to first look to other organisms for similarities. In this way, we can understand how other organisms transform the energy that humans perceive as the visual world. In doing this, we would discover that some characteristics of the visual world, such as color, are perceived differently by different organisms. From an evolutionary perspective, we would want to know not only how a given visual system works, but also why it might have evolved in this way. We could also ask at what point in evolutionary time a particular species became sensitive to particular wavelengths of light. In this way, you can track when organisms moved from perceiving the world in only black and white to being sensitive to increased numbers of frequencies (i.e., colors). For example, the genes involved in humans experiencing red and green are located on a different chromosome than those involved in seeing blue. This suggests that red and green perception evolved at a different time than did blue perception. Further, in science, similar processes should be explained by the same fundamental principles. This, of course, is one of the cornerstones of the scientific method.

Another hallmark of the scientific method is that it helps us to know when we are wrong. Thus, we not only want to create hypotheses in order to understand our data, but we also want to consider what type of finding would show that our hypotheses are wrong. In the early 1900s, Rudyard Kipling wrote "just so" stories in which he told how the camel got his hump or how the alphabet was made. Although the stories are good literature that children love, they are not, and were never meant to be, good science. If someone told you that he gets up every morning and yells to keep the tigers away, you would probably laugh. What if he further told you that it works because if you look around you, you will not see any tigers? You, of course, know that he was using an invalid form of logic. When asking "why" questions in evolutionary psychology, it is critical that we not only consider what evidence supports the hypothesis under study, but also what evidence would be required to refute the hypothesis. By logically evaluating our ideas in light of the data, we come to see which hypotheses better help us to understand the processes we are studying. Thus, science gives us a method for directing our research and a means of self-correction.

As the philosopher of science Thomas Kuhn (1970) has pointed out, at any moment in the history of science some questions are overemphasized and others ignored. Kuhn called the topics we study and the types of questions we ask a **paradigm**. Whereas Charles Darwin's thought greatly shaped the scientific paradigm of psychology in the latter part of the 19th century, in the 20th century that paradigm was replaced by a focus on environmental factors and their influence on learning. This new perspective included an assumption that organisms come into the world largely as a blank slate (*tabula rasa* in Latin), which is written on by experience. Experience, in turn, completely influences the directions and choices that a person makes. From this perspective, humans are completely malleable. This view has been referred to as the Standard Social Science Model (SSSM). Those who have adopted this view have emphasized the plasticity of humans and the ability to learn and unlearn almost any human process. Although psychology gained from the study of environmental conditions, this is not the complete picture of human development (see Pinker, 2002 for an extended discussion of the role of blank slate models in psychology and the neurosciences).

Psychology is now returning to a more complete picture of human behavior and experience. As the 20th century came to a close, psychology began to integrate some of the conceptual insights of the 19th century with the empirical focus of the 20th century. In the 21st century, we are seeing the beginning of a willingness to reconsider the evolutionary significance of cognitive, emotional, and instinctual processes. This includes a reorientation and willingness to consider their functional significance. The value of Darwin's ideas is again returning to a place of importance in psychology. Additionally, psychology, in its willingness to draw from the neurosciences and genetics, is again finding value in biological thinking and its understanding of the evolutionary perspective. This has allowed us to ask different types of questions, such as what an infant's preferences are immediately after birth. For example, studies show that newborn infants have a preference for human faces, especially ones that continue to look at them. Infants are also expert at copying the facial expressions of adults. Just stick out your tongue at a baby and see what happens. Even infants without the ability to hear initially babble and coo as do hearing babies. All of this suggests that humans come into the world with a variety of programs already built into our system. However, many of these programs are modified by our environmental experiences. For example, a variety of studies have shown us that experience, particularly early in life, helps to determine how much of your brain is devoted to a particular process. If you have played a violin since you were young, the area in your brain that controls your left hand is larger than the area that controls your right (Elbert, Pantev, Wienbruch, Rockstroh, & Taub, 1995). This, of course, results from the fact that when playing a violin, your left hand requires fine responses to control the strings whereas the right hand only has to move the bow. Thus, there is also plasticity in our developmental processes. The important point is that human beings are more than just inborn processes, in the same way that they are more than environmental influences alone. We will come to see that there is a rich interconnectedness between our internal and external worlds, including the culture in which we live. What you and I will be examining in this book is the psychological perspective as informed by evolutionary and cultural perspectives as well as relevant research from the neurosciences.

The Evolutionary Approach

One fundamental process that we will consider in this book is evolution. Like Newton, who helped to formalize our understanding of the physical world, Charles Darwin helped to formalize our understanding of organic change over time. Natural selection is the simple but elegant idea that Darwin used to unite the great variety of data available for understanding life on earth. Thus, I begin with Darwin and examine his theory of natural selection. As we continue throughout this book, we will consider how evolutionary perspectives help us to understand psychological processes such as cognition, emotions, and behavior. At times, in order to complete this task, I will draw from the neurosciences and its close connection to biology. In the process, I will also reexamine various perspectives in the history of psychology in terms of the evolutionary perspective. As we begin, we should remember that there is no single theory of evolution, especially as related to psychology, but a general set of principles that determine the scientific questions we ask and the manner in which we perform our research. Below is a list of these principles.

1. All life is related, in that it is made up of the same components (cells, genes, DNA, and other organic structures).

2. Organic life has shown an increase in complexity over evolutionary time; change and time are critical components of the natural world.

3. Organisms can be organized in terms of similar physiological processes (e.g., mammals are organisms that feed their young with breast milk from the female).

4. Life evolves using previous organic systems.

   a. In cold-blooded animals, sperm is developed in the body cavity. In the transition from cold-blooded to warm-blooded animals, the testes moved outside the body because sperm develop best when the temperature is lower than internal body temperature.
   b. The human eye is sensitive to light, which will pass through water; the anatomy of receptors in the eye shows a building out. If you were an engineer asked to design an eye, you would probably not place the blood vessels and the nerves between those photosensitive cells that are sensitive to light and the source of the light itself. Yet, this is what we see in vertebrate eyes.
   c. The general view is that the present-day eye evolved from a structure that probably detected gross changes in light, not the specific images and colors we see today.
   d. The same structures are used by a variety of species (e.g., limbs; see Figure 2.2).

5. Organisms may retain previous physiology that is neither adaptive nor functional. These are called *vestigial structures.* For example, human babies can grasp and hold their own weight. Some people can wiggle their ears. This probably remained from other mammals that make ear movements to localize sounds. Human babies in the womb may also show tails at the end of the spinal cord, which disappear before birth.

6. The basic evolutionary processes take place outside the awareness of the organisms involved (e.g., people will choose sweaty t-shirts on opposite-sex individuals due to immune system functions, but they cannot articulate why they make their choices; human females may dress to show more skin when they are most likely to conceive, but they will not be aware of their clothing choices).

7. Organisms have only a limited amount of energy at any one time, and this results in tradeoffs (e.g., energy used to fight disease cannot be used for growth).

8. Species also show tradeoffs in their evolution (e.g., eating protein such as meat reduces the size of the gastrointestinal system; a small birth canal results in more dependency of the child on the mother).

Figure 2.2   Similar limb structures are seen in a variety of species.

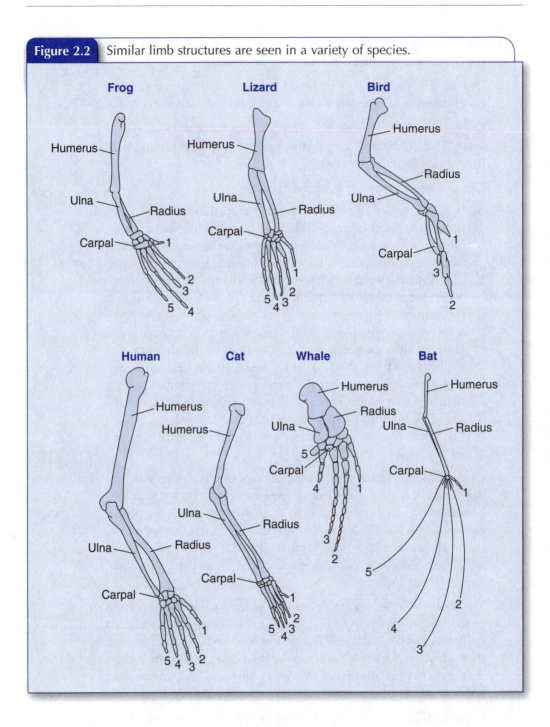

9. An adaptation that increases abilities on one level may reduce them on another (e.g., bright colors in male birds may increase sexual attraction but reduce protection from predators).

10. There are limits to the evolutionary process (e.g., **variation** is needed; selection can only work when there is variation; evolution

cannot work outside the laws of nature—physics, chemistry, biology, and psychology).

11. There are key questions that organisms seek to answer:
    a. How to survive,
    b. How to reproduce,
    c. How to organize society.

CHARLES DARWIN

In this section, I want to spend some time introducing you to Charles Darwin and his work. He is a scientist who is not discussed in detail in many psychology books, yet his work had a tremendous influence on the emergence of scientific psychology. When we think of Darwin, we generally think of his theory of evolution by natural selection. However, seeds of his theory had been available for at least two thousand years and were actively discussed in Darwin's time—the middle of the 19th century. In fact, Alfred Russel Wallace independently developed a theory of evolution similar to Darwin's. Both Wallace and Darwin based their theories on their travels studying the plants and animals of the world. Their theories were published at about the same time. However, whereas Darwin sought to apply the theory of evolution to all life on earth, Wallace saw humans as more difficult to conceptualize within evolutionary terms, which was consistent with the intellectual thought of his day. What Darwin did was give us a logically reasoned presentation supported by relevant data and careful observation. This came at a time in which fields such as geology also were describing long-term changes in the earth's crust, as well as attempting to understand the nature and location of newly discovered fossils. The intellectual thought of the time was focused on historical change, and Darwin brought forth a theory to understand change as applied to organic life on the planet.

All his life Darwin was interested in nature. As a youth, he collected shells, eggs, and minerals and liked watching insects. Given parental pressures and the need to find an occupation, at age 16, Darwin went to medical school. Not liking the medical procedures of his day, which was prior to the development of anesthesia, Darwin decided being a country pastor would be a better calling. Two years later, he transferred to Christ's College, Cambridge. Throughout his life he was interested in natural history, and even during his study of theology, Darwin gravitated to professors with similar interests. After three years at Cambridge, Darwin was given the opportunity to be part of an expedition to survey the coast of South America, including Patagonia, Tierra del Fuego, Chile, and Peru. The map of his travels is shown in Figure 2.3. This allowed Darwin to pursue his real interests, and so he sailed on the HMS *Beagle*. This voyage marked a turning point for Darwin and later scientists concerning the way they thought about animals and plants on this planet.

Figure 2.3 Map Showing Darwin's Trip Around South America Including Patagonia, Tierra del Fuego, Chile, and Peru. The Galápagos Islands are located about 600 miles northwest of Lima, Peru.

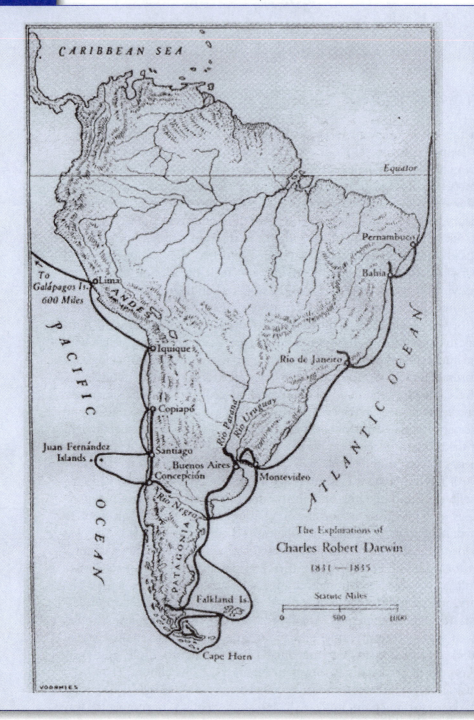

Sailing of the HMS Beagle

At the beginning of the voyage, Darwin, like others, assumed that life came from a limited number of locations on earth. By the end of his travels, Darwin realized that the environment plays an important role in producing variations in species of plants and animals. Darwin further understood that *adaptation* on the part of species is crucial to the great variations seen on earth. Darwin helped to make a radical shift in the thinking of the period by suggesting that life on earth is not static. According to Darwin, an important aspect of life on earth was change through adaptation to the environment. During his trip to the coast of South America, Darwin read carefully the work of Sir Charles Lyell, especially his *Principles of Geology*. Lyell suggested that the earth's physical features could be understood in terms of geological and climatic processes that had occurred continuously and uniformly over very long periods of time. During his trip, Darwin recorded in his notebooks the manner in which the white cliffs he viewed at St. Jago could have been created by small volcanic eruptions followed by slow elevation of mass and erosion by rain and the ocean over a long period of time. In many ways, Darwin took this idea and applied it to life processes. Clearly, ideas concerning evolution can be found previous to Darwin's work. What makes his books seminal is the well-organized presentation of data in support of his theory. These data were initially collected on his travels to the Galápagos Islands.

The Galápagos Islands

During September, 1835, the HMS *Beagle* arrived at the Galápagos Islands, which are approximately 600 miles off the coast of Ecuador. What was amazing to Darwin was the number of plants and animals that existed nowhere else on earth. In fact, he estimated that of the 185 species of flowering plants that he found, some 100 existed only on these islands. Even more amazing for Darwin was the discovery that species of birds found on one of the 10 islands were different from those found on the rest of the islands. Particularly intriguing were the differently shaped beaks of finches from the different islands. Why would finches on one island have thick, strong beaks while those on another island had slender beaks? Darwin later suggested that environmental conditions played a crucial role. Another question for Darwin was why apparently different plants and animals would occupy identical habitats on the east and west sides of an island. Darwin realized that not only is variation a crucial aspect of nature, but that great variation can exist in a relatively small geographical area.

Darwin continued discussing and refining these ideas, but it would be some 28 years from the time that the *Beagle* initially set sail until November, 1859, when his book *On the Origin of Species* was published.

During this period, Darwin by chance read *An Essay on the Principle of Population* by Thomas Malthus (1826), in which the struggle for existence was presented as a principle ruling human populations, especially as they increase in number. Darwin adopted this idea and incorporated it into *On the Origin of Species. Origin* represents, according to Darwin, one long logical explanation of the way in which natural selection accounts for the diversity of life found on our planet.

Variation in Nature

Variation was to become one of the major components of Darwin's thinking concerning evolution. In fact, he began with the assumption that heritable variations can and do occur in nature. Darwin then presented the important realization that not all plants or animals that come into existence survive. Many organisms (e.g., sea stars) produce millions of eggs, of which only a small number survive. Depending on climate conditions, food supply, predator population, and a host of other factors including disease, only a limited number of births survive to maturity. Consequently, Darwin suggested, there is a recurring struggle for existence. Who is to survive in this struggle? Darwin suggested that if an individual has even a slight variation that helps it to compete successfully for survival, then over time, the species will be made up more and more of members with these characteristics and less and less of individuals lacking them. Darwin referred to this process as *natural selection*:

> Owing to this struggle for life, any variation, however slight and from whatever cause proceeding, if it be in any degree profitable to an individual of any species, in its infinitely complex relations to other organic beings and to external nature, will tend to the preservation of that individual, and will generally be inherited by the offspring. The offspring, also, will have a better chance of surviving, for, of the many individuals of any species which are periodically born, but a small number can survive. I have called this principle, by which each slight variation, if useful, is preserved, by the term Natural Selection, in order to mark its relation to man's power of selection. (Darwin, 1859, p. 61)

Natural Selection

Let's stop for a moment and understand what Darwin suggested. Darwin saw that in each generation there are variations that appear to happen randomly. Darwin knew this because many of the animal and plant breeders of his time capitalized on this knowledge to breed animals or plants with particular characteristics. He saw this same process happening naturally on the Galápagos Islands. Some of the finches had long, thin beaks and others had small, thick, hard beaks (see Figure 2.4). Imagine that on the rocky island on which these birds live there is very little rain, and the trees that produce the seeds that the birds eat produce a bad crop year after year. Initially, all birds can grab the seeds as they fall to the ground. However, after all the easy-to-find seeds have been eaten, there would only be seeds in hard-to-reach places, such as cracks in the rocky surface of the island. Which finches would have an advantage? Of course, it would be those with long, thin beaks that can reach between the rocks for the seeds to eat. We could also think of other situations, such as environments having trees that produce thick, hard seeds, that would favor birds with small, strong beaks. In Darwin's view, small variations such as the length or thickness of the beak can influence survival. The obvious realization is that the individuals that survive are also the ones that live to mate. It is their characteristics that are passed on to the next generation. On the other hand, the characteristics of the individuals that do not survive are lost. One implication of this reasoning is that even if all the finches on the Galápagos Islands came from the same set of parents originally, particular environmental conditions at specific locations on each island could lead to very different species of finches arising over time.

| **Figure 2.4** | Examples of Beak Variation Seen in Finches on the Galápagos Islands |

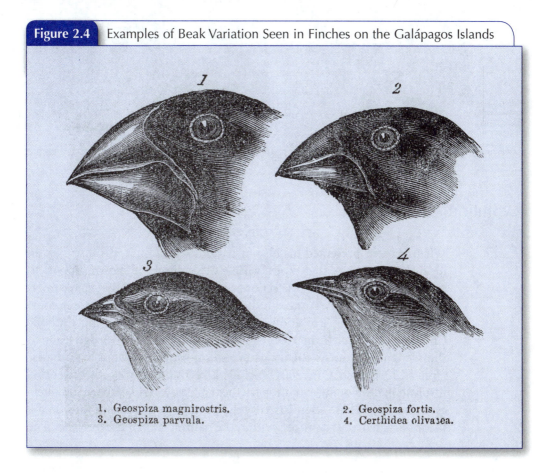

1. Geospiza magnirostris.
2. Geospiza fortis.
3. Geospiza parvula.
4. Certhidea olivasea.

There are actually 13 different species of finches on the Galápagos Islands (see Figure 2.5). For your information, the biological concept of *species* suggests a group that only breeds among the group and does not seek to breed with other groups (Mayr, 1963). This has been observed in the differing species of finches on the Galápagos Islands. More technical definitions of species include the concept of a common gene pool for a population that differs from that of another group. In terms of the finches, diversity then becomes the product of evolution, and the mechanism Darwin proposed was natural selection through an interaction with the environment. Of course, for natural selection to work, the particular characteristic or trait of the individual must be heritable. We will discuss this in greater detail in Chapter 3.

Figure 2.5 These species of finches live on the Galápagos Islands.

Evolution After Darwin

When Darwin presented his idea of natural selection, it was just that, an idea. However, since that time a variety of studies have shown support to such an extent that natural selection is now seen as one of the major unifying factors in biology. Although there has been debate in the wider community concerning evolution, even the former Pope of the Catholic Church, John Paul II, in 1996 concluded that "new knowledge leads to the recognition of the theory of evolution as more than a hypothesis" (Jones, 2000; also Orr, 2005, p. 52). Likewise, many of the scientists involved in developing evolutionary theory, like Darwin, also had an interest in religion. These scientists view the theory of evolution as they do the theory of gravity: as a process within the natural laws of the universe. The point to be made is that evolutionary theory reflects mechanisms by which life on earth changes and adapts to its environment. You are free to see that mechanism as ultimately related to your personal theological conceptualization or not, but either way, that is a leap of faith on your part and not part of the scientific understanding of evolution.

One animal commonly used to illustrate natural selection is the peppered moth in England. The peppered moth rests motionless on trees during the day and feeds and mates at night. The wing color of these moths ranges from light gray to almost black, although before 1850 the dark-colored moths were less common. The moths are colored in a camouflage-like pattern, which makes them almost invisible when on the tree trunk during the day, an advantage because otherwise they would be eaten by a variety of birds. On many of these trees grew a light-colored lichen—a fungus and an algae together. Lichens can be seen in this country on stones as well as trees. In the 1850s, the industrial revolution began in England. Soot and pollutants from factories began to kill the lichens and make the tree trunks dark. Under these conditions, it was the dark moths that had the advantage of being hidden from birds on the dark trunks of trees. The light moths were more likely to be eaten and, as a result, would be unable to reproduce and pass on their characteristics. Indeed, during this time, this was what was observed. The dark moths, which had previously been rare, now increased in number. A hundred years later in the 1950s, with the introduction of pollution controls, the reverse happened. Lichens made a comeback, tree trunks no longer were affected by soot, and light-colored moths increased in number. This is a simple, clear example of how environmental changes favor certain traits in a population and influence which traits will be passed on to the next generation. As we saw with the peppered moths, the exact meaning of what was "fit" at any one moment changed as the environment changed.

EVOLUTION IS STILL TAKING PLACE

More recent research suggests that changes of the kind Darwin described can actually take place over short periods of time, that is, within a few generations. During the last part of the 20th century, Peter and Rosemary Grant continued Darwin's study of the 13 species of finches on the Galápagos Islands (see Weiner, 1994 for an overview of the early work). Methodologically, they caught and placed bands on many of the birds so that they could follow their life cycles as well as those of their offspring. During the period in which the Grants performed research on the islands, a number of significant environmental changes took place, including a severe drought. Food supplies decreased, and the finches were forced to eat seeds with tougher hulls. The finches with the strong, thick beaks could open the seeds and survived. The ones with the longer, thinner beaks could not and died in greater numbers. As Darwin suggested, it is the finches with strong beaks that have an advantage and survive to mate. Examining the next generation, the Grants found more offspring with that type of beak. Although evolution is generally thought of as a slow process, this is one case in which the adaptation took place in one generation. However, there was more to the story: The climate of the Galápagos Islands then changed drastically to one of heavy rains. With the rains came floods that washed away larger seeds to leave only small seeds that were able to lodge between the rocks. In a turn of events, it was the finches with the long narrow beaks that were best adapted for the new environmental conditions. Species react not only to environmental conditions such as weather, but also to competitors. In 1982, a species of finch from one of the other Galápagos Islands began breeding on another of the islands named Daphne Major (Grant & Grant, 2006). A different species of finch already existed on this island. Both species competed for some of the same food. However, the newly arrived species consumed twice as much of one of the important seed foods as did the existing species of finch, which resulted in a reduction in food supply. Further, the new species was also able to chase the other species away. The Grants were interested in whether this would result in a change in the physical characteristics of the original species of finch. Indeed, by 2004, the beak size of the species originally on the island was reduced, suggesting that evolutionary changes had taken place. Similar to the peppered moth and pollution story, environmental conditions, including the presence of competitors, rewarded differential characteristics in terms of adaptation. What is most intriguing is the speed at which natural selection was seen to work. Changes were noted after one generation. Technically, the situation in which a single species develops into multiple species, as in the case of the finches depending on ecological niches, is referred to as "adaptive radiation."

Although I have presented the story of natural selection in simple terms, we must also realize the complexity of the situation. Darwin said it in this way:

> Let it also be borne in mind how infinitely complex and close-fitting are the mutual relations of all organic beings to each other and to their physical conditions of life; and consequently what infinitely varied diversities of structure might be of use to each being under changing conditions of life. (Darwin, 1872/1998, p. 61)

What this passage clearly suggests is that life on earth is closely interconnected and represents a complex process that is difficult to study in simplistic terms. For example, one cannot consider the pepper moths without also considering the birds that eat them and the environment in which both live. Likewise, one cannot consider the birds that eat the pepper moths without considering the dangers these birds face. As Darwin said, it is extremely complex. Darwin continues the passage above by reaffirming that any slight variation that helps the individual survive would be continued in future generations and that those that do not help it survive would be lost. The complexity, of course, is that changes are taking place constantly in all species and in the environment. As we shall discuss later in this book, humans' environment extends beyond the natural world and includes the world of culture and the societies in which we live.

SEXUAL SELECTION

Darwin later extended the theory of natural selection to include **sexual selection**, or the manner in which males and females choose a mate. This work is described in his book *The Descent of Man and Selection in Relation to Sex* (1874). *The Descent* was divided into three parts. The first part expanded on the theory of natural selection and more explicitly set out the case for the similarity between humans and other animals. The second and third parts of the book examined sexual selection in relation to animals (Part II) and in relation to humans (Part III). In the second and third parts of the *Descent*, Darwin notes that males and females not only differ in their organs of sexual reproduction but also in secondary sexual characteristics, such as mammary glands for the nourishment of infants in females and physical size in males. According to Darwin, sexual selection depends on the success of certain individuals over others of the same sex. Darwin also saw that besides same-sex competition, there is also competition to attract members of the opposite sex. As you can imagine, there has been continuous debate and research concerning what attraction means for males and females. We will look at this in detail in later chapters. It is a somewhat complicated story, but we know that males compete against other males for "attractive" females and that females compete among themselves for "attractive" males. We also know that some secondary sex characteristics, such as the color of the tail of the peacock, supply additional information, such as information about the health of the male. Other mechanisms, such as entrainment of the menstrual cycle in animals, may aid the dominant female in having her choice of mates by ensuring a common period of receptivity. We will return to questions of attractiveness and mechanisms of sexual selection later.

To summarize, Darwin suggested two mechanisms that influence which physical characteristics are passed on to the next generation: The first is natural selection. Natural selection is composed of a number of steps. First, natural selection is focused on characteristics that vary in a given species, such as the physical size of the finch's beak or the color of the moth. Second, natural selection focuses on those characteristics that help an organism survive in the context of its particular environment. Third, an organism that survives can mate and thus pass on those characteristics, whereas organisms that do not survive cannot. Thus, even slight changes in the environment can influence characteristics of future generations. The second mechanism is sexual selection. Sexual selection takes place on two levels. First, characteristics that make one more attractive to a mate will be passed on to future generations. Thus, if female peahens like male peacocks with larger and more colorful tails, then through mating, these characteristics will be passed on to future generations. Second, within the same sex, characteristics such as strength or cunning that allow one to compete and control reproduction will also have a greater chance of being passed on to future generations because animals without these characteristics will have less opportunity to mate. Generally, when we think about characteristics in relation to natural selection and sexual selection, we think in terms of physical characteristics. But what about cognitive characteristics?

PSYCHOLOGICAL PROCESSES

Darwin began the *Origin* with the question of natural selection especially as it related to animals. In the *Descent*, he expanded these ideas to humans and also examined the question of sexual selection. In other works, such as his notebooks, he extended his thinking to cognitive and emotional processes. The broad question is, How might psychological functions have evolved? One answer he gives, which we will discuss in later chapters, is that living in social groups produces an increase in cognitive ability. Darwin also presents notes on memory and habit, imagination, language, aesthetic feelings, emotion, motivation, animal intelligence, psychopathology, and dreaming (Gruber, 1974). As pointed out by Gruber, Darwin was interested in showing the evolutionary continuum between humans and other animals in two ways. First, he suggested that nonhuman animals show rudimentary examples of problem solving and consciousness. This view helped to establish research in comparative psychology at the beginning of the 20th century. Also, research by the Gestalt psychologists in the 20th century showed that primates can solve insight problems in ways similar to humans. Further, research suggests that humans are not the only species to use tools. For example, a number of primates use sticks to pull termites from their nests. How about using napkins when eating? Surprisingly, orangutans use leaves as napkins. Thus, many of the characteristics we see in humans are also found in other species. Second, Darwin suggested that human action is not always fully guided by conscious rational thought. Darwin noted in his notebooks the manner in which humans make selections and classifications outside of awareness. In other words, humans are not always logical or rational in the manner in which they behave or experience the world. This, of course, is a topic of current research in a variety of areas of psychology, ranging from the speed at which we form an opinion about another person to the irrational way we choose to take gains and losses in the stock market. Part of Darwin's method was to explore and note the similarity of psychological processes in animals and humans.

Summary

Darwin did two things that greatly advanced intellectual thought. First, he linked all life on earth, including human beings, with other life forms. In doing this, he suggested the advantage of looking across species for similar processes and physiological mechanisms and asking how certain processes in complex life forms may have evolved. The great intellectual advantage to this procedure is that one does not need to suggest different mechanisms of form, physiology, or behavior for each species. As you will learn in Chapter 3, all life on this planet uses the same basic set of building blocks or genes. Second, Darwin suggested a close and complex relationship between life on earth and the planet itself. That is to say, environmental factors shape the evolution of life, and it is impossible to fully understand life without understanding the environment in which life takes place.

Cartwright (2000, 2001) has suggested that the essence of Darwin's theory of evolution can be summarized in eight propositions and a ninth expectation:

1. Individuals can be grouped together into species on the basis of such characteristics as anatomy, physiology, and behavior. By definition, members of a species can breed with each other to have fertile offspring.

2. Within a species, individuals are not all identical. There is variation. Individuals will differ in physical and behavioral characteristics.

3. Some of these differences are inherited from the previous generation and may be passed to the next. We now know physical and behavioral traits are expressed by information carried by DNA. Humans inherit DNA equally from each parent.

4. Sexually reproducing species such as humans produce offspring that are not identical to either parent. This makes every individual genetically unique.

(Continued)

(Continued)

Variation is enriched by the occurrence of spontaneous but random novelty. A feature may appear that was not present in previous generations or may be present to a different degree.

5. Resources required by organisms to thrive and reproduce are not infinite. Competition must inevitably arise, and some organisms will leave fewer offspring than others.

6. Some variations will confer an advantage on their possessors in terms of access to these resources and hence in terms of leaving offspring.

7. Those variants that leave more offspring will tend to be preserved and gradually become the norm. If the departure from the original ancestor is sufficiently radical, new species may form, and natural selection will have brought about evolutionary change.

8. As a consequence of natural selection, organisms will become adapted to their environments in the broadest sense of being well-suited to the essential processes of life, such as obtaining food, avoiding predation, finding mates, competing with rivals for limited resources, and so on. Through this process of adaptation, organisms will appear to fit closely with their environment.

9. The human body and mind, through their long evolutionary history, are structured in ways that promote survival and reproduction.

As you think about the complexity of the interaction between organisms and the immediate environment in which they exist, you will realize that there is constant change, but this change does not necessarily suggest a particular ultimate outcome. Rather, evolution, as Darwin described it, keeps organisms changing and constantly adapting to their environmental conditions, but with little suggestion that this change necessarily will result in improvement. As seen in the example of the peppered moths, being dark in color is an advantage in times of factory pollution, and being light colored is an advantage in times of no pollution, but neither is better than the other in isolation.

In the Tradition of Darwin

As we consider evolutionary psychology in this book, it will be useful to understand some of the intellectual roots that have influenced present-day psychology. The influence of Darwin on the psychological perspectives taken during the end of the 19th century and the beginning of the 20th century is seen by some as basically shaping the field of psychology as it exists today (Murphy & Kovach, 1972). This next section will focus on some of these historical underpinnings and the manner in which evolutionary thought influenced and informed a variety of intellectual and scientific research programs. This is a not an easy task because Darwin created the intellectual roots of a research tradition that cuts across a number of traditional disciplines, ranging from biology to anthropology to ecology to genetics to medicine to neuroscience and, more recently, to evolutionary psychology. This section of the book is not designed to give an in-depth history of the period following Darwin's writings, but rather to consider how the theorists of that period incorporated evolutionary thought into their work.

RESEARCH ACROSS SPECIES AND COMPARATIVE PSYCHOLOGY

In *The Descent of Man,* Darwin (1874) clearly states that not only are humans descended "from some less highly organized form" but that we share similar structures and processes with other animals. Even more important was the suggestion that humans and other higher mammals have similar mental faculties. For Darwin, humans and other animals differed only in degree of functioning. We saw one example of this in Darwin's discussion of the expression of emotions in animals and humans. The implication of this way of thinking is that all animals are the proper study of a psychological science. This was in opposition to Descartes, who stated that animals and humans were qualitatively different. If, however, animals share both physiological and cognitive processes with humans, then the scientific study of these processes would be an important undertaking. Indeed, Darwin encouraged such a comparative psychology when he gave the British physiologist George Romanes (1848–1894) his notebooks on animal behavior. Romanes focused on the question of animal intelligence and examined the behavior of a variety of species including ants, spiders, reptiles, fish, birds, elephants, and monkeys, as well as domestic animals. The result of this work was what came to be regarded as the first comparative psychology textbook, *Animal Intelligence,* published in 1883. The main thesis was that there was a similarity in intellectual reasoning between humans and other species. Although Romanes helped to set the stage for a future comparative psychology, many have been critical of his scientific methods. For example, Romanes often accepted anecdotal stories of animal achievements from others without verification. He also used anthropomorphic thinking, in that he assumed that animals reasoned as he did. If a cat, who Romanes thought to be the most intelligent of animals, could open a latched stable door, then it must have achieved this feat through reasoning. This led other pioneers in comparative psychology, such as Lloyd Morgan (1852–1936), to suggest a more conservative and scientific approach. Morgan is best known for what came to be called Lloyd Morgan's Canon. This is similar to the suggestion of parsimony made by Newton in the 1680s, which directed that scientific explanation should be as simple as possible. Morgan suggested that in assessing animal intelligence, one should not ascribe particular actions of an animal to higher mental states if these actions could be explained by lower mental processes. Other investigators began to ask questions of the animal mind and the mental processes illustrated in insect and animal colonies. Although Descartes justified the study of animal behavior by noting its dissimilarity to human processes, it was Darwin who reunited them through his emphasis on similarity across species. As we will see in later chapters, animal models have helped us make significant progress in understanding areas as diverse as mother-infant attachment and health psychology.

UNDERSTANDING INDIVIDUAL DIFFERENCES AND DEVELOPMENT

Francis Galton

Francis Galton (1822–1911) initially received medical training in London and then pursued studies in mathematics at Cambridge University. The ability to combine these two fields gave Galton the resources necessary to study variation and adaptation in relation to human abilities. When Darwin, who happened to be Galton's cousin, published the *Origin*, Galton turned his attention to the study of individual differences, especially those related to intellectual abilities. Galton published his book *Hereditary Genius* (1869) ten years after the publication of the *Origin*. Galton begins this book by saying, "I propose to show in this book that a man's natural abilities are derived by inheritance, under exactly the limitations as are the form and physical features of the whole organic world" (p. 1). His main thesis was that intellectual abilities can be found in families with a frequency that cannot be explained by environment alone. What became crucial for psychology was Galton's suggestion that not only did genius run in families, but specific abilities were inherited. In doing this, Galton laid the ground work for the future study of individual differences in ability. Galton also developed important methodologies still in use today. His desire to make the study of ability more quantitative resulted in the development of the **correlation coefficient.** He was particularly interested in physical traits such as the relationship between the height of parents and the height of their adult children. These were plotted in a scatter plot.

Drawing a best-fit line through the values created what we now call a **regression line**. Although the mechanisms of heredity were not well understood in Galton's time, it was known that twins had greater resemblance than non-twins. Using this fact, Galton collected information on twins as a way of understanding the effect of inheritance and the environment on individual characteristics.

Development

Infant development was actually a topic Darwin himself had carefully observed. In an article published in the journal *Mind* (1877), Darwin described the developmental processes of his infant son. Following Darwin, both James Angell (1909) in the United States and Ernst Heinrich Haeckel (1905) in Germany wrote papers on Darwin's influence on psychology. Both authors not only made links between mental processes and physiological processes, they called attention to the manner in which evolutionary thought emphasized developmental processes and fostered studies in the area. Haeckel, a zoologist, had shown the difficulty of differentiating human embryos at various stages of development from those of other animals. He made the overall suggestion that the development of a human, beginning with conception (**ontogeny**), could be seen as paralleling the evolutionary history of the species (**phylogeny**). That is to say, the development of an advanced species such as humans passes through steps represented by adult organisms of more primitive species. This became known as the *biogenetic law*, stated as "ontogeny recapitulates phylogeny."

UNDERSTANDING PSYCHOPATHOLOGY

Sigmund Freud

Sigmund Freud trained as a zoologist before he completed medical school. The nature of the neuron was just being discovered, and Freud based his early theories on the neuroscience of his day. Freud was an enthusiastic reader of Darwin and credited his interest in science to an early reading of Darwin. A number of Freud's ideas can be seen as coming from Darwin (Ellenberger, 1970; Sulloway, 1979). Although Freud incorporated Darwin's emphasis on **instinct** into his work, he emphasized sexual selection over natural selection. For Freud, the sexual instinct was the major driving force for human life and interaction. Some evolutionary researchers suggest that Freud misread Darwin, especially in relation to parent-offspring relationships, and that Darwin never suggested these represented sexual rivalry (Daly & Wilson, 1990). Others have also suggested that Freud based his theories on a Lamarckian mechanism of evolution, which suggested that incorporation of certain behaviors by one generation would result in future generations displaying these behaviors (Hogenson, 2001). The Lamarckian view was discredited during the time of Darwin. Regardless of mechanisms, Freud did adopt Darwin's interest in morals. Freud saw these as developing from more instinctive processes related to early tribal groups, rather than personality processes. Freud was also influenced by the suggestion of the neurologist John Hughlings Jackson that in our brains there are more primitive brain areas underlying more advanced ones. Thus, it is quite possible for the psyche to be in conflict with itself, or at least to have different layers representing different processes. To understand the nature of these more primitive processes, Freud looked to the description of dreams and wish fulfillment. One of his works, *The Project for a Scientific Psychology* (1895/1954), utilizes these ideas and sought to place psychology on a firm scientific basis. The *Project* was based on three separate ideas. The first was **reflex processes**. For example, organisms withdraw when confronted with unpleasant stimuli. Freud extended this idea to cognitive and emotional processes to suggest that, mentally, humans avoid ideas or feelings that are unpleasant to them. The second principle Freud used was **associationism**: Ideas that are presented together in time will be mentally called forth together. Freud suggested that if, as a child, you are in a fearful situation such as an automobile accident, then riding in a car could make you feel fearful or anxious. The third idea is that the nervous system is capable of retaining and discharging energy. This energy was initially called "Q" but later came to be known as **libido** or **sexual energy**. This psychic manipulation of energy allowed for the possibility that higher cortical processes could inhibit the experience of lower ones, a process that would come to be called **repression**. The overall statement of the psychoanalytic perspective is that our evolutionary history has emphasized survival and sexual activity and built these instincts into our brain. Anxiety is the result of society and culture having inconsistent rules for the expression of sexuality and aggression. This anxiety and our inability to acknowledge these instinctual experiences lead to defense mechanisms and neurosis. The *Project* sees the brain as basically a blank slate upon which experiences become connected with one another, driven by instinctual processes of sexuality and self-preservation. The human, for Freud, becomes the real-life laboratory in which nature and nurture struggle.

Carl Jung

Whereas Freud emphasized the drives of the sexual and self-preservation instincts in the context of experience, Jung viewed human behavior and experience in much broader terms. Jung asked the question, In the same way that there is an evolutionary history of the body, is there also one of consciousness? He spent a great amount of time examining old myths, stories, and artifacts in an attempt to reconstruct a history of the psyche.

Jung was particularly interested in the close connection between instinctual processes and the environmental factors that influence them. In many ways, Jung was actually closer to current thinking than Freud. He stated,

> The psyche has two conditions, two important conditions. The one is the environmental influence and the other is the given fact of the psyche as it is born. The psyche is by no means a *tabula rasa* but a definite mixture and combinations of genes, and they are there from the very first moment of our life, and they give definite character, even to the little child; and that is a subjective factor, looked at from the outside. (Evans, 1990)

Like Darwin, Jung was particularly interested in human universals and spent time in Africa, the American Southwest, and other non-European areas to determine whether the psychic structure of all humans was similar. For example, one question that Jung asked was, Do individuals throughout the world have similar dream patterns? He answered this question in the affirmative and suggested few differences in the psychic structure of humans throughout the world. Jung referred to this structure as the **collective unconscious,** or the manner in which all humans are similar. The collective unconscious reflects the manner in which the expressive predispositions of current-day humans are the result of evolutionary pressures on our ancestors. This collective unconscious is passed on to generations across time. Jung referred to the universal patterns available to all humans as **archetypes.** These are not unlike the action patterns seen in animals, which was an important concept to the ethologists discussed in Chapter 1, although for Jung, archetypes took place on a more psychic level and represented ways in which our brain organizes particular perceptions and our responses to events. We see many of these archetypes depicted in Hollywood films. For example, we know the task of the hero and see it portrayed in *Star Wars* by the character of Luke Skywalker or the Harry Potter character in the *Harry Potter* series of films. We also see in *Star Wars* the archetypes of the wise old man and the guru in Obi-Wan Kenobe and Yoda. At times, an actor can even become identified with an archetype, as was the case with John Wayne. He became the hero personified in his many movies in the middle of the 20th century. Not only are there physiological similarities between individuals, we also share certain predispositions for behavior and experience.

THE VALUE OF UNDERSTANDING FUNCTION

William James

William James, who is credited with establishing the first psychological laboratory in the United States at Harvard University, had studied

Darwin and was influenced by his work. Similar to Darwin, James was particularly interested in the functional aspects of psychological processes, asking the question, What purposes do they serve? In his major works, he distinguished between the long-term cause or function of a behavior and the immediate cause of a behavior. Today, evolutionary psychologists also talk about ultimate causes, which reflect the long-term evolutionary history and selective pressures on a particular trait, and proximate causes, which reflect the conditions of one's lifetime. Functional approaches are also distinguished from structural ones as a way of describing behaviors. European psychology during James's time emphasized structure and sought to take a behavior and decompose it into its components. For example, a reaction time measurement to a blue rather than a red light could be decomposed into the time required to see that the light had been turned on plus the time required to distinguish blue from other colors.

Whereas Freud had emphasized two broad instincts, sexuality and self-preservation, James examined a large variety of instinctual processes, such as how a silk worm "knows" how to make a cocoon or a bird flies south in the winter without previously being taught. James discusses these instincts in his chapter on "Instinct" in *The Principles of Psychology* (James, 1983). Instinct, according to James, was the "faculty of acting in such a way as to produce certain ends, without foresight of the ends, and without previous education in the performance" (p. 1004). Physiologically, James describes the nervous system as a pre-organized bundle of reactions that are called forth by particular sensory stimuli. Specifically, James described the situation as follows:

> The neural machinery is but a hyphen between determinate arrangements of matter outside the body and determinate impulses to inhibition or discharge within its organs. When the hen sees a white oval object on the ground, she cannot leave it; she must keep upon it and return to it, until at last its transformation into a little mass of moving chirping down elicits from her machinery an entirely new set of performances. The love of man for woman, or of the human mother for her babe, our wrath at snakes and our fear of precipices, may all be described similarly, as instances of the way in which peculiarly conformed pieces of the world's furniture will fatally call forth most particular mental and bodily reactions, in advance of, and often in direct opposition to, the verdict of our deliberate reason concerning them. The labours of Darwin and his successors are only just beginning to reveal the universal parasitism of each creature upon other special things, and the way in which each creature brings the signature of its special relations stamped on its nervous system with it upon the scene. (James, 1884, p. 191)

In reaction to those who suggested humans are different from other animals in terms of a lack of instincts, James (1983) suggested that "Man has a far greater variety of *impulses* than any lower animal; and any one of these impulses, taken in itself, is as 'blind' as the lowest instinct can be" (p. 1010). However, James suggested that because humans have a sense of memory and can consider the outcome of their actions we act out responses for the sake of the results: "It is obvious that *every instinctive act, in an animal with memory, must cease to be 'blind' after being once repeated*" (p. 1010). Thus, according to James, given that humans have memory, a power of reflection, and the ability to draw inferences, then once instincts combine with experience, the resulting actions can be modified. In a rather complex process, James suggested that reason itself cannot inhibit instincts. Through imagination, cognitions can bring forth an opposite **impulse,** which can neutralize the original impulse. Thus, if someone cuts you off on a freeway, you may not be able to not react, but you can create a new impulse that would reduce or eliminate the original reaction. That is to say, environmental stimuli may bring forth a range of impulses, which may actually be contradictory to each other, but, given that they are initially unstable, they can be modified by other impulses created in reaction to our cognitive processes. To put this in a broad perspective, James saw humans as beginning life with a large number of reflexive actions, from sneezing, hiccupping, and startling to moving limbs when touched or stimulated. Later, emotional and sexual impulses as described by Darwin come forth and, with experience, humans begin to modify and even create situations for bringing forth instinctual experiences. In the final analysis, these impulses are used in the service of human purposes and goals. Thus, you yell at a football game to bring forth impulses in your team to make them play better and to confuse their opponents.

James also saw evolution extending beyond physiological processes. In a lecture delivered before the Harvard Natural History Society, "Great Men, Great Thoughts, and the Environment," James (1880) begins with the statement, "A remarkable parallel, which I think has never been noticed, obtains between the facts of social evolution on the one hand, and of zoological evolution as expounded by Mr. Darwin on the other" (p. 441). By this James is comparing the spontaneous variation of physiological features, such as the beak of the finch, with the spontaneous arising of individuals with new ideas about society and intellectual thought. In essence, according to James, the environment "adopts or rejects, preserves or destroys, in short *selects*" the fate of the person with new ideas and, in turn, those ideas that are selected modify the current environment, "just as the advent of a new zoological species changes the faunal and floral equilibrium of the region in which it appears." That is to say, according to James, the individual who brings forth new ideas for society parallels Darwin's concept of spontaneous variation. At the end of this essay, James presents an even more intriguing idea: He suggests that evolution occurs within individuals as much as it occurs between individuals and their environment. The implication is that our internal physiological processes and our current set of thoughts, feelings, and actions serve as an environment for natural selection in terms of spontaneously arising internal impulses. Thus, evolution in humans can operate at multiple levels simultaneously, using Darwin's principles of variation and the complex relationship between an organism and its environment.

Ignoring Evolutionary Thinking

JOHN WATSON

Whereas others at the beginning of the 20th century had utilized and emphasized various aspects of Darwin's work, John Watson basically ignored it. His work set psychology on the course of emphasizing environmental explanations for behavior and rejecting the theoretical value of internal concepts such as instincts. This called into question the value of studying such topics as consciousness and other internal processes. John Watson set the course of only studying observable behavior with his 1913 paper *Psychology as the Behaviorist Views It.* Although he endorsed Darwin's thesis that there were no fundamental differences between human behavior and animal behavior, Watson's other points were in direct opposition. Specifically, Watson suggested that the proper study of psychology was behavior and not the mind. Further, Watson saw the goal of psychology as identifying environmental conditions that direct behavior. Under no circumstances should the theory make reference to consciousness, mind, or other internal unobservable events. Partly as a reaction against those who sought to infer conscious processes from behaviors in animals, and partly from the failure of introspection in humans as a technique for describing mental processes, Watson created a psychology based on observable behaviors alone. This position allowed for and supported the development of a strong stimulus-response psychology. Watson's statement emphasizing the role of the environment in development is well known:

> Give me a dozen healthy infants, well-formed, and my own specified world to bring them up in and I'll guarantee to take any one at random and train him to become any type of specialist I might select—doctor, lawyer, artist, merchant-chief, and yes, even beggar-man and thief, regardless of his talents, penchants, tendencies, abilities, vocations, and race of his ancestors. (Watson, 1930, p. 82)

As the quote implies, Watson assumed that there existed "talents, penchants, tendencies, abilities" that were part of an individual, but that these could be overridden by environmental factors. In fact, Watson demonstrated that an 11-month-old infant named Little Albert could be conditioned to fear an animal such as a lab rat that the infant had previously enjoyed playing with (Watson & Rayner, 1929). The procedure was to create a loud noise when the infant was observing the animal. The pairing of the aversive noise and the animal led to conditioned fear. Watson's demonstrations with Little Albert appear in many introductory textbooks. However, what is left out is the finding that fear conditioning did not always work, was of short duration, or worked better with evolutionally relevant objects, such as animals, but less so with a bag of wool or with person-made objects such as a wooden toy (cf., English, 1929; Watson & Rayner, 1920). Further, if the infant was able to self-regulate through such procedures as sucking his thumb, then fear conditioning did not work.

B. F. SKINNER

B. F. Skinner became the 20th century's most vocal proponent of behaviorism. Beginning with his 1938 book, *The Behavior of Organisms*, Skinner played a significant role in experimental psychology until his death in 1990. His exemplar experimental procedure was to demonstrate that an animal, generally the laboratory rat or pigeon, could be taught to make specific responses if, after the occurrence of the desired response, the animal was given a reward, generally food. This procedure came to be known as **operant conditioning**. The basic procedure noted that behavior could be elicited or shaped if **reinforcement** followed its occurrence. Consequently, if these behaviors ceased to be rewarded, their occurrence would decrease. Thus, the emphasis was on behaviors and the rewards that follow them, as opposed to the environmental stimuli evoking them. What was often ignored in the larger theory was that operant procedures required the organism to be in a deficit state, such as hunger. Nevertheless, the theory was often applied to larger societal and human conditions. For example, in a highly controversial book, *Beyond Freedom and Dignity*, published in 1971, Skinner suggested that such concepts as freedom, will, dignity, and other concepts referring to the mind or internal states have no explanatory value. One should only be interested in the relationship between behavior and consequences, according to Skinner. Even processes such as language learning were seen to be the result of words being reinforced and learned one at a time. In this manner, any type of complex behavior was seen to be the result of learning simple behaviors that were then chained together. Although Skinner saw both operant and classical conditioning as products of evolution, his larger metatheory suggested the individual was shaped by environmental conditions (Skinner, 1981). The larger implication was that humans came into the world ready to be influenced by the reinforcement contingencies of the environment to determine their development and actions in the world. Both Skinner and Watson left us with a psychology that emphasized the environment and ignored any discussion of internal processes or mechanisms for understanding life. However, even during this period, there were others who noticed the inability of behaviorism to examine common phenomena encountered in everyday life.

Return to Evolutionary Thinking

Broadly, the behaviorist paradigm suggested that there were few patterns of responding that were not learned in a step-by-step manner. The metaphor used was a blank slate. The meaning of this metaphor was that nothing was known that was not first learned through experience. As we will see throughout other chapters of this book, a variety of researchers found their results inconsistent with this formulation of the brain. In terms of perception, the Gestalt movement demonstrated the variety of visual processes that work in an automatic manner. In their theories, they also anticipated current work on infant perception of faces and sounds (Murray & Farahmand, 1998), which has shown that from birth, infants react differently to certain sounds or faces, a position inconsistent with Watson's suggestion that infants come into the world as basically blank slates. In terms of emotional expression, Paul Ekman (1973) has demonstrated that facial expressions and their interpretation appear similar throughout the world, in spite of the culture in which one has grown up. John Bowlby (1969, 1982) studied the emotional attachment of children who grew up in orphanages during World War II. These children, although they had their physical needs met, responded differently to interpersonal human contact than did children raised with a loving, giving caregiver. This is clearly in opposition to the Watson position that children do not need emotional responses in infancy. Harry Harlow (1959; Harlow, McGaugh, & Thompson, 1971) followed up on this work experimentally in his study of monkeys raised in isolation with artificial mothers formed of either wire mesh alone or wire mesh covered in terrycloth. Even though feeding was associated with the wire mesh mother, the infant monkeys would still run to the cloth one when they were afraid. All of this research runs counter to the behaviorist position that learning is not related to the evolutionary significance of the stimuli. Even those who studied learning in rats were punching holes in the behaviorist paradigm. For example, Garcia, Kimeldorf, and Koelling (1955) demonstrated a type of one-trial learning that can be best understood in terms of its evolutionary significance. In a series of studies, Garcia and colleagues paired a particular food with radiation, which produced sickness in the animals. In this situation,

the rats would no longer eat that food. Thus, only a single trial could produce food avoidance. Pairing other stimuli, such as lights or sounds, with
the nausea could not produce the same effects. The one-trial avoidance of
foods associated with nausea is also a common occurrence in humans. We
have all eaten a food, become sick a few hours later, and then felt repulsed
by that food afterward. The work of Garcia and others helped psychology
ask why certain processes were special and could be learned so quickly, or
even why certain processes exist at all. One important answer to these
types of questions led to the re-emergence of the evolutionary perspective.

Except for the period following World War II, with social psychology's
emphasis on group behavior in terms of team processes, obedience, and
persuasion, psychology has largely focused on the individual and his or her
relation to the environment. The evolutionary perspective invites greater
consideration of individuals in groups as well as the functioning of group
behavior. If you think about it, you will realize that humans have always
lived in groups with other humans. Thus, not only do individuals live in a
natural world, but they also live in a culture, and this social world is an
additional coupling that the human organism experiences. For example,
we know that such seemingly different human activities as religious cere-
monies and the production of beer and wine have been a part of human
history for thousands of years. Yet, psychology rarely considers the role
these processes have played in human behavior and experience. The evolutionary perspective helps us to see such activities in a different light.
From this perspective, we can consider how today's football games or rock
concerts are similar to gatherings in the coliseum in Ancient Rome or even
earlier gatherings of human beings.

SUMMARY

The study of evolution is the study of the various pathways that lead to the current structure and function of a specific organism. It asks both "how" and "why" questions in relation to our evolutionary history. An understanding of evolution begins with the idea that
all life on earth is related. Part of the focus of evolution is to understand the pathways
various organisms followed over time, including where their energy was expended in order
to ask three major questions. The first question is how to survive. The second is how to
choose a mate and reproduce. And the third is how to relate to others and the calculus of
social relationships. The major scientist associated with the development of the field of
evolution is Charles Darwin. His travels around South America in the 1880s enabled him
to formulate his ideas about natural selection and sexual selection and the role of variation
and adaptation in nature. Although Darwin influenced psychological theories up until the
20th century, there was a period beginning in the early part of the 20th century when
evolutionary thinking was largely ignored. Only at the end of the 20th century was psychology influenced by evolution and the neurosciences.

STUDY RESOURCES

Review Questions

1. What is evolution?

2. What are the types of problems we have to solve today? How are these similar to and different from those of our ancestors?

3. What is the difference between proximate questions and ultimate questions? Give an example of each from an evolutionary perspective.

4. What does it mean to say that science is a way of knowing? What are some ways that the scientific method has been applied to the study of evolution and evolutionary psychology?

5. There is no single theory of evolution, especially as related to psychology, but there is a general set of principles to guide research. This chapter lists 11 of these principles. What are they?

6. In what way is the work of Charles Darwin critical to the foundations of a scientific psychology?

7. Define the following concepts introduced by Darwin's theory of evolution: natural selection, species, environment, adaptation, variation, sexual selection. How has our understanding of these concepts changed since Darwin's time?

8. How does Cartwright summarize the essence of Darwin's theory of evolution?

9. Many scientists since Darwin's time have incorporated evolutionary thought into their work. What are the contributions of the following scientists to the development of an evolutionary perspective of human psychology: George Romanes; Lloyd Morgan; Francis Galton; Ernst Heinrich Haeckel; Sigmund Freud; Carl Jung; William James?

10. At the beginning of the 20th century, the behaviorist perspective stood in opposition to the evolutionary perspective. Who were two of its major proponents, and what was their concept of the proper study of human psychology?

11. What recent research results can you cite that show inconsistencies—or incompleteness—in the behaviorist perspective?

For Further Reading

Barkow, J., Cosmides, L., & Tooby, J. (Eds.). (1992). *The adaptive mind.* New York: Oxford University Press.

Darwin, C. (1859). *On the origin of species by means of natural selection.* London: J. Murray.

Dawkins, R. (2009). *The greatest show on earth: The evidence for evolution.* New York: Free Press.

Gruber, H. (1974). *Darwin on man: A psychological study of scientific creativity.* New York: Dutton.

Mayr, E. (2001). *What evolution is.* New York: Basic Books.
Sulloway, F. (1983). *Freud: Biologist of the mind.* New York: Basic Books.
Weiner, J. (1994). *The beak of the finch.* New York: Alfred A. Knopf.
Zimmer, C. (2001). *Evolution: The triumph of an idea.* New York: HarperCollins.

Key Terms and Concepts

- What is evolution?
- How and why questions
- Understanding behavior from an evolutionary perspective
- Science as a way of knowing
- The evolutionary approach
  - Charles Darwin
    - Sailing of the HMS *Beagle*
    - The Galápagos Islands
    - Variation in nature
    - Natural selection
- Evolution after Darwin
  - Evolution is still taking place
  - Sexual selection
  - Psychological processes
- In the tradition of Darwin
  - Research across species and comparative psychology
  - Understanding individual differences and development
    - Francis Galton
    - Development
  - Understanding psychopathology
    - Sigmund Freud
    - Carl Jung
  - The value of understanding function
    - William James
- Ignoring evolutionary thinking
  - John Watson
  - B. F. Skinner
- Return to evolutionary thinking

SAGE Study Site

Visit the study site at **www.sagepub.com/ray** for chapter-specific study resources.

Glossary Terms

- Archetypes
- Associationism
- Collective unconscious
- Correlation coefficient
- Evolution
- Impulse
- Instinct
- Libido
- Ontogeny
- Operant conditioning
- Paradigm

- Phylogeny
- Proximate questions
- Reflex processes
- Regression line
- Reinforcement
- Repression
- Sexual energy
- Sexual selection
- Ultimate questions
- Variation

Genetic Perspectives 3

Think about who you are. What do you look like and what psychological traits do you possess? Do you have blue eyes? Are you color blind? Is your skin black or brown or white or yellow or some combination? Although we don't often think in these terms, it should be obvious that the way you answer these questions has a lot to do with decisions your parents made. Actually, decisions your parents' parents made, and their parents, and so on likewise play a role. Who your ancestors mated with determined many of your characteristics today. If they mated with someone who had a variation in a single gene—MC1R, for example—you would have red hair and find it difficult to tan when in the sun. Evolution works by genetic transmission. This is the focus of the present chapter. However, to form a complete evolutionary psychology, we must also consider other ways that information is passed from generation to generation. In addition to genetic transmission, information can be transferred by epigenetic, behavioral, and symbolic means (for an in-depth discussion, see Jablonka & Lamb, 2005). For example, as we will also see in this chapter, it is possible for behaviors that your parents, or even grandparents, engaged in to influence you. This is not actually the result of changes in your genes but changes in the mechanisms that turn your genes on and off, a process called *epigenetics*. In later chapters, I will discuss other ways that information can be acquired through learning and imitation as well as cultural processes.

In his theory of natural selection, Darwin stressed variations in heritable traits and the manner in which different environments place specific traits at an advantage. What Darwin did not know at the time he was writing was the specific unit involved in this process, which today we call the **gene**. Genes carry the instructions that direct the expression of particular traits. As we begin to understand the role of genes, we see how this is critical to our understanding of evolution. In fact, one view in the history of science is that the loss of interest in evolutionary approaches during the first half of the 20th century was due to the lack of an articulated connection between genetics and evolution. This has historical precedence. Although they were unknown to each other, at about the same time Darwin was working, the initial mechanisms by which genes work was being described by Gregor Mendel. Mendel worked in a monastery in a city near Vienna, which is now part of the Czech Republic, and Darwin worked on his farm in Down, England. During the latter part of the 19th century, the work of Darwin and Mendel and their followers occupied parallel tracks. It was with the publication of Dobzhansky's *Genetics and the Origins of Species* in 1937 that these two lines of research came together in what is now referred to as the modern synthesis (Huxley, 1942/2010; Mayr, 1942).

WHAT GENES DO

Almost daily we hear about how a person was cleared of a crime because of DNA testing or learn that a suspect was linked to a crime scene using DNA found in skin cells on a steering wheel, pet hairs on clothing, or saliva on a cigarette butt (see Jobling & Gill, 2004). In medicine, new discoveries relate a person's genetic makeup to certain diseases. Contemporary textbooks in behavioral genetics point to important new research showing which psychological traits appear to be genetically linked and which are not (cf. Plomin, DeFries, McClearn, & McGuffin, 2008). We discover in children that ADHD (attention deficit hyperactivity disorder) is heritable but that aggressive and disruptive conduct is not. We also learn that early Alzheimer's disease is related to a particular gene on chromosome 14. The critical question is the manner in which genes and behavior are related.

Sometimes we see the work of genes in everyday life but never realize what we are seeing. Take diet, for example. When you go to a traditional Chinese restaurant, there is very little in the way of dairy products, whereas you see cheeses, sauces with cream, and other forms of dairy products in a traditional French meal. Why is this so? Of course, one explanation could be that the cultures just developed different preferences, and it has nothing to do with genetics. However, you might reconsider this idea if you knew that Northern Europeans have a gene that enables them to continue digesting milk products after the traditional time of weaning. A person with such a gene would have had an advantage in Northern Europe because dairy products are a high quality food source and over time, probably less than 10,000 years, that advantage would have allowed these genes to be passed on to almost all the European population. Other work has shown that agricultural societies and hunter-gatherers in arid environments who consume food with a large starch content have accumulated extra copies of a particular gene (AMY1), which is related to a protein in one's saliva that breaks down starch (Perry et al., 2007). Rainforest hunter-gatherers and other groups that eat foods with less starch do not show these extra copies of the gene. Overall, these types of studies suggest that in evolutionary time, diet can play a role in genetic selection.

An important question is, How many generations does it take for genes to change? An interesting study has shown that ethnic Tibetans split from Han Chinese fewer than 3,000 years ago (Yi et al., 2010). Tibetans have the ability to work at high altitudes with low oxygen levels. This suggests that, as with European milk-digesting abilities, genetic mutations may be involved. The Tibetan study compared the genomes of 50 Tibetans and 40 Han Chinese and discovered that a variety of genes related to how oxygen is used by the body were different in the Tibetans as compared to the Han Chinese. One of these genes is referred to as EPAS1 and is also seen in individuals with high-level athletic performance. What is interesting is that the genetic changes happened in fewer than 3,000 years.

Many people are under the impression that if a person has a particular gene, then whatever activity is connected with that gene will be seen. It could be a negative experience, such as cancer or alcoholism; it could also be a positive experience, such as long life or a strong immune system. However, it is just not that simple. There is a complex pathway between genes and behavior that can be influenced by a variety of factors. To begin with, a gene is simply a part of the total length of DNA. As we shall see later, genes or sequences of DNA tell the body how to manufacture particular proteins. In newspaper and television descriptions of genetic discoveries, the complex turning on and off of our genes is often ignored, especially in relation to disease. What we are led to believe instead is that particular genes produce particular disorders. The problem, of course, is that genes do not exist to make people or animals sick. The manner in which we become sick or display disease is a complex process that involves our genes, but it also involves a variety of environmental factors. As we will see, except for blood type, very few traits are displayed by genes without a complex input and interaction with the environment. Striking examples exist in nature, such as the Squinting Bush Brown butterfly (*Bicyclus anyana*), which is brightly-colored if born in the rainy season, but gray if born in the dry season. The side-blotched lizard of the Mojave Desert will also have different colorings depending on its environment. It will be black if it is raised in a habitat of black lava flow and lighter if raised in light desert sand. The advantage of this tight coupling with the environment is that it offers a means of protection. Environmental couplings may also promote health and well-being. With some disorders, simply changing the environmental conditions in terms of the types of food a person eats can actually prevent the negative outcomes of a genetic disorder. Even more surprising is that if you are a mouse, what your mother ate can influence the color of your fur and the diseases you are susceptible to. As we begin to study the genetic relationships with those aspects of behavior and experience that psychologists consider most crucial to study, it becomes even more complicated. In considering the role of genetic and environmental factors in behavior and experience, we can recall Darwin's (1859) reminder that "how infinitely complex and close-fitting are the mutual relations of all organic beings to each other and to their physical conditions of life" (p. 80). That is, genetic and environmental factors are mutually dependent upon one another.

One striking example of the manner in which cultural and environmental change can be mapped along with genetic change is that of lactose tolerance (Wade, 2006; Tishkoff et al., 2007). Lactose is a sugar found in milk. The infants of most mammals, including humans, can no longer digest milk once weaned. What gives infants the ability to digest lactose are certain enzymes in the milk of their mothers, which work with the infant's own genes to break down the lactose. Actually, it is a single dominant gene that is involved in the production of the enzyme that breaks the milk sugar down. Without the enzyme, anyone drinking milk can feel sick with symptoms including cramps, diarrhea, and nausea. However, some humans currently living in Europe, India, and sub-Saharan Africa and their descendants continue to be able to drink milk into adulthood. How did this happen? It appears that when cattle were first domesticated some 9,000 years ago, humans began to eat their meat and drink their milk. Some of the people living at that time had a mutation that kept the gene involved in producing the enzyme that enabled the individual to digest milk sugar permanently switched on. Given that these individuals did not become sick from drinking milk, they had a certain advantage, particularly in difficult times such as droughts. In fact, it is has been estimated that individuals with the mutation were able to leave almost 10 times as many descendants as those without it (Tishkoff et al., 2006). This is demonstrated today by the fact that almost all of the citizens of the Netherlands and Sweden, the area where cattle were originally domesticated in Europe, are lactose tolerant. Further, it is thought that lactose tolerance developed independently in different parts of the world. Overall, this shows the manner in which cultural and environmental changes can produce a shift in the genetics of a specific population.

As psychologists, we are particularly interested in the manner in which genes influence developmental processes by influencing interactions with the environment. Likewise, environmental conditions influence which genetic programs are expressed. A basic distinction in terminology is made between the genotype and the phenotype. The **genotype** consists of what is inherited through the sperm and the egg at the moment of conception. The **phenotype** represents the observed traits of the individual including morphology, physiology, and behavior. The focus of psychology has largely been the study of the phenotype. In this chapter, I want to begin on the level of the genotype and describe the factors that lead from the genotype to the phenotype. I'll begin with a discussion of the **genome**, or the complete set of human genes. We care about the complete set of human genes because of its ability to carry the recipe of life from generation to generation. This is the biological mechanism by which evolution works. The process is described in a number of basic biology books (e.g., Starr & Taggart, 2006), genetics texts (e.g., Cummings, 2009), DNA texts (e.g., Micklos & Freyer, 2003), and behavioral genetics texts (e.g., Carey, 2003; Plomin et al., 2008).

FUNCTIONS OF GENES

Let us first look at the players in the drama of life and then the mechanisms by which inheritance takes place. One of the founders of the field of molecular biology, Max Delbrück (1949), suggested that when we look at living cells, what we are seeing is the result of billions of years of experimentation. All of us begin as a single fertilized egg, which by the time of birth has given us a body with about one trillion cells (that's 1,000,000,000,000 cells)! These cells can be differentiated in terms of structure and function. The cells in your muscles do different things from those in your brain. The same can be said of those of your liver or heart. However, in each of the cells there is a nucleus that contains the genome, which in humans is the set of some 20,000 genes along with some additional material. Other organisms have a different number of genes, although the basic mechanism is similar across species. In fact, many of our genes are also found in other organisms and perform similar functions. The job of a gene is to lay out the process by which a particular protein is made. Said technically, each gene is able to encode a protein. I will describe how this is accomplished later, but for now, what is important is that the output is a protein. Proteins are involved in a variety of processes. Functionally, proteins in the form of enzymes are able to make metabolic events speed up, whereas structural proteins are involved in building body parts. Similar proteins in insects are involved in creating such structures as spider webs, butterfly wings, and feathers. Proteins are diverse and complex; they are found in the foods we eat and are made by our cells from some 20 amino acids. Proteins serve as signals for changes in cell activity, as illustrated by hormones. Proteins are also involved in health and disease as well as development and aging. Thus, proteins do the work of the body and genes influence their production.

Although the cells in the body carry the full set of genetic information, only a limited amount related to the function of the cell is expressed at any one time. That is to say, although a large variety of proteins could be produced at any one time, there is selectivity as to what is produced related to internal and external conditions. Further, the location of the genes makes a difference, in that cells in your brain produce different proteins from those in your muscles, liver, heart, and so on.

GENES AND THEIR EXPRESSION

Before continuing, let's think about some of the implications for a gene encoding a protein. First, a gene does not produce a protein constantly: Protein is produced in the context of a complex physiological system influenced by internal bodily processes and by events in the external environment. Thus, we can think of a gene being turned on (produce the protein) or turned off (do not produce the protein) relative to specific events. The bottom line is that just because a person *has* a specific gene does not mean that it will necessarily be *expressed*. Second, the environment in which a person develops and lives plays an important role in gene expression. Even identical twins with the same genotype can display different phenotypes if their environmental conditions differ during their development. For example, if one was to grow up in a high mountain range and the other in a below-sea-level desert, important physiological differences, such as lung capacity and function, would be apparent. Thus, as we will see, there are few human processes that can be explained by genetic factors alone. It is equally true that few human processes can be explained entirely by the environment. Third, although I will attempt to make human genetics understandable and attempt to keep it simple, we should remember that there are few human factors of interest to psychologists that can be explained entirely by a single gene. Rather, what we view in human processes represents not only a complex interaction between a person's genetic makeup and the environment, but also a complex expression of many genes. Fourth, thinking of a gene's ability to encode a protein, we should also realize that we should not speak of a gene *producing* a behavior. Rather, we must remember that a gene encodes a protein, which can have *implications* for actions, feelings, and thoughts. Although there are implications, it does not necessarily follow that the behavioral outcome was the result of a genetic plan alone. This is a complex process that involves a variety of levels, especially in humans. Even in insects, there are a variety of steps involved in most behavioral processes. For example, if the appropriate genes in a spider do not produce certain proteins, then through a series of steps, the web will end up misshapen. Given the various mechanisms involved, it is really not accurate to talk about "a gene for" misshapen spider webs. Thus, when we hear or read about the gene for misshapen spider webs or disorders or any of the other traits, we must consider what protein was produced under what conditions, as well as the steps required. We will have the opportunity to reconsider these questions in greater detail in other chapters in this book (see Chapters 5 and 14). At this point, it will be useful to move to a structural level in our consideration of genetics. Let us begin with DNA.

DNA

The events leading James Watson and Francis Crick to discover the double helix structure of DNA in 1953 is a well-known story (Watson & Crick, 1953a, 1953b). Watson and Crick wrote fascinating narratives describing how this discovery came about (Crick, 1988; Watson, 1968, 2007) as well as a number of books concerning DNA (Watson, 2000, 2003). In 2003, a number of journals celebrated the 50th anniversary of this event with special editions. Before describing the event, let's see how we got to that discovery. In 1868, almost 100 years before Watson and Crick, a physician named Johann Friedrich Miescher collected cells from the pus of open wounds as well as the sperm of fish. Miescher was interested in identifying the chemical composition of the nucleus of the cell. What he discovered was an organic compound with the properties of an acid, which he called *nuclein.* Today we know nuclein as DNA, the storehouse of information concerning heritable traits (see Dahm, 2008, for a history of Miescher's discovery of DNA).

Not much was made of the discovery in Miescher's day, which coincidently happened within 10 years of both Darwin's and Mendel's publications. Later, during the first part of the 20th century, the basic chemistry of nuclein was worked out, with two forms differentiated in terms of sugar composition. Those forms were **DNA** (deoxyribonucleic acid) and **RNA** (ribonucleic acid). With the developments of physical chemistry and X-ray crystallography, the stage was set for Watson and Crick's discovery. The work that led to the discovery of the structure of DNA included the work of Linus Pauling describing chemical bonds. Later, Pauling and R. B. Corey measured a helical structure, and Maurice Wilkins and Rosalind Franklin created X-ray diffraction photographs of DNA. At this point, the challenge for Watson and Crick was to create a structure that conformed to the laws of physical chemistry and, at the same time, could function as a gene, the carrier of heredity. The answer was a double helix, with each individual rung being made up of a pair of nucleotides that were not similar. I will go into the specifics later.

In one of the more understated pronouncements in the history of science, Watson and Crick (1953a) noted in their *Nature* paper, "It has not escaped our notice that the specific pairing we have postulated immediately suggests a possible copying mechanism for the genetic material" (p. 737). With this discovery, the mechanism by which the hereditary processes suggested by Mendel worked could now be explained. As we shall see, DNA is important for its ability to reproduce itself and its role in producing proteins.

OVERVIEW OF DNA AND RNA

Let's begin with a general description of the process and then become more specific. Overall, DNA provides information necessary to produce proteins. We can think of proteins as a link between the genotype and the phenotype. The question arises, How do we get from information, which is what DNA and RNA are all about, to actual physiological changes? This is accomplished in two steps. First, the information in DNA is encoded in RNA. Second, this information in RNA determines the sequence of amino acids, which are the building blocks of proteins. Technically, the DNA synthesis of RNA is called **transcription**, whereas the step from RNA to protein is called **translation**. RNA is like DNA, except its structure is that of a single strain whereas DNA has a double strain. Once encoded, the RNA goes to a part of the cell capable of producing proteins. Proteins are produced by putting together amino acids.

STRUCTURE OF DNA

To be more specific, DNA contains the chemical building blocks, or nucleotides, that store information. DNA molecules are composed of two strands, which twist together in a spiral. Each strand consists of four types of nucleotides, which are the same except for one component, a nitrogen-containing base. The four bases are adenine, guanine, thymine, and cytosine. They are generally referred to as A, G, T, and C. The nucleotides are linked by a sugar-phosphate backbone.

Although you can visualize DNA as two strains of beads with four different types of beads, the beads cannot appear randomly. Because of the shape of the molecules in one half of the spiral, they can pair with only certain ones in the other half. Adenine generally pairs with thymine; that is, A pairs with T. Likewise, guanine pairs with cytosine: G with C. These bases A, T, G and C, are repeated millions of times in one long strand to form a chromosome. The particular order of these four bases is called a *sequence*. Using names based on structure, the beginning of a DNA strand is called 5' (five prime) and the end 3' (three prime). The two strands of the double helix contain the same information, albeit in opposite directions. That is, one strand in the DNA molecule runs 5' to 3', and the other runs 3' to 5'. To give you some sense of size, each full twist of the DNA double helix is 3.4 nanometers (i.e., one billionth of a meter). Said in other terms, if we took the DNA in the 46 chromosomes of a single human cell and stretched it out, it would be around 6 feet long (see Figure 3.1).

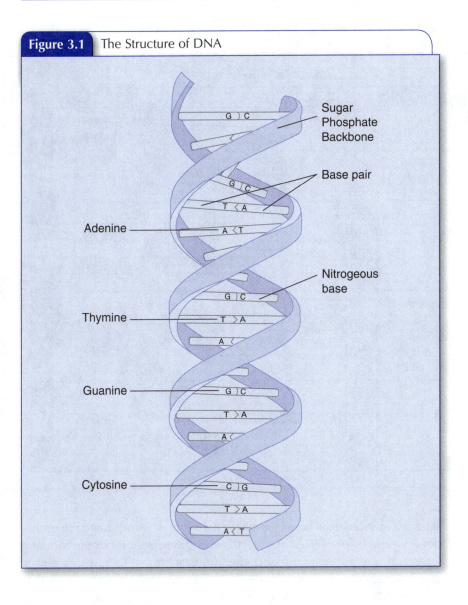

Figure 3.1 The Structure of DNA

STRUCTURE OF RNA

Like DNA, which contains the four bases adenine, guanine, thymine, and cytosine, RNA also contains four bases. However, in RNA the thymine has been replaced with uracil, which is referred to as U. The RNA code is a sequence of three of these letters along a single RNA strand, which specifies one particular amino acid. This sequence of three bases is called a **codon**. These sequences determine which of 20 amino acids are put together to form a specific protein. The table of correspondences between codons and amino acids is called the **genetic code**. As you can see in Figure 3.2, there can actually be more than one codon for the same amino acid. There are also sequences that signal the beginning and end of the protein chain, called

Figure 3.2   Table of Human Amino Acids

First base of codon	Second base of codon				Third base of codon
	U	**C**	**A**	**G**	
U	UUU UUC Phenylalanine phe UUA Leucine leu UUG	UCU UCC Serine ser UCA UCG	UAU Tyrosine tyr UAC UAA STOP codon UAG	UGU Cysteine cys UGC UGA STOP codon Tryptonphan trp UGG	U C A G
C	CUU CUC Leucine leu CUA CUG	CCU CCC Proline pro CCA CCG	CAU Histidine his CAC CAA Glutamine gin CAG	CGU CGC Arginine arg CGA CGG	U C A G
A	AUU Isoleucine ile AUC Methionine met AUA AUG {start codon}	ACU ACC Threonine thr ACA ACG	AAU Asparagine asn AAC AAA Lysine lys AAG	AGU Serine ser AGC AGA Arginine arg AGG	U C A G
G	GUU GUG Valine val GUA GUG	GCU GCC Alanine ala GCA GCG	GAU Aspartic acid asp GAC GAA Glutamic acid glu GAG	GGU GGC Glycine gly GGA GGG	U C A G

start and stop codons. There is some thought that RNA originated in evolutionary time before DNA, in that it is also the genetic molecule in many viruses. It also possesses a higher mutation rate than DNA, which means that it can change its form quickly. The practical implication of this is that viruses such as HIV (human immunodeficiency virus) are difficult to control because they have the ability to change quickly.

DNA, which is the information storage molecule, transfers information to RNA, which is the information transfer molecule, to produce a particular protein. Further, change in the rate at which RNA is transcribed controls the rate at which genes produce proteins. The expression rate of different genes in the same genome may vary from 0 to approximately 100,000 proteins per second. Thus, genes not only produce proteins, they do so at different rates. The crucial question becomes what causes a gene to turn on or turn off.

Jacques Monod and François Jacob, in classic research performed in the 1960s, came to an initial understanding of how genes turn on and off (see Jacob, 1998; Monod, 1972 for overviews). The particular organism they were studying was the bacterium *Escherichia coli*. This organism can switch from a diet of sugar (glucose) to milk sugar (lactose) if glucose in its environment becomes scarce. To make this happen, these bacteria must produce an enzyme that breaks down lactose. What Monod and Jacob discovered was that an environmental event, the presence of lactose and the absence of glucose, would cause the genes to turn on and the enzymes to be produced. When this environmental condition was not present, these enzyme-producing genes were inhibited and thus not allowed to turn on. Said in the language of genes, the transcription of the DNA into RNA and the resulting proteins were repressed when the environmental condition of lactose presence and glucose absence existed. This tells us that genes are designed to perform specific tasks depending on the presence of certain internal or external environmental conditions. Thus, we cannot have a complete picture of behavior and experience without understanding both the genetic and environmental conditions. Even larger organizational structures, such as whether an organism becomes male or female, in some species relates directly to the environmental conditions during its development and the genes that are turned on and off.

METAPHORS OF DNA

As we talk about DNA, we should realize that scientists use various metaphors to describe its function. Dorothy Nelkin (2001) has reviewed these different metaphors, which range from "master molecule" to "blueprint of life." One common metaphor is that of a language and particularly that of a code. This is an easy metaphor to adopt given that the chemical bases are designated by letters and that the particular order of the DNA information determines the genetic information encoded. A blueprint or plan used to construct a building is also a common metaphor. Because the chemical composition of DNA is represented by letters, some researchers describe our DNA as a book, with chromosomes analogous to the chapters and genes to the particular paragraphs. Another metaphor used by Richard Dawkins in *The Selfish Gene* (1989) and Matt Ridley in *Nature via Nurture* (2003b) is that of a recipe. Each of these metaphors is a useful way to help us reduce complex processes to an analogy we can understand. One problem, of course, is that metaphors may lead us to think about a concept in ways that may not be accurate. Previously, scientists described the brain as a telephone switchboard and the eye as a camera. Neither of these metaphors proved to be an adequate description. In addition to linguistic metaphors, scientists also use various graphic representations of DNA, as can be seen in Figure 3.3.

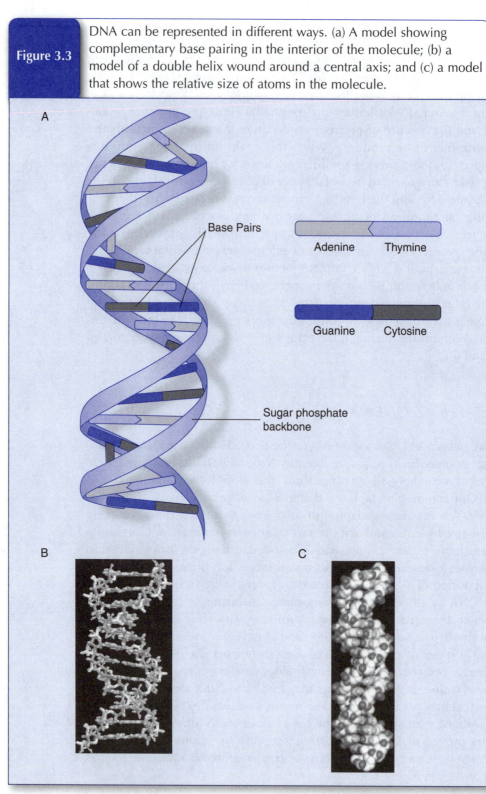

Figure 3.3 DNA can be represented in different ways. (a) A model showing complementary base pairing in the interior of the molecule; (b) a model of a double helix wound around a central axis; and (c) a model that shows the relative size of atoms in the molecule.

A

Base Pairs

Adenine   Thymine

Guanine   Cytosine

Sugar phosphate backbone

B

C

From Proteins to Structure and Behavior

In terms of behavior and experience, the production of proteins can be transitory. For example, touching a rat's whiskers causes changes in gene expression in the cells of the sensory cortex of the brain (Mack & Mack, 1992). This is just a momentary change. Changes can also be long term. As we will see when we discuss development, turning on one set of genes may have lasting influence on the ability of other genes to produce specific proteins. For example, when a songbird first hears the specific song of its species, a particular set of genes comes into play that, when once set, determines the song produced by that bird for its entire life. This process has been mapped by a variety of researchers (cf. Mello, Vicario, & Clayton, 1992; Ribeiro & Mello, 2000). Likewise, raising mice in an enriched environment—that is, one with lots of toys and stimulation—will cause increased gene expression in genes that are associated with learning and memory (Rampon et al., 2000). How do we know which genes are involved? In this study, the genes of mice in enriched environments were compared with those of control mice who did not have this experience. Another way to know which genes are involved in a process is to actually change the genes in a particular organism. So-called "knockout" mice are genetically engineered mice in which particular genes have been turned off by breeding them in specific ways. Research shows that simple genetic changes made experimentally in animals can result in protein changes that influence social behavior. Some examples of such behaviors are increased fear and anxiety, increased grooming, hyperactivity, and even increased alcohol consumption when stressed.

In terms of physical development, there are specific genes, called **homeotic genes** or **Hox genes**, that control the timing of development of our body parts. What is fascinating about these Hox genes is that they lay out the basic body plan during development for all species. The same Hox genes that determine where the body parts go in the mouse also do so in the fly and in the giraffe. They do this by switching on other genes during development. The location of these genes along the chromosome corresponds to the body from front to back. That is to say, the first Hox gene develops the front aspects of the body, continuing in order until the final Hox gene develops the posterior aspects of the body. What is intriguing is that these genes are similar across species in such a manner that the first Hox gene, for example, in the fly and mouse are more similar to each other than they are to other genes in the same species (Smith, 1998). What is even more interesting is that Hox genes can be swapped between species with little obvious effect on physical development. This suggests that the same basic genetic developmental system has been retained across a variety of species. What has changed between species is the specific genes that these Hox genes influence. These other genes cause the physical structure of one species to be quite different from another. However, on the level of the Hox gene, the basic mechanism has been retained across species. This has been demonstrated when researchers have inserted the gene responsible for making eyes in mice into a fruit fly and produced the compound eye of the fly. Thus, it is not the basic genes that are different, but their interaction and regulation. In this elegant system, the same basic genes that give the giraffe a long neck give the mouse hardly any neck at all.

GENETICS AND EVOLUTION

One of the real scientific contributions of DNA analysis has been the realization of how similar organisms are in terms of DNA structure. All organic life on this planet shares DNA similarities. Humans have DNA, chimps have DNA, bacteria have DNA, and even flowers have DNA. Given that all organisms have DNA, it is possible to compare how similar different organisms are and, from this, make inferences about common ancestors. We know, for example, that the structure of DNA in chimps and humans is about 97% the same. However, that 3% makes all the difference in the world.

MAPPING THE GENOME

Whereas DNA science began with Watson and Crick, it has come of age with the publication of the map of the human genome in 2001. A DNA molecule along with the proteins that are attached to it is called a **chromosome.** In humans there are 23 separate pairs of chromosomes, making 46 in all. Each chromosome has a unique appearance. The chromosomes are numbered in approximate order of size, with 1 being the largest and 22 being the smallest. These 22 are referred to as **autosomes**. The remaining chromosome pair is called the *sex chromosome* because this chromosome differs in males and females. Females carry two copies of the X chromosome, whereas males carry one X and one Y (see Figure 3.4). By treating the cells with particular dyes, chromosomes can be seen under a microscope. They appear as long, banded cylinder-like structures that are pinched in at one point along their length (see Figure 3.5). The pinched-in region of the chromosome is called the **centromere** and the ends are called **telomeres.** Because the centromere does not equally divide the chromosome, the resultant appearance of a long and short arm is referred to by the letters q (long arm) and p (short arm). The banding patterns of the chromosome are described by number, with the lowest numbers being nearest the centromere. In this system, the chromosome number comes first, followed by the long or short arm designation and then the banded region number. Thus, you would use 7p22 to represent region 22 on the

Males and females have 22 pairs of identical chromosomes, which are numbered by size. Chromosome pair 23 in females has 2 X chromosomes and in males has an X and Y chromosome.

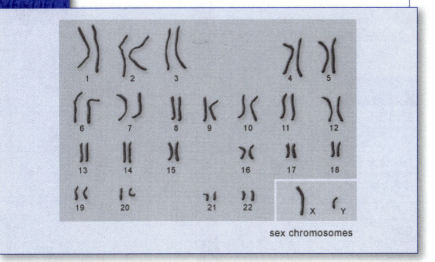

Figure 3.5 Image of Human X and Y Chromosomes

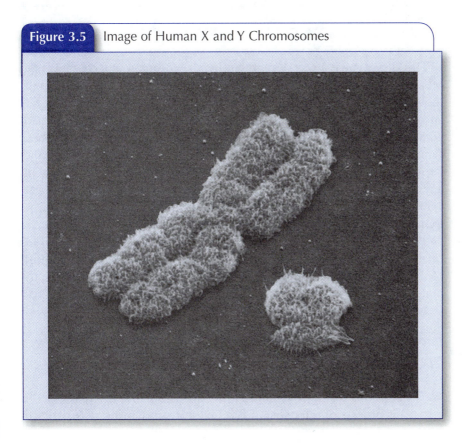

short arm of chromosome 7. A number of websites, such as that of the National Library of Medicine, illustrate each chromosome. The website of the University of Washington Pathology Department (http://www.pathology .washington.edu/galleries/Cytogallery/) shows different methods of illustrating chromosomes. Although similar in structure, other organisms may have more or fewer chromosomes than humans; for example, a fruit fly has 4 and a dog has 39 (see Figure 3.6).

Figure 3.6	Number of Chromosomes in Various Organisms
Goldfish	94
Dog	39
Elephant	28
Chimpanzee	24
Human	23
Guppy	23
Rabbit	22
Cat	19
Fruit fly	4

The **karyotype** is a way of representing the chromosomal contents of a cell, including the number of chromosomes followed by a description of the sex chromosomes. Thus, a human male karyotype would be 46, XY and a human female 46, XX. Each of the chromosomes has been associated with different physiological processes, particularly in terms of genes. Genes are particular stretches of chromosomes that contain all of the heritable bits of information necessary to produce a new individual. On any one chromosome there can be anywhere from a few hundred to almost 3,000 genes. Specific genetic information for each chromosome can be found at http://www.ornl.gov/sci/techresources/Human_Genome/launch pad/. In 1990, the Human Genome Project was started with the goal of cataloging the genetic information found in humans. At this point, most of the approximately 20,000 human genes have been described. The current research related to the project can be seen at http://www.ornl.gov/sci/ techresources/Human_Genome/home.shtml.

CELL DIVISION

We all began as a single cell and ended up with about a trillion (10^{14}) cells. This process of cell division is called **mitosis**. During mitosis, each chromosome is first replicated to form identical pairs that are joined at the centromere. These are referred to as sister **chromatids** until they become separated to form pairs of identical chromosomes.

The cell then divides in such a manner that each new cell has a copy of the original chromosomes. Thus, when a cell divides, the new cell contains the same genetic information as the old. One intriguing and extremely important feature for DNA molecules is that they can replicate themselves. As we have seen, hereditary information is encoded in the particular sequence of the four bases, which forms a unique code that appears to determine species-specific information. DNA structure is important in that it helps to explain how it is replicated before the cell divides. Before division, DNA is replicated by an unwinding of the double-stranded molecule. As this happens, a new complementary strand is assembled piece-by-piece on the exposed bases of each parent strand. That is to say, the parent DNA remains intact but unwound from its pair. A new strand of DNA is then formed on each of these parent strands, which produces two double helixes; half of each is old and half new (see Figure 3.7). This process continues not only during development but throughout life as DNA is replaced and repaired.

VARIATION IN DUPLICATION

The DNA that is duplicated is generally exactly the same as the original DNA. However, there are times that slight variations develop. Mechanisms within our bodies called "proofreading proteins" detect most of these changes and actually correct them. However,

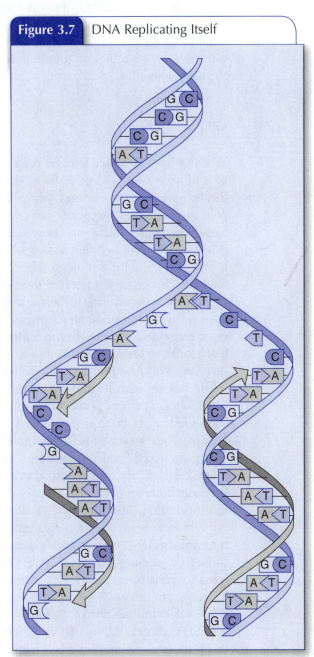

Figure 3.7   DNA Replicating Itself

changes can take place, and these are called **mutations**. Some of these changes in DNA can be slight, as with the alteration of a single base letter, while others can be more extensive. These apparently random mutations, if passed on to the next generation, cause changes in evolution to take place. Changes can also take place as a result of environmental events. Some of these, such as exposure to radiation or toxic chemicals, produce genetic mutations, usually with negative consequences. However, positive consequences are also possible. As we shall see, because of their genetic makeup, some individuals are less likely to contract certain diseases. Thus, within a given individual, mutations may have positive, negative, or neutral effects. For a mutation to influence evolution, it must be passed on to the next generation.

SEXUAL REPRODUCTION

What we have discussed thus far refers to *somatic cells,* which are all of the cells of your body except those related to sexual reproduction. We now look at **germ cells** or **gametes**, which refer to your father's sperm cells and your mother's eggs. In your father's sperm and your mother's egg there is a single copy of the genome, referred to as **haploid**. The production of the gametes is somewhat different from that of mitosis, in that the DNA must be replicated and the diploid number of chromosomes must be reduced to haploid. This process is referred to as **meiosis**.

How does this work? To begin, a germ cell duplicates its DNA. Each duplicated chromosome now consists of two DNA molecules. As in mitosis, these remain attached at the centromere and are called sister chromatids. Unlike mitosis, these chromosomes proceed through two consecutive divisions. We know that each duplicated chromosome migrates within the cell to line up with its partner. At this point, each chromosome is replicated to form pairs of sister chromatids. Then each chromosome becomes connected to its homologue so that all four chromatids are intimately aligned. Thus, we have four DNA molecules, which may later develop into four gamete cells and function in sexual reproduction. However, before that takes place, the chromosomal material is almost randomly exchanged between homologues. This process of gene swapping is referred to as **recombination**. After this process, the chromosomes are no longer identical to those inherited from the parents. Rather, each of the four strands of recombinant DNA contains some material originating from the father and some from the mother (see Figure 3.8). It is this process that eventually leads to variation in the traits of the offspring. To be more specific, a human germ cell has 23 pairs of homologous chromosomes. Thus, 2^{23} or 8,388,608 combinations of chromosomes from a mother and father are possible each time a human germ cell gives rise to sperm or eggs. Without this process everyone would be exactly like his or her parents.

Figure 3.8   Graphic Presentation of Mitosis and Meiosis

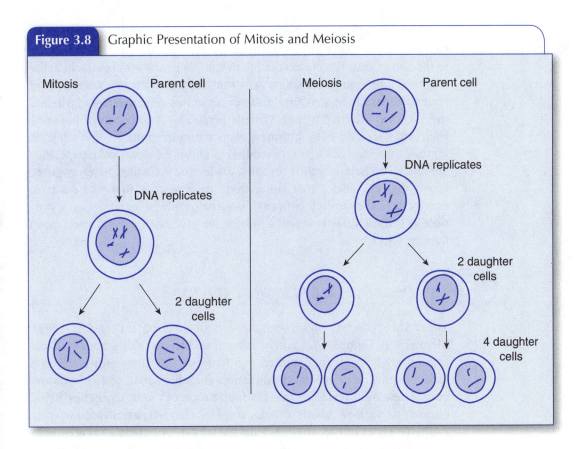

The single cell (soon to be you) that is produced by your mother's egg and your father's sperm is referred to as a **zygote**. To summarize, this single cell divides into two more cells and then these divide, resulting in a ball of eight nearly identical cells. These cells change into a more flattened shape with additional layers forming, which results in eventual formation of body parts such as limbs and organs. This unfolding, especially as related to the development of our brains, will be examined in the next chapter.

VARIATIONS IN GENES

Genes form the blueprint to describe how you are to become. Over our evolutionary history, a majority of our genes reflect little variation. This is why all humans have two eyes and one nose and one mouth. However, perhaps a fourth of all genes allow for variation. What makes things interesting is that the two genes of these pairs are usually slightly different. The technical name for the unique molecular form of the same gene is an **allele**. It has been estimated that of our approximately 20,000 genes, some 6,000 exist in different versions or alleles (Zimmer, 2001). Thus, in each sperm or egg, the alleles inherited from the mother may express different characteristics than those from the father. It is these structural differences that determine many of your characteristics, from the shape of your face to the size of your fingers to whether or not your earlobes are attached. For example, although it is a single gene that determines the development of your earlobes, slight structural differences in this gene determine whether they develop attached or not. When a person has two copies of the same allele, they are said to be **homozygotes** or **homozygous** for that allele. If, on the other hand, they have two different alleles for a particular gene, they are said to be **heterozygous** for those alleles and are called **heterozygotes**. Given that the alleles that come from your mother may not result in exactly the same characteristics as those from your father, variation is possible. It is these variations that allow for the process of natural selection to have its effect.

MENDEL AND INHERITANCE PATTERNS

The study of genetics begins with the work of Gregor Mendel (1823–1884). Mendel was a monk who taught natural science to high school students (see Figure 3.9). Having studied mathematics as well as grown up on a farm, Mendel had a special combination of abilities that led to his discoveries. These discoveries became the foundation of modern genetics. Being curious as to how plants obtain atypical characteristics, Mendel performed a series of experiments with the garden pea plant. Peas are a self-fertilizing plant, which means that the male and female aspects needed for reproduction develop in different parts of the same flower. Therefore, successive generations of peas are similar to their parents in terms of particular traits such as the color of their flowers. Mendel wondered what would happen if he cross-bred pea plants that have one particular trait (e.g., white flowers) with those of another trait (e.g., purple flowers).

During Mendel's lifetime, scientists did not understand the manner in which male and female parents pass traits to their offspring or whether one parent contributes more than the other. Another question of the time was whether the characteristics of the parents actually blended, so that combining a white flower with a red flower would produce a pink flower. In performing his experiments, Mendel was able to clarify these questions and explain the manner in which information is transmitted from parent to offspring. Mendel accomplished this by transferring pollen from one plant's flower

Figure 3.9 Gregor Mendel, whose work with pea plants provided the foundation for the modern study of genetics.

to the flower of another plant. In one series of experiments, Mendel found that when he combined peas with white flowers with those with purple flowers, the next generation had all purple flowers. Allowing this generation to self-fertilize brought forth plants that had purple flowers but also some that had white flowers. Mendel explained these findings by suggesting that a plant inherits information from each parent, the male and female aspect. Mendel was hypothesizing that information must be conveyed. He further suggested that one unit of information could be dominant in comparison to the other, which we now call recessive. In this case, the unit of information that coded for purple would be dominant.

MENDEL'S EXPERIMENTS

By performing numerous experiments on a variety of traits, Mendel noted the relative occurrence of the dominant and recessive information. As Mendel determined the relative frequency of the traits related to hereditary units (what were to be called dominant and recessive genes), he realized that these frequencies could be thought of in terms of the laws of probability. Given two units of information (i.e., genes) related to flower color, one from each parent, we would see the following possibilities:

Purple   Purple

Purple   White

White   Purple

White   White

If purple represented the dominant piece of information, the outcome would be:

Information from Parent		Results in Flower Color
Purple	Purple	Purple
Purple	White	Purple
White	Purple	Purple
White	White	White

Thus you would find the purple flowers 75% of the time and white ones 25%. Of course, as with tossing a penny, the laws of probability would suggest that, in any one generation, the percentage would not be precise.

If you are interested in more than one trait, such as both flower color and height (e.g., dwarf and tall), then you need to consider the probability for each of the outcomes. You first want to know which is dominant and which is recessive. Tallness is dominant and dwarfism recessive. This can be diagrammed as follows:

Information From Parent				Results in Flower Color & Height
Color		Height		
Purple	Purple	Tall	Tall	Purple Tall
Purple	White	Tall	Dwarf	Purple Tall
White	Purple	Dwarf	Tall	Purple Tall
White	White	Dwarf	Dwarf	White Dwarf
Purple	Purple	Tall	Dwarf	Purple Tall
Purple	White	Dwarf	Tall	Purple Tall
White	Purple	Tall	Dwarf	Purple Tall
White	White	Tall	Dwarf	White Tall
Purple	Purple	Dwarf	Tall	Purple Tall
Purple	White	Tall	Tall	Purple Tall
White	Purple	Tall	Tall	Purple Tall
White	White	Tall	Tall	White Tall
Purple	Purple	Dwarf	Dwarf	Purple Dwarf
Purple	White	Dwarf	Dwarf	Purple Dwarf
White	Purple	Dwarf	Dwarf	Purple Dwarf
White	White	Dwarf	Tall	White Tall

Simply counting the four possibilities, we can see that purple-flower tall pea plants happen 9 out of 16 possible times, purple-flower dwarf plants 3 out of 16 times, white-flower tall plants 3 out of 16, and white-flower dwarf pea plants only once out of 16 possible times.

Mendel did not known about genes, but he hypothesized the existence of a specific structure he called "elements." From his experiments, he determined the basic principle that there are two elements of heredity for each trait (e.g., color in the previous example). Mendel assumed that one of these elements can dominate the other, and if it is present, then the trait will also be present. Mendel also suggested that these elements can be nondominant, or recessive. For the recessive trait to appear, both of these nondominant elements must be present. These ideas are referred to as the **law of segregation** or **Mendel's first law**.

Put in today's language, Mendel suggested that alleles of a specific gene exist that account for variations in inherited characteristics and that an

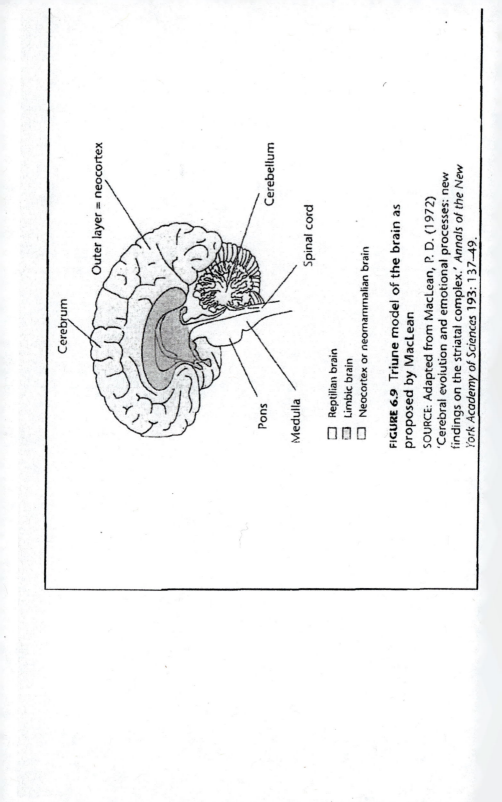

Cerebrum

Outer layer = neocortex

Cerebellum

Spinal cord

Pons

Medulla

☐ Reptilian brain
☐ Limbic brain
☐ Neocortex or neomammalian brain

FIGURE 6.9 Triune model of the brain as proposed by MacLean

SOURCE: Adapted from MacLean, P. D. (1972) 'Cerebral evolution and emotional processes: new findings on the striatal complex.' *Annals of the New York Academy of Sciences* 193: 137–49.

Reptilian brain: Consists of the brain stem, medulla, pons, mesencephalon, basal ganglia, reticular activating system, midbrain and the cerebellum. Its purpose is related to physical survival: digestion, reproduction, breathing, circulation and the execution of the fight or flight response are housed here. Area responsible for basic drives, repetitive and ritualistic forms of behaviour. Involved in 'innate' disposition to establish hierarchies. Also possibly storage of learnt forms of behaviour.

Old mammalian (limbic system): Contains a number of areas concerned with fighting, feeding, self-preservation, sociability, feelings, and affection for offspring. It includes the amygdala ▬▬, the hypothalamus, the mammillary body, the anterior thalamus, the cingulated cortex and the hippocampus. Linked with emotionally charged memories, links emotion and behaviour and so can override the habitual reactions of the reptilian brain. Linked with activities related to food, sex and emotional bonding.

Neomammalian (neocortex): Relatively recent in evolutionary time. Well-developed neocortex found only in higher mammals. Thin sheet of neutrons but highly convoluted. Makes up about two-thirds of brain mass in humans. Receives information from eyes, ears and body wall. Responsible for higher mental functions, well developed in primates, especially humans where it constitutes about five-sixths of the human brain. Processes sensory information and coordinates and plans voluntary movements.

organism receives one allele from each parent. Further, one of these alleles can be dominant or recessive, which determines which characteristics are expressed. Mendel also realized that the inheritance of the gene of one trait is not affected by the inheritance of the gene for another trait. In the previous example illustrating the inheritance of color and height, those factors influencing color do not affect height, and vice versa. That is, the probability for each occurs separately. This fact is known as the **law of independent assortment** or **Mendel's second law**.

Today, the general notation for denoting dominant and recessive traits is to use an uppercase letter to represent a particular dominant trait and a lowercase letter to represent a recessive trait. In our previous example, given that purple flowers and tallness are dominant traits, then a purple-flowered tall pea would be AABB (two pairs of genes are dominant), a purple-flowered dwarf pea would be AAbb, a white-flowered tall pea would be aaBB, and a white dwarf would be aabb. A different way to diagram this situation is called the *Punnett-square method*. The advantage of this method is that it is easier to keep track of all of the possible combinations by noting them in a square. This is shown in Figure 3.10.

In the previous example, you may have noticed that adding a second gene did not just double the number of possible combinations; it produced an exponential increase. If we just consider the possible combinations of a single gene, we have AA, Aa, aA, aa. However, because Aa and aA would result in the same outcome, we actually have three possible genotypes. Adding a second gene would give us nine. The general mathematical rule for any number of gene pairs is 3^n, where n is the number of gene pairs. One important implication of this rule is that complexity increases quickly as the number of gene pairs increases. For example, only 12 gene pairs will produce more than half a million possible genotypes—531,441 to be exact!

Mendel's mathematical calculation performed the critical work to form the basis for modern genetics. He was able to show that traits from the

Figure 3.10	Results of Mendel's Cross-Fertilization Experiments Examining Plant Color and Plant Height			
Punnett Square	**AB** ¼	**Ab** ¼	**aB** ¼	**ab** ¼
AB ¼	AABB 1/16	AABb 1/16	AaBB 1/16	AaBb 1/16
Ab ¼	AABb 1/16	AAbb 1/16	AaBb 1/16	Aabb 1/16
aB ¼	AaBB 1/16	AaBb 1/16	aaBB 1/16	aaBb 1/16
ab ¼	AaBb 1/16	Aabb 1/16	aaBb 1/16	Aabb 1/16

parents do not blend—that is, a red flower and a white flower do not produce a pink one—rather, they remain unchanged in the offspring. This suggested to Mendel that traits were inherited as if they were separate units. He was also able to show that it did not matter whether the traits came from the male or female parent; they combined in the same manner. With the later discovery by others of the main structural unit of inheritance (i.e., the gene), Mendel's work took on great scientific significance.

OVERVIEW

Since Mendel's time we have learned a great deal concerning the process of inheritance. What he referred to as elements or units of information we now call genes. We also know that genes can have alternative forms, which we call alleles. Independent researchers Walter Sutton (2003) and Theodore Boveri (1904), working independently in the U.S. and Germany, suggested the now-accepted fact that genes are carried on chromosomes. We now know that each of the approximately 20,000 human genes occurs at a specific site, called a locus, on one of our 24 different pairs of chromosomes. As genetics progressed in the 20th century, it became clear that it was necessary to go beyond the two laws suggested by Mendel to a more complex understanding of how traits are passed from generation to generation. For example, if two genes are located close to one another on the same chromosome, then the result is different from that predicted by Mendel's second law. As you remember, Mendel's second law as illustrated previously with flower color (Trait A) and tallness (Trait B) would predict offspring representing all four types in terms of the dominant and recessive aspects of these two traits (AB, Ab, aB, ab). However, if the genes are close together on the same chromosome, the result would violate Mendel's second law and produce only two types, dominant for both and recessive for both (AB and ab). The advantage here for scientists is that the logic also works in reverse. That is, when one encounters genes that violate Mendel's second law, it suggests that they reside close together on the same chromosome. This phenomenon is referred to as **linkage**. Let us now turn to other ways of passing genes from generation to generation that do not strictly conform to Mendelian laws. As we examine these non-Mendelian methods of transmission, you will note that the field began with the study of individuals with clearly identifiable disorders (see Ostrer, 1998 for additional information).

Sex-Linked Inheritance

Males and females have partially different genomes; the sex chromosomes are inherited differently for males and females. Females have two X chromosomes and males have an X and a Y chromosome. One implication of this is that genes on the Y chromosome are expressed only in males. Another implication is that some genes on the X chromosome may be expressed at a higher level in females. Researchers are just beginning to understand which characteristics of males and females are influenced by genes on the X and Y chromosome, besides the actual physical differences in terms of sexual organs. Given that females have two X chromosomes, they transmit an X chromosome to all of their offspring whether they are males or females. Thus, everyone receives an X chromosome from his or her mother. Males, on the other hand, transmit an X chromosome to their daughters but not to their sons. Thus, sons cannot inherit an allele on the X chromosome from their fathers. These male offspring receive only a Y chromosome. Because the X and Y chromosomes are different and do not contain identical genes, this sets up the possibility for transmission of traits that can be different for males and females. One implication is that recessive traits on the X chromosome will be expressed in males but not as frequently in females. One common X-linked recessive trait is color blindness. The most common form results in the individual being unable to see red or green as distinct colors (see Figure 3.11). Because this is caused by a recessive allele on the X chromosome, females would need to inherit the allele on both X chromosomes

Figure 3.11   A person with normal color vision can see the number 74 in this Figure.

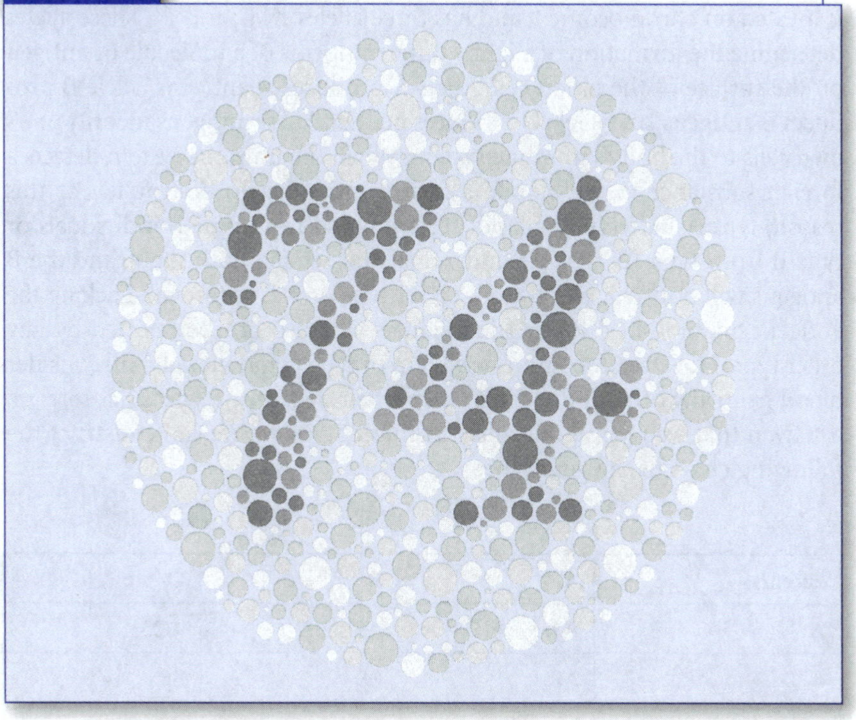

Note: The actual image used in color blind tests will be in color.

for them to be color blind whereas males, having only one X chromosome, would only need to inherit one recessive allele. Sex-linked traits also have different patterns of inheritance throughout generations for males and females. Since fathers do not pass X chromosomes to their sons, a color blind father and a non-color blind mother are not likely to have a color blind son. They might, however, pass the allele on to their daughter whose son could be color blind. That is to say, the daughter would not be color blind but would be a carrier of the color blind allele whereas the grandson would be color blind. In this manner the trait would skip a generation.

CODOMINANT ALLELES AND HUMAN BLOOD TYPING

Blood type is one of the few characteristics that is passed on genetically and is not influenced by the environment. As we will see later in the chapter, this fact offers some advantages for tracing lineage. Most of us learned about blood type in relation to blood transfusions. Although blood transfusions had been used since the early 1800s, it was not until the early 1900s that Karl Landsteiner at the University of Vienna was able to determine why some individuals given a blood transfusion would die while others would survive. His discovery of **blood typing** helped us to understand who could receive blood from which other person. We now know there are four major blood types—A, B, AB, and O. In terms of inheritance, the gene (I) for blood type is located on chromosome 9 and has three alleles I^A, I^B, and I^O. These alleles determine the formation of slightly different forms of a molecule or antigen on the surface of the blood cell. Allele A produces A antigens, allele B produces B antigens, and allele O produces neither. These antigens identify one's own cells to the body's immune system. When the immune system detects a foreign substance in the blood, it creates antibodies to destroy it. For this reason, type A individuals cannot receive blood from type B individuals or type B from type A. Type AB individuals possessing both the A and the B antigens will not treat blood from either type A or B as foreign. Lacking the antigen, the blood of Type O individuals will also not be rejected by any other type. However, the immune system of type O individuals will consider blood from any other individuals except their own type (type O) as foreign.

Given that we receive one allele from each parent, we can construct the following chart of the genotype:

Parents	A	B	O
A	AA	AB	AO
B	AB	BB	BO
O	AO	BO	OO

The expression of these genotypes into phenotypes is more complicated. The A and B alleles are dominant over the O allele. Thus, the AO genotype will result in the A phenotype and the BO genotype will result in the B phenotype. That is to say, you can have type A blood either from receiving an A allele from each of your parents or an A from one and an O from the other. The same is true for type B blood. However, if you receive an A allele from one parent and a B from the other, what blood type would you have? In this situation, both A and B alleles are expressive, a condition referred to as **codominance**. That is, rather than one allele being dominant and one submissive with a single phenotype being expressed, codominance is the situation in which nonidentical alleles produce two separate phenotypes at the same time, which results in blood type AB. Finally, because the O allele is recessive, you will only have type O blood if both your parents have type O blood. We can now complete the previous table to include both genotypes and phenotypes.

Parents	A	B	O
A	AA = Type A	AB = Type AB	AO = Type A
B	AB = Type AB	BB = Type B	BO = Type B
O	AO = Type A	BO = Type B	OO = Type O

Before leaving the question of blood types, I can use this example to illustrate some additional points. First, genes may have more than the two alleles we discussed with the work of Mendel. You may have also considered that the *I* gene had three alleles but that a given individual can carry only two alleles. Thinking about the manner in which genetics works, it is necessary to also consider the population of individuals and the manner in which many alleles of a given gene can exist. Second, it is at the population level that the work of natural selection takes place. Given that different blood types are associated with a differential susceptibility to particular diseases, it is possible for this factor to influence which genes are passed on to the next generation. Third, although genes may be associated with the presence or absence of a certain disease, you should not think of this in terms of a "gene for cancer" or a "gene for schizophrenia." Genes do not exist to give us diseases. Also, the story is extremely complicated, as we shall see. For example, people with type O blood are less likely to develop certain cancers of the esophagus, pancreas, and stomach than people with type A. However, people with type O blood are more susceptible to infection from cholera, whereas people with type AB are less likely to get certain types of diarrhea.

Blood type is also a way to study genetic variation in populations. Although beyond the scope of our present discussion, it is interesting to see how the distribution of blood types differs in various parts of the earth and consider what information this may tell us about historical migrations of people. For example, the distribution of the type B allele suggests a migration of people from Central Asia into Europe. Looking at the maps of blood types in Figure 3.12, we might also conclude that the O blood type is older than either A or B. How might one come to that conclusion? One answer is that there is no place on earth where there are no individuals with the O blood type, but there are places where you cannot find type A or B. Since it exists all over the world, one would assume type O is the oldest.

GENETIC INFLUENCES

One important research topic has been the manner in which genes may protect one from or make one susceptible to certain diseases. Genes that appear to be protective for one disorder may make one more susceptible to another. For example, in the next section we discuss the genetic disorder sickle cell anemia. Although sickle cell anemia can cause a variety of physiological problems, its presence also confers a resistance to malaria. Because sickle cell anemia is most often seen in individuals whose ancestors lived in parts of West Africa, lowland regions of Sicily, Cyprus, Greece, the Middle East, and India, where malaria exists, it is assumed that its presence is a result of natural selection. In terms of diseases such as sickle cell anemia, the same genes can have negative, positive, or neutral effects on the individual, depending on the situation. An important topic just now beginning to be researched extends the study of the genetics of physical disorders to those of psychological disorders. As we will see, a variety of research studies have sought the genetic components of psychological processes. It is also possible to ask the analogous question, Are there psychological disorders that are associated with a resistance to other problems? I will consider this question in the final chapters of this book.

As suggested, the environment may play a differential role in the expression of the phenotype. In the case of blood typing, environmental influences play no role, whereas other physiological and psychological mechanisms are greatly influenced by environmental factors. For example, the common garden plant hydrangea will produce different flower colors depending on how acidic the soil is. In this situation, the alleles are identical but interact with an environmental factor. This is also true of a certain type of rabbit whose fur color is determined by the temperature of its different body regions. The Himalayan rabbit's ears, which are cooler, will have darker fur than the warmer body regions. Finally, although we were only

| Figure 3.12 | These three maps show the percentage of native populations in various parts of the world who have Type A, Type B, and Type O blood. |

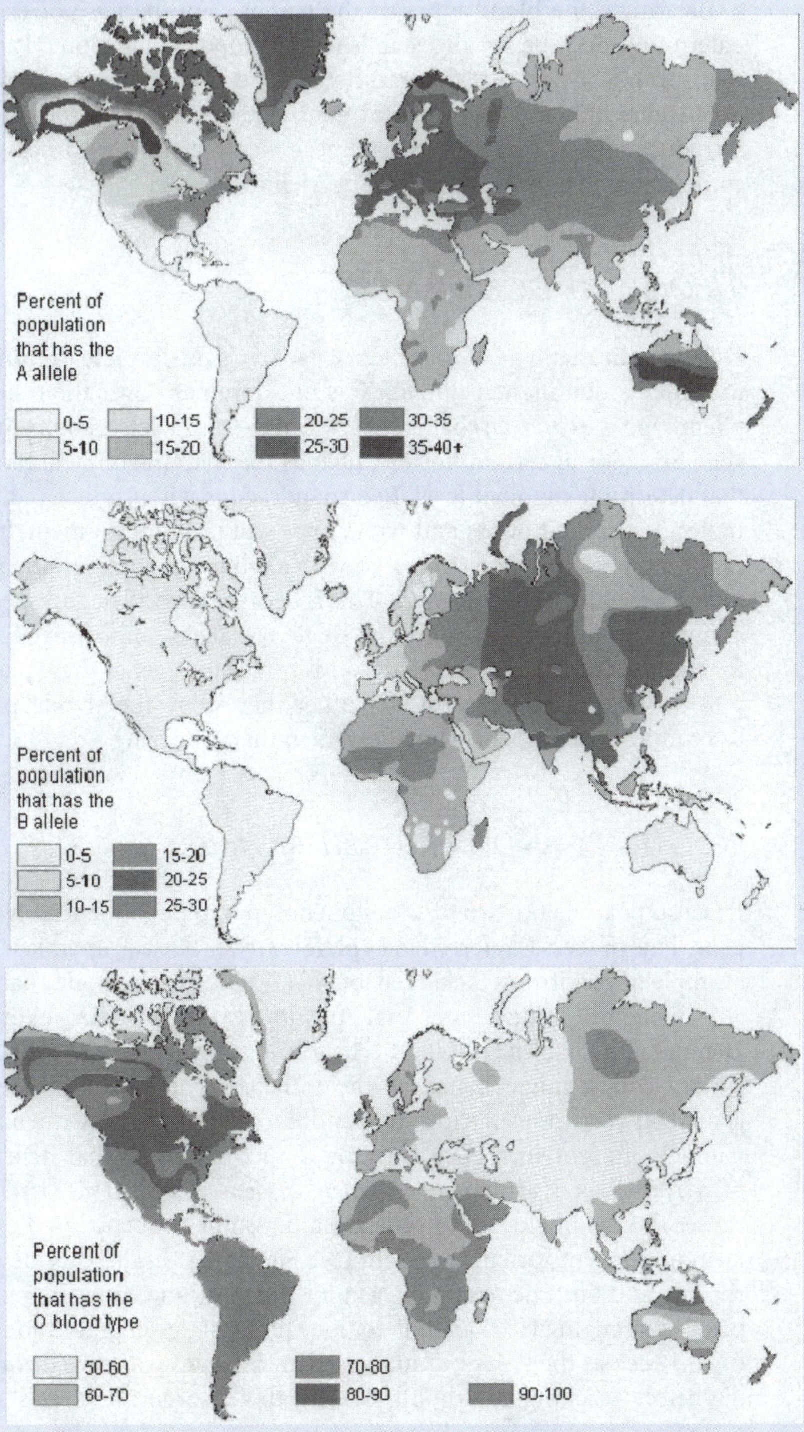

Percent of
population
that has the
A allele

☐ 0-5   ☐ 10-15   ■ 20-25   ■ 30-35
☐ 5-10   ■ 15-20   ■ 25-30   ■ 35-40+

Percent of
population
that has the
B allele

☐ 0-5   ■ 15-20
☐ 5-10   ■ 20-25
■ 10-15 ■ 25-30

Percent of
population
that has the
O blood type

☐ 50-60   ■ 70-80
■ 60-70   ■ 80-90   ■ 90-100

interested in illustrating codominance in discussing blood types, it should be noted that the story may be more complicated because there are exceptions to these rules. That is, knowing the blood type of a child may help you to determine the blood types of the parents, but, because of exceptions, paternity cannot be legally established by blood typing alone. Part of this stems from the fact that the traditional genetic relationships described by Mendel are only the beginning of the story. In the next section, I want to introduce you to some types of inheritance that involve processes more complicated than those described by Mendel.

INCOMPLETE DOMINANCE

One complicated type of inheritance pattern is **incomplete dominance**. In incomplete dominance, one allele is not dominant over the other, and a phenotype is expressed that is in between the two alleles. For example, the gene for color in certain flowers, such as the snapdragon, will have alleles that determine pigment level. Red snapdragons will produce red pigment molecules in the flowers and white ones will produce pigment-free flowers. If a red snapdragon is crossed with a white snapdragon, the resulting offspring will have pink flowers. This is because each allele can specify only a limited amount of pigment; the single red allele cannot specify enough for the flower to be red, so the flower is pink. However, if these plants with pink flowers are crossed with each other, they follow the Mendel principles to produce red, pink, or white flowers in their offspring.

PLEIOTROPY AND SICKLE CELL ANEMIA

It is also possible for two or more phenotypes to be influenced by a single gene. This process is referred to as **pleiotropy**. Sickle cell anemia is a classic example of pleiotropy. Sickle cell anemia results from a single change in an 861-nucleotide-long gene that produces the protein hemoglobin. Hemoglobin enables red blood cells to carry oxygen. Some people have a variant with a single change in the 15th base pair of the β-hemoglobin gene. This variant results in a slightly different amino acid sequence for the hemoglobin protein, which tends to produce molecules that stick together in a rod-shaped arrangement when oxygen is low. This arrangement causes the red blood cell to collapse and assume the shape of a sickle, the farm implement for cutting grain (see Figure 3.13). These sickle cells can rupture and limit necessary oxygen for the body and result in a variety of problems ranging from anemia to poor physical development to failure of organs such as the kidney. If untreated, individuals with this disorder may die before reaching adulthood. Clearly, this disorder illustrates a case in

Figure 3.13 Normal red blood cells, shown on the left, are flat, disk shaped, and indented in the middle. Blood cells characteristic of sickle cell anemia are more elongated and fragile.

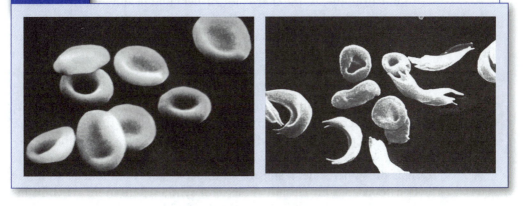

which the expression of the alleles at a single gene location can have dramatic effects at a variety of locations. The allele that controls this aspect of hemoglobin is located on chromosome 11 and is recessive. Thus, both parents must transmit the allele to the offspring for sickle cell anemia to be manifested. What is intriguing about the gene that produces sickle cell anemia is that although it produces a sometimes life-threatening disorder, the gene also protects the person, to some extent, from malaria.

EPIGENETIC PROCESSES

One basic idea from Mendelian genetics was that genes are not changed by experience. What is passed on, except in the case of damage to the gene, is exactly the same gene that was received by the organism from its parents. This came to be called the "central dogma" of molecular biology, as described by Francis Crick. He basically stated that information flow was unidirectional. That is, it went from the gene to the protein. What came to be called "reverse translation" was seen as impossible. Thus, the gene could not be influenced or changed by changes in proteins. This was the basic view from the 1950s until even today. However, as researchers became interested in how genes turn on and off and what factors influence this, it became apparent that the story was more complicated. They discovered that the processes that determine which genes turn on and off could themselves be passed on to the next generation. Of course, the factors that turn the genes on and off are largely influenced by the environment of the organism. Thus, although DNA itself could not be influenced by the environment, it was possible for the environment to influence future generations by changing those processes that turn genes on and off.

This possibility of another form of inheritance came to be called **epigenetic inheritance** (see Hallgrímsson & Hall, 2011 for an overview). A variety of studies have shown that the diet of a mouse mother before conception can influence the hair color of her infants and even her infants' infants (e.g., Cropley, Suter, Beckman, & Martin, 2006). One interesting aspect of this research is the suggestion that a mother's diet can influence future generations, independent of later changes in diet. It has also been shown that a mouse will develop a diabetes-like disease if her father's diet before her conception was high in fat (Skinner, 2010). Fathers can also influence their offspring. If a mouse father is overweight, then gene activity in the pancreas of his offspring is abnormal (Ng et al., 2010). Because the pancreas makes insulin, which regulates blood sugar, the father's obesity may set up the possibility of future diabetes. The opposite is also the case. If the father's diet results in an underweight condition, genes in the liver associated with fat and cholesterol synthesis are more active in his offspring (Carone et al., 2010). Another study suggests that whether a human father smoked early in life was associated with his sons being heaver in weight at age 9 (Pembrey et al., 2006). Overall, this type of research suggests that behavior and experiences at critical periods could later influence characteristics for generations to come. Current health research related to such disorders as diabetes and cancer, as well as types of psychopathology, is suggestive of such a relationship (see Katsnelson, 2010; Os, Kenis, & Rutter, 2010 for overviews). Thus, epigenetic inheritance, which involves tags or markers that determine when genes are turned off or on, offers a parallel track to traditional Mendelian inheritance for influencing phenotypes. Further, a new area of research uses identical twins to study specific epigenetic mechanisms with the goal of determining how genetic and environmental factors influence epigenetics (e.g., Bell & Spector, 2011). This approach may offer better insight into the expression of complex traits.

MITOCHONDRIAL INHERITANCE

Mitochondria are structures within a cell that are involved in the production of energy. It is assumed that mitochondria descended from bacteria that began to live inside single-celled organisms more than a billion years ago. As such, mitochondria have their own DNA (mtDNA), which contains 13 coding genes with about 16,000 base pairs. Thus, a given cell in your body contains both the nuclear DNA that I discussed previously and hundreds of mitochondria and their DNA. What is interesting is that generally mitochondrial DNA is inherited only from your mother, clearly a violation of Mendelian inheritance. This helped researchers to discover the genetic link of certain disorders that show maternal or **mitochondrial**

inheritance patterns, such as Leber's hereditary optic neuropathy, a disorder that results in rapid loss of vision beginning in adolescence. Because mtDNA does not recombine sections of DNA from your mother and father, it is very stable and mutates very slowly. This gives mitochondrial DNA a special application in the study of evolution.

It is possible to use mtDNA to trace evolutionary time over the generations. For example, we could ask how similar in mtDNA were two women, one who lives in Europe and another who lives in Japan. We could also ask how similar are women living in any given country. Researchers have determined that there is more diversity in mtDNA in women living in sub-Saharan Africa. What does this mean? This finding suggests that given that mtDNA changes by mutation alone and very slowly, this location is the place that human females have lived the longest. In fact, researchers suggest that it is possible to trace the mitochondrial DNA present today in humans back to a single female who lived some 150,000 to 200,000 years ago (e.g., Stoneking, 2008). This female has been referred to as "Eve." This is not to suggest that there was only one female at the time. John Maynard Smith suggests that there were approximately 5,000 males and 5,000 females at the time who have contributed to our present genetic makeup (Smith, 1990). However, through a variety of circumstances, the other women did not contribute to modern-day mtDNA. Only Eve's daughters survived. That is to say, somewhere in the generations of offspring from other women of the time, there was a generation with no females. Of course, genetic material from other females could have been passed on through their sons, but this would have no influence on mtDNA. When later genetics of a larger population can be traced to a limited number of individuals, this is referred to as a *founder effect.* Founder effects can also be seen in modern-day communities such as the Amish in Pennsylvania, in which a few individuals created a community that has remained isolated, with intermarriage being common.

In summary, we can use various analytical techniques to compare the mtDNA of two females to determine how similar they are. If they are identical, we would assume that the individuals are related in some manner. However, if they are dissimilar, we would assume that their last common maternal ancestor lived some time ago. One example of this was an examination of Neandertal bones from nine individuals from 43,000 years ago. These were found in a cave in Spain (Rosas et al., 2010). Researchers found similar mitochondrial DNA for three adult males, two teenage males, and one child. However, three adult females were each found to have a different lineage of mtDNA. This suggested that Neandertal males lived in small groups of closely related males, whereas females in the group were from other clans. We can perform these comparisons not only between humans but also between other species. Thus, using mtDNA, it is possible to determine how similar organisms are to one another. For example, you could ask what animals in the wild are most like your pet dog and at what point did they become domesticated. The answer is that grey wolves show a close relationship to dogs (Vilà et al., 1999). Surprisingly, the initial domestication of dogs from wolves appears to have begun 15,000 years ago in Southwest Asia, although dogs and wolves may have separated some time earlier. In a similar way, we can ask whether early humans were similar to Neandertals (Serre et al., 2004). Mitochondrial DNA from Neandertal fossils from a variety of areas show similarity to one another but not to that found in early human fossils, although other research, which I will discuss later, shows that humans and Neandertals may have mated. Also, using mtDNA, one can construct a map of early human migration over time, as shown in Figure 3.14.

You can also see a Web-based presentation of the migration from Africa at http://www.bradshawfoundation.com/journey/. These migration patterns have also been supported in some unexpected ways, such as by human tooth decay. It turns out that the bacterium that causes tooth decay is passed from a mother to her infant during birth. By examining the DNA of the bacteria, it is possible to trace its lineage in Africa, Asia, Europe, and the Middle East (Caufield, Saxena, Fitch, & Li, 2007). Similarly, the bacterium that can cause ulcers is found in the stomachs of half the humans on earth. This bacterium, which appears to have originated in Africa, also seems to have spread out of East Africa around 58,000 years ago, which is one estimate of the beginning of human migration. Today, some five different DNA versions of the bacterium can be found (Linz et al., 2007). In fact, researchers suggest that these genetic bacteria markers are actually better than traditional human genetic markers for determining lineage (Wirth et al., 2004).

The Y chromosome may also show slight variations that can be used to identify descendants of an individual whose Y chromosome is somewhat distinctive. One famous example of this is Genghis Khan. Khan was born around 1162 and established a large empire in Asia. As part of his conquest, he would slaughter those who were conquered and take his pick of the remaining women. He also ruled over a civilization in which harems and concubines were the norm. Khan and his sons were also characterized as being highly prolific. Researchers have examined the Y chromosome of individuals from Asia (Zerjal et al., 2003). In the area that would have been the empire of Genghis Khan, they found a Y chromosomal lineage with several unusual features, which they referred to as "star-cluster chromosomes." It was found in about 8% of the men in that region but less than ½ of 1% of men worldwide. They concluded that it originated about 1,000 years ago and that its rapid spread could not have happened by chance alone. This suggests that Genghis Khan possessed the star-cluster chromosome and that he and his sons helped to establish the current genetic makeup of the men in that area. This is not to suggest that the star-cluster

DNA migration pattern map created from compiled research on DNA populations around the world. The first humans originated in Africa more than 100,000 years ago. Group L3 populated the rest of the planet during early human migrations. Northern Europeans (Groups H, T, U, V, W, and X) and Southern Europeans (Groups I, J, and K) migrated out of Africa some 45,000 years ago. Asian populations migrated out of Africa about 70,000 years ago and populated the Americas by crossing the Bering Strait in three different migrations. The first migration into the Americas was 10,000–20,000 years ago, the second was about 12,000–15,000 years ago, and the third was about 7,000–9,000 years ago. The data also demonstrate a possible fourth migration that took place about 15,000 years ago when Scandinavian Vikings crossed the Atlantic and mixed with Native Americans who crossed the Bering Strait (haplogroup X).

originated with Genghis Khan but that he received a mutation, at least from his father and grandfather, that he and his sons rapidly gave to future generations. What is amazing is that as a result of a time-limited conquest of an area, a large number of men over generations received and passed on this mutation. The current geographical distribution of star-clustered chromosomes is shown in Figure 3.15.

In this section, we have examined only a limited number of exceptions to Mendel's fundamental laws of genetics. There are other processes, such

Figure 3.15

Geographical Distribution of Star-Cluster Chromosomes. The shaded area of the map represents the extent of Genghis Khan's empire. The darker segments of the circles represent the proportion of the local population who have star-cluster chromosomes.

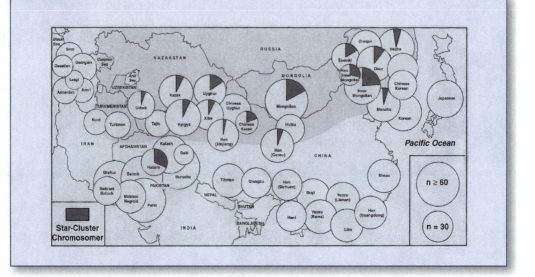

as **epistasis**, which is the situation in which alleles of one gene mask the expression of another gene's alleles such that an expected phenotype does not appear, as well as its opposite, in which the interaction between two gene pairs results in a phenotype that neither pair alone can produce. In the next section, we will examine research that seeks to differentiate the role of the environment and that of genes from human behavior.

Behavioral Genetics

Behavioral genetics is the study of genetic and environmental contributions to organisms' behavior (see Carey, 2003, DiLalla, 2004; Plomin et al., 2008; Kendler, Jaffee, & Romer, 2011 for overviews). One large question is the manner in which genes and the environment work together to shape behavior. To answer this question, researchers use a variety of behavioral genetic approaches to quantify the amount of variance that can be attributed to genetic influences and the amount attributed to environmental influences.

One traditional distinction made is between gene by environment interaction (G x E) and gene by environment correlations (see Plomin, DeFries, & Loehlin, 1977). *Gene by environment interaction* refers to the possibility that individuals with different genotypes may respond to the same environment in different ways. For example, a study of how children with different genotypes respond to the traditional school system would examine gene by environment interaction. A *gene by environment correlation* concerns the way certain genotypes and certain environments occur together. For example, sensation seeking as a personality trait has been shown to be inherited. Those individuals who are sensation seekers are more likely to put themselves in high risk environments, such as mountain climbing or auto racing. In this example, it is more difficult to determine the amount of variance attributed to genetic influences and environmental influences as separate factors. Thus, it is possible for genetic and environmental factors to influence each other in subtle ways.

One of the main approaches of behavioral genetics is twin studies. Twins offer an occurrence in nature that enables researchers to study critical factors related to genetic influences. There are two types of twins: Monozygotic (MZ) twins are identical twins, which occur when the zygote (fertilized egg) divides during the first two weeks of gestation. Because they both come from the same egg, their genes are identical. Dizygotic (DZ) twins, on the other hand, come from two different eggs fertilized by two different spermatozoa. They are called *fraternal twins* because they share approximately 50% of their genes, which is the same percentage as any two siblings. DZ twins can be either same sex or opposite sex, whereas MZ twins must always be the same sex. By comparing the psychological traits of MZ and DZ twins, it is possible to obtain an estimate of heritability.

A classic research design is to compare the responses of MZ twins with DZ twins on particular behavioral traits, such as intelligence or personality characteristics. Because it is assumed that both DZ and MZ twins would have had similar environmental influences in their family, differences between MZ and DZ twins would be the result of genetic influences. For example, Gottesman (1991) has studied schizophrenia with this research design. In these studies, a particular MZ twin was more likely to have schizophrenia if the other twin also did. In DZ twins this was not the case. Researchers examine the statistical degree to which twins are identical to each other as a function of genetic influences and environmental influences. That is to say, you create correlation coefficients for MZ twins and for DZ twins. This tells you how similar each type of twin is on a particular trait. From this, it is possible to determine the percentage of contribution to the trait that comes from environmental influences and the percentage that comes from genetic influences. For example, personality factors such as extraversion have been shown to have a 50% contribution of genetic factors and a 50% contribution of environmental factors.

Another important type of study is the adoption study of DZ and MZ twins who have been raised apart. During World War II for example, children from England were often sent to Canada to allow them to grow in a less dangerous situation. Because the children were raised in different environments, it was possible to better determine the environmental and genetic influences. In the United States since 1979, a series of twins who were separated in infancy and reared apart have been studied by researchers at the University of Minnesota (see Bouchard, Lykken, McGue, Segal, & Tellegen, 1990 for an overview). In work with more than 100 pairs of twins, these researchers found that about 70% of the variance in IQ could be associated with genetic factors. Later studies have supported this finding. However, if the child's family lived in poverty, the degree of association dropped drastically. Although it is not surprising to find IQ or temperament to have genetic associations, it was intriguing to see that the leisure time interests of each twin in the pair were similar, whether the twins were reared together or reared apart.

A third type of study is referred to as the *linkage analysis*. Linkage analysis examines generations of families and looks for the association between particular DNA marker alleles and particular traits. This is commonly done for psychological and physiological disorders that run in families, such as depression or bipolar disorder.

As I conclude this chapter on genetics, it can be noted that evolutionary psychologists and behavioral geneticists are just beginning to integrate and draw on each other's research. As you read the remaining chapters, you will see the manner in which behavioral genetics contributes to the important ideas (e.g., altruism) of evolutionary psychologists.

SUMMARY

All living organisms and plants contain genes. In each cell of a human there is a set of some 20,000 genes along with some additional material. A gene carries information related to the production of proteins in the body. Only a limited amount of genetic information is acted on at any one time, related to the function of specific cells. Liver cells produce different proteins than brain cells or those in muscles. A gene does not produce a protein constantly; it is produced in the context of a complex physiological system influenced both by internal bodily processes and events from the external environment. Genes can be turned on (produce the protein) or turned off (do not produce the protein) relative to specific events. In 1953, James Watson and Francis Crick discovered the double helix structure of DNA. DNA contains the chemical building blocks, or nucleotides, that store information. DNA molecules are composed of two strands which twist together in a spiral. Each strand consists of four types of nucleotides, which are the same except for one component, a nitrogen-containing base. The four bases are adenine, guanine, thymine, and cytosine. They are generally referred to as A, G, T, and C. The nucleotides are linked by a sugar-phosphate backbone. DNA, which is the information storage molecule, transfers information to RNA, which is the information transfer molecule, to produce a particular protein. Change in the rate at which RNA is transcribed controls the rate at which genes produce proteins. The expression rate of different genes in the same genome may vary from 0 to approximately 100,000 proteins per second. Homeotic or Hox genes control the timing of development of body parts. Hox genes lay out the basic body plan during development for all species. A DNA molecule along with the proteins that are attached to it is called a chromosome. The 20,000 human genes occur at a specific site, called a locus, on one of our pairs of chromosomes. In humans there are 23 separate pairs of chromosomes making 46 in all. The first 22 pairs are the same in males and females. In number 23, females carry two copies of the X chromosome whereas males carry one X and one Y. Over evolutionary history, a majority of human genes reflect little variation. As such, all humans have two eyes and one nose and one mouth. However, perhaps a fourth of all genes allow for variation. The two genes of these pairs are usually slightly different. The technical name for the unique molecular form of the same gene is an allele. It has been estimated that of our approximately 20,000 genes, some 6,000 exist in different versions or alleles. Gregor Mendel (1823–1884) performed a series of experiments with the garden pea plant to determine which dominant and recessive genes influence offspring. Epigenetic processes reflect the possibility for the environment to influence future generations through changes to those processes that turn genes on and off rather than changing the DNA itself. Mitochondria are structures within a cell that are involved in the production of energy. Mitochondria have their own DNA (mtDNA), which contains 13 coding genes with about 16,000 base pairs. Mitochondrial DNA is inherited only from the mother, which is a violation of Mendelian inheritance. It changes slowly over evolutionary time and has been used to trace human evolution. Behavioral genetics seeks to describe the relative influences of genes and environment on behavior. Twin studies involving monozygotic (MZ) and dizygotic (DZ) twins are one technique for examining genetic and environmental influences.

STUDY RESOURCES

Review Questions

1. What are genes? What is their role in evolution?

2. What is the difference between genotype and phenotype?

3. Can a gene produce a behavior? If not, what is the pathway from gene to behavior?

4. Describe the structure and function of DNA and RNA. What is the relationship between them?

5. What causes a gene to turn on or turn off?

6. What does the homeotic or Hox gene do? What is its importance from an evolutionary perspective?

7. What does "mapping the genome" mean? What do we know about the human genome?

8. There are two types of cell division. What are they and how do they function? What is their impact from an evolutionary perspective?

9. How does a mutation occur? Do mutations always impact evolution? Why or why not?

10. The majority of our genes show little variation. How is variation accomplished in our remaining genes and what is its role in evolution?

11. The modern science of genetics started with Mendel. What were the two laws he derived from his experiments with trait inheritance in pea plants?

12. What are some examples of genetic inheritance that don't follow Mendel's laws?

13. Can a gene cause a disease? If not, what are some of the pathways from gene to disease?

14. What is epigenetic inheritance? What is its implication for the relationship between an organism's genetics and environment? What is its implication for the genetics of future generations of organisms?

15. What are some of the critical findings researchers have made by using the distinctive nature of the inheritance pattern of mitochondrial DNA?

16. What is behavioral genetics? Why are twins and families studied so extensively in this field?

For Further Reading

Ridley, M. (2003a). *The agile gene.* New York: Perennial.
Ridley, M. (1999). *Genome.* New York: Perennial.
Rutter, M. (2006). *Genes and behavior: Nature/nurture interplay explained.* Malden, MA: Blackwell Publishing.
Watson, J. (1968). *The double helix.* New York: Atheneum.

Key Terms and Concepts

- Evolution and genetics
  - What genes do
  - Functions of genes
  - Genes and their expression
- DNA
  - Overview of DNA and RNA
  - Structure of DNA
  - Structure of RNA
  - Metaphors of DNA
- From proteins to structure and behavior
  - Genetics and evolution
  - Mapping the genome
  - Cell division
  - Variation in duplication

- o Sexual reproduction
- o Variations in genes
- o Mendel and inheritance patterns
- o Mendel's experiments
- o Overview
- Sex-linked inheritance
  - o Codominant alleles and human blood typing
  - o Genetic influences
  - o Incomplete dominance
  - o Pleiotropy and sickle cell anemia
  - o Epigenetic processes
  - o Mitochondrial inheritance
- Behavioral genetics

SAGE Study Site

Visit the study site at **www.sagepub.com/ray** for chapter-specific study resources.

Glossary Terms

- Allele
- Autosomes
- Blood typing
- Centromere
- Chromatids
- Chromosome
- Codominance
- Codon
- DNA
- Epigenetic inheritance
- Epistasis
- Gametes
- Gene
- Genetic code
- Genome
- Genotype
- Germ cells
- Haploid
- Heterozygotes
- Heterozygous
- Homeotic genes
- Homozygotes

- Homozygous
- Hox genes
- Incomplete dominance
- Karyotype
- Law of independent assortment
- Law of segregation
- Linkage
- Meiosis
- Mendel's first law
- Mendel's second law
- Mitochondria
- Mitochondrial inheritance
- Mitosis
- Mutations
- Phenotype
- Pleiotropy
- Recombination
- RNA
- Telomeres
- Transcription
- Translation
- Zygote

Basic Human Function and Process

Evolution of Brain and Function

4

All living things have much in common, in their chemical compo-
sition, their germinal vesicles, their cellular structure, and their
laws of growth and reproduction. Therefore I should infer that
probably all the organic beings which have ever lived have
descended from some one primordial form.

Darwin (1859, p. 484)

As students of evolution, we are faced with the challenge of understanding both the similarity and diversity of life on earth. One basic
approach has been to focus on the cellular structure across evolutionary
time and to make inferences concerning how simple organisms billons of
years old developed into the complex structures we see today. Unfortunately,
soft tissues that comprise nervous systems do not leave the same type of
record as do the fossils of hard tissue structures. Thus, we need to look for
other approaches. An alternative approach is to examine organisms existing today that are known to be modern descendants of earlier organisms.
Beginning on a basic level, we can look for similarity in physiological processes across species. What we discover is that even simple organisms such
as single-cell protozoa share sophisticated behavior processes with higher
level organisms. Three such behaviors are appetitive behaviors, which supply energy, defensive behaviors, which protect the organism, and reproductive behaviors, which perpetuate the species (Swanson, 2003). We also
know that the basic building block of nervous systems, which supports
these behaviors, is the neuron. In large part, the neuron has not changed
over evolutionary time. What has changed is the complexity of nervous
system organization (Swanson, 2003).

In studying nervous system complexity we can also note how different
parts of the brain have evolved. Brains appear to change in nonrandom ways
as they increase in size. For example, in higher organisms over evolutionary

time, the neocortex has shown greater increases in size in comparison to the brain stem. As well, early primates have more neocortex in comparison to other early mammals (Kaas & Preuss, 2008). They also have more of the brain devoted to visual processing. Further, with the increase in complexity of processing, different types of organization are required. Whereas simple reflexes such as the startle response may rely on only a few neurons connected to one another, higher level processes require complex networks that are capable of being modified as conditions change.

We can also look for changes in genetic structure across species. For example, there is a particular gene (MYH16) that influences the jaw muscles in humans and monkeys. Stedman and his colleagues (2004) found that nonhuman primates have an intact version of the gene, which gives them strong jaws. Humans, on the other hand, have a mutation in this gene, which gives us smaller jaw muscles. Based on a variety of evidence, it is suggested that this mutation appeared some 2.4 million years ago. This was the period just before the modern cranial form began to appear. The interesting hypothesis raised by this work is that the presence of smaller jaw muscles allowed for more of the area of the skull to be devoted to the brain. That is, smaller muscles could, in turn, require less bone to support them, and this could allow for more area for the brain. For the MYH16 mutation to be adaptive, this would also require other changes to be taking place at the same time, such as a shift to using the hands rather than the teeth in food preparation and/or a change in diet, such as eating more meat (Currie, 2004).

Overall, we look for common pathways by which organisms solve problems of survival and adapt to their environment. This also leads us to diversity as we consider alternative ways organisms have adapted to an ever-changing environment. This, in turn, has led to a variety of evolutionary pathways. What adds complexity to our search is that changes over time are uneven and may appear in a burst of activity as well as gradually. For example, fossil records show that around 530 million years ago there was an explosion in the diversity of organisms. No one knows why this is so, although data suggests there was also a shift in the orientation of the poles of the earth about that time. This would have resulted in climate shifts, which would require new adaptations by the earth's organisms (Kirschvink, Ripperdan, & Evans, 1997). Although fossil records exist for many of these changes, fossil records mainly tell us the structure of the organism. As psychologists, we are primarily interested in the behavior and experience of organisms. We are left with the task of inferring information concerning evolutionary changes from a variety of sources of indirect evidence.

One of these lines of evidence comes from comparing a variety of living organisms with one another. For example, humans and chimpanzees are 97% similar in genetic structure. Humans are more genetically different from gibbons and even more from Old World monkeys. The basic assumption is that these similarities in molecular structure can help us to know the relative point at which species separated from one another. For example, Old World monkeys separated from other primates more than 25 million years ago, whereas gibbons separated from other primates between 15 and 20 million years ago. We can also compare one type of organism, such as humans, with another that is believed to be older and thus more primitive, such as sea coral. Sometimes this results in surprising findings, as when we discover that sea coral shares a number of gene sequences with humans (Kortschak, Samuel, Saint, & Miller, 2003). For some scientists, these types of findings support the idea that in terms of evolutionary history, humans have a close connection with the sea. For example, humans today share a number of characteristics with sea mammals, such as having little body hair, chubby babies, voluntary control over breathing, and subcutaneous body fat (Morgan, 1997). It can also be noted that the human brain contains proteins that are more similar to those found in shellfish than to any other known food source. This suggests to some that shellfish was an important part of the human diet in an earlier period.

Another line of evidence involves examining brain processes in a variety of species. We can look at the brains of various species and infer what cortical processes are available to that species. Again, if the fossil evidence suggests that there has been little change in physical structure over time, we might infer that behavioral processes have remained fairly stable also. As we will see later in this chapter, we can also consider the amount of energy needed to support various brain processes. This can help us to infer, among other things, the type of diet that would be required to supply this energy, given the available food sources in the organism's environment.

The Brain in Evolution

One common conviction of neuroscientists is that there is something unusual about the human brain that enables us to perform a variety of tasks (Kaas & Preuss, 2008; Northcutt & Kaas, 1995; Preuss, 2009; Preuss & Kaas, 1999). The human brain has been estimated to contain 100 billion neurons and more than 100,000 kilometers of interconnections (Hofman, 2001). Estimates in mammals suggest that a given neuron would directly connect to at least 500 other neurons. This, in turn, would suggest there are 50 trillion different connections in the human brain! Regardless of how exact this estimate may be, we still come away with the conclusion that the human brain has an extremely complex set of networks. How these networks are formed is a fascinating story. A somewhat strange part of this story is that as an adult, you actually have fewer neurons than you did as an infant. This is a normal condition that is connected with a variety of processes, including incorrect wiring patterns in the brain as well as use. For example, if a child is born unable to hear, the normal initial babbling behaviors will be produced but then lost.

In terms of brain structure, the thin outer shell of the brain consists of dark-colored cells called **gray matter**. Underlying this are the **axons**, which transfer information throughout the brain. Their **myelin sheaths** are lighter in color, and thus these areas are referred to as **white matter**. Myelin is made up of fats and proteins and wraps around axons like insulation does around electrical cables; it results in an increased speed of information transmission. A basic distinction is made between the brain's neocortex and the allocortex. The **neocortex** includes regions devoted to sensory and motor processing and higher cognitive processes. The neocortex both sends and receives information from different areas within itself and to and from **subcortical structures**. These connections are largely made through **pyramidal cells**, which release an excitatory transmitter substance such as glutamate. There are also **non-pyramidal neurons,** which serve the purpose of making short-term connections in the cortex. These can be either inhibitory or excitatory. The neocortex has six layers; each layer is composed of specific cell types and connections. In evolutionary terms, the neocortex is considered the most recent structure to evolve. The **allocortex** is older and includes the **hippocampus**, **olfactory cortex**, and other related areas. As we shall see, the allocortex can be further divided into the **archicortex** and **paleocortex**. One main feature of the allocortex is that it does not have the six-layered structure of the neocortex.

THE BRAIN STRUCTURE OF MAMMALS

Let's begin with some simple terms. The front of the brain is referred to as **anterior** while the back is called **posterior**. You will also see the Latin terms **rostral** and **caudal** used in the same way. You can remember that the speaker's *rostrum* is in the *front* of the room, if you want a way to remember this difference. The brain appears symmetrical from the top, with a **left hemisphere** and a **right hemisphere**. Structures closer to the **midline** dividing the left and right hemispheres are referred to as **medial structures,** whereas those farther away from the midline are called **lateral structures**. Looking at the right hemisphere from the side, we can describe four **lobes**: the **frontal lobe,** which is at the front; the **parietal lobe**, which is toward the back and at the top; the **occipital lobe** near the back of the brain and toward the bottom; and the **temporal lobe**. Looking at the brain, you can see that the frontal and temporal lobes are separated by a deep groove, which is called the **sylvian fissure** or **lateral fissure**.

Figure 4.1   The Major Lobes of the Human Brain

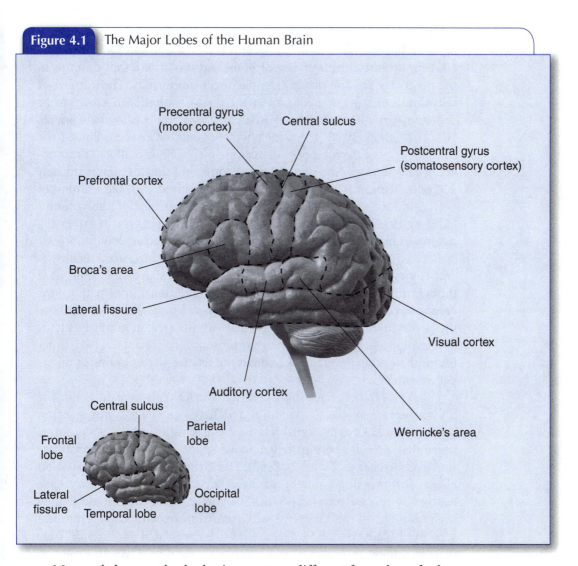

Mammals have evolved a brain structure different from that of other organisms—the six-layered neocortex. Each of these layers has a distinct neurological organization and connections. The bottom layers (5 and 6) have neurons that project to subcortical structures. The next layer (4) contains local circuit neurons. The next three layers (1, 2, and 3) have neurons that project to other cortical structures and receive information from layer 4. Although the neocortex is consistent in structure, among mammals there is great variation in cortical size, organization, area devoted to different types of cortical processing, and connectivity in network connections. Separate cortical areas are devoted to processing specific types of information, such as color or motion, which is later put together to give us a coherent image. If we compare the brains of rodents to those of humans, we find only 5 or so cortical areas devoted to different types of visual processing in rodents, whereas humans have more than 30.

The traditional view of brain structure and evolution emphasizes the basic uniformity of structure of the neocortex across species (see Preuss, 2001 for an historical overview of brain and evolution). Cell columns in the neocortex are one classic example of this uniformity. The number of cells found in any given column in the neocortex has been shown to be approximately 110, regardless of where in the cortex it is located (Rockel, Hiorns, & Powell, 1980). This same number of cells has also been found to be constant across different species of mammals. The only exception is the number of cells found in the primary visual cortex in primates—approximately 270 cells. Thus, it is assumed that the brain evolved with the addition of new columns, rather than by changing the structure of the columns (Allman, 1999). It is also assumed that the human brain grew by increasing neuron number rather than increasing neuron size (Kaas, 2008).

Based on this type of uniformity in cortical structure, many neuroscientists view evolution in terms of increasing the size of the brain. It is thought that this increase in size allows for additional information processing to take place. However, it should be noted that humans do not have the largest brain, nor do we have a brain with the greatest number of folds or convolutions. Whales, dolphins, porpoises, and elephants all have larger brains than humans. Figure 4.2 shows the relative size of brains of different mammals.

Other researchers have suggested that cortical enlargement is not the only process available to evolution and have even called into question some of the exact cell counts described previously. Further, it should be noted that as brains become larger across species, their internal organization tends to change (Striedter, 2005). This change in internal organization allows for the development of new cortical networks, which have evolved to process novel capacities. Language in humans would be one such example. In this chapter, I will draw from research using both perspectives because definitive data are yet to be presented. In fact, it is likely that both these processes have taken place over time. Overall, I want to

Figure 4.2   The Relative Size of Brains From a Variety of Mammals

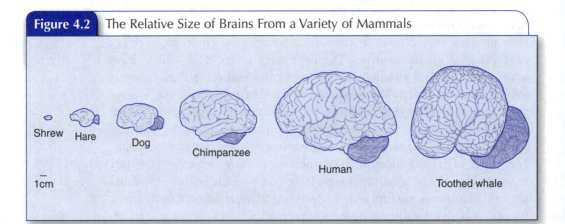

Shrew   Hare   Dog   Chimpanzee   Human   Toothed whale

1cm

examine the manner in which our physiology in general, and our brain in particular, may have evolved. I will also note the factors that influence the growth of the brain. For example, if a brain increases in size, there must also be an increase in energy and ways to supply that energy. Although our human brain is only about 2% of our body weight, it uses some 25% of our energy. The brain of a newborn uses more than 80%, which reduces to less than 45% by the age of 5. Further, the brain is efficient in terms of its operation and designed to conserve space, materials, time, and energy (Laughlin & Sejnowski, 2003). However, as a brain evolves to solve challenges of life, the complexity of the neuronal networks and processing times may be limiting factors (Hofman, 2001). That is to say, there is a point at which energy requirements and the ability to connect ever-increasing numbers of neurons and their networks in an efficient manner may reach a limit.

There are a variety of research approaches that we can use to inform the study of brain evolution. We can utilize the methods of comparative psychology and neuroscience to illustrate similarities between physiological structures for performing basic sensory and cognitive processes. We can also compare genetic organization to further see how similar various species are in terms of their genetic makeup. From an evolutionary perspective, we can follow changes over evolutionary time. For example, it is thought that brains first appeared about 500 million years ago. We can also consider at what point in time particular structures or processes began to be seen. For example, we know from the fossil record that about 300 to 400 million years ago, there was a split between mammals and their closest vertebrate relatives, reptiles and birds. With this separation, there was a gradual change in mammals that resulted in such characteristics as hair, sweat glands, and mammary glands. Characteristics such as teeth became more specialized for slicing, piercing, and grinding. Mammals further evolved mechanisms for maintaining constant body temperature. More recently in evolutionary time, about four million years ago, a species of primates began spending most of its time walking on two feet. This change enabled them to use their hands—objects could now be manipulated, which allowed for a great variety of tasks to be performed differently. This led to the development of tools some two million years ago. The fossil records suggest that these primates knocked rocks together to create sharp-edged stones that could be used for a variety of purposes, including cutting up meat (Olson, 2002). This species also used bones as hammers and anvils. It is this species that scientists first refer to as part of the genus *Homo*. Within this genus, a new group appeared between 100 and 200 thousand years ago. This was the species *Homo Sapiens,* from whom we are all descended. The Latin word *sapiens* refers to being wise or knowing. As the name implies, it is our cognitive flexibility that characterizes human behavior and experience.

In considering these long timeframes of evolution, scientists often make a distinction concerning the timeframe of characteristics. If a particular characteristic was present in the ancestors of the group we are studying, then it is said to be a **primitive characteristic** or an **ancestral characteristic**. On the other hand, if the characteristic has evolved in the group under study, it is said to be a **derived characteristic** or **specialized characteristic**. In a species such as humans, there is, of course, a combination of primitive and derived characteristics. One focus of evolutionary research has been to trace the development of these primitive characteristics. In making these tracings, Darwin (1859) reminds us to consider primitive and specialized characteristics as a **tree branching** rather than a direct and single line (p. 129). Using this metaphor, we realize that different species can have unique histories of evolution. For example, on the genetic level, when Kortschak, Samuel, Saint, and Miller (2003) looked at the genes of coral, they found genetic sequences shared by humans and coral that were not found in either worms or fruit flies. Thus, knowing that an organism such as the fruit fly has a complex nervous system, at least compared to coral, does not permit you to assume evolutionary development in a simple linear fashion. There are many different branchings possible between primitive organisms and later, more complex ones.

The study of the evolution of the nervous system carries with it particular challenges. Because brain tissue is destroyed over time, it cannot be studied from fossil records like the evolution of teeth or bones. At best, fossil records can offer gross estimations as to the size of the brain. However, it is possible to bring together a variety of indirect techniques to help us answer questions of brain evolution. One of the best techniques is to compare one living species with another living species. This comparison allows us to infer the manner in which development may have taken place, on a variety of levels ranging from the genetic to the behavioral. In making such comparisons, the question arises as to the nature of any similarity observed. If the observed similarities are due to a shared evolutionary history—that is to say, they were inherited from a common ancestor—it is referred to as **homologous similarity**. However, similarities may be due to an independent evolutionary history. That is to say, rather than have a common ancestor, different species may independently evolve similar characteristics. In this case, these characteristics are called **analogous similarity**. Thus, similar characteristics in two different species can come from either a common ancestor or from a process of parallel evolution.

It is also possible for both processes to take place, but during different time periods. For example, both bats and birds inherited forelimbs from a common ancestor that did not fly. However, the modifications of the forelimbs that enabled bats and birds to develop wings that fly developed independently. Thus, the forelimbs are homologous, whereas the later-evolved wings are analogous (Preuss & Kaas, 1999). What this tells us is that there are a variety of pathways for developing similar structures. This can lead to some surprising results, which take us beyond what we see before us. For example, the forelimbs of bats and whales are homologous, whereas the forward-looking eyes of cats and primates are analogous. We are just beginning to understand the manner in which human brain evolution is built upon a vast history of organic development. At this point, because our understanding is incomplete, scientists have developed large conceptual frameworks upon which to build testable hypotheses. Two of these were the work of Hughlings Jackson in the 1800s and the 20th-century work of Paul MacLean and his conception of a triune brain.

HUGHLINGS JACKSON

In the 1800s, the neurologist John Hughlings Jackson began to examine the brain from a developmental and evolutionary perspective. Over evolutionary time, the brain developed higher level functions by superimposing them on lower level function. He spoke of the brain having three levels of functioning. The most basic level involves vegetative functions such as reflexes, sleep, and temperature regulation that would involve the spinal cord and brain stem. The next level would include the basal ganglia and its involvement in a number of movement-related processes. The highest level was associated with higher cortical processes.

In the process of this research, Hughlings Jackson suggested two principles based partly on evolutionary analysis. The first principle is **hierarchical integration** through inhibitory control. By this he means that the various levels of the brain, such as the brain stem, the limbic system, and the neocortex, are able to interact with each other. Further, the type of interaction from the higher levels is that of restricting or inhibiting the lower levels. Current research has supported this by showing many more inhibitory pathways going from the higher brain levels to the lower brain structures than vice versa. A simple example of this is that when a human infant is first born, she or he shows a variety of simple reflexes. One of these is the Babinski reflex. If you take your finger and run it along an infant's foot, the toes will curl up. As the infant matures, the reflex disappears. If there is higher cortical damage at a later point in life, then this reflex can reappear. Hughlings Jackson assumed that the higher level structure, which evolved later than the reflexive ones, serves the purpose of inhibiting and modulating these basic reflexes.

Mental illness was also seen to result from the situation in which higher level processes become disordered. Symptoms such as illusions, hallucinations, or delusions are seen as lower level processes. What happens when the higher level processes in the brain no longer function correctly? The answer, for Hughlings Jackson, is that the midlevel processes continue to function normally and produce phenomena such as hallucinations. Thus, the symptoms of mental illness can be seen as particular brain areas functioning without higher level control. Support for this type of thinking is seen in the normal process of sleep and dreaming. Current neuroscience research suggests that the experience of dreaming results from a reduction of inhibition of higher level cortical areas on emotional limbic processes.

Hughlings Jackson's second principle is **encephalization**. This is the principle by which special-purpose control systems are taken over by a general-purpose control system over evolutionary time. That is, more recently evolved higher level centers control the older lower level centers. Over evolutionary time, sensory processes are gradually transferred from the lower centers to higher centers in the brain. For example, lateral inhibition (the tendency for activity in one area of processing to reduce activity in another area) takes place in the eye of birds but not in the brain of humans. Thus, over evolutionary time, human brains have developed a more general-purpose processing system without replacing the earlier special-purpose processing mechanisms.

TRIUNE BRAIN

In the 20th century, one of the major programs for understanding cortical and behavioral processes from an evolutionary perspective was developed by Paul MacLean (1990, 1993). Examining fossil records along with brains of a variety of organisms, MacLean suggested that our current brain can be viewed as having the features of three basic evolutionary formations—reptiles, early mammals, and recent mammals. MacLean notes that these three systems vary greatly, both in chemistry and structure. This, in turn, results in the three having different forms of memory, motor functions, and understanding of time and space. MacLean's formulation, which is referred to as the **triune brain**, suggests that through rich interconnections, our brains can process a variety of information in three somewhat independent, although not autonomous, ways (see Figure 4.3).

The first level is the **reptilian brain** or **R-complex,** involving the **brain stem** and **cerebellum**. This level processes major life requirements such as breathing, temperature regulation, and sleep-wake cycles. Also involved in this level is olfaction (olfactory bulbs) and instinctive motor processes (basal ganglia). This level of processing represents fairly structured behavioral patterns involving basic activities such as territoriality, courtship, and hunting and also includes patterned displays related to these behaviors.

The second level of the triune brain is the **paleomammalian brain**. Anatomically, this level includes the limbic system and its involvement in emotional processing. The limbic system was initially described by Paul Broca in the 1870s. Broca (1878) noted that the "the great limbic lobe" exists as a common denominator in the brains of all mammals, and he described its location and structure in a variety of mammals. More recently, the limbic area has been associated with changes in mammalian evolution. MacLean (1990) points to three developments that took place evolutionarily in the transition from reptiles to mammals. Although mammals have

| Figure 4.3 | Diagram of MacLean's Triune Brain |

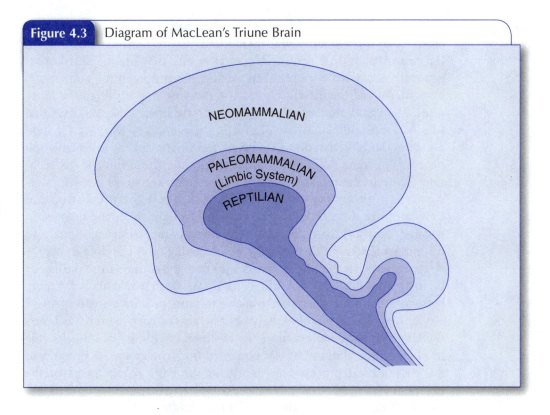

been seen as evolving from reptiles, there are stark contrasts in three types of behaviors. First, whereas reptiles such as lizards lay their eggs and the offspring must fend for themselves, mammalian offspring have a close connection with their mothers. As you may know, nursing in conjunction with maternal care is the source of the term "mammal." Over the past 50 years, it has been shown that damage to one area in the limbic structure, the **cingulate**, results in disrupted maternal behaviors. Second, mammals use audio-vocal communication, which maintains maternal-offspring contact. Most mammalian young will voice a separation cry if separated from their mothers. The origin of these cries may have been related to the early mammal being nocturnal, which would emphasize vocalizations over vision. These cries may also represent the earliest and the most basic mammalian vocalizations from which language could develop. Summarizing the function of the limbic area, MacLean suggests that the structures in this area function as a type of volume control for modulating affective feelings in relation to self-preservation and the preservation of the species. The third type of behavior that mammals demonstrate that is not seen in reptiles is play behavior. Not only do you see human children playing on the playground, but also in lower mammals, such as the hamster, you can observe play behaviors including play fighting. There are a variety of theories related to the role of play behavior, and most theories stress its role in developmental processes.

The third level of the triune brain is the **neomammalian brain**, which is related to the neocortex and **thalamic structures**. As the name implies, the neocortex and its related structures is the "new brain." This level is generally associated with problem solving, executive control, and an orientation toward the external world with an emphasis on linguistic functions. From an evolutionary perspective, it is the level of the neocortex that would be most influenced by cultural processes and new learning. It would also be at this level that processes involving self-control and self-regulation become apparent. Although MacLean describes these three levels separately in an evolutionary sense, it is important to recognize the rich interconnections that allow for information exchange between the structures that comprise the various levels. In fact, MacLean notes the manner in which neocortical structures may be involved in regulating emotional and instinctual functions. Structurally, an interesting recent finding in neuroscience research is that there are more inhibitory pathways from the higher brain areas to the lower ones than vice versa, which would allow for more behavioral flexibility than that available to more primitive organisms.

One basic idea that evolutionary psychologists can derive from MacLean's thinking is that as one examines the evolutionary history of humans, one must also think about what was borrowed from earlier species in terms of the physiological processes necessary for the basic requirements of the organism. As organisms became more complex, new structures evolved that took advantage of the previous developments. Also, with this complexity in mammals in general, and humans in particular, came relationship processes, which many see as the basis of all human activity. With these higher order brain structures came the ability to display choice in one's actions. Humans not only live in the context of genetically structured programs for self-preservation, preservation of the species, and social processes, we live with culturally modifiable behaviors and experiences. That is to say, whereas there is little flexibility in how one responds when faced with a loss of oxygen, there is considerably more choice in how humans respond to each other, although evolutionary predispositions still play a role. Although MacLean's anatomical framework is highly schematic, and more detailed analysis is required to understand exactly how mammalian self-regulation achieved the advances in behavioral flexibility and social coordination, his approach has been highly influential in emphasizing the integral social basis of the evolution of higher levels of psychological function. For example, thinking in these terms, we would conclude that such processes as a sense of control as well as conscious self-awareness would come late in evolution.

One implication of the triune brain theory is that we would expect to find simpler systems for solving similar problems on a variety of levels. We would also expect to find that only the most sophisticated of these systems has direct access to conscious awareness. In this manner, we would expect to find simple perceptual systems, for example, on the lower levels. This is indeed what we find in terms of the visual system. This was dramatically demonstrated in the second half of the 20th century, through a variety of experiments that demonstrated the ability of humans to make use of information obtained without conscious awareness. I will now discuss two of these: blindsight and hemispheric lateralization.

Blindsight

Blindsight is the name given to a process in which individuals report an inability to see objects but can accurately "guess" the location of the object. It is generally found in people who have had brain damage. It was first named by Larry Weiskrantz in the 1970s (see Weiskrantz, 1986 for an overview). Individuals with this condition say they cannot "see" an object such as a cursor on a computer screen. However, if the cursor is moved, the individual can report the direction of the movement. Thus, the person has no conscious awareness of his or her perception but can accurately describe the motion. It is assumed that different visual pathways in the brain are at play in blindsight than those involved in vision with awareness.

Hemispheric Lateralization

In the 1960s and 1970s, an operation was performed to reduce frequent and uncontrollable epilepsy. The initial operations cut the fiber tract, the corpus callosum, which connects the left and right hemispheres of the brain (see Figure 4.4). By performing this operation, doctors could prevent epileptic seizures from spreading over the entire brain. These patients were referred to as "split brain" patients. Overall, following the operation, these patients showed a drastic reduction in seizures. Surprisingly, cutting the corpus callosum, which contains some 200 million nerve fibers, did not appear to cause any changes in the patients' everyday behavior or experience. However, with more extensive experimental procedures, a different picture emerged. This picture suggested that the left and right hemispheres of the human brain are specialized for different tasks. The left hemisphere is involved in language processing and other serial processes, and the right hemisphere processes spatial tasks and other global processes. This work was initially performed by Roger Sperry and his colleagues (see Springer & Deutsch, 2001 for an overview).

Sperry and his colleagues devised experimental techniques that limited the information flow to just one hemisphere. One of these techniques was to present visual information for less than 1/5 of a second. This is faster than your ability to make an eye movement, which could result in the information going to both hemispheres. What they found was that when information was presented to the left hemisphere of the split brain patients, they reported seeing it and could identify it verbally. However, if the information was presented to the right hemisphere, patients would say

Figure 4.4 A diagram of the human brain showing the corpus callosum, which transfers information between hemispheres.

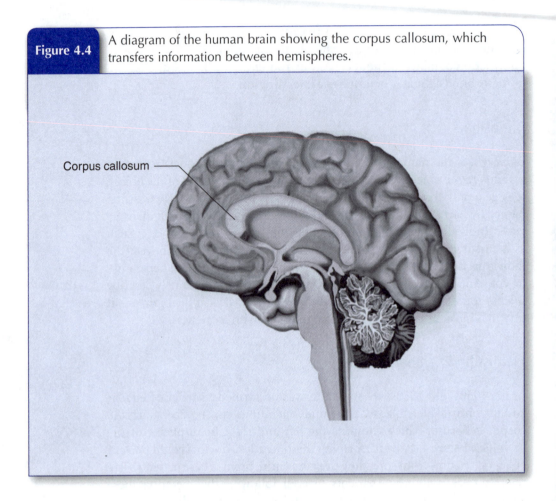

Corpus callosum

they saw nothing. Further, if asked to point to a series of objects with the left hand, which is controlled by the right hemisphere, they were able to do it correctly. This led Sperry to suggest that split brain patients possessed the equivalent of two minds, each with its own separate consciousness.

A particularly intriguing outcome of these "two minds" is the manner in which the conscious, verbal left hemisphere appears to fill in gaps in information. In this research, a snow scene was flashed to the right hemisphere of the patient and a chicken claw to the left hemisphere. The split brain patient was then shown the pictures presented in Figure 4.5.

The person was asked to point with each hand to an image that was related to what had been seen. The right hand, which is controlled by the left hemisphere, pointed to a chicken. The left hand, which is controlled by the right hemisphere, pointed to a shovel, which would be used to shovel snow. The person was able to observe where each hand pointed, although the verbal left

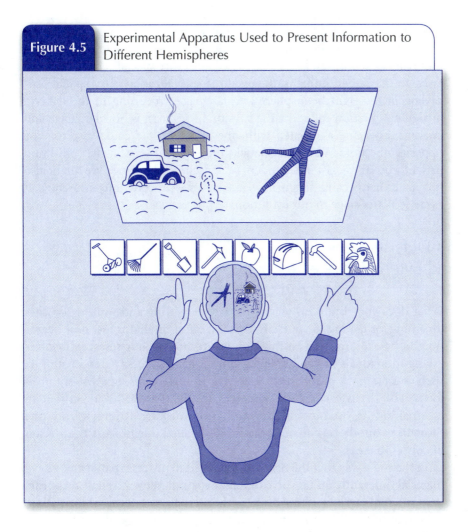

Figure 4.5 Experimental Apparatus Used to Present Information to Different Hemispheres

side would not have been aware of seeing the snow scene because information seen by the left eye went to the right hemisphere. When asked why he pointed where he did, the patient's verbal response from the left hemisphere was "I saw a claw and I picked a chicken, and you have to clean out the chicken shed with a shovel" (Gazzaniga & LeDoux, 1978).

How should we understand this? Gazzaniga and LeDoux (1978) suggest that the left hemisphere acts as an interpreter of action and creates views of one's behavior that fit a consistent scheme. In addition, these researchers suggest all humans do this, not just split brain patients. That is to say, it is part of our nature to fill in the gaps and create explanations for our actions. It is assumed that filling in the gaps is the result of neural network integration, which integrates information from a variety of cortical areas. In terms of evolutionary time, as the brain areas of the two hemispheres increased, the density of interconnections between the two was actually reduced (Striedter, 2005). That is to say, as brain size in primates increases over time, the corpus callosum, and thus the relative number of interconnections, does not increase proportionally. Thus, each hemisphere is able to function more independently and also able to become more specialized for different tasks. In the case of humans, the resulting specialization is for spatial processing in the right hemisphere and language processing in the left. An intriguing question raised by the split brain research is how language and awareness became associated with one another. One could also ask the opposite question: Why does spatial processing, at least in the split brain patient, appear to exist independent of conscious awareness? We might also speculate that because language is associated with conscious awareness, it came at a later stage in our evolutionary process.

The Brain's Default Network: Internal and External Processes

What does your brain do when you are just sitting and waiting, or daydreaming, or talking to yourself? This is a question that is just now beginning to be explored. If you think about it, most of our research involves asking individuals to cognitively or emotionally process external stimuli, such as a face or a problem to be solved. In these cases, one's attention is focused on the external world. However, we all know that even without an external task to do, our mind is constantly working. It jumps from one thought to another. William James (1884) called this process the **stream of consciousness.**

In the same way that the brain is organized to process spatial and verbal material differently and involve different cortical networks, it also appears that different circuits are involved with internal vs. external information. A variety of studies have examined brain imaging procedures in which individuals performed internal tasks vs. external tasks (e.g., Ray & Cole, 1985). The neural networks that are active during internal processing are called the brain's **default network** (see Buckner, Andrews-Hanna, & Schacter, 2008 for an overview). Buckner and his colleagues describe the default network as separate from, but similar to, other networks, such as those involved in visual perception or motor activities. That is to say, the default network is made up of a set of interacting brain regions, shown in Figure 4.6. The areas were identified from brain imaging data of individuals not engaged in any active task.

A variety of studies suggest that the default network is most active when individuals are engaged in private thoughts or left to think alone about both real and hypothetical events, such as what one would do in the future or what another person is thinking. Figure 4.7 on page 134 displays those areas of the brain that are active when a person engages in some of these conditions. The top image (A) displays areas active when people were asked to remember specific events from their past. Below this is an image (B) found

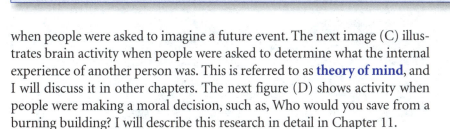

| Figure 4.6 | Meta-analysis of nine PET studies involving 132 participants. Default network areas shown as darker. The darker areas were more active during passive tasks. |

when people were asked to imagine a future event. The next image (C) illustrates brain activity when people were asked to determine what the internal experience of another person was. This is referred to as **theory of mind**, and I will discuss it in other chapters. The next figure (D) shows activity when people were making a moral decision, such as, Who would you save from a burning building? I will describe this research in detail in Chapter 11.

Buckner and his colleagues (2008) suggest that the default network is involved during internal or private considerations that do not require

Activation of the default network from a variety of internal tasks including remembering oneself in the past, imagining the future, considering how someone else would experience the world, and making moral decisions.

A.   **AUTOBIOGRAPHICAL MEMORY**

B.   **ENVISIONING THE FUTURE**

C.   **THEORY OF MIND**

D.   **MORAL DECISION MAKING**

processing external sensory information. In fact, it appears as if there is a negative correlation between activities in the default network and networks associated with processing information from the environment. Overall, this suggests that separate brain mechanisms evolved for dealing with information involving the external environment as opposed to considerations internal to the person.

HIGHER COGNITIVE PROCESSES

As psychologists, we are concerned with the question of the evolutionary substrate of higher cognitive processes. In many ways, this question returns us to the question of physiological mechanisms because the human brain's cognitive mechanisms are built upon underlying circuits. We know, for example, there are at least 31 separate areas in the occipital cortex whose cells are sensitive to various types of visual information, such as color or shape or angle. The same also is true for other forms of sensory and perception information. In order to think, feel, or move, we must integrate information from a variety of locations in the brain. These circuits can be found in different levels in the brain, ranging from higher level cognitive processes, to more mid-level emotional processes, to the basic vegetative processes associated with the brainstem reticular system. Although specific studies of brain anatomy and function are solid, understanding evolutionary changes as well as the mechanisms of cognitive processes is more speculative. In fact, it has been noted that there has been limited research concerning the manner in which the human brain organization differs from that of other species (Preuss, 2000).

DEVELOPMENT OF THE NERVOUS SYSTEM

In this section, I begin by taking a broad view of development and later focus on the brain and spinal cord (see Allman, 1999; Rakic & Kornack, 2001; Stiles, 2008; and Williamson & Allman, 2011 for an extended discussion). As described in Chapter 3, there is a common set of genes, the Hox genes, that controls development across species. What is fascinating about these Hox genes is that they lay out the basic body plan during development for all species. In an amazing manner, these genes are expressed in the embryos across species in the same nose-to-tail arrangement as their order in the chromosomes. That is, the first Hox gene develops the front aspects of the body, continuing in order until the final Hox gene develops the posterior aspects of the body (see Figure 4.8). As noted previously, these genes can be swapped between species with little obvious effect on physical development. For example, the Pax-6 gene controls formation of the eye in fruit flies, mice, and humans. Research has demonstrated that the mouse

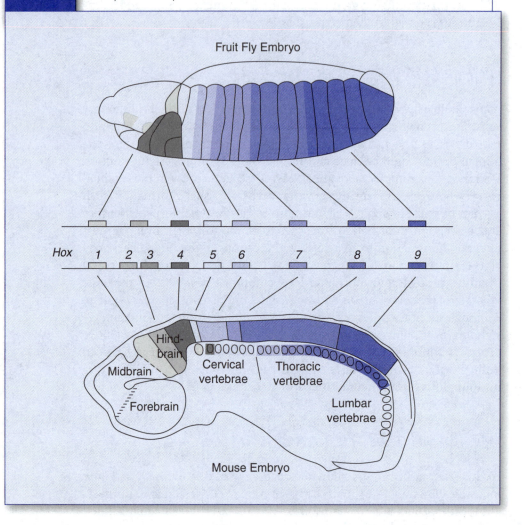

Figure 4.8

Hox genes determine body parts in similar ways across species. They have the unusual characteristic that spatial location in the genome is reflected both in the embryo and the adult animal. Shown are embryos for a fly and a mouse.

Fruit Fly Embryo

Hox   1   2   3   4   5   6   7   8   9

Hind-brain
Midbrain
Forebrain
Cervical vertebrae
Thoracic vertebrae
Lumbar vertebrae

Mouse Embryo

version of this gene can be placed in a fruit fly and will produce normal eyes in fruit flies. How is this possible? It appears that these genes turn on other genes, which in turn produce body parts related to a given species. Thus, they give the basic instruction, such as "build an eye," and turn on specific genes that create the structure of the body part for that particular organism. Given this manner of functioning, it is assumed that Hox genes existed in a common ancestor prior to both flies and mice. Using such a mechanism, it is possible for the same basic genetic developmental system to have been retained across a variety of species, although the actual structures produced will appear quite different.

An interesting finding is that genes from a mother and father differentially influence the development of the brain (Keverne, Fundele, Narasimha, Barton, & Surani, 1996a). In mice, genes from the father contribute to the development of such basic forebrain structures as the hypothalamus and septum, but not the cortex. Genes from the mother, on the other hand, contribute to the development of the cortex as well as striatum and hippocampus, but not to the basic forebrain. Said in other terms, maternal genes influence the more executive aspects of the brain, whereas paternal genes influence the more emotional aspects of the brain (Keverne, Martel, & Nevison, 1996b). In primates, it is the more executive aspects of the brain that have shown the greatest changes across species. Keverne and his colleagues suggest that over evolutionary time, the controlling mechanism for behavior became more centered in executive function. This is not to say that the motivational aspects of the emotional brain have decreased, but that more control of an intellectual or strategic nature has evolved in larger-brained primates.

The **central nervous system**, which includes the brain and spinal cord, develops during the first month of pregnancy. About 14 days following conception, a process referred to as **gastrulation** occurs. Gastrulation leads to the development of three different cell lines from undifferentiated embryonic tissue. Each of these cell lines is capable of producing cells that will make up different organs in the body. At about 18 days post conception, a process begins that results in the creation of the neural tube from which the brain and spinal cord develop. Literally, a structure of cells begins to develop a groove, which closes over itself to form the neural tube. This tube then sinks inside the embryo. The anterior part of the neural tube increases in size as new cells develop. It is from these structures that the neocortex and its cerebral hemispheres eventually develop. Unlike some other organisms, humans appear to develop all of their cortical neurons by the sixth month of pregnancy. In an amazing manner, neurons migrate during development to form connections and pathways. Structurally, the most anterior end of the neural tube becomes the forebrain, the midbrain, the cerebellum, and the hindbrain. The remaining part of the tube becomes the spinal cord (see Figure 4.9). Different parts of the tube expand differently in different animals under the control of specific genes. For example, as compared to other organisms, primates, including humans, have an extremely large neocortex, which develops from the most anterior part of the neural tube. In mammals, there are extreme differences in the number of neurons and in the surface area of the neocortex. For example, the surface area of a macaque monkey brain is some 100 times that of the mouse. The human brain has about 1,000 times more surface area than the mouse brain and about 10 times more than the monkey brain (Blinkov & Glezer, 1968). Along with the expansion of the surface area of the brain during evolution, there was also an increase and expansion of areas involved in processing information. As noted previously, humans have more than 30 areas devoted to visual processing, whereas rodents have only 5. As evolution produced greater diversity in cortical

Figure 4.9 Illustration of Brain Development in the Human Fetus

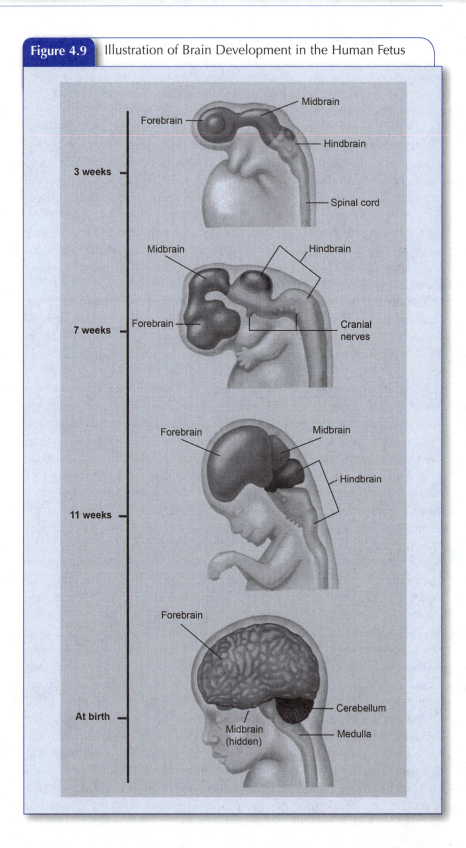

structure, there remained a similarity in the manner in which the nervous system functioned. As everyone learns in beginning psychology and neuroscience courses, the basic unit of signal transmission is the axon and the action potential that is generated within it.

EVOLUTION OF BRAIN SIZE

As psychologists, our interest is not so much in the development of the brain per se, but in how this relates to behavior. In the 1940s, the brain scientist Karl Lashley (1949) suggested that the only neurological characteristic for which there was a strong correlation with behavioral abilities was the size of the brain in relation to the size of the body. Of course, by this Lashley did not mean that there were no other relationships between the brain and behavior. Rather, he was interested in what aspects of brain structure mirror changes in cognitive ability across species. Lashley's answer was that the size of the brain in relation to body weight gave such a measure. Jerison followed up this idea in a now classic work, *Evolution of the Brain and Intelligence* (1973). Jerison made a number of suggestions for using brain size to understand cognition. First, he suggested that brain size could be used to estimate other structural parameters, such as the density of neurons, the number of folds in the cortex, and the size of other neural structures. One exception to this involves the sense of smell—the olfactory bulbs appear to have little relationship to the size of other brain structures. Second, he suggested that the amount of information processed by a particular brain area is reflected in the size of that area. And third, he was able to show that, in vertebrates, as body size increases across species, brain size expands in a mathematically predictable manner. Specifically, Jerison reported that each unit increase in the average body size for a species results in a .67 increment in the size of the brain. More recent work has shown the number to be slightly larger: .75 (Martin, 1996).

In the context of physical evolution, Jerison (1973) also considered the evolution of cognitive processes. He speculated that early mammals that were known to be nocturnal could not rely on visual stimuli. Instead, they needed to integrate information from their auditory system with that of olfaction. Hearing told them that something was present and where it might be, and smell told them what it was. According to Jerison, this was the beginning of a nervous system that moved beyond the simple stereotyped responses of reptiles to various types of visual stimuli. The nervous system of nocturnal mammals encouraged the evolution of spatial maps, which he speculated would later evolve into humans' ability to create internal representations of external events. Over time, as mammals moved from being active at night to being active during the day, a more complex visual system also developed, which carried with it these previous capacities for spatial representations as well as the need for integration of information from a variety of sensory modalities. One important development, according to Jerison, came with the larger brain in primates, including humans. This was the ability to connect information processing with time. Thus, such an organism could not only integrate information from a variety of sources, it could be aware of temporal contingencies. This eventually led to a sense of self in humans—a self that integrates information and has a history that it remembers.

Nicholas Humphrey (1976) asked an interesting question. He wanted to know why great apes performed laboratory tests in a way that suggested they possess more intelligence than would be required for obtaining food in the wild. His answer was that the intelligence was needed for social processes. According to Humphrey, there is a dynamic tension in social groups, in that individuals seek both to preserve the overall structure of the group and outmaneuver others in it. That is, social groups lead to both cooperation and competition. In the sense that social intelligence also contributes to survival and reproduction, it becomes a force in the evolution of cognitive processes. Through this mechanism, the intelligence of a species can be increased. This has come to be called the **social intelligence hypothesis** or the **Machiavellian intelligence hypothesis** (cf. Byrne & Whiten, 1988). As we will see in later chapters, researchers have used social intelligence as a way to study such topics as deception, social learning, and the ability of one organism to understand the motivation and thinking of another.

How might you study social intelligence and brain size? One approach has been to simply look at group size. However, group size alone has not been shown to be strongly related to brain size across a variety of primate species (Dunbar, 2004). If you think about group size, you may realize this is more a measure of potential interactions than actual interactions. For example, because primates groom one another, a measure of actual social interactions would be the size of the grooming group or clique. Indeed, this measure does correlate positively with relative brain size (Kudo & Dunbar, 2001; see Figure 4.10).

OTHER FACTORS RELATED TO THE BRAIN

Scientists have taken two complementary approaches to the study of brain evolution and size (Kaskan & Finlay, 2001). The first, which is sometimes referred to as the **allometric approach**, focuses on the entire brain or large subdivisions. Jerison's (1973) work illustrates this tradition. A second approach, which is sometimes referred to as the **neuroethological approach**, examines the relationship between specific behaviors and underlying cortical structures. For example, you could ask whether one of the brain structures involved in spatial maps, the hippocampus, is larger in organisms that have a large territory that they explore than in those who do not. You could also ask whether the number of songs that an organism

| Figure 4.10 | Relative Brain Size vs. Mean Size of the Grooming Clique |

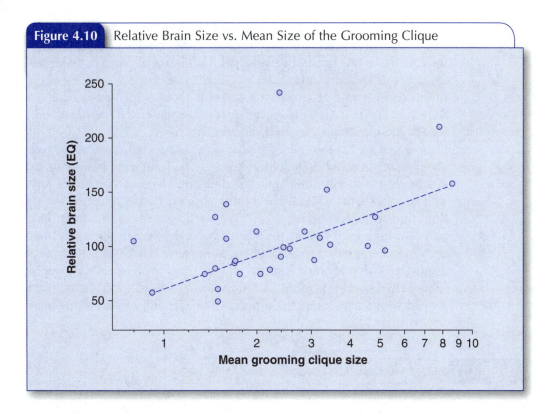

can produce is related to the number of neurons in the areas of the brain that control singing. Research shows that primates who are primarily nocturnal have larger olfactory structures, whereas those who are awake in the day have larger primary visual areas in the brain. Looking at a longer evolutionary perspective, it appears that in primates, there has been a persistent tradeoff between olfaction and vision. Newer research has also shown this to be true on the genetic level (Gilad, Wiebe, Przeworski, Lancet, & Pääbo, 2004). From examining genetic structure across a wide variety of species, these authors concluded that the evolution of color vision occurred in humans and other primates genetically similar to us as olfactory abilities were declining. This, of course, was not true in primates such as new world monkeys, which have not developed color vision.

As we look at the size of brains across species, we notice that organisms with big brains are rare. Why would this be? The common answer is that big brains require more energy than small brains. It is estimated that compared to the same amount of muscle tissue, brain tissue requires a metabolism that is more than 22 times faster (Aiello, Bates, & Joffe, 2001). When we look at mammals, we observe that primate brains tend to be 2.3 times larger than brains of nonprimates with the same body weight. When we observe humans, we discover that, given our body mass, our brains are some three to five times the size that would be expected in comparison to other mammals. How did humans, over the course of evolution, come to support such a big brain? One quick guess might suggest an increase in metabolism. However, humans support their brains without a large increase in the rate of basal metabolism. That is, metabolism in mammals appears to vary with body size, not brain size. For your information, metabolism or rate of energy use scales at about ¾ of body weight, as shown in Figure 4.11. This Figure shows the relationship between body weight and metabolism across a variety of species.

Now that we have examined body weight and metabolism, we can ask about brain size and metabolism. Whereas body weight shows a direct relationship to metabolism, brain size does not. The inconsistent relationship between brain size and metabolism suggests that, throughout evolution, human metabolic requirements may have been constrained. This may also have implications for adaptation and behavior. As we will see, such an increase in brain size must have been related to other factors, such as the types of foods early humans ate, the types of activities we engaged in, as well as the competition for food sources between infants and others around them. This competition between infants and others in turn may

| Figure 4.11 | Organisms' Metabolic Rate vs. Body Weight |

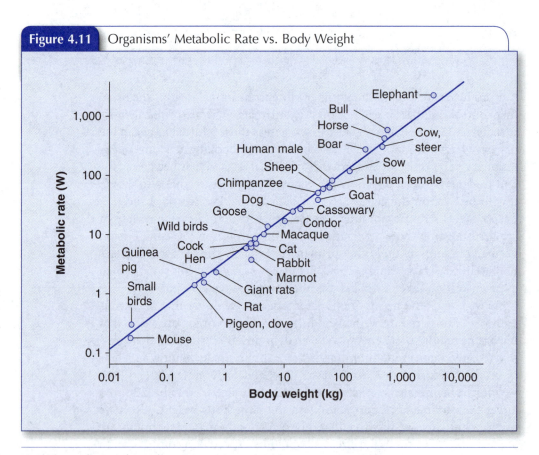

Note: The graph uses a log scale.

have limited the number of offspring humans produced as well as shaped the role of caregivers and extended families in providing food.

The development of human brains and their complex wiring both take more resources and a longer period of dependency than is seen in other species, which has significant implications for parent-child dependency and interactions. In terms of resources, newborns use 87% of their resting metabolism for brain growth and functioning, compared to 44% at age five and 25% in adulthood (Bogin, 2000). These percentages are more than twice those found in chimpanzees. Some researchers have suggested that the way humans have adapted to a larger brain is to give birth earlier. That is, compared to other mammals, human are not fully developed when we are born. In fact, it has been estimated that about half of all synapses in humans are formed after birth (see Changeux, 2004 for an overview). Human birth occurs during a phase in which it has been estimated that synapses are formed at the rate of 40,000 per second, which would be 2,000,000 each minute (Bourgeois, 1997). Compared to chimpanzees, whose cranial capacity increases 1.6 times after birth, the cranial capacity of humans increases 4.3 times. Unlike nonhuman primate brains, the brains of human infants continue to grow at pre-birth rates for about 13 months after birth. If the growth rate of humans actually matched other primates, then the human infant would remain in the womb 21 months! Of course, an infant of this size could not pass through the birth canal, given the size of a human female's pelvis. The pelvis, in turn, is constrained by require- ments associated with walking upright on two feet. Thus, evolution appears to have made a tradeoff between the requirements of walking upright and the development of a large brain. The tradeoff resulted in an infant who is born less well-developed and in need of more support, com- pared to other primates. It also resulted in human births taking longer and placing the mother in more risk than is seen in other primates. As we will see in later chapters, this need for support for both infants and mothers in turn requires a social system, which greatly shapes human development (see Cartwright, 2000 for additional details).

Returning to the question of brain size, we can also examine the rela- tionship between brain weight and body weight. As body weight increases, brain weight also increases. Figure 4.12 shows this relationship. Note in the Figure that humans and dolphins have a brain weight that is larger than that predicted from the regression line based on body weight.

Allman (1999) has modified the graph of primate body weight by brain weight to include what the primates eat (see Figure 4.13 on page 145). What he notes is that primate species that eat mainly leaves have smaller brains than those that eat fruit. This is, of course, related to a variety of factors. One of these is that leaves require more energy to digest than fruit. Thus, energy that is used for digestion cannot be used by the brain. This type of thinking is also supported in evolutionary terms because there appears to be an inverse relationship between the size of the brain and the digestive organs of

Figure 4.12   Brain Weight vs. Body Weight in a Variety of Species

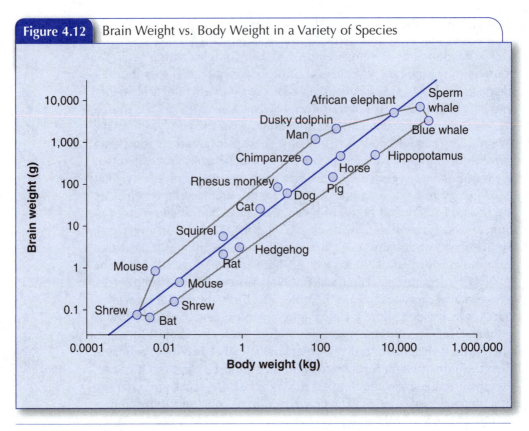

Note: The graph uses a log scale.

the gut. In humans, there appears to be a gram-for-gram tradeoff over evolutionary time between the increase in brain size and the reduction of human digestive organs as compared to apes. Allman further suggests that although its evolutionary development must have been highly interactive, fruit eating requires larger and more complex brains because an organism must know where the fruit trees are and also anticipate when they will be producing ripe fruit. A brain capable of noting color would also be beneficial for assessing the ripeness of the fruit. Further, the limited amount of ripe fruit must have resulted in greater competition than would be the case for leaves, which are more readily available. This same type of thinking would also apply to meat eating in humans because meats are easier to digest than leaves, and hunting for meat sources requires a variety of complex cognitive processes and may be best accomplished in groups.

Allman (1999) further examined the relationship between brain weight and life span in humans, gorillas, orangutans, and chimpanzees. There is a strong relationship between brain size and longevity, which in turn is related to food source. For example, the gorilla, which eats leaves and plants, has a relatively smaller brain and shorter life span compared to other primates.

Figure 4.13 Brain Weight vs. Body Weight for Species That Consume Different Types of Food

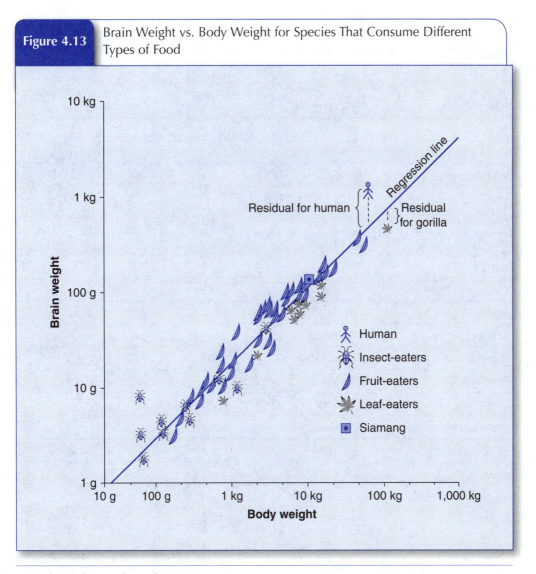

Note: The graph uses a log scale.

Among primates, humans have the longest life span and the largest brains. Unfortunately, these data were not extended to other mammals known for life spans similar to humans, such as horses, whales, and elephants.

The question of importance to psychologists relates to the evolution of cognitive processes. In our previous discussions, we have considered brain weight in relation to an organism's body weight, which some refer to as the **Encephalization Quotient (EQ)**. Figure 4.14 shows brain weight and EQ for a variety of mammals.

Research suggests that it is not EQ but absolute brain size that better predicts mental abilities (Gibson, Rumbaugh, & Beran, 2001). This is consistent

| Figure 4.14 | Brain Weight, Encephalization Quotient (Brain Weight/Body Weight), and Number of Cortical Neurons in Various Species | | |

Animal taxa	Brain weight (in g)	Encephalization quotient	Number of cortical neurons (in millions)
Whales	2600–9000	1.8	
False killer whale	3650		10 500
African elephant	4200	1.3	11 000
Man	1250–1450e	7.4–7.8	11 500
Bottlenose dolphin	1350	5.3	5800
Walrus	1130	1.2	
Camel	762	1.2	
Ox	490	0.5	
Horse	510	0.9	1200
Gorilla	430e–570	1.5–1.8	4300
Chimpanzee	330–430e	2.2–2.5	6200
Lion	260	0.6	
Sheep	140	0.8	
Old world monkey	41–122	1.7–2.7	
Rhesus monkey	88	2.1	480
Gibbon	88–105	1.9–2.7	
Capuchin monkey	26–80	2.4–4.8	
White-fronted capuchin	57	4.8	610
Dog	64	1.2	160
Fox	53	1.6	
Cat	25	1.0	300
Squirrel monkey	23	2.3	480
Rabbit	11	0.4	
Marmoset	7	1.7	
Opossum	7.6	0.2	27
Squirrel	7	1.1	
Hedgehog	3.3	0.3	24
Rat	2	0.4	15
Mouse	0.3	0.5	4

with brain imaging work from the neurosciences, which shows that the actual size of a body part does not map directly to the size of its representation in the brain. Rather, it is the sensitivity or acuity of the sensory and motor processes that reflect the amount of cortical tissue devoted to those processes. Thus, our hands and tongue have more cortical areas devoted to them than do our feet, for example, even though our feet are larger than our hands. Across species there is differential representation of body parts in the brain depending on their utilization. For example, the hands of raccoons, the tails of spider monkeys, the snouts of coatimundis, and the lips of llamas all have increased cortical areas devoted to their control. Thus, greater sensitivity in the sensory and motor system results in larger cortical areas devoted to those tasks.

Some higher cognitive tasks that humans perform, such as speaking language, require a motor component, whereas other higher level tasks, such as memory, do not. When we consider complex cognitive tasks, the nature of the relationship between cognitive abilities and brain areas becomes more complex. There are two primary ways of conceptualizing this relationship. The first is the **mental module model** or **Swiss army knife model**. This model has been proposed by a number of researchers interested in evolutionary psychology (Cosmides & Tooby, 1992; Pinker, 1997). The model suggests that the brain, like a Swiss army knife, contains a number of modules devoted to specific tasks. Thus, there would be a module for language, a module for spatial abilities, and so forth. Underlying this model is the suggestion that evolution of cognitive abilities carried with it the requirement for a new neural module in the brain. The **alternative to the mental module model** suggests that increased abilities come with a global increase in neurons and their interconnectedness within the brain that allows for greater information processing. Most neuroscientists today favor the second model, although there may be a greater relationship between these two models than can be seen at first appearance because as the brain increases in size, there is a limit to the number of neurons that any one neuron can connect to. This, in turn, allows for the fragmentation of functions, or processing nodes, to be developed. Indeed, as brains grow larger over evolutionary time, there tend to be proportionately more connections with neurons within the region and fewer from those outside. That is to say, there are more short-distance than long-distance connections in the brain. Additionally, there can be temporal delays in neurons' signal transmission between regions. For example, as the primate brain has enlarged, the proportional number of connections through the corpus callosum between the left and right hemispheres has been reduced (Striedter, 2005). This, along with temporal delays through the corpus callosum, has been seen as the basis for hemispheric specialization, in which the left and right hemispheres in humans differ in their ability to process language and spatial relationships, as discussed previously. Overall, the implication for brain size is similar in both models. That is, both models suggest that, over evolutionary time, the development of higher cognitive processes required an increase in cortical tissue. Of course, an increase in cortical tissue would require a larger skull area to house the brain. This gives us an opportunity to create a gross estimate of cognitive abilities from the fossil record by examining the cranial capacity of a species.

In primates, not only is there a relationship between body size and brain size, but there is also a relationship between brain size and underlying brain tissue. For example, gray matter in the brain, which is composed of cell bodies and dendrites, is directly related to the overall volume of the brain across primate species. That is, across primates, the percent of gray matter remains basically constant. As a generalization, you may say that gray matter is involved in the processing of information, whereas white matter is involved in moving information from one area of the brain to another. Unlike gray matter, white matter, which is composed of axons with myelin sheaths, increases as brain size increases. That is, whereas about 9% of the brains of lower primates are composed of white matter, 34% of the human brain is white matter, while gray matter remains a constant percentage.

An intriguing challenge is how to understand sex differences in brain size. There is ample data to show that human adult male brains are larger than those of adult females (Falk, 2001). In fact, the brain size of males is approximately 100 g larger than that of females, when adjusted for body weight or for height (Ankney, 1992). These same gender differences in brain size have also been reported in children. Recent research suggests one way to understand these differences may lie in the manner in which male and female brains are "wired." Examining the white matter of the brain, gray matter of the brain, and cerebrospinal fluid, Gur and his colleagues (1999) found differences in their distribution in the brains of males and females. Females had a higher percentage of gray matter (55% vs. 51%) whereas males had a higher percentage of white matter (40% vs. 38%). Males also had more cerebrospinal fluid (CSF) in their **sulci**, the depressions or fissures on the surface of the brain (8% vs. 6%). Further, males and females showed different patterns in relation to the two hemispheres of the brain. Males had more gray matter in the left as compared to the right hemisphere and more CSF in the right as compared to the left hemisphere. Females, on the other hand showed no differences in gray matter, white matter, or CSF between the two hemispheres of the brain. One implication of these findings for cognitive processing is that females have more tissue available for computational processes, whereas males have more for the transfer of information across different regions of the brain. The greater lateralization in males as compared to females is also consistent with the lateralization of function literature. In terms of function, it has been shown that language is more lateralized to the left hemisphere and spatial processing is more lateralized to the right hemisphere in males as compared to females, who show less lateralization of function.

The question arises as to how the differences in gray matter, white matter, and CSF are related to performance. As would be predicted from brain size alone, performance on spatial tasks correlate with volume of gray matter and white matter for both males and females. Further, performance on verbal tasks correlate with volume of white matter, but not gray matter. However, the lateralization differences in the Gur et al. study did not predict performance on cognitive tasks.

Evolution of Sensory Systems

Scientists have also considered how neural networks evolved to give us sensory information. We know that the task of sensory systems is to derive meaning from energy that exists in the external world. All sorts of energy exists in our universe, but humans have receptors for only a small portion of the electromagnetic spectrum. We experience these as sights and sounds. We don't see, hear, or feel information coming from frequencies in the radio or TV or microwave bands, although these are physically similar to the frequencies in the visual range, but on a different frequency. Why is this? One answer can be found by examining the evolution of our sensory systems in response to environmental conditions.

Let us take vision as an example. As you remember, a little more than 500 million years ago, there was an increase in the diversity of life forms of earth. Organisms existing at that time lived in water. One characteristic of water is that it transmits some frequencies in the electromagnetic spectrum better than others. As Figure 4.15 demonstrates, those frequencies that are least affected when passed through water correspond to those that our visual system is most sensitive to. Thus, although the visual system continued to evolve as organisms lived outside of water, the physical frequencies processed by our visual system harken back to adaptations manifested more than 500 million years ago. By the way, you may have also noted in Figure 4.15 that low frequencies (approximately 100 Hz) were also transmitted without reduction in water. These are frequencies used by electric fish to probe and sense their environment.

It appears that during this period of increasing diversity more than 500 million years ago, new genetic variations developed that produced different types of photoreceptors. One type of photoreceptor was sensitive to low light and evolved in the rods in our eyes, which allow us to see in dim light. Another type of photoreceptor was produced that required greater illumination. Over time, the receptors of this system became sensitive to different frequencies in the visual spectrum. These were the forerunners of the cones in our visual system, which allow us to experience colors. These genes for cones differ in different species, resulting in different sensitivity to different parts of the visual spectrum.

Figure 4.15

Graph Showing the Ability of Different Frequencies to Pass Through Water. The graph shows the most reduction (attenuation) at frequencies outside the wavelengths processed by the human visual system.

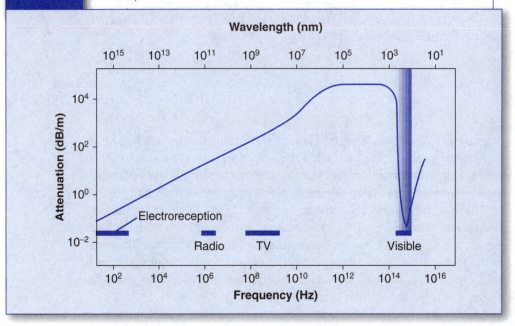

The visual system evolved to solve a variety of tasks. We rarely think about how stable the world stays as we turn our heads and move through space. However, our vestibular system senses movement and sends this information to the hindbrain, which in turn sends signals to the eye muscles. This enables our eyes to move in the opposite direction from our movement, in order to compensate for that movement and leave the image on our retina stable. Further corrections take place in the cerebellum, which compares changes in eye velocity and head velocity. The front-facing location of our eyes enables us to determine depth, which would have been helpful for both eye-hand coordination as well as catching prey.

As primates evolved, there has been a shift from reliance on the olfactory system to reliance on the visual system. In fact, the olfactory bulb is smaller and simpler in humans than in other primates. The question that evolutionary psychologists have been interested in is, How do we determine what information we should be paying attention to? The most basic answer is that we pay attention to those aspects of the environment that have signals of value to us. Loud noise, which may signal danger, is one such example. However, because humans have never been a solitary species and have always lived in social groups, a further answer is that we pay particular attention to the cues of others, especially facial expressions. Humans not only have carefully tuned visual systems for noting changes in facial expressions, we also have large cortical areas that produce facial expressions (e.g., directing muscles that retract the corners of the mouth and smooth or wrinkle skin around the eyes). Part of the limbic system, the **amygdala**, receives input from areas of the cortex involved in facial expression. We know this because damage to this area results in the lack of ability to detect emotional expression, even though the person can identify the face. We not only watch the expressions of others, we are also attuned to their movements. In fact, when we are watching someone perform a task, there are neurons in specific areas of our brain that fire as if we were performing the task ourselves. These are called **mirror cells** and may be involved in observational learning as well as development of an understanding of others.

Hominin Evolution

The majority of this chapter examined the evolution of the brain across a variety of species. Scientists have discovered that as humans evolved, our brains become relatively larger as a result of our neocortex becoming larger (Striedter, 2005). Although as we have seen, humans do not have the largest brain either in absolute or relative terms, humans do have the largest number of cortical neurons (Roth & Dicke, 2005). This results from the high density of neurons in the human brain. It is particularly interesting that the neocortex evolved an amazing level of direct access to the motor neurons of the medulla and spinal cord. This enables humans to have a high degree of dexterity in our hands as well as to control the muscles of our eyes, jaws, face, tongue, and vocal cords. Humans also have better control over their breathing than do most other species. The obvious advantage of this arrangement is the ability it gives humans to produce vocal sounds as well as facial expressions. The enlargement of the frontal areas in humans also gave us the ability to exert voluntary control over responses, rather than just respond automatically to stimuli. Surprising as it may seem, the modern human brain does not appear to contain any areas not found in other primate species. However, humans use these areas for different purposes. For example, similar areas to those humans use for language, such as Broca's and Wernicke's areas, are also found in other primates.

At this point, let us take a brief look at hominin evolution (see Figure 4.16). **Hominin** refers to a number of species including humans. The older word was **hominid,** which was replaced in order to be more precise in naming species, although there is still confusion concerning the terms, and you will see both. In order to understand the evolutionary relationship of these species, it is necessary to draw information from a variety of sources including paleontology, comparative anatomy, anthropology, and embryology. The picture is, of course, incomplete. Even fossil records that

Figure 4.16   Timeline Showing Species That Are Part of the Human Family. The *Ardipithecus* provides a link between earlier and later hominins.

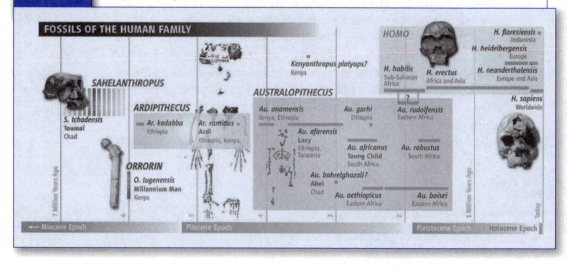

are the most solid are incomplete, given the time frame under study. As with other lines of evolution, you should not think of these species forming a straight line. Rather, they are best represented by branches on a bush (see Figure 4.17).

In 1974, a discovery was made in the remote desert region of Ethiopia: a skeleton of a human ancestor that lived some 3.2 million years ago. She was the first *Australopithecus afarensis* discovered and was called "Lucy" after the Beatle's song—*Lucy in the Sky With Diamonds*. Lucy walked on two legs, although she had a more ape-like head, long arms, and a brain about ¼ the size of current-day human brains. Findings have suggested that Lucy's species had a fourth metatarsal and arches in their feet, similar to modern-day humans (Ward, Kimbel, & Johanson, 2011). Thus, they were able to walk upright.

A discovery of an even earlier hominin was report in 2009 and described in the journal *Science* (see Gibbons, 2009 for an overview). This discovery pointed to a hominin called *ardipithecus* that lived before the time of Lucy, 4.4 million years ago in an area of Africa that is now Ethiopia. The amazing part of the discovery was that a more complete skeleton was found, which included most of the skull, teeth, pelvis, hands, and feet. This skeleton provides an unexpected picture. Some scientists expected that the species before Lucy would represent a transition point between primates and humans. However, *ardipithecus* does not resemble a chimpanzee, gorilla, or other nonhuman primate. Rather, this was a species that was neither chimpanzee nor human. The skeleton found was a female, and she was about four feet tall and weighed about 110 pounds. This is about the size of a chimpanzee, with the brain size to match. Based on her skeleton, she is assumed to have walked upright and planted her feet flat on the ground. It is also assumed that she could

Figure 4.17 Timeline Depicting Early Human Species

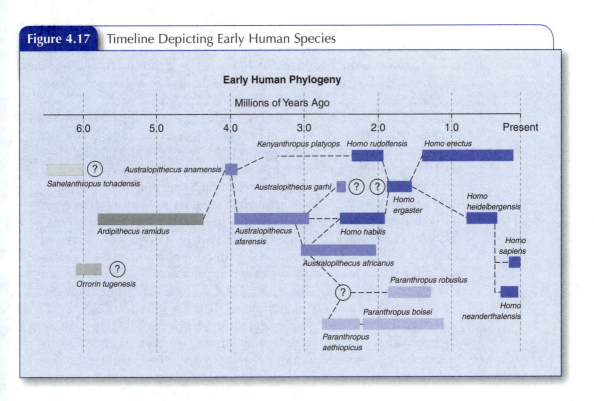

move through the tops of trees because she had an opposable big toe, which could grasp limbs. Other evidence suggests that she lived in woodlands rather than grasslands.

The next oldest hominin species that we know about is the *australopithecine* that appears to have walked upright between three and four million years ago. By this time, they had lost the opposing big toe, which is seen in other apes. We know they walked upright from fossil records of footprints found in Tanzania and the structure of the skeleton—mainly the pelvis, spine, and feet. Their hips and legs appear better suited for walking on the ground than on tree limbs. This would also make it easier to walk in open woodlands as opposed to dense forests. The best-known example of this species is Lucy. Some researchers consider it important that the ability to walk upright came some time before changes in brain size. Australopithecines overlapped with another species of the genus *Homo,* classified as *Homo habilis.*

Homo habilis lived from 2.4 to 1.6 million years ago. It was given the name "handyman" because of the tools that have been found with it. The first specimens of this species were discovered by the Leakeys in Africa in the 1960s. Its arms were somewhat long and its legs somewhat short. This species had hands like we do today, with opposing thumbs. Opposing thumbs enable you to easily pick up objects and to do precise work with your hands. Tools found at these sites were basically stones with a sharp edge. Consistent with tools that could be used with food preparation was the discovery that this species had smaller teeth. That is, if you can use your hands and tools to prepare food, then there would be no advantage to having large teeth. The height of *Homo habilis* is thought to be around five feet, with a weight of 100 pounds. The brain size of this species was around 650 cc.

During this same period another species of *Homo* appeared—*Homo erectus.* Dating from around 1.8 million years ago, *Homo erectus* used more sophisticated tools and probably fire. They were also thought to make containers for food and water. Interestingly, once the tools appear in the fossil record, they remain largely unchanged, suggesting that the species lacked innovation. There has been some suggestion that this species was tall (at least six feet) and slender and may have been more efficient at walking than current-day humans. This species had a brain size of around 1,000 cc, which is about a third less than current-day humans. What is intriguing is that fossils of *Homo erectus* are found not only in Africa, but also in Asia and Europe. This suggests that this was the first of the hominins to migrate out of Africa. A little less than a million years ago, the ice age began with alternating periods of greater and lesser cold. This isolated the populations in Europe, Asia, and Africa. The Asian group evidently became extinct. The European group evidently led to *Homo Neanderthalensis* and the African group led to *Homo sapiens.*

In 1856, near the time Darwin was preparing to publish his book *On the Origin of Species*, a German school teacher found some human-like bones in a cave in the Neander Valley. Although some debate ensued, it became clear that these bones, and others found previously in Belgium as well as other parts of Europe and the Middle East, were different from modern humans. These individuals had a broad rib cage, wide pelvis, large protruding jaws, large nasal area, long thick skulls, and projecting brow ridges. The brain size of 1,450 cc may have been slightly larger than modern humans but is also consistent with a bulkier body size. The body type is associated with colder climates, as opposed to the slender humans of Africa. Named for the valley in which this German specimen was found, *Homo Neanderthalensis* was considered to be a distinct species of humans who lived between 230,000 and 30,000 years ago. Because the spelling of the German word for valley was changed from *thal* to *tal* in the early 1900s, today you will see both the old spelling *Neanderthal* and the new spelling *Neandertal* when referring to this species of hominin. Judging by the variety of tools and weapons found with them, it is likely the Neandertals were formidable hunters. Their tools appear to have been made for specific purposes. They were the first human-like species to have been found to bury their dead—one burial site dates from about 100,000 years ago. They also decorated their bodies with pigments. Until 2010, it was thought that although Neandertals overlapped with *Homo sapiens* in Europe and they probably came in contact with one another, there was little in the way of mating between the two groups. However, as

I will discuss in more detail in the next chapter, more recent DNA analysis gives a different picture and suggests that mating did take place (Gibbons, 2010).

Also in 2010, a finger bone was discovered in the Denisova cave in southern Siberia that suggests that another *Homo* group existed along with both the Neandertals and modern humans. DNA analysis indicates that this group, called the Denisovans, diverged from Neandertals about 640,000 years ago. About 300,000 years ago, the Neandertals went into ice-age Europe, whereas the Denisovans went east. There is also evidence to suggest that the Denisovans were present in Asia about 45,000 years ago. This is shown by the fact Denisovans share DNA mutations with people from Papua, New Guinea, with 4% to 6% of their DNA in common. This suggests complex interactions between early humans, the Neandertals, and the Denisovans. This story is still being articulated.

Modern humans, referred to as *Homo sapiens*, are thought to have appeared in Africa somewhere between 195,000 and 160,000 years ago, although the exact date varies depending on the research method used. The brain size of modern humans is somewhere around 1,350 cc. *Homo sapiens* are characterized by a small pelvis area, a prominent chin, and a forehead that rises sharply. Evidence suggests that humans began to migrate out of Africa around 90,000 years ago, although recent findings suggest it might have been earlier, initially through the Middle East. *Homo sapiens* are associated with sophisticated tool use. Beginning about 80,000 years ago, bone harpoon points appear. By 40,000 years ago, a wide variety of materials such as flint and bone were used for tools such as needles and fishhooks. Also, clothing and art began to appear. This included objects worn as decoration on the body. From a psychological standpoint, symbolic behavior is seen for the first time. A variety of art objects dating from around 30,000 years ago have been discovered. In Germany, a series of animal figurines from about 34,000 years ago were discovered. These included figures of a lion, panther, bison, horse, reindeer, and mammoth. Carved from ivory, they were discovered in the caves of Vogelherd. In France, a series of cave paintings depicting a variety of animals dating from 32,000 years ago were discovered. These can be seen at http://www.culture.gouv.fr/culture/arcnat/chauvet/en/index.html as well as http://www.bradshawfoundation.com/france/index.php. The exact meaning of the cave painting of this era is unknown, although some scholars have suggested a religious significance. Based on these types of behavioral changes, it is argued that the archeological record has changed more in the last 40,000 years than it had in the prior million years (Klein, 2000). Compared to other human species, *Homo sapiens* have modified their environments in ways not seen previously and in a relatively short time. Some researchers speculate that one aspect associated with these changes some 50,000 to 40,000 years ago was changes in neural capacity that allowed for language.

SUMMARY

The human brain has been estimated to contain 100 billion neurons and more than 100,000 kilometers of interconnections. The thin outer shell of the brain consists of dark-colored cells called *gray matter*. Underlying this are the axons, which transfer information throughout the brain. Their myelin sheaths are lighter in color, and thus these areas are referred to as *white matter*. Mammals have evolved a brain structure different from other organisms— a six-layered neocortex. There is great variation among mammals in cortical size and organization. Separate cortical areas are devoted to processing specific types of information. The human brain is about 2% of body weight, but it uses some 25% of our energy. In the 1800s, Hughlings Jackson developed two principles based on evolutionary analysis, hierarchical integration and encephalization. Paul MacLean developed the idea of the triune brain. There are a variety of processes that show humans can process information outside of conscious awareness, including blindsight and split brain research. The brain has evolved a network for processing task-related information and a separate network for processing internal processes such as mind wandering. One area of study has been the relationship between evolution of brain size and cognitive processing. It is possible to describe early human species prior to present-day humans and examine their evolution.

STUDY RESOURCES

Review Questions

1. Why is studying evolution through cellular structures a difficult undertaking? What alternative approaches have researchers used to study the pathways of evolution?

2. The human brain has an extremely complex structure. Construct a set of high-level maps of the human brain showing the relationship of functional building blocks such as axons and neurons, the location of "geographical areas" such as the lobes, and a timeline of the evolution of different levels such as the limbic system.

3. What is the difference between homologous similarity and analogous similarity?

4. What are the evolutionary advantages of hierarchical integration and encephalization proposed by Hughlings Jackson?

5. From an evolutionary perspective, what are some of the implications of the triune brain, a concept developed by MacLean?

6. Describe two simple perceptual processes that operate in humans below the level of conscious awareness and support the coexistence of perceptual systems on multiple levels.

7. What is the function of the brain's default network?

8. Describe the development of the central nervous system in the human fetus. How does it differ from other species, both primate and nonprimate?

9. What evolutionary advantage does having a larger brain provide? What tradeoffs were required to support the development of a larger brain?

10. Describe the two primary models for conceptualizing the relationship between cognitive abilities and brain areas. Which do you find most compelling? What evidence can you cite to support your answer?

11. What sex differences have been found in terms of brain size?

12. What evidence is there to support the evolution of our visual system?

13. How do we determine what information we should be paying attention to?

14. The evolution of hominin species has been described as best represented by branches on a bush. What were the different hominin species that have been discovered to date and what have they contributed to the homo sapiens of today?

For Further Reading

Allman, J. (1999). *Evolving brains.* New York: Scientific American Library.
MacLean, P. (1990). *The triune brain in evolution.* New York: Plenum.
Olson, S. (2000). *Mapping human history.* Boston: Houghton Mifflin.

Key Terms and Concepts

- Evolution of brain and function
- The brain in evolution
  - The brain structure of mammals
  - Hughlings Jackson
  - Triune brain
    - Blindsight
    - Hemispheric lateralization
- The brain's default network—internal and external processes
  - Higher cognitive processes
  - Development of the nervous system
  - Evolution of brain size
  - Other factors related to the brain
- Evolution of sensory systems
- Hominin evolution

SAGE Study Site

Visit the study site at **www.sagepub.com/ray** for chapter-specific study resources.

Glossary Terms

- Allocortex
- Allometric approach
- Alternative to the mental module model
- Amygdala
- Analogous similarity
- Ancestral characteristic
- Anterior
- Archicortex
- Axons
- Brain stem
- Caudal
- Central nervous system
- Cerebellum
- Cingulate
- Default network
- Derived characteristic
- Encephalization
- Encephalization Quotient (EQ)
- Frontal lobe
- Gastrulation
- Gray matter
- Hierarchical integration
- Hippocampus
- Hominid
- Hominin
- Homologous similarity
- Lateral structures
- Left hemisphere
- Lobes
- Machiavellian intelligence hypothesis
- Medial structures
- Mental module model

- Midline
- Mirror cells
- Myelin sheaths
- Neocortex
- Neomammalian brain
- Neuroethological approach
- Non-pyramidal neurons
- Occipital lobe
- Olfactory cortex
- Paleocortex
- Paleomammalian brain
- Parietal lobe
- Posterior
- Primitive characteristic
- Pyramidal cells
- R-complex
- Reptilian brain
- Right hemisphere
- Rostral
- Social intelligence hypothesis
- Specialized characteristic
- Stream of consciousness
- Subcortical structures
- Sulci
- Swiss army knife model
- Sylvian fissure
- Temporal lobe
- Thalamic structures
- Theory of mind
- Tree branching
- Triune brain
- White matter

Developmental Aspects 5

T he picture we have of our human ancestors begins more than 150,000 years ago in the high grasslands and wooded slopes of Eastern Africa, which today would be the countries of Ethiopia, Kenya, and Tanzania (Olson, 2002). It is assumed that those humans looked much like we look today. Early humans lived in groups and gathered nuts, fruits, and seeds. They obtained meat by hunting gazelles and rabbits as well as scavenging carcasses of animals killed by other predators. Because hunting was successful only about 20% of the time, gathering food was extremely important. Most reconstructions of this period suggest a division of labor, with females caring for infants and gathering food and males hunting but also involved in gathering.

A vexing question is why our species of humans replaced other human-like species such as the Neandertal people who came before them. Evidence suggests that modern humans and Neandertals lived near each other for thousands of years. It was initially believed that they did not interbreed. However, the sequencing of the Neandertal genome was completed in 2010, and we now know that Neandertals and modern humans did mate with each other (see Gibbons, 2010 for an overview). We know this from examining DNA from bones of Neandertals and comparing it with DNA from our own species. Specifically, the DNA of three Neandertal females was compared to the complete genomes of five living humans from around the world, and it was discovered that Europeans and Asians share 1% to 4% of their nuclear DNA with Neandertals. Africans, however, do not show shared DNA. This suggests that early humans interbred with Neandertals after the migration out of Africa. Other research suggests that our early ancestors did not fight with the Neandertals, but lived within proximity of them (Olson, 2002). For whatever reason, the Neandertals disappeared, and we became the single species of humans. Our similarity as a species is clearly demonstrated by the fact that humans from any country or race can breed with any other human on earth. In fact, there is less variation in the genes of humans than in those of other species.

One explanation for this lack of human genetic diversity is the occurrence of specific events in human history that reduced the size of the population of humans on earth. These events are referred to as *bottlenecks*. One such event happened about 70,000 years ago when the Toba supervolcano erupted in Indonesia, resulting in a 10-year winter that may have reduced the human population on earth to fewer than 15,000 individuals.

It is commonly assumed that somewhere around 100,000 years ago, some humans moved north along the Nile valley and then settled in the Middle East. Moreover, artifacts found in Crete also suggest that early humans reached this island around the same time (Strasser et al., 2010). Some 60,000 years ago, humans began to populate India and southeastern Asia and sailed to Australia. Human culture was also changing by this time, and people were wearing jewelry made from shells, bones, and animal teeth. They also created smaller and better stone tools. With the settlement of Europe around 40,000 years ago, we also see a species capable of producing art and technology. This is illustrated by sculptures of animals and human figures and the various cave paintings found throughout the world (Lewis-Williams, 2002). Manufactured objects such as projectiles, harpoons, awls, buttons, needles, and ornaments have been dated to this same period (Ambrose, 2001). About this time, eastern Asia was being settled. It was not until about 10,000 years ago that North and South America were inhabited by individuals thought to have come through a wide plain, which at that time joined Siberia with Alaska. One important change of lifestyle was the development of agriculture around 10,000 years ago, with its more fixed communities. However, it is generally argued that 10,000 years is too short a period for natural selection to have substantially affected our social and cognitive abilities in a simple genetic fashion, which has led researchers to look for epigenetic and other factors.

If we begin with the relatively recent period of about 5,000 years ago, when written language was developed, we realize that in a relatively short period of time, humans have modified their environment with the development of cities, technology, and, more recently, communication systems that link the world. Most researchers look to culture as one of the driving forces behind these changes. From this perspective, some developmental psychologists (e.g., Bjorklund & Pellegrini, 2002; Geary, 1995) have suggested that cognitive abilities should be considered as biologically primary or secondary abilities.

Biologically primary abilities are abilities such as language that have been part of human life from the earliest times. Biologically primary abilities develop effortlessly, and they universally follow a typical pattern of development in children. You do not need to formally teach a child language; he or she just picks it up. Every 2-year-old can do it. Secondary abilities, on the other hand, such as reading or higher mathematics, actually require effort and are of relatively recent origin. These secondary abilities generally require more extensive practice to master and may be taught at different times in different cultures. As you differentiate primary and secondary abilities, you must also consider the question of which of our psychological processes reflect more stable or invariant processes, and which are less fixed and open to modification. The term that is often used to describe conditions in which processes are open to modification is **plasticity**. In terms of development, a variety of studies have shown that human and other primate infants who are initially deprived of social and emotional stimulation show difficulties in these areas. However, these difficulties can be reversed if the infants are placed in a more caring and stimulating environment. Thus, humans and other organisms possess mechanisms that enable plasticity in developmental processes.

The complexity and plasticity of human beings is partly related to our large brains. Another important aspect is our extended juvenile period: We are born immature and continue to develop for the next 15 to 25 years. In describing development, evolutionary psychologists ask what role evolved psychological mechanisms have played in adapting infants and children to their physical and social environment (see Ellis & Bjorklund, 2005 and Bjorklund & Blasi, 2005 for an overview). For example, human children around the world spend a considerable amount of their available energy playing. As we consider play, we can consider how it helps children in their current social, emotional, cognitive, and physical development, as well as how it prepares them for future roles in society. Thus, this perspective helps us to think about how adaptations of infants and children impact adult development. This is a complicated question because it forces us to think about the interaction between adaptations of childhood, their impact on adulthood, and the manner in which they are passed to the next generation.

We begin with the manner in which children relate to their environment at different ages. As we do this, we find ourselves constantly asking the question, What factors underlie these interactions? In proposing answers to this question, we find ourselves looking at the context of the situation on a variety of levels, from the genetic to the cultural to even the environmental level, including weather and physical terrain. There is, of course, no one answer, but a complex interaction of factors involving multiple layers of analysis. However, it might be useful to think of an infant as constantly giving itself experiences based on its genetic programming and environmental situation. In this spirit, evolutionary psychology has allowed us to make some predictions and test hypotheses that psychology without an evolutionary perspective did not consider.

We begin at the beginning. We also begin with the obvious: Human infants cannot survive alone. They are dependent on a caregiver to take care of their needs. This caregiver, in turn, is most likely dependent on a larger community. Moving to an evolutionary level, we discover that there has not been a time in human history when human infants were not dependent upon caregivers. Thus, we assume that a critical question for humans has related to nurturing infants, and that our evolutionary history has made this a critical issue. To help us think about dependency, we can also consider alternative ways for infants to develop. Some fish, for example, will produce hundreds of offspring that, after birth, are at the mercy of the environment. These newborns are literally left to swim for themselves. Humans, on the other hand, generally give birth to one infant at a time. Although the brain of this infant develops at the same rate as that of other primates such as chimpanzees or gorillas, the human brain grows to about four times its birth size, whereas primate brains only double in size. Clearly, human infants are born in an undeveloped state compared to other species. Also, human females carry a risk of death when giving birth. Consider that a 200-pound female gorilla gives birth to a 4-pound baby, while a human female of half to two-thirds that weight gives birth to a 6- to 9-pound baby. The implications of this for both the baby and the mother are that mechanisms are needed to ensure the survival of the mother as well as the protection and development of the infant. Historically, it is the group that has given this support. Of course, humans are not unique in this: Other primates show caregiving behavior similar to our own.

In order to understand caregiving, we can also consider what happens when events such as war or natural disasters interrupt the normal caregiving pattern. John Bowlby (1969) sought to determine what would happen if a young child had its physical needs, such as food and housing, satisfied, but did not experience a close emotional connection. Where could he find such children? Unfortunately, there were children who became orphans during World War II. They were physically cared for, but they lacked the emotional attention from a caregiver, such as a mother dealing with her own infant. I will examine in some detail the results and implications of Bowlby's research later in this chapter. As terrible as events such as wars, floods, fires, hurricanes, as well as disease and accidents are to individuals, they are not uncommon events in human history. From an evolutionary perspective, we expect there to exist universal patterns of responding to such universal events through mother-infant interactions. We would also assume that we could find patterns for common alternatives to the more expected pattern, such as when the mother is not present because of death or sickness and is not available to the child. For example, Jay Belsky (2007) suggests different infant attachment styles may be productive in difficult environments and may adapt children to life in a world where people and resources are unpredictable, leading to different mating and parenting strategies than are found in children raised in more supportive environments. Thus, you would expect different types of relationships when times are good versus when they are difficult. To answer such questions, we search for alternative patterns displayed in a subgroup of individuals that are related to specific changes in the environment. We want to consider both the short-term and long-term patterns displayed.

Mother-Child Interactions

Whether we look at human or nonhuman primates, we observe a close bond between mothers and their infants. This is not surprising because infants, even before birth, are able to recognize their mother's heart rate and voice. The mother and the infant undergo a variety of physiological processes that aid in creating a bond. For example, infants show a "rooting" reflex when their lips are touched, which helps a new mother begin to produce milk. However, it is also true that the experience a new mother and infant have with each other is a process of learning and conditioning. For example, through classical conditioning, the hungry cry of an infant will result in the mother "letting down" or producing milk in preparation for feeding. There are, of course, a variety of events, such as physical contact, which are experienced as pleasurable by both the mother and infant. Thus, we see both internal and external processes and their constant interplay leading to mother-infant bonding. Bowlby (1969) named this process "attachment" rather than the traditional term used in psychoanalysis, which was "object relations." Bowlby saw the process of attachment as a social-emotional behavior equally as important as mating behavior and parental behavior. He saw attachment as a multifaceted process that involves a variety of developmental mechanisms during the first year of life. Attachment, according to Bowlby, was a process in which the mother was able to reduce fear by direct contact with the infant and provide support, called a "secure base." This secure base would allow for later exploratory behaviors. Bowlby suggested that there were five universal attachment behaviors in human infants:

1. sucking,

2. clinging,

3. crying,

4. following,

5. smiling.

It was assumed by Bowlby that the relative immaturity of the human infant resulted in attachment being a slower process in humans than in other primates.

Similar attachment mechanisms are also found in other primates (see Suomi, 2002 for an overview). Rhesus monkeys, along with a great variety of other animals, show attachment processes that parallel those seen in humans. In the wild, animals who become separated from their mother die. Thus, it is not surprising that a variety of infants, including humans, have the ability to cling tightly immediately after birth, as shown in Chapter 1 (Figure 1.6). Behaviors such as suckling, clinging, and following keep both the human and nonhuman primate infants in close contact with the mother. Suomi has suggested that the attachment bond in rhesus monkeys is like no other social relationship it will experience in its lifetime. Initially, it is the mother who offers a "secure base" to her infant in terms of food, comfort, and protection. As the infant begins to explore on its own, she monitors its behaviors and typically keeps it within arm's length. When they are between two and three months old, infant monkeys develop social fear. A similar process is seen in human infants at about nine months and is commonly called "stranger anxiety." After this point, it is the infant who maintains proximity and physical contact with the mother. As they explore, the infant monkeys return to the mother when distress is experienced. If the infant does not establish an optimal attachment relationship, it will actually explore less.

Bowlby (1969) focuses on four primates—chimpanzees, gorillas, baboons, and rhesus macaques—in considering the evolutionary origins of the human experience. In the decades since Bowlby published his classic book *Attachment*, scientists have studied a variety of other primates. Sarah Hrdy (2009) reviews this work and suggests that there is no one universal pattern of infant care among primates. There are even a few species of monkeys (e.g., *Callicebus*) in which the father carries the baby around when it is not nursing, and the infant shows more distress from being separated from the father than the mother. Hrdy also notes that among primates, continuous care with lots of contact does not appear to be a universal hardwired trait. In fact, primate mothers tend to cut corners and rely on shared care of their infants, a condition she likened to the human use of day care. The point to be made is that the primate ancestors of humans show no one pattern of child rearing that was passed on to us in a hardwired manner. If anything, there are a variety of patterns, including mothers who abandon their infants under certain conditions, as humans have been known to do. The larger picture is one of infants eager to make contact with other humans in their world and a variety of others, historically family, seeking to reciprocate.

RESEARCH CONCERNING ATTACHMENT

Today we know there is an evolutionary calculus that tends to support the physical and emotional climate for human development. However, in the 1950s there was a real debate between whether the infant's response to its mother is learned or whether certain inherent properties of the mother elicit infant attachment (Harlow et al., 1971). To better understand the nature of attachment in monkey infants, Harry Harlow (1959) first placed monkey infants in isolated cages after birth. In the cage were two surrogate mothers—one made of wire and the other made of terrycloth. The wire surrogates had bare bodies of welded wire, whereas the cloth surrogates were covered by soft, resilient terrycloth. Both surrogates had long bodies that could be easily clasped by the infant rhesus monkey (see Figure 5.1).

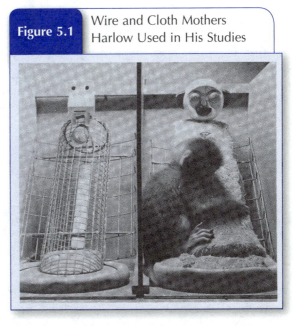

Figure 5.1 Wire and Cloth Mothers Harlow Used in His Studies

For half of the infants, a nipple by which they could feed themselves was attached to the wire surrogate, and for the other half the nipple was attached to the terrycloth surrogate. In either surrogate mother, the infants had the nutrition that they needed. If attachment was entirely learned through reinforcement, then the infant monkeys should go to the surrogate that fed them. What do you think happened? What happened was a finding completely contrary to the learning theory interpretation. As the infants who fed on the wire surrogate grew, they showed decreasing responsiveness to her and increasing responsiveness to the cloth surrogate, even though this surrogate had no food to offer (see Figure 5.2). From this, Harlow concluded that it is the contact comfort and not the feeding per se that binds the infant to the mother.

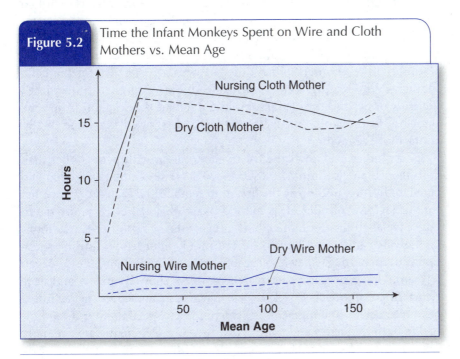

Figure 5.2 Time the Infant Monkeys Spent on Wire and Cloth Mothers vs. Mean Age

Note: Nursing was not a factor for which mother was chosen.

In the illustration from Harlow's work in Figure 5.3, the infant monkey can be seen to surround itself with a cloth diaper.

| Figure 5.3 | Infant Monkey Wrapped in Cloth Diaper |

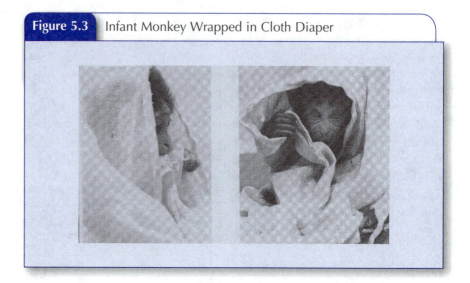

Harlow (1959) understood that mother-infant bonding is a complex process and sought to determine additional factors that influence its process. For example, he found that infants preferred a surrogate mother that rocked over one that was stationary (see Figure 5.4). Harlow also examined the role of temperature. He compared a warm wire mother with a cool cloth one and found that, initially, the infant monkeys preferred the warmth. However, after 20 days, they showed a preference for the cloth mother. Even creating a cloth surrogate "monster mother" who rocked violently or produced violent air blasts did not keep the infants from staying close to the cloth surrogate mother. This showed the value of this contact for the infant.

Later studies examined rhesus monkeys raised with peers rather than with their biological mothers (Suomi, 2002). These infants were fed and cared for by humans during the first month of life and then raised together for the next five months. At six months of age, the infants were moved into larger social groups containing both peer-reared and mother-reared monkeys of the same age. The peer-reared monkeys developed strong social bonds to each other. They also showed normal physical and motor development. However, these peer-reared monkeys showed anxiety and were reluctant to approach novel objects. They also appeared shy in initial encounters with unfamiliar peers. Overall, their social abilities were limited in both frequency and complexity. For example, the males were more impulsive and the females groomed less with their peers than mother-raised monkeys. These types of studies have led researchers to suggest that

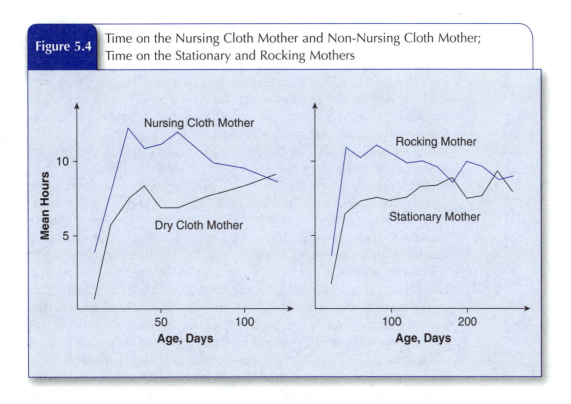

Figure 5.4 Time on the Nursing Cloth Mother and Non-Nursing Cloth Mother; Time on the Stationary and Rocking Mothers

early attachment relationships can have an important bearing on the development of interpersonal skills.

Part of Bowlby's interest in attachment came from observations of children in orphanages following World War II. Like the peer-reared monkeys, these children had all of their physical needs met, but they lacked a form of emotional and social connectedness. Following Darwin's lead, Bowlby carefully observed children and recorded his observations in a series of books and articles focused on secure attachment as well as loss and separation anxiety (Bowlby, 1951, 1969, 1988). Bowlby had been influenced by ethology. Thus, he interpreted attachment from an evolutionary perspective, emphasizing the survival value of attachment, especially as the human infant is beginning to crawl or walk on its own. In terms of the general characteristics of attachment, Bowlby reported that children who develop a secure bond or attachment with a caregiver or parent, who is usually their mother, display patterns of activity in relation to that caregiver that are especially strong from the end of the first year of life until about 3 years of age. First, the infant will show distress when the caregiver leaves. Second, the infant smiles, makes noises, or shows other signs of pleasure when the caregiver returns. Third, the infant shows distress when approached by a stranger, unless the caregiver encourages the interaction. And fourth, the infant will show more exploratory behaviors in an unfamiliar situation when the caregiver is present.

Based on infants' reactions to their caregiver, Mary Ainsworth developed the "strange situation" to research attachment patterns experimentally (Ainsworth, Blehar, Waters, & Wall, 1978). The basic procedure is to bring the infant and his or her mother into an unfamiliar room with toys. With the infant and mother alone, the infant is allowed to explore without the mother being involved. At this point, a stranger enters and talks with the mother and then approaches the infant. During this time, the mother leaves inconspicuously. The stranger reacts to the infant as appropriate. The mother then returns and greets and comforts the infant. Following this, the mother leaves the infant alone in the room, and the stranger returns. The mother then returns again and greets and picks up the infant while the stranger leaves. During this procedure, the researchers observe the infant's reaction to the return of the mother. Initially, Ainsworth et al. described three patterns of attachment styles. The first pattern, which is referred to as *secure attachment*, is characterized by the following pattern: the infant (1) engages in active exploration; (2) is upset when the mother leaves; and (3) shows positive emotions when the mother returns. The second pattern is called *avoidant style*. In the avoidant style, the infant shows more interest in the toys than the mother and shows less distress when the mother leaves and less positive emotion when she returns. The third attachment pattern is referred to as *anxious/ambivalent*. In this pattern, the infant appears preoccupied with having access to the mother and shows protest on her separation. When she returns, the infant may show anger or ambivalence toward her. More recently, other researchers have suggested that a fourth pattern of attachment may exist, which is characterized by disorganization. Of course, infants do not grow up in a vacuum, so it is also important to characterize the mothering style of the caregiver. With infants displaying secure attachment patterns, the style of the mother is consistent and responsive to her infant's signals. On the other hand, mothers of infants showing avoidant patterns tend to be more rejecting and rigid and, in general, insensitive to the infants' signals, including requests for bodily contact. Anxious/ambivalent patterns tend to be associated with inconsistent mothers who may be intrusive. Of course, the complexity of the situation is highlighted by the fact that some infants are easier to care for than others. That is to say, some infants appear to be temperamentally more irritable than others, and thus they could be more difficult for a caregiver to approach positively. Current research suggests that training mothers with irritable infants to develop a more secure relationship can, indeed, result in more secure attachment when the infants are later tested in the strange situation (van den Boom, 1994). Current research is also moving beyond the idea of a single attachment figure and considering the possibility that an infant can have different attachment relationships with a variety of people (see Hrdy, 2009; Van Ijzendoorn & Sagi, 1999). In Chapter 10, I will discuss in greater detail the manner in which a variety of caregivers can be involved in the attachment relationship.

GENETIC ASPECTS OF ATTACHMENT

Additional evidence to suggest a genetic component of attachment comes from work with the vole, a small rodent that is like a mouse. One type of vole, called a prairie vole, creates monogamous pair bonds for producing and rearing infants, whereas another type, the montane vole, does not. Examining the DNA of these two species, researchers have found differences in the region of the gene responsible for specific neuropeptide receptors, especially vasopressin and oxytocin (Insel, 2010; Insel & Hulihan, 1995; Insel & Winslow, 1999). Insel (2003, 2010) also suggests that the same brain circuits related to pleasant feelings, such as those following a reward, may also be related to the development of social attachment, and that these may be gender specific. This is particularly intriguing because other work with humans has suggested that oxytocin is related to the expression of affiliative or social behaviors in females (Taylor et al., 2002; see Taylor, 2002 for an overview).

Differential Susceptibility to Rearing Influences

In trying to understand why children raised in similar environments may actually show greater diversity than those raised in different environments, the developmental psychologist Jay Belsky (2005, 2007) suggests that children display a large variation in the degree to which they are influenced by their parents. That is to say, some children show a close coupling between their behavior and the manner in which they are reared, whereas others do not. Belsky suggests that natural selection has produced these differences in response to rearing pressures because this ensures that a variety of styles are available to unpredictable future events. We tend to think of evolutionary pressures happening in the present. However, we can also think of childhood as a time to prepare for future requirements. With a variety of styles available, some of one's offspring are more likely to survive, no matter what the conditions.

There are two types of research support for the idea that children show differential responses to parental influences. One is genetic. There is a MAOA gene located on the X chromosome that makes certain neurotransmitters inactive and has been associated with aggression in mice and humans. Specifically, this gene encodes the brain enzyme monoamine oxidase (MAOA) and makes such neurotransmitters as serotonin, norepinephrine, and dopamine inactive. Following a large number of boys over a long term, Caspi and his colleagues (2002) found that mistreatment as a child influenced some boys differently than others later in adulthood. Those boys who were mistreated in childhood and had a particular form of the MAOA gene were more likely to be violent and engage in a variety of antisocial behaviors as adults, including conflicts with law enforcement officials. Those without this particular form of the gene did not display antisocial behaviors, even if they had been mistreated as children. Thus, environmental influences such as maltreatment would be modulated by the presence of certain genetic structures. The other type of research support is behavioral. Belsky (2005) has reviewed a variety of these studies. What is surprising is that the infants who are most inhibited, fearful, and display negative emotions are the ones most affected by positive parenting.

Life History Theory

Every species has a different life history, although every species must deal with questions of birth, death, mating, living conditions, and survival. Different species answer these questions differently. Some species produce hundreds of offspring at a time, while others produce only one. Historically, organisms that have evolved to produce lots of offspring have been said to adopt an *r-selection strategy*, whereas those that produce few offspring have developed a *K-selection strategy*. These two strategies have been seen as end points on a larger r-K continuum. In difficult environments, which include the possibility that offspring will die or be eaten, the r-selection strategy is optimal. In more stable environments, the K-selection strategy has evolved. Although this continuum is used less today in life history theory, it did help to note a variety of differences in species. For example, some species have a short life span, while others have a long one. Some species mate early in the organism's development, while others do not. Some organisms die after their ability to mate and reproduce have ceased, while others, like humans, continue to live even though they can no longer produce offspring. Some species have a short development history, while others, like humans, have an extended period of development during which they are taken care of by parents. It is possible to graph a variety of these differences for various species. Hill (1993) graphed the average female adult lifespan by female age at maturity. These data are shown in Figure 5.5.

Each of the activities that an organism engages in requires that the organism convert energy from a variety of sources, including food, into energy that can be utilized. However, there is a limited amount of energy and resources that any given organism can utilize. Thus, there are always tradeoffs between the activities an organism will engage in. Extended developmental periods for children may reduce the amount of energy a parent can devote to his or her own activities. It would also limit the energy available to produce and care for additional children. Not only do species differ in terms of their life history, but they also can find themselves in either stable or fluctuating environments. Life history theory was developed in

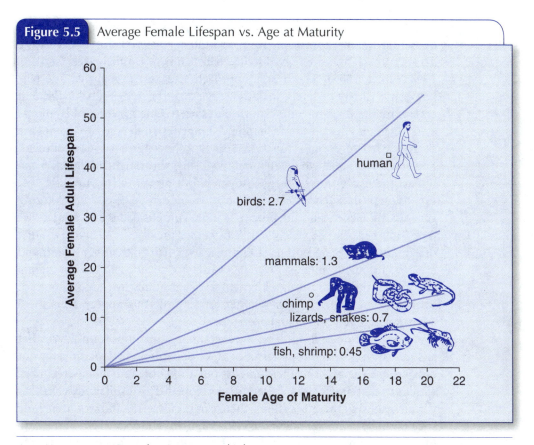

Figure 5.5 | Average Female Lifespan vs. Age at Maturity

Note: Humans approximate the same curve as birds.

biology to understand the evolved strategies including behavioral, physiological, and anatomical adaptations that influence survival and reproduction. Researchers have extended this thinking to a variety of fields, including psychology and anthropology (see Hill, 1993; Kaplan & Gangestad, 2005; Nylin & Gotthard, 1998; Ricklefs & Wikelski, 2002; Stearns, 1977; Strassmann & Gillespie, 2002 for overviews). Overall, life history theory offers a means of considering various evolved traits by articulating the cost, benefits, and tradeoffs of different patterns of development.

Developmental Psychology From an Evolutionary Perspective

Important debates have centered on the driving mechanisms and the flexibility of expressed behaviors, such as the gender differences seen in play. For example, boys show more rough and tumble play than girls. Why might this be? One theory that has attempted to describe the close relationship between genes and the environment in relation to development is the **developmental systems approach** (see Bjorklund & Blasi, 2005 for an overview). This approach was initially developed by Gilbert Gottlieb (see Gottlieb, 1998; Miller, 2007). The overall approach sees development as interplay between a variety of levels, including genes; neural activity; behavior; and environment, which includes culture and society. One key concept is epigenesis, which was discussed in Chapter 3. **Epigenesis** refers to the emergence of new structures and functions during the course of development. Epigenetic rules relate to the manner in which environmental influences can impact the expression of the genome without directly changing the DNA, even though these patterns of gene expression can be passed on to future generations. Genetically, the process is more complicated than a simple "we have traits because of a gene" view, as discussed previously. As noted, the diet of a mouse before conception can influence the hair color of her infants and even of her infants' infants. Overall, a variety of genetic and environmental factors may influence any developmental trait, resulting in a large amount of variability in when, or in what manner, certain traits may appear. Thus, there are patterns to developmental processes.

According to developmental systems theory, one important factor that ensures species-specific patterns of development is that organisms not only inherit the genes of their parents but also come into an environment similar to that in which their parents developed. This similar environment is seen by developmental systems theory in broad terms and would include such physical characteristics as gravity, air, light, and also water, in the case of aquatic animals. The human developmental environment generally includes nine months in a protective womb, an affectionate mother who feeds the infant, a father and kin to provide additional support, and peers later in childhood. Thus, an infant not only inherits a specific set of genes associated with its species but also an environment in which these genes play out the developmental process.

Gottlieb (1992, 1998) emphasized the point that although we may think experience is not necessary for such instinctual processes as attachment or imprinting, this is not exactly the case. In terms of attachment, for example, a new mother and infant may go through a series of encounters as they become more comfortable with one another. Thus, it is not the case that attachment works without any place for experience. To understand the role of experience in imprinting experimentally, Gottlieb modified the prenatal experience of ducklings. In a series of experiments, Gottlieb showed that if a newborn duck is placed in a round tub with audio speakers playing duck sounds from different species, the newborn duck will go toward the sound of its own species. Because the duck is newly born, most individuals would view this as an example of innate behavior. However, Gottlieb wondered whether other factors could play a role. In order to test this idea, Gottlieb first removed the eggs from the nest and separated them, so that the unborn ducklings could not hear the sounds of the mother or the other ducklings still in the egg. In this case, newborn ducks would still go toward the sound of their own species. In the next experiment, he used a reversible procedure that prevented the duckling from making sounds. Thus, the ducklings heard neither their own sounds nor those of other ducks. With this procedure, the ducklings showed no preference for sounds of their own species compared to that of other species. What this shows is that environmental factors are able to influence developmental processes from the earliest manifestation of the organism. As a practical matter, this means that we need to rethink the time periods during which various factors can influence development. This, of course, is consistent with the perspective presented in the earlier chapters, which suggests that all genetic processes in humans, except blood type, can be influenced by environmental factors.

Joe Campos and his colleagues have shown that infants do not show fear of heights until they are able to crawl (Campos, Bertenthal, & Kermoian, 1992). The fear of heights emerges as a complex interaction involving the visual system, the motor system, the feedback and experience that the infant receives as he or she begins to crawl, and the genes that prepare the organism to develop coordination and seek to crawl. All of these factors are further influenced by such environmental factors as when the baby is born. For example, babies born in the winter crawl sooner than those born in the summer because they begin learning to crawl during the summer, a time when parents are more likely to let them play on the floor.

TENETS OF EVOLUTIONARY DEVELOPMENTAL PSYCHOLOGY

Bjorklund and Blasi (2005) suggest there are at least six basic assumptions or ideas that underlie evolutionary developmental psychology:

1. It is necessary to describe the manner in which evolutionary principles apply to adults and the manner in which these principles influence the patterns and development of infants and children.

2. It is important to consider the manner in which the activities of children are the expression of evolved epigenetic programs.

3. Children show a high degree of plasticity and are able to adapt to a variety of initial environments. The assumption is that children will be able to adjust their behaviors to a particular environment in a way that will be to their best advantage. In order to do this, infants and children must be sensitive to the present context and perform self-regulation processes consistent with a particular context. One example of this is the finding that children reared in an environment with inadequate resources, such as a high-stress situation with rejecting

and harsh parents, will mature faster than children reared in a low-stress, well-resourced home with warm and sensitive parents (Ellis & Garber, 2000). Further, later mating strategies can be influenced by supportive and nonsupportive environments (Belsky, Steinberg, & Draper, 1991). Children reared in well-resourced environments tend to show more long-term, enduring relationships with their partner, have children at a later age, and are more invested in their offspring, whereas children reared in a less supportive environment show the opposite. That is, they have children at an earlier age, have less stable relationships with their partners, and are less invested in their children.

4. The extended childhood of humans allows the child to understand the complexities of human social communities and incorporate cultural traditions. A variety of researchers have noted that humans have a longer juvenile period than any other species. We are born incapable of taking care of ourselves and require an extended period of care until adulthood. One implication of this situation is that we spend a large amount of time with other members of our species during our youth. In this context, infants and children interact with a variety of others as well as observe the interactions of others. It is in these interactions that children incorporate the complex structures of social relationships. Because children also exist within the larger social environment, they also take in the rules of their culture.

5. Many aspects of childhood serve as preparation for adulthood and were selected over the course of evolution. One implication of this is that we must consider how particular behaviors or processes might prepare a child for actions in the future, rather than just the present. Play is one example of such a behavior. Certain gender differences seen in children's behaviors may play a similar role. Characteristics that serve later adult development are referred to as **deferred adaptations.**

6. Not all characteristics of infants and children are preparations for adulthood. Some characteristics of infants and children were selected to serve an adaptive function at a specific time in childhood. Characteristics that serve only the developmental period are referred to as **ontogenetic adaptations.**

Developmental Theories

As evolutionary perspectives have developed, researchers have reconsidered some of the classic theories in developmental psychology (Bjorklund & Blasi, 2005; Bjorklund & Pellegrini, 2002; Burgess & MacDonald, 2005).

MacDonald and Hershberger (2005) emphasize the importance of domain-specific mechanisms. As developmental processes unfold in an infant, they are directed at specific tasks. In other words, there is a hierarchy of needs, such as food and comfort, that an infant seeks and that take priority over other needs or desires. The infant possesses intrinsic motivation. The infant, and then the child, is a curious and interested explorer of the world, rather than a passive recipient of environmental influences. The infant actually seeks new information including motor, emotional, and cognitive responses. He or she feels happy when solving a problem or learning something new. This, in turn, enables the infant to have a close relationship with its environment and to learn accordingly. As psychologists, we tend to focus on the cognitive and emotional levels, but we must realize that the infant's nervous system is constantly asking questions concerning what it needs next. We know, for example, if children lack a certain nutrient in their diet, they will modify their diet to increase those foods in which they are deficient. Overall, this suggests that infants come into the world with a series of genetic procedures ready to be exploited for his or her own benefit.

SENSORY DEVELOPMENT

Human newborns show the ability to make a variety of sensory differentiations (Rakison, 2005). For example, they prefer the taste and smell of sweet nourishment and can differentiate a variety of tastes. Newborns can identify the scent of their mother and prefer it to that of a stranger. They can also recognize their mother's voice, which they prefer. Newborns demonstrate a rooting reflex, which facilitates nursing, as well as protective reflexes such as coughing, sneezing, and blinking. In terms of visual perception, newborns prefer looking at a representation of a face—a head-sized paddle with eyes, eyebrows, nose, and mouth—rather than a paddle with these same features arranged in a non-face-like way. Overall, research suggests that newborns come into the world with mechanisms that predispose them to look at faces. Human newborns also respond to motion and are able to track moving objects. This, of course, is an evolved ability seen across a variety of species, which would help track predators and thus increase an organism's chance of survival.

MEMORY AND COGNITION

Memory is often thought of in domain-specific terms. Squirrels appear to possess a specialized memory system for identifying the location of previously stored nuts. Some people say they can't remember names; others don't remember how to spell certain words; still others can't remember where they parked their car in a parking lot. Developmentally, human infants have an amazing capacity for remembering spoken words and songs as well as faces. One influential idea is that with environmental experience, human infants develop the nervous system processes that make memory possible. Specifically, it is suggested that memory and cognitive systems are organized around the experience of events, including interactions with others (Nelson, 2005). Flavell (2000) has suggested four ways in which the early predisposition and abilities of infants involve other humans:

1. Human infants find human faces, voices, and movements highly interesting.

2. Infants can perceptually analyze and discriminate human stimuli.

3. Infants seek to attend to and interact with other humans.

4. Infants respond differently to humans than they do to objects.

Infants are capable of memory processes requiring procedural memory, priming, and perceptual representations. In terms of procedural memory, if an infant has learned to solve a simple puzzle, he or she shows improvement when presented with the same puzzle a second time. Priming effects are also seen, as when you begin a nursery rhyme and the infant says the next word. By age 2, toddlers show the ability to use semantic memory processes and can begin simple narratives. This is illustrated by saying to a 2-year-old, "Tell Mommy what you just did," and she says, "I threw the ball." By age 3 to 5, most children can describe events and display episodic memory. True episodic memory is more than just recalling your participation in a particular event; it also includes the ability to do this without any situational cues for its recall in the present. That is to say, you can recall at will particular events in your life at almost any of your previous ages. This, of course, requires that organisms have a sense of time—past, present, and future. Some researchers view episodic memory as unique to humans, like language.

CHILDREN AND ANIMALS

Children are fascinated by things that move. If you take a 2-year-old to a park or woods, she will quickly notice the birds, squirrels, and anything else that moves. Children not only watch the animals but want to know about them—what is it called? What does it do? How does it look? This is true whether the 2-year-old is from the country or the city. According to many evolutionary psychologists, this interest not only reflects evolutionary pressures but is also the basis of cognitive development (Barrett, 2005).

PLAY

Play is seen in all human cultures and across a variety of animal species (Burghardt, 2004; Göncü & Gaskins, 2007; Smith, 2005). Play, like babbling, appears to be preparation for future developmental stages, although the participants remain unaware of its future potential. They enjoy it for what it is. Play can be simple or it can be extremely complex, as when individuals take on roles and act them out. Even animals will sometimes shift roles, as when a dominant individual "loses" in order to keep the game going. Given its ubiquitous nature, especially in mammals, play is thought to be important and have profound value for the individual.

Burghardt (2004) suggests five criteria for characterizing play:

1. Play is not fully functional in the context in which it is expressed. That is to say, engaging in play does not contribute to an organism's survival at that moment.

2. Play appears to be spontaneous, engaged in voluntarily, pleasurable, and done for its own sake.

3. Play tends to be characterized by incomplete, exaggerated, and sometimes awkward movements. In this sense, it differs from behaviors performed in the service of more serious processes seen in adults related to survival and sexuality. Further, in some species, play is only seen in juveniles.

4. Play occurs repeatedly in a similar form. This repetition of patterns is seen in play and games in both humans and other animals.

5. Play tends to take place when organisms are well-fed, healthy, and free from stress. It has been observed that play is one of the first types of behavior to drop out when animals are hungry, threatened, or in a difficult environment.

Overall, organisms appear to have fun during play and do not engage in it if a positive emotional experience is not possible.

Play has been divided into three types: rough-and-tumble play, object play, and pretend or role play. Rough-and-tumble play may look like real fighting or conflict, but it can be differentiated from these in a number of ways (Smith, 2005). First, rough-and-tumble play is usually engaged in by friends. Second, it does not begin with a threat and usually ends with other social activity. Third, the participants usually appear to be enjoying themselves. And fourth, the roles played appear to be flexible and there is sensitivity to environmental restraints. Developmentally, rough-and-tumble play changes in focus from the elementary to high school years. In elementary school, rough-and-tumble play is centered on friendship themes; by adolescence, dominance becomes a more common theme. Strong gender differences in rough-and-tumble play are found across all cultures. More males than females engage in rough-and-tumble play. One common theory of rough-and-tumble play suggests it is preparation for later dominance challenges.

A modern example of object play is children playing with toys. Both anthropological and archeological studies suggest that object play is found in a variety of cultures across time. Unlike rough-and-tumble play, object play is engaged in equally by both males and females.

Pretend or role play is seen across cultures and often reflects tasks that the children observe their parents or elders engaging in. Since the peak period of pretend play occurs in children between 3 and 6 years of age, there is some suggestion that pretend play is related to theory of mind. That is to say, pretend play helps children understand what can happen and how others may react to these changes. Watching children of this age, you can observe how often they refer to other people and how the other people might feel.

DEVELOPMENT OF AGGRESSION

How do we understand aggression? What factors produce it in humans? A variety of longitudinal studies are beginning to give a clearer picture of aggression (see Tremblay, Hartup, & Archer, 2005 for an overview). Given the importance of dominance throughout the animal kingdom, you might expect a similar process in humans. However, the picture shown by the current studies is just the opposite. That is, rather than learning to be aggressive as one grows throughout childhood, children learn not to be aggressive and to inhibit these impulses. What happens to children who cannot inhibit aggressive impulses? These individuals are referred to as "antisocial." Especially for males, physical aggression during childhood predicts which individuals become antisocial during adolescence. Another picture that is emerging is gender differences in aggression. Boys show more aggression from infancy to adolescence than do girls. However, females show more indirect forms of aggression than males, which may include talking about others in a negative way.

Theory of Mind

When scientists consider the differences between humans and other primates, the differentiation generally focuses on social aspects of human interaction (see Dunbar, 2000 for an overview). In particular, two important distinctions are the utilization of language and the ability of humans to infer another person's mental state and intentions. Later, I will discuss language, and here I will focus on inferring another's state of mind. Theory of mind is the study of one's ability to understand one's own or another person's mental state. For example, if I show you a box of cereal and ask you what is in it, you would probably say "cereal." However, if I opened it and pulled out ribbons, you would no longer say it contained cereal. What if I asked you what friends of yours would say? You would, of course, say "cereal" because they did not see the ribbons being pulled out of the box. However, young children, as well as individuals with autism, would not give this answer. They would say "ribbons" because they are unable to understand that what someone else knows could be different from what they know. This ability to take another's perspective is referred to as *theory of mind* or *mind reading.* It is an ability that develops during the preschool years, generally between 3 and 5 years of age. Theory of mind has also been seen as a prerequisite for the ability to engage in pretend play and the ability to lie.

Theory of mind was initially researched by Premack and Woodruff in 1978 and continues to be an important topic in developmental psychology (see Call & Tomasell, 2008 for their review 30 years later). Included in theory of mind is the capacity to infer another's mental state from his or her behavior. Mental state can include purpose, intention, knowledge, belief, thinking, doubt, pretending, liking, and so forth. Some researchers have suggested that only humans possess this ability which makes possible sophisticated social interactions. One line of thinking suggests that this ability initially develops as the mother and her infant attempt to understand each other's internal states. This attempt may be improved as children begin to interact with a variety of peers and adults. At some time during the preschool years, children demonstrate their ability to act as if they understand their own mental state as well as that of others. One aspect of theory of mind has been called *belief-desire reasoning* (Wellman, 1990). **Belief-desire reasoning** suggests that you understand another person by inferring what they desire or what they believe. That is, you infer their motivations. Further, by knowing your own motivations, you can understand that you and another person may be motivated by different beliefs and desires.

The experimental procedure with the cereal box is formally called the "false-belief" task and has been used to assess theory of mind. In this procedure, a cereal box is shown to the child. The child is then asked what is in the box. Of course, the child responds by naming the type of cereal, such as Cheerios. The experimenter then opens the box and shows the child it contains something else, such as ribbons. The child is then asked what another child out in the hall would think is in the box. Three-year-old children tend to respond, "ribbons," whereas 4-year-olds would say, "Cheerios." Thus, the 4-year-olds understand what others would believe, whereas 3-year-olds do not. In the final part of the task, the experimenter asks the child what he or she initially thought was in the box. Four-year-olds say, "Cheerios," whereas 3-year-olds say, "ribbons." When theory of mind tasks have been given around the world, it is observed that the ability develops at about the same age in all cultures. Few 3-year-olds correctly understand what another knows, and few 5-year-olds are incorrect in their ability to understand what another child would experience.

Researchers have sought to theorize the developmental aspects of inferring mental states in another person. Simon Baron-Cohen's (2005) model suggests five components. The first aspect that the child begins to develop during the first nine months of life is an intentionality detector. What is meant by this is that an infant tends to interpret movement in a two-person relationship as desire and goal directed. The second aspect that begins to develop during this time is an eye direction detector. The infant infers that another person is looking at him or her vs. looking at something else. The third aspect is seen at the end of the first year of life. This aspect is referred to as a *shared attentional mechanism*. The infant is aware that the mother, for example, knows where she is looking. If the infant could put this into adult language, she would say something like, "Mother sees that I see the cup." In real life, infants during the second year of life are not surprised when their mother notices that they are looking at a particular object. Built on these aspects, the fourth mechanism, a theory of mind mechanism, is seen after at least 2 years of age. This enables a child to infer what one knows by observing what one sees. For example, if one child sees another child watching an adult hide a toy under the pillow, then the first child could infer that the second child knows where the toy is.

In order to understand the development of empathy in children, Simon Baron-Cohen (2005) has suggested two additional aspects in the theory of mind model: an emotion detector and an empathy system. The emotion detector develops during the first year of life and recognizes emotional signs in another person. The empathizing system goes beyond recognition of emotion; it is the ability, on some level, to know how another person feels. This, of course, signals the beginning of empathy. In Chapter 11, I will introduce how this aspect of the theory of mind has been used to understand the lack of empathy seen in some disordered individuals, such as children with autism and psychopathic individuals.

Another non-exclusive line of reasoning points to the extent that humans rely on social exchange and the historical importance of understanding another's intentions. These intentions could be either to support you or to cheat you. Anyone who can successfully make this distinction would clearly have an advantage. Additionally, although it is clear that primates can be influenced by seeing the actions of others, some researchers suggest that only humans actually instruct their young with the conscious purpose of teaching them new information.

Personality

What is personality? Generally, we think of personality as that which gives individuals particular characteristics—more outgoing, more shy, more concerned with others, and so forth. Typically, personality refers to behaviors that are consistent over time. The ancient Greeks talked about personality in terms of the four humors—choleric, sanguine, phlegmatic, and melancholic. Individuals who were quickly aroused were called choleric, which was associated with the circulatory system and blood. Easygoing and sociable individuals were sanguine, which was associated with yellow bile. Calm, controlled individuals were referred to as phlegmatic, which was associated with phlegm in the body. Melancholic individuals were those who were serious and worried and were represented by black bile.

Carl Jung (1968) talked about personality in terms of a particular sensitivity that one had. If you went into a room of people, what would you pay attention to? Who was there? What they wore? The purpose of the event? The way the room was designed or decorated? Or what the event would mean to you? These are all different perspectives which, for Jung, represented a sensitivity that directs one's values in the world. Jung described personality in terms of a sensitivity in four different realms: intellect, feeling, sensation, and intuition. *Intellect* sees the world through analysis and asks what something is. *Feeling* asks whether something is agreeable. *Sensation* asks how it works. And *intuition* asks what pattern is represented in a series of events. Each of these four represents different ways of understanding ourselves and the world. Jung further suggested that these four sensitivities can refer to the external world or the internal world. He invented the words "introversion" and "extraversion" to describe these points of reference. From this, Jung derived eight different personality styles.

In the 20th century, Kretschmer (1931) in Germany, and later Sheldon (1942) in the United States, sought to develop a personality system that combined physical body type with temperament. Sheldon suggested that an individual could be described as one of three types: endomorph, mesomorph, or ectomorph. The endomorph body type is soft and round, with a relaxed and sociable temperament. The mesomorph body type is muscular, strong, and low in fat, with an energetic and assertive temperament. The ectomorph body type is long and thin, with a cerebral and introverted temperament. Later in the 20th century, Hans Eysenck (1967) translated the idea of Greek humors into modern psychological language in terms of two dimensions. The first dimension ranged from extraversion on one end to introversion on the other. The second dimension ranged from stable to unstable. This second dimension also included the idea of emotionality, in that *unstable* was seen as including negative emotionality and neuroticism. A variety of factor analytic studies consistently demonstrated the dimensions of extraversion and neuroticism to be the same across a variety of cultures.

During the 20th century, a psychometric approach directed by Robert McCrae and Paul Costa (1987) extended the factor analytic approach to personality, including the work of Raymond Catell (1950), which pointed to five major personality dimensions. These five dimensions include

Eysenck's initial two dimensions of extraversion and neuroticism and add openness, agreeableness, and conscientiousness. Openness as a personality trait is associated with curiosity, flexibility, and an artistic sensitivity, including imaginativeness and the ability to create a fantasy world. Agreeableness is associated with being sympathetic, trusting, cooperative, modest, and straightforward. Conscientiousness as a personality trait is associated with being diligent, disciplined, well-organized, punctual, and dependable. The five-factor personality work has also demonstrated the stability of these personality traits across a variety of cultures (McCrae, 2002). In one study, McCrae, Costa, and their colleagues (1998, 1999) in five other countries gave personality measures to individuals across the lifespan. They found that there were changes in levels of the five factors over the lifespan and that these differences were found in all of the cultures studied. Overall, lifespan data suggest that from age 18 to 30, individuals show declines in neuroticism, extraversion, and openness to experiences and increases in agreeableness and conscientiousness. McCrae and Costa (1996, 1999) suggested that the five factors of personality be considered as biologically based tendencies, as opposed to culturally conditioned characteristic adaptations.

Nettle (2006) has examined the McCrae and Costa dimensions, called the Big Five, in relation to an evolutionary perspective. He suggests that each of the dimensions has a particular advantage given certain environmental conditions. Extraversion, for example, is associated with success in mating, having social allies, and exploration of the environment. Neuroticism, on the other hand, is associated with greater vigilance and labeling situations as dangerous. In time of little stress, extraversion would be a successful strategy. However, in dangerous times, it may not afford the necessary caution that would be found with neuroticism. Nettle's summary of the costs and benefits of each of the Big Five dimensions is presented in Table 5.1.

From an evolutionary perspective, theoretical aspects of the development of personality are still being articulated (see Figueredo et al., 2005; Buss & Hawley, 2011 for an overview). Initial speculation, such as that of Tooby and Cosmides (1990), did not emphasize personality because personality differences did not fit into a search for universal human traits. Buss (2009), however, suggested that personality theory needed an evolutionary perspective and that personality traits represent distinct adaptive strategies.

Research that has looked at more than 100 species suggests that personalities are also a widespread phenomenon in the animal kingdom (see Wolf, van Doorn, & Weissing, 2008 for an overview). Wolf and his colleagues emphasize that one important personality variable across species is the degree to which individual behavior is guided by environmental stimuli. Even in simple tasks such as running a maze, some mice and rats differ in their sensitivity to changes made to the task. Some individuals form routines and display consistent behavior even when changes to the

Table 5.1 Summary of Hypothesized Fitness Benefits and Costs of Increasing Levels of Each of the Big Five Personality Dimensions

Domain	Benefits	Costs
Extraversion	Mating success, social allies, exploration of environment	Physical risks, family stability
Neuroticism	Vigilance to dangers, striving and competitiveness	Stress and depression, with interpersonal and health consequences
Openness	Creativity, with effect on attractiveness	Unusual beliefs, psychosis
Conscientiousness	Attention to long-term fitness benefits, life expectancy, and desirable social qualities	Missing of immediate fitness gains, obsessionality, rigidity
Agreeableness	Attention to mental states of others, harmonious interpersonal relationships, valued coalitional partner	Subject to social cheating, failure to maximize selfish advantage

Source: Nettle (2006, p. 628).

task are made. We all know humans who develop routines and rarely change their behaviors even when the world around them is changing. A critical question for evolutionary psychology is why responsive and unresponsive individuals coexist within a population. A second related question is why some individuals show this consistency over time and situations. If we think about being responsive to the environment, we realize that this involves some costs in the form of effort and the inability to spend the energy in other ways. However, we can also imagine that paying attention to, and being influenced by, the environment could bring us some benefits. Wolf and his colleagues suggest that for responsiveness to spread throughout a population, the benefit of the behavior must be greater than the cost. Otherwise, unresponsiveness would spread. Further, responsiveness appears to spread when it is rare, but not when it is common. An analogy would be a store having a sale. If only a few individuals pay attention to the sale, then their effort pays off. Indeed, this would support future efforts to pay attention to sales. However, if everyone in a population pays attention to the store's announcement of a sale, then the effort would not pay off because of long lines and limited goods. These individuals would be discouraged from going to future sales.

Another question is what leads to the stability of personality traits across generations. One possible mechanism suggested by a variety of environmental researchers is assortative mating. **Assortative mating** suggests that humans do not randomly choose partners but choose partners who are like themselves on some selected traits. If those traits could be represented by the personality characteristics of the five-factor model, then the traits would be more likely to be passed on to the couples' children. That is to say, if extraverts found themselves attracted to other extraverts, then the genetic predisposition for the temperament associated with extraversion would be passed on. The data related to attractiveness according to the five-factor model shows mainly positive correlations between one's own traits and those one finds attractive in others, supporting an assortative mating model.

The actual manner in which personality develops appears to be a complicated question. Most theoretical explanations suggest that, by the age of 5 or 6, personality characteristics are becoming stable. McCrae and Costa (1999) suggest that the five factors develop out of temperament and that this development is not influenced by environment. An alternative model would suggest that personality is like language, in that the basic predisposition is present which carries with it a universal grammar, but the environment influences which domains of personality become predominantly activated for a given individual. The research on attachment suggests one way in which environmental factors can lead to more enduring traits. In either case, having a variety of styles available would ensure survival in a great variety of situations.

JUDGMENT OF PERSONALITY

A recent development in the consideration of personality from an evolutionary perspective is the idea that humans have evolved an ability to judge the personality of others (Haselton & Funder, 2006). Part of this idea is based on the variety of social psychological research studies that have shown that humans are able to make quick judgments concerning the attributes of other humans. Not only are humans able to make quick judgments, but these judgments reflect an accuracy of processing that one would not expect, given the limited experience with the person and the complex possibilities available. Haselton and Funder suggest that we should think about this ability in the same way we consider a child's ability to develop language. That is to say, in the same way that children are able to learn language quickly because their brain has evolved for this purpose, human brains also contain the basic categories necessary for personality judgment. This would mean that this ability does not have to be formally taught. Specifically, Haselton and Funder suggest that the ability to judge personality can be considered in terms of four basic hypotheses.

Hypothesis 1: People should be naturally proficient in personality judgment.

Hypothesis 2: Personality judgment abilities should form a distinct part of the phenotype.

Hypothesis 3: The ability to form personality judgments should emerge without explicit training and perhaps in spite of incompatible social inputs.

Hypothesis 4: Personality judgment should be ubiquitous.

According to Haselton and Funder (2006), support for these hypotheses can be found in a variety of studies showing that people almost cannot stop themselves from judging others in terms of personality features. Further, these judgments occur quickly and are made without conscious reasoning. Children begin to use trait-like terms by age 3, and by age 5 they are able to note that different individuals may have different traits across a number of dimensions, including being shy, honest, or selfish. Given that the Big Five Personality Dimensions framework just described has been observed across cultures, it might be expected that these dimensions would form an important part of personality judgment.

SUMMARY

Humans require a longer period of care than many other species. This may have resulted in the evolution of attachment mechanisms, which are also seen in other species. Bowlby first described attachment in humans. Harlow experimentally studied attachment in monkeys. Ainsworth developed a "strange situation" to research types of attachment patterns in humans. Gottlieb saw development as interplay between a variety of levels, including genes, neural activity, behavior, and environment, which includes culture and society. He also performed early studies of epigenetics. Bjorklund and Blasi suggest there are at least six basic assumptions that underlie evolutionary developmental psychology. One important theme in developmental evolution is the manner in which human children are able to take the perspective of another person. This is called theory of mind. Children also develop a personality, which has certain benefits and costs. Humans are also able to judge characteristics of another's personality.

STUDY RESOURCES

Review Questions

1. How has the notion of mother-infant interaction changed over time? Consider Bowlby's attachment theory; Hrdy's research with patterns of infant care among primates; Harlow's research with infant monkeys; Bowlby's observations of orphanages after World War II; and Ainsworth's "strange situation" research.

2. What evidence can you cite to support the view that children raised in similar environments may actually show greater diversity than those raised in different environments?

3. Give some examples to support Gottlieb's developmental systems approach that sees development as interplay between a variety of levels, including genes, neural activity, behavior, and environment, which includes culture and society. How has this research expanded our prior notions of genetic inheritance?

4. What are the six basic assumptions underlying evolutionary developmental psychology as proposed by Bjorklund and Blasi?

5. Play is seen in all human cultures and across a variety of animals. Because play appears to be preparation for future developmental stages, it has received a lot of study. What are the five criteria for characterizing play that Burghardt suggested? What are the three types of play that have been identified?

6. How do we understand aggression? What factors produce it in humans? Are they the same factors that produce it in other species?

7. What is theory of mind? What are its developmental stages in humans? Are humans the only species with this capability?

8. How would you define personality? Others defined it in different ways: the ancient Greeks; Carl Jung; Kretschmer and Sheldon; McCrae and Costa. How are these definitions similar? How are they different? Are humans the only species with a personality?

For Further Reading

Bjorklund, D., & Pellegrini, A. (2002). *The origins of human nature: Evolutionary developmental psychology*. Washington, DC: American Psychological Association.
Bowlby, J. (1969). *Attachment and loss: Vol. 1. Attachment*. London: Hogarth.
Geary, D. (2005b). *The origin of mind: Evolution of brain, cognition, and general intelligence*. Washington, DC: American Psychological Association.
Gottlieb, G. (1992). *Individual development and evolution*. New York: Oxford University Press.

Key Terms and Concepts

- Mother-child interactions
  - Research concerning attachment
  - Genetic aspects of attachment
- Differential susceptibility to rearing influences
- Life history theory
- Developmental psychology from an evolutionary perspective
  - Tenets of evolutionary developmental psychology
- Developmental theories
  - Sensory development
  - Memory and cognition
  - Children and animals

- ○ Play
- ○ Development of aggression
- Theory of mind
- Personality
  - ○ Judgment of personality

SAGE Study Site

Visit the study site at **www.sagepub.com/ray** for chapter-specific study resources.

Glossary Terms

- Assortative mating
- Belief-desire reasoning
- Deferred adaptations
- Developmental systems approach
- Epigenesis
- Ontogenetic adaptations
- Plasticity

Emotionality 6

One important aspect of being human is our ability and desire to communicate with one another. In this chapter, I will emphasize an evolutionary understanding of communication in terms of emotionality and language. Although later chapters will include information on social aspects of communication, it is important to remember the broader context in which communication takes place. Let's begin with emotion. In 1884, William James published an article titled "What Is An Emotion?" More than 100 years later we still do not have a definitive answer to his question. As noted by many authors, emotionality is a difficult concept to define. Everyone seems to know what it is until asked. To complicate matters, everyday English does not clearly distinguish between feelings, moods, emotions, passions, affects, and motivations. However, we can speak of specific emotions such as anger, fear, and happiness. What underlies such specific emotions is a topic of current debate (see Barrett, Mesquita, Ochsner, & Gross, 2007; Ortony & Turner, 1990; Russell, 2003). Research has not found exact autonomic nervous system or brain patterns that completely differentiate one specific emotion from another. This suggests to some authors that a more dimensional, rather than basic categorical, approach should be taken. I will discuss these alternatives later in the chapter.

For now, it can be noted that the dimensional explanation of emotionality derives from a structural attempt to break down emotional experiences into their component parts, such as positive or negative emotionality. The basic emotion approach described by Darwin, which emphasized specific emotions such as anger or sadness, was a more functional approach to the topic. These two approaches, although different, should not be seen as oppositional; rather, they offer different types of information. For example, our visual experience of color is the result of our nervous system transforming a continuous electromagnetic spectrum of light into specific colors. Receptors in our nervous system are tuned to three major frequencies, which we experience as blue, green, and red. These three basic receptors give us the experience of a large variety of colors. If our experience of emotionality is similar, then it is possible for networks involved in the experience of basic emotions such as anger or sadness to create blends of emotionality. This would suggest that it is quite possible to have a dimensional approach that results in experienced categories. This, in turn, would speak against adopting a position that states that only a dimensional approach is accurate.

From an evolutionary perspective, I want to ask the functional question, What is the role of emotionality in our human history? In doing this, we can divide the concept of emotion into emotional recognition, emotional production, and even the nature of emotions themselves. We can also describe the external aspects of emotions and consider the situations that evoke particular emotional processing. We can also consider the internal aspects and describe the internal recognition and experience of emotionality. Current research also suggests that our ability to quickly make trait assessments of other people in social situations, such as their trustworthiness, may have evolved from our ability to analyze emotional expressions (Todorov, 2008). Thus, it may turn out that different emotions, as well as the social and experiential aspects of emotionality, may have evolved at different times and in different ways.

Darwin and the Expression of Emotions

Almost every author who discusses Darwin's work speaks of him as being a close and careful observer. In *The Expression of the Emotions in Man and Animals*, Darwin (1872/1998) not only reveals a careful observation of emotionality but also seeks to understand underlying patterns of responding. Throughout his book, Darwin presents drawings and photographs of people and animals as they express different emotions. The common theme is that emotions are universal and represent an example of evolution through natural selection.

Ekman (2009) suggests Darwin made a number of important contributions to our study of emotions:

1. Darwin saw emotions as discrete. That is to say, we experience fear, anger, disgust, and so forth as distinct entities.

2. Darwin emphasized the human face in the expression of emotions, as illustrated by the photographs of human faces he used in his book (see Figure 6.1).

| **Figure 6.1** | Photographs Darwin Used to Describe the Facial Muscles Involved in the Expression of Emotions |

3. One of Darwin's main ideas is that emotional processes are innate and found across a variety of species, including humans. Darwin clarified this idea by suggesting that although facial expressions are universal, gestures may be specific to a given culture.

4. Darwin's fourth idea is that emotions are not unique to humans and may be found in a variety of species.

5. Particular muscle movements may signal a particular emotion.

You will see these five themes described throughout this chapter.

We begin with the understanding that there are more than 50 muscles in the human face, far more than is needed for eating, language, or closing the eyes. Why do we have these muscles in the face? The answer, for evolutionary psychologists, is that these muscles have evolved for the expression of emotion. As we will see, the ability to quickly express emotion and to recognize these expressions gave humans an important means of communication. Darwin (1872/1998) suggests that these expressions are displayed involuntarily and also exist in nonhuman animals for purposes other than social communication. Darwin emphasized that facial expressions play an important role in preparing an organism for taking in information from the environment and acting on that information. Thus, facial expressions of emotions have a long evolutionary history that predates social communication. Darwin begins his book on emotions with three principles: (1) the principle of serviceable associated habits; (2) the principle of antithesis; and (3) the principle of direct actions of the nervous system.

The **principle of serviceable associated habits** refers to the situation in which ritualized behaviors are performed in response to a particular internal state. In discussing this principle, Darwin (1872/1998) describes a variety of situations that must have been protective for our ancestors and have become part of our human reflexive behaviors. For example, when falling, most individuals protect themselves by extending their arms. We continue to engage in this behavior even when it is not necessary. For example, falling voluntarily on a soft bed will elicit this behavior. Darwin described his own attempts not to express this reflex:

> I put my face close to the thick glass-plate in front of a puff-adder in the Zoological Gardens, with the firm determination of not starting back if the snake struck at me; but, as soon as the blow was struck, my resolution went for nothing, and I jumped a yard or two backwards with astonishing rapidity. My will and reason were powerless against the imagination of a danger which had never been experienced. (pp. 43–44)

Clearly, in this paragraph Darwin understands that certain behaviors, especially those that had increased survival value in the past, may take precedence over willed or planned behaviors. His example also illustrates the evolutionary principle that behaviors that were protective over time do not quickly change with the introduction of modern technology. In this case, the technology was the glass of the snake enclosure.

The second principle is **antithesis**. As the name implies, this principle suggests that opposite internal states produce the opposite external movements from those of the first principle. That is to say, we shrug our shoulders when we feel helpless because it is the opposite set of movements from when we feel aggressive. As can be seen in Figure 6.2, a hostile dog has its ears up, its tail up, its eyes fixed, its back elevated, and so forth. The opposite internal state, according to Darwin (1872/1998), would result in the opposite external manifestation, with its ears down, its tail down, its back down, and so forth. However, as Darwin noted, these responses may be species specific. For example, although dogs and cats have different postures for fear and aggression, each species displays the opposite response for the opposite emotion.

This principle has more to do with how Darwin believed the nervous system, and thus emotionality, was organized than with natural selection.

Figure 6.2 Drawings Darwin Used to Illustrate Hostile and Affectionate Postures

Darwin assumed that these opposite responses did not themselves serve our ancestors in terms of survival.

The third principle is **direct actions of the nervous system**. With this principle, Darwin (1872/1998) is acknowledging that emotional expression can result from the structure of the nervous system. For example, when a person is enraged, the face becomes red with the veins on the forehead and neck distended. Monkeys also redden from passion. When frightened, various species of animals, including humans, experience the hairs of their arms standing upright. Darwin also notes that with different emotions, the heart rate speeds up, which in turn influences the brain, which in turn influences the heart. The idea that there are specific physiological reactions for different emotions, and that the cardiovascular and cortical system mutually interact with one another, are two of Darwin's ideas that were considerably ahead of their time. Darwin further notes that anger, rage, and indignation are displayed in a common manner throughout the world. In this way, it is not voluntary action, previous learning, or habit that influences the expression of emotion, but the organization of the nervous system.

Even today, these three principles drive research in the neurosciences (e.g., Susskind et al., 2008). Susskind and his colleagues examined two emotional expressions—fear and disgust. Fear is an emotional response that has been associated with greater perceptual attention, whereas disgust has been associated with sensory rejection. Given that these emotional responses reflect opposite types of sensory processing, the principle of antithesis would suggest that their expression would involve opposite responses. Indeed, when Susskind and his colleagues examined how the skin of the face changes as a result of fear and disgust, they found the skin deforms in opposite ways, as shown in Figure 6.3.

Figure 6.3 Facial Expressions of Fear and Disgust. Facial features move in the opposite direction to create these expressions.

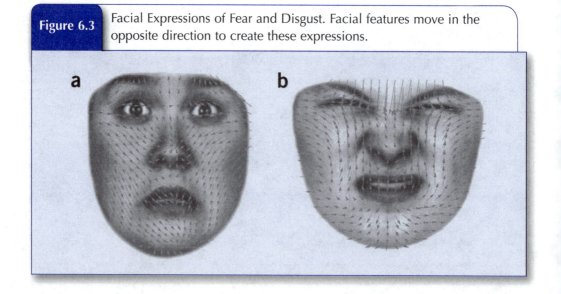

Susskind et al. (2008) next looked at three different physiological measures during the expression of fear and disgust: (1) how much air an individual was able to breathe in during each of these emotions; (2) how fast the eye was able to move; and (3) how large an area individuals were able to see. Again, fear and disgust resulted in opposite measures; individuals were able to take in more air, move their eyes faster, and see a larger area during fear than during disgust. These researchers see their research supporting Darwin's idea that not only does emotional expression enable social communication, it also modifies our ability to prepare for perception and action. The connection between facial expressions and physiological changes suggests that facial expressions are more than just social signals, important as that is; they also offer biological advantages in terms of potential perception and action.

Returning to Darwin (1872/1998), we see the basic theme throughout *The Expression of the Emotions in Man and Animals* to be that emotional expression is universal, shaped by natural selection, has survival value, and is found in humans and a variety of animal species. Darwin also helps us to think about larger "why" questions, such as why do a number of species, including humans, touch one another when feeling affectionate, or weep when feeling grief, or show their teeth when angry? Using careful observation, Darwin sought to describe the specific muscles involved in many facial expressions, including surprise, fear, helplessness, disgust, guilt, love, suffering, shame, and blushing (see Figures 6.1 and 6.4).

As a scientist, Darwin (1872/1998) also sought to demonstrate the universality of emotion recognition by showing different emotions to people. For example, he showed pictures displaying surprise to some 24 people; all but two reported seeing some variation of surprise or astonishment (p. 279). Darwin was clearly using his work to forward his argument of universal expression of emotion, as he said in the concluding chapter, "I have endeavored to show in considerable detail that all the chief expressions exhibited by man are the same throughout the world" (p. 355).

By the end of the 20th century, researchers such as Paul Ekman (1973) had followed Darwin's tradition by studying facial expressions cross-culturally and demonstrating the universality of emotional expression. For example, Ekman performed interesting research in New Guinea by showing individuals different facial expressions and asking them to tell a story about what caused the person to look the way he or she looked in the picture (Ekman & Friesen, 1971). He also performed the research in a reverse manner, in which a story was told without using emotional terms. The person was then asked which of a series of emotional faces would best represent the person in the story. This type of research supported the idea that both emotional recognition and emotional expression were universal.

Darwin (1872/1998) interprets the universality of emotional response as support for the idea that all humans are descended from a "single parent stock" (p. 355). Darwin further suggests that certain of our emotions, such

Figure 6.4 The photographs used by Darwin to illustrate what he called "low spirits" included images of grief and despair.

as joy or fear, developed early in our evolutionary history, while others, such as contempt or disdain, would have come later. Darwin also speculates that early emotions, such as disgust, share the same facial expression as the motor action of vomiting. What could this mean? To Darwin, it meant that emotional expressions such as disgust previously accompanied acts such as vomiting. Over evolutionary time, the expression of disgust came to be a response of its own without the gastrointestinal motor component. In this sense, our emotional expressions can be seen as coming from primitive motor processes and representing uncompleted actions.

Look at Figure 6.5. The task is to name the emotion that is displayed on each of the faces.

Figure 6.5 These photographs of emotional expressions were used by Paul Ekman and his colleagues to determine emotional recognition across a variety of cultures.

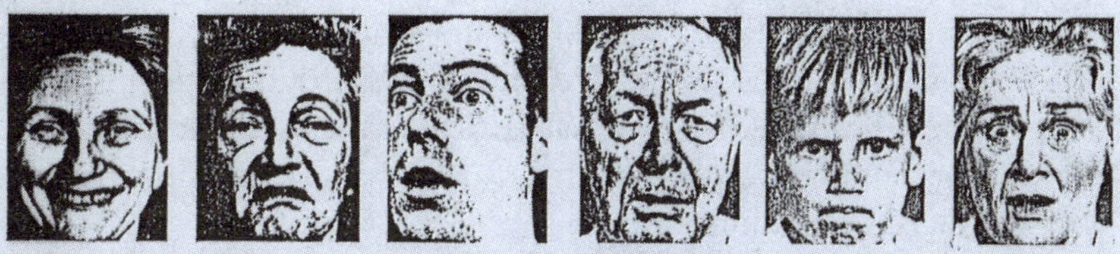

	Happiness	Disgust	Suprise	Sadness	Anger	Fear
United States (N=99)	97%	92%	95%	84%	67%	85%
Brazil (N=40)	95%	97%	87%	59%	90%	67%
Chile (N=119)	95%	92%	93%	88%	94%	68%
Argentina (N=168)	98%	92%	95%	78%	90%	54%
Japan (N=29)	100%	90%	100%	62%	90%	66%

Before you look at the common answers, let's think about the task. How did you recognize the facial expressions depicted in Figure 6.5? It has been estimated that human faces can produce more than 10,000 different expressions (Ekman, 2003b). Clearly, this is partly due to experience. You hear others commenting on someone's expression and giving it a label. However, if your recognition of emotions were entirely a result of your culture, as some researchers thought, then we might expect to see different cultures using different expressions, even for such basic emotions as fear or disgust or surprise. In the 1950s, Paul Ekman (along with many in psychology at that time) assumed facial expressions to be socially learned and largely influenced by culture (Ekman, 1957). However, his own cross-cultural work and that of others forced Ekman to adopt the opposite position. Ekman asked whether emotional expression differed across cultures (see Ekman, 1999b for an overview). He presented a series of emotional faces to people in five different countries: Chile, Argentina, Brazil, Japan, and the United States. What Ekman found echoed what Darwin had suggested years earlier: Facial expressions are universal. As noted previously, Ekman later confirmed this by observing facial expressions displayed by isolated tribes in New Guinea who had no contact with Western culture and had never seen television, movies, or photographs. Because he was studying individuals without a written language, Ekman created stories and asked people to pick from a variety of pictures the facial expression that would be displayed by the person in the story. As also suggested by Darwin, individuals across cultures display similar expressions when experiencing similar emotions. There is also compelling evidence that these expressions are part of our evolutionary history. One such set of studies examined individuals who were born congenitally blind. What one finds in these studies is that blind individuals display spontaneous emotions similar to those of sighted individuals, although their expressions are not as well articulated (see Galati, Scherer, & Ricci-Bitti, 1997). Clearly, internal emotions are articulated using facial expressions whether one has seen facial expressions or not.

Wait a minute, you might say, I have seen people who don't always smile when they are happy or frown when they are sad. Yes, that is true. There is more to the story. In a clever series of studies, Ekman and others have shown that, although the ability to recognize an emotional expression may be universal, people do not always allow themselves to make the expression. Ekman (1999b) showed films of surgery and accidents to American and Japanese individuals. When they were viewing the films alone, people from both cultures displayed the same facial expressions. However, the Japanese, more than the Americans, would not fully display their emotional reactions if there was an experimenter in the room while they were watching the films. Thus, situational and cultural factors can influence emotional expression. These are called **display rules**.

If you can control whether or when an emotion is expressed, can you also lie? Of course, this is what great actors or con-people do all the time. Now, the more interesting question: Can you learn to recognize when someone is lying? From an evolutionary standpoint, the detection of someone who was lying to the group would be a critical task. Ekman (2003a) believes that facial expressions associated with lying are different from those that portray true emotions. He suggests that when one attempts to produce an emotional expression that differs from one's internal experience, there will be leakage in the form of microexpressions that quickly convey the hidden emotion. These quick (less than a fifth of a second) expressions can be recognized in some individuals, but not easily. What can be recognized is whether a smile is the result of a natural event—a person hearing a joke or an infant seeing his mother—or an attempt to voluntarily smile. This distinction is attributed to

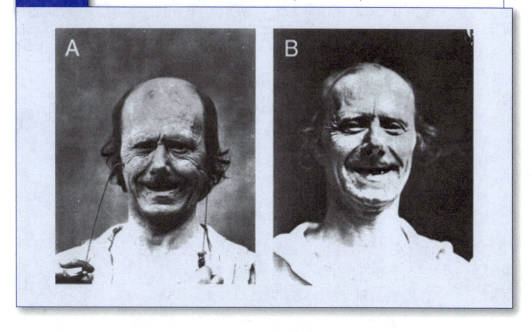

Figure 6.6 The smile in photograph A was produced by electrical stimulation to the cheek muscle and the smile in photo B is spontaneous.

Duchenne, who took the photographs in Figure 6.6. Duchenne produced two types of smiles, one that resulted from the person hearing a joke (picture B) and the other from electrical stimulation of the zygomatic (cheek) muscle in the face (picture A). When you hear a joke or see someone you care about, you move both the zygomatic and the orbicularis oculi (eyelid) muscles. When you try to smile, you just stimulate the zygomatic muscle because the orbicularis oculi muscle is difficult to voluntarily manipulate. A number of studies have also shown that there is a more symmetrical response in the face during spontaneous smiling as compared to forced smiles.

The basic perspective from the standpoint of evolutionary psychology is that emotions evolved for their adaptive value in dealing with fundamental life tasks (Ekman, 1999a). **Fundamental life tasks** are universal human predicaments such as losses, frustrations, and achievements. Specially, these events can include fighting, falling in love, escaping predators, and a variety of other tasks (Tooby & Cosmides, 1990). The important implication is that our current emotional expression and experience is directly influenced by our ancestral past. In general, similar cortical and neurochemical mechanisms involved in emotional experience and expression can be found across a variety of species. For example, current research suggests facial expressions seen in primates during play and during submission map onto the human expressions of laughter and smiling, respectively (de Waal, 2003).

The Nature of Basic Emotions

What is a basic emotion? One way to answer this question is to consider what criteria are common to all emotions. Ekman (1999a) suggested a set of characteristics common to all emotions:

1. distinctive universal signals,

2. emotion-specific physiology,

3. automatic appraisal mechanism,

4. universal antecedent events,

5. distinctive appearance developmentally,

6. present in nonhuman primates,

7. quick onset,

8. brief duration,

9. unbidden occurrence,

10. distinctive thoughts and memory images, and

11. distinctive subjective experience.

The first characteristic is *distinctive universal signals*. Ekman is referring to a distinctive facial expression that goes with each of the basic emotions. As illustrated by the facial expressions presented by Darwin (Figures 6.1 and 6.4) and the experimental procedure described by Ekman (Figure 6.5), a specific facial expression is associated with each of the basic emotions. The second characteristic, *emotion-specific physiology*, means that underlying emotional states are distinctive patterns of physiological activity expressed in the central and autonomic nervous systems. Indeed, in a variety of studies it has been shown that autonomic nervous system activity displays different patterns for anger, fear, disgust, and sadness. The third characteristic, *automatic appraisal mechanism*, means that there is a very fast, usually out-of-awareness, process that allows for appraisal of both internal and external stimuli. LeDoux (1996), for example, describes the presence of a second visual system in rats that runs through the midbrain and allows for quick responses without the visual clarity of the rat's normal visual system. Such a system might cause the rat to jump if it sees a snake-like structure on the ground. It is only through the slower normal visual system that the rat can distinguish whether what it saw was a snake or a stick. In humans a variety of cortical networks are involved in affective processing (Pessoa & Adolphs, 2010). From an evolutionary self-preservation perspective, it is better to be wrong and think a stick is a snake than vice versa. The fourth characteristic of all emotions is *universal antecedent events*. A person feels sadness, for example, after a loss of someone or something significant to the person. The fifth characteristic is *distinctive appearance developmentally*. This suggests that each emotion may develop in individuals in the same order. A sixth characteristic is that these emotions are also *present in nonhuman primates*. Current research, as well as Darwin's observations, suggests that nonhuman primates share most, if not all, emotional expression with humans. The seventh and eighth characteristics of basic emotions are that they have a *quick onset* and are of *brief duration*. The basic idea is that emotions are quick and that is their survival value. You see something disgusting, have a reaction, and move away. For clarity, it is important to distinguish emotions from moods, which are more long-lasting. It is also possible to turn an emotion into a mood by the continued presence of the stimulus or by talking to yourself about the situation. The ninth characteristic is unbidden occurrence. This simply means that individuals do not plan to have an emotional reaction. The last two characteristics suggest that each basic emotion has associated with it *distinctive thoughts and memory images* as well as *distinctive subjective experiences*.

One important idea that has driven research on emotions is that there is a finite number of basic emotions (Tomkins, 1965). Various researchers have described these in slightly different terms, although most include anger, disgust, fear, happiness, sadness, and surprise. Sometimes contempt is included, although this shows less universality across studies (Elfenbein & Ambady, 2002). The analogy to this approach is similar to seeing colors. With colors, there are basic primary colors recognized by all people, from which combinations may be made. Similarly, basic emotions can form into complex blends or combinations.

Silvan Tomkins (1962) articulated the basic theoretical ideas that directed emotion research during the last quarter of the 20th century. One idea is that affect is a separate system and works as an amplifier, giving a sense of urgency to basic cognitive processes, such as memory, perception, thought, and action. A variety of studies of memory, for example, have shown that you remember an event better if there was an emotional reaction initially. Another of Tomkins' ideas was that the body response produced by emotions is centered on the face. Classic studies in facial recognition conducted by Paul Ekman and Carrol Izard and others over the past 40 years suggest universality in emotional facial recognition in both literate and preliterate cultures. A meta-analysis covering almost 100 separate studies with more than 20,000 participants further supports the existence of these emotional universals (Elfenbein & Ambady, 2002). As would be expected, emotions are most accurately rated if they are judged by the same national, ethnic, or regional groups that expressed the emotion. As with language, environment plays a role in shaping the expression and recognition of basic emotions.

Underlying Dimensions of Emotionality

In the late 1800s, Wundt sought to find the elements that underlie emotionality (Wundt, 1896). He constructed three dimensional variables. The first was a dimensional scale ranging from pleasure to displeasure. The second was a scale ranging from tension to relief, and the third was a scale ranking from excitation to calm. Over the years, these dimensions have come to be described as *valence, arousal,* and *power.* Most recent utilizations of this approach have emphasized valence (positive-negative) and arousal (activation-deactivation) as underlying the experience of emotionality (Russell, 1980, 1997, 2002, 2003). This can be diagrammed as shown in Figure 6.7.

Figure 6.7 A dimensional representation of affect. The horizontal line represents the dimension ranging from displeasure to pleasure. The vertical line represents arousal ranging from sleep to high arousal. Any feeling can be displayed within the circle based on the various dimensions.

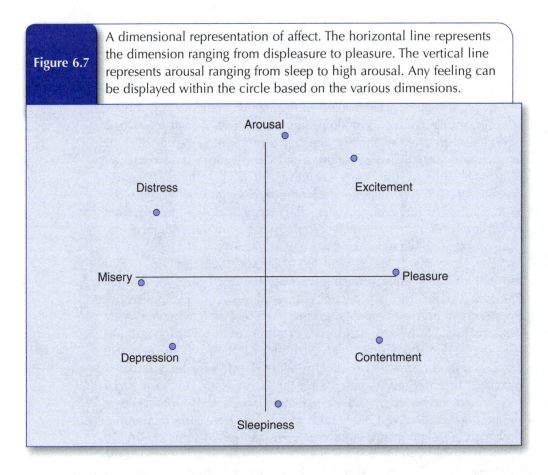

In order to test this, Russell (1980) asked individuals to rate a variety of emotional words. These results are shown in Figure 6.8. Russell's model suggests that the experience of any emotion reflects a point related to the degree of arousal and the degree of pleasure.

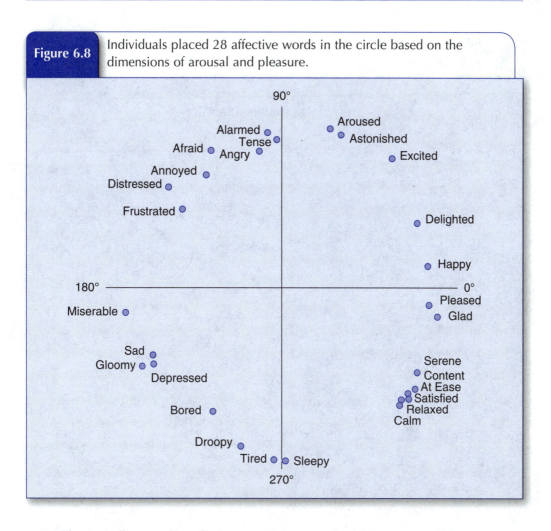

Figure 6.8 Individuals placed 28 affective words in the circle based on the dimensions of arousal and pleasure.

Besides Russell, a number of other emotion researchers have presented circumplex models of emotionality. These have been described by Yik, Russell, and Barrett (1999) and are diagrammed in Figure 6.9.

Using data from individuals in Canada and the U.S., Yik et al. (1999) suggest that it is possible to construct a single two-dimensional structure that incorporates the four different models of affect shown in Figure 6.9. The combined model is composed of two dimensions—degree of activation (deactivation-activation) and pleasure (unpleasant-pleasant). This resulting model is shown in Figure 6.10 on page 205.

Understanding Categorical and Dimensional Models of Emotion

In the history of emotion research, there has been much debate considering the nature of emotions. One position in this debate is that emotions can be categorized, as suggested by Darwin, and that particular emotions,

Figure 6.9 Four research groups found that experimental participants represented affect in similar ways utilizing arousal and pleasantness dimensions.

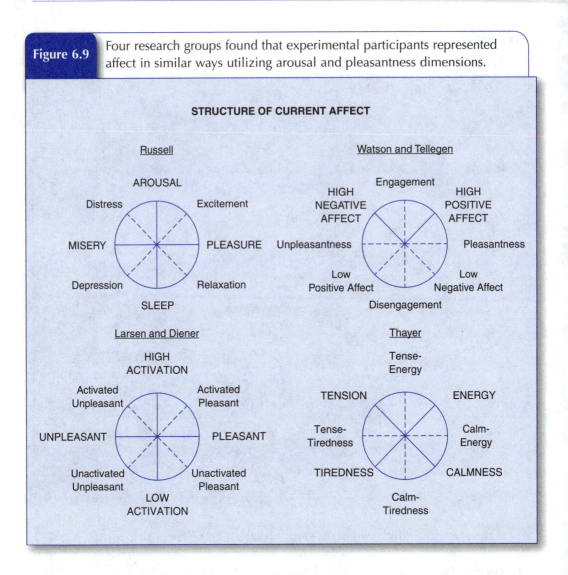

STRUCTURE OF CURRENT AFFECT

such as fear or anger, are basic. Much of the research we have discussed in this chapter subscribes to this view. Discovering that throughout the world the same set of facial muscles is responsible for the same emotions lends strong support to the basic emotion position. The finding that emotions can be represented in terms of a finite number of dimensions, as discussed in the previous section, suggests an alternative approach. Underlying this debate is the idea that emotionality cannot be categorical (e.g., fear, sadness, anger) and dimensional (e.g., varying in activation and pleasantness) at the same time. Typically, the dimensional researchers suggest that there are problems or exceptions in the research performed by the categorical researchers. This is further complicated by suggestions that the underlying debate is actually a nature-nurture question, which leaves people speaking at cross purposes (see the September, 2007 issue of *Perspectives on Psychological Science* for a series of debates on the nature of emotion).

Figure 6.10 Two-dimensional structure that incorporates the four different models of affect shown in Figure 6.9. The combined model is composed of two dimensions—degree of activation (deactivation-activation) and pleasure (unpleasant-pleasant).

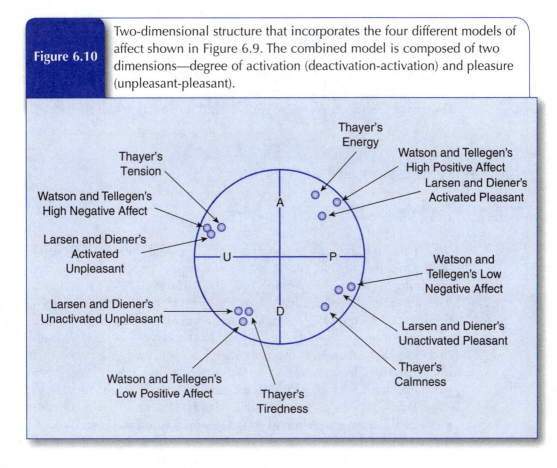

As you know, there are many ways—genetic, epigenetic, modeling, and culture, to name four—that humans develop processes, including emotionality. I will suggest to you that, at this point, we do not understand the nature of emotionality to the extent that we can describe all of the mechanisms involved and make a final decision concerning categorical and dimensional approaches. In fact, both approaches offer important, but different, information concerning the nature of emotionality. One problem with both approaches results from our inability to specify exactly what an emotion is and how emotional processes should be measured. Carroll Izard (2007) asked more than 30 experts in the field of emotional research to define *emotion*. He found no consensus, and some even said it was not possible to define the term. It may be the case—as in many debates in science—that we will discover that both positions are correct, but under different conditions. For example, the creation of ice and steam—categorical states—are best understood by their relation to an underlying dimension: temperature or, more specifically, the kinetic theory of heat. Likewise, our visual system transforms a continuous electromagnetic spectrum into discrete colors, such as red, green, and blue. Of course, experiencing emotions may not be like perceiving colors.

Öhman (1999), for example, has suggested that different emotions should be viewed as independent from one another, in that they may possess different evolutionary histories. This would suggest that fear could have evolved at a different time and under different conditions than sadness. From an evolutionary perspective, the critical question is the manner in which emotions evolved and the function that they serve.

Emotional Expression and Recognition

CORTICAL NATURE OF EMOTION

What parts of the brain are important for processing emotional information? A number of studies of a variety of species, including humans, are beginning to answer this question (Bennett & Hacker, 2005). As we begin, it is important to realize that the neural organization involved in emotionality can span multiple regions of the brain, depending on the nature of the emotional response (see Tucker, Derryberry, & Luu, 2000, for an overview). For example, at the brain stem level (including the pons), one can see basic representations of laughing and crying. Even in rare cases when an infant is born with only a brain stem, he or she is still able to show facial displays of pleasure and distress. The brain stem controls many of the basic physiological processes involved in movement, chewing, eye movement, and facial expression as well as levels of arousal involving the sympathetic and parasympathetic nervous systems. At this level, it is difficult to distinguish emotional responses from those involved in motivational processes. In fact, some researchers have suggested that emotion is always involved in motivation to action or its inhibition. These more fixed types of responses are different in nature from higher level situations, when we remember and re-experience a previous emotional experience. In this section, I want to introduce you to examples of how emotionality is processed in the brain so that you can see the different levels of processing.

One approach to understanding emotionality and brain processes is to look for core processes across species (Panksepp, 1998, 2004, 2006). The basic idea is that core emotional tendencies emerged from ancient brain processes shared by all mammals. Panksepp proposes that these systems are anger, fear, sexual lust, maternal care, separation distress, and social bonding, as well as playfulness and a resource acquisition system. Let's look at these briefly.

1. Anger or rage is evoked when there is stiff competition for resources. This system can also be aroused by restraint, frustration, and other irritants.

2. Fear is evoked when the organism is in the presence of danger. This system will produce freezing at low levels of arousal and flight at higher levels. Research suggests that external stimuli may be processed at a fast, but less conscious, level through low-level brain circuits, or at a slower, but more accurate, level at higher cognitive levels.

3. Sexual lust becomes manifest during puberty, although the basic components of the system exist early in the development of the organism.

4. Care systems are designed to allow us to nurture one another.

5. Separation distress is seen when a young organism is separate from its mother. In a variety of species, the infant will cry out in these situations, and in extreme cases will panic. Panksepp suggests that this feeling of abandonment may be built on early pain circuits.

6. Play is seen in a variety of species and is often accompanied by expression of joy and laughter. As we will see, play is an important preparation for later social life.

7. The seeking system controls our desire to find and harvest the fruits of the world. In humans, it is connected with goal-directed urges and positive expectation concerning the world. Across species, it is related to the motivation to obtain resources from the environment. In humans, it is also connected with awareness and appraisals of the world.

As you can see, Panksepp (2004) builds the emotional responses of the organism on top of basic instinctual processes. As you remember from Chapter 4, Paul MacLean (1990, 1993) also argued that emotional processing in the brain is built upon the more primitive reptilian brain. According to MacLean, emotional processes involve the limbic area, the main structures of which are the amygdala, hippocampus, and insula. The medial frontal cortex is also believed to have a role in emotional decision making, and the orbital prefrontal cortex is involved in evaluating emotional contingencies, especially in relation to social and moral judgments. Research using such techniques as fMRI has indeed shown these areas to be involved in emotional processing, although specific emotions have not been linked to specific brain areas (see Phan, Wager, Taylor, & Liberzon, 2002 for a review). It should also be noted that some studies suggest a difference in the cortical processing of emotions related to social processes and those that are not (Britton et al., 2006). I will discuss the nature of social emotions later.

The amygdala is one of the main structures involved in emotion (see Adolphs & Damasio, 2000 for an overview). The amygdala, as its Latin name implies, is an almond-shaped structure. It is a subcortical area found in the frontal part of the temporal lobe. The amygdala receives processed sensory information and also has a direct connection to the olfactory bulb. Structures involved in memory and attention, such as the hippocampus, basal ganglia, and basal forebrain, connect to the amygdala. The amygdala also has direct connections with the frontal lobes, which are involved in planning and decision making. Given these connections, the amygdala sits between external information brought in through our sensory systems and the necessary attentional, memory, and emotional responses. In electrophysiological studies with primates, the amygdala shows the highest levels of response to threatening face displays. On the other hand, scenes of grooming or huddling show less response. With humans, brain imaging studies show greater left amygdala activity when viewing fearful faces as opposed to happy ones. Also, the level of change in amygdala activity correlates with the intensity of the expression. Both humans and monkeys who have had damage to this area do not respond appropriately to fearful faces. Humans normally remember emotional material better than nonemotional material. With damage to the amygdala, this is not the case. An interesting case study describes a woman, "SM," whose amygdala was damaged and who reported feeling no fear, although she fully understands the concept of fear (Feinstein, Adolphs, Damasio, & Tranel, 2010). However, SM does experience other emotions. Most recent research with the amygdala indicates that it is involved in any event that may have major negative significance for an individual. In nonhuman primates, there is a long tradition showing the role of the amygdala in social processes, especially those related to dominance. Monkeys normally establish dominance hierarchies with an alpha male in charge. Following damage to the amygdala, the alpha monkey would no longer display any aggressive behavior. Overall, the amygdala is seen to play an important role in the evaluation of both emotional and social processes.

The amygdala has projections that go to the temporal lobe. This allows it to be involved in both emotional face perception and emotional memories. The area of the right temporal lobe, the fusiform gyrus, appears to respond selectively to faces as compared to other types of complex visual stimuli, and networks with the amygdala are thought to process the emotional content of the face. In terms of memories, scientists make the distinction between explicit memories and implicit memories. Implicit memories would involve the internal feeling of a particular situation, and explicit memories would involve details of the external situation. These two aspects of emotional memory are influenced differently by damage to the amygdala and areas of the temporal lobes (Bennett & Hacker, 2005). Damage to the amygdala interferes with emotional memories that are implicit, but not explicit. On the other hand, damage to areas of the temporal lobe does the opposite: It interferes with explicit memories, but not with implicit ones. Thus, with temporal lobe damage you could remember feeling a certain way but not remember the situation in which it occurred.

Another part of the brain involved in emotional processes is the prefrontal cortex, especially the bottom one-third of it, which is called the orbitofrontal cortex (see Berridge, 2003 for an overview). In a variety of studies, the left frontal areas have been seen to mediate positive affect, whereas the right is related to negative affect. Neurons in the prefrontal cortex have been shown to fire when the organisms see foods they like. However, unlike the amygdala, damage to the prefrontal cortex does not result in a loss of emotional reactions. The involvement of this area in emotionality appears to be of a higher level. For example, individuals with damage to this area appear not to incorporate the emotional consequences of their own actions into their everyday behaviors. It has also been suggested that this area is related to our ability to induce an emotion in ourselves through cognitive means or to reduce an emotional reaction.

As we saw in Chapter 4, the complexity of the human brain has allowed for a type of emotional functioning different from that of other animals. We can think about our emotions. We can inhibit them. We can voluntarily create them. As Hughlings Jackson noted, our higher level cognitive processes can re-represent, and thus transform, the lower level emotional processes. In such a process, we can add new features to an emotional reaction. We can also experience emotional responses to symbolic objects such as the flag of one's country or religious symbols, as well as music and art.

Emotional Development

Anyone who has watched an infant develop realizes the crucial role that emotions play in this process. From the very beginning, infants share their emotional worlds through facial expressions such as smiles and frowns. These expressions show their reactions to their environment and communicate these states to those around them. In fact, these reactions can be seen not long after birth by placing a sweet or sour substance on an infant's tongue. What is even more intriguing is research using ultrasound techniques that shows that even before birth, the fetus will react to emotional events (Salisbury, Yanni, LaGasse, & Lester, 2004).

As with motor and cognitive processes, it is assumed that emotional processes have been part of our evolutionary history. This suggests that examining emotionality in nonhuman organisms, including the manner in which brain processes lead to emotional processing, is an important endeavor (cf., Panksepp & Smith-Pasqualini, 2005). For example, across a variety of species, separation of an infant from its mother will lead to distress. Newborn rodents will emit vocalizations in the ultrasonic range when separated from their mother. The mother, in turn, will retrieve the infants that produce these calls. In a newborn baby chick, separation will lead to cries that continue for hours. Placing the chick in human hands will result in what has been called a comfort response. The chick will close its eyes, lower its head, and fall asleep. This response appears to be mediated by the release of the molecule oxytocin, which has been associated with bonding in a variety of species.

Based on research from the neurosciences, Panksepp (2004) suggests the existence of at least six core emotional systems: fear; rage; panic, which includes separation distress; care, which includes maternal care; play; and seeking.

Emotional Development of Facial Expression

At least since the time of Darwin's careful observation of his own son's emotional development, research studies have found that the facial expressions of infants are similar to our own (Dunn, 2003). These studies suggest that the basic emotions of happiness, anger, fear, sadness, and disgust are present in infants in the first weeks of life. Clearly, an infant's expression of distress, happiness, and anger can be discriminated early. What about the ability of infants to recognize the emotional expression of others? Research suggests that at about 3 months of age, infants begin to differentiate facial expressions and can tell surprised from happy and sad. By 4 months, infants can discriminate joyful faces from angry ones, and by 5 months of age they can discriminate among different types of negative emotions such as sad, fearful, and angry. As infants reach 1 year of age, they begin to notice the intensity of emotional expressions. From an evolutionary perspective, the communicative nature of emotionality is critical—it helps the helpless infant to survive and understand danger. For example, studies show that year-old infants will look to their mother's emotional expression to determine their reaction to novel toys. Clearly, infants begin life with an impressive set of emotional behaviors that signal to others to provide nurturance and soothing (Kopp & Neufeld, 2003).

Human emotional development happens in the context of social development, especially in relation to the baby's caregiver, who is usually the mother. In fact, by the fifth or sixth week of life, babies become as interested in the person feeding them as they do in the feeding itself. Another interesting aspect of an infant's emotionality is her ability to respond to the emotionality present in her environment. For example, young infants will often cry if other infants around them begin to cry. Beginning in the third month, infants will begin to differentiate emotional expressions of others. Most of the research has examined an infant's response to the emotional expressions of her mother. Generally, if she smiles, then the infant will also show signs of happiness. Anger, on the other hand, will generally result in less interest on the part of the infant.

The overall picture is that the infant comes into this world able to express emotionality. What an infant finds emotional is a little more complicated. As noted, infants may look to their caregiver to tell them about the emotional valence of an object. In one study, 1-year-old infants were allowed to crawl across a table with a piece of glass representing a "visual cliff" segment. If the mother made a fearful expression, the infant would avoid that part of the table. If the mother expressed happiness, then 74% of the infants would crawl across the glass. It is assumed that these responses are somewhat plastic and the mother could influence future behaviors by changes in her expression. However, the development of some emotional responses appears to be of a one-time nature. This is particularly true of distress, happiness, and anger. At this point, the evidence points to a universal basis for the expression and experience of emotionality.

In order to understand human emotional development, Bard (2005) suggests the importance of examining emotional development in other species. For example, chimpanzee infants, like human infants, show some emotional expressions in the first few hours of birth and other expressions as they develop.

Vocal Expressions of Emotion

All species except humans have established predators. For example, vervets—a small monkey from the African savannah—are prey to eagles, snakes, and leopards. What is amazing is that vervets have developed a vocal alarm system specific to each of these predators. In fact, if recordings of those animals are played, the monkeys will respond as if that specific predator were present (see Snowdon, 2003; Seyfarth & Cheney, 2003 for an overview). Ground squirrels also have different calls whether a predator is on the ground or in the air, and they will even modulate their calls to reflect the degree of danger. That is, a predator that surprises a squirrel on the ground would be more dangerous than one flying at a distance in the air. Even more amazing is the chickadee. Black-capped chickadees are common song birds found in North America. In the nonbreeding season, they form flocks of six to eight birds and use a system of vocalization both to mediate social interactions and to warn about predators. The system of vocalization is elaborate in that the chickadee calls reflect the state of the predator (in flight or on the ground) and the size of the predator. One set of research studies examined the response calls to some 15 different predators and found variation on at least two dimensions. It is assumed that these calls convey both the location of the predator and the danger faced (Templeton, Greene, & Davis, 2005). Given the self-preservation nature of this information, it is assumed that there exist few vocalizations in these species that do not contain some emotional content. What is intriguing is that the calls of the various species gave more than just emotional information. There was also reference to objects and events in the environment, such as what type of predator it is, where the predator is, and the degree of danger. This has led researchers to suggest that human language evolved from an emotional vocalization system, although there are still many questions to be answered.

The complexity of emotional vocalizations was shown by an analysis of the brain's involvement in vocalizations in monkeys (Ploog, 1981). Ploog showed that these vocalizations reflected involvement at the most basic level with the motor cells in the lower brain stem. At the next level, these motor nuclei came under the control of the midbrain to produce patterned responses that were species-specific. If the calls had an emotional component, then structures in the limbic system, such as the amygdala and hippocampus, became involved. If the call was of a more voluntary nature in the service of a goal, then higher cortical structures became involved. This suggests that, over evolutionary time, basic structures become involved in more complex tasks and become controlled by higher cortical processes. If this is correct, what would we expect in terms of emotional responses in humans? One implication is that if there is damage to higher cortical structures, then we would expect to see less inhibited displays of emotional processes. This is indeed what is seen. This would also suggest that the structures that evolved for emotional expression in a variety of species could also lie at the heart of our involvement with both music and language.

MUSIC

It is only recently that the evolution of music has been studied with some seriousness (e.g., Hauser & McDermott, 2003; see Mithen, 2006 for an overview). This is somewhat surprising considering some of the earliest human artifacts are musical instruments. Music is also found in all cultures throughout the world and has been played and enjoyed by individuals across the globe. As they do with language, children seem to absorb and produce music in an effortless way without any formal training. This suggests that music is not an adaptation like writing, which takes considerable effort. However, neuropsychology research suggests that those parts of the brain involved in music are somewhat independent from those involved in language (see Mithen, 2006 for an overview).

Part of the lack of formal study from an evolutionary perspective may be related to the difficulty seeing the adaptive value or functional significance of music, although some have connected it with emotionality. Clearly, humans use music to induce emotional moods in themselves and others. Darwin referred to music as "mysterious" because it apparently lacked any functional significance in our daily life, although he did relate it to sexuality. Darwin (1874) suggested that music and rhythm were precursors to the use of language in charming and expressing mutual love to a member of the opposite sex (p. 572). More recent work has studied the role of music in creating and maintaining social bonds. A variety of reports from around the world suggest that making music with others leads not only to positive emotional feelings but also a sense of connectedness with others. One possible physiological mechanism associated with these experiences may be the release of oxytocin in the brain during music making (Freeman, 2000). As you remember from the last chapter, oxytocin is associated with pleasant feelings and social attachments. Overall, the number of people who produce or listen to music daily suggests it has an important connection to human functioning, although its exact evolutionary history and function remains less clear.

From an evolutionary standpoint, it has been suggested that mothers singing to their babies may be the forerunner of speech (Falk, 2004). Mothers and others also use a sing-song type of communication called *baby talk* when communicating with their infants. Some researchers suggest that baby talk differs from normal language in terms of its sing-song or musical characteristics such as pitch and tempo. It has been pointed out that in baby talk, it is the melodic and exaggerated rhythmic patterns that interest infants rather than the meaning and grammar. Thus, there are at least three functions of baby talk. The first is to strengthen the mother-child connection. The second is to comfort the infant so the mother can also perform other tasks. Other primate infants just cling to their mother's back, which humans do not. And third, because baby talk is characterized by an exaggerated production the infant can better differentiate the sounds of his or her future language.

SUMMARY

Darwin studied the development of emotions from an evolutionary perspective. First, Darwin saw emotions as discrete, as exemplified by fear, anger, and disgust. Second, Darwin emphasized the human face in the expression of emotions. Third, one of Darwin's main ideas is that emotional processes are innate and found across a variety of species including humans. Fourth, emotions are not unique to humans and may be found in a variety of species. Fifth, particular muscle movements may signal a particular emotion. Darwin described three principles: (1) the principle of serviceable associated habits; (2) the principle of antithesis; and (3) the principle of direct actions of the nervous system. Research supports the idea that emotions are universal and are expressed and recognized similarly across all cultures. Emotions have also been studied in a dimensional manner. Panksepp suggested that core emotional tendencies could be seen to emerge from ancient brain processes shared by all mammals. It is possible to see brain areas involved in emotional processing, such as the amygdala. Other systems that contain emotional expression include music.

STUDY RESOURCES

Review Questions

1. What were the five important contributions Darwin made to our understanding of emotions?

2. Describe the three principles Darwin uses to frame his study of emotions and give an example of each.

3. What does it mean to say that emotional expression is universal?

4. Where do display rules come from, and how do they impact the expression of emotion?

5. What are fundamental life tasks, and how are emotions related to them from an evolutionary perspective?

6. Ekman developed a set of characteristics common to all emotions. List them and give an example of each characteristic.

7. Currently, there is a debate in emotion research as to whether to study emotions in terms of categories, following Darwin's lead, or in terms of their underlying dimensions. What are the advantages and disadvantages of each perspective? Can you suggest a way to integrate them?

8. What parts of the brain are important for the processing of emotional information?

9. What role do emotions play in the early development of an infant?

10. Researchers have suggested that human language evolved from an emotional vocalization system found in other species. What evidence do they point to in support of this position? Give some examples of the situations in which other species use their emotional vocalizations.

For Further Reading

Darwin, C. (1998). *The expression of emotions in man and animals* (3rd ed.). New York: Oxford University Press. (Original work published 1872)

Ekman, P. (2003). *Emotions revealed.* New York: Times Books.

LeDoux, J. (1996). *The emotional brain.* New York: Simon & Schuster.

Pinker, S. (1994). *The language instinct.* New York: William Morrow.

Key Terms and Concepts

- Darwin and the expression of emotions
- Nature of basic emotions

- Underlying dimensions of emotionality
- Understanding categorical and dimensional models of emotion
- Emotional expression and recognition
  - Cortical nature of emotion
- Emotional development
- Emotional development of facial expression
- Vocal expressions of emotion
  - Music

SAGE Study Site

Visit the study site at **www.sagepub.com/ray** for chapter-specific study resources.

Glossary Terms

- Antithesis
- Direct actions of the nervous system
- Display rules
- Fundamental life tasks
- Principle of serviceable associated habits

Language 7

One important aspect of being human is our ability and desire to communicate with one another. In this chapter, I will emphasize an evolutionary understanding of language. Like emotion, everyone knows what language is, but no one can define it. In 1866, the Linguistic Society of Paris banned papers or debates regarding language because no one could agree on the nature of language. Even today it has been suggested that linguists will not be able to understand evolutionary questions related to language until they are able to define what language is (see Locke, 2010 for an overview). Without a definition of language, it is difficult to answer such questions as "Do animals have language?" We know that bees perform a "dance" that tells other bees where to find nectar. Is this language? Or, should American Sign Language (ASL) used by deaf humans be considered a language?

As you will see in this chapter, there has been considerable debate about the nature of language and its relation to evolutionary processes. Some researchers emphasize the social nature of language and its importance in group dynamics and look to the history of social interactions as an important evolutionary driving force (Dunbar, 1996). Others have emphasized the manner in which language may have been important in sexual selection and see its evolution from this standpoint (Miller, 2000). Still others suggest there is nothing special about language. That is to say, language is like many cultural processes that we learn from our society, but there is nothing biologically special concerning its acquisition and production (Skinner, 1957, 1986). This is countered by those who see language as different from other learning (Chomsky, 1959) and part of our evolutionary history, even to the extent that language can be considered a trait or instinct (Pinker, 1994). In fact, some researchers have suggested that language is the key to what makes us human (Bickerton, 2009).

From an evolutionary perspective, one can ask, "Does language have the earmarks of an adaption?" Hauser and Fitch (2003) suggest it does. In particular, they suggest that language has its own particular design features:

1. It is present in all humans.

2. It is mediated by dedicated neural circuits.

3. It exhibits a characteristic pattern of development.

4. It is grounded in a suite of constraints that can be characterized by formal parameters.

They further suggest that if we consider language to be an adaptation, it becomes fruitful to study it neuroscientifically and as an evolutionary process that can be examined across a variety of species. I begin with the nature of language. Later chapters will include additional information on social and sexual aspects of communication.

The Nature of Language

It is challenging to understand human language in the context of evolution. Since 1990, a large number of scientific articles and at least one book a year have been devoted to the theme of language evolution (see Bickerton, 1995, 2009; Christiansen & Kirby, 2003; Deacon, 1997; Locke & Bogin, 2006; Pinker, 1994, 2007). As humans, we understand language and speak without effort. In an amazing manner, a human infant can acquire any of the more than 6,000 existing languages on earth. Environmental factors, of course, determine which languages any of us learn. We appear to be the only species that speaks. However, a variety of species, including certain marine mammals, parrots, hummingbirds, and songbirds, have the ability to imitate sounds, which is necessary for the evolution of language, whereas primates do not (see Berwick, Okanoya, Beckers, & Bolhuis, 2011; Bolhuis, Okanoya, & Scharff, 2010; Hillix & Rumbaugh, 2004 for overviews).

Darwin noted the parallels between language learning in infants and song learning in birds. Current research suggests that there are a number of similarities in vocal learning between humans and songbirds (Berwick et al., 2011; Bolhuis et al., 2010). One parallel is the way human infants learn to speak and songbirds learn to sing. In both cases, learning results from an interaction of internal programs and specific experiences. Songbirds can imitate a variety of sounds, although they generally imitate songs heard from their own species. Human infants are quick to imitate other humans, even though other sounds are available to them from pets and other sources. If songbirds are reared in isolation, their singing does not develop normally. Abnormal language development is also seen in the few cases of humans who developed without access to human language. Thus, in both songbirds and humans, there is a critical period after which vocal learning becomes more difficult. This can be seen in humans who try to learn another language after puberty. In both the human infant and young songbird, a listening phase precedes a production phase. The initial stage of the production phase is not like the adult vocal productions (e.g., the babbling stage in human infants). Further, for both humans and songbirds, vocal learning is enhanced by social interaction. The parallels of human and bird vocal learning suggest the possibility of parallel brain and genetic mechanisms underlying this learning.

At least since the writing of Condillac in the 1700s until the present day, scientists have noted the large gap between the types of communication patterns seen in humans and those of other organisms. In terms of complexity, including vocabulary, grammar, and the range of ideas that can be expressed, there is nothing like human language in other species. Humans communicate with language in a way that is different from every other species. In other species, communication systems tend to be mapped in a one-to-one manner. A chickadee, for example, can produce a sound directly related to the size and location of a predator. Vervet monkeys will emit different alarm calls depending upon whether they see an eagle, a leopard, or a snake. However, these species have only one way of saying what was said. Even songbirds do not have the ability to combine sounds to create new meanings. With human language, on the other hand, there are a variety of ways of conveying the same information. If there is a dangerous fire, you can say "leave," "run," "get out of here," "there is a fire," "there is danger," and so forth. Pinker (2003) suggests that the most powerful aspect of language is its ability to convey an unlimited number of ideas from one person to another using only a stream of sounds.

Honey bees are one species that does appear to have a more complex system of communication. Bees can use their sensory systems to determine color, scent of flowers, locations, and other factors as they gather food. What is interesting is that once they locate a food source, they return to the hive and use various types of movements to communicate to the other bees the direction, distance, and quality of food. These movements or dances were carefully studied by the Austrian ethologist Karl von Frisch (1967). Von Frisch was able to determine the meaning of these bee movements, and in 1967 he won the Nobel Prize along with Nikolaas Tinbergen and Konrad Lorenz. Although the communication system involving movement is complex, it is also limited in vocabulary or concepts. For example, one of von Frisch's assistants placed a food supply in a tower that the bees were able to discover. These bees then returned and described the location of the food to the other bees, who then went to the location. They discovered the tower but not the food, which was higher up. Thus, it appears that the communication system of the bees is two-dimensional and has no means to communicate height. Although von Frisch called his book *The Dance Language and Orientation of Bees,* there are those who question whether this is really a language. Let us now turn to the nature of human language.

There are at least four questions that can be asked from an evolutionary perspective (Kirby, 2007):

1. Structure: Why is language the way it is and not some other way? How can an evolutionary approach explain the particular language universals we observe?

2. Uniqueness: Why are we unique in possessing language? What is so special about humans?

3. Function: How could language evolve? What were the selective pressures involved?

4. History: What is the evolutionary story for language? When did it evolve? Were there intermediate stages?

These questions reflect the different approaches a variety of researchers have taken over the years. However, at this point we do not have clear answers to these questions. In this chapter, I will help you understand what we have discovered thus far.

THE EVOLUTION OF LANGUAGE

What is the function of language and how did it evolve? Darwin viewed language as the result of an evolution that began with inarticulate cries, gestures, and expressions, as seen across a variety of species, followed by a series of steps in which humans moved to an articulated language. Indeed, one hypothesis suggests that a common origin for vocalization evolved more than 400 million years ago in fish. We usually do not think of fish vocalizing, but some are able to do so with the aid of an air sac that is used for buoyancy. Using muscles associated with the air sac, these fish are able to vibrate the air sac in such a way that it functions as a resonance chamber and amplifies sound. These vocalizations are related to mating and defense of territory. Researchers have been able to examine the brain circuits related to these sounds (Bass, Gilland, & Baker, 2008). What is intriguing is that the organization of these circuits is consistent with vocal systems in frogs, birds, and mammals, suggesting a common body plan for vocalization. The relation of this type of social vocalization to speech in humans is still being determined.

It has been suggested by a variety of authors that the expanded childhood of humans set the stage for language learning. That is to say, the longer contact of the child with its family and the need for complex communication would support the development of language. This, in turn, is followed by a period of adolescence, with the pressures of social interactions (Locke & Bogin, 2006). Surprisingly, a variety of research studies from numerous cultures suggest that one main topic of language is social relationships—generally referred to as gossip. What do you talk to your friends about? The answer is usually other people. In this sense, one function of language is to keep the connection in social relationships. What do other primates do to bond social groups? The answer is grooming. By analogy, Dunbar (1996, 2003, 2004) suggested that language is to humans what grooming is to other primates. Actually, he suggests that language evolved in a series of stages, with grooming at the earliest stage, followed by vocal chorusing as a way of bonding a group, followed by a socially focused language, and finally the metaphoric and technical language we use today (Dunbar, 2003). Although we don't pick small insects from each other's heads, we do gossip. It is clearly a way we bond with each other. Walk across a college campus and notice what most people are saying to each other on their cell phones. They are usually talking about other people and, of course, themselves.

The idea of language as grooming might also support the idea that language evolved from basic motor processes (Lieberman, 2000, 2006). For example, think about the importance of using our hands as we talk to others. It might also suggest that language is an extension of the basic mating dances seen in a variety of species. Rather than perform a mating dance, we "chat someone up," as the British say. Further, language is used to convey a variety of underlying processes. Sometimes we use sounds as a place filler, such as "uhhh" or other sounds. Also, there are numerous types of logic that underlie our words. Teenagers tend to reason by analogy: They will, like, say that, like, everything is like something else. Scientists use more formal logic to rule out alternative hypotheses. We also use language to describe empathetic reasoning, to show we understand another person's experience. The point is that language can describe a variety of internal and external processes. It is this cumulative process that enables languages and their derivatives (spoken and written forms) to set the stage for culture to play a role in human history that is very different from that of other species.

THE STRUCTURE OF LANGUAGE

When we think about language, there are at least five factors that should be considered. First, a language is regular and has rules, which we call a *grammar*. Second, it is productive. That is to say, there are an almost infinite number of combinations of words that can be used to express thoughts. Third, words in a language are arbitrary, in that across languages any word can refer to any thing. For example, the words "dog," "chien," "perro," and "hund" all refer to the same animal but in different languages

(English, French, Spanish, and German). As far as anyone can tell, there is an arbitrary relationship between words and their meanings. An exception to this is onomatopoeia, which refers to a word that imitates the sound it represents, such as "tick tock" or "cuckoo." Fourth, languages are discrete, in that sentences can be divided into words and then into smaller bites of meaning called *morphemes* and then into sounds. And fifth, languages are linear, in that words are presented one after the other. Further, language can help us to describe both the internal world that we experience personally and the external world that we experience around us.

Researchers interested in language separate it into levels of analysis. All languages begin with sounds. The basic sound of a language is referred to as a **phoneme**. The study of the ways phonemes can be combined in a language is called **phonology**. There are approximately 100 different phonemes used in all languages around the world. English uses approximately 40 phonemes. For example, the phoneme "ba" associated with the letter "b" is an element unto itself. By itself, it has no meaning other than the sound we process. As we will see, every infant can recognize and reproduce all of the 100-plus phonemes. As we grow older, we lose this ability and are limited to the phonemes in the languages we learned early in our lives. For example, Japanese does not have the "qu" phoneme associated with the initial sound in the English word "quack," and Japanese speakers find it almost impossible to pronounce that word. Of course, English speakers have similar problems when repeating phonemes in other languages, such as the "ch" sound in German. What is interesting in terms of language learning is that we rarely hear these basic sounds in isolation.

The next level of analysis is a **morpheme**—the smallest meaningful unit of a language. Morphemes can be words (e.g., "cat," "house," or "paint"). Morphemes that can stand alone are called *free* morphemes. Morphemes can also be *bound*; that is, they cannot stand alone. Examples of such morphemes are tense markers on verbs (e.g., paint-ed, drive-s), number markers on nouns (e.g., boy-s, child-ren, church-es), prefixes on adjectives (e.g., un-believable, in-tolerant, co-worker), suffixes on nouns and adjectives (e.g., boy-hood, formal-ity, good-ness), and so forth. Words can become quite complex morphologically, even in a language like English, which is not known for its morphological makeup. For example, a word (morpheme) like *form* can be suffixed to form an adjective (*form-al*), prefixed to become the opposite (*in-form-al*), turned into another noun (*in-form-al-ity*), then pluralized with yet another suffix (*in-form-al-iti-es*), with the final outcome containing five morphemes.

The next level of analysis is **syntax**—the structure of a sentence and the rules that govern it. For example, one rule is that sentences must have both a noun and a verb. Finally, **semantics** is the study of meaning. That is, how do we understand what is being said? A critical question in the study of language is how humans are able to move between the levels of meaning and syntax.

What Is Language?

In the 1960s, Noam Chomsky (1966, 1968) helped to establish many of the ideas and debates that today influence how we think about language. He suggested that all humans have a set of innate principles and parameters, which he called *universal grammar*. The **universal grammar** describes the total range of morphological and syntactic rules that can occur in any language. Chomsky's original goal was to describe the manner in which spoken language is mapped onto meaning. The actual spoken word, with its grammatical structure, is called "surface structure," whereas the meaning of the speech is called "deep structure." As illustrated previously with the example of a dangerous fire, there are a variety of ways (surface structure) of saying this, which would convey the same meaning (deep structure). An extension of this idea is shown with bilingual individuals who often will remember an event or idea but cannot remember in which language they learned about the event.

Chomsky (1966, 1968) was interested in describing the rules by which deep structure is transformed to speech, and vice versa, by investigating the rules shared among all languages and those that are language-specific. Related to the notion of universal grammar is the critical idea that language is generative. This suggests that there exists a learnable finite system of rules that can generate an infinite number of sentences. The basic observation is that we can generate sentences we have never uttered before, as well as understand sentences we have never heard before. By the age of 3, children are fluent speakers of their language without any formal instruction in the nature of grammar. Even more impressive is their ability to invent languages that are more systematic than the ones they hear and to follow subtle grammatical principles for which there are no examples in their environment (Pinker & Bloom, 1990). Listen to what you say to your friends. Each time you speak, you generally use a sentence you have never used before. Sure, the meaning is similar to other times you have spoken, but the exact wording is different. Without thinking, you produce the sentences and you understand the sentences. What is more, you extract meaning even when there is ambiguity. A sentence like "Flying planes are dangerous" or "The sailor passed the port" is simple for humans to understand, given a context, but difficult for a computer to understand due to the ambiguous nature of the sentence. Further, we extract meaning from language in a way that is not always logical: "We park in a driveway and drive on a parkway." Although children learn to speak a language and use the rules of grammar so quickly, Chomsky was not convinced that language could be explained by Darwin's understanding of evolution. According to Chomsky, language may have appeared as our brains became larger and more complex. Thus, language learning was not a product of natural selection but an emergent property of brain complexity. It is unclear why Chomsky rejected language being influenced by natural selection, unless it was his view that language is somehow different from other human faculties. However, he still saw language facility as an inborn ability and referred to language learning in humans as the innate *Language Acquisition Device* or LAD.

One language researcher who does see language as shaped by natural selection is Steven Pinker. Pinker (1994) begins with the suggestion that the process of language learning must be innate. In this way, language can be considered the same as any sensory process or instinct whose development can be viewed from an evolutionary perspective. In fact, Pinker suggests that language possesses the same type of design features as physical structures such as the eye. What is especially intriguing to Pinker is that in teaching a language, parents give children examples of language through their speech but do not teach rules per se. However, children are able to infer the rules and apply them automatically. One example of this in English is when children say "he runned" or "she goed," rather than "he ran" or "she went." Clearly, the child is applying a past tense rule rather than just repeating what his or her parents said. The fact that children apply such language rules suggests innate mechanisms for language learning based on universal principles, rather than just copying what a parent says. In this sense, Pinker asks us to look to biological predispositions, rather than culture, in order to understand language learning.

One fundamental question of language relates to its role in the natural world (Pinker & Jackendoff, 2005). That is to say, how should we consider the evolution of language in relation to our biological processes as well as that of other species? Pinker and Jackendoff suggest that language is like other biological systems in that it has evolved by natural selection and shows signs of complex adaptive design. In particular, Pinker and Jackendoff suggest three specific questions to answer in this regard. First, which aspects of language are learned from environmental input, and which aspects arise from the design of our brains? Second, which parts of a person's language ability are specific to language per se, and which parts belong to more general abilities? And third, which aspects of language are uniquely human?

Over the years, it has been argued by such researchers as Alvin Liberman (1985) that speech is special. That is to say, humans are able to recognize certain sounds used in human speech in ways that other species cannot. However, other research has suggested that certain other species are also able to make these discriminations and that human language may not be special (see Pinker & Jackendoff, 2005 for an overview). This would suggest that the ability to perceive speech-like sounds predates the evolution of language in humans. The picture is complicated by the fact that humans use different areas of their brains for perceiving speech versus other auditory sounds. In fact, there is a certain type of brain damage called "pure word deafness," in which a person can hear environmental sounds but not analyze speech. There is also the opposite condition, in which a person can analyze speech but not recognize environmental sounds.

PRIMATES AND LANGUAGE

If language is special for humans, what aspects of language represent this specialness? We know that human infants, raised in an environment in which they are introduced to language, will perceive and produce language generally before age 3. We also know from some tragic situations that human children raised without exposure to language will never develop normal language abilities. It is also clear that other species do not develop the major aspects of human language in the wild. What would happen if a chimp, who is our closest genetic relative, were reared in an environment in which language was present (see Hillix & Rumbaugh, 2004 for an overview)?

In the 1960s, Allen and Beatrix Gardner raised a chimp named Washoe in their home. She was born in Africa and brought to the United States. Beginning when she was 10 months old, she was taught ASL, as if she were a deaf child. She had her own space in a house trailer in the Gardner's backyard. She actually wore clothes and shoes and learned to use a spoon and a cup. She was with adults who used sign language both with each other and with her. By the end of her first year with the Gardners, she knew about 50 words in sign language. What was intriguing was that Washoe was able to combine signs, such as YOU ME DRINK. Her level of sign language equaled that of human infants who lived in a household in which sign language was used. At one point, she dropped a toy down a space in her trailer when another assistant was taking care of her. When Allen Gardner came to the trailer, she signed the word OPEN at the place where the toy had fallen behind the wall. She is also reported to have signed WATER BIRD when she saw ducks on a pond. These examples would suggest that Washoe was doing more than just presenting information that had been previously learned. However, at about age 2, human infants show an increased learning of language not seen in Washoe. After about five years, Washoe's vocabulary was about 140 words. In comparison, a human first grader would know about 10,000 words, which would increase to 50,000 by the fifth grade.

In the 1980s, Sue Savage-Rumbaugh took a somewhat different approach to teaching communication to a bonobo, also referred to as a pygmy chimpanzee. This bonobo was named Kanzi (see Figure 7.1). What was really interesting was that Kanzi learned his first words by watching the researchers try to teach language to his mother. He actually displayed knowledge of words without ever being asked. The idea with Kanzi was to teach him to communicate. Like Washoe, Kanzi played with toys and was involved in

> **Figure 7.1**   Sue Savage-Rumbaugh and Kanzi

Source: http://www.primatesworld.com/TalkWithChimps.html

conversations taking place around him. He was also taken on walks around the research center, during which he was spoken to. However, this time the conversations were in spoken English and not sign language. There are a number of videos showing Kanzi responding to such English sentences as "Take off Sue's shoe" by performing the requested action. Also, Kanzi could respond by pointing to symbols. Each symbol represented an English word. Given Kanzi's ability to perform acts and respond to English questions, many researchers suggest he was able to understand sentence structure. For example, he was correct 75% of the time when given sentences like "place the book on the rock" as opposed to "place the rock on the book." However, he had more difficulty when asked to do two activities, such as "give Sue the bottle and the cup." He could do one, but not both.

Like Washoe, Kanzi's comprehension of language appeared to be comparable to that of a 2 ½-year-old child. If you would like to read an interview with Dr. Savage-Rumbaugh about primate language, you can go to http://pubpages.unh.edu/~jel/512/chimps/SSR.html and http://www.ted.com/talks/lang/eng/susan_savage_rumbaugh_on_apes_that_write.html. The research involving primate language suggests that basic linguistic abilities of some form existed before the evolution of human speech. What allowed humans to develop speech and move beyond the level of a 2-year-old child is still a hotly debated question (see Deacon, 1997; Lieberman, 2000 for overviews).

A different approach to teaching primates language was adopted by Ann and David Premack (Premack, 1976). The Premacks were more interested in cognitive processes and intelligence than language per se. However, their work helps inform animal language studies. They worked with a young female chimpanzee named Sarah. Ann Premack was born in China and drew from Chinese pictograms to create a similar set of pictograms for English (see Figure 7.2). These symbols could be placed on a magnetic board. The basic procedure was to study how Sarah learned a specific linguistic function. They were particularly interested in (1) how word meaning was related to existing knowledge; (2) how the primate learned such concepts as name of, color of, same and different, and other such concepts; and (3) rules for relating words to one another, including word order. Although size of vocabulary was not the focus of their training, they reported similar vocabulary size (approximately 130 words) as found with Washoe. Further, the Premacks suggested that language training actually changed cognitive abilities. For example, when shown an apple, a space for another object, and a cut apple, the language-trained primates could correctly pick out that a knife, as opposed to other objects, should be put in the space. Non-language-trained primates could not perform this task. They were also able to show that primates could learn same, different, and similar concepts. For example, big and small red squares would be seen as similar. In terms of language, the Premacks suggested that although primates could show some forms of reasoning and reading of symbols, they do not possess the ability to construct sentences or understand grammar as do humans. One critical part of this work was to show the connection between language and cognitive processes.

Duane Rumbaugh spent more than 30 years teaching animals to learn aspects of language (Hillix & Rumbaugh, 2004). One important primate in this work was a chimpanzee named Lana. Lana was taught through a key press board to name objects and ask for things (see Figure 7.3 on page 229). Each key was a lexigram that stood for a word. The keys were color coded: red lexigrams represented edibles and violet ones stood for the name of a person. It was also possible to reposition the lexigrams on the board, so that Lana was actually learning the lexigram rather than just its position. There was also a period key that would end and erase the sentence. Lana not only learned to ask for different types of food but also to push the period button if she made a mistake in her request or the sequence of key presses and wanted to start over. Interestingly, it was reported that Lana was 95% correct in completing valid sentence stems and rejecting those with fatal grammatical flaws. For example, she loved

Figure 7.2 The plastic symbols that the Premacks used with Sarah and other chimpanzees. These could be placed in various orders on a metallic board.

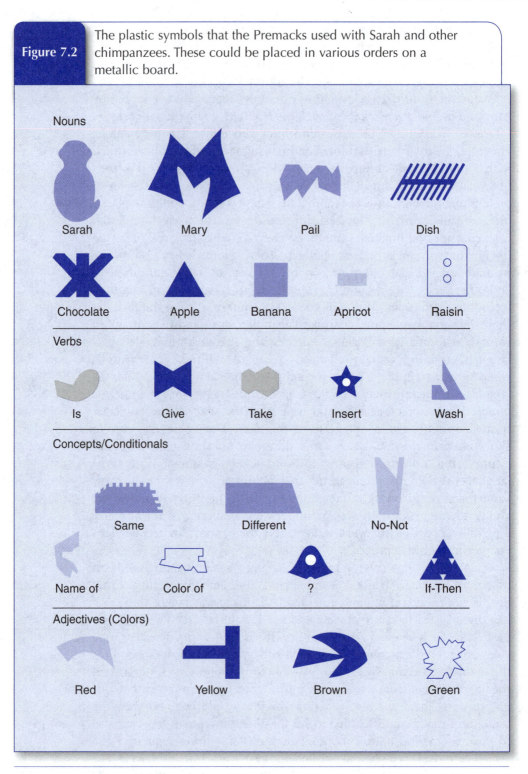

Source: Hillix and Rumbaugh (2004, p. 114).

the drink Coke and over the years would ask for it in different ways, such as YOU GIVE COKE IN CUP TO LANA as well as YOU GIVE CUP OF COKE TO LANA. Equally interesting is that over the years, Lana was able to give names to things that had never been named. For example, she called a cucumber a BANANA WHICH IS GREEN and the citrus fruit orange the BALL THAT IS ORANGE. Although initially it took Lana 1600 trials to learn to distinguish the names for M&Ms and banana slices, later differentiations took much less time. Rumbaugh suggests that Lana learned the concept that everything has a name, and this made later naming tasks easier. What is most intriguing is that if the researchers did not give her what she wanted, she would engage in a conversation with them through the lexigram board until she received something she would accept.

Some current language research using primates can be found at http://www2.gsu.edu/~wwwlrc/

Figure 7.3 Lana in front of her board on which she could press the keys to point to objects and to ask for things. Once pressed, the key would remain lit. In this way, she did not need to remember which keys had been pressed.

Source: Hillix and Rambaugh (2004, p. 129).

STRUCTURE OF VOCAL CORDS

Most nonhuman primates have the larynx higher in the throat than do humans. This enables them to breathe and drink at the same time, but not to make speech sounds. The human infant actually begins life with the larynx high in the throat. This also enables breathing and drinking at the same time. In about the third month of life, their vocal tract begins to descend and they can begin to produce a unique set of vowels, as would be found in words such as see, saw, and sue. These three vowel sounds are arranged at maximum distance from each other in the oral cavity, thus allowing for maximum discrimination. Also, humans have a larger area of the spinal cord necessary for breath control in producing speech than other primates, as well as an auditory system tuned to the predominant frequencies found in speech. It has also been noted that, during the first year of life, the human face changes from one with the features found in Homo erectus and Neandertals to that of modern humans (Lieberman, 2006). In Figures 7.4 and 7.5, you can see the location of the larynx in a chimpanzee and in an adult human.

How do humans make sounds that we hear as speech? We do it with our larynx, which also contains a cartilage we call our Adam's apple. By having

Figure 7.4 The head and neck of an adult male chimpanzee. Note the high position of the larynx, the long oral cavity, and the position of the tongue in the mouth.

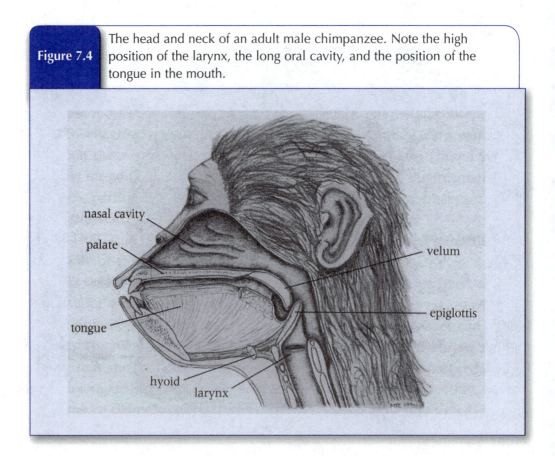

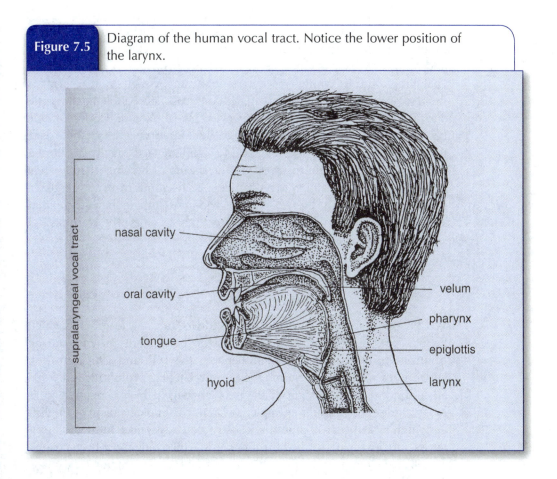

Figure 7.5 Diagram of the human vocal tract. Notice the lower position of the larynx.

supralaryngeal vocal tract

nasal cavity

oral cavity

tongue

hyoid

velum

pharynx

epiglottis

larynx

your larynx low in your throat, you are able to make a wider range of sounds than other species can produce. To make a sound, the vocal cords in our larynx move in and out, modifying the continuous flow of air from our lungs into puffs of air. We also use our tongue and lips to modify speech sounds. Notice how your tongue is in different places and also has a different shape and manner of contact when you say "to" than when you say "shoe."

INFANT VOCALIZATION

One approach to understanding human vocalization has resulted from the study of the development of speech in human infants and young children (Oller & Griebel, 2005). During the first month of life, the human infant produces a wide variety of sounds that are assumed to be precursors to speech. These sounds may be uttered in any context—when the infant is alone, when he or she is with caregivers, and so forth. By the second month, the infant produces "cooing" sounds, especially in the context of interactions with others. Of course, throughout these periods, caregivers spend considerable time talking to the infant. During the next three months, children expand their range of sounds to include squeals, growls, and more vowel-like sounds, as their vocal cords begin to change. These "babbling" sounds contain both consonant and vowel sounds. What is interesting is that deaf and hearing infants coo and babble at the same ages. By about 10 months of age, however, the babbling of hearing infants becomes more like their native language. Deaf infants begin to babble with their hands if they have been exposed to sign language. Finally, at about a year of age, words begin to appear in the speech of hearing infants. They also begin to lose the ability to recognize speech sounds from any language other than their own. By two years of age, most infants have combined simple words and continue during the next year to reflect the grammatical rules of their language.

CREOLE LANGUAGES

What happens when a group moves or is moved to a new location in which people speak a different language? This was particularly the case during colonization by the major powers between the 16th and 19th centuries. Without formal language training in the new language, colonized individuals utilized a simple version of the new language, which is referred to as *pidgin.* Pidgin English, for example, was a much simpler version of English and often lacked correct grammatical structures as well as future and past tenses. Linguists have studied the manner in which pidgin has been created as well as the manner in which the children of these immigrants learn language. What is surprising is that the children do not just copy the pidgin of their parents, but instead create a new type of language with specific grammatical rules. This more structured form of the original pidgin is referred to as *Creole.*

It has been suggested that Creole languages throughout the world use a very similar grammatical structure. The structure is not related specifically to the new language; it appears to be universal. The argument that has been made by a variety of researchers is that the similarity of structures from a variety of Creole languages throughout the world is reflective of a biological program for language. This suggests that language is created in the brain by a set of biologically determined rules, rather than just copied by children from their parents. If Creole was just copied by the children from the parents, then you would expect that the children would speak the same pidgin that their parents spoke. One important statement of this position is that of Derek Bickerton (1984). He studied Hawaiian Pidgin and Hawaiian Creole and suggested that in this case, the movement from pidgin to Creole was accomplished in a single generation. He further suggests that this supports the idea suggested by Chomsky that there exists a modular organization of language, rather than a general process of the brain not related to language per se.

GENETICS AND LANGUAGE

There is a rare language disorder called *developmental verbal dyspraxia* (DVD) that is inherited and has been linked to an allele of the FoxP2 gene on chromosome 7. Humans with this allele show problems in articulation, production, comprehension, and judgments related to grammar. The normal version of the gene is found universally in humans but not other primates. However, the gene is found in songbirds and has been related to song production. In humans, the gene is related to vocal learning and the integration of auditory and motor processes. Some estimates suggest that this gene appeared within the last 200,000 years. At present, this research is in the early stages and there is controversy concerning the exact genetic basis of language.

BRAIN INVOLVEMENT

The traditional model of language processing in the brain dates back to the 1800s. The French neurologist Pierre-Paul Broca had a patient who had a stroke. The damage to the brain resulted in the patient having difficulty in producing speech, but not in understanding it. This type of language disorder has come to be called *Broca's aphasia,* and the left frontal area of the brain affected is called *Broca's area.* In 1887, about 25 years after Broca described his patient, the German neurologist Carl Wernicke described the opposite condition, in which a person could produce speech, but it lacked coherent meaning. This disorder came to be called *Wernicke's aphasia,* and the left posterior area generally affected in the brain is known as *Wernicke's area* (see Figure 7.6). The basic idea is that spoken language is first perceived in Wernicke's area, which is related to the processing of auditory information. This information is then transmitted by pathways to Broca's area. Broca's area is related to speech production. Studies of individuals with some form of brain damage suggest that Broca's area is involved in not only the production of speech but also syntax, which includes grammatical formations involving verbs. Individuals with damage in Wernicke's area do not have similar problems producing speech, but they have difficulty with those aspects related to the meaning of the words, especially nouns. More recent brain imaging studies have asked individuals either to read or to repeat spoken words. These studies show brain activation in the individual's left hemisphere in those areas associated with motor responses, such as the primary motor cortex, the premotor cortex, and the supplementary motor cortex, as well as areas in both hemispheres around Broca's area. However, Philip Lieberman (2000, 2006) cautions against seeing language as encapsulated in just Broca's and Wernicke's areas. He has described the evolution of language in terms of its connections with early motor processes, especially subcortical structures such as the basal

Figure 7.6   The Major Language Areas of the Brain

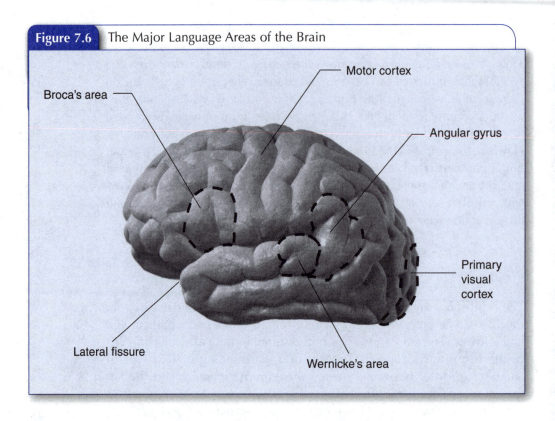

ganglia. Lieberman further notes that most language disorders include these subcortical structures along with Broca's and Wernicke's areas.

In terms of the evolution of language, there has been a debate as to whether it arose gradually over time or arose very quickly with the anatomical changes that give humans linguistic abilities (see Ghazanfar, 2008 for an overview). In a variety of human traits such as color vision, there is clear evidence for a gradual evolution. However, others have argued that language is totally human and happened quickly. Although the question is not settled, brain imaging studies are beginning to suggest a gradual development of language. For example, James Rilling and his colleagues (2008) examined the differences in the way fiber tracts connect the frontal and temporal lobe in humans and other primates. This is an important pathway in the brain for language. Damage to this pathway in humans leaves the person with the ability to understand speech but unable to repeat what was said. As can be seen in Figure 7.7, this pathway is different in humans compared to chimpanzees and macaque monkeys. However, it is more developed in the chimpanzee than the macaque. Because chimpanzees come between humans and macaques in terms of primate lineage, this suggests that language development may, indeed, have been a gradual process. This is further supported by the finding that all of these primates have areas in their cortex that are sensitive to the sounds of other members of the species (Petkov et al., 2008). However, this area in humans involves different circuits than that of other primates, as can be seen in illustration "b" in Figure 7.7. This suggests that, like human vision, human speech and language are the result of modifications to existing structures.

Figure 7.7
(a) Humans, chimpanzees, and macaques have circuits in the brain for recognizing sounds from their own species. (b) The voice area in macaques is located in a different place than would be predicted from the location of the human voice area.

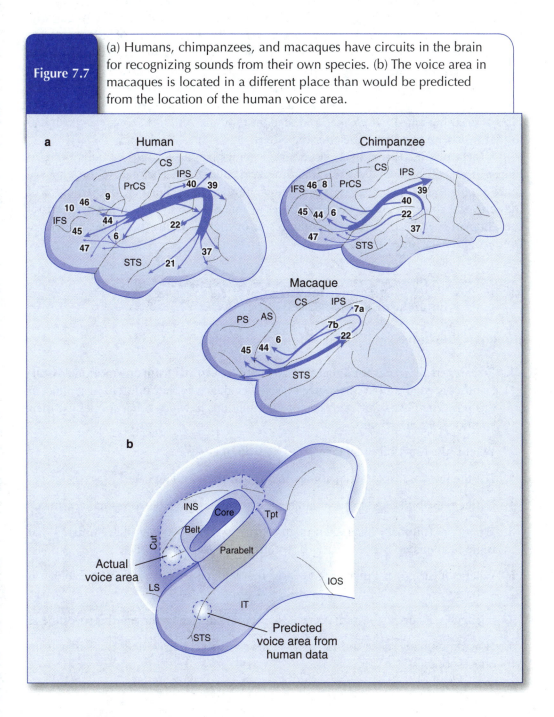

SUMMARY

Language plays an important role in the life of humans. Evolution offers a lens by which to view language. Hauser and Fitch (2003) suggest that language can be considered an adaptation in evolutionary terms. Darwin noted parallels between language learning in infants and song learning in birds. The human developmental sequence allows for long periods of interactions with others, which supports the development of language.

From a structural sense, there are five factors of language. First, a language is regular and has rules, which we call a grammar. Second, it is productive. Third, words in a language are arbitrary in that across languages any word can refer to any thing. Fourth, languages are discrete in that sentences can be divided into words, and then into smaller bites of meaning called *morphemes,* and then into sounds. And fifth, languages are linear in that words are presented one after the other.

A variety of studies sought to determine whether language could be taught to primates. In general, none of these research programs could teach a primate to use language more sophisticated than that of a 3-year-old human child. Further, the structure of human vocal cords differs from that of other primates. In terms of human brain structure, human speech and language is the result of modifications to existing structures over evolutionary time.

STUDY RESOURCES

Review Questions

1. Researchers have suggested that human language evolved from an emotional vocalization system found in other species. What evidence do they point to in support of this position? Give some examples of the situations in which other species use their emotional vocalizations.

2. What is the function of language and how did it evolve?

3. List the five core factors that comprise our definition of language.

4. Define these building blocks of language structure: phoneme, morpheme, syntax.

5. What does Chomsky mean by humans having an innate universal grammar? What is the relationship between surface structure and deep structure?

6. What evidence does Pinker cite to show that language evolves like other biological systems?

7. If language is special for humans, what aspects of language represent this specialness?

8. How do humans make sounds that we hear as speech? How does this differ from other species?

9. Describe the stages of infant vocalization.

10. What does recent brain research tell us about the evolution of language?

For Further Reading

Bickerton, D. (1995). *Language and human behavior.* Seattle: University of Washington Press.

Bickerton, D. (2009). *Adam's tongue: How humans made language, how language made humans.* New York: Hill & Wang.

Deacon, T. (1997). *The symbolic species: The coevolution of language and the brain.* New York: Norton.

Hillix, W., & Rumbaugh, D. (2004). *Animal bodies, human minds: Ape, dolphin and parrot language skills.* New York: Kluwer.

Pinker, S. (1994). *The language instinct.* New York: William Morrow.

Pinker, S. (2007). *The stuff of thought: Language as a window into human nature.* New York: Viking.

Key Terms and Concepts

- The nature of language
  - The evolution of language
  - The structure of language
- What is language?
  - Primates and language
  - Structure of vocal cords
  - Infant vocalization
  - Creole languages
  - Genetics and language
  - Brain involvement

SAGE Study Site

Visit the study site at **www.sagepub.com/ray** for chapter-specific study resources.

Glossary Terms

- Morpheme
- Phoneme
- Phonology
- Semantics
- Syntax
- Universal grammar

Sex and Gender 8

Imagine that as you walk across campus, a person of the opposite sex walks up to you and says, "I have been noticing you around campus. I find you very attractive." She or he then says to you, "Would you go out with me tonight?" What would you do? If you were similar to the students who actually participated in this study, about half of you would say "yes," which also means that about half of you would say "no." Would it matter if you were a male or a female? No, the same percentage of men and women agreed to (or turned down) the request for a date. Now, what if the person who found you attractive asked you to come over to his or her apartment that night? Would you agree? What if he or she directly asked you to go to bed with him or her that night? What would be your response then? Would you expect males and females to answer these last two propositions differently? The answer is, of course, yes. In two separate studies, about 70% of the males agreed to either go to the female's apartment or to go to bed with her (Clark & Hatfield, 1989). No female, on the other hand, agreed to go to bed with the male who told her she was attractive. A few women (6% in one study and 0% in the other) agreed to go to his apartment that night. Clearly, there are gender differences in our willingness to make ourselves available to another, especially for sexual activity. Why is this?

In this chapter, I will consider what an evolutionary perspective can tell us about mating preferences and behavior. As we will see, looking across species can give us a picture of the variety of ways in which different species engage in mating. However, we can also note ways in which humans appear to be distinctive. We are, for example, almost the only species that has sex face to face. The bonobos, a species of small ape, is another species that has intercourse facing one another. How this type of sexual activity relates to sharing between partners and other social aspects of a species is, of course, an interesting question. As we consider mating preference and sexual activity, we will also note that not all species require males and

239

females for mating. As we shall see, there is even a species of lizard in the western United States that is composed of only females. However, humans do have different genders, and we want to understand the predispositions we have in seeking a mate. We begin by considering Darwin's view of sexual selection.

Darwin and Sexual Selection

In addition to natural selection, which emphasized the manner in which organisms adapt and survive in relation to a changing environment, Darwin (1874) also developed a theory of sexual selection. His theory of sexual selection emphasized the manner in which organisms have evolved not only to survive but also to reproduce. One of the themes of the theory of sexual selection was competition—that males compete with other males, and that females compete with other females, for access to a mate. As we will see, sometimes the competition takes the form of outright fighting, as in the case of male elephant seals or reindeer. At other times, the competition is to determine who has the brightest colors, as seen in a variety of male birds and fish. I will also note the manner in which females compete with one another for access to males, although in most species this is less overt.

What does competition contribute? The big-picture view suggests that organisms compete to ensure that high-quality genes are passed to the offspring. What are high-quality genes? According to evolutionary theory, they are genes that are associated with factors such as health and caring, which in turn ensure a newborn can survive, be taken care of, and mature to an age at which he or she can contribute to future generations. How can an individual in a species know this information? This is a question that scientists have been particularly interested in answering. When there is direct fighting between the males, as in the case of elephant seals, then it is more obvious that the one who wins would be the one that is more physically fit. However, what about the display of bright colors? Take the peacock, for example. The peahen is most attracted to the peacock with the brightest spots on his tail. But what is the advantage of choosing a male with a bright tail? The answer is that there is a direct relationship between the male's tail and his health. Thus, by picking a peacock with a bright tail, the peahen also chooses a healthy male. Of course, for this system to work, it is necessary that the winner of the competition be able to mate and produce offspring at a greater rate than the losers. Studies in a variety of species have shown this to be the case. The winners of physical competitions have been shown to mate more frequently. Likewise, there is a direct relationship between the number of eyespots on a peacock's tail and mating success. What about human mating patterns? In Chapter 9, I will present some of the characteristics human males and females look for in mates and how this may increase the survival of the infant and continuation of the species. As we will also see, this may result in males and females seeking different characteristics in a mate.

A particularly important question for Darwin was, What happens when the pressures of natural selection and survival are at odds with those of sexual selection and reproduction? Clearly, what makes a brightly colored male bird attractive to a female also makes it more visible to predators. Again, let's consider the peacock. The male has a large tail that fans out, whereas the female does not (see Figure 8.1).

According to Darwin, the tail of the peacock put it at a disadvantage in terms of survival. Having a large heavy tail would make it difficult to escape a predator. What Darwin concluded was that although both survival and reproduction are primary pressures, in most cases, if they are pitted against each other, evolution will favor reproduction over survival. In some species, the act of reproduction is literally at odds with survival. Salmon, for example, starve to death while breeding. There is also the sad tale of the male praying mantis that has his head bitten off by the female during the act of copulation.

| Figure 8.1 | Peahen Observing Peacock Display His Tail |

Sexuality

What is the sex drive and how does it work? Most humans experience it without noticing the manner in which it colors our existence. Sexual strategies are generally not consciously considered, and we may not even be aware of some aspects. Given that we are a species composed of males and females who have sex, it is somewhat surprising that so little research has been devoted to the topic. The World Health Organization estimates that each day, there are 100 million acts of human sexual intercourse, yet there are fewer than a million conceptions. Thus, sex must play an important role in the life of humans beyond conception. When asked about their reason for having sex, many people just report that it feels good or that they do it in order to have children. However, it is an extremely complex behavior. In fact, it is only recently that we have attempted to study the multiple factors involved in sexuality and our choice of mates.

As we look across species, we realize that if there are males and females, then a number of processes must be at work. First, of course, males and females need a way to come in contact with each other. Organisms must also be able to recognize who is a male and who is a female. Further, organisms need a way to signal to each other interest in the other and one's own availability. In some species this is accomplished through pheromones: molecules whose scent carries an important sexual message. Other species, such as the monkey, have areas of skin that change color to signal receptivity. Auditory signals may also be used. As we watch males and females come together, we see a courtship ritual in many species. Some birds, for example, perform a mating dance. When courtship leads to mating, relationships during gestation, birth, and parenting can be examined. In this exploration, we will see both the competition and cooperation required between males and females to ensure the preservation of the species. We will also note what factors males and females consider in making these decisions. Overall, we will consider how males and females differ and how they are the same.

Biological Sex and Sexuality

I begin with the realization that the mechanisms of reproduction differ in males and females. In mammals, males produce small mobile sperm in large numbers, whereas females produce a relatively limited number of large eggs. One important pressure on the female is that she carries the fertilized egg to the birth of the offspring. The male, on the other hand, is not required to be temporally and spatially involved in the development of the fetus in the same way as the female. Thus, it is potentially possible for a given male to be involved in the production of many more offspring than a given female. Further, during both the time in which the female carries the fetus and after birth, the female must find resources such as food to supply the energy requirements of both herself and her offspring. Because this asymmetry between males and females is seen across species, we might think that all species would mate and care for offspring in a similar manner. Of course, this is not the case. In fact, there is great variety in types of social and sexual relationships across species.

The evolutionary story begins with the realization that not all organisms use sex between a male and female to produce offspring and thus pass on their genes. Some simple organisms, such as protozoa and bacteria, just divide. The one organism simply becomes two. For example, the paramecium's single-celled body just becomes longer as the genetic material doubles and divides. At this point, what was previously one long organism is now two. However, nothing is ever quite that simple. For example, if environmental conditions are those of hardship, such as when the ponds in which these organisms live begin to dry up, then another process takes place. One paramecium joins with another so that the two organisms become joined internally. Then these joined paramecia divide as normal, resulting in four organisms containing a combination of the genetic material of the original two. For now, just note that in times of hardship, a genetic mixing takes place, whereas in normal times the organism just divides. Eventually, we will come to see changes in sexuality as another response to hardship.

Nonsexual reproduction is not limited to lower organisms; it can also happen in vertebrates. For example, there is a type of whiptail lizard in the western U.S. that is only female, and the offspring are all females. The eggs that the female produces require no fertilization by sperm, and each offspring is a genetic duplication of the mother. This type of reproduction is referred to as **parthenogenesis** (virgin birth). If this is the case, why do we need sex? The general answer given is that sexual reproduction through its recombination of genes produces changing genotypes, allowing for adaptation to a changing environment. Thus, sex gives us flexibility. However, it comes with a cost (Price, 1996). First, the environment must support ways for males and females to come in contact with each other. Second, it is inefficient, in that sexual reproduction requires twice as many offspring as asexual reproduction to accomplish the same end. That is to say, whereas the whiptail lizards can produce females who, in turn, can produce more females, sexual reproduction requires two different individuals, a male and a female, to produce the same number of offspring. And third, because males compete with each other for females, or females compete for males, there is a considerable amount of energy used. This energy could be used for other tasks. Also, with the loss of energy, the animals may be at risk from either their own species or from predators.

Given these costs, there must be advantages to sexual reproduction. One current theory emphasizes how sexual reproduction is a response to changing environmental conditions, especially diseases. One analogy used is the lottery. Based on the work of George Williams (1966), this analogy suggests that asexual breeding is like buying many tickets for a national lottery, but all of them have the same number. Sexual reproduction, on the other hand, is like giving everyone a different number, and having a variety of numbers increases the odds that someone will win. In this case, "winning" is the ability to survive particular parasites that could wipe out a species if every member were the same. Thus, sexual reproduction gives a species an advantage over disease by increasing the variety of genes that can be passed to the next generation (Hamilton, 1967).

Interestingly enough, some species, such as the aphids on your rose bushes, use both sexual and asexual techniques for reproduction. Again, we see environmental conditions playing a role. In the summer when environmental conditions are supportive, aphids use asexual means of reproduction. With the coming of winter and its bleak conditions, aphids change to a sexual means of reproduction. In the laboratory, aphids will switch to sexual reproduction if they experience overcrowding. Although sexual reproduction between males and females of a species gives an advantage, it is an advantage that must be repeated over and over in a constant struggle to survive. For humans, who have no natural predators, the struggle is against ever-changing diseases and the parasites that produce these diseases. It is not progress but a struggle to stay the same. With every reduction of one disease, another appears. This situation is illustrated by The Red Queen hypothesis.

RED QUEEN HYPOTHESIS

The Red Queen hypothesis is one explanation of why sexual reproduction is so common in nature. As you remember, in the story of Lewis Carroll's book *Through the Looking Glass* (1872/1946), Alice meets the Red Queen. They begin to run across the chessboard but never seem to get anywhere. Alice says to the Queen that in her country, if she runs fast, she ends up in another place. The Queen responds by saying, "Now, *here*, you see, it takes all the running *you* can do, to keep in the same place. If you want to get *somewhere else*, you must run at least twice as fast as that" (see Figure 8.2). The Red Queen hypothesis was developed by Van Valen (1973) to reflect the process of evolution he saw in the fossil record. At any one time there are multiple forces in the environment influencing a species, ranging from predators to parasites. A species must keep changing just to survive and avoid extinction. William Hamilton suggested that sex might provide an advantage to organisms in that they could change faster than the parasites trying to adapt to them. That is to say, sexual reproduction increases the

| Figure 8.2 | Image of Alice and the Red Queen From Lewis Carroll's *Through the Looking Glass* |

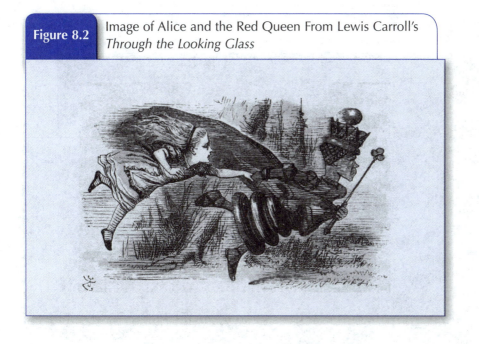

genetic variety of offspring in a manner that parasites cannot duplicate. The Red Queen theory is that with every advance in the species, there may also be a change in its environment, which includes its predators. The species changes, but the relationship to the environment stays the same.

Biological Foundations

Let us now turn to some basic physiological differences. We begin with the simple biological fact that a male sperm is always smaller than a female egg (ovum). This is true across all species, as shown for hamster ovum and sperm in Figure 8.3.

Although sperm carries the same amount of genetic material from the father as the egg does from the mother, it is the fact that the mother's egg provides the nutrients necessary for the initial development of the organism that accounts for the difference in size. It is the task of the sperm to find and fertilize an egg. It is somewhat surprising that millions of sperm are released in humans, for example, but fewer than 20 reach the site where fertilization takes place. What are the characteristics of that single sperm that performs the fertilization and the ones that don't?

Well, first we need to realize that competition between males continues after sexual relations. In the 1970s, Geoff Parker suggested that if two or more males mate with the same female, their sperm could compete with one another to fertilize the egg (see Wigby & Chapman, 2004, for an overview).

| Figure 8.3 | Image of a Sperm and Egg |

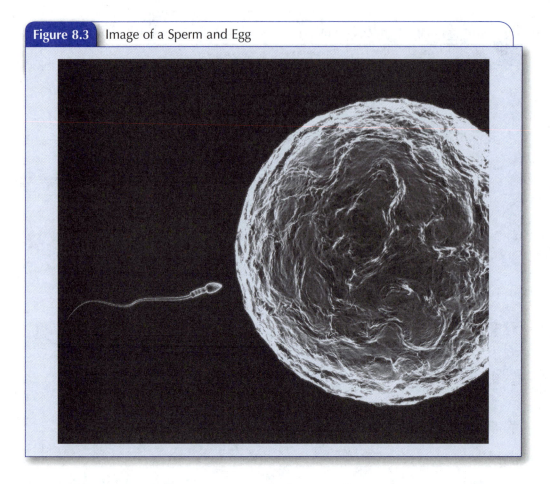

The process has been referred to as *sperm wars*. Although a somewhat surprising idea at the time, research has continued to suggest it is a reality. Further, surveys of a variety of animals including humans suggest that there are different types of sperm (Baker & Bellis, 1995). These different types of sperm, and the proteins contained within the ejaculate, serve at least three purposes. The first is to penetrate and fertilize the egg. These sperm are designed to swim quickly up the female reproductive tract to fertilize the egg. It has been estimated that only a small percentage of all sperm released at a given time serve this purpose. A second purpose seen in some species is coagulation and forming a plug in the female reproductive tract that interferes with the entrance of new sperm from another partner. This is supported by research with primates showing higher coagulation rates in species in which females have multiple partners, and lower rates in those that do not (Dixon & Anderson, 2002). A third purpose is destroying existing sperm found in the female reproductive tract. Basically this type of sperm, which is sometimes called *kamikaze sperm,* has the job of destroying sperm from a different male. What is intriguing is that some studies suggest that the composition of the ejaculate is determined by existing environmental conditions. For example, in chimpanzee troops in which promiscuity is observed, a greater number of kamikaze sperm will be released. A similar situation has been observed in human males when the female might be expected to have had sex with another man. The type of sperm and also the amount of sperm seems to vary in relation to mating conditions. For example, if a human male has been separated from his stable mate for a period of time, the volume of sperm produced may increase by a factor of 3 the next time they have sex. This does not happen if the man was in the proximity of the mate but did not have sex during a similar time period. Why would this be? One possible answer is that human male sexuality evolved to respond to the possibility that his mate had a relationship with another male during his absence. Other studies have shown sperm volume to be higher in those primate species that have multi-mating patterns as opposed to single-partner patterns. This would suggest that physical characteristics evolved in relation to patterns of mating behavior. Indeed, male chimps who share females with other males have larger testicles compared to their body size than do male gorillas, whose testicles are comparatively tiny but who are assured of paternity. In terms of genetic changes, it has been found in a variety of species that genes related to sperm production evolve faster than other genes. Comparing humans with chimps and gorillas, results suggest that sexual genes in humans and chimps are evolving at about the same rate, but at a faster rate than sexual genes in gorillas (Wyckoff, Wang, & Wu, 2000). Overall, this suggests that mating patterns drive physiological changes on a variety of levels. The question also arises whether female physiological changes can influence the sperm within a woman's reproductive system. Presently, there are some speculative studies that this can occur, although these studies are just beginning to be conducted.

Differential Evolutionary History

The basic approach of evolutionary psychology is to consider the manner in which particular behaviors enable one to solve the problems of life, including mate selection, reproduction, and parenting. We can also consider how these tasks may have been different for males and females. That is, in what ways have males and females faced different adaptive problems over evolutionary time, and how can this analysis help us to understand sex differences? Thinking about sex differences from the evolutionary perspective, we would expect to see the greatest differences in areas in which males and females have faced different adaptive problems. Conversely, with challenges that males and females alike faced, we would expect to see fewer sex differences. Males and females have experienced different roles in reproduction and parenting throughout evolutionary time. In turn, males and females have faced different challenges, which have led to different processes in structure and function. This may have also led to different priorities in accomplishing these goals. In many ways, scientists are just beginning this exploration, and thus many important factors have yet to be articulated.

Using research as a guide, it is clear that gender differences exist in some areas and not in others. Since gender differences began to be reported in psychological research, there has been a fierce debate as to the nature of these differences. In this rhetoric, a number of important points have been missed. One of these is that researchers have not been directing their comments to the individual level. Group differences never dictate what any one person will or can do. Second, many of the arguments on either side of the gender debate have adopted a simplistic version of human behavior and experience. For example, they have ignored the ability of humans to experience a variety of seemingly complex and contradictory feelings and thoughts. Anyone who has set an alarm to wake up early to prepare for an exam knows that you can experience both the desire to stay in bed and the need to get up at the same time. The same is true in a variety of aspects related to mate selection, sexuality, and parenting. Third, the debates often ignore the fact that feelings do not always lead to actions. That is, we may feel a certain way, but that does not mean that we will necessarily act on those feelings.

Underlying many of these debates is often a naïve version of psychological theory that says that humans are either totally controlled by biological factors or totally controlled by social construction. Throughout this book, I have clearly demonstrated through a variety of types of research that this is not the case. In this regard, psychological mechanisms, including those related to sexual selection, should not be viewed as hardwired, fixed, or unmodifiable. In fact, experience can "rewire" the brain (Hass et al., 2000). As we have discussed throughout this book, there is such a rich and complex interaction between one's biological heritage and one's cultural and social influences that it is impossible to determine a "cause" in most cases. In fact, it is most often the case that biological predispositions interact complexly with environmental conditions as well as with other biological conditions.

Even in species with patterned mating responses, complexity still exists. For example, there is an Australian bird known as the satin bowerbird, a particular favorite of Darwin. The males are brightly colored a brilliant purple-blue, with blue eyes and yellow beaks. To attract females, they build a U-shaped structure of straw called a bower (see Figure 8.4). The male further decorates the bower with found blue objects such as feathers, glass, and even plastic bits. During mating season, the female will stand inside the bower and watch the male perform for her by strutting and singing mating songs. Actually, it is a little more complicated than that. The female first visits a number of these bowers when the male is not present and carries out an inspection. She then returns to a subset of these structures when the male is present to see him strut and sing. If she finds his performance acceptable, she then builds a nest. Although she may build nests at different bowers, she finally makes a choice and mates with a single male. With these birds, it is the female that appraises the male's constructions and performances and makes a selection.

A recent study sought to understand the nature of the female selection process in these bowerbirds (Coleman, Patricelli, & Borgia, 2004). For identification purposes, these researchers first placed leg bands on about 90 wild male and female bowerbirds and set up video cameras. The researchers were also able to determine the age of the female, so they knew whether this was the first year she had mated, the second, or the third. They then gave the males at 14 of the 28 bowers extra decorations, which the birds incorporated into their structures. Thus, half of the bowers contained extra decoration, and half did not. In this way, the researchers could determine whether the extra decoration influenced the female's selection. Indeed, this was the case. However, it was more complicated than the female bowerbird choosing the male with the most decorated bower. Females at every age were more likely to return to the bowers that were more decorated than those that were not. What these researchers found, however, was that

Figure 8.4   Male and Female Bowerbirds, With the Female in the Bower

females at different ages relied on different factors for their choices. Now, what factors do you think determined who mated with whom? Here, age played an important role. The older females based their decisions on the intensity of the male's performance during the second stage of courtship when the male struts and sings. The younger females, however, based their decision on the first stage, that is, how decorated were the bowers. One possibility suggested by the researchers is that the younger females were afraid of the intense performance of the males. Whatever the case, this research demonstrates the complexity of mate choices, especially as related to age, as has also been shown in other species. As we will see in this chapter, we are just beginning to understand factors related to sexual preferences and mate choices in humans, much less the potential complexity that may exist.

Overview of Gender Differences

Because we are just beginning to understand human sexuality, we need to find models that may help us describe the processes under study. The learning of language is one such model. Across cultures, the timing of language learning is universal, whereas the particular language learned is determined by the society in which one is reared. Evolutionary psychologists ask what historical factors could have led humans to have a propensity for experiencing the world in a certain way. Social constructivist theories, on the other hand, focus on the current social pressures experienced by the individual. There is no doubt that humans live in culture as much as animals live in nature. As I discuss in the final chapter of this book, we are influenced by our culture, but this does not remove the possibility that predisposition and preferences were shaped throughout our evolutionary history. One way these apparently competing theories have been differentiated is to stress their emphasis on the temporal dimension. That is, the evolutionary perspective views time from a broader perspective, whereas the social theories have focused more on the present societal and cultural conditions. The fundamental question lies in whether one sees gender preferences and predisposition as shaped through evolutionary adaptation or regenerated from the societal conditions in each generation. Of course, the answer is in some ways both, depending on which particular behavior is under study. In this book, I am emphasizing the former, although the latter must also play a role. I emphasize the former by asking how a particular set of behaviors allows one's genes greater possibility of being passed to the next generation. Overall, both approaches offer a functional analysis of behavior, which involves adaptations to environmental conditions. Both have noted the existence of particular mediated gender differences, such as males possessing greater size and strength and females being involved in child bearing and lactation (Eagly & Wood, 1999). More important, neither limits the individual's ability to exercise preferences and choices that manifest his or her greatest potential.

Clear differences between males and females are portrayed in the popular media, whether it is TV shows or books, that suggest that males and females are from different "planets." The question for scientists is which of these portrayed differences are real and which, like urban myths, just get repeated without any underlying evidence. For example, the differences between men and women portrayed in the early 1900s were shattered when it was demonstrated that women could perform the abilities ascribed only to men equally well. In the 1970s, various types of ability differences were claimed because no female had been an astronaut, a rabbi, an attorney general of the U.S., a general in the U.S. armed forces, a secretary of state, or a Supreme Court Justice. Of course, since then women have held each of these positions. As scientists began to look at gender differences, some differences, such as differential achievement scores, have been shown to be small or nonexistent.

In the area of sexuality, the research of Masters and Johnson (1966) in the middle of the last century demonstrated that sexual attraction and sexual response exist in both males and females. Although it may seem like a quaint attitude today, at one time females were viewed as uninterested in sex, and males were told to eat cornflakes to help reduce their sexual desire. As we shall see, other gender differences, such as attitudes toward specific aspects of sexuality, have been shown to be more enduring and robust (Oliver & Hyde, 1993). At this point, scientists are just beginning to gain a clearer perspective on gender differences, especially those related to sexuality and mate preference. Thus, this initial research has tended to focus on universals found in most individuals across most cultures. However, there are always exceptions, and thus this research should not be seen as limiting individuals in their attitudes and behaviors or as prescribing how one must act or feel. Additionally, the evolutionary perspective should not be seen or used as a way to remove individual human responsibility in our interactions with one another. As scientists gain a clearer perspective, it is clear that in the area of gender differences, as with other evolutionary differences, there is a close coupling and interaction with the environment that may lead to both flexibility and more structured preferences in sexuality. We have noted similar processes in a variety of areas such as the learning of language, in which the stages of language learning appear to be structured, whereas the content of the language is dependent on the environment. This is also true with sexuality. For example, E. A. Westermarck (1921) noted in the early part of the 20th century that individuals brought up together show a reduced sexual desire toward one another. That is, you have different sexual feelings toward your brother or sister than you do toward their friends. More recent research has shown unrelated individuals raised together in a kibbutz also tend not to marry (see Lieberman, Tooby, & Cosmides, 2003 for an overview). To test attitudes toward sexual relationships, Lieberman and her colleagues asked 186 college students to rank-order 19 acts, including sexual relationships and marriage between siblings, in terms of morality. The findings support the Westermarck hypothesis and show a relationship between duration of living together and strength of the relationship, even when the individuals are not related. There is also evidence to suggest that relationships with parents during childhood may influence the future type of sexual relationships that one has. However, that is getting ahead of the story.

Let us begin by noting that a large variety of studies have suggested four important differences in sexuality between males and females (Peplau, 2003). What I wish to accomplish in this section is to present a description of these four differences. Later, I will connect these behaviors with an evolutionary perspective.

SEXUAL DESIRE

The first gender difference in sexuality is sexual desire. Overall, men show more interest in sex than do women, and this can be seen in a variety of ways. For example, males report thinking about sex more often than females, including having more sexual fantasies and feelings of desire. Males are also more interested in visual sexual stimuli. They like looking at sexually orientated magazines or Internet sites and are also more willing to spend money to obtain such stimuli. This is less true with females. Recent brain imaging research has shown that males produce greater activation of the amygdala and hypothalamus than females in response to viewing sexual stimuli, although both males and females showed similar responses in areas of the brain associated with reward, and both rated the material as equally arousing (Hamann, Herman, Nolan, & Wallen, 2004). In actual sexual behavior, there are also gender differences, with males seeking sex more often than females. This is also true with same-sex orientation, as seen in comparisons of gay and lesbian couples. That is, homosexual couples report having sex more often than lesbian couples. In one meta-analysis of 177 studies examining gender differences in a variety of sexual behaviors and attitudes, incidence of masturbation showed the largest difference (Oliver & Hyde, 1993). The gender differences found in sexual desire or behavior cannot be related to satisfaction of experience because this meta-analysis also found no differences in level of sexual satisfaction between males and females.

COMMITMENT

The second gender difference in sexuality is commitment. This is true for both attitudes and behavior. When asked about sexual desire, males are more likely to emphasize physical desire and intercourse, whereas females are more likely to describe relationship elements. Likewise, in fantasies, females tend to include familiar partners and commitment, whereas males are more willing to include strangers and emphasize specific sexual acts. Males are also more willing to engage in premarital and extramarital sexual behaviors than females.

SEXUALITY AND AGGRESSION

The third gender difference in sexuality relates to aggression and sexuality (see Campbell, 1999 for an overview). Human males have been shown to engage in aggression more often than human females, from about age 2 onward. Such data as police records from a variety of cultures universally show males to be more aggressive than females. Not only are males more aggressive, but they commit more serious crimes, including almost 90% of the murders reported in the United States. When asked to describe their own sexuality, males are more likely than females to include a dimension involving aggression, power, and dominance (Andersen, Cyranowski, & Espindle, 1999). Men are also seen as taking the lead in early stages of dating relationships, and although females do initiate sexual behaviors, they do so less frequently than their male partners (Impett & Peplau, 2003). Finally, using physical force to initiate sexual intercourse is primarily a male behavior (Felson, 2002).

FLEXIBILITY IN SEXUALITY

The fourth gender difference in sexuality relates to the manner in which external factors can influence attitudes and behaviors (see Baumeister, 2000 for a review). The research suggests that males are less sensitive to situational factors than females in terms of sexual behaviors. In reviewing this research, Baumeister describes three basic themes. One theme is that once a male's sexual predispositions or tastes emerge, they will remain stable. Another theme is that a female's predispositions will be more influenced by her culture and society than will a male's. From this one would predict that females would vary from one culture to another in terms of sexual predispositions. The final theme is that the relationship between one's attitudes toward sexuality and one's behavior will be different for males and females. That is to say, females should show higher correlations between cultural attitudes and sexual behavior than males, whereas males should show higher correlations between their own sexual attitudes and behaviors.

In terms of flexibility, an interesting study suggests that gender differences in sexual predispositions can not only be seen in other species, but can be manipulated as well (Kendrick, Hinton, Atkins, Haupt, & Skinner, 1998). In this study, newborn sheep and goats were exchanged. The goats were raised by sheep and the sheep by goats. After these animals became adults, they were returned to their own species. The researchers then observed social and mating preferences of these returned animals: The males preferred to socialize and mate approximately 90% of the time with their adoptive species. This preference did not change even after they were returned to their own species and lived there exclusively. The females, on the other hand, showed a lower frequency (69%) of socialization and mating, which was reversible within one to two years of living with their own species. This suggests that, in these species, male sexuality and socialization is related to early environmental influences. The authors of this research suggest that this resulted from an imprinting or attachment-like mechanism in males involving the adopted mother. This mechanism, when fixed, created social and sexual predispositions that could not be changed. Females appear not to be influenced in the same manner and thus show more flexibility in their preferences.

Types of Mating Relationships

As we look across different species, we see a variety of male and female mating relationships. **Monogamy** is the situation in which one male and one female are paired more or less exclusively during the mating season. Species such as migratory songbirds, for example, remain together during the mating season but live apart during periods of migration. There are also species, such as swans and some types of wolves, in which monogamy can be seen across the entire lifetime of the individuals. Often a distinction is made between **social monogamy,** in which a male and a female of a species live together, and **sexual monogamy,** in which the male and female only mate with each other. With the advent of genetic testing, it is now possible with great certainty to determine the parents of particular offspring. As we shall see, this has led to the discovery that, even with species that are socially monogamous, sexual monogamy is not always the rule.

In contrast to monogamy, **polygamy** is the general term used to describe the situation in which one member of one sex is paired with more than one member of the opposite sex. These pair bonds can be successive (an individual has a number of mates in succession) or they can be simultaneous (an individual has a number of mates at the same time). The more specific term **polygyny** is used to describe the situation in which one male mates with multiple females. Northern elephant seals who mate on Año Nuevo Island off the coast south of San Francisco illustrate this mating style. These huge male seals, which look like the character Jabba the Hutt from *Star Wars,* fight with each other until a dominance hierarchy is established. Females, who are much smaller than the males, arrive during the winter. They then give birth because they were pregnant when they arrived.

At the end of the nursing period of about 28 days, the females become available for mating. The dominant male seals create harems, which they protect from other males. One research study observed that the 5 highest ranked males (of 115) performed 123 of the 144 observed copulations (Le Boeuf & Peterson, 1969). A variety of mammalian species are polygynous. The case in which one female is associated with multiple males is referred to as **polyandry**. Polyandry is seen in some quails, pheasants, and a variety of shorebird that breeds primarily in the Arctic Circle. In these shorebirds, the female seeks out and courts the males. Once she has laid eggs, the male incubates the eggs, while the female seeks out and courts additional males.

Given the asymmetric relationship of males and females to the production and care of offspring, one important topic of study has been the development of monogamy. How did it arise? It appears that there is not one simple answer to this question. There are multiple pathways on which the evolution of a mating relationship takes place in a species (see Reichard & Boesch, 2003 for an overview). Let us begin with social monogamy. The basic theory is that for monogamy to have developed, it must contribute to male reproductive success in a way that is greater than mating with a variety of females. Current thinking suggests that various factors are important in the evolution of social monogamy, although the importance of each may vary by species (Low, 2003; Reichard & Boesch, 2003). The main point is that the social and mating relationships found in different species, even if the same, may have evolved by different pathways.

One of these important factors is the necessity of having two parents. It has been hypothesized that the requirement of two parents led to socially monogamous relationships. That is, if having a second parent helps to increase the likelihood that the offspring will survive, then the tendency to form socially monogamous relationships would increase reproductive fitness. What this suggests is that certain traits that support monogamous relationships would be passed on to the next generation. What would such traits be? One example in humans would be males who assist in the parenting of children. If this were the case, then we would predict that human females would prefer mates who show willingness to care for and parent children. We would also assume that females would prefer males who possess resources, especially those that would benefit, either directly or indirectly, the production and care of offspring. For males, it is suggested that monogamy arose in situations in which staying with one female offered reproductive benefits that would not be found otherwise.

Are mating patterns also related to other abilities, including cognitive abilities? Although a seemingly strange question, answering it may help us to better understand the gender differences that may exist. Let us return to the vole that we discussed in Chapter 5 in terms of the genetic aspects of attachment. This mouse-like animal may give us a clue to this question. Two types of voles, the prairie and the pine vole, are monogamous. Males and females stay together in one territory. In these species, males and females occupy the same-sized territories. The meadow vole, on the other hand, is polygynous. Males travel over a number of territories to mate with different females. In fact, a male may visit territories more than four times the size of a given female's territory. In order to determine whether mating patterns were related to spatial abilities, Gaulin and FitzGerald (1986) tested males and females from all three species of voles on their ability to learn mazes. What they found was that, in the monogamous species, there were no differences in spatial ability between males and females. However, among the polygynous meadow voles, the males made fewer errors in learning the mazes than the females. This might make one think that types of sexual activity influence cognitive abilities. In this case, those voles that would be the most successful in mating would be those with the best spatial abilities. If fact, it has been shown that, in the meadow vole, brain structures related to spatial processing, such as the hippocampus, are larger in males than in females. However, there is more to the story. For example, if a male vole comes from a litter in which the other voles are mainly male, he will perform better on spatial measures than if the others in the litter are female (see Alcock, 2001 for a review). This suggests that sex hormones in the womb also are able to influence the development of spatial abilities.

Primate Mating Systems

Because primates are genetically closest to humans and have evolved complex social systems, we might expect we could gain some insight from them concerning human mating patterns. We can, of course, gain insight, but it is not as simple as some would like you to believe. What we quickly discover is that different species have very different patterns (see Falk, 2000; Daly & Wilson, 1983 for an overview). Although it is difficult to know which came first, it has been suggested that the distribution of food and the manner in which it is obtained may lead to the mating patterns observed (Miller, 1998). Let us begin by looking at the species of primates that are most similar to humans: gibbons, gorillas, chimpanzees, and bonobos.

GIBBONS

Gibbons are found in Southeast Asia and, along with siamangs, are referred to as *lesser apes*. Gibbons spend part of their days moving through the canopies of trees foraging for food as well as just resting. They are one of the few primate species that is socially monogamous. Gibbons have been observed to mate both from the rear and face to face and even while hanging from trees. They produce a whining squeal at the end of copulation that is thought to reflect ejaculation. Either sex may initiate mating, and there appears to be no specific season in which mating takes place. Males and females are characterized as establishing joint male-female territories and staying together for decades. During this time they produce about 10 offspring. Opposite-sex pairs establish a territory that other pairs do not enter. It appears that calls from the pair keep others away from their territory, and there is less aggression than is seen in other primate species. Also, there appears to be little competition between males for mates. Some scientists have considered the lack of competition between males to be one reason for the lack of difference in size between males and females. That is, without competition, there was no advantage for males to evolve a larger body size. Males also have been observed to spend more time grooming and playing with their offspring than do females.

GORILLAS

Gorillas are found in equatorial Africa and referred to as *greater apes.* Unlike the gibbon, there are great differences in size between male and female gorillas. Whereas the female may average 175 pounds, the typical male would weigh 380 pounds. Perhaps because of their size, gorillas spend less time in trees and more time moving around using all four limbs, also referred to as *knuckle walking.* Gorillas have also been observed standing on two legs and beating their chest, especially when they become excited. Their diet is mainly leaves, shoots, and stems of a large variety of plants. About 45% of a gorilla's day is spent feeding. Gorillas live in fairly stable groups composed of one male and several adult females with their young. In general, aggression is seen only when an outside male tries to attract a female from an established group. Within the group, females have been observed to solicit mating more than males by presenting themselves. Mating is both back to back and face to face, with the average duration of intercourse lasting about a minute and a half.

CHIMPANZEES

Chimpanzees are also found in Africa. They have been described as smart, social, sexual, and political, as well as a species that fights, reconciles, makes tools, hunts, makes war, and can also practice infanticide and cannibalism (Falk, 2000). Jane Goodall (1990) was one of the first to describe chimpanzees using tools as she watched a chimp take a stem of grass and modify it to so he could poke it into a termite mound to catch food. Since that time, a variety of tool use has been observed, including using leaves for a drinking cup, picks to extract marrow from bones, and stones to open nuts. Chimps live in social groups of around 50 animals, which frequently divide into smaller groups and then come back together at a later time. In the social groups, chimpanzees can be seen to touch, hug, and even kiss, and offer a variety of vocalizations. Males remain in the group in which they were born, whereas females move to other groups around the time of sexual maturity. Unlike gorillas, male chimpanzees are only slightly larger than females. Males establish a dominance hierarchy, although females also play a part in this process. The dominant male seeks to limit access to the females in his group. However, the females often mate with a number of males during estrus.

BONOBOS

The bonobo is a type of chimpanzee that also lives in central Africa. It has recently gained notoriety based partly on the role of female sexuality in this species (de Waal & Lanting, 1998; de Waal, 1997). Bonobos appear to become aroused easily and engage in sex often. They utilize a variety of couple combinations, with males inviting females and females inviting males, as well as sexuality involving members of the same sex. De Waal (1995) also reports observing sporadic oral sex, massage of another individual's genitals, and intense tongue-kissing. Unlike other mammals that show sexual activity only during a few days of the female's cycle, female bonobos are almost continuously sexually active. Although bonobos engage in a variety of sexual relationships more often than other primates, they give birth at about the same rate as other species of chimpanzees. Thus, it is suggested that bonobos have sexual relationships for a variety of reasons. It has also been suggested that the bonobo uses sexuality in place of aggression. This is not to say that there is no aggression, but that aggression sometimes ends with sexual activity. In bonobos, sexual and social relationships are largely intertwined. Like other chimpanzees, bonobo society is described as *fission-fusion*. That is, bonobos move in small groups that may constantly change during the day. However, unlike other ape species in which the males will dominate or chase off females for food, the bonobo female will not be chased off. Rather, she will band with other females to chase off the male. Bonobo females have also been observed to trade sexual relations for food.

SUMMARY

Darwin studied sexual selection and the characteristics of males and females. There are a variety of mechanisms utilized to continue a species. Sexuality between males and females is only one such mechanism. Sexuality between males and females may offer advantages to future offspring by increasing genetic variation. Males and females have experienced different pressures during evolutionary time in terms of desire, commitment, sexuality and aggression, and flexibility. Across all species, there are a variety of mating relationships including monogamy, polygamy, and polyandry. Nonhuman primates display a variety of mating systems.

STUDY RESOURCES

Review Questions

1. In the faceoff between natural selection and survival in one corner and sexual selection and reproduction in the other, which pair wins, and why?

2. Nonsexual reproduction is not limited to lower organisms. If this is the case, why do we need sex? What evolutionary advantage does it provide?

3. What is the Red Queen hypothesis, and what critical role does it play in the survival of a species?

4. What is the concept of sperm wars, and how does it extend the concept of competition between males in sexual relations?

5. In what ways have males and females faced different adaptive problems over evolutionary time, and how can this analysis help us understand sex differences?

6. As we have discussed throughout this book, there is such a rich and complex interaction between one's biological heritage and one's cultural and social influences that it is impossible to determine a "cause" in most cases. What evidence is presented in this chapter in support of this perspective as it relates to sex and gender differences?

7. Does adopting an evolutionary perspective remove our individual human responsibility in our interactions with one another? How would you integrate these ideas?

8. Describe the four important differences in sexuality between males and females suggested by Peplau, and give evidence from research supporting each one.

9. Describe the variety of male and female mating relationships that exist in different species.

10. Given the asymmetric relationship of males and females with the production and care of offspring, how did monogamy develop?

11. Given that primates (e.g., gibbons, gorillas, chimpanzees, and bonobos) are closest to humans in terms of genetics and have evolved complex social systems, how can we characterize their mating patterns, and what insights can we gain from them concerning human mating patterns?

For Further Reading

Deacon, T. (1997). *The symbolic species.* New York: Norton.

Geary, D. (1998). *Male/female.* Washington, DC: APA Press.

Miller, G. (2000). *The mating mind: How sexual choice shaped the evolution of human nature.* New York: Random House.

Ridley, M. (1993). *The red queen: Sex and the evolution of human nature.* New York: Penguin Books.

Key Terms and Concepts

- Sex and gender
- Darwin and sexual selection
- Sexuality
- Biological sex and sexuality
  - Red Queen hypothesis
- Biological foundations
- Differential evolutionary history
- Overview of gender differences
  - Sexual desire
  - Commitment
  - Sexuality and aggression
  - Flexibility in sexuality
- Types of mating relationships
- Primate mating systems
  - Gibbons
  - Gorillas
  - Chimpanzees
  - Bonobos

SAGE Study Site

Visit the study site at **www.sagepub.com/ray** for chapter-specific study resources.

Glossary Terms

- Monogamy
- Parthenogenesis
- Polyandry
- Polygamy
- Polygyny
- Sexual monogamy
- Social monogamy

Sexual Selection 9

The general picture of natural selection presented by Darwin was that traits that would be an advantage to the organism would win out over those that would not. Darwin noted that a certain-shaped beak evolved because of the advantage it gave the organism in finding food. Darwin further extended his thinking and distinguished between those traits that are necessary for survival and those involved in mating and rearing of the young. In fact, some traits that help with gaining a mate, such as the beautiful tail of the peacock, may actually place an organism at a disadvantage in terms of survival. In other words, such traits as the peacock's tail should not have evolved in the normal process of evolution because it did not benefit survival. However, he observed that the peahen did pay attention to the peacock tail in her choice of mate. In this sense, it was the female that was choosing which traits would evolve. Thus, there was a second process involved in evolution—sexual selection. In the 1930s, the statistician Ronald Fisher (1930/1999) followed up on this idea with the concept of **runaway sexual selection.** The concept basically suggests that if a female is more willing to mate with a male with a certain trait, then that trait will be favored and passed on to the next generation. The outcome of such a process could eventually be an exaggeration, as in the case of the peacock's tail.

According to Darwin, sexual selection involved two different processes. One was same-sex competition, which is most obvious in male-to-male competition. From this process would evolve characteristics, such as antlers on deer, that would enable one male to dominate another, and thus have the advantage. It would be the dominant male that would mate, and thus these characteristics would be passed on to the next generation. The second process involved selection of a mate, which Darwin sometimes described as *female choice*. The female makes a choice among males, as when the peahen chooses the most-adorned peacock. Thus, the process of sexual selection produced characteristics that would help in domination and characteristics that would help in ornamentation. In his observations of animals, Darwin asked why males and females were different in both structure and behavior. In most species including humans, the male is larger and more muscular than the female, who is smaller and has more body fat. Darwin differentiated between primary and secondary sexual characteristics. Primary characteristics are those aspects of sexuality that are physiologically primary, such as organs for the production of sperm or eggs. Secondary characteristics are those that are not required for sexual reproduction but have evolved to support the acquisition of mates, such as bright plumage in birds.

Body Size and Mating Patterns

We now know that many of the physical sex differences in males and females are related to the mating patterns of the species. In species in which males compete with each other for control of a large number of females, the body size of the males is larger than that of females. The northern elephant seal is a good example: Males can grow to 13 feet in length and weigh 4,500 pounds, whereas females grow to 10 feet and 1,500 pounds. Male northern elephant seals compete with one another to become the dominant male. The winner of these competitions will have a harem of 30 to 100 females. The logic of this is that the larger and stronger male tends to win and pass on his genes, giving future generations these characteristics. Given the nature of genetics, some of these characteristics are also passed on to the females, and they likewise increase in size, but not to the extent of the males. In those species in which females compete for males, such as certain small birds, it is the male that is smaller. In species in which males and females form more monogamous relationships, the size of the males and females tends to be more equal.

How about humans? How do males and females of our species differ, and what does this suggest about our evolutionary history? Humans show sexual differences in several traits (see Miller, 1998; Geher & Miller, 2008 for overviews). Human males are taller and heavier than human females, have more upper body strength, higher metabolic rates, more facial and body hair, deeper voices, larger brains, riskier lives, and earlier death. The slight differences between human male and female body size compared to other primate species suggests that humans evolved under a moderately polygynous mating system. It also suggests that males directly competed with other males, more than females competed with other females, for mates. When comparing humans to other primates, human differences suggest sexual selection has played an important role. For example, unlike other primates, human females have enlarged breasts and buttocks, a greater orgasmic capacity, and the ability to be interested in sexual activity throughout the monthly cycle. What are the differences thought to be evolved through sexual selection? They include more hair on our heads, whiter eyes, longer noses, larger ear lobes, and more expressive faces. Males, on the other hand, have long, thick, and flexible penises and more facial hair. An important consideration in understanding the evolution of male genitalia is female choice (e.g., Eberhard, 1985). Gorillas, orangutans, and chimpanzees have thin penises less than three inches long when erect, while human male penises are generally more than five inches long. This is not related to sperm competition, which would require larger testicles, as is seen in the chimpanzee. Rather, it is suggested that females chose the males they mated with based on physical characteristics, and these characteristics were passed to future generations. Before leaving this section, it should also be noted that some researchers suggest that human mating patterns may have changed with the advent of agriculture about 10,000 years ago and the need for humans to remain in one location.

Mate Choice and the Evolution of Mental Abilities

There is a variety of evidence that mate choice influences the evolution of physical characteristics of males and females. The intriguing question is whether sexual selection also had a hand in producing changes in our mental processes (see Miller, 1998; Geher & Miller, 2008 for overviews). As I introduced in Chapter 2, Darwin wrote of the possibility that cognitive and emotional processes were influenced through evolutionary processes. Until recently, many authors believed this happened through natural selection rather than sexual selection; however, today this view is changing. The logic of sexual selection influencing cognitive and emotional processes is straightforward. As with physical characteristics, if an individual would rather mate with someone he or she finds intelligent, funny, and creative, then these characteristics, to the extent they are genetically related, would be passed on to future generations. Thus, research that seeks to understand preferences in a mate would be critical. I will introduce you to this type of research later in the chapter.

Theoretical Perspectives on Sexual Preferences

A critical question found in evolutionary thinking has been what drives mate preferences (Gangestad, 2000; Gangestad & Simpson, 2000). Two theories have emerged in this quest, which should not be seen as either/ or but as examples demonstrating different mechanisms available for mate selection.

GOOD GENE THEORY

The first theory is the **good gene** perspective. The basic idea is that females choose males who possess indicators of underlying genetic fitness. How can a female know about underlying genetic fitness? The answer is by its outward manifestations, called "indicators" (Miller, 2000). Take the peacock, for example. Females will always choose males with the brightest and best-looking tails. In fact, peahens appear to comparison shop until they determine which peacock has the most elaborate tail (Petrie, 1994). Why would this be so? Recent research has shown a direct relationship between tails and health: Characteristics of the plumage are an "indicator" of disease resistance and thus of good genes.

There is additional data to suggest that females are seeking good genes even when they are in a monogamous relationship. In some species of birds in which the males and females stay together to take care of the young and appear to be monogamous, there are sexual relationships outside the social relationship. That is to say, pairs that are socially monogamous are not sexually monogamous. In these species, it has been estimated that 10% to 20% of the offspring in the nest were not fathered by the male of the pair. The current thinking is that this is a mechanism by which the female ensures good genes in her offspring. In these "monogamous" mating species of birds, a large proportion of males of reproductive age will find a mate. Thus, some females will be mating with males who are lower in genetic fitness. If females have extra mating with more genetically fit males, then the overall level of fitness will increase. Of course, for females to be able to select in terms of fitness, there must exist variability among genes. Indeed, it has been observed that higher numbers of these extra relationships are associated with greater genetic diversity (Petrie, Doums, & Møller, 1998). Additionally, it has been noted that fitness-related traits may have more variation in underlying genetic structures than other traits (Gangestad, 2000).

GOOD PROVIDER THEORY

The second theory concerning mate preferences is the **good provider** theory. It is not just producing offspring that is key in evolutionary thinking, but also the conditions necessary to nurture these offspring to adulthood so they can also reproduce. This theory suggests that females choose males who possess traits that either enhance the female's own survival or enhance the survival of the offspring. Resources such as food, protection, or care of the young would be examples of such traits.

PARENTAL INVESTMENT AND SEXUAL STRATEGIES

The concept of **parental investment** was advanced by Robert Trivers in 1972. The basic idea is that the sex that invests the most in its offspring will evolve to be the most discriminating in selecting its mating partner. Investments, in this case, are factors such as time, energy, and effort that increase the offspring's chances of survival. It should also be noted that when an organism is investing in an offspring, this reduces its ability to produce additional offspring. Thus, there is a tradeoff between investment in offspring and mating success. The concept of parental investment further suggests that the sex that invests the least will be less discriminating in mate choices. However, if that sex is to mate, then it must compete with its own sex, if it is to be available to the opposite sex for mating. That is to say, if a female of a species sought a male who controlled territory to mate with, then the males must compete to achieve territory if they are to mate. Overall, Trivers related differences in parental investment to sexual selection, and thus to mating strategies.

Indeed, a variety of studies have shown that the sex less invested in the offspring do show differential mating patterns. In general, the sex less invested will mate more quickly, at a lower cost, and with more partners than the sex that is more invested. It has also been shown that the less-invested sex is also more competitive and aggressive in its competition with members of its own sex (see Schmitt et al., 2003 for an overview). As you were reading this, you probably thought of females as being the most invested, which is the case with mammals. However, remember that in some species, such as crickets, seahorses, and some fish, males display more investment in the offspring. The female seahorse lays her eggs in a special pouch on the male's chest. The male then carries the eggs until they hatch. In these species, as the theory suggests, it is the females who compete for the males. Trivers' theory is supported by data from species in which males make the larger contribution to offspring and from species in which females make the larger contribution.

Let us return to mammals. For mammals, including humans, the number of offspring that a female can produce is limited. This results from the fact that a female cannot conceive while she is carrying a fetus. Also, lactation reduces the chance of a pregnancy. Parental investment theory would suggest that females would be the choosier in selecting mates. It would also suggest that, in mammals, males would compete among themselves more than females. One implication of this is that males should have evolved greater skills in relation to competition. Another implication is that females should have evolved better abilities to discriminate characteristics that would be associated with reproductive success and survival of the offspring. A variety of empirical studies have supported these implications across a variety of species (Trivers, 1985).

ADDING THE FEMALE PERSPECTIVE TO DARWIN: ALTERNATIVE TO THE COY FEMALE

Darwin originally suggested that males compete among themselves for access to females. It is then the female who chooses the best male. Darwin presented an asymmetrical picture of mating, with the female being less eager to mate than the male. Darwin (1874) actually described the female as "coy" and requiring courtship (p. 273). In Darwin's time, not only was the female seen as coy, but some could not even envision a world in which female choice was equal in importance to male competition, much less the possibility that females may also compete in various ways. This resulted in an asymmetrical picture of sexual selection. Recently, a number of scientists have looked more carefully at the mating patterns of males and females, especially nonhuman primates. One of these is Sarah Hrdy (1999). Hrdy argues that there is a problem with generalizing from average behavior, which misses some underlying tendencies, especially as it relates to monogamy. The problem is that we miss the variety of ways in which males and females engage in sexual selection. She believes from her studies that primate females, including humans, evolved a tendency to seek extra-group males. Similar behavior is also seen outside of primates. As we shall see, in some birds that are socially monogamous, it is the female who seeks males from outside this relationship. The quick story is that these females seek males for extra relationships who are most unlike their own mates genetically, and the extra mating allows for improvement in their offspring. The longer story, according to Hrdy (2000), is the possibility that females might benefit from polyandrous mating.

To support her theory, Hrdy (2000) examined data from a variety of species. The first question she asked is whether females seek novelty. Examining data from pseudoscorpions (a small scorpion-like arachnid), the answer is yes. Females of this species show eagerness to mate after 48 hours, but they require at least an hour and a half before mating again, if it is with the same male. However, females with a different male were as likely to accept mating after an hour and a half as after 48 hours. In this species, the male did not show the same desire for novelty, as they remain eager to mate repeatedly with the same female. Another question relates to the benefits of mating with more than one male. The evidence from species such as prairie dogs shows that females who seek extra mating are more fertile and their litters more healthy. Further data from chimps suggest that a third to a half were sired by males outside the troop. Seeking novelty outside standard male mating partners would have evolved only if it produces more benefits to the species than detriments. What would those benefits be? One benefit is better genetics in the offspring.

SEXUAL SIGNALS

One of the indicators of sexual availability in primate females is **sexual swelling,** which is often accompanied by a change in color. Sexual swelling is thought to have evolved at three different times and is found in some 25 species of primates (Hrdy, 2000). It has been estimated that a maximally swollen female chimpanzee mates one to four times an hour with as many as 13 or more partners. Hrdy modified the traditional idea that suggested that each female was selected to mate with the one best male. Rather, she suggested that females evolved to mate with a variety of males. Sexual swelling advertises to the males that the female is available. Clearly one purpose of such behavior is conception. However, could there be more than this?

One approach was to examine primates in terms of social groups. Female macaque monkeys do not show sexual swelling, but rather signal their willingness to mate in other ways. When female macaque monkeys were housed with a single male, mating took place during the mid-cycle period of estrus when the animal was most likely to become pregnant. However, if the females were housed with multiple males, then things changed. The mating patterns were more flexible in that the females solicited sex throughout the follicular phase of the cycle, during which they were less likely to become pregnant. It was also the case that the dominant females took precedence over the subordinates in mating with the most males (Wallen, 1990).

Throughout the primate literature, it is apparent that sexual signals mirror the underlying changes that take place during the periodic estrus cycle. Could this also be true for the menstrual cycle of the human female? As we shall see when we discuss attraction later in the chapter, females do, indeed, change their preferences in terms of male facial features during different periods of the menstrual cycle. Females also show differential reaction to male body smells during the period. In what have been called "t-shirt" studies, females were asked to rate the smell of t-shirts that males had slept in the night before (Gangestad & Thornhill, 1998). During the ovulation phase of the menstrual cycle, when females are most likely to become pregnant, females choose shirts that belong to males with symmetrical bodies. As noted, symmetrical bodies have been associated with greater health. Overall, this suggests that females seek males with the best genes at times that correspond with their greatest probability of becoming pregnant.

What type of man does a woman who is already partnered prefer? Strange as it may seem, human females appear to have preferences in males similar to that seen with birds. As you remember, many female birds who form monogamous relationships will still seek extra partners to mate with short term, if that partner displays characteristics of better genes than her current partner. It turns out that human females may do the same. In one study, titled "The Best Men Are (Not Always) Already Taken," the researchers studied 110 women who had a partner and 110 who did not (Bressan & Stranieri, 2008). The women in the study were asked to rate the photographs of 12 males who varied in degree of masculinity and attractiveness, although all males were rated as physically pleasant. The participants were told to imagine they were at a party with their partner, if they had one. They were then to imagine seeing the man in the photo. Each photo was accompanied by one of four labels. The labels said, "this person is single," "this person is in love," "this person has a girlfriend," "this person is married." The photos and labels were presented in a different random order for each participant. The researchers were also able to determine where the women were in their menstrual cycle and thus establish a measure of conception risk. What these authors found was that conception risk is an important variable in rating a potential partner. Women with a partner rated the photos of men who were described as attached more highly than men described as single, if their conception risk was low. However, the opposite was found if the conception risk was high. Additionally, the preference for single men during fertile days was related to how masculine the face of the man appeared: The women preferred the single men whose faces were masculine. It has been suggested that masculine appearance is reflective of good genes. Thus, the women with a partner were reflecting a preference for potentially diversifying the genetic composition of their offspring. How about the rating of women without a partner? Overall, they rated all men as more attractive than did the partnered women. Further, they did not show any effect related to their menstrual cycle. Bressan and Stranieri suggest their results support the idea that human females have evolved a dual mating strategy. For long-term relationships, females prefer a male who will take care of them and their offspring. However, for short-term relationships, females seek genetically superior males.

Not only do females seek males with the best genes, but they also seek males whose genes are different from their own (see Wedekind & Penn, 2000 for an overview). Studies in mice have shown that both male and female mice prefer to mate with mice that have genes (major histocompatibility complex genes—MHC) that are different from their own. By mating with genetically different partners, it is possible to increase resistance to infectious disease in the offspring. Indeed, greater differences in MHC genes are related to a greater resistance to HIV and also to hepatitis. In humans, t-shirt studies have also shown that women prefer the odor of MHC-dissimilar men. In fact, the women judged the odor of the t-shirts of men with genes similar to their own as less pleasant. Other research has shown that men also prefer t-shirts from women who are genetically different from themselves. It has also been shown that just the act of smelling a female's t-shirt will increase a male's testosterone levels (Miller & Maner, 2010). Further, if the t-shirt was from an ovulating woman, the men showed a higher level of testosterone than if the t-shirt was from a nonovulating woman. Clearly, factors related to olfaction create a channel of communication in humans that may influence mating preferences and choices.

It also appears that women, through olfactory information, can influence each other's timing of menstrual cycles, at least if they live in close proximity. What was noticed in the now classic work of Martha McClintock (1971) was that, over three or four cycles, roommates begin to see their menstrual cycles synchronize. In her original research, she compared 135 women who lived together in a female dorm of a women's college. She compared the women who were roommates and together socially with the same women placed statistically in random groups. This helped to rule out common factors experienced by all of the women in the college, such as eating the same food, or the weather, or such other factors. The question arises as to what factors led to the synchrony of the women's menstrual cycles. In the original study, all that was known was that women who live together tend to have menstrual cycles in synchrony. Since it is known in animals that pheromones can influence a variety of sexual responses, including menstrual synchrony, this seemed like a good place to start.

Pheromones are chemicals released into the air that have been shown to signal to other members of a species various aspects of sexuality, including when a female is receptive. In this next study, compounds were taken from under the arm at two different phases of a woman's menstrual cycle. The first was while the egg was being developed—the follicular phase. The second phase sampled was just after the egg was released—the ovulatory phase. One of these sets of compounds was presented to the women in the study each day for the duration of two menstrual cycles (Stern & McClintock, 1998). Most of these women could not smell the substance and thought they were in a control group. When the women were exposed to the compounds from the follicular phase, their cycles became shorter. When, on the other hand, they were exposed to those from the ovulatory phase, their cycles were longer. This research also suggests that humans have not lost the ability to be influenced by pheromones. Thus, information concerning the menstrual cycle can be signaled to other women, but what could the functional significance be?

Two suggestions have emerged from the animal literature. The first suggests that infants born at the same time from a number of mothers are healthier and survive better until weaning than one infant born alone. Thus, there is safety in numbers. Early human history, with groups of humans living together, is consistent with this suggestion. The second suggestion sees synchrony as a way for the dominant female to make sure that she will be receptive at the same time as other females, so that she can mate with the male of her choice. The existence and function of synchrony in humans is still under some debate.

The major theme from this research is that a variety of species, including humans, possess mechanisms that seek to increase the survivability of the offspring. In many species, one important channel for communicating this information is odor. As humans moved over evolutionary time to a reliance on vision, it was assumed that odor played less of a role in mating. However, the research just discussed suggests this is not entirely the case, and we will have to wait for more systematic studies to understand the full story.

ENSURING PATERNITY

Another question asked by Sarah Hrdy (1979) was whether sexual relations with a female will alter the male's behavior toward her offspring. The answer is yes. However, this is not always for the better. To ensure that a female's offspring is their own, males may actually kill the mother's unweaned infants. This behavior has been seen in at least 34 different species of primates so far. In the langur monkey, it has been reported that a third of all infants die by being killed when their mothers are intercepted by males they have never mated with. These males never kill their own offspring, so it is not just a case of males being aggressive. As shown by behavioral observation and DNA testing, it is the offspring of others that they kill.

SEXUAL STRATEGIES THEORY

In humans, the female conceives the child internally, gives birth, and has the ability to nurse the infant. This is not to deny that many males are heavily invested in the emotional, social, and cognitive development of their children. However, the obligation and requirement of investment is greater in the human female than the human male. This obligation has existed at least since the beginning of our mammalian ancestors and helped to shape the differential evolutionary histories of males and females. It follows that part of this differentiation was related to sexual selection and mating. **Sexual strategies theory** was developed by David Buss and David Schmitt (1993) as an extension of Robert Trivers' parental investment theory applied to humans. The basic idea is that males and females have evolved a variety of mating strategies, especially in terms of the perceived length of the relationship. That is, if the person sees the future of the relationship to be short term, a different strategy would be adopted than if she sees it as a long-term relationship. In long-term mating, males are hypothesized to place a greater premium on signs of fertility and reproductive values such as youth and physical appearance. Females are seen to place value on factors related to a male's ability to take care of the family, including such factors as the male's status, resources, and maturity. The underlying theme is that each of the values for males and females has been shaped over time as an adaptive response to environmental situations. As such, we would expect many of these preferences to be obvious to us and others to be less within our awareness. However, we should be able to conduct research that allows us to understand these preferences. Let us begin with the preferences we can tell to another.

What characteristics do you look for in someone to go to a party with? What if you want to spend the rest of your life with that person? David Buss (2000) was interested in how undergraduates would answer these questions. If, indeed, male and female responses could be explained by evolutionary theory, then we would expect the responses to be consistent with reproductive success. Buss asked individuals to rate 76 different qualities that they would seek in someone they might marry. Buss found that the females valued financial resources in a mate significantly more than the males did. Females also sought characteristics that would lead to these resources, such as ambition, industriousness, education, and social status. The males, on the other hand, reported valuing good looks and physical attractiveness. Why would this be the case? There is, of course, a variety of reasons why any one group of individuals would prefer one characteristic over another.

Evolutionary psychologists would emphasize the requirements that are needed to produce large-brained infants, especially in terms of resources. The emphasis would be on characteristics that represent sexual success for the production of the offspring. From this perspective, human females, who invest more than males in human infants, would seek males who would aid with the survival of the offspring. There are a variety of ways in which males could aid with the survival, including resources such as housing and financial goods. Males, on the other hand, would seek females who would be healthy and be able to give birth and support an infant. Resources on the part of males and health and the ability to produce infants on the part of females would create differential age desirability between male and female mates: Males would seek younger women and females would seek older men. Overall, what is being suggested is that mating patterns for male and female long-term relationships center on the creation and support of future humans.

How might one test these ideas? One approach is to ask individuals which characteristics they seek in a long-term mate. Do you care if he is handsome or wealthy or can solve crossword puzzles? Does it matter what area of expertise a woman has or if she is beautiful or can run fast? Should either own a fast car or a big house? As you think about these characteristics, you may realize that some of these characteristics in your ideal mate could have been shaped by evolution and others not. Strength, for example, could have evolved simply by the fact that stronger individuals were the ones that mated and passed on these genes to their children. On the other hand, the love of crossword puzzles itself could not have evolved because written language is a relatively recent development, but the desire to solve cognitive problems may have evolved because this is a skill that would aid in survival. Thus, as one begins to test mate preferences, it is important to present the characteristics in terms that are consistent with genetic transmission. It is also important to consider traits that can vary and thus have the potential to give an individual a selective advantage. Further, given the manner in which a particular culture, including media sources, can influence what humans see as important characteristics in a mate, it is important to rule out competing hypotheses. For example, research has shown that females are more likely than males to seek a mate who is wealthy. One alternative explanation is that in many societies, females have fewer material resources than males. Thus, they are trying to gain something (i.e., money) that they do not have. If this were true, then we would expect females in a given society who are themselves wealthy to choose a mate on grounds other than wealth. However, research suggests that wealthy females place more, rather than less, emphasis on the financial status of their mate, a finding consistent with evolutionary theory (Wiederman & Allgeier, 1992).

In contrast to asking individuals about their mate preferences, another approach is to see what they do in the real world. The real world, in this case, is the "Personals" section of newspapers and magazines. One study looking at personal ads from a variety of newspapers found data consistent with the evolutionary perspective (Waynforth & Dunbar, 1995). That is, females tended to seek partners who were slightly older than themselves, whereas males sought partners who were younger. Females also sought resources significantly more often than males (18% vs. 4%). Males, on the other hand, sought attractiveness more often than females (44% vs. 22%). Comparing good looks to resources, it was determined that more than 40% of the male ads sought females with good looks, whereas less than 5% of the ads sought females with resources. Females, on the other hand, requested good looks only slightly more often than resources (22% vs. 18%). Thus, females sought good looks in a mate less than males and resources more. On the other hand, females offered good looks more often than resources, whereas males offered resources more often than good looks. This type of research helps us to understand what males and females are seeking in a mate.

A related question is why males and females use the "Personals" column and what this tells us about mating. One possible answer is that personal ads tell us how available males and females are. That is, if it were easy to find a mate, then there would be less pressure to seek a mate through a

"Personals" column. By looking at the age of the person being sought in ads and dividing that by the number of people seeking mates, it would be possible to determine demand and availability of males and females in different age groups. Following this line of thinking, some researchers have developed a measure of the "market value" of males and females based on both number and characteristics of mates sought (Pawlowski & Dunbar, 1999). In this report, it was determined that males in their late thirties have the highest market value, whereas females in their twenties are most in demand (see Figure 9.1).

Another approach that would help to rule out alternative hypotheses would be to examine mate selection across a wide variety of cultures, with the goal of determining universal characteristics. Buss and his colleagues performed such a survey and sought to determine if universal characteristics in mate selection existed. That is to say, do males and females in a variety of cultures value similar characteristics in a mate? In order to answer this question, 10,047 individuals in 37 different cultures located on six continents and five islands valued the characteristics of a potential mate. As found in the previous study, Buss and his international collaborators

| **Figure 9.1** | Market Value of Males and Females vs. Age. Males have a higher market value later in life and females earlier in life. |

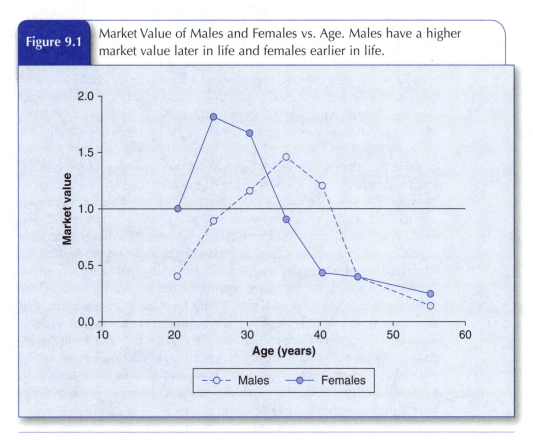

Source: Pawlowski and Dunbar (1999, p. 283).

found two clusters of sex differences. He found that females more than males in these 37 cultures valued financial prospects in a mate. He also found that males more than females valued physical attractiveness and youth. The researchers also found a variety of characteristics that both males and females valued in a mate. These include mates who were kind, understanding, intelligent, exciting, healthy, and dependable.

In the multicultural study, Buss (1989) also asked the individuals at what age they preferred to marry. Males, on average, preferred to marry at 27.49 years of age to a female who was 2.66 years younger. This age is, indeed, near the age of a female's peak fertility. Do individuals from a variety of cultures actually marry at the preferred ages? The answer is yes. Further analysis showed that males, on average, marry when they are 28.2 years of age to females who are 25.3 years of age. This suggests that males both had a preference for females who were at the height of their potential fertility and also acted on their preference in terms of actual marriages. An interesting test of this hypothesis would be to ask males in their teens who they saw as attractive. If the evolutionary psychology hypothesis is correct, then we would expect teenage boys to also find females in their 20s to be attractive. Kenrick and Keefe (1992) performed such a study. What they found was that 17-year-old males did, indeed, find females who were 6 years older than them most attractive. For completeness, it should be noted that 12- to 16-year-old males found women who were 3 to 4 years older to be most attractive. It is hard to argue that the basis for these preferences would be experience because most teenage boys would have had limited contact with females in their 20s, as compared to females of their own age. Overall, these data support the idea that an important consideration that is part of our evolutionary history is maximal opportunity for preservation of the species.

Sexual relationships between males and females can range from lifetime commitments to brief encounters, with a wide range of possibilities in between. The question arose as to the types of characteristics that males and females would value in long-term vs. short-term relationships. Based on Trivers' (1972) concept of investment, we would predict that females would be more discriminating than males in both long-term and short-term relationships. This is exactly what has been found in a variety of studies. Females incur the same potential costs of creating and raising infants whether the relationship is a long-term or short-term one, and thus there is no potential value to having different standards, although, as we shall see, the story can be more complicated. Because males will potentially invest more in a long-term than a short-term relationship, we would expect to see greater differences in this comparison. In fact, that appears to be the case. In one study, the values that males sought in short-term mates were significantly lower in 41 of 67 variables.

There are three properties of short-term mating, according to sexual strategies theory:

1. Males possess a greater desire than females for a variety of sexual partners.

2. Males will consent to sexual intercourse in a shorter time period than females.

3. Males more actively seek short-term mates than females.

Although these ideas have been supported by research in the U.S., Schmitt and 118 colleagues (2003) extended this work into 10 major world regions, surveying 16,288 people. Schmitt and colleagues found that the desire for sexual variety is greater for males in all cultures. This was true regardless of whether the men were married or single, heterosexual or homosexual. Further, among all individuals who were actively seeking short-term mates, more than 50% of the males and less than 20% of the females were seeking more than one sexual partner in the next month. When the time frame was increased to the next 6 months and the next year, the percentage of males desiring more than one sexual partner increased to 69% and 75%, respectively. For females, the percentage increased only marginally. Overall, these results support the first hypothesis of sexual strategies theory, that males possess a greater desire than females for a variety of sexual partners.

The second hypothesis suggested that males would consent to engage in sexual activity in a shorter time span than females. Previous research performed in the U.S. had shown that males, on average, would consent to having sex after knowing a female for about a week (Buss & Schmitt, 1993). Females, on the other hand, would not consent to sex until they had known the partner for about 6 months. Given these results, it is no surprise that if a male were asked whether he would engage in sex after he knew his partner for one month, the answer would be yes. Likewise, a female would say no. These are exactly the results others have found (Schmitt, 2003). In extending this to the 10 regions of the world, Schmitt and colleagues (2003) had males and females rate the likelihood of having sex on a scale that ranged from +3 (definitely would have sex) to -3 (definitely would not have sex). The general findings across regions showed results similar to the previous U.S. studies. Although in every region males reported a greater likelihood of having sex than females, there were some differences by region. These differences are assumed to have resulted from differences in cultural, religious, and social roles in these communities. As we have discussed previously, evolutionary predispositions should interact with environmental conditions to produce the final results.

The third hypothesis suggested that males would more often actively seek short-term mates as compared to females. The basic idea suggested by Buss and Schmitt (1993) is that males, as a group, tend to spend more effort on short-term mating because their strategy is based on attracting a larger number of sex partners than do females. This, of course, is not to say that, for various reasons, females do not seek short-term relationships or that males do not wish for long-term commitments. Rather, it is a statement that males have more of a predisposition than females to seek short-term mates. That is exactly the results seen in the 10-world-region study. Males would more actively seek short-term relationships than females. As you think about this result, you might ask, What if the individuals were married, or living together, or just dating one person, or not dating at all? To answer this question, the researchers looked at individuals who scored above +1 on the likelihood of having sex scale in the four groups. As you might expect, a larger percentage of both males and females who were not currently in a relationship were seeking short-term mates. However, even in this case, a larger percentage of males (79%) than females (64%) scored above +1. This also was true for the other three categories. That is, more married men (25%) than women (10%); more cohabiting men (39%) than women (16%); and more men (45%) than women (27%) who were dating one person exclusively were seeking short-term relationships. These data clearly demonstrate that males, more than females, seek mates for short-term relationships. What is even more compelling is that the results found with married couples (25% vs. 10%) mirrors other data on the percentage of American males and females who have engaged in extramarital sexual relationships (24% vs. 12%; Wiederman, 1997).

Overall, the 10-world-region study presented data to show that males and females differ in the desire for sexual variety, differ in the time required to agree to sexual intercourse, and differ in their desire for short-term relationships. Further, the results suggest that this is a universal phenomenon. Overall, the basic idea is that males and females have evolved somewhat different strategies for both long-term and short-term relationships. Because there is some variation in the responses of men and women in the surveys, as well as in their actual behavior in real life, a future challenge for evolutionary psychology is to understand this variation.

Attraction

What physical features do you look for in a mate? How do you judge attractiveness in anyone? Recent research is beginning to describe features that characterize attractiveness in males and females (Thornhill & Gangestad, 2004; Little & Perrett, 2011). Like the peacock's tail, physical features in humans also appear to reflect health and reproductive success. For males, facial features associated with the sex hormone testosterone, such as high cheekbones, strong jaws and chins, and large noses, are seen as attractive. For females, facial attraction has been related to large eyes, small noses, and full lips. In both males and females, symmetry is seen as an important feature of attractiveness. The basic idea is that the features of perceived beauty reflect an underlying physiological process associated with reproductive success and health. Thus, in terms of evolutionary psychology, what you view as attractive and beautiful is not arbitrary, but reflects important markers that have evolved over human history. As with many markers, these can be greatly influenced by environmental conditions. For example, attractiveness becomes more important in a mate when there is a greater prevalence of infectious diseases (Thornhill & Gangestad, 2004).

Overall, it has been suggested that there exist three main domains that are involved in determining attractiveness: averageness, symmetry, and secondary characteristics of males and females. Averageness, as the name implies, simply asks the question, How similar is a given face to all other faces? A variety of studies have shown that average faces are rated as more attractive than faces with more extreme characteristics. One method of performing this research is to take pictures of a number of individuals and then use a computer program to morph these into a single face. Why would a face that represents the average of all human faces be seen as more attractive? One possibility may be that those with an average face would also have genes that represent those found in the population in general. In normal times, this genetic diversity would also be associated with a general resistance to disease and thus health. Although this hypothesis is still being tested, there are studies that show that nonaverage facial features are negatively correlated with health. Another facial feature that is associated with attractiveness is symmetry. Symmetry is determined by drawing a vertical line from the forehead through the nose and ending in the chin. From this line, measurements can be made on the left and right side of the face in relation to the eyes, ears, edge of nose, and lips to determine whether there are right and left differences. Overall, a variety of studies show that ratings of attractiveness are positively associated with symmetry. The third domain is gender related. A variety of studies have shown that males who have characteristics such as high cheekbones, strong jaws and chins, and large noses are rated by females as attractive. When males rate females, facial attraction has been related to large eyes, small noses, and full lips.

The principal male sex hormone testosterone stimulates fat deposits in the abdominal region and inhibits it in the thighs. The principal female sex hormone, estrogen, on the other hand, inhibits fat deposits in the abdominal region and stimulates fat deposits in the thighs. Thus, measurements of the hips and waist could give indications of hormonal processes. In fact, a variety of studies have shown the waist-to-hip ratio to reflect female reproductive status, including reproductive capability and health (Singh, 1993). If, indeed, attractiveness is reflective of reproductive success, then we would expect males to rate females differentially in terms of their hip-to-waist ratio. This is indeed what Singh found, regardless of whether the figures were underweight, normal weight, or overweight. Using the stimuli presented in Figure 9.2, Singh asked college males to

Figure 9.2 Figures used to represent body weight categories: (I) underweight, (II) normal weight, and (III) overweight. Waist to hip ratio shown under each figure.

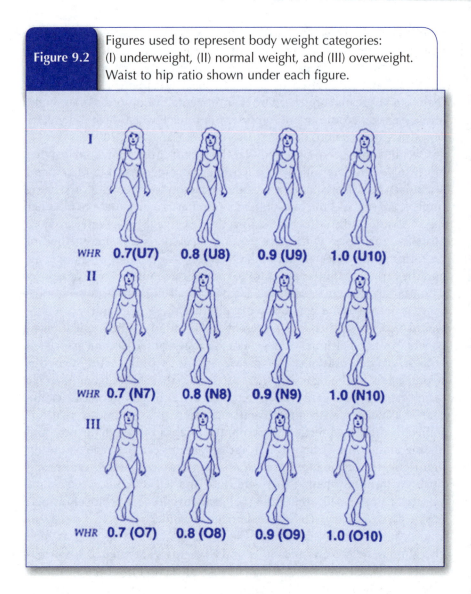

rate the figures in terms of four characteristics: (1) attractive and sexy; (2) healthy; (3) youthful looking; and (4) desire and capacity for having children. In general, the .70 hip-to-waist ratio was rated highest for all four measures, regardless of whether the figure was under, over, or of normal weight. Further, when this research was extended to older men, the results were the same.

Since Singh's (1993) original work, there has been some debate as to the validity of the waist-to-hip ratio theory (e.g., Tassinary & Hansen, 1998). One criticism is that the original work confounded waist-to-hip ratio with weight. To help evaluate this work, Streeter and McBurney (2003) replicated the original work with photographs rather than line drawings. The authors used a photo of a woman and manipulated waist, hip, and chest widths using Photoshop software. These authors also used a wider range of hip-to-waist ratios than in the previous work. Both males and females who took part in the research were asked to judge the attractiveness and the weight of the person in the various figures in a random order. As in previous research, Streeter and McBurney found that both males and females rated the images with the waist-to-hip ratio of .70 to be the most attractive, with males in general rating the images as more attractive overall. (see Figure 9.3). In terms of the independent manipulation of chest, waist, and hip, images with medium chest size, medium hip size, and medium waist size were judged the most attractive. Further, statistically removing weight from the data did not remove the effect of waist-to-hip ratio.

The association between waist-to-hip ratio and attraction has led a number of researchers to ask why this should be. The general answer is that attractiveness is related to fitness. Like the peacock's tail, the waist-to-hip ratio gives a visual estimate of health and fertility. This ratio has also been seen as related to critical fat reserves that a mother would need to sustain fetal and infant brain development. One hypothesis has suggested that upper body fat has a negative effect and that lower body fat has a positive effect on the supply of polyunsaturated fatty acids required for this development (Lassek & Gaulin, 2008). Based on this hypothesis,

| Figure 9.3 | Attractiveness as a Function of Waist-to-Hip Ratio |

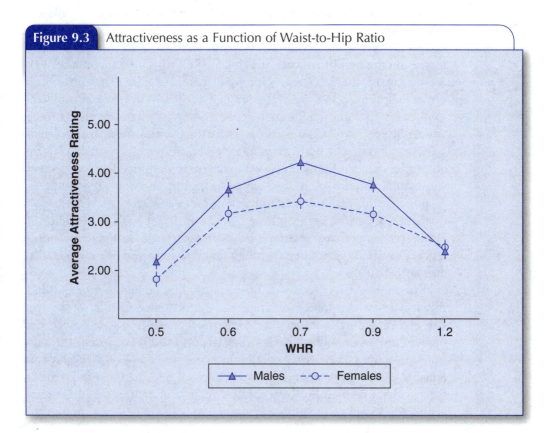

Lassek and Gaulin suggested that the waist-to-hip ratio would predict cognitive development. What these researchers found was that women with lower waist-to-hip ratios had higher cognitive tests scores, as did their children, even after controlling for other factors such as education, income, and age.

If a teenage girl were to become pregnant, nutrients would be needed for both her own development and that of her fetus. Thus, there is a trade-off between resources she needs for her brain development and resources for her developing fetus. In this group, Lassek and Gaulin (2008) found that women with lower waist-to-hip ratios and their children were protected from the cognitive decrements associated with teen birth. These results for both teen mothers and older mothers were seen for waist-to-hip ratio but not for body mass index (ratio of weight to height). Overall, these studies suggest that waist-to-hip ratio not only signals health but also future cognitive development.

Although these waist-to-hip ratio studies point to an underlying factor related to attractiveness, there were a variety of possible confounds in their interpretation, including (1) a confound of body weight and waist-to-hip ratio, in that individuals with smaller waists could also be perceived as lighter; (2) limited ecological validity because the images were not real figures of women; and (3) the ratio of the 2D images is a measure of width and not circumference, and it is circumference that is correlated with fertility. Rilling and his colleagues sought to clarify these issues by presenting images of real women rotating in three-dimensional space, as well as increasing the number of measures taken (Rilling, Kaufman, Smith, Patel, & Worthman, 2009). These additional measures and their relation to physiological processes are presented in Table 9.1. What these researchers found was that the abdominal depth and waist circumference of the women were the strongest predictors of attractiveness, even stronger than waist-to-hip ratio or body mass index (ratio of height to weight). These authors concluded that women with shallow abdominal depth and small waist circumference are more likely to be healthy and non-pregnant, suggesting that this may be an adaptive male preference that has been shaped by natural selection. Leg length was also a consistent positive predictor of attractiveness, perhaps because it has been correlated with biomechanical efficacy or healthy prepubertal growth that is unhindered by nutritional or energetic deficiency.

If we look across a variety of species, including humans, we would find that female mating preferences change as a function of such factors as age, size, and reproductive status. I have described tendencies, such as with the peahen and peacock, that have a direct benefit to the offspring through immunological competence resulting in better health. What about human females? If evolutionary tendencies were to play a role, then we would expect there to be a relationship between preference and conception, or at least expect it to vary with the probability of conception. Let us look at one recent

Table 9.1   Developmental and Endocrine Characteristics of Selected Anthropometric Measures

Measure	Measurement Rationale
Abdominal depth	Negatively correlated with adult estrogen levels
Acromial height	Negatively correlated with pubertal timing
Chest-to-underchest ratio	Positively correlated with adult estrogen levels
Hip circumference	Positively correlated with fat stores used in reproduction
Second to fourth digit ratio	Negatively correlated with the ratio of fetal testosterone to fetal estrogen, and adult estradiol
Leg-to-stature ratio	Leg length is positively correlated with health and nutrition throughout childhood
Mid-arm circumference	Positively correlated with body fat stores and peripheral fat patterning
Pelvic width	Positively correlated with extent of estrogen exposure at puberty and fetal outcomes
Shoulder width	Positively correlated with extent of androgen exposure at puberty
Sitting height	Positively correlated with health and nutrition in infancy and puberty
Stature	Positively correlated with pre-adult nutrition and health and life expectancy
Waist circumference	Negatively correlated with adult estrogen levels
Waist-to-hip ratio	Negatively correlated with adult estrogen and progesterone levels; positively correlated with androgens and health risk
Weight	Negatively correlated with adult estrogen and progesterone levels; positively correlated with androgens and health risk
BMI (body mass index)	Curvilinear correlation with nutritional status (under- and overnutrition) and health

Source: Rilling et al. (2009, p. 23).

study that examined reproductive status in human females. One way research in this area has been performed is to study the attraction of a male to a female at different phases of the menstrual cycle. Because the follicular phase of the menstrual cycle is the time when females are most likely to conceive a child, this phase is often compared with other phases of the cycle in which there is a low probability of conception. In one such study, male faces that were modified to be either more masculine or feminine in shape were presented to Japanese women in their early 20s (Penton-Voak et al., 1999). The faces were of both male Japanese and Caucasians. Although females generally prefer slightly feminized male facial shapes, there is a connection between more masculine features and immunological competence. Thus, if females were choosing males for their ability to offer better genes to the offspring, then more masculine faces would be selected during periods in which conception was more likely. This is exactly what was found in the study. Japanese women preferred male faces that were more masculine during the phases of their menstrual cycle in which they were most likely to become pregnant, as compared to other phases of their cycle. The actual origin of the males, either Japanese or Caucasian, did not affect the female's choice.

What if you let females create the face they think is most attractive? In one study, British females in their 20s were able to change the masculine and feminine characteristics of a male's face (Little, Jones, Penton-Voak, Burt, & Perrett, 2001). These females were asked to choose the face they found most attractive for a long-term relationship and for a short-term relationship. For a short-term relationship, the results were the same as in the Japanese study. Females found more masculine faces more attractive during those times in their menstrual cycle that they would be more likely to become pregnant. However, for a long-term relationship, face preferences were not related to phase of the menstrual cycle. One way of interpreting these data is to suggest that females seeking short-term relationships look for males who are most likely to produce the best offspring genetically. This, of course, would be support for the good gene theory.

If you think about preferences of males and females from a Darwinian perspective, you realize that there is a more significant decision taking place: Characteristics that are sought after will also be those that are passed on to the next generation.

SUMMARY

Darwin described same-sex competition for a mate and the factors that influenced selection of a mate. A further differentiation can be made between primary and secondary sexual characteristics. Primary characteristics are those aspects of sexuality that are physiologically primary, such as organs for the production of sperm or eggs. Secondary characteristics are those that are not required for sexual reproduction but have evolved to support the acquisition of mates, such as bright plumage in birds. Body characteristics in males and females of a species are reflective of their mating patterns. Two theories have been suggested to reflect mating preferences: the good gene theory and the good provider theory. Trivers suggested parental investment determines sexual selection and mating behavior. The basic idea is that the sex that invests the most in its offspring will have evolved to be the most discriminating in selecting its mating partner. There are a variety of ways that mates signal sexual readiness to each other. Sexual strategies theory suggests that males and females have evolved a variety of mating strategies, especially in terms of the perceived length of the relationship. In long-term mating, males are hypothesized to place a greater premium on signs of fertility and reproductive values such as youth and physical appearance. Females are seen to place value on factors related to a male's ability to take care of the family, including such factors as the male's status, resources, and maturity. Males, but not females, show differences in short-term strategies. There are a variety of factors that define attraction.

STUDY RESOURCES

Review Questions

1. What is sexual selection and how does it relate to natural selection? How does the concept of runaway sexual selection extend the notion of sexual selection?

2. How do human males and females differ, and what does this suggest about our evolutionary history? Which differences are thought to have evolved through sexual selection?

3. Describe the good gene theory and the good provider theory as alternative perspectives on what drives mate selection.

4. What is the relationship between parental investment and sexual selection strategies?

5. Darwin originally described the female as "coy" and requiring courtship. What was Hrdy's criticism of this perspective? How has she expanded our understanding of male and female sexual selection?

6. Sexual signals are indicators of sexual availability. What are the results of some of the recent research studies that help us understand the ratings and preferences of potential mating partners?

7. Buss and Schmitt developed the sexual strategies theory concerning the basic idea that males and females have evolved a variety of mating strategies. The chapter cites a wide range of studies to support this theory. Which three studies do you find most compelling to show that males and females differ in their sexual strategies?

8. What do you look for in terms of physical features in a mate? How do you judge attractiveness in anyone? In terms of evolutionary psychology, what you view as attractive and beautiful is not arbitrary, but reflects important markers that have evolved over human history. Give examples of some of the physical features that have been studied and the underlying evolutionary advantage they represent.

For Further Reading

Barash, D., & Lipton, J. (2001). *Myth of monogamy: Fidelity and infidelity in animals and people.* New York: W. H. Freeman.

Dixon, A. (2009). *Sexual selection and the origins of human mating systems.* New York: Oxford University Press.

Trivers, R. (1985). *Social evolution.* Menlo Park, CA: Benjamin/Cummings.

Key Terms and Concepts

- Back to Darwin
- Body size and mating patterns
- Mate choice and the evolution of mental abilities
- Theoretical perspectives on sexual preferences
    - o Good gene theory
    - o Good provider theory
    - o Parental investment and sexual strategies
    - o Adding the female perspective to Darwin: Alternative to the coy female
    - o Sexual signals
    - o Ensuring paternity
    - o Sexual strategies theory
- Attraction

SAGE Study Site

Visit the study site at **www.sagepub.com/ray** for chapter-specific study resources.

Glossary Terms

- Good gene
- Good provider
- Parental investment
- Pheromones

- Runaway sexual selection
- Sexual strategies theory
- Sexual swelling

Kin and Family Relationships 10

I f someone asks you about your relationships with others, how do you answer? Do you talk about your romantic relationships, your friendships, or your family? From an evolutionary psychology perspective, each of these relationships is qualitatively different and regulated by different processes (Daly, Salmon, & Wilson, 1997). In this chapter, I will emphasize family relationships. Although we all talk about our families, it is rare that you read about family relationships in psychology or the neurosciences, partly because it is not the type of research conducted in most psychological laboratories. However, this is changing as evolutionary psychology considers the importance of family and kin relationships (see Bjorklund & Pellegrini, 2002; Burnstein, 2005; Kurland & Gaulin, 2005; Salmon & Shackelford, 2008).

Various studies, including large-scale cross-cultural studies, point to the importance of family and family relationships throughout the world. The human family is extraordinary and unique in many respects (Flinn, Ward, & Noone, 2005). One aspect of this is the long period of childhood experienced by humans, with its extensive social relationships. Humans are suggested to be the only species to live in multi-male and multi-female groups with complex coalitions and extensive parental care. One key here is that most human infants have caregivers from multiple generations. Grandparents and aunts and uncles are important people in the lives of many children. Another important aspect is the extensive parental care given to human infants by both parents. In other primate communities, the almost exclusive focus of the males is on mating. It has been estimated that male parenting is found in less than 5% of mammals. Some researchers have even suggested that the idea of cooperative males should be considered an evolutionary puzzle (Flinn, Quinlan, Coe, & Ward, 2008). How these relationships came about and the meaning of kin have been important questions for evolutionary psychology.

What factors might be involved in the development of family relations? One critical factor that drives human kinship dynamics is the fact that the human infant is born less mature than other species and requires a long period of care for maturation. This makes an infant's family crucial in its well-being and survival. This, in turn, suggests that genetic structures supporting parental investment will be passed on to future generations. That is to say, those infants who are cared for during this extended maturation will survive and thus pass on their genes, whereas those who are not cared for will not. Thus, it is in the interest of the infant to seek care and in the interest of the parents to give care. As we will see in this chapter, there is also reason to believe that the need for human infant support extends beyond the parents and may have driven the involvement of grandparents in infant care.

On a more basic level, another crucial determination of kin relationships is the manner in which individuals can ensure that their genetic material, or material similar to their own, is passed on. Thus, in addition to self-preservation, family relationships also appear to influence who you choose to partner with in later life and the nature of those relationships. On a social level, genetic decision-making strategy, as suggested by Hamilton (1996), is at the basis of a variety of processes, including who helps whom and to what extent, who shows violence to whom, and what categories of relationship take precedence over others. These are some of the issues that will be considered in this chapter.

Kinship and Altruism

Altruism and its relation to kinship has been a fundamental question for understanding family relationships. I begin here because the work of W. D. Hamilton (1996) laid a scientific basis for understanding important aspects of family relationships. In terms of kin, it is possible to know who is related to whom and in what way. Categorizing kin relationships may follow separate rules than other forms of categorization studied by cognitive and social psychology, and it is these rules and their resulting relationships that are important to evolutionary psychologists. It may seem surprising that these rules can be thought of in mathematical terms and that they can accurately describe your behavioral patterns with relatives, but that is exactly the case.

This key discovery was the work of W. D. Hamilton (1963, 1964). You first encountered Hamilton in Chapter 1. As you remember, Hamilton was interested in why organisms would perform actions that did not directly benefit themselves. This problem came to be referred to as *altruism*. The naïve view was that natural selection would always reward selfish behavior, and thus it was difficult to explain why an organism would engage in behaviors that had a cost. Hamilton suggested that the situation was more complicated than this. He suggested that organisms would perform altruistic acts if those acts led to genes similar to their own being passed on. That is to say, you are more likely to perform altruistic acts if the person who benefits is kin rather than a stranger. Further, you are more likely to aid those kin who are more closely related to you genetically. Although most of us never consciously realize the exact calculus we are using, it is possible to describe this in mathematical terms. Basically, Hamilton suggested that a behavior will evolve if the cost to the individual is outweighed by the gain to another multiplied by the degree of genetic relationship. Mathematically, this is stated as the following relationship:

$$C < R \times B$$

Cost to the individual is less than the degree of relationship times the benefit.

This relationship came to be known as *Hamilton's rule* and forms the basis of kin selection theory. Hamilton's work helped us understand how altruism could have evolved, as well as dispel the naïve idea that natural selection only supports selfish behavior. Genes that support altruistic behavior will be more likely to be passed on when the benefit and the degree of relationship are higher than the cost. However, if the opposite is the case, the genes that support selfish behavior will be passed on. Hamilton expanded upon Darwin's original concept of fitness. This expanded view came to be called *inclusive fitness*.

Inclusive fitness includes both the Darwinian idea of fitness and the manner in which altruism contributes. Overall, Hamilton's work helped to establish that there are behavioral decision rules for relationships. As psychologists we are interested in describing the psychological mechanisms related to Hamilton's work and performing research to test its implications. For example, we would want to know how individuals assess C (cost), R (degree of relationship), and B (benefit). That is, what factors lead them to determine that someone is kin, and what parameters influence how they assess cost and benefit? Included in this search will be the question of the appropriate models for understanding relationships as we move to a psychological level.

A useful place to begin the extension of Hamilton's work would be to develop some possible hypotheses. Kurland and Gaulin (2005) suggest seven outcomes that we would expect to see:

1. Altruistic nuclear family relations will dominate kin relationships. This hypothesis suggests that in comparison to other types of relationships, family will tend to support the success of the infant's development.

2. Determinate maternal and probabilistic paternal links will lead to a female laterality bias. This hypothesis suggests that because it is easier to know exactly who the mother of an infant was than the father, it is more likely that more altruistic behaviors will be shown by the mother.

3. Conflict will increase and cooperation will decrease with decreasing relatedness. This hypothesis reflects the direct result of Hamilton's kin selection theory. Altruism is expressed for those whom one is most closely related to.

4. Kin will track relatedness differences within the family. This hypothesis suggests that across all cultures, individuals will know how they are related to others in their family.

5. Kin will track the benefit-to-cost ratio of interactions. This hypothesis suggests that the kin selection rule will determine the behaviors of a person in relation to his or her relatives, although the person may not be able to consciously acknowledge these relations.

6. Reciprocity will increase as relatedness increases between kin. This hypothesis suggests that family members will help each other in relation to their genetic relatedness.

7. Deceit, manipulation, and exploitation will increase as relatedness decreases among kin. This hypothesis reflects the opposite of altruism: that a person will exploit and manipulate those who are least related to him or her.

Overall, the Hamilton approach suggests that genetic relatedness is an important factor in determining both positive and negative relationships. Kurland and Gaulin (2005) spell out this relationship in terms of the seven hypotheses above. As we move through this chapter, you can determine how the research supports kin selection. It should also be noted that kin selection moves our understanding of evolution beyond a self-centered approach that suggests that every person is out for himself or herself.

How Do We Determine Relationships?

An important question is how do I know whom I am related to? Evolutionary psychologists suggest we are able to process a variety of kin relation information outside our awareness. This ability relies on specific decision rules. In relation to the decision rules, Burnstein (2005) has suggested that we consider our brain as being evolved to compute two types of relationships: first, our brain is able to categorize individuals in terms of their relatedness to ourselves, and second, it is able to compute the costs and benefits of interacting with these individuals. The manner in which we make these decisions must take place on a variety of levels. Genetically, a variety of studies have suggested that we tend to marry others who are, overall, more similar to ourselves, and that our friends are also more genetically similar to us than randomly matched pairs (see Rushton, 1989 for an overview).

At this point, research is unclear as to whether we choose people more like ourselves in terms of observable cultural and interpersonal characteristics and these, in turn, carry with them genetic similarity, or, as with t-shirt studies, we are actually influenced by underlying genetic makeup. It is also possible that who we want to spend time with and who we mate with may be decided by different behavioral decision rules. Further, there are also data from birds that suggest some preferences, such as plumage color, may be related to experience during development. In these cases, birds select mates of the same color as experienced in the family in which they were reared. Other research suggests more basic factors are involved. With ground squirrels, for example, the female may mate with a number of males in rapid succession. This results in the possibility that her infants may be either full or half siblings because they could have the same or a different father. Even though the infants were litter mates, they were able to discriminate these relationships, as shown by the fact that when they became adults, there was greater cooperation and less competition between full siblings than between half siblings (Holmes & Sherman, 1982). These authors suggested it was through odors, which would have a genetic basis, that the identification was made. In humans, there are data to suggest that genetic factors that influence facial characteristics may be important markers for indexing kinship. For example, in computer simulation games, it has been shown that people who look more like yourself, as would your relatives, are trusted more than those who do not (DeBruine, 2002).

What about infants? Do you think men or women would be better able to pick out their resemblances in an infant? Why would we even expect a difference? From an evolutionary perspective, we begin with the idea just discussed: that both males and females seek to ensure that their genes are passed on. We might expect a sex difference because males and females have different degrees of certainty in knowing whether a child is their own offspring or not. With males, there is potential uncertainty whether his partner's child is really his own. Women, on the other hand, know for certain whether a child is their own. This would suggest that males would have evolved strategies for ensuring paternity, whereas females would have less pressure to evolve such abilities.

One such possibility would be the ability to recognize physical characteristics of an infant shared with the parent. To answer this question,

Platek et al. (2002) morphed the faces of males and females involved in the research with those of 2-year-old strangers. Morphing is a computer technique in which photos of two faces are combined in varying percentages of one or the other face. In this study, the authors morphed the faces at a 50:50 ratio, such that 50% of the face was the participant's and 50% was a child's face. Additionally, an equal number of males and females were morphed into a face of either a male or female child. As you can imagine, if the composite picture contains a large percentage of your picture, then it is relatively easy to recognize yourself. However at 50%, none of the participants in the study could pick out their own morphed picture. Thus, they saw themselves as a 2-year-old, but they did not realize it was them. The task in the research was to view five faces, including the morphed one of them, and answer a question (see Figure 10.1).

One question was "Which one of these children would you be most likely to adopt?" The results showed that 90% of the men and 35% of the women picked the child image that included a morph of their own face. Other questions showed similar results. When asked which face they found most attractive, the men chose their own face 85% of the time, whereas the women chose their face only 35% of the time. When asked which child they would spend $50 on, if only one, the men chose their image 80% of the time, vs. 40% for the women. It was also the case that

| **Figure 10.1** | Faces Used in the Platek et al. (2002) Study |

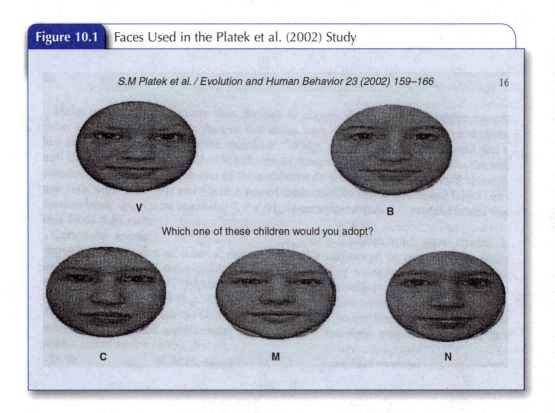

S.M Platek et al. / Evolution and Human Behavior 23 (2002) 159–166   16

V

B

Which one of these children would you adopt?

C

M

N

men made their decisions quicker than women. The authors interpret these results to suggest that males have evolved the ability to identify their own children, whereas females have not. They further suggest that this process works outside awareness.

You might be thinking that males may just be better at assessing physical resemblance no matter what the task, and thus the results are not directly related to paternity. In order to answer this question and understand more concerning the mechanisms of facial self-recognition, a follow-up study was performed (Platek et al., 2003). This study sought to distinguish between two alternatives. Were men more sensitive to their own resemblances and thus able to recognize them more quickly, or did men give more weight to them in decisions related to parental investment? In the follow-up study, the self-images were morphed with the child image in differing percentages (50%, 25%, 12.5%, 6.25%, and 3.125%). Seven faces were presented and a question similar to the previous study was asked. For example, when asked, "Which one of these children would you be most likely to adopt?" 80% of the males and 45% of the females chose their own image at 50% morphing. At 25% morphing (25% of their image and 75% of the child's image), 75% of the males and 35% of the females chose their own image. When the percentage of their image dropped below 25% in the morphed face, neither males nor females chose their own face at rates greater than chance. With another group of participants, individuals in the study were asked to match the morphed pictures of infants to adult pictures of themselves or to pictures of other adults. Both men and women were equally able to match the child pictures to the adult if the morph contained at least 50% of the adult facial features. The interesting part of the results was for images that contained less than 50% of the adult. Below 50%, men were unable to match the child to the adult. Even though men could not pick themselves out in the child images at 25%, they still chose those children as the ones they would choose to benefit. The authors conclude men are able to process facial resemblances without awareness. These results suggest that men could not consciously recognize aspects of their own resemblance better than women, but on some level they were able to use these aspects in making decisions that would potentially benefit their own children.

The Structure of Relationships

An important question is whether relationships between individuals could be structured like language. If this were so, it would contradict the traditional Standard Social Science Model, which suggests all relationships are learned and structured by custom. Of course, just as it does when you are learning a language, the environment in which you develop has an important role to play in your relationships. But evolutionary psychologists suggest that this is not the total story. Evolutionary processes may have created preparedness for certain types of information in terms of relationships. If this position is true, then we could expect to find some underlying universal constraints that direct the types of relationships that we have. These cognitive universals of kinship would be like a linguistic grammar structure that sets up the rule structure for relationships, in the same way that grammar describes language constraints such as that sentences need a noun and verb. Can a small set of principles describe what we observe in seemingly complex relationships?

Doug Jones (2003) suggests this is a real possibility. Jones begins by noting that different cultures in widely separated areas show similar systems to classify relationships involving kin. *Kin classification* refers to how relatives are classified. In English-speaking cultures, for example, there is only one mother and one father, but we do not distinguish between a mother's mother and a father's mother. They are both called "grandmother." Likewise, a mother's sister and a father's sister are both referred to as "aunt." The important question for an evolutionary psychology is Do these linguistic distinctions also reflect important deep-structure processes, such as genetic relatedness? That is to say, is what appears to be an environmentally arbitrary or pragmatic scheme for denoting kin relationships actually reflective of deep-structure rules?

Kin classification, from this perspective, appears to be derived from three larger principles: genealogical distance, social rank, and group membership (Jackendoff, 1994; Jones, 2003). Genealogical distance tells us who is related to us and what this entitles us to do or prohibits us from doing with these individuals. Not only do adult humans have a clear distinction of the meaning of kin, but young children reflect the understanding of this concept (Hirschfeld, 1989). Primates can also recognize kin relationships (Dasser, 1988). Social rank or dominance teaches us hierarchies and when these are important or can be ignored. To help you understand this, you might think of situations in which you would tell a person what to do, as opposed to request that they perform a particular act. Group membership tells us what groups we can belong to and who the members of these different groups are. Who is invited to a family picnic is one expression of group membership principles.

Jones (2003) suggests that these three principles have deep evolutionary roots. Based on the work of Hamilton in terms of kin selection, we know that organisms will more often act altruistically to organisms who are genetically related to them than to those who are not. As described in Chapter 1, altruism benefits the genes and ensures that genetic material more like your own is passed on. Thus, the first principle of genealogical distance appears to be a surface structure reflection of the underlying degree of genetic relatedness. The second principle, social rank, has direct adaptive value in knowing who are the higher ranking individuals.

PARENTAL INVESTMENT THEORY

Parents in different species invest in their young in a variety of ways. Mothers nourish the young during gestation or egg production. Both parents may protect the young from potential dangers. During development in social species, parents directly or indirectly help the young to establish their place in the social hierarchy. Human parents actively teach their children skills necessary to successful development and incorporation within the social group. Robert Trivers (1972), who we discussed in Chapter 1, defined parental investment as any investment by the parent in an individual offspring that increases the offspring's chance of surviving. Survival, in turn, carries with it the implicit idea that a particular offspring will potentially be able to reproduce. Further, if a parent gives resources to one offspring, he or she may be less able to invest in other current or potential offspring. From an evolutionary perspective, there are tradeoffs between being a parent, which requires a certain amount of energy and time expenditure, and other opportunities, such as mating or acquiring additional resources. If parental investment did not benefit the offspring in terms of better survival rates, then it would not survive as a feature of a particular species. Given that some species do not engage in parental care, evolutionary scientists assume that the reproductive benefits must have been great enough to outweigh the costs, including physical resources (food, shelter, protection) as well as success across the lifespan.

If you look at a variety of species, you observe a range of styles in terms of parental investment in infants (Geary, 2005a). Some species put no investment at all into their young. Young are just born and literally left to sink or swim. Others place more effort into raising their young. In fish, for example, one crucial condition is whether internal or external fertilization of the eggs takes place. External fertilization enables males to know the paternity of the newborns, whereas with internal fertilization it is more difficult. Although birds produce young by internal fertilization, parental certainty appears to be an important factor in parental investment. In fact, in birds, there appears to be a relationship between the degree of investment that male birds make in their offspring and the chance that the infant could have been fathered by another, although there are exceptions to this relationship.

Mammalian species show a different style of parental investment. For over 95% of mammalian species, females provide care while males provide little direct investment. This is true for chimpanzees and bonobos—two species closely related to humans. Given this background, one might expect that human males would not invest in their infants, but the picture is more complex than that.

COOPERATIVE BREEDING MODEL

The cooperative breeding model has been developed by Sarah Hrdy (e.g., 2008, 2009). This model suggests that during the Pleistocene period, the era before the development of farming 10,000 years ago, a human infant needed the attention of a number of individuals in order to survive. Hrdy refers to these nongenetic parents as *alloparents*. With the assistance of other caregivers, human mothers could have additional children without having to increase the period of time between each child. This model helps to explain the paradox that a human mother is able to produce children at short intervals even through these infants are costly to maintain in that there is a long period of development required. The assistance from alloparents may have allowed humans to migrate, as was seen in the exodus from Africa into Asia and Europe. One byproduct of infants having additional support would be an increase in their ability to note who would take care of them as well as note the intentions of others. This type of parenting over an extended period of time is not seen in other primates. Based on Hamilton's rule, one would expect the most involved alloparents to be genetically related.

SPECIFIC CAREGIVERS

Before I describe specific individuals known to function as parents and alloparents, let's look at questions of gender roles in infant care. The question of the roles of human men and women in taking care of their children has brought forth comment from scientists, the legal profession, and social activists, to name a few. The answers given have varied. A common approach has been based on gender equality. This view suggests that men and women should contribute equally, although equally may be defined in a variety of ways including in terms of time, resources, commitment, closeness, and so forth. Legal views have sought to determine what is good for the family as a unit and the infant's well-being. These and other approaches have sought to describe what "ought" to be. Evolutionary psychologists have focused more on the question of what "is" in terms of propensities to act in certain ways and what adaptations in the past have led us to these various styles of investment in parenting. It is only through a clear understanding of the data and knowledge of the evolutionary pressures that a society is able to make informed social policy.

Fathers

When comparing the human male to males of other mammals, a different picture of care emerges. In fact, some have even considered the behavior of the human father to be a scientific riddle to be solved (Geary, 2008). The human male interacts with, and provides resources to, his children to a greater extent than other mammals. One benefit of this attention is physical well-being. In a variety of studies, physical well-being has been shown to increase when the human father is present (Geary, 2000). This is true in present-day hunter-gatherer societies as well as industrial societies, although socioeconomic status also has an important influence in industrial societies. In the traditional tribal and hunter-gatherer groups, the father is often present because much of his time is spent in camp. In fact, anthropological studies have shown that fathers in hunter-gatherer societies actually spend more time with their children than those in more modern Western societies, although Western fathers have doubled the amount of time they spend with their children over the last 40 to 50 years (see Hrdy, 2009). It has been suggested that the presence of the father increases social and emotional well-being by teaching the children the nature of play and competitiveness. Females who have a warm relationship with their father tend to experience menarche later than girls with an emotionally distant father or one who is absent. One factor associated with male parental investment in humans is the quality of the marital relationship. Men in satisfying relationships show higher levels of parental investment. An interesting interaction in terms of a father's parental investment is what has come to be called *female laterality*. When female marital infidelity is frequent, men invest in their sister's, rather than their wife's children. Other studies have also shown that stepchildren are much less likely to receive resources, such as money for college, than genetic children (see Salmon, 2005 for an overview). Of course, as with all forms of parental investment, this is consistent with Hamilton's original formula in terms of effort spent. In light of mammalian reproduction patterns, one extraordinary feature of human parental care is men's parenting. This may also be related to human patterns of teaching children, which some scientists assume is unique to humans.

Mothers

Although human fathers give attention to their children, human mothers provide the majority of support and care to their children. This relationship is found in all cultures around the world (see Bjorklund & Pellegrini, 2002 for an overview). An important part of the mother-infant relationship is attachment, which I discussed in Chapter 6. Other studies have also shown that early physical contact has implications for emotional development throughout a child's life. Childhood experiences in the family have also been shown to have an impact on later attitudes and behaviors (see Bereczkei, 2007 for an overview). As we have seen throughout this book, children appear ready to take in a large variety of information from their environment, including language and family rules. Given the historical resources that mothers have given to their children, it is surprising that psychology has not paid more attention to this relationship (Daly, Salmon, & Wilson, 1997).

Grandparents and the Grandmother Hypothesis

The grandmother hypothesis was presented in response to the question of what advantage is conferred by human females not having the ability to bear children approximately halfway through their life (Hawkes et al., 1998; see Peccei, 2001 and Hawkes, 2003 for a review). This situation seems unusual because females of most species continue reproduction until death. The most common idea, as suggested by Williams and also Hamilton, relates to inclusive fitness. Basically, the grandmother hypothesis suggests that menopause and the resulting end of producing offspring evolved as a means of increasing the survival odds of children related to an older woman. That is to say, if a grandmother can help take care of her daughter's children and increase the likelihood of their survival, this would be an advantage. Related to this is the idea that were the grandmother to continue having children herself, these children would be at greater risk because infants of older-age women are more likely to die or have other complications. The grandmother hypothesis brings together four distinctive features of human life histories (Hawkes, 2003):

1. longevity,
2. late maturity,
3. midlife menopause,
4. early weaning.

Early weaning may be followed by another offspring before the prior human infant can actually feed himself. Overall, the grandmother hypothesis is a means of explaining one factor that led to these four conditions evolving. Some have even suggested that this is an important factor that gave humans an advantage over other homo species and has enabled us to survive. Indeed, a variety of studies show that the presence of a grandmother increases the survival odds of an offspring.

KIN RELATIONSHIPS DETERMINE HOW WE REASON

Of course, we can't do research that systematically varies life and death situations, but we can examine situations where this happened naturally.

We can also simulate these situations, which a number of researchers have done (see Burnstein, 2005 for an overview). For example, in one study individuals were asked their willingness to help in either a high-cost or low-cost scenario (Bornstein & Ben-Yossef, 1994). In the first scenario, a relative was asleep in a burning house and would die unless something was done. The second scenario suggested that the relative had forgotten something while shopping and asked whether the participant would be willing to be late to a meeting in order to help the relative. Further, the characteristics of the relative in the scenarios were varied in terms of age, sex, health, and degree of kinship. As would be predicted, no matter what the situation, individuals are more willing to help a close relative than a distant one. In terms of gender, female relatives were more favored than male relatives by participants of both sexes. In terms of age, there was a U-shaped function, with the very young and the very old receiving the most help. The authors also reported that there was an interaction of helping and health. That is to say, in a life and death situation, individuals were more likely to help someone in good health, but in the everyday situation, they were more likely to help someone in poor health. What this study shows is that individuals have a calculus in which they make decisions related to helping their kin.

If our decision-making processes are related to our evolutionary history, then one possible distinction would be group size. That is to say, until recently humans have never lived in communities of more than a few hundred individuals, and most kin relationships are fairly small. Thus, we might make decisions using group size as an important variable. Wang and his colleagues (1995) studied this possibility. They begin with a cognitive phenomenon referred to as the *framing effect,* in which tasks show a nonlogical reversal depending on how they are worded. Below is one example.

Imagine 600 people are infected by a fatal disease. There are two medical procedures that can be used. If procedure A is used, 200 people will be saved for certain. If procedure B is used, there is a one-third probability of saving all 600 people and a two-thirds probability that none will be saved.

Which one would you choose? Most people given this choice will choose procedure A, which is a sure thing. Now let's look at another alternative.

Imagine 600 people are infected by a fatal disease. There are two medical procedures that can be used. If procedure A is used, 400 people will die for certain. If procedure B is used, there is a one-third probability that none will die and a two-thirds probability that all 600 people will die.

What would you do in this case? Most people will choose procedure B. The general way of describing these decisions is that under positive framing, individuals are risk averse, but under negative framing, they are risk seeking.

Wang and his colleagues asked individuals to solve one of the above problems for groups of 6,000, 600, 60, or 6 people (see Wang, 1996, 2002). With groups of 6,000 or 600, the individuals in the study responded in the same way as found in a variety of cognitive research studies. They chose certainty under positive framing and risk under negative framing. However, with a group size of 60 or 6, the probabilistic risk procedure was chosen by 70% of the people, whether the task was presented in a positive or negative manner. Further, if the individuals were told that the 6 individuals were kin, the number choosing risk increased to more than 90% (see Figure 10.2). This research shows that we make decisions differently when we are considering kin as opposed to strangers. This work also supports the idea that our evolutionary history favors making decisions related to our historical group size of fewer than 200. Decisions involving larger numbers appear to use a different set of considerations.

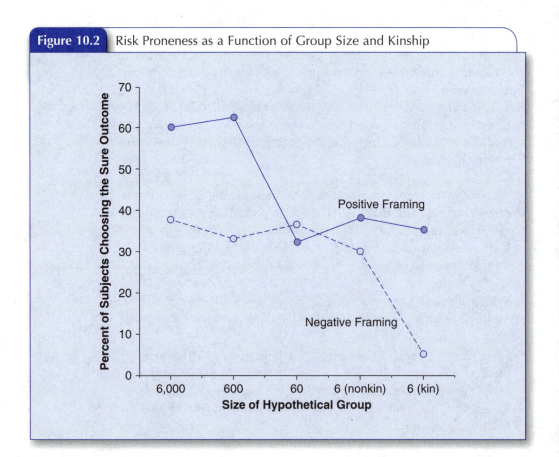

| **Figure 10.2** | Risk Proneness as a Function of Group Size and Kinship |

CONFLICT IN THE FAMILY

Robert Trivers (1974) addressed the question of parent and offspring conflict. At its heart, this considers the situation in which a parent and his offspring, who shares 50% of his genes, are both seeking to optimize their resources. Most of the time the interests of both overlap, and they engage in behaviors that each desires. However, this is not always the case. One clear example is that of weaning, in which the mother may wish to wean the child before the child wants to be weaned. The mother may wish to use her resources for other activities, such as her own interests or her other children. Of course, the basic idea of parent-offspring conflict can be extended to any kin as well as describe issues of sibling conflict. A sibling can benefit if it is able to direct resources toward itself. The manner in which siblings seek resources for themselves is an important question in itself.

VIOLENCE IN THE FAMILY

It has been suggested that other than the police or military, the human family and the human home are the most violent social settings in human society (Straus & Gelles, 1986). Is this really the case, and if so, does it follow the overall decision rules suggested by Hamilton in terms of inclusive fitness? Hamilton was previously discussed in terms of altruism, that is, who you would help. However, this type of thinking should also give us some perspective in answering the opposite question. That is, who would you not help or even hurt? In order to answer this question, Daly and Wilson (1998, see also Daly, 1988) reviewed the literature related to homicide risk and kin relations (see also Salmon, 2005). They first noted that family homicide consists primarily of spousal homicide and that this rate is higher than homicide involving children. Spousal homicide is usually men killing women, although this is not always the case. Second, they reported that the homicide rate for people living in the same household, but not genetically related, was greater than that for genetically related individuals. It was actually 11 times as great in one study. They further noted that this was not just the result of spousal homicide—roommates and boarders showed similar results. Third, they reported that in cases where parents were involved in killing their child, stepfathers were implicated in clearly half the cases. In one particular study involving the town of Hamilton, Ontario in Canada, the risk of a preschool-age child being killed was 40 to 100 times higher for stepchildren than for children living with two genetic parents. Overall, these data suggest that a human is less likely to display violence toward someone who is genetically related to them than those who are not (see Figures 10.3 through 10.7).

Figure 10.3 The ratio of the risk of being killed by a person *in loco parentis* to the victim in a stepparent-plus-natural-parent home over the risk in a two natural-parent home, in relation to the child's age. Canada, 1974–1983.

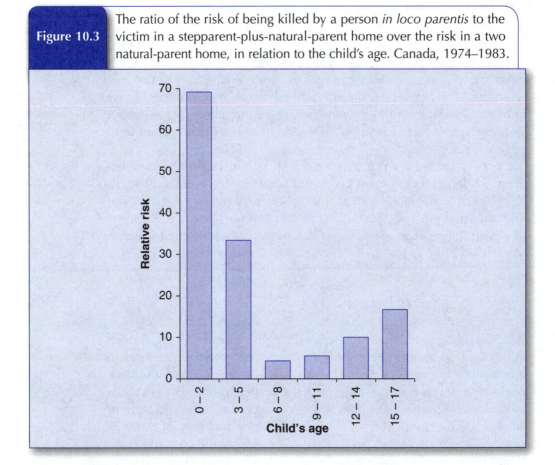

Figure 10.4 The ratio of child abuse risk in a stepparent-plus-natural-parent home over the risk in a two natural-parent home, in relation to the child's age. (a) United States, 1976. (b) Hamilton, Ontario, 1983.

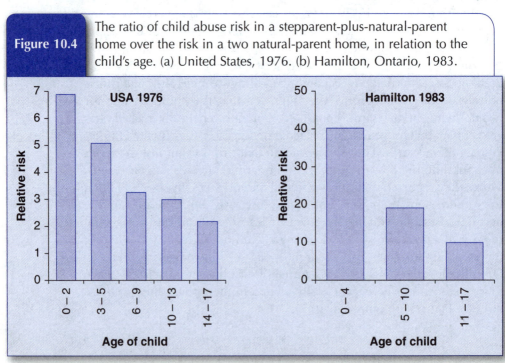

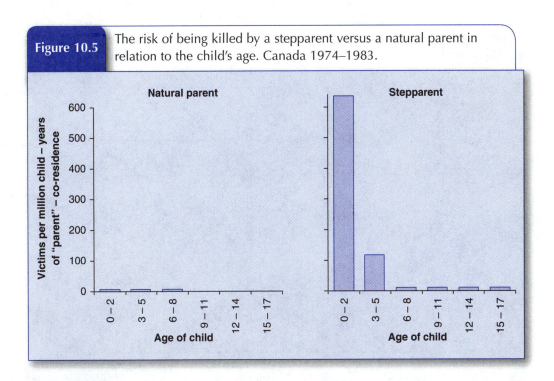

Figure 10.5 The risk of being killed by a stepparent versus a natural parent in relation to the child's age. Canada 1974–1983.

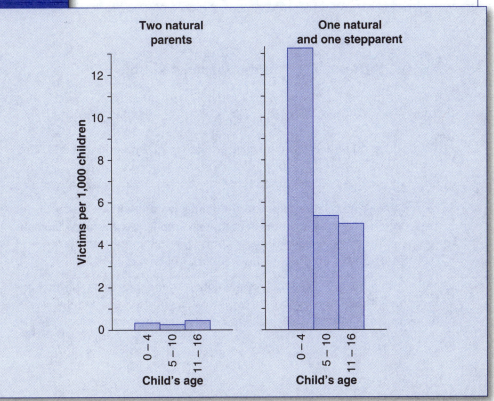

Figure 10.6 Per capita rates of child abuse cases known to children's aid societies and reported to a provincial registry. Hamilton, Ontario, Canada, 1983. (Modified from Daly & Wilson, 1985.)

| Figure 10.7 | A child's risk of homicide at the hands of mother versus father as a function of the child's age. Canada 1974–1983. |

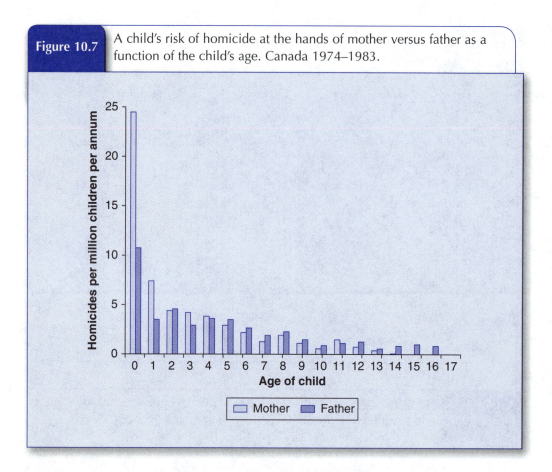

Universal Features of Human Kinship

After reviewing the literature on human kinship, Daly, Salmon, and Wilson (1997, p. 281) suggest 13 universal principles:

1. **Ego-centered kindred terminologies are universal.** Around the world, family relationships are described in relation to a particular individual. If you say "my mother," you are describing only one person in the entire world.

2. **Parent-offspring relationships are the fundamental building blocks of this ego-centered structure, so the terminology implies a genealogy.** Humans describe their family relationships in terms of offspring. You say "my brother" to refer to another individual who was born from your mother.

3. **All kinship systems include terminological (and practical) distinctions according to sex.** Throughout the world, all languages make family distinctions in terms of gender. Daughters are distinguished from sons and husbands from wives.

4. **All kinship systems include terminological (and practical) distinctions according to generation.** Likewise, daughters are distinguished from mothers and sons from fathers.

5. **Kin relations are universally understood to be arrayed along a dimension of closeness.** There is an expectation that kin relations reflect a closeness that is not expected in non-kin relationships, and degree of relationship parallels global expressions of closeness.

6. **This dimension of the characteristic closeness of kinship categories is always negatively correlated with the characteristic number of genealogical links defining them.** The degree of genetic relationship parallels the expectation of closeness.

7. **There is everywhere a strong positive correlation between the average or characteristic of kinship categories and the levels of solidarity and cooperation among those so related.** This points out that brothers, for example, cooperate more than cousins and are willing to tolerate inequalities that would be considered exploitative in a friendship. Humans universally turn to kin in times of need and are less likely to harm genetic kin when the data are controlled for proximity and frequency of contact.

8. **In all societies, persons related by marriage are deemed to be in a sort of quasi-kinship relationship.** This suggests that in all cultures the act of marriage moves their relationship into one more like kin. Languages reflect this with such terms as "brother-in-law," and so forth.

9. **In all societies, people are motivated to inquire how strangers and new acquaintances might be genealogically linked to people they already know and feel that they have acquired useful social information when such links are uncovered.** This suggests that humans seek to know who is related to whom and by what degree.

10. **In all societies, certain people make it their business to know genealogies and to educate others, especially their relatives, about exactly how they are related to one another.** Although humans in general seek to know about genealogy, there is universal support for certain individuals to be experts.

11. **In all societies, one's beliefs about one's genealogical links are core components of the phenomenology of self.** Who I am is strongly related to who my relatives are. The idea of tribe is also related to one's core identity. This is possibly reflected in adoptive children wanting to know their original parents at some point in their life.

(Continued)

(Continued)

12. **In all societies, some kinship terms incorporate more than one genealogical relationship, but people are nowhere oblivious to the distinctions that terminology obscures or ignores.** One example of this is when a man or woman with children remarries and refers to the new partner as "your dad" or "your mom."

13. **In all societies, kinship terms are extended further still, being deployed figuratively rather than literally, for evocative and propagandistic purposes.** Even though many cultures use such phrases as "He is my brother," humans within that culture can easily distinguish what is expected of that person and what is not.

SUMMARY

The long period of childhood experienced by humans, with its extensive social relationships, means that humans may be the only species to live in multi-male and multi-female groups with complex coalitions and extensive parental care. Kinship and altruism are two aspects of this situation. Based on Hamilton's work, Kurland and Gaulin suggest seven outcomes that we would expect to see. An important question is how we determine who we are related to. Three principles are genealogical distance, social rank, and group membership. Parental investment theory and the cooperative breeding model are important. There are a variety of caregivers including mothers, fathers, and grandparents. Research has examined conflict and violence in the family.

STUDY RESOURCES

Review Questions

1. What is Hamilton's rule? How does it help us understand altruism, inclusive fitness, and kin selection theory within the evolutionary perspective?

2. List the seven predicted outcomes that Kurland and Gaulin developed as an extension of Hamilton's approach that genetic relatedness is an important factor in determining both positive and negative relationships.

3. How do I know who I am related to? How is our brain able to categorize individuals in terms of their relatedness to us? How is it able to compute the costs and benefits of interacting with these individuals? What are the differences between males and females in these abilities?

4. Is there a structure for kin relationships similar to the grammatical rules we have for language? If so, is it based on local cultural factors or on universal evolutionary factors?

5. What is parental investment theory? What are its tradeoffs from an evolutionary perspective? List some different styles of parental investment found across species.

6. Parental investment is not just for mothers any more. What are the primary characteristics of each of the following in terms of parental investment: alloparents, fathers, mothers, grandparents?

7. What is the grandmother hypothesis and what evolutionary advantage does it provide?

8. Kin relationships determine how we reason. What evidence is presented in this chapter to support that statement?

9. We have seen that kin and family relationships play an important role in altruism through the concept of inclusive fitness. If that's true, how can we understand conflict and violence in the family—who would you not help or even hurt?

10. What are the 13 universal features of human kinship proposed by Daly, Salmon, and Wilson?

For Further Reading

Hrdy, S. (1999). *Mother nature.* New York: Pantheon Books.
Hrdy, S. (2009). *Mothers and others.* Cambridge, MA: Harvard University Press.

Key Terms and Concepts

- Kinship and altruism
- How do we determine relationships
- Structure of relationships
  - Parental investment theory
  - Cooperative breeding model
  - Specific caregivers
    - Fathers
    - Mothers
    - Grandparents and the grandmother hypothesis
  - Kin relationships determine how we reason
  - Conflict in the family
  - Violence in the family
- Universal features of human kinship

SAGE Study Site

Visit the study site at **www.sagepub.com/ray** for chapter-specific study resources.

Social Relations   11

Humans are social creatures. There has never been a time in history when humans have lived alone. Of course, a given individual here and there has gone off on his or her own, but as a species, neither males nor females are solitary. From the earliest times as hunter-gatherers, we have lived in social groups that gave the environmental impetus that shaped our skills and abilities to this today. For example, as humans, we are quick to make judgments of other individuals. Our brain focuses on perceptual qualities related to the appearance and behavior of others. We not only make appraisals of appearance, but also of intention. We are able to make quick estimates of someone's intentions and prepare to respond appropriately.

From an evolutionary standpoint, Lorenz (1970) has reminded us that the environment of every species includes a social system. Certain tasks were required from earliest human history. One important task, as we have seen in previous chapters, is decrypting information from another's face. As we have seen, we can identify emotions in someone's face without problem, unless, of course, if it is upside down as we saw in Chapter 1. We have also found it important to know the intentions of other people: Are they going to help us or use us? We have come to understand that certain types of processing are given priority over other types. Things that represent a danger are processed faster and receive a high priority of action. This has led to a distinction between implicit and explicit processes in social cognition (see Frith & Frith, 2008 for an overview).

Implicit processes are fast, largely automatic, and usually occur with little awareness. We meet someone new and immediately have a feeling of whether we like this person or not. In the next chapter, I will present you with some moral dilemmas; for example, if you could save only one person in a burning building, would it be a baby or an 85-year-old man? Most people answer these types of questions quickly without consciously thinking. However, some social considerations are more explicit, and we use mental effort to come up with a solution. What we pay attention to is clearly part of evolutionary history. Equally a part of this history are the aspects of our culture we incorporate into our worldview. Like children's ability to efficiently absorb the language around them, as humans we absorb the social norms of our culture, and the ability to use this effectively is an advantage (Simon, 1990b).

In this chapter, I emphasize social relationships, such as cooperation and competition, which have been an important focus of evolutionary psychology. It is clear that a variety of abilities and development trajectories of humans support a high level of social interaction for an extended period of time. Humans have the ability to use language with ease, which fosters social interactions. Some researchers see language and social cognition as closely linked (see Fitch, Huber, & Bugnyar, 2010 for an overview). That is to say, language is acquired in a social context and, in turn, this social context allows for the development of social cognition on both a local level and in larger cultural contexts. As noted, we are particularly sensitive to emotional cues, which deepen social interactions. Also, as discussed in terms of developmental processes, humans can infer the intentions and behaviors of others from limited information. Human infants, children, and adolescents remain dependent in a variety of ways that encourage social interactions. Not only do we enjoy and seek social contact, but the denial of this contact leads to pain. For example, using fMRI, it has been shown that the same areas of the brain that are active during physical pain are also active when people experience being socially excluded (Eisenberger, Lieberman, & Williams, 2003). This type of research helps us to understand the manner in which these processes may have evolved. It also helps us to discover which of our social processes are domain-specific and which are parts of general processing facilities. As you will recall, domain-specific brain mechanisms are activated only in certain types of processes, whereas general processes are activated in a variety of situations.

What it means to be social and how we evaluate our social relationships will be important questions to consider in this chapter. Many things we do as humans are done in the service of social interactions. As infants we not only pay attention to others, we are eager to connect with them, to imitate them with both sounds and movements. This continues throughout our lives. We can note the manner in which humans have taken modern technology, such as the cell phone or the Internet, and placed it in the service of social interactions. Text messaging is one clear example of using technology to keep connected socially.

The evolutionary perspective helps to understand the manner in which blogs on the Internet or staying in touch on cell phones or even eBay are consistent with our ancestral past. Does trading on eBay make you smarter? The answer is yes, as every social exchange has the potential to increase your awareness of others and their intentions. What is necessary when you trade on eBay or buy stocks or a used car? You need to know quickly what something is worth. By making trades, you quickly learn that some people are out to deceive you and others to help you. Thus, you not only need to make cognitive and emotional decisions as to what something is worth, and what it is worth to you, you also need to consider the nature of the social relationship you have entered into. These types of considerations have been with us since our earliest human history. From this perspective, social processes may have influenced the evolution of our higher level cognitive abilities, including mathematics. The pressures of living in close social groups are seen by some evolutionary psychologists to have driven the increasing complexity of social facilitation and also to have increased our cognitive abilities (Adolphs, 2003, 2010; Dunbar, 2003). In fact, across nonhuman primate species, brain size is related to the size of the social group each individual interacts with. In a complex fashion, this increase in cognitive abilities and social facilitation in humans lies at the basis of our development of culture. I will discuss culture in more detail in Chapter 15.

The Social Brain Hypothesis

The social brain hypothesis was developed in the 1980s to suggest that primates, including humans, differed from nonprimates principally in the complexity of their social skills. Prior to this, it was generally assumed that human intellectual abilities were the result of the skills required for hunting and other tool use. In reviewing the literature, Dunbar (2003) points out that at least five separate measures of social complexity have been shown to correlate with neocortex volume in primates (see Figure 11.1):

1. social group size,

2. grooming clique size,

3. extent to which social skills are used in male mating strategies,

4. frequency of tactical deception,

5. frequency of social play.

Particular areas of the brain show higher correlations to social group size: the frontal lobes, the part of the amygdala that has direct neural connections to the frontal lobe, and the temporal lobe. As you remember, the frontal lobes are used in planning and executive function, and the amygdala is involved in emotional processing. Studies have shown that in both humans and nonhuman primates, amygdala volume is related to the size and complexity of social networks. The temporal lobe is involved in sensory processing, including face recognition. I will come back to brain involvement in social interactions shortly. As you can see in Figure 11.1, the mean social group size of humans is 150. This is roughly the number

Figure 11.1 Mean Social Group Size for a Variety of Primates Including Humans vs. The Size of the Neocortex Divided by Size of the Rest of the Brain

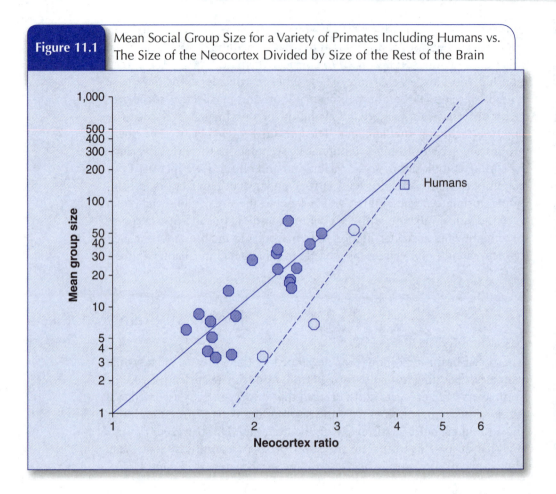

of people you have a personal connection with—or the number of people you could ask a favor and expect it to be granted.

Thus far, we have considered a variety of examples of how the brain pays particular attention to certain types of stimuli. This is especially true in self-preservation. We find ourselves quicker to respond to potential danger than almost any other type of information. We also pay attention to a variety of sexual signals. As we will see in this chapter, we are also more sensitive to certain types of social information than to others. It is one task of evolutionary psychology to identify these social domains and articulate the underlying rules that are involved in our interactions with each other.

Social Relations

One theory related to the domains of social living in humans is Alan Fiske's (1992). Fiske begins with the assumption that humans are fundamentally sociable and that societies throughout the world can be understood in regard to how people organize their relations with other people. That is to say, as humans we seek to relate to others in some basic and fundamental ways. These fundamental ways of relating have basic rules, in the same way that language has a grammar to guide its construction. Based on a variety of research studies, Fiske suggests that everyday life can be seen as involving four basic social-cognitive processes:

1. **Communal sharing** is the type of relationship in which a community treats material objects as belonging to all. This type of relationship is seen with family members who share holiday meals or religious groups in which everyone is seen as equal. In these relationships, people take what they need and contribute as they can. As with a party punch bowl or a shared meal, there are no predefined allotted shares and no one monitors who takes what. Decisions in these types of groups are often made by consensus, with collective discussions but no vote on the matter at hand. Historically, this type of relationship has been seen with people genetically related, either in terms of family or culture. Those outside of the kin are seen as the Other or "they" and collectively viewed as different from "we." This type of relationship is often seen at sporting events where everyone for our team is viewed as one, of us and everyone for the other team is viewed as not one of us or "the enemy." As we discussed in Chapter 1, Hamilton's idea of kin selection or inclusive fitness suggests an evolutionary basis for communal sharing. That is to say, we treat others as equivalent to ourselves if they share similar genetic material. Communal sharing is not limited to humans and is seen in other species. What is not known at this time is whether genetic similarity is a limiting factor in humans or we have evolved to have a more global psychological mechanism with greater flexibility than is seen in other species.

2. **Authority ranking** is the type of relationship in which people are ranked according to some linear hierarchy. The military presents the prototypical example of this type of relationship. Everyone has a rank and thus a place in the hierarchy. Typically, in authority ranking relationships, individuals higher in the rankings have more prestige, prerogatives, and privileges than those lower down the hierarchy. In describing the hierarchy, spatial metaphors are often used, with individuals being described as "higher up" or "lower down." As in the case of tribal leaders or kings and queens, those in charge make decisions or rulings that influence those lower in the hierarchy. However, in many cultures, those higher up are also expected to take care of, and look out for, others lower down. In other species, such as nonhuman primates, dominance hierarchies

are a common feature of the community. What is intriguing in hierarchical social relationships is that one's rank in the hierarchy also influences a variety of other processes. For example, as male mandrills move up and down the dominance hierarchy, there is also a change in sexual characteristics. With a rise in rank, there is a rise in testicular volume, an increase in circulating testosterone, and increased reddening of the sexual skins. With a fall in rank, the opposite is seen. Psychologically, Gur and Sackeim (1979) reported that humans expand their view of themselves when they are succeeding and shrink their view of themselves when they are failing.

3. **Equality matching** can be thought of as "tit-for-tat" relationships. That is, you do something for me, and I do something for you. The basic idea is that each person is entitled to an equal amount in the relationship. "If you invite me to your house, then I should invite you to mine" would be one common manifestation of this type of relationship. Part of the calculus of this type of relationship is determining what is equal to what. "If you give me a ride to school every day, then I should buy your gas" could be one typical outcome. Competitive sports display this type of relationship in that each team has a turn to score, equal opportunity in terms of equal team size, and other structures that place neither team at a disadvantage. Thus, the structure of equality matching relationships is balancing. Later in this chapter, I will review a variety of studies examining tit-for-tat relationships.

4. **Market pricing** attempts to determine through ratios and rates the value of some aspect of the relationship. For example, if I own 75% of a business, then I would expect to receive 75% of the profits. The most common examples of market pricing relationships involve money and typically require a detailed analysis of the situation. This type of relationship is often referred to as *cost-benefit analysis.* For example, if you decide to buy a car with payments of $540 a month, then you determine that you will not have enough money to go to Europe for a vacation. As we will see later in this chapter, a new field has developed, referred to as *behavioral economics,* which studies the manner in which humans calculate market pricing relationships. Overall, these types of relationships have not been reported in other species.

One aspect of these four types of relationships, according to Fiske (1992), is that they correspond closely to the four scales of measurement described by Stevens (1946, 1951, 1957; see also Ray, 2012). These four scales of measurement are nominal, ordinal, interval, and ratio scales. *Nominal scales* utilize the property of identity and refer to categories. Examples such as telephone numbers or diagnostic categories point to differences of kind and not of degree. You can't say, for example, that someone with the number 12 on his sports jersey is twice as good as someone with the number 6. Likewise, communal sharing relationships involve categories but do not distinguish differences within the relationships. *Ordinal scales* involve both identity and magnitude. Class standing and a horse's placing in a race are examples of this type of scale. Knowing that a horse finishes first or second or third will tell you its rank in the hierarchy, but nothing about the differences between ranks. Likewise, authority ranking relationships give one a linear understanding of where one falls on a hierarchy. *Interval scales*, as illustrated by temperature measurements, represent equal intervals. Unlike telephone numbers or class standing, there is a precise relationship between 55° and 56° Fahrenheit. Likewise, equality matching relationships allow for mathematical reasoning in the form of "I did you two favors and you did me one, so you owe me one." Finally, *ratio scales* are similar to interval scales, but they have an absolute zero point, which allows for extended mathematical calculations. For example, market pricing relationships can be considered in terms of ratios and rates. Overall, what this suggests is that the four types of social relationships are different and utilize different types of reasoning, which can be related to properties of measurement. Although not discussed by Fiske, one implication of this way of thinking is that the evolution of mathematical abilities in humans may have had its origin in different types of social relationships. This is evidenced by the fact that quality matching and market pricing relationships are only seen in humans.

Brain Processes Involved in Social Relations

In his textbook of social psychology first published in 1908, William McDougall (1908) suggested that an evolutionary psychology should underlie the study of social processes. However, this suggestion was largely ignored in the social psychology of the later 20th century. Currently, researchers are beginning to connect social psychology with neuroscience, especially in terms of brain function, which has enabled them to ask questions related to evolutionary psychology (Adolphs, 2003; Johnson, 2005). As we discovered earlier, our present-day emotionality has largely evolved within a social context. Many of the brain structures involved in the processing of emotion are also important for social behavior. Brain structures involved in social interactions can be organized in terms of three processes (Adolphs, 2003; Brothers, 1990). The first process involves higher level neocortical regions that process sensory information. This is how we know what we experience through vision, hearing, touch, and so forth. Research suggests when we look at a face, we process broad categorizations related to gender and to the emotion expressed before we complete the detailed construction of the entire face and determine who we are seeing.

Second, our sensory system also helps us to predict what people will do socially, based on their physical movements. When we see a social interaction, what happens in the brain? What happens first involves the amygdala, striatum, and orbitofrontal cortex. The amygdala, as you remember, is involved in processing the emotional significance of an event. I told you about the amygdala's activation while viewing a fearful face. Activation also takes place if a person looks untrustworthy. This determination occurs independent of gender, race, eye gaze, or emotionality expressed. For example, Dimoka (2010) experimentally manipulated trust and distrust characteristics of sellers on eBay by manipulating the ratings and text comments on their feedback page. The participants in the study were asked to rate trust and distrust characteristics of sellers while in an fMRI. She found different patterns of brain activation when participants viewed sellers who were trustworthy and those who were not, in comparison to neutral sellers. The amygdala was one of the areas of the brain that differentiated sellers who were trusted from those who were not. The fMRI results are shown in Figure 11.2. As you look at Figure 11.2, remember that the top series of images shows the areas of the brain that were activated when the participants viewed information about a high-trust seller compared to a neutral-trust seller. The bottom series shows a high-distrust seller compared to a neutral seller. This suggests that trust and distrust are processed by different areas of the brain.

Figure 11.2

The top series of fMRI images show the areas of the brain that were activated when the participants viewed information about a high-trust seller compared to a neutral-trust seller. The bottom series shows a high-distrust seller compared to a neutral seller.

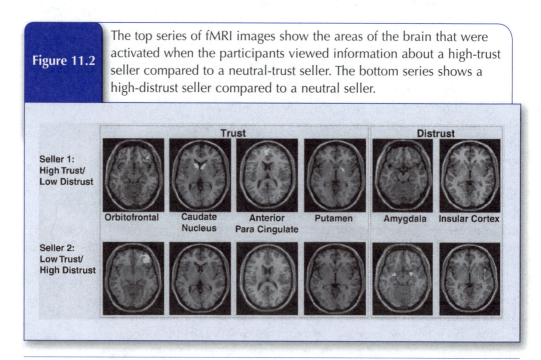

Note: This suggests that trust and distrust are processed by different areas of the brain.

Through its connections to other areas, the amygdala also can influence memory, attention, and decision making. Overall, these areas help us to know the emotional context of our perceptions and what we need to do about them.

The third process involves the higher cortical regions of the neocortex. These are the regions that let us construct an inner model of our social world. Included in this model would be some social understanding of others, their relationship with us, and the meaning of our actions for the social group. As we saw in Chapter 6, these areas are most likely associated with "theory of mind"—our ability to attribute mental states to other people. Indeed, damage to the orbitofrontal cortex does reduce our ability to detect a faux pas in a given situation. The prefrontal cortex has also been shown to be activated during humor, social-norm transgressions resulting in embarrassment, and so-called moral emotions. With damage to this area, individuals have difficulty knowing that another is being deceptive. Although there is limited research currently directed at the topic, it may turn out that we have not only evolved systems for determining the basic emotions, such as fear, joy, or anger, but also for the more socially related ones, such as guilt, shame, embarrassment, jealousy, and pride. The prefrontal cortex appears to be involved in various aspects of social relationships, social cooperation, moral behavior, and social aggression. Overall, Adolphs (2003) describes a three-part brain system in which sensory information is processed in the sensory cortex, its emotional value determined in structures such as the amygdala, and the social implications determined by the prefrontal cortex. Of course, given the rich interconnected networks of the brain, it probably does not work in quite this simple a linear manner. Figure 11.3 shows the major areas of the brain involved in social processes.

Imitation Learning and Mirror Neurons

What happens in your brain when you see someone wave or clap her hands? One intriguing answer to this question comes from research that suggests the neurons in your brain fire as if you had performed the same actions. These neurons are called *mirror neurons*. Mirror neurons were first discovered in monkeys. They were shown to fire both when the monkey performs a particular action and when it observes another monkey, or even human, perform that action. Mirror neurons are in an area of the brain referred to as *F5*, which is a part of the premotor cortex. Some researchers suggest that this brain process may be the basis of imitation learning as well as other human social phenomena, including language (Rizzolatti & Craighero, 2004; Rizzolatti & Fogassi, 2007).

To summarize, mirror neurons discharge when an organism makes a particular type of movement. These neurons were first studied in monkeys,

Figure 11.3 Important regions of the brain involved in social cognition including the medial prefrontal cortex (mPFC) and temporoparietal junction (TPj), which are involved in thinking about mental states. The posterior superior temporal sulcus (pSTS) is involved in facial processing. Other regions include the amygdala, anterior cingulate cortex (ACC), and the anterior insula (AI), which are also involved with social cognition.

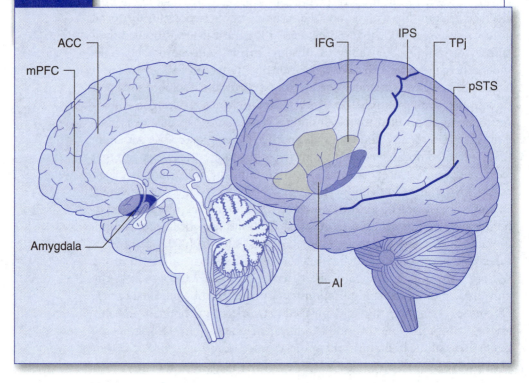

and shown to discharge when the primate made a goal-related motor act such as grasping, holding, and manipulating objects. It should be noted that these particular neurons do not fire when simple movements are made. Further, it was observed in monkeys that mirror neurons also discharge when the monkey watches another monkey, or a human, perform a grasping action. The basic idea is that these neurons help primates, including humans, to understand the actions of others. How does this happen? Rizzolatti and Craighero (2004) suggest the following. Each time an individual sees an action by another, the neurons that would be involved in that action are activated. This, in turn, creates a motor representation of the observed action. That is, we see an action and consider how we might make it ourselves, although we don't do this consciously. In essence, the observer's brain turns a visual image into a motor plan. This process can explain one aspect of how imitation learning can take place. That is, by seeing something, I also understand how I can do it. Even more important for Rizzolatti and Fogassi (2007) is that such a network gives the organism an advantage because this network helps the organism understand not only "what" others are doing, but also "why" they are doing it. If my brain works similarly to another's brain, I have some understanding of what he or she is experiencing. Overall, the mirror neuron system offers a basis of imitation and understanding of another's action. In the same way that individual neurons in the visual system fire to specific features of a stimulus and these, in turn, become integrated into a larger perception, the mirror neuron system can be seen as part of a larger cortical network involved in person perception. This, in turn, could form the basis of interpersonal relationships and more complex social interactions.

Social Interactions in Nonhuman Primates

Primates other than humans are also social beings. They show achievement motivations in their attempts to secure mates and be part of the social hierarchy. In this process, they must be calculating in terms of probable losses and gains, as well as possess the cognitive abilities required to remember dominance hierarchies, know who is having what type of relationship with whom, and use this information for their own advantage (de Waal, 2002; Ghazanfar & Santos, 2004; Byrne & Bates, 2011). As noted, such requirements associated with social processes may have been one important driving force in the evolution of intelligence. Beginning in the 1960s, a variety of researchers, including Jane Goodall, began to observe chimpanzees in their natural environments. Chimps live in groups ranging from 20 to 120 individuals. Their society has been referred to as *fission-fusion*. This refers to the fact that individuals spend time alone as well as join and leave subgroups of the larger group (Pusey, 2001). How chimps spend their time is related to whether they are male or female. Females tend to spend more time alone with their dependent offspring in geographical areas that overlap, but are different from, those of other females. Males tend to spend less time alone (about 18% of their time). The overall geographical territory of the group is defended by the males, although not necessarily in a group or cooperative manner. Hunting by both males and females does appear to be a social activity, although 90% of the hunting is performed by male chimpanzees. Because the size of the territory is related to food availability and, indirectly, health, protecting territory increases the reproductive rates of the resident females. As they grow, almost all male chimpanzees remain in the group in which they were born. The females, on the other hand, leave the community to go to others. As would be expected, DNA relationships are closer between males than females in a community. Males in the community form a dominance hierarchy in which there is clearly one alpha male, with the other males placed along the hierarchy. Compared with other species, such as the baboon, male chimpanzees are friendlier to each other and more apt to use cooperative alliances to maintain positions along the hierarchy. In fact, the alpha male has been seen to give meat to his allies and withhold it from his rivals. Some researchers view the meat as a primitive form of currency, which may give us clues to the roots of human economic behavior. Males will groom one another frequently and also display a variety of techniques for social appeasement, reassurance, and reconciliation. More recent research has begun to examine female hierarchies and their effect on reproductive success. These results show that high-ranking females tend to live longer, their infants survive better, and their daughters mature as much as four years earlier than those of low-ranking females (Pusey, Williams, & Goodall, 1997). This is seen to be related to both the fact that high-ranking females are able to occupy areas with better food and the observation that they will kill newborn infants of low-ranking females.

Understanding Another Primate's World

An intriguing question asks whether chimps reflect any of the characteristics we discussed earlier in terms of theory of mind (see Byrne, 2001; Byrne & Bates, 2010 for an overview). A variety of observations suggest that chimps are able to understand, to some extent, what another chimp might know. One situation used with laboratory animals is to place two monkeys who have a close relationship, such as friends or a mother and daughter, together. Then something, or someone, that they would find dangerous is introduced. In one condition, one of the monkeys could see a "predator," but the other could not. In a second condition, both could see the "predator." The question asked was, In which condition did the chimp give an alarm call? If the chimp gave the alarm call in both conditions, then he or she would be reacting to the predator alone. However, if the chimp gave the alarm call only when the other could not see the predator, then the chimp would be assumed to have some understanding of the other's perspective and realize that the other chimp does not know about the danger. It was found that chimps, but not all other primates, gave the alarm call only when the other could not see the "predator." This suggests that chimps can understand the visual perspective of another chimp.

Further evidence in terms of understanding relationships is found in vervet monkey mothers who not only respond to a recorded cry of their own infant, but if played a call of another infant, look toward that infant's actual mother. When vervet monkeys hear calls of other monkeys, their reaction depends on whether the other monkey is higher in rank or lower in rank. They give a more agitated reaction to more dominant monkeys and largely ignore the calls of subordinates.

Evidence also suggests that primates are able to recognize dominance relationships that extend beyond themselves and can recognize relationships between third parties.

A related question relates to deception. A variety of observations in the wild suggest that monkeys use deception to get what they desire. For example, one female gorilla living in a small group with a dominant male would restrict her sexual encounters to lower-ranking males in the group. She was seen to "get left behind" so that she was out of the dominant male's sight. She would then choose one of the lower-ranking males and socialize or copulate with him. What adds to the deception is that she would not emit the normal copulation calls, but would remain quiet. In other situations, young baboons have been seen to "cry wolf" in order to get food. In experimental situations, chimps can recognize themselves in a mirror. Chimps, but not all monkeys, will touch their foreheads if they see a red dot on it in the mirror (Gallup, 1970). Self-recognition in the mirror is shown by chimps, bonobos, orangutans, and some gorillas.

Cooperation—Competition

Understanding cooperation was initially a daunting task for evolutionary psychology. If we just pay attention to natural selection and sexual selection, where does cooperation fit in? One answer to this question was found during the 20th century as scientists began to examine a variety of species. From this examination, it became clear that a variety of species displayed cooperation. This was seen in bees that collect pollen for the whole hive, mole rats that build elaborate tunnels for the whole community, meerkats that risk their lives to guard a common nest, and vampire bats that will feed other bats when there is need. There are even cases of altruism: whales and dolphins have been seen to help members of another species (Trivers, 1985). With the extensive research on bees, ants, and other species, it became clear that, in addition to self-preservation and sexuality, there were also instinctual programs for social processes. The task was then to understand the details of these programs.

STRONG AND WEAK ALTRUISM

If someone stops you on campus and asks you to help them do something, what do you do? "Depends upon what I am asked to do" is probably your first answer. If it really does not cost you anything, then you will most likely say "yes." This is what Donald Campbell (1983) called **weak altruism**. If it costs you something, he referred to it as **strong altruism**. For example, a honeybee worker will sting an intruder to save the group, even if this results in death for the bee. How do we calculate whether helping is going to cost us something or not? One answer is, Does it benefit our family? If the person who asks you is related to you, then you are more likely to help, even if it costs you something.

To reiterate, as you read in Chapter 1, the theory of kin selection was developed by William Hamilton in the 1960s. The basic theory suggests that we help relatives because it increases the chances that genes similar to our own will be passed on. The outcome of the theory is that the more related we are genetically, the more we will help. As noted, altruistic behavior is seen across all species. Technically, altruism was a problem for Darwin, which Hamilton helped to solve. Darwin was concerned that altruistic behavior could not be explained by natural selection because altruism did not appear to aid a given organism's fitness. Hamilton saw that altruism could evolve if it aided the organism's genetic kin to pass on their genes. Included in these genes would be the mechanism for altruism among kin. Hamilton suggests that by acting altruistically, the organism ensures that genetic material more similar to its own is passed on. That is to say, if a behavior helps to ensure the passing on of genes similar to one's own, then this behavior would be favored. Hamilton's answer to the question of altruism came to be called *kin selection* or *inclusive fitness*. Inclusive fitness as a property can be measured by considering the reproductive success of the individual plus the effects of an individual's actions on the reproductive success of one's relatives.

What about unrelated individuals? Do we help them? We help unrelated individuals if we can reasonably expect them to help us in turn. This is the theory of **reciprocal altruism**, which was developed by Robert Trivers in the 1970s. The basic idea is that our own fitness, in an evolutionary sense, can be increased if we can expect others to help us sometime in the future. Trivers saw this tendency growing out of our evolutionary past, in that humans lived in small groups and it was possible to note who helped whom or not. Those who helped were helped in return and thus had a greater chance of surviving and passing on the genes related to these processes. Because one condition of this theory is that the individual is able to recognize and remember who had helped in the past, reciprocal altruism should be limited to species with these abilities. Primates, including humans, would fit this qualification for weak altruism. Strong altruism, or kin selection relationships, on the other hand, can be found across a wide variety of species.

Before examining some of the research related to cooperation, it is important for you to realize that a distinction is made not only between strong and weak altruism but also between altruism and cooperation. The traditional definition of altruism, as defined by E. O. Wilson (1975), for example, included the idea that altruistic behavior needs to be self-destructive for the person performing the task. Cooperation, as defined by Cosmides and Tooby (1992), for example, does not require any costs to the person performing the task, only that the behavior benefits another. Thus, as you read the literature, you should note whether costs to the person are incurred.

USING GAMES TO STUDY COOPERATION

How can we study our tendencies to cooperate with another? One answer to this question is games. One of the best studied games is known as *the prisoners' dilemma*. Imagine two individuals are imprisoned and accused of committing some crime together. The police hold the two suspects in separate cells. In their dealings with the prisoners, the police attempt to have each individual give evidence about the other's involvement in the crime. The police say, "If you implicate the other person, you not only can go free, but you will receive a reward." In this case, the other individual would go to jail. If both individuals implicated each other, then both would go to jail, but the sentence would not be as great as if one had refused to testify. However, if neither person implicates the other, both will go free. What would you do if you were one of these individuals? Of course, if you could talk to your acquaintance, then you would agree to cooperate with each other and not talk to the police so both of you would go free. However, you are not allowed to have this conversation. What to do? If you just said, "I will take care of myself," you would implicate the other, and perhaps you would receive a reward and go free. Traditionally, some economists would say this is the rational thing to do because it potentially maximizes gain for a given individual. However, reciprocal altruism, in which you cooperate, would enable you both to gain. The game can be diagrammed as shown in Table 11.1.

If you were to play the game only once, it would be difficult to know what to do. However, in real life, our dealings are not just about one-time encounters, but repeated interactions with people we know. By analogy, it is also assumed that social dealings that humans have had with one

Table 11.1   The Prisoners' Dilemma Diagram

		Prisoner B	
		Cooperation *It was neither of us*	Defection *It was her*
Prisoner A	Cooperation *It was neither of us*	Reward for mutual cooperation	Sucker's payoff and temptation to defect
	Defection *It was her*	Temptation to defect (reward for turning the other person in) and sucker's payoff	Punishment for mutual defection

Source: Adapted from Axelrod and Hamilton (1981).

another over evolutionary time were with others we knew by acquaintance. Thus, the most realistic way of playing the game would be to repeat it a number of times. We might assume that playing the game a large number of times in the laboratory would model the situation that humans evolved over our evolutionary time. That is to say, there would have been a variety of situations in which we needed to know whether to cooperate with another or not. The prisoners' dilemma models these situations.

Using the prisoners' dilemma game, Axelrod and his colleagues (see Axelrod, 1984 for an overview) looked at the evolution of cooperation. They suggested that the evolution of cooperation can be conceptualized in terms of three questions related to robustness, stability, and initial viability. The *question of robustness* asks what type of cooperative strategy can best survive given the wide variety of alternative strategies. The *question of stability* asks under what conditions such a strategy, after it has been established, can resist invasion by mutant strategies. And finally, the *question of initial viability* asks how cooperative strategies could come to play a role in environments that are predominantly noncooperative.

What is the best strategy for playing the prisoners' dilemma game? To help answer this question, various academics from around the world were asked to submit procedures for playing the game that could be computer-tested against each other. Although many of these were very complicated, a simple procedure worked best. The answer has been called **tit-for-tat** and was submitted by a Canadian named Anatol Rapaport. Tit-for-tat has only two rules: (1) On your first move, you should cooperate; (2) on every move after that, do what the other person did on the last trial. Embedded in this second rule is a flexibility that ensures that if the other person changes from defection to cooperation, then you will also. In terms of Axelrod and Travis's other questions, it was found that tit-for-tat is an extremely stable strategy once it is established and that it is possible for it to be started even in noncooperative environments. Trivers (1985) has restated the rules to read first, do unto others as you wish them to do unto you, but then do unto them as they have just done unto you.

Does tit-for-tat work in the real world? One answer to this question came from a place we would not expect cooperation, war. Axelrod (1984) has argued that in the trench warfare of World War I, the soldiers on each side acted as if they were playing the prisoners' dilemma game. The soldiers, who could literally see each other across the battle lines, adopted a "live and let live" strategy, which is another way of saying tit-for-tat. It was reported that soldiers shot at the other side, but purposely missed. If soldiers on one side were killed, then an equal number on the other side would be killed. In actuality, the strategy was broken only when the officers ordered raids behind the enemy lines.

Another place we might not expect cooperation is among birds. Using blue jays, Stephens, McLinn, and Stevens (2003) created a simplified version of the prisoners' dilemma game. Two blue jays were placed side by side in two separate parts of a V-shaped apparatus. A series of levers and chutes enabled a blue jay to either put a small piece of food in its own dish or a larger piece in the other's dish. If performed as a single trial event, blue jays, like humans, are more likely to take the immediate reward. To make it more than a single trial event, the food was dispensed into a transparent tray so that the bird could see food accumulate. In this study, the bird could eat the food after playing the game four times. To gain experimental control, one of the blue jays responded freely, whereas the other's response was programmed to be either all cooperative (put food in the other's dish) or all defecting (put food in its own dish). Experimentally, this was a 2×2 design in which the bird could eat the food immediately or had to wait four trials and experienced either all cooperation or all defecting. What did they find? When the other bird always defected, cooperation declined toward zero. It did not matter whether the food could be eaten on each trial or it accumulated. When the other bird always cooperated, the experimental bird showed high levels of cooperation also. However, in this situation, the cooperation was highest (between 60% and 70%) when the food was allowed to accumulate. This suggests that the timing of when one receives benefits makes a crucial difference to the level of cooperation, at least with birds. Further, the researchers noted that these birds were extremely forgiving and would continue cooperating at rates near 50% even after they had been suckered.

Indirect Reciprocity

Would you help someone you would never see again? If so, why would you? To help us understand why one person helps another, we can look at another game. This game is called *the trust game*. In the game, one of two anonymous players is given a sum of money. The player with the money has a choice: she can give the other player nothing or any percentage of the money she wishes. The other player then receives twice the amount suggested by the first player and has the opportunity to return some of the money. How much would you return, given that you would never see this person again? It turns out that more than half of the people involved returned some of the money. In order to understand the motivations to give some of the money back, researchers have modified the game so that the players are no longer anonymous or, in other cases, play a series of these games. With these modifications, the number of individuals who will give some money back increases. This has led some researchers to suggest that reputation—that is, to be known as a charitable person, someone who will help—is a key motivation for cooperation (Nowak & Sigmund, 2004; Wedekind & Milinski, 2000).

One model based on reputation is *indirect reciprocity* (Alexander, 1987). The advantage of this model is that it helps to account for helping behavior even in situations in which individuals may not see each other again. Underlying the model is still the desire to increase one's own fitness. That is, if I act in such a way as to be seen as charitable, another person will, at some time in the future, be more likely to help me out, which will thus increase my evolutionary fitness. If indeed this is the case, then these experimental games help us see a link between action as means of increasing fitness and manipulating our image of ourselves. We will return to images and attitudes later. Now, let's look at the opposite of being charitable, that is, being a cheater.

Cheaters

What if someone offers to paint your neighbor's house for a low price—that would be a benefit to your neighbor. However, while he is painting, he is also stealing items from inside the house. What do you do? Let's go back to playing games for an answer. We know that people will give others money just to be known as cooperative, but will they also spend some of their money to punish those who cheat? The answer is yes. This came to be called *altruistic punishment*. In one study, Fehr and Gächter (2002) tested this using a public goods game. They created groups of four individuals. Each member of the group received 20 money units, of which they could contribute between nothing and 20 to a group project. Whatever a given individual did not contribute, he could keep. Thus, if you gave nothing, you would have 20 money units for yourself. However, if you contributed 1 money unit, then you and everyone else in the group would receive 4 money units. Let's consider for moment what would happen if no one gave anything. Then, everyone would keep their 20 money units. However, if everyone gave everything (20 money units), then each person could earn more than he or she began with because each money unit was multiplied by four. In the game, everyone is free to give what he or she wishes, and everyone must make his or her decision at the same time. What this sets up is the possibility that someone who gave nothing could receive money from those who did contribute. In one condition of the game, once the individuals knew what the others in their group had contributed, they had the opportunity to punish them by taking away some of their money. However, in order to take away 3 money units from the other person, you would also have to give up 1 money unit of your own. Thus, it costs you to punish another. What would you do?

Of the 240 individuals who played the game six different times, more than 84% punished at least once, and 34.3% punished more than five times in the six games. There was also a clear pattern in the way punishment was carried out. It was generally enacted by those who had contributed more than the average amount of money units on those who had contributed less than the average. Also, the less someone gave, the more he or she was punished. These results are shown in Figure 11.4.

How did the ability to punish another or not influence how much an individual contributed? As can be seen in Figure 11.5 on page 326, if the person was not able to punish those who contributed less, then his own level of giving decreased over the six trials. However, if punishment was available, then the level of giving increased over the six trials. It did not matter whether a participant in the experiment started with the ability to give punishments or not.

How do we understand these results from an evolutionary perspective? Fehr and Gächter (2002) suggest that when we see others getting something for free, this arouses negative emotions in us and results in the desire to punish the free rider. Given that contributions were actually larger over time when participants had punishment as an option, this suggests punishment may actually play a role in the development of cooperation.

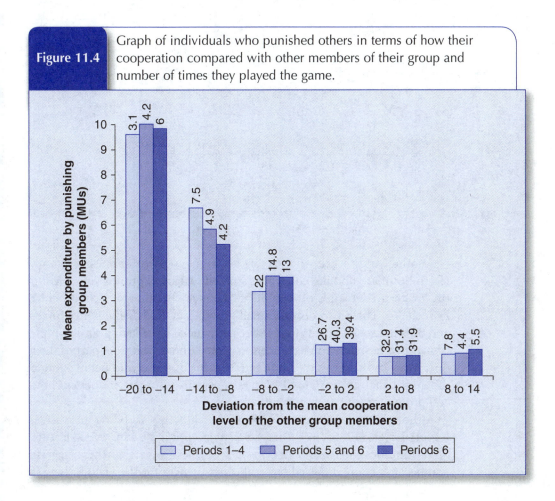

Figure 11.4 Graph of individuals who punished others in terms of how their cooperation compared with other members of their group and number of times they played the game.

Figure 11.5 Graph showing trend of mean cooperation over periods with punishment possibility coming first (a) or last (b).

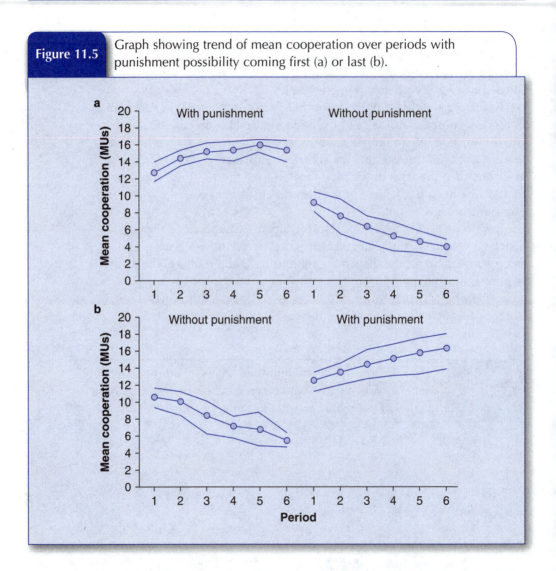

Another study asked what factors determine who you punish and how. Helen Bernhard and her colleagues studied two small groups who lived in the Western Highlands of Papua New Guinea (Bernhard, Fischbacher, & Fehr, 2006). These two distinct small groups lack traditional police forces and thus use social norms to regulate their social life. Playing similar punishment games, individuals tended to protect those who were part of their own social group and give more punishment to those who belonged to a different tribal group. Thus, your relationship to others influences how you protect, as well as punish, others.

Although we don't usually think of cheating as being pervasive, Robert Trivers (1985, 1991) suggests that deception is a widespread feature of communication within many social species. Trivers further suggests that because being deceived has real consequences for the victim, there is evolutionary pressure to develop better means of detecting deception. He further suggests that over evolutionary time, selection to spot deception may also have improved cognitive capacity, including simple ability to count. Clearly, we pay closer attention to someone if we are not sure of the transaction that is taking place. We also assume that deceiving another requires a greater amount of effort than just engaging in normal social interaction. For this reason, deception may evoke changes in the voice, facial expressions, and body movements of the person trying to deceive another.

Self-Deception

We can deceive others; can we also deceive ourselves? What are the mechanisms involved in self-deception? Without a doubt our sensory system can be fooled, as illustrated by visual illusions. In earlier chapters, we even saw situations, such as with blindsight or split brain patients, in which individuals claimed they saw nothing, yet the information influenced their decisions outside their awareness. Gur and Sackeim (1979) suggested that self-deception can be understood in three ways. First, true and false information is simultaneously stored in a single person. Second, the true information is processed out of awareness, whereas the false information is described consciously. And third, self-deception is motivated in relation to other individuals. They performed an experiment to demonstrate these three characteristics. They began with the fact that normal individuals respond on a physiological level to hearing their own voice. Galvanic skin responses (GSR) are stronger in response to your own voice than to the voices of others. In the experiment, Gur and Sackeim asked people to rate whether voices they heard were their own or others'. What made this study interesting was that before the individuals rated the voices, they were given an "intelligence" test, which was manipulated such that some people did well and others poorly. Although both groups showed similar GSR responses to their own voice, conscious recognition was worse in the group that did poorly on the test. One important implication of the Gur and Sackeim study is that humans can process information on a variety of levels, and this processing can be influenced by environmental events. Why might this be?

To answer this question, we can look to the work of Robert Trivers (1985; von Hippel & Trivers, 2011). He suggests that self-deception is hiding truth from the conscious mind. What advantage is there to deceiving oneself? The answer is that by deceiving oneself, it is also easier to deceive others. As I pointed out, deception is common in plants and animals in terms of camouflage and mimicry. Some animals are able to inflate themselves to appear larger, or produce a low, loud sound to suggest they are larger than they really are. With the advent of language in humans, deception became possible to an even greater extent. However, as we saw with the work of Paul Ekman and others, humans also give subtle clues when they are being deceptive. These clues include forced smiles, which used different muscles than involuntary smiles, eye movements, sweaty palms, and changes in voice intonation. If an individual did not realize that he or she was being deceptive, then it is possible that the message given to another would lack these subtle clues of deception and would appear more believable. Thus, if you want to deceive someone else, it helps to deceive yourself also. In this sense, there would have been an evolutionary advantage in developing self-deception, as strange as it seems to the conscious mind.

Brain Activity in Playing Games

You may think that playing games is not part of the real world, but our brain doesn't know this. Recent research has begun to examine how our brains respond when we are playing the prisoners' dilemma or ultimatum game. In the ultimatum game, two players have the possibility to split a sum of money. One player offers an amount to be split between the two of them. The other player can either accept or reject the offer. If the offer is accepted, the money is split as suggested. However, if the offer is rejected, neither receives any money. What would you do? If you were trying to maximize your gain, you would offer as little as possible. Likewise, if given a choice, you might assume that the other person would take whatever was offered because otherwise, he or she would receive nothing. This is what economists claim is the rational thing to do. What do you think people really do? It turns out when you look at a wide variety of studies in various countries, the most frequent offer made is around 50% of the money. If the offer is much lower than this, say around 20% of the total, it has about a 50% chance of being rejected. Why is it rejected? Because the offer is believed to be unfair. It is suggested that this is an emotional response in which the person feels angry and seeks to punish the other person because of the low offer. In one brain imaging study (Sanfey, Rilling, Aronson, Nystrom, & Choen, 2003), fair (split 50% of the money) and unfair offers (split 10% or 20% of the money) resulted in differential brain activation. Unfair offers, in comparison to fair offers, showed greater activation of the bilateral anterior insula, dorsolateral prefrontal cortex, and the anterior cingulate cortex. Remember that these are brain areas involved in the processing of emotional information. Further, that these findings were the result of a human social reaction was demonstrated by the fact that the insula showed greater activation when the participants thought they were playing against real people as opposed to a computer. Overall, these data suggest that emotionality lies at the basis of our social interactions.

SUMMARY

Humans have always lived in social relationships. Some researchers suggest this has driven brain evolution. There exist a variety of ways in which social relations are structured. Four of these, according to Fiske, are communal sharing, authority ranking, equality matching, and market pricing. Adolphs suggests that three brain processes are involved in social behavior. The first process involves higher level neocortical regions in the processing of sensory information. The second suggests that the sensory system helps to predict what people will do socially, based on their physical movements. The third process involves the higher cortical regions of the neocortex. Adolphs describes a three-part brain system in which sensory information is processed in the sensory cortex, its emotional value determined in structures such as the amygdala, and the social implications determined by the prefrontal cortex. Mirror neurons may lie at the basis of imitation and empathy. A distinction is made between weak and strong altruism. Researchers have used games to examine cooperation, reciprocity, as well as determine cheaters.

STUDY RESOURCES

Review Questions

1. What is the social brain hypothesis and to which groups is it applied? List the five measures of social complexity proposed by Dunbar.

2. Describe Fiske's four fundamental types of social relationships and provide an example of each. What is their relationship to social reasoning and mathematical calculation?

3. Adolphs describes a three-part brain system in which sensory information is processed in the sensory cortex, its emotional value determined in structures such as the amygdala, and the social implications determined by the prefrontal cortex. Give an example of how each of these systems is involved in social relations.

4. What are mirror neurons and what evolutionary advantage do they provide?

5. This chapter proposes that primates other than humans are also social beings. Do you agree? What evidence would you cite to support your answer?

6. Understanding cooperation was initially a daunting task for evolutionary psychology. If we just pay attention to natural selection and sexual selection, where does cooperation fit in?

7. What are the differences among weak altruism, strong altruism, reciprocal altruism, and cooperation?

8. How does Hamilton's concept of kin selection or inclusive fitness help us understand the role of altruism?

9. What is the prisoners' dilemma? What types of situations is it used to research? What is the best strategy for playing the game?

10. What other games are used to research different social situations? What have we learned from them from an evolutionary perspective?

11. How do Gur and Sackheim suggest that we can understand self-deception? What evolutionary advantage in developing self-deception does Trivers suggest?

For Further Reading

Dugatkin, L. (2006). *The altruism equation: Seven scientists search for the origins of goodness.* Princeton, NJ: Princeton University Press.

Ridley, M. (1996). *The origins of virtue: Human instincts and the evolution of cooperation.* New York: Penguin Books.

Key Terms and Concepts

- The social brain hypothesis
- Social relations
- Brain processes involved in social relations
- Imitation learning and mirror neurons
- Social interactions in nonhuman primates
- Understanding another primate's world
- Cooperation – competition
  - o Strong and weak altruism
  - o Using games to study cooperation
- Indirect reciprocity
- Cheaters
- Self-deception
- Brain activity in playing games

SAGE Study Site

Visit the study site at **www.sagepub.com/ray** for chapter-specific study resources.

Glossary Terms

- Authority ranking
- Communal sharing
- Equality matching
- Market pricing
- Reciprocal altruism
- Strong altruism
- Tit-for-tat
- Weak altruism

Making Social Decisions

Social Contract Algorithms and Hazard Management Systems

In Chapter 1, I introduced you to the Wason selection task. The original task was developed by Peter Wason in the 1960s in order to study how humans perform logical operations. One version of the task includes four cards, as shown below. Each card has a square with or without the word "think" on one side and a triangle with or without the word "think" on the other. The question asks which of the cards would you have to turn over to determine whether every card that has a "think" square on one side has a triangle with "think" on the other.

Square with think	Triangle with think	Square without think	Triangle without think

If you are like most people, you chose the first and the last card. You may be in good company, but you are wrong. The correct answer is the first and second card. For most people, this is a difficult exercise in propositional logic. The same problem can be presented in a less abstract way, as you saw in Chapter 1. Let's repeat the task to remind ourselves. The task is as follows:

> Part of your new job for the City of Cambridge is to study the demographics of transportation. You read a report on the habits of Cambridge residents that says, **"If a person goes into Boston, then that person takes the subway."**

The cards below have information about four Cambridge residents. Each card represents one person. One side of a card tells where a person went, and the other side of the card tells how that person got there. Indicate only those card(s) you definitely need to turn over **to see whether any of these people violated the subway rule.**

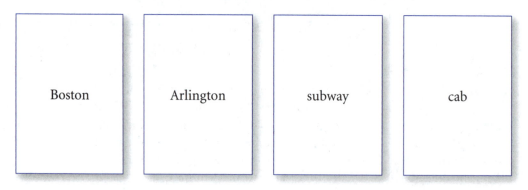

From a logical point of view, the rule has been violated whenever someone goes to Boston without taking the subway. Hence the logically correct answer is to turn over the *Boston* card (to see whether this person took the subway) and the *cab* card (to see whether the person taking the cab went to Boston). More generally, for a rule of the form *If P then Q*, one should turn over the cards that represent the values *P* and *not-Q*. In the previous example using the word "think", the "think square" would be *P* and the "think triangle" would be *not-Q*.

The Wason selection task has been used extensively by Leda Cosmides, John Tooby and their colleagues to study social exchange. *Social exchange* is cooperation for mutual benefit. Social exchange is generally of the form, "if I do this, then you will give me a benefit" or "if you give me a benefit, then I will do this." Examples include economic trades, reciprocal gift giving, and helping with the expectation that someday the favor will be returned. If these types of social exchange have been important throughout our evolutionary history, then we should be sensitive to those who accept benefits without fulfilling their side of the exchange. These individuals have come to be called "cheaters." It is assumed that we have evolved a cognitive mechanism that is sensitive to cheating. This has been referred to as the "cheater detection module" (Cosmides, 1989). Cheater detection is aimed at individuals who break the rules of a social interaction.

In Chapter 1, you saw the Wason task reworded in a social exchange manner. The social exchange problem would be worded, "If you are to eat those cookies, then you must first fix your bed." This problem would be presented as follows:

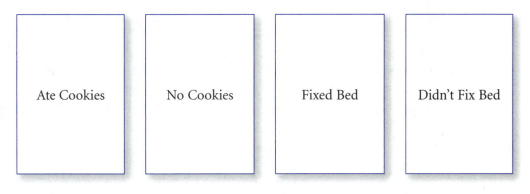

In studies of this type, around 75% of participants get the correct answer, which is the cards that say "ate cookies" and "didn't fix bed." As noted in Chapter 1, individuals got the social exchange problem correct three times more often than when the problems was presented in a logic format. This suggests that human brains evolved to value social interactions more than logical ones.

Another version of the task is as follows:

In its crackdown against drunk drivers, Massachusetts law enforcement officials are revoking liquor licenses left and right. You are a bouncer in a Boston bar, and you'll lose your job unless you enforce the following law: **"If a person is drinking beer, then he must be more than 20 years old."**

The cards below have information about four people sitting at a table in your bar. Each card represents one person. One side of a card tells what a person is drinking and the other side of the card tells that person's age. Indicate only those card(s) you definitely need to turn over to see whether any of these people are breaking the law.

One criticism of the cheater detector module interpretation has to do with familiarity. That is to say, being 21 years old to be able to drink is a rule all college students are familiar with, whereas some of the other non-social tasks may be less familiar. To answer this, Leda Cosmides (1989) asked participants to imagine being part of a Polynesian island culture with strict sexual mores, including no sex between unmarried individuals. For background, you should know that when a man is married in this culture, he receives a facial tattoo. There is also a root—cassava root—that makes a man irresistible to women. Given that this root works so well, many bachelors are tempted to cheat. Assume each card represents one of four men. Again, the task is to determine which cards you need to turn over in order to determine who is cheating. The proposition for you to determine would be "If a man eats a cassava root, then he must have a tattoo on his face."

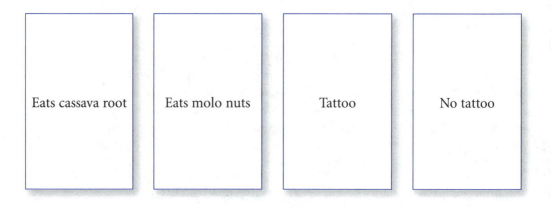

This social problem was paired with a non-social problem. Imagine you are an anthropologist studying a hunter-gatherer group that likes to eat the meat of a small antelope called a duiker and uses ostrich eggshells to carry water. It turns out that duiker meat and ostrich eggshells are often found together. The proposition to determine was "If you eat duiker meat, then you have an ostrich eggshell."

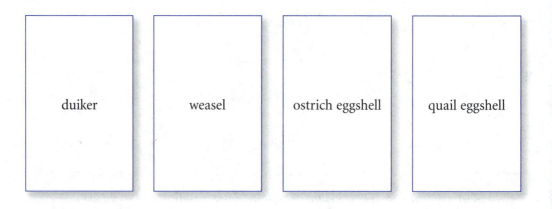

As in the previous experiments, about 75% of the participants were able to correctly solve the social problem, whereas only about 21% could solve the non-social version. These types of studies have been taken to support the idea of socially sensitive logical processing in humans that is more accurate than traditional Aristotelian logic alone.

To make the point that humans have evolved mechanisms for understanding social exchange, it is important to show similar processes across a variety of cultures. Indeed, Wason-type tasks have shown similar results in North America, Europe, and Asia. In all of these areas, people were better able to solve social exchange problems than non-social exchange problems. However, these tests were all performed in economically developed literate cultures. What would happen if isolated non-Western cultures were presented with social exchange tasks? To answer this question, Lawrence Suglyama, John Tooby, and Leda Cosmides (2002) presented a graphic version of the Wason task to an isolated rural group of inhabitants of the Ecuadorian Amazon, the Shiwiar. They found that the Shiwiar performed similarly to Harvard undergraduates in their ability to detect violations of social requirements, that is, to detect cheaters. This adds support to the idea that, over evolutionary time, humans have evolved a sensitivity to social exchange relationships, and this sensitivity is universal among all humans.

To summarize, using a computational metaphor, it has been suggested the human brain contains an expert system designed for reasoning about social exchange (see Cosmides & Tooby, 1992; Fiddick, Cosmides & Tooby, 2000 for an overview). Social exchange is cooperation for mutual benefit. Social exchange is generally of the form, "if I do this, then you will give me a benefit" or "if you give me a benefit, then I will do this." Some examples include economic trades, reciprocal gift-giving and helping with the expectation that some day the favor will be returned. If these types of social exchange have been important over our evolutionary history, then we should be sensitive to those who accept benefits without fulfilling their side of the exchange. These individuals have come to be called "cheaters." It is assumed that we have evolved a cognitive mechanism that is sensitive to cheating. This has been referred to as the "cheater detection module" (Cosmides & Tooby, 1992). Cheater detection is aimed at individuals who break the rules of a social interaction. Support for this position is our ability to perform the Wason selection task more accurately when social exchange is involved than when non–social exchange examples are used. Needless to say, there has been some debate as to whether an actual part of our brain is dedicated to cheater detection. Further, factors that influence the results on the Wason selection task have not been completely detected (Atran, 2001; Buller, 2005; Fodor, 2000; Sperber, Cara, & Girotto, 1995). Thus far, Cosmides, Tooby and their colleagues have been able to show the domain-specific nature of human reasoning when related to social interactions, although the debate is not completely resolved.

Social Exchange and the Brain

An intriguing question would be whether the brain responds differently to social exchange problems than to more logical ones. What areas of the brain would you think would be involved? One answer to this question has come from patients who have various forms of damage to the brain. In a variety of studies, patients with frontal lobe lesions perform poorly on social exchange Wason tasks as compared to individuals without brain damage. If you are just asked to solve the logical problem, then you would see activation of the prefrontal areas, particularly on the left side of the brain. One patient, called R. M., had a bicycle accident when he was 25 years old that resulted in damage to the limbic system, including the orbitofrontal cortex and anterior temporal cortex (Stone, Cosmides, Tooby, Kroll, & Knight, 2002). The temporal damage was actually severe enough to disconnect the amygdala on both the left and right sides. His performance on three types of Wason problems was compared to a group of individuals without brain damage. The first type of task was a non-social exchange descriptive task. One example would be "if a person had arthritis, then that person must be over 40." The second task was of a social exchange nature: "If you go canoeing on the lake, then you have to have a clean bunk house." The third task was of a protective social nature. An example would be "if you work with toxic chemicals, then you have to wear a safety mask." As expected, everyone did worse on the logical descriptive tasks compared to the social ones. In terms of the social tasks, the individuals without brain damage did equally well on both the social exchange tasks and the social protection tasks, which is consistent with a number of other studies. However, R. M. did worse on the social exchange task but equally well as others on the social protection task. This suggests that particular areas of the brain are involved specifically in detecting people who break social rules. To further determine what these areas are, Canessa and his colleagues (2005) asked individuals to solve Wason-type problems while brain imaging measurements were taken. As with other studies, they found left hemisphere activation while participants solved the descriptive logical task. The regions involved were areas of the brain important for word tasks, for integrating information, and for looking at the larger picture while solving a smaller task. Overall the left hemisphere activation is consistent with solving logical problems. However, during the social exchange task, they saw left hemisphere activation and also saw activity in the right hemisphere of the brain. Clearly, our brain is designed to put more resources into problems that involve social relations.

The Logic of Cooperation

The logic of cooperation is based on two ideas. The first is that our evolutionary social history resulted in our interacting with a limited number of individuals with whom we would interact on a variety of levels. Some estimates suggest the average size of these groupings was between 100 and 150. The second idea is that, given time, we can become sensitive, on a variety of levels, to identifying individuals who would cooperate with us or cheat us. This would allow us to have preferences in whom we interacted with. Of course, the ability to identify such individuals would not only have implications in the social realm, but also in terms of self-preservation and sexuality, including the nurturance of children.

As a thought experiment, let's ask what would happen if the two ideas just discussed were not true. In order to do this, imagine an environment in which there were an equal number of cooperators and defectors in prisoners' dilemma terms (Frank, 2004). Further, imagine that you could tell the two groups apart immediately. If your interactions with various members of these two groups were accidental and of a one-time nature, what would happen? As we know from the prisoners' dilemma game, the single-time strategy would benefit the defectors. The defectors would end up controlling the resources, and the cooperators would die out. If, on the other hand, we could identify the defectors on first sight, then cooperators would only deal with each other and defectors would die out. We might also imagine that if defectors were to die out, then those abilities such as detecting cheaters would also die out as they would no longer give certain individuals any advantage. Neither cooperators nor defectors have died out. Thus, we might assume that the defector and cooperator aspects of individual behaviors have remained in a form of equilibrium or dynamic tension, which can be called forth depending on environmental conditions.

Implications in Social Psychology and Economics

Why study economics from an evolutionary perspective? One important answer is that these types of choices lie at the basis of a variety of decisions we make, including how we save, how we use credit cards and debt, our choice of jobs, our eating habits, and even marriage decisions (Fehr, 2002; Zak, 2004). Before we look at these types of decisions in humans, let's look at economic processes in other species. Other species, such as pigeons, make economic-type decisions all the time, especially those involving time. Pigeons, for example, prefer a smaller reward arriving sooner than a larger one arriving later. In one experiment, the pigeon could press one key which would immediately give the animal 2 seconds of access to a full grain hopper. If it pressed another key, the pigeon could have 4 seconds of access to the grain, although it would have to wait 4 seconds for the hopper to open. Almost all of the animals chose the key that gave immediate access. Before you decide that pigeons just can't wait, let's look at another experiment. In this experiment, the outcome was the same but a 28-second wait was added to each of the choices. In this case, the pigeons chose the longer wait for the greater reward. By pushing the reward time out into the future, the pigeon optimized the gain. Humans, as we shall see, also prefer smaller, immediate rewards to larger, later ones. We will choose to spend a small amount of money today rather than save it and have a larger amount later. However, like the pigeons, if you ask workers whether they would be willing to have a larger part of future salary raises go toward their retirement fund, they will perform the necessary action for this to happen.

Historically, the field of economics has viewed humans as rational in their economic behaviors. The rational person and his or her self-interest has been the traditional model of study. That is, it has been assumed that in any transaction you would only be concerned with your self-interest. However, a variety of studies over the past 50 years have shown that rationality is only one concern on the part of a human being. As we just discussed, humans also care about cooperation. Even when others are not involved, humans are not totally rational in their economic dealings. For example, would you drive an extra 10 miles if you could get an item for $5 that was selling for $15 just down the road? Most people will say yes, they would. What if you could get a $310 item for $300? In this case, most humans would say no, they would not drive the extra distance. Why the difference when in each case the saving is $10—the same saving for the same effort? It would be rational to use the same amount of effort for the same amount of saving. If indeed humans, or other animals for that matter, display a nonrational set of rules when entering economic transitions, this would suggest that factors other than traditional logic come into play. An important question is what is the nature of these factors? As evolutionary psychologists, we would assume that economic transactions reflect exchange processes that have been with humans since our early history and that our history reflects greater certainty for immediate gains than for delayed rewards.

BOUNDED RATIONALITY

Herbert Simon (1956) was a researcher who was interested in how humans make decisions. For this work, he won the Nobel Prize for Economics. **Bounded rationality** was the term he chose to reflect a process lying between the rational and the psychological (Simon, 1956). Before this, a variety of fields assumed that humans made their decisions in a rational way without the constraints of time, knowledge, or limited cognitive processes. Simon suggested that one could learn about human decision making by noting how the environment in which these decisions must be made can allow for simplifications in adaptive decision making. His metaphor was that of a pair of scissors; one blade is the environment and the other is the cognitive limitations of humans. By this he meant that humans with limited time, knowledge, and other resources can rely on the environment to aid in decision making. With this conceptualization, a variety of researchers began to study how humans make decisions. The procedures for arriving at a decision are called **heuristics**.

HEURISTICS

A *heuristic* is a set of rules that help us to understand how people make decisions. The term became known in psychology through the work of Newell and Simon (1972), who saw it as a way to avoid complex algorithms. It was defined by Simon (1990b) as "methods for arriving at satisfactory solutions with modest amounts of computation" (p. 11). This suggests that heuristics help humans perform a task with reduced effort (Shah & Oppenheimer, 2008). Although initially viewed within a cognitive domain, from an evolutionary perspective, you can see that a variety of tasks can be thought of as heuristics. Some heuristics involve decisions such as how do you determine who to help or who to save in a burning building. Most individuals will choose to save a child rather than an older person, and they make this decision quickly. Heuristics can be outside your awareness, as when you determine how to catch a baseball that is hit into the outfield. Heuristics can also be of an emotional nature, as when we see our relationships as more positive than those of others. A large number of social psychology studies have shown that there is a consistent tendency for individuals to view themselves, their world, their friends, and other aspects of themselves in an overly positive manner. Not only do we categorize whether another individual is like us (our in-group), we also determine who is not like us (our out-group). We tend to see people in our out-group in more negative terms, as less deserving, and as more responsible for any negative event in their life. If, indeed, they were able to accomplish something positive, we would call it luck. However, if you happen to be in our in-group, then the opposite attributions are made. You are responsible for your successes and situations are responsible for your failure. There are also heuristics related to effort. Do you read material if it is not going to be on the test? Herb Simon (1990a) suggests that our ancestors thrived to the extent that they were socially docile. By this he means that they were receptive to social influence. Many of the classic social psychology experiments of the 20th century demonstrated the manner in which humans would conform to the group. In terms of cognitive and emotional effort, Simon suggests it is cheaper and better to do what other people say than to figure out the way to do something on your own.

How do heuristics work? Shah and Oppenheimer (2008) suggest that all heuristics rely on one or more of five basic principles:

1. Examining fewer cues,

2. Reducing the difficulty associated with retrieving and storing cue values,

3. Simplifying the weighting principles for cues,

4. Integrating less information,

5. Examining fewer alternatives.

As various fields, such as economics and political science, have incorporated evolutionary factors in their attempts to understand human decision making, they have moved away from a traditional rational view of decision making toward a more domain-specific set of problem-solving strategies. In doing so, some common themes have become important. First, with domain-specific strategies, consistency is no longer a hallmark of successful decision making. As has been pointed out throughout this book and I will discuss in the next section, we are not consistent in our decision processes across all situations. Second, most decisions humans make are performed quickly and with limited information. When you meet someone new, what do you do? If you are like others, you immediately form an opinion of the other person. Do I like him? Will he be helpful to me? Is he being honest? Research in social psychology has shown that we form immediate impressions of other individuals and that these social categorizations, as they are called, endure well after the initial meeting (see Krebs & Denton, 1997 for an overview). In fact, these first impressions color later interactions. Third, these decisions are based on evolutionarily earlier events or base rates for particular happenings rather than ones seen in our present environment. That is, if you hear a noise late at night in your house, you may initially feel afraid although it is more likely to be something benign than something dangerous. Said in other words, you don't react in terms of actual probabilities but in terms of potential dangers. Fourth, whether a person makes a decision alone or with others influences the decision.

FRAMING

Kahneman and Tversky (1979) showed that people make economic decisions differently depending on how they are framed. In their study, identical outcomes were framed as either gains or losses. In the positive or risk-averse framing, someone is told she can receive $1500 as a sure thing or flip a coin, which would determine whether she receives $1000 or $2000. When the offer is framed this way, the majority of people choose the $1500. However, if they are offered $2000 and then told that they either give up $500 or flip a coin to see if they must give $1000 or nothing, they choose the coin toss. As you can see, the situations are exactly the same in terms of money received. Thus, humans are not basing their decisions on logical or mathematical determinations. It is a psychological decision based on the framing. Why would this be so? One possibility is that in the context of our evolutionary history of social bargaining, it would be seen as a sign of weakness to relinquish prior gains and may even invite future demands for concessions (Daly & Wilson, 2001). Another possibility is that a quick reaction does not lead to careful mathematical analysis, which results in the first framing appearing to be more certain than the second. This is illustrated by consumers who more often pick the package of meat that says 80% lean as opposed to 20% fat, even though they mean the same thing.

DECISION MAKING AND THE BRAIN

Most recently, researchers have sought to determine which brain areas are involved in making decisions related to framing. De Martino and his colleagues used a framing situation similar to that just described while participants were involved in a brain imaging study (De Martino, Kumaran, Seymour, & Dolan, 2006). In the study, participants were placed in an fMRI and informed that they had to choose between two options in relation to their money, a "sure" option and a "gamble" option. The "sure" option was framed in two ways. The amount of money received was framed either in terms of the amount of money gained (you can keep $20 out of $50 you receive) or in terms of money lost (you will lose $30 out of the $50 you receive). The "gamble" option was presented graphically. The individuals were presented with a pie chart that represented the probability of winning it all or losing it all. On a given trial, they were presented with the amount of money they had and then presented with the "gain" or "loss" framing, followed by the decision to either go for a "sure" thing or gamble in an all-or-none fashion. As with previous studies, individuals in the study were risk averse with the "gain" framing and were less likely to gamble. The participants were also more willing to gamble if the information was presented within a loss frame. Because this study was performed in a brain imaging device, it was possible to determine which brain areas were active during each type of decision. One area of the brain involved in these tasks was the amygdala, an area we discussed earlier, which is associated with personal emotional information processing. Increased activation in the amygdala was associated with being risk averse within the "gain" frame and risk seeking within the "loss" frame. These results suggested to the authors that at the basis of the framing effect is an emotional or value-related response to keeping gains and taking risks when losses are perceived. This is the traditional behavioral response. However, if the participants in the study chose to go against the traditional response and gamble with a sure thing, or not take a risk with a perceived loss, then the amygdala was silent. The area of the brain that was active was the anterior cingulate cortex (ACC), which is known to be involved in conflict detection. In other studies, the ACC was also active when a person perceived he or she had made an error. Overall, these results demonstrate that the brain is sensitive not just to the emotional implications of the frame, but also to the person's decision on how to respond. From an evolutionary perspective, the authors suggest that adding social and emotional cues to one's decision offers an advantage that goes beyond a purely rational decision.

Do you think other species also rate sure things versus gambles in the same way? In order to answer this important question, you could look at the manner in which a variety of species make similar loss and gain decisions. Animals don't use money; however, they do have other resources. Given that food is a resource, you could examine animal behavior to better understand the calculus of obtaining food. For example, seed-eating birds, as well as rats, generally adopt a risk-averse strategy in terms of foraging. However, this strategy switches to risk proneness if their caloric intake is reduced or their physiological level of substances, such as blood sugar, needed to sustain life is modified to imply starvation. This type of behavior is broadly paralleled in humans. In seeking resources, later-born children, who were historically least likely to be the ones to receive the inheritance or land, grew up to be the ones who became explorers, warriors, or migrated to another land (see Daly & Wilson, 2001 for an overview).

SOCIAL AND MORAL EMOTIONS

As researchers studied emotional processes, it became clear that there was an additional type of emotional processing that generally appeared in the context of social interactions. What happens if you say something stupid or call your current boyfriend by the name of your previous boyfriend? You feel embarrassed. Just as with basic emotions, you have physiological responses: your face turns red, you avert your eyes, you touch your face. It feels like a basic emotion. However, it is different in that it requires the presence, or the imagined presence, of another person. In this sense, embarrassment is a social emotion. The evolutionary perspective allows us to think about emotions such as fear as satisfying a self-preservation function and emotions such as embarrassment, guilt, or shame as serving a more social function. Because these social emotions also require a more developed sense of self, we would also predict that they appeared later in our evolutionary development. Let us look at these social emotions.

Embarrassment is a social emotion easily understood by lay people that has been observed in a variety of cultures (Keltner & Buswell, 1997).

In terms of understanding the situational nature of embarrassment, Iranian and Japanese children classified the causes of embarrassment in similar ways. Embarrassment is commonly reported in response to physical mishaps such as spilling something on someone, cognitive mistakes such as forgetting someone's name, loss of body control such as belching, or finding oneself the center of undesired attention as with teasing. Surprisingly, embarrassment has been less well studied by those interested in basic emotions, although Darwin did describe blushing in relation to a violation of etiquette, which he saw as a type of shame. However, patterns of embarrassment satisfy the nine requirements of a basic emotion suggested by Paul Ekman in Chapter 5. These include being automatic, of quick onset, with a specific physiology, and found across cultures. Another of his requirements was that the emotion be seen in nonhuman species. Embarrassment-like body movements, including gaze aversion, smiling, head movement, self-touching, and grooming are seen in nonhuman primates in appeasement displays, in which one individual seeks to pacify the other and keep the social bond intact. Thus, embarrassment may have had its origins in appeasement.

Embarrassment is usually short-lived with minor consequences, but other social emotions may be more long lasting. Guilt and shame are two examples. Social psychologists see these as two separate, although similar, emotions (Eisenberg, 2000). Guilt is described as an emotional state associated with other people objecting to your actions, inactions, or intentions and may be preceded by lying, cheating, stealing, infidelity, and neglecting duties (Keltner & Buswell, 1997; McCullough, Kilpatrick, Emmons, & Larson, 2001). Research suggests that individuals' shame experiences are more painful and intense than guilt experiences (Eisenberg, 2000). Shame also involves the opinion of others to a greater extent. Overall, shame appears to involve our entire concept of ourselves, whereas guilt is more distinct from the self. Guilt involves feelings of tension, remorse, and regret without involving our core identity. One distinction that has been made is that shame is associated with the desire to undo aspects of the self, whereas guilt involves the desire to undo aspects of behavior. Because guilt and shame involve transgression against the conventions of the group, they have been called *moral emotions*. Feelings of sympathy and guilt have been seen to motivate cooperative behavior and altruism (Trivers, 1971). Additionally, guilt appears to help individuals keep commitments and thus maintain relationships.

MORAL JUDGMENTS

How do you make a moral judgment? That is to say, how do you decide whether something you observe is wrong? If you watch someone hurt a helpless animal, how do you respond? If you see someone help someone who is helpless, what is the difference in your response? Where does this response come from? Is it like a preference? That is, do we have some sort of code in our heads that says helping is good? Or, perhaps, do we have an internal feeling, such as the feeling of being satisfied? The origin of moral judgment has recently become of interest to evolutionary psychologists.

How do you make a moral judgment? A variety of studies suggest that moral judgments happen quickly (see Miller, 2008 for an overview). It is a matter of an emotional or gut reaction to the situation. If asked, "Why did you make that decision?" most individuals will either say, "I don't know; it just felt right" or try to create a cognitive reason to justify the decision. There is also research to suggest that creating a feeling of disgust in a person will increase their sense of moral outrage or immorality.

Steven Pinker (2008) suggests that the nature of moral judgments is different from other types of thinking. Think of a food you dislike. Do you care whether someone else eats that food? No! We may like chocolate ice cream but would not be upset if someone else had strawberry. However, you don't say, "It is fine with me if you want to hurt someone." Thus, moral judgments are not like preferences. Pinker also suggests moral judgments are not a matter of fashion. You may think that bell-bottoms are out of style, but we don't consider it doing harm to another to go in and out of style. Pinker also makes a distinction between moral judgments and what is imprudent. We tell others not to scratch mosquito bites, but this is different from saying you should not randomly kill others.

Pinker (2008) further suggests that there are two important hallmarks of moral judgments. The first is that these judgments are felt to be universal. Someone who thinks that rape or killing is wrong does not think that this only applies to his hometown but to the entire world. In this sense, moral judgments are experienced differently from cultural ones. The second hallmark is the belief that committing immoral acts should be followed by punishment. People often say it is wrong to let someone "get away with it." Thus, according to Pinker, humans not only make moral judgments but also believe that immoral behavior should be punished.

There are a variety of ways to study moral judgment in the laboratory. Most research uses hypothetical scenarios, such as, "If you could only save one person, who would you save in a burning building, a young child or an old man?" Most everyone would say the young child, without a second thought. Another scenario is referred to as the trolley problem (Figure 12.1). In this case, you are a trolley driver. You lose your brakes and are headed for five workers on the tracks in front of you. The only way to save the lives of these workers would be for you to hit a switch on the control panel that would send the trolley down another set of tracks. If you did this, you would kill a single worker on those tracks. What would you do? Most individuals would say it was OK to kill the one person if that meant five people would be saved. This type of scenario is generally classified as *low conflict* because most individuals agree with the moral decision.

Figure 12.1 The trolley problem: Would you change the trolley's direction to kill one person rather than four persons?

Now let's consider a higher conflict situation (Figure 12.2). What if you were on a bridge above the track and you saw the runaway trolley coming. The only way you could stop the trolley would be to push a large person off the bridge in front of the trolley.

What would you do in this case? This scenario produces much less agreement that it is OK to push the man off the bridge, even though the result is the same as in the previous scenario, that is, saving the lives of five people at the cost of one.

To understand how high- and low-conflict situations involve emotional circuits in the brain, Koenigs and his colleagues (2007) presented these problems to individuals who had damage to an area of the brain involved in emotional action (Koenigs et al. 2007). The area was the ventromedial prefrontal cortex, which is an area in the front of the brain involved in

Figure 12.2 The trolley problem: Would you push a person off the bridge to save four people?

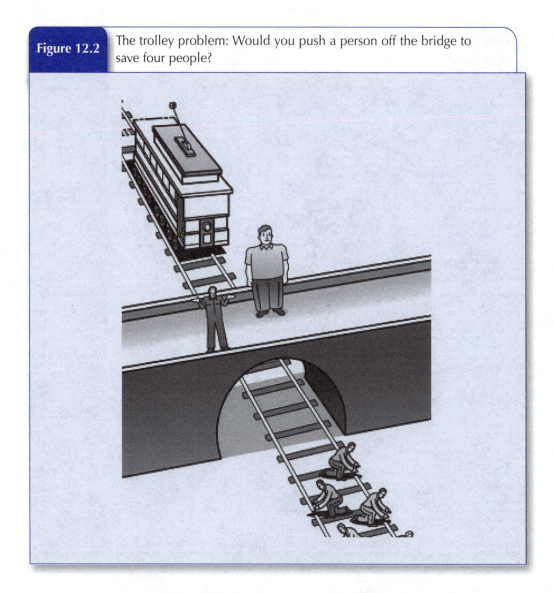

encoding the emotional value of sensory information, as well as emotional components of human actions. What these researchers found was that individuals with damage to these frontal areas of the brain were less likely to show differences between high- and low-conflict scenarios. That is to say, they made their decision on the utilitarian premise that in each case five individuals would be saved. Overall, this suggests that moral judgments rely on emotional processing in the brain. In other research, the ventromedial prefrontal cortex has been shown to be activated when someone chooses to give money to charity or views pictures of hungry children.

A variety of studies have asked whether children below the age of 6 differentiate between a moral judgment and a conventional one. An event that would require a moral judgment would involve aggression, such as hitting or biting another; stealing, such as taking another child's posses-sion; and psychological harm, such as teasing. Events related to a conven-tional judgment would include not being neat or making a mess and breaking school rules, such as playing in an area off limits. In a classic study, preschool children were asked to evaluate naturally occurring and hypothetical events involving moral and conventional transgressions (Smetana, Schlagman, & Adams, 1993). These researchers found that pre-school children did make a distinction between the moral and the conven-tional events. The moral events were seen as more serious, wrong, and more deserving of punishment than the conventional events. Evolutionary psychologists view these types of results as suggesting that cultural and moral judgments rely on different systems of judgment and that moral transgressions are seen as more serious offenses than cultural ones.

Interpersonal and Intragroup Violence

As we look at recorded human history, there appears not to be a time when wars or conflict were not taking place somewhere on earth. Even limiting our observations to the last 100 years, we still find a world in which war is the common, not the unique, event. Initially, it was assumed that war was somehow unique to humans and perhaps resulted from the development of weapons or the denseness of the population. However, with the obser-vation that chimpanzees also engage in lethal attacks on one another, this view changed. The question arises as to how to understand warfare from both a comparative and evolutionary standpoint (see Wilson & Wrangham, 2003 and Jones, 2008 for overviews). Since the 1960s, some 11 different communities of chimps and bonobos have been studied. As noted previ-ously, chimps live in communities of around 150 individuals following a fission-fusion pattern in which smaller subgroups are constructed and disbanded. Across all sites, chimps will show hostility when they detect other chimps who are not part of their community. Initially, this hostility is of a vocal nature and may turn into physical encounters. The level of hostility appears to be different between females and males of the same community. Females, especially if they have infants, tend to avoid encoun-ters with neighboring groups. Other females have been seen to be more aggressive. Males, however, are the most aggressive. They typically show fear or hostility to strange males, but they will retreat if they are outnum-bered. If the males from each community are evenly matched, the attacks tend to be vocal with some charging. These situations typically end with less than severe injuries. If, however, a group of males finds a lone male from the other community, this results in severe injuries including death. If males encounter other females, they will often attack them and may kill their infants. Male chimps generally do not attack females who show signs that they are in estrus, such as sexual swelling, but rather will attempt to mate with them.

Wilson and Wrangham (2003) complete their review of chimpanzee aggression by asking how this might relate to humans. In terms of humans, it should be noted that aggression between hunter-gatherer groups has existed within a fairly stable pattern. The most common pattern was for a party of men from one group to launch a surprise attack on the other group. These attacks were typically set up so that the attackers were less likely to be harmed. In comparing hunter-gatherers to chimps, Wilson and Wrangham suggest both share three tendencies. First, they both show a tendency to respond aggressively in encounters with members of other social groups. Second, they both avoid intensive aggressive confrontation by retreating. And third, they both take advantage of imbalances of power when males kill members of neighboring groups. Interestingly, bonobos do not appear to conduct any type of lethal violence, although they defend their territories.

Today, there is continuing debate as to whether humans evolved an inclination to kill. However, even if this were true, there is also evidence to suggest that humans have evolved an ability to live life without killing, given certain circumstances (Jones, 2008). It has been suggested by a number of researchers that the availability of resources is one set of circumstances that reduces the incidence of killing. Correlational research suggests that, over time, as opportunities for acquiring necessary resources increase within a population, killing decreases. For example, the murder rate in Europe has dropped since the Middle Ages, when there was greater inequality. It decreased from 32 killings per 100,000 people in the 1200s to 1.4 killings per 100,000 in the 20th century (Eisner, 2001).

A number of social psychologists have begun to look to evolution as a means of integrating a variety of findings in the field (see Schaller, Simpson, & Kenrick, 2005 for a large-scale overview of this perspective). Traditional social psychology has been described as consisting of a loosely connected set of nonintuitive and curious effects (Haselton & Funder, 2006). One of the best known of these is the *fundamental attribution error*. This occurs when an individual infers that the behaviors of another are directed by trait-like processes. For example, if a car almost hits you as you are about to cross the street, you might say that the driver "is really stupid." However, if you were driving and almost hit someone, you would probably explain your behavior in situational terms and not as due to personality characteristics. For example, you might say the sun was in your eyes or that another person distracted you. In this book, I described such processing of interactions under the rubric of heuristics. Traditional social psychology has also directed its research and theory at such topics as how one develops attitudes, how one perceives oneself and others, what factors lead to conformity, and helping and aggression. As described by Schaller et al. (2005), the evolutionary perspective allows for a framework to bring these topics together. For example, the evolutionary perspective gives greater insight into the question of altruism or why we may help someone even if it puts us at an apparent disadvantage. As we shall see in the last chapter of this book, understanding our commitment to cooperate with others, to understand and spend time with others, and to consider our society from a larger perspective are some of the basic building blocks of moving beyond the individual level and creating a culture.

SUMMARY

The Wason selection tasks have been used to evaluate logic versus social logic. Research has identified brain differences when the problem has a social dimension. In order to solve problems, humans use a variety of strategies including bounded rationality, heuristics, and framing. These procedures enable us to examine fewer cues, reducing the difficulty associated with retrieving and storing cue values, simplifying the weighting principles for cues, integrating less information, and examining fewer alternatives. Moral judgments use a different calculus than would be required for a similar logical problem. Violence continues to be an important aspect of human behavior.

STUDY RESOURCES

Review Questions

1. What is the cheater detection module, and why is it important in social exchange?

2. What evidence can you cite from Wason selection task research and brain research that helps us understand the difference between social exchange logic and traditional Aristotelian logic domains?

3. Explain the human decision-making concepts of bounded rationality, heuristics, and framing. Give an example of each in social relations and explain what benefits they provide from an evolutionary perspective.

4. How do individuals process decisions differently when presented with a "gain" framing versus a "loss" framing?

5. How are social and moral emotions different from the basic emotions? What role do they play in social relations from an evolutionary perspective?

6. How are moral judgments different from other types of judgments? Describe Pinker's two important characteristics of moral judgments.

7. As we look at recorded human history, there appears not to be a time when wars or conflict were not taking place somewhere on earth. Is war unique to humans? Is it a necessary part of human evolutionary history? What evidence would you cite for your answer?

For Further Reading

Newell, A, & Simon, H. (1972). *Human problem solving.* Englewood Cliffs, NJ: Prentice-Hall.

Key Terms and Concepts

- Social contract algorithms and hazard management systems
- Social exchange and the brain
- The logic of cooperation
- Implications in social psychology and economics
  - Bounded rationality
  - Heuristics
  - Framing
  - Decision making and the brain
  - Social and moral emotions
  - Moral judgments
- Interpersonal and intragroup violence

SAGE Study Site

Visit the study site at **www.sagepub.com/ray** for chapter-specific study resources.

Glossary Terms

- Bounded rationality
- Heuristics

Applications

PART III

Health 13

T his chapter looks at some of the implications of our evolutionary
history as it relates to health. In doing so, we will cover a variety of
topics drawn from medicine and psychology. Studying human health, like
all of evolution, requires us to consider the relationship between the environment in which we live and our bodily states. This exploration takes
place on a number of levels, ranging from pathogens to social relationships. As you will see, a variety of psychological factors influence health.
These factors include attachment relationships and social support as well
as dominance hierarchies. We will also consider health differences in
males and females. On an even higher level, you will see how culture
influences health.

Although most of us think of health improvement as coming from
medical breakthroughs, history suggests that this is only one part of the
picture. Actually, it is often changes in sanitation and food supplies that
produce the greatest improvement. For example, in the last century,
human health was improved greatly by societal changes such as utilizing
resources to ensure clean water, sanitation, and improved hygiene. This
has led to an increase in expected lifespan in the U.S., from 46.6 years for
men and 48.7 years for women in 1900 to 74.3 years for men and 80.9
years for women some 100 years later. If you are interested, current life
expectancy data can be found at http://www.cdc.gov/nchs/fastats/lifexpec
.htm. Also, medical research on the development of vaccines and other
medicines has played an important role in health. Likewise, prevention
programs and careful attention to workplace accidents have also changed
health outcomes. One result of this is that humans are living longer than
at any time in our evolutionary history.

How do we understand life expectancy and aging from an evolutionary
perspective? Actually, **senescence** is the more technically correct term for
aging (see Crews, 2003 for an overview). We know, for example, that there

is less genetic diversity among humans who live past the age of 70 than among those who do not. That is to say, the genetics of those who live past 70 years of age are more similar compared to the genetics of everyone who is 30. A variety of researchers, including Sir Peter Medawar (1977), R. A. Fisher (1930/1999), and W. D. Hamilton (2002), have shown that as one becomes older, the influence of natural selection lessens. This simply means that your ability to influence future generations decreases as you become older. That ability is, of course, greatest during the peak reproductive years. Genetically, because natural selection diminishes with age, any alleles that have little effect on the person during child-bearing years can be passed on. However, it is possible for these alleles to have negative effects on health in later years. One possible explanation is that alleles that are beneficial to reproduction in early years actually have a negative effect on one's later health. This was the idea of George C. Williams (see Nesse & Williams, 1994 for an overview). Another way of saying this is that nature favors reproductive success over long life.

Why do we get sick? When you consider health and disease from an evolutionary perspective, you may ask why disease exists at all. As you have seen throughout this book, if a gene or series of genes are related to a trait that gives an organism an advantage in terms of survival and/or reproduction, then that gene is more likely to be passed on. Conversely, genes related to nonadaptive traits should not be passed on because the individuals and their offspring who carry those genes would be less likely to survive over evolutionary time. Thus, from this simple perspective, we might expect that diseases would slowly die off. However, we know this is not the case. One factor that complicates the picture is that humans are not the only biological organism that experiences the pressures of evolution. Specifically, pathogens, such as viruses, that are related to our diseases are also changing in relation to evolutionary factors. In fact, they are capable of changing faster than we are, and we end up with another "Red Queen" story in which we have to constantly change in order to stay still (see Chapter 8). That is, the faster we come up with responses to pathogens, the faster the pathogens change. It is clearly not a simple story. Thus, I begin with the critical question of how to understand disease and health from an evolutionary perspective.

We think of being sick as a bad thing and, of course, no one wants to be sick. You might expect that, over evolutionary time, disease would have disappeared because those who were able to stay healthy would have had the advantage. Included in this line of reasoning is the finding that most species select mates, at least in part, based on signs of health, such as the color of peacock feathers. Thus, we might expect health and less disease to pass on to future generations. However, disease has not disappeared over time and is found in all species. How are we to understand this? Let's begin this consideration by asking what makes us vulnerable to disease.

Vulnerability to Disorders

Let's begin by considering how the relationship between health and disease evolved. Nesse (2005) suggests that there are six ways to think about this question from an evolutionary standpoint:

1. Mismatch: The Body and the Environment Do Not Match

Mismatch is based on the idea that evolutionary changes in our bodies happen slowly, whereas cultural changes may happen quickly. This, in turn, results in some unexpected consequences. Basically, Nesse (2005) suggests that our bodies were not designed for the modern environments in which we now live. For example, the diet that most modern individuals eat is high in certain types of fats, which leads to such disorders as atherosclerosis. In the past, such naturally occurring substances as sugars were more difficult to obtain, and thus an individual would have a limited amount of sweet food he or she could eat. With the processed foods of today, this is not the case, and it is easy take in large amounts of calories.

Culture also creates situations that allow for previously unrecognized conditions to be seen. That is to say, certain technologies need to be developed before the disorder is actually noted. As a culture develops reading, for example, disorders such as nearsightedness, which is genetically passed on, become more obvious. As you read in Chapter 3, it is also possible that genetic changes in a particular group of individuals may lead to a mismatch between individuals without this genetic structure and their environment. One classic example is the ability to drink milk throughout adult life—a characteristic of people of Northern European descent. These individuals, as you remember, do not lose the ability to digest lactose, as do most humans. Thus, were a person from Asia to drink milk, he or she would feel ill and have symptoms of bloating and diarrhea resulting from a mismatch between his or her genetic makeup and the food source, whereas those from Northern Europe would not.

2. Infection and Coevolution

In terms of infection, it is not only humans that are evolving, but also bacteria and viruses. The problem for humans is that pathogens evolve at a faster pace than the ability of our bodies to change and destroy them. The AIDS virus is one case in point. It can also be the case that the very systems that are designed to destroy pathogens may themselves cause problems. Such autoimmune disorders as allergies and asthma are examples of this situation.

3. Tradeoffs: Every Trait Is a Tradeoff

We also have tradeoffs, including the situation in which the very process that is protective also causes problems. Our autoimmune system is designed to destroy pathogens. However, asthma and a variety of other disorders result when the autoimmune system overreacts. Likewise, our body produces antioxidants, which promote health. However, when antioxidants are out of balance, the result can be gout produced by uric acid or childhood jaundice related to the production of bilirubin. Tradeoffs also occur during the development of the fetus. When there is insufficient food, the human fetus develops more slowly. It is assumed that growing more slowly, with a reduced birth weight, enables energy and resources to be diverted to the development of critical organs such as the brain. It has also been suggested that, evolutionarily, an organism is prepared to live in the same environment in which it develops. Thus, if one is born into a time of fewer resources, such as famine, one's physiology is best suited to continue that condition. Were the person to find himself in a different environment in which foods were readily available, that person's physiology and environmental conditions would not match. That, in turn, can result in a greater frequency of certain diseases. For example, low birth weight is often associated with insulin resistance, a condition that in later life can lead to type 2 diabetes, especially in individuals with a certain genetic structure. Were such individuals to live with insufficient food, then diabetes would develop more slowly, or not at all. However, if rich foods become abundant, then the possibility of diabetes becomes greater. The basic idea is that there is a close connection between the environment and the manner in which the organism develops, and this is used by the organism to predict future conditions and needs. When this prediction is not met and the organism finds itself in a different environment, then nonoptimal conditions, including disease, may result.

4. Constraints on Natural Selection

Our physiological structures have developed over a long period of evolutionary time. At times, new structures are simply added to the old. Thus, these newer structures are constrained by what was there previously. As was noted previously, the arrangement of our retina is the exact opposite of what one would do when designing an eye. The wiring comes out into the eye rather than being behind it. That is to say, the photoreceptors that are sensitive to light are behind the horizontal cells, which are behind the amacrine cells and bipolar cells, which are behind the ganglion cells, which send information to the visual areas in the brain. It is as if one were adding electricity and Internet lines to a castle built years ago. One would be forced to run the wires along the walls rather than behind them. That is similar to what happened with our retina.

5. Organism's Selection Is for Reproductive Success, Not for Health

As you read previously, there is an important connection between reproductive processes and health. Mate choices are often driven by signs that denote a healthy organism. Clear skin, symmetrical facial features, and other such features are seen as signs of attractiveness in humans. They are also related to health. Although this relationship exists between sexual attractiveness and health, Nesse (2005) points out that reproductive success still carries the most weight in evolutionary terms. Nesse suggests that perhaps this pressure is part of the reason men do not live as long as women. That is to say, those factors that support reproductive success in males may actually be at odds with longevity.

6. Defenses and Suffering

No one wants to be sick or to experience nausea, vomiting, diarrhea, fever, or cough. Yet, from a health perspective, many of the things we think are bad may be good. They are actually ways in which our bodies protect themselves. They are basic defense mechanisms. They are designed to remove or kill the pathogens. Like many other protective mechanisms, such as reacting to a stick as if it were a snake, sickness-related mechanisms err on the side of being overprotective. At times, this leads to an immune system response that is actually greater than necessary for the challenge. However, Nesse (2005) refers to this as the "smoke detector principle," in which it is better to have a sensitive smoke detector than to miss even one fire. In young children, the response to pathogens also serves another purpose. It enables the immune system to create a "memory" of the pathogen, so that it knows how to respond at its next occurrence. This, of course, is the basic principle underlying vaccinations.

Bodily Defenses

Let's continue our discussion of bodily defenses and think about the role of such responses as fever and pain. As we do this, you may come to realize that, from an evolutionary perspective, we may not want to remove every negative experience that we have in relation to our health. The fever clearly serves a purpose—to kill germs. To reduce the fever through available medications may actually lengthen the time that one is sick. Thus, just because a symptom, such as fever, appears at the same time as the disease, it does not mean it is part of the disease. It can be our body's attempt to fight off the disease. Of course, not all forms of bodily defenses that result in fever and pain are beneficial. To this end, it is useful to distinguish between a defect and a defense (Nesse & Williams, 1994). A *defect* is a physiological manifestation that serves no purpose. A seizure may be an example of such a process. A *defense*, on the other hand, serves an initial purpose. A cough, for example, is a defense designed to expel foreign material from the respiratory tract. As you saw in Chapter 3, some defenses, such as those that protect against malaria, also allow for other disorders such as sickle cell anemia.

In 2002, a provocative study was published in the *New England Journal of Medicine* that asked the question, "Is the decreased incidence of infectious diseases causally related to the increased incidence of immunologic diseases?" In this study, Jean-Francois Bach (2002) examined the decrease in common infectious diseases such as measles, mumps, and rheumatic fever. What is intriguing is that, as these disorders decreased, largely through widespread immunization of children, another set of disorders, including multiple sclerosis, Crohn's disease, asthma, and type 1 diabetes, increased. This can be seen in Figure 13.1. The larger question is did the traditional infectious diseases, such as measles and mumps, for example, influence our immune system and, in turn, reduce our chance of developing asthma, Crohn's disease, type 1 diabetes, and multiple sclerosis?

Figure 13.1   Graph A shows incidence of infectious diseases from 1950 to 2000. Graph B shows increase of immune disorders during the same period.

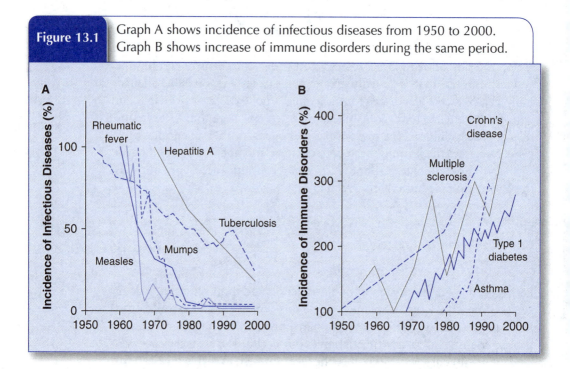

Gene-Environment Interactions

Throughout this book I have emphasized Darwin's idea of a close connection between genetic and environmental influences. A variety of examples show that changes in the environment are related to developmental changes that persist over a lifetime. For example, there is a fly called the dung fly because the female lays her eggs on cattle dung. The dung provides food for the hatched larvae. The amount of dung available varies due to a number of environmental factors. When there is ample dung, the flies take longer to mature and grow larger than when dung is less available. With less available dung, the flies accelerate development and grow to a smaller body size. In essence, there is a tradeoff between growth and the ability to reproduce. Another example of this is coat thickness in the offspring of meadow voles. If they are born in the spring, their coats are thinner than if they are born in the autumn. This, of course, makes sense because thicker coats would be needed for the winter as compared to the summer. However, it is not the outside temperature that determines the thickness, but rather the mother's hormonal responses to changes in the length of the day. A final example is the locust. Locusts respond to overcrowding and lack of food by migrating. However, if they are to migrate they need to have a different wing shape and metabolic rate. When you realize that the changes must take place early in development, then some interesting questions arise. One has to do with the relationship between the current environment and the future environment in which the developing organism will live. That is, does an organism prepare her offspring for a future environment that may be different than the current one? The answer appears to be yes.

Do these same factors relate to human health and disease? The answer also appears to be yes. In the early 1960s, in what was to become the **thrifty genotype hypothesis**, James Neel (1962) suggested that certain genes may be advantageous in times of famine, in that they reduce energy expenditure and thus are thrifty. This was expanded by David Baker to the **thrifty phenotype hypothesis**, which suggests that a mother's nutrition during early pregnancy could influence both fetal and infant growth and, in turn, create a situation in which obesity and diabetes would result later in life (see Hales & Barker, 2001 for an overview). As with other organisms, human infants are prepared for the environment in which the mother lives. If a mother eats less food or less nutritious food, the infant develops in a way that gives it the ability to require less. This is generally apparent in body size and physiological mechanisms that conserve energy. That is, the infant's metabolism is thrifty. Thousands of years ago, a mother eating less was more likely to reflect her immediate environment in terms of availability of food. Today, however, food is more abundant. Thus, it is possible for a fetus to develop today as if there were restricted availability of food in its environment, when in fact the opposite is the case. A conservative physiology, along with plentiful food, can lead to obesity and related diseases, such as diabetes.

What present-day support can we find for the idea that early life changes occur to increase the survival potential of an individual? To help answer this question, researchers have looked for situations in which there had been drastic changes in the human environment. One of these was the Dutch

Hunger Winter of 1944/1945. In November of 1944, Nazi occupiers of Holland sought to punish the population for war resistance activity. To do this, the food supply was cut such that the mean caloric intake went from approximately 2,000 calories a day to less than 800. This food shortage ended when the Allies liberated Holland some seven months later. Using birth data from the hospitals during that period, it was possible to determine which mothers had a limited diet at the beginning of their pregnancies and which ones became undernourished only at the end of their pregnancies. Fetuses that were undernourished late in pregnancy had a reduced birth weight. Fetuses that were undernourished early in pregnancy had a normal birth weight but were later shown to develop obesity and insulin resistance. Later tests also show these individuals to have higher plasma glucose concentrations after a standard glucose tolerance test. The basic idea is that a brief period of intense deprivation, in an otherwise well-nourished population, results in a mismatch and leaves these individuals susceptible to future obesity and diabetes. Thus, the mother's dietary intake during pregnancy can program metabolism without altering birth size. This idea is further supported by examining longer periods of dietary restrictions. One such period was the siege of Leningrad (St. Petersburg, Russia) during World War II, which lasted from 1941 to 1944. With children born during this period, there was less obesity and diabetes in later life.

Gluckman and Hanson (2005) have extended these ideas to suggest that organisms make **predictive adaptive responses** (PAR) based on expectations about the environments their offspring will live in. These PARs can have important implications for future health and disease. To summarize, current environmental conditions produce changes in an organism's development that will help the organism match future environmental factors. It is suggested that PARs have seven basic characteristics (Gluckman and Hanson, 2005):

1. PARs are induced by environmental factors early in life as a predictive response in expectation of some future environment.

2. PARs result in permanent changes in physiology or structure.

3. These changes can be accomplished by multiple pathways at different times in development.

4. PARs occur across the full range of fetal environments.

5. PARs will confer a survival advantage in the predicted reproductive environment.

6. The PAR defines an environmental range in which the organism can optimally thrive until, and through, the reproductive phase of its postnatal life.

7. PARs can lead to disease or disadvantage when the predicted environment does not occur.

Gluckman and Hanson (2005) suggested that obesity in humans is one example of a health condition that results from PARs. They first suggest that humans evolved in a nutritional and energy environment that was different from the one we live in today. This was the environment of hunter-gatherers. In the same way that camels evolved humps to store fat for lean times, humans evolved mechanisms for storing fat in the abdomen. When there were changes in the environment, PARs would result in changes in fetal development to help the infant match these changes. For example, times of difficulty in finding food would result in a slower metabolism and a potentially smaller infant. Today, food is generally readily available. This sets up two conditions. First, our bodies are still programmed for less abundant times, and thus our craving for tastes such as sweetness leads to obesity. Second, if there is less nutrition available to a fetus because of environmental conditions or behaviors of the mother, such as smoking, the PARs prepare the infant for tough times. This causes those particular individuals to be more likely to develop obesity.

Internal Milieu

In the early 1900s, the French physiologist Claude Bernard (1927) came to the realization that the brain had circuits that were specialized for monitoring and controlling internal events, which he referred to as the "internal milieux." These internal states included physiological processes such as thirst, temperature, and metabolism. In 1915, Walter Cannon at Harvard developed the concept of **homeostasis**, reflecting the manner in which a physiological system tended to center on a set point. Canon saw mechanisms in physiological systems that were similar to a thermostat that regulates temperature in a building. "Stress," according to Cannon, was the situation in which these systems deviated away from the set point.

Initially, many of the systems described in this chapter, such as the autonomic nervous system, the endocrine system, and the immune system, were seen to function independently. However, we now know that not only do internal pathways exist to allow for communication among the systems, but external psychological and cultural influences can also play a role. This has led to the realization that daily stressors can influence these systems (see Cacioppo & Berntson, 2007 for an overview).

Stress

The evolutionary logic of survival is one of the easiest to comprehend. If an organism is not able to successfully respond to threat, it can be hurt or killed. If it is killed, its genes can not be passed on. If it is hurt, it may become a less appealing mate or not be allowed to seek mates. Thus, it is expected that organisms will have evolved sophisticated mechanisms that benefit survival. The basic mechanisms include the autonomic nervous system; a network of hypothalamic, pituitary and adrenal responses; the cardiovascular system; metabolism; and the immune system. The brain has two major pathways by which it influences peripheral physiology. The first is the autonomic nervous system, which innervates a variety of organs including the adrenal medulla, which results in the release of catecholamines (norepinephrine and epinephrine) from the terminal of sympathetic nerves. As described below, the basic consequence of this action is to prepare the body for action. The second pathway involves cells in the hypothalamus, which are released into the bloodstream and go to the pituitary gland. This causes the pituitary to release hormones that influence other hormones, which in turn influence peripheral organs such as the adrenals, as well as cells in the immune system. Simply said, this system helps to convert stored fats and carbohydrates into energy that can be used immediately. Because, historically, survival processes that would activate this system would have involved conflict and fights, it was important that the immune system also be activated to protect the organism from wounds. This hypothalamus, pituitary, and adrenal pathway is called the HPA axis (see Figure 13.2). In psychology and physiology, these mechanisms have been studied under the rubric of stress.

The stress response was initially described by Walter Cannon as a bodily response to danger. Although Cannon originally studied animals, research since his time has shown the basic stress response also applies to humans. The overall stress reaction has been referred to as the **fight-or-flight response** (Cannon, 1932). What happens when you are faced with a potential threat? According to Cannon, your body prepares you either to fight or to leave the scene. How does it do that? Since the time of Cannon, we have learned that the stress response is accomplished by a variety of interacting systems including the amygdala and other cortical systems, which result in the hypothalamus activating the sympathetic nervous system and the hypothalamic pituitary adrenal (HPA) axis (Ulrich-Lai & Herman, 2009). Basically, your brain, through the hypothalamus, produces a substance referred to as CRH (corticotropin-releasing hormone), which in turn produces ACTH in the pituitary. ACTH in your blood, in turn, results in the adrenal glands producing cortisol. Research studies will often use a measure of cortisol to reflect the stressfulness of a situation. The sympathetic nervous system releases norepinephrine and epinephrine (noradrenalin and adrenalin) into your blood stream. During this activation, your heart rate is increased such that blood moves to your legs and arms so you can be ready to fight or flee. Other sympathetic responses include the dilation of the pupils, which enables you to see better in shadows and darkness, increased

Figure 13.2 The figure on the left shows the basic sympathetic and parasympathetic response to stress. The right side of the figure shows HPA activation during stress. In general, the sympathetic and HPA axis show similar reactions to stress.

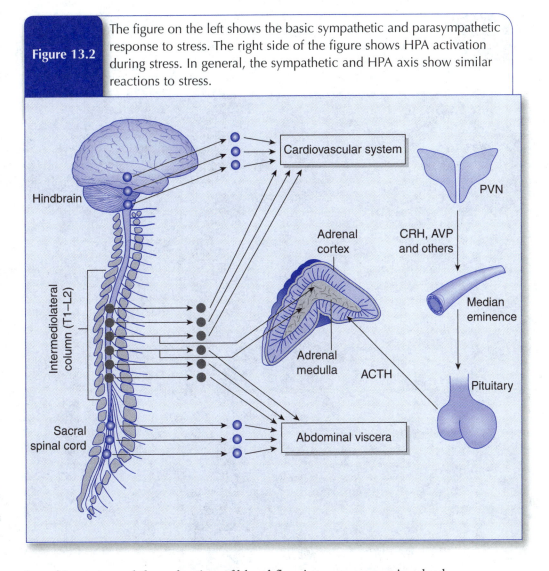

breathing rate, and the reduction of blood flow into organs not involved in action (see Figure 13.3).

One of the major figures in the history of stress research was Hans Selye (1956). It was actually Selye who borrowed the term "stress" from physics. In physics, stress refers to the strain placed on a material. Selye used the term as a way of organizing physiological responses to a variety of challenges, including heat, cold, pain, noise, hard work, and so forth. One of Selye's early findings was that the body reacts similarly to a variety of these different stressors. Selye called this response the General Adaptation Syndrome (GAS). The GAS was seen to involve three stages: (1) the alarm stage was an initial reaction to the stress, which involved an increase in adrenal activity as well as sympathetic nervous system reactions, such as increased heart rate; (2) the resistance stage represented an adjustment to

Figure 13.3 Graphic illustration of the autonomic nervous system. The sympathetic system is on the left and the parasympathetic is on the right.

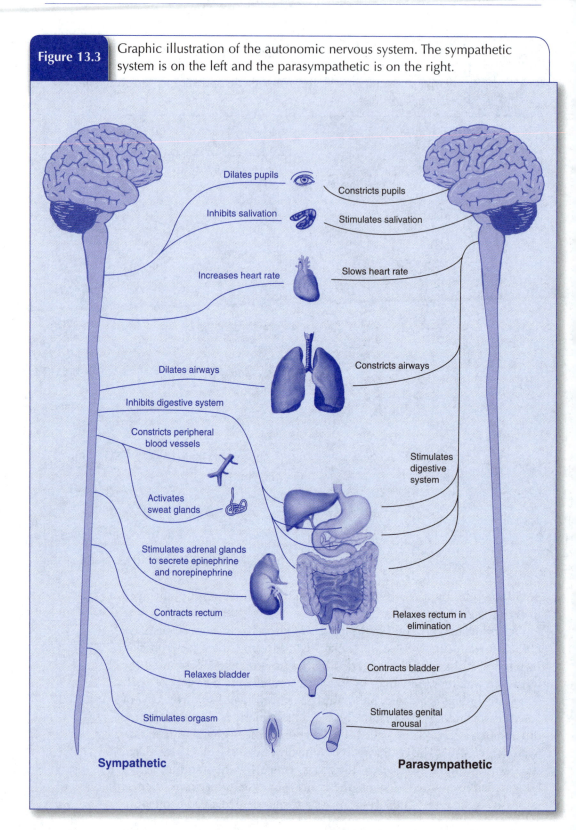

the stress, which included the availability of additional energy resources and mechanisms for fighting infection and tissue damage; (3) the exhaustion stage was the final stage, in which bodily resources were depleted. One of the paradoxes that Selye recognized was that the physiological stress responses that protect and restore the body can also damage it. However, Selye also reported that repeated exposure to a particular stress situation could also increase the organism's ability to withstand that same stress in greater amounts.

More recently, Bruce McEwen (2002) has begun to address the paradoxical nature of the stress response. He begins by suggesting part of the problem in understanding stress is the ambiguous meaning of the term *stress*. He suggests that the term *stress* be replaced with the term *allostasis*. **Allostasis** refers to the body's ability to achieve stability through change. Allostatic systems are thus systems designed to adapt to change. Traditionally, for humans, change related to stress has a broad range of possibilities, including dangerous situations, crowded and unpleasant environments, infection, and performing in front of others. Some researchers even suggest that stress may be greater for humans than other animals because we are also able to use our cognitive abilities to increase the experience of stress through imagination. The overall stress response involves two tasks for the body. The first is to turn on the allostatic response that initiates a complex adaptive pathway. Examples of this turning on are the fight-or-flight and the tend-and-befriend (discussed later in this chapter) responses. Once the danger has passed, the second task is to turn off these responses. Research suggests that prolonged exposure to stress may not allow these two mechanisms to function correctly and, in turn, may lead to a variety of physiological problems. This cumulative wear and tear on the body as a result of responding to stressful conditions is called *allostatic load*.

Allostatic load has been discussed by McEwen (1998) in terms of four particular situations: The first situation reflects the fact that allostatic load can be increased by frequent exposure to stressors. These stressors can be physical or psychological. A variety of psychological studies have shown an association between worry, daily hassles, and negative health outcomes. One of the most studied areas is cardiovascular risk factors, with stress showing a strong association with heart attacks and the development of atherosclerosis. The second condition for the increase in allostatic load is when an individual does not adapt or habituate to the repeated occurrence of a particular stressor. Some people, for example, continue to show larger physiological responses to everyday situations like driving a long distance or taking an airline flight, even though the data suggest there is limited risk in these situations. Asking individuals to talk in front of a group also induces stress-like responses in many individuals. The third situation reflects the fact that not all individuals respond the same to changing situations. In particular, some individuals show a slower return to the nonchallenge physiological condition, once the initial threat is removed. These individuals appear to be more at risk for developing health-related conditions. Some researchers suggest that high blood pressure is associated with a normal stress response not being turned off. The fourth condition discussed by McEwen reflects the situation in which a nonresponse to stress produces an overreaction in another system. That is, if one system does not respond adequately to stress, then activation of another system would be required to provide the necessary counterregulation and return the system to homeostasis. Overall, McEwen emphasized the importance of individual differences and the variety of ways in which perceived stress can influence future health. His graphic depiction of the allostatic system is seen in Figure 13.4.

Figure 13.4 The stress response and development of allostatic load. Perception of stress is related to experience, genetics, and behavior. Over time, allostatic load can accumulate and lead to disease.

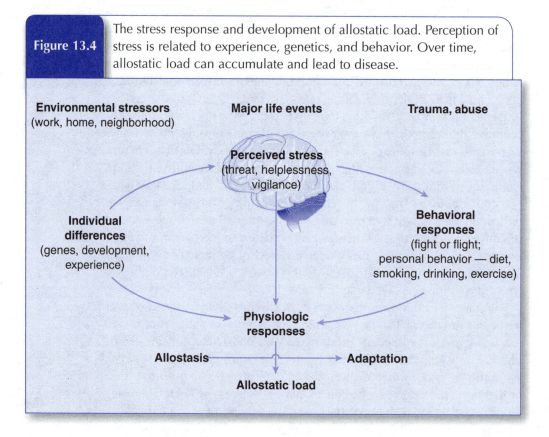

SOCIAL STRESS

Not only does our stress system respond when we are faced with threatening situations from our environment, it also responds to challenges in our social world (see Flinn, 2007 for an overview). Just being asked to stand up and talk in front of a group of people will produce characteristic stress responses. Given the social nature of human beings, it is not unreasonable to assume threats to our social system would be important. However, the evolutionary link that connected social challenges with the stress system for life-and-death situations is less well understood. One would assume that, as with many other evolutionary processes, nature used systems already available.

Flinn (2007) reviews the idea that the adaptive value of the social stress response begins in childhood. Studies across a variety of species have shown that early exposure to stress will modify how the stress response is expressed in later life. It appears that children who experience trauma in the form of abuse, the death of a parent, or divorce show larger stress responses to social stress later in life. It is not the case, however, that early physical stress, such as experiencing hurricanes or political upheaval in one's country, results in a differential stress response.

UNCONTROLLABLE STRESS

Another critical factor in how we experience a situation is whether we feel that we are in control or not. Over the past 50 years, a variety of studies have shown that individuals who experience high demands in their jobs but have little control over how and when they perform their work display more symptoms of a variety of disorders, including heart disease. Those individuals who felt that they had control, even though they may have had demanding jobs, displayed fewer symptoms.

Jay Weiss examined the results of uncontrollable stress in experimental animals. Stress procedures included subjecting animals to electric shock and placing organisms that did not like water in small pools where they were required to swim. It became apparent in this research that uncontrollability produced both health problems (e.g., gastric ulcers) and depressive symptoms. What was intriguing was that the depressive symptoms in animals were very similar to clinical definitions of human depression. According to the *Diagnostic and Statistical Manual of Mental Disorders,* which is used by psychologists and psychiatrists in the United States and other parts of the world, depression includes such symptoms as loss of appetite, psychomotor retardation, fatigue, disrupted motivation, sleep disturbances, and reduced capacity for attention. These were exactly the symptoms that Jay Weiss and his colleagues found in the organisms they studied (See Weiss, Demetrikopoulos, McCurdy, West, & Bonsall, 2000 for a review). The intriguing question, of course, is: Does clinical depression in humans result from stress?

DOES FIGHT-OR-FLIGHT APPLY
EQUALLY TO MALES AND FEMALES?

Health psychology has emphasized the fight-or-flight response as a critical mechanism for responding to stress. The problem for current-day humans is that many of the stressors we face do not require a fighting or fleeing response. For example, imagine that you are working in a large company where there are rumors that a number of people are being laid off. Your boss calls you into the office. Your initial response is probably to feel stress because you could be the next to be fired. As you go in, you can feel your heart pounding. At this point, your boss says, "You have been doing a great job and I want to ask your opinion on another project." The threat is gone, but your body is still reacting. This fight-or-flight reaction has been critical throughout our evolutionary history, but today, in our different social structure, it may lead to stress-related disorders. I will return to this question later in the chapter.

In many ways, males and females have had different evolutionary pressures on them, including the manner in which they respond to various challenges. After examining a variety of studies, Shelley Taylor and her colleagues (Taylor, 2002; Taylor et al., 2002) suggest that the fight-or-flight response better described a human male's response to stress than a female's. For females, they suggest a better descriptor is **tend-and-befriend response**. What do they mean by this? First, they suggest that, over evolutionary time, females have evolved behaviors to maximize the survival of both themselves and their offspring. Second, when stressed, females respond by nurturing offspring as well as displaying behaviors that protect them from harm. These tending behaviors have also been shown to reduce the presence of stress hormones in the infants. Third, like fight-or-flight, these behaviors are associated with particular neuroendocrine responses, although different hormones are involved. These responses make up the tending response. The tending response activated by stress is seen as part of the larger attachment process, which we discussed in Chapter 6. The befriending response involves a large social group. Females under stress seek contact with their social group, which is also protective in survival terms.

It is intriguing that the basic neuroendocrine responses to stress appear to be similar in males and females (Taylor et al., 2002). They are initially a sympathetic response, as described previously. What is different is that these hormones affect males and females differently. Human males show the sympathetic response of activation and increased arousal, which can lead to aggression—the fight part of fight-or-flight. The male brain appears to be organized to give aggressive responses in the presence of substances such as testosterone that are less present in the female brain. Present in the female brain is the hormone oxytocin, which is released in larger amounts in females compared to males. Oxytocin has been found in a variety of animal studies to reduce anxiety and to calm the organism. According to Shelly Taylor and her colleagues, oxytocin leads females to quiet and calm down offspring in response to stress. Thus, whereas males are seen to produce more sympathetic responses to stress, females show more parasympathetic responses. Oxytocin is believed to lie at the basis of these responses for females—the tend-and-befriend response.

Additional support for the presence of gender differences in response to stress has come from the work of Repetti (1989). She examined the behaviors of fathers and mothers following a stressful work day. Whereas fathers tended to isolate themselves at home following stress, mothers tended to be more nurturing and caring toward their children. Further, differences also are found in the larger social networks: Stressed females tend to seek out other women for comfort and support. Compared to females, males seek support from same-sex friends less often. A variety of anthropological studies suggest that males and females form groups for different purposes. Male groups tend to be larger and directed at well-defined tasks such as defense. Female groups tend to be smaller and carry with them social and emotional connections to a greater degree.

Why did researchers initially not see differences in male and female responses to stress? The answer is simple. During most of the 20th century, females were not studied in this research. Even the animal studies typically used males. Once females were studied more thoroughly, these differences emerged. If you think about it, you can see that these stress response differences are consistent with mating differences and investment in the care of offspring. That is to say, given that the female typically has a greater role in caring for offspring, her response to stress should not jeopardize herself or her offspring, as might be the case with fleeing or fighting.

What is less well known is that stressful events activate the same immune and brain circuits as do infections (Maier & Watkins, 2002). Why is this so? Maier and Watkins suggest that the immune system first evolved to be sensitive to pathogens such as those associated with disease or the common cold, for example. In evolutionary time, the immune system is seen to have evolved before such responses as fight-or-flight because all organisms have mechanisms for dealing with pathogens.

Immune System

The immune system comes into play both in terms of specific pathogens, such as viruses, and also in terms of stress. There are two major types of immunity that protect the organism (see Folds, 2008 for an overview). The first system is general and involves those processes of the immune system that are present at birth. This system responds to a variety of pathogens, including bacteria and other toxic organisms. It tends to be fast-acting, non-specific, and usually of short duration. The second type of immunity begins to develop after birth. This type of immunity is involved in recognizing specific pathogens such as bacteria, viruses, or toxins after initial contact and remembering their structure. This system is longer lasting and contains a memory of a specific pathogen. This system is also the basis of immunizations for preventing specific diseases. Basically, the immune system learns to recognize the presence of a specific pathogen. Today, measles, chicken pox, mumps, diphtheria, whooping cough, yellow fever, and polio have all been prevented by vaccines that activate the immune system. Overall, the two immune processes, innate prevention and learned, are what we usually consider in discussions of the immune system fighting infections. However, it is even broader than that. The immune system is designed to attack whatever is not you. That is why you have allergies. Allergies are simply your immune system attacking what it considers a pathogen. It is also why so much care must be taken in organ transplants. The immune system realizes the transplanted organ is not yours and may even attack it. Although we experience the effects of the immune system, especially with allergies, most of what it does takes place outside of awareness. Let's look at the immune system itself (see Maier & Watkins, 2002 for an overview).

The immune system evolved to help organisms protect themselves from pathogens. These defense mechanisms appear to be some of the earliest to have evolved. One important task of the immune system is to determine what is foreign and what is part of the organism. These foreign substances include bacteria, viruses, and parasites that enter our system and are detected by the immune system. Antibodies, which are produced by our immune system, can detect literally millions of different foreign substances and engage in a process that, hopefully, leads to their destruction.

There are a variety of types of immune cells. In general, immune cells originate in the bone marrow (see Henderson & Baum, 2004 for an overview). Some of these cells migrate to the thymus and develop into T-cells. T-cells circulate through blood and lymph as well as exist in the lymph nodes. There are also other types of cells, such as the B-cell, which produce antibodies. Both B- and T-cells require prior exposure to the pathogen to produce an immune response. Other natural killer cells (NK) do not require prior exposure and form a first line of defense against pathogens. In addition to attacking pathogens, immune system responses are also associated with the experience of feeling ill. From an evolutionary perspective, feeling ill would be protective because it would result in withdrawal from dangerous situations as well as allow for rest.

At one time, the immune system was viewed as a separate system that functioned independently. However, since the 1970s, a variety of studies have demonstrated that the immune system is influenced by the brain, and vice versa. In particular, it has been shown that stress can influence the immune system, such that an organism is more likely to become ill following stress. Robert Ader was also able to show that the immune system could be classically conditioned (Ader, 2002; Ader & Cohen, 1993). These types of studies helped to create the field of psychoneuroimmunology (see Kemeny, 2007 for an overview). Psychoneuroimmunology is the study of how psychological factors can influence the immune system. More recently, it has also become apparent that not only does experience influence the immune system, but the immune system can influence the brain and thus behavior. Some of the psychological factors that can influence the immune system are loneliness, poor social support, negative mood, disruption of marital relationships, bereavement, and natural disasters (Cohen & Herbert, 1996).

Sickness Behavior

What do you do when you get a cold? You engage in activities that have come to be called **sickness behaviors**. You typically want to eat less, you feel depressed, you have little desire to be aggressive, and you want to withdraw to a comfortable place, usually alone. Robert Dantzer and his colleagues suggest that sickness behavior should be viewed as a motivational state (Dantzer, O'Connor, Greund, Johnson, & Kelley, 2008). They further suggest that sickness behaviors are the normal response to infection, just as fear is a normal response of an organism to a predator. What happens when you get an infection? Your body produces changes in the endocrine system and the autonomic nervous system, which are reflected in your behavior and experience. Specifically, the changes are mediated by the activation of your immune system at the site of the infection in response to whatever pathogen is encountered. The behavioral changes are believed to enable ill individuals to cope better with the infection.

What do you do when you feel psychological stress? Many people experience similar responses to those of illness. According to Maier and Watkins (2002), that is not just a coincidence. They suggest that what were initially mechanisms for fighting infection became co-opted to respond to all types of stress. Thus, your immune system becomes involved through the pathways from the brain to the immune system in all types of stress. This may also help to explain why many processes that involve psychological stress, such as taking a test, also change the functioning of your immune system. Or, why you get sick when you go home after final exams are over.

Social Support Research

Do you ever take a friend with you when you are about to do something that you imagine will be stressful? If the answer is yes, then you may be preventing or reducing the normal stress response. A variety of studies show that if a friend is present, you experience less stress than when you perform a task alone (see Knox & Uvnäs, 2002; Taylor, 2007 for an overview). Various studies have shown that following disasters and other negative events such as terrorist attacks, humans turn to others for comfort. What this suggests to a number of researchers is that we should view social relationships and bonds as a protective mechanism. That is to say, whereas different organisms have a variety of protective mechanisms, including camouflage, thick skin, sharp teeth, and quick reflexes, in humans, social relationships serve a similar function (Taylor & Gonzaga, 2006). The opposite has also been shown to be the case. Social isolation is shown to be unhealthy and associated with a risk for disease and early mortality.

One of the first forms of the social bond that humans experience is attachment. Although I discussed attachment with you in Chapter 5, attachment is usually not discussed in terms of its health benefits. However, a variety of studies suggest that early attachment relationships help to influence later reactions to stress (Taylor & Gonzaga, 2006). For example, rat pups that received positive maternal care showed fewer negative hormonal responses to stress. These animals also showed more open field exploration, suggesting less anxiety on their part. In another study, monkeys were raised in one of three environments (Rosenblum et al., 1994). In the first environment, food was readily available, and the mothers were attentive to their young. In the second environment, food was less readily available, but the mothers were still attentive to their offspring. In the third environment, food was sometimes available and sometimes not. This condition resulted in the mothers being more harsh and inconsistent in their mothering. The offspring in this third condition displayed more clinging behaviors to their mothers and lower levels of exploration and social play. As adults, these monkeys displayed more extreme HPA-axis responses to stress. They also appeared more fearful and lacked the normal social responses. In humans, similar responses are seen in response to difficult rearing environments. For example, in a study of 13,494 adults, a relationship was found between exposure to abuse and household dysfunction and adulthood negative health outcomes (Felitti et al., 1998).

Based on the studies examining social relationships and health, Taylor and Gonzaga (2006) developed a social shaping hypothesis. This hypothesis suggests that early social relationships can shape a person's biological, social, and behavioral responses to a variety of situations, including stressful ones. According to these researchers, social shaping has three functions. First, early relationships can calibrate how the systems involved in stress responses will develop. Second, social relationships help regulate the stress response in terms of day-to-day experiences. Social relationships tend to buffer stress responses, whereas the lack of social relationships tends to exaggerate the responses. And third, social relationships can serve as a source of information as to the nature of the environment. The information can be presented directly or indirectly.

In summary, the research suggests that people with social support live longer and that those who are isolated display more detrimental health problems. For example, a variety of studies show a strong relationship between social isolation and subsequent cardiovascular morbidity. Social support reduces cardiovascular reactivity to acute stress, and lack of social support is associated with increased resting levels of sympathetic activation. Thus, lack of social support may itself be a stressor. One hormonal mechanism that may underlie social support is oxytocin. It has been found to be released in both males and females in response to touch, warm temperature, and massage. Similarly, the infants of female baboons who are social are more likely to survive to their first birthday than those of nonsocial females (Silk, Alberts, & Altmann, 2003). These researchers, using 16 years of data from a well-studied population of wild baboons, suggested that social support is an adaptive mechanism that cannot be explained by dominance rank, group membership, or environmental conditions.

Coronary Heart Disease as a Means to Understanding Psychological Factors

Coronary heart disease is a significant cause of death in the United States. Physiologically, coronary heart disease is related to atherosclerosis, the buildup of lipid deposits in the arteries of the body. Gender differences are found across the lifespan for coronary heart disease. For humans in their 40s, the death rate from coronary heart disease is five times higher for males than females. By age 60, it drops to two times higher. The common theory for these differences is that estrogen protects premenopausal women from coronary heart disease and atherosclerosis. This is supported by a higher death rate in women who go through an early menopause. It is also supported by animal research in which egg-laying hens, for example, show less coronary artery atherosclerosis compared to roosters.

However, coronary heart disease has also been shown to be influenced by a variety of psychological factors (Kaplan et al., 2002). One of these is hostility. Men with "Type A" behavior patterns, who are quickly angered, show greater incidence of coronary heart disease than the less hostile "Type B" individuals. Type A individuals are seen as competitive, time urgent, hostile, and angry. Friedman and Rosenman (1959) first suggested this behavior pattern was related to coronary heart disease (see Friedman, 1996 for an overview). They developed a structured interview to assess "Type A." "Type B" originally was seen as an absence of "Type A" characteristics. However, research suggests positive qualities of humor, forgiveness, self-esteem, autonomy, and balance may also be important in preventing coronary heart disease.

Dominance

In a variety of species, dominance relationships have been shown to be an important part of sexual selection. A further question asks how dominance relates to health. Dominance relationships, and their effect on the individual monkey, have been manipulated in a variety of studies (see McGuire & Troisi, 1998 for an overview in relation to health). In one study, the dominant male monkey was removed. As expected, the other subordinate males competed to become the dominant male. What is interesting is that the male who became dominant not only changed behaviors, as would be expected, but also his physiological profile changed, especially peripheral serotonin levels. The relationship of serotonin levels to dominance is further demonstrated by the fact that the original dominant male that was removed from the group will show a decrease in serotonin if he is not returned to the group within two weeks.

Because dominance also carries with it features of resources and control, this has been an important paradigm for studies of health. Kaplan, Manuck, Clarkson, Lusso, and Taub (1982) studied the complex patterns of social interactions and hierarchies of macaque monkeys. In a classic laboratory study, they placed the monkeys in two groups with 15 monkeys in each group. The monkeys were allowed to establish dominance hierarchies in two conditions. The first condition was a stable environment, in which the membership of the group did not change over the two years. The second condition was an unstable environment in which membership of the group changed every one to three months. During the study, the monkeys were fed a typical American diet that was high in fat.

The study reported that competitiveness and aggression in the form of dominance predispose individuals to cardiovascular problems, especially when they live in a stressful environment and eat a high fat diet. In the stable environment, it was the subordinate monkeys that showed the most pathology (see Figure 13.5). There have been similar findings with humans. Studies of British postal workers show that individuals in low-level positions have more health problems.

A follow-up primate study examined the role of sex differences by placing male and female monkeys in single-sex groups of four. Again, these monkeys were fed a diet high in fat and cholesterol. They also created a measure of competitiveness and submission by placing grapes in each group and rating how many grapes a particular monkey took. For both males and females, the more competitive monkeys showed less atherosclerosis than the less competitive ones. There was also a general sex difference, with males showing

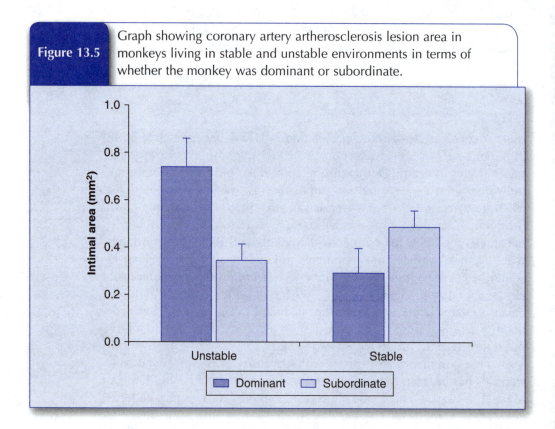

Figure 13.5 Graph showing coronary artery artherosclerosis lesion area in monkeys living in stable and unstable environments in terms of whether the monkey was dominant or subordinate.

more atherosclerosis than females. A follow-up meta-analysis of a variety of studies from their lab showed that dominant males developed more extensive atherosclerosis than subordinates when housed in unstable environments (Kaplan, Chen, & Manuck, 2009). Further, dominant females developed less atherosclerosis than subordinates.

Cultural Changes in Health

What do you think has made the greatest change in the health of humans in the last 100 years? Most people will answer medical breakthroughs in the form of new miracle drugs or procedures. However, as noted previously, they would be wrong. As important as these are, they have not caused the major improvements in health in the last 100 years. The greatest change has been caused by improvements to the environment, in the form of safe water supplies, better sewage treatment, improved diet, and so forth. These changes, in turn, led to a decrease in infectious diseases and an increase in life expectancy. Between 1750 and today, life expectancy has more than doubled. Today it is more than 80 years in some countries. Further, in just the last 100 years, infant mortality has dropped from more than 19% of all infants to less than 8% today. These are data from the more developed countries, as some African countries still show rates in the range of 150 to 180 deaths per 1,000 live births. Also, developed countries tend to show only a slight increase in deaths if these statistics include those 5 and under, whereas less developed countries show a large increase (see Figure 13.6).

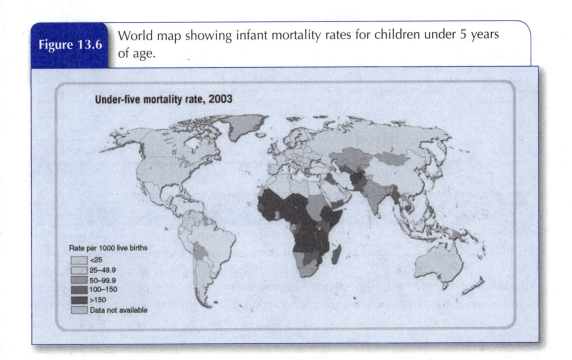

Figure 13.6 World map showing infant mortality rates for children under 5 years of age.

Under-five mortality rate, 2003

Rate per 1000 live births
<25
25–49.9
50–99.9
100–150
>150
Data not available

It should be noted that, statistically, life expectancy increases as infant mortality drops. Table 13.1 shows changes in life expectancy and infant mortality over the last 100 years. Table 13.2 shows the leading causes of death in the U.S. in 1900 and 2000.

Table 13.1 Changes in Life Expectancy and Infant Mortality

- U.S. Life expectancy   males   females
  - 1750   33.7   36.6
  - 1900   46.3   48.3
  - 2000   74.1   79.5
- U.S. Infant mortality
  - 1900 – 192 deaths per 1000
  - 1950 – 33 deaths per 1000
  - 2000 – 7.3 deaths per 1000

Table 13.2 Leading Causes of Death in the U.S. in 1900 and 2000

1900		2000	
Cause of Death	**Deaths per 100,000**	**Cause of Death**	**Deaths per 100,000**
Cardiovascular diseases	345	Cardiovascular diseases	331
Influenza/pneumonia	202	Cancer	201
Tuberculosis	194	Pulmonary diseases	41
Stomach-related	143	Accidents	34
Accidents	72	Influenza & pneumonia	33
Cancer	64	Diabetes	23
Diphtheria	40	Suicide	11
Typhoid fever	31	Kidney disease	10
Measles	13	Liver diseases	9.3

SUMMARY

Health and disease are important aspects of the evolution of humans. Nesse suggests six ways to consider disorders. These are a mismatch between the body and its environment, the coevolution between infections and humans, the tradeoffs between humans and their environment, the constraints on natural selection, the emphasis on reproduction over health, and the relationship between suffering and defenses. Environmental conditions play a role in health and disease, as suggested by the thrifty genotype hypothesis. An expansion of this idea is the predictive adaptive response. The body has information from both external factors and internal factors. Stress has been an important concept for health. McEwen replaced the term stress with the term allostasis. Social stress functions similarly to physical stress. There are gender differences in response to stress. The immune system is the basic response to stress. Heart disorders illustrate the relationship of psychological factors to health and disease. Human life expectancy has increased over the last 100 years.

STUDY RESOURCES

Review Questions

1. Nesse proposes six ways to think about what makes us vulnerable to a disease or disorder from an evolutionary perspective. Describe each of these and provide an example of each.

2. Focusing on issues surrounding human health and disease, use Neel's thrifty genotype hypothesis and Baker's expanded thrifty phenotype hypothesis to explain how an organism can prepare her offspring for a future environment that may be different from the current one.

3. What are the seven basic characteristics of predictive adaptive responses (PARs) that Gluckman and Hanson proposed organisms make, based on their expectations of the environments offspring will live in?

4. What is the stress response? What are the primary physiological systems that interact in activating this response?

5. Why does McEwen suggest that the term stress be replaced by *allostasis* and *stress response* by *allostatic response*? What two tasks does the allostatic response include? What is allostatic load?

6. What is meant by fight-or-flight response and tend-and-befriend response? How are they similar? How are they different?

7. How are social stresses different from physical stresses in our responses to them?

8. Describe how a variety of factors (e.g., exposure, control, gender, social support, dominance) impact the ways in which individuals respond to stress.

9. What is the role of the immune system? In what ways does it interact with the brain, behavior, and the environment?

For Further Reading

Nesse, R., & Williams, G. (1994). *Why we get sick: The new science of Darwinian medicine.* New York: Vintage.
Taylor, S. (2002). *The tending instinct.* New York: Henry Holt and Co.

Key Terms and Concepts

- Vulnerability to disorders
- Bodily defenses
- Gene-environment interactions
- Internal milieu
- Stress
  - Social stress
  - Uncontrollable stress
  - Does fight-or-flight apply equally to males and females?
- Immune system
- Sickness behavior
- Social support research
- Coronary heart disease as a means to understanding psychological factors
- Dominance
- Cultural changes in health

SAGE Study Site

Visit the study site at **www.sagepub.com/ray** for chapter-specific study resources.

Glossary Terms

- Allostasis
- Fight-or-flight response
- Homeostasis
- Predictive adaptive responses (PAR)
- Senescence
- Sickness behaviors
- Tend-and-befriend response
- Thrifty genotype hypothesis
- Thrifty phenotype hypothesis

Psychopathology   14

O ne of the main themes of evolution is the manner in which organisms are in close connection with their environment. It is this close
connection that allows for change—including the turning on and off of
genetic processes—to take place. In humans, there is another layer of complexity involved in the process. Part of this complexity comes from the fact
that humans are born less fully developed at birth than many other species, and thus we are more sensitive to changes in their environment as we
continue to develop. Our environment includes our relationships with our
family and others we come in contact with at an early age. As humans, we
develop societal and cultural perspectives that become the backdrop of
our environment. Unlike animals that live in nature, humans, for the most
part, live within our culture. Another part of human complexity is our
ability to reflect on ourselves and our world. In this way, a layer of thought
can be injected between the person and the environment. This allows for
expectation and even imagination to play a role in human behavior and
experience.

In this sense, our inner world of thoughts and feelings becomes another
environment in which we live. For example, you can tell yourself you are
wonderful or you are stupid and there is no one there to dispute it. One
positive aspect of this is that your inner world enables you to plan future
actions and reflect on past ones, but it can also be experienced as distress
when your internal thoughts reflect such states as anxiety or hopelessness.
As we shall see in this chapter, our internal thoughts at times may lead to
interpretations of the environment or ourselves that may not be productive. What should lead to successful survival, sexuality, and social relations
leads instead to interactions that reduce the close connection between the
person and his or her internal and external environment. This lack of connectedness lies at the heart of psychopathology.

Humans not only consider themselves; they also consider others. A
positive side of this, as noted previously, is the ability to understand the

internal experiences of another. This enables us to experience empathy. We can also consider how we appear to others and other questions of self-image. One aspect of this is related to the sexual instinct. That is, we can say or do things that make us more attractive to a mate. In terms of self-preservation, humans also have a personal history that enables each person to learn from the past and develop strategies for living life. These strategies tend to protect us and even may have saved our lives, in exceptional cases. However, it is also possible that the strategies that work in one environmental situation will not work in another. When a person loses contact with the current environment and applies strategies that worked perhaps in an earlier time, then unsuccessful adaptation is the result. This lack of connectedness to our environment may take place on both external and internal levels. On an external level, the person finds herself different from the group or even seeks to be separate from others. As I have noted throughout this book, living as isolated individuals is not our historical experience. As a species we have always lived in close contact with other humans, which led to the development of societies and cultures. In fact, many of the specific abilities of humans are geared to social interactions on a variety of levels. When we no longer have a connection with the group, we experience a sense of loss. This loss often carries with it the experience of negative affect and depression and a need to withdraw. On an internal level, humans often have the need to explain to themselves the events that have just occurred, which may include anger, distorted perceptions, or a genuine plan for recovery. In this chapter, I want to consider these types of processes and how they may have evolved. We refer to the extreme cases as *psychopathology.*

What is psychopathology? Although there is no single definition of abnormal processes, five ideas have been critical.

1. The processes involved in psychopathology are maladaptive and not in the individual's best interest.

2. The processes cause personal distress.

3. The processes represent a deviance from both cultural and statistical norms.

4. The person has difficulty connecting with his or her environment and also with himself or herself.

5. Individuals with a mental disorder are unable to fully consider alternative ways of thinking, feeling, or doing. That is to say, they often do not see, feel, or think there are alternatives. This results in their psychological processes being rigid and patterned. Having fewer alternatives also suggests that they have less freedom in any given situation.

Models of Psychopathology From an Evolutionary Perspective

As with other psychological processes I have discussed in this book, an evolutionary perspective on psychopathology goes beyond traditional psychological and physiological considerations. One question might be how long, in terms of our human history, a particular psychopathology has existed. Let's take schizophrenia as an example. A World Health Organization (WHO) study examined the presence of schizophrenia in a number of countries with very different racial and cultural configurations (Sartorius et al., 1986). If schizophrenia had an important environmental component, then one would expect to see different manifestations of the disorder in different cultures. What these authors found was that, despite the different cultural and racial backgrounds surveyed, the experience of schizophrenia was remarkably similar across countries. Likewise, the risk of developing schizophrenia was similar in terms of percentage of the total population—about 1%. Further, the disorder had a similar time course in its occurrence, with its characteristics first being seen in young adults.

If you put these facts together, it suggests that schizophrenia is a disorder that has always been part of the human experience. The fact that it manifests throughout the world in strikingly similar ways suggests that it existed before humans migrated out of Africa. The genes related to schizophrenia were carried by early humans who migrated from Africa, and thus its presence is equally likely throughout the world. Given these estimates on the history of the disorder, one might ask why schizophrenia continues to exist. We know that individuals with schizophrenia tend to have fewer children than individuals without the disorder. Thus, we might assume that schizophrenia would have disappeared over evolutionary time because it reduces reproductive success and has a genetic component. However, this is not the case.

This creates a mystery for evolutionary psychologists to solve. In order to answer this question, we can draw on many of the considerations presented in the discussion of health. Perhaps, in the same way that sickle cell anemia is associated with a protection against malaria, schizophrenia protects the person from another disorder. Or perhaps, like the reaction of rats to stress that results in depression-like symptoms, the symptoms of schizophrenia are the result of a long chain of stressful events in which the organism breaks down in its ability to function. Psychopathology could even go in a more positive direction and be associated with creative and nontraditional views of the world. For example, there are a variety of accounts that have noted greater creativity in families of individuals with schizophrenia.

The evolutionary perspective enables us to ask questions such as what function a disorder might serve as well as how it came about. In the same way that pain can be seen as a warning system to the body to protect it from tissue damage, anxiety may have evolved to protect the person from other types of potential threats. For example, many of the outward expressions of social anxiety parallel what is seen in dominance interactions in primates. Submissive monkeys avoid contact with most dominant monkeys, as do individuals experiencing social anxiety. This suggests the possibility that anxiety may have its evolutionary origins in dominance structures. If this were the case, then we might expect to see some relationship to sexual instinctual processes, as is the case with dominance. Indeed, social anxiety begins to manifest just prior to the onset of puberty, around 8 years of age. The evolutionary perspective can also help us think about how psychopathology should be treated. These are some of the questions I will discuss in this chapter.

What function does psychopathology play? What models should we use when we think about psychopathology? For example, does posttraumatic stress disorder (PTSD) work like the Garcia effect with food? In describing the Garcia effect, which involves one-trial learning with a particular food, we noted how eating a food that made us sick was followed by revulsion to that food for months, if not years (see Chapter 2). Clearly, this had great survival value at an early period in our history. Could the same principle work with psychological processes and PTSD? That is, could remembering and reliving overwhelming events in basically neutral situations be protective in the same way that one avoids even the smell of food that makes one sick? Thus, one-trial learning may be one model for psychopathology. Another model might be the exaggeration of a normal process. For example, consider basic attentional factors. Clearly, in a variety of situations, it is protective for humans to scan the environment for danger. However, if this behavior is exaggerated, as seen in some forms of anxiety disorders with a constant screening of the environment, then this takes protection to the extreme and limits full human functioning. Developmentally, there is some suggestion that the scanning of the environment seen in some individuals with generalized anxiety disorder is associated with being required prematurely as children to play a responsible parental role for others. That is, if your mother was disorganized when you were a child, you may have needed to watch out for your own needs and maybe even those of your mother as well.

Another model suggests that we consider psychopathology as reflecting a lack of functioning in a normal process, in the same way we think of color blindness as a special case of color vision. In this situation, psychopathology results when the physiological networks are not functioning correctly or are missing some critical element. Using this perspective, it has been suggested that the auditory hallucinations of schizophrenics result from a breakdown in a mechanism that identifies whether an action was produced by the self or another (Frith, 1992). How do we actually know whether what we experience as a voice in our heads came from ourselves or from someone in the external world? We have a variety of clues, such as whether we produced it and whether we can control the voice. However, if the mechanisms that give us these experiences were not functioning, what would our experience be? Perhaps, like people with schizophrenia, we would not be able to tell the difference between external voices and internal voices. Two additional possibilities are present when seemingly positive traits become associated with negative outcomes: There is a suggestion that genetic processes associated with creativity and intelligence may also be related to psychopathology. This is seen in the case of bipolar disorder, in which there is a statistically greater number of artists who experience this disorder than would be expected by chance. The second model uses the analogy of sugar and obesity as its basis. Humans and many other organisms enjoy sweet-tasting foods. Thousands of years ago this was not a problem because sweet foods were not easy to come by. However, today sugar is readily available in a large variety of foods, which in turn may lead to obesity when we overindulge our cravings. Drug addictions may follow a similar model. Overall, the evolutionary perspective helps us better understand psychopathology by creating innovative predictions to be tested. In summary, below I list seven potential models that may describe the development of psychopathology.

1. One-trial learning, similar to the Garcia effect with food;

2. Overemphasis of a normal process, such as scanning the environment;

3. Loss of a sense of agency, such as not knowing whether voices are internal or external;

4. Developmental processes leading to later problems, such as anxious attachment leading to anxiety;

5. Disorder as a byproduct of another type of protection, as when protection of malaria leads to sickle cell anemia;

6. Highly adaptive traits that lead to a potential for pathology, such as creativity leading to manic depression and schizophrenia;

7. Previously adaptive mechanisms now leading to pathology, as when the attraction to sweet tastes leads to health problems.

One perspective of the evolutionary approach has been to redirect psychology to the basic processes of human existence, such as survival, sexual processes, and social behavior. We can then ask what types of disorders are found within each broad category. We can also consider the developmental and social processes I discussed in previous chapters and ask how these processes may be involved in psychopathology. Thinking in these terms, we may discover that disorders that have very similar end states—depression, for example—may have developed from distinctly different beginning conditions. As described in the previous chapter, depression can result from extreme stress that elicits self-preservation instincts. Depression can also result from the loss of significant other people in one's life. Further, loss of social status is also associated with depression. Thus, what appear to be similar symptoms, as in the case of depression, may have been produced by separate and distinct trajectories.

Another disorder that has been approached from an evolutionary perspective is personality disorder. Personality disorders reflect a rigid approach to dealing with social relationships. Two commonly discussed personality disorders are psychopathic personality and hysteria. Psychopaths are described as manipulative, callous, dishonest, and self-centered. They are antisocial in the sense that they display no need to follow the traditional rules of a society and display little remorse or guilt for their actions. For example, they would contract and collect money for a job without completing it. They would clearly qualify as "cheaters." On the other hand, individuals with a histrionic personality disorder constantly seek the attention of others and are very emotional in their reactions. They can be manipulative in their interpersonal relationships.

Harpending and Sobus (1987) suggest that the psychopath and the hysteric represent different adaptive strategies in relation to sexuality. Both these personality types are viewed by Harpending and Sobus as "cheaters." Given that it is more common to see male psychopaths and female hysterics, these researchers suggest that the disorders result from different reproductive strategies. A male cheater in a sexual relationship should be able to persuade a female to copulate with him while deceiving her about his commitment to her and his willingness to offer resources for the offspring. A female cheater, on the other hand, would exaggerate her need for the male and make herself appear helpless and in need, so that he would give her additional attention and resources. She would also be willing to put her own needs ahead of her offspring, even to the extent of abandoning them. The work of Harpending and Sobus shows how evolutionary thinking can help to explain both the motivational factors of a particular disorder and the demonstrated gender differences.

Let's look at another well-studied process—sleep—as a model for thinking about psychopathology. Because sleep disturbance is associated with a variety of psychopathological disorders, we can study it to consider how normal processes may be influenced to appear pathological. Many people would like to go to sleep when they want to and not be awakened during the night. However, evolution is not always about what makes us feel good. The critical question, from an evolutionary perspective, is what function does sleep play? Has sleep been shaped by natural selection? Some researchers answer yes to this question (Nesse & Williams, 1994). They offer at least five reasons for why this is so.

1. Sleep is found in a variety of organisms and is perhaps universal among vertebrates. However, not all animals sleep in the same way. Elephants and cows spend most of their sleep time standing up. Dolphins sleep with one half of their brain while the other half remains awake.

2. All vertebrates share similar mechanisms that control sleep and dreaming. These mechanisms are found in the more primitive areas of the brain.

3. The pattern of sleep seen in mammals, with periods of rapid eye movement and faster EEG activity during the sleep period, is also seen in birds. The fact that the evolution of birds went down a different pathway before the time of dinosaurs suggests that sleep is a very primitive and basic mechanism.

4. When one examines the sleep patterns across species, there appears to be support for the idea that these patterns adapted to match the ecological niche of each particular animal.

5. All animals show deficits in response to a lack of sleep.

Currently, a variety of researchers are seeking to determine the function of sleep. The best evidence suggests that it allows for restoration of certain physiological processes. There is also evidence that sleep consolidates information learned during the waking hours. One conceptual idea is that, given the light/dark cycle produced by the earth's rotation around the sun, sleep developed as a protective mechanism during the night.

In summary, we can ask critical questions concerning psychopathology that relate to other evolutionary processes:

1. Is the experience of mental illness universal? If it were not universal, then it would be difficult to argue that we should study psychopathology from an evolutionary perspective. If it is a universal process, such as emotionality or language, then we can begin to ask what the nature of mental illness is and how its existence fits into our history as humans.

2. Is there an adaptive value to the behaviors and experiences displayed in psychopathology? It is easy to see that there is a value in not trusting what someone tells you some of the time, but is there any adaptive value in not trusting what anyone tells you all of the time or to thinking that everyone is always out to get you?

3. Is there evidence of psychopathology across human history? This includes the question of whether we see signs of psychopathology in nonhuman species.

4. What is the nature of psychopathology? That is to say, should we consider psychopathology to be qualitatively different from normal functioning, or is it the situation in which normal processes have been taken to the extreme? We know, for example, that allergic reactions are situations in which our immune system is overreactive. We also know that fever is the process in which body temperature is raised to fight infection. However, the fever uses energy and can damage the body.

5. Is psychopathology protective in some manner? Like sickle cell anemia, does having schizophrenia or depression, for example, make you less likely to experience another disorder?

6. Is psychopathology a recent process? That is, should we consider psychopathology to be the result of a mental system designed in the stone-age interacting with a fast-paced modern environment? For example, aggression in teenage gangs may reflect behaviors that were adaptive in previous times but are no longer adaptive for society today.

These questions are not mutually exclusive. As you will see, they also represent some of the ways in which scientists and others have sought to understand psychopathology. From an evolutionary perspective, the study of psychopathology begins with the three instincts of survival, sexuality, and socialness. From this perspective, psychopathology becomes a disruption of these instinctual processes.

Universal Psychopathology?

If psychopathology is part of our human makeup, then we would expect to see similar manifestations of it worldwide. One classic study in this regard was performed by Jane Murphy (1976) of Harvard University. During the 1970s, mental illness was thought to be related to learning and the social construction of norms. In fact, some suggested that mental illness was just a myth developed by Western societies. According to this perspective, neither the individual nor his or her acts are abnormal in an objective sense. One important implication of this view was that what would be seen as mental illness in a Western industrial culture might be very different than what was seen as mental illness in a less-developed rural culture. That is to say, mental illness was viewed as a social construction. The alternative to this perspective is more similar to what we saw with human processes, such as emotionality, in which humans throughout the world show similar expression of the basic emotions.

If mental illness is part of our human history, as evolutionary psychologists would suggest, then we would expect to find it across a variety of cultures. Dr. Murphy (1976) first studied two geographically separate and distinct non-Western groups, the Inuit of northwest Alaska and the Yoruba of rural tropical Nigeria. Although many researchers at that time would have expected to find that the conceptions of normality and abnormality were very different in the two cultures, this is not what she found. She found that these cultures were well acquainted with processes in which people were said to be "out of their mind." This included doing strange things and hearing voices. Jane Murphy concluded that processes of disturbed thought and behavior similar to schizophrenia are found in most cultures, and most cultures have a distinct name in their language for these processes.

Additionally, Murphy (1976) reported that these cultures had a variety of words for what traditionally is referred to as neurosis, although today we would refer to them as *affective disorders.* **Affective disorders** include feeling anxious, tense, and fearful of being with others as well as being troubled and unable to sleep. One Inuit term was translated as "worrying too much until it makes the person sick." Thus, it appears that most cultures have words for what has been called "psychosis," "neurosis," and "normalcy." What is also interesting is that many cultures also have words for describing people who are out of their mind, but not crazy, such as witch doctors, shamans, and artists. Violation of normal states of consciousness appears to be an important distinction for this concept. To add evidence to her argument that psychopathology is indeed part of our human nature, Murphy also reviewed a large variety of studies that looked at how common mental illness was in different cultures. The suggestion here is that if its prevalence is similar in cultures across the world, then it is more likely to be part of the human condition rather than culturally derived. What these studies suggest is that common forms of mental illness, such as schizophrenia, are found at similar rates the world around. Overall, this research established that mental illness was not a concept created by a given culture, but rather part of the human condition in both its recognition and its prevalence. This set the stage for a development that came to be known as **evolutionary psychopathology** or **Darwinian psychiatry.**

During the 20th century, learning theory played a large role in the conception of psychopathology. Fears were seen to be the result of classical conditions, as illustrated in the "little Albert" studies described in Chapter 2. If the fear or phobia was the result of learning, then it should be possible to unlearn the problem behavior. Thus, therapy should follow an extinction procedure. However, even during this period, it became clear that not all fears could be extinguished. Evolutionary perspectives give insight into why certain fears would have more potency than others.

Historical Perspective on Psychopathology

We have discussed the general question of how we should understand psychopathology from an evolutionary perspective. We can also be more specific. Ask yourself what you are afraid of. As you think about the answer, it becomes apparent that most of what we fear has been with us throughout our evolutionary time. Many individuals will describe the fear of heights, dark, deep water, small spaces, blood, or certain animals such as spiders and snakes. Most individuals will not say they are afraid of more recent inventions, such as cars or computers. However, we are all at much greater risk from being hurt by a car than by snakes or spiders. It is easy to see why fear of spiders or heights would be protective at one time in our evolutionary history. From this perspective, we might think of psychopathology as a normal process that has gone astray or is used at the wrong time. We might also use basic evolutionary processes to organize considerations of psychopathology. Using this organizing principle, we could describe disorders of self-preservation, disorders of sexuality, and disorders of social processes.

The modern study of psychopathology is generally dated to the late 1700s. As with the move toward experimentation and empiricism in physics and chemistry, the study of psychopathology initially began with careful description. There was also a shift away from external explanations, such as possession by spirits, toward an explanation in terms of natural processes. With this shift came a differentiation between patients in mental hospitals who experienced mental disorders and those who were just misfits in their society. Marquis de Sade, who wrote novels of a sexual nature, was released by the director of a mental hospital in Paris during this period with the statement, "He is not mad; his only madness is vice." (Szasz, 1970). The difference between vice and madness was one of many dichotomies that has plagued the study of psychopathology over the centuries; it continues to this day as a larger intellectual and societal question. For example, is drug addiction a pleasure-seeking mechanism that is being overused? It was only at the end of the 20th century that addictions such as alcoholism were officially viewed by the federal government as physiological disorders rather than a problem of will.

Underlying many of these dichotomies is the dualism associated with the French philosopher Descartes who, in the 1600s, described human beings as influenced by both physiological processes, such as the body, which could be measured scientifically, and mental processes, including the soul, which follow different laws. Even without the religious questions of Descartes' time, this dichotomy reflected in a mind/body differentiation has influenced psychopathological research. A separate but related question is the extent to which psychopathological symptoms are to be viewed as representing underlying brain pathology or an exaggeration of everyday behavior. "Both" is the answer underlying current therapeutic approaches. This implies that psychosis is the result of a brain disorder, whereas affective disorders such as generalized anxiety disorder are seen as exaggerations of normal processes. Evolutionary perspectives offer the opportunity to move beyond these current dichotomies by focusing on the manner in which psychopathology developed within the context of our evolutionary history.

HUGHLINGS JACKSON AND MACLEAN

Before continuing, let me bring you back to the brain and evolution work of John Hughlings Jackson in the 1800s and Paul MacLean in the 1900s. Although I previously discussed their work in Chapter 4 in relation to brain evolution, it is also important in relation to mental disorders (Ploog, 2003). As you remember, Hughlings Jackson introduced the idea of different functional levels in the nervous system. The higher levels of the cortex were seen to inhibit the lower subcortical ones. Hughlings Jackson further saw the lower levels as more structured, in the sense that they performed fixed processes. One example of such a fixed and automatic process is the startle reflex. We all jump when we unexpectedly hear a loud noise. The higher centers, on the other hand, are more flexible in how they deal with information and include voluntary components in their response. According to Hughlings Jackson, evolution was the development over time of these higher and more complex centers. Evolution was the movement from the more automatic centers of lower brain processes to the more voluntary ones. Hughlings Jackson believed that in mental disorders such as schizophrenia, the higher systems were no longer inhibiting the lower ones, resulting in illusions, hallucinations, and delusions. Disorders such as epilepsy occurred when the lower center lacked inhibition. Without inhibition, lower brain processes can propagate unchecked. This results in the large EEG waves seen in epilepsy. Hughlings Jackson called this process "dissolution of the nervous system."

In a paper on mental disorders, Jackson (1932) stated,

Disease is said to "cause" the symptoms of insanity. I submit that disease only produces negative mental symptoms answering to the dissolution, and that all elaborate positive mental symptoms (illusions, hallucinations, delusions, and extravagant conduct) are the outcome of activity of the nervous elements untouched by any pathological process; that they arise during activity on the lower level of evolution remaining. (p. 46)

In his view of a hierarchical representation of the brain, Hughlings Jackson was a forerunner to Paul MacLean and his concept of the triune brain. The theory of the triune brain, as I described in Chapter 4, suggested that from an evolutionary perspective, the brain could be seen as consisting of three major components. The first component was involved in the regulation of basic systems such as temperature, breathing, and sleep, as well as fixed types of displays seen in relation to self-preservation and sexuality. This is a large part of the forebrain in reptiles and birds. The second component related to emotionality and came with the development of the limbic system. As pointed out earlier, the transition from reptiles to mammals included three important processes associated with the development of the limbic system: (1) nursing of the infant in the context of maternal care; (2) oral communication for maintaining mother-child contact; and (3) play and its role in social development. Finally, the third component of the triune brain was the neomammalian brain. It is this aspect of our human nature that enables us to consider future possibilities, have extensive knowledge of and relationships with our external environment, and perform a large variety of cognitive and social processes. Given these separate components and types of information, there is the possibility that conflict within the brain can result. For example, what may be important for you on a higher level may be at odds with your initial basic reaction. The basic idea that ties the triune brain to psychopathology is this potential conflict between cognitive, emotional, and reptilian responses.

FREUD

Sigmund Freud was greatly influenced by Darwin. In fact, Freud quotes Darwin in many of his written works (Bailey, 1987; Sulloway, 1983). On some topics, such as the development of emotions, including fears, in children, Darwin and Freud followed parallel tracks. One important theme in their work was the role of instinctual processes in child development. As we have discussed throughout this book, Darwin emphasized two main instinctual processes—self-preservation and sexual selection. Similarly, Freud said that he began his studies with the idea that hunger and love are what moves the world. However, in his writings Freud emphasized sexual processes over those of self-preservation. As Freud described in his early work, he viewed instinctual energy as a form of biological energy that could build up unless it was in some way expressed. The lack of expression of sexual energy, for example, was seen to be the basis of various types of psychopathology. Likewise, the experience of sexual and self-preservation instincts, when in conflict with the restrictive rules of a particular society, were seen to lead to anxiety. Overall, Freud saw neurosis as an attempt by individuals to treat the problem they were experiencing. For example, anxious individuals often worry too much about problems or events that could happen in the future. Although consideration of future problems may be helpful in problem solving, constant consideration or worry is not.

JUNG

Carl Jung was, in many ways, a forerunner of the modern evolutionary psychology perspective. He understood that humans came into the world with a variety of instinctual processes and that there was an important genetic component to human behavior. Like Paul MacLean, Jung viewed humans as influenced by an evolutionary history that could manifest on a variety of levels that were capable of conflicting with one another. One important emphasis of Jung's work was his suggestion that all humans were similar in their psychological processes and that these processes were based in our evolutionary history. To demonstrate this, Jung collected dreams and stories from around the world that, he suggested, showed similar patterns of relationships. Jung was also interested in symbols and the manner in which humans have used symbols to represent and generate artistic and religious meaning. Jung was also important for his conceptualization of psychological development across the lifespan. He described the manner in which each stage of life brings forth a particular pattern of functioning, which he called an archetype.

BOWLBY

From a development perspective, John Bowlby laid out in great detail the manner in which evolutionarily significant processes, such as attachment, could, in certain circumstances, lead to anxiety rather than comfort. As we have seen, attachment is the situation in which a caregiver and an infant establish a close psychological and physical relationship, which protects the infant and allows for optimal development. The model that Bowlby articulated was that if an emotional caregiver were not present or a close connection could not be established, then the result was distress. Initial distress can be seen as an attempt to reestablish the connection. Continued distress is seen to lead to fear and anxiety of an enduring nature. Current research with affective disorders such as anxiety has shown a relationship between the degree of anxiety and the type of attachment relationship in childhood. Other researchers have suggested that apparently "abnormal" types of attachment may represent strategies that offer infants a way to obtain resources from their caregivers in difficult situations (Belsky, 1997, 1999).

JAAK PANKSEPP

As described in Chapter 6, Jaak Panksepp suggested that there are seven basic systems from which emotions develop: anger, fear, sexual lust, maternal care, separation distress and social bonding, playfulness, and resource seeking. He further suggests that these can also be seen as related to particular psychopathologies. Below I will review the emotional systems and the psychopathologies that develop from them.

1. Anger or rage is evoked when there is stiff competition for resources. This system can also be aroused by restraint, frustration, and other irritations. Out of this system can emerge irritability, contempt, and hatred. Psychopathologies associated with this system would be those involving aggression, such as conduct disorders in children, psychopathic tendencies, and personality disorders.

2. Fear is evoked when the organism is in the presence of danger. This system will evoke freezing at low levels of arousal and flight at higher levels. Research suggests that external stimuli may be processed quickly, but less consciously, by low-level brain circuits or slower, but more accurately, by high cognitive levels. Out of this system can emerge simple anxiety, worry, and psychic trauma. Psychopathologies associated with this system include generalized anxiety disorder (GAD), phobias, and various forms of PTSD.

3. Sexual lust manifests during puberty, although the basic components of the system exist early in the development of the organism. Out of this system can emerge erotic feelings as well as jealousy. Psychopathologies associated with this system include fetishes and sexual addictions.

4. Care systems are designed to enable us to nurture one another. Out of this system can emerge nurturance, love, and attraction. Psychopathologies associated with this system include dependency disorders, attachment disorders, and aloofness.

5. Separation distress is seen when a young organism is separated from its mother. In a variety of species, the infant will cry out in these situations. Extreme cases result in panic. Panksepp suggests that these feelings of abandonment may build on early pain circuits. Out of this system can emerge sadness, guilt, shame, and shyness. Psychopathologies associated with this system include panic attacks, pathological grief, depression, agoraphobia, and social phobia.

6. Play is seen in a variety of species and is often accompanied by the expression of joy and laughter. As we saw earlier, play is considered an important preparation for later social life. Out of this system

can emerge joy and happy playfulness. Psychopathologies associated with this system include mania and disorders of hyperactivity, such as ADHD.

7. The seeking system controls our desire to find and harvest the resources of the world. Across species, it is related to the motivation to obtain resources from the environment. In humans, it is connected with goal-directed urges and positive expectations concerning the world, as well as with awareness and appraisals of the world. Out of this system can emerge interest, frustration, and caring. Psychopathologies associated with this system include obsessive compulsive disorders, paranoid schizophrenia, and addictive disorders.

Psychopathology in the Context of Natural Functioning

Mental disorders can be considered a failure of psychological adaptations to perform their natural function. In thinking about psychopathology from this evolutionary perspective, Wakefield (1992) first suggests that we need to understand natural function as well as its opposite, dysfunction. Natural function is what a particular process has evolved to do. For example, the heart is designed to pump blood. Other processes, such as the sounds that the heart makes, are byproducts of this purpose. Thus, it would not be suggested that the heart evolved to make sounds. In this example, dysfunction would be the situation in which the heart could not adequately pump blood. Similarly, the visual system processes external stimulation, whereas a dysfunction in this system could lead to visual hallucinations. Likewise, fear serves a natural function by protecting an organism in dangerous situations. However, when fear is manifested in situations in which there is no clear danger, then there is a dysfunction. In terms of traditional psychopathology, the person in such a situation would be described as a displaying a phobia. Phobias, such as the case in which a person refuses to leave his house, would be considered dysfunctional. Wakefield concluded that a condition is a mental disorder if two conditions are met: First, the condition causes harm to the person, and second, the condition results from the inability of some mental mechanism to perform its natural function. The emphasis is on what the mechanism evolved to do and whether there is a problem in accomplishing this task.

This type of thinking can be further clarified by asking three questions (Nesse, 2005): (1) Are the cognitive and brain mechanisms normal or defective? If the brain mechanisms are defective, as might result from accidents or trauma, then an evolutionary analysis of psychopathology would be inappropriate. (2) Did the symptoms arise from novel aspects of the environment? As we have seen, there are novel aspects of modern environments that may evoke responses that would have been appropriate in an earlier time, but not in modern society. (3) Are the symptoms in the interest of the individual, his or her genes, or neither?

From these three questions Nesse (2005) developed a categorization system to consider psychopathology. He first looks at emotional, cognitive, and behavioral responses that arise from normal systems. He suggests that there are five conditions in which these responses may arise.

1. There are normal responses that may be useful to the person, such as anxiety or anger, but which can be experienced as aversive.

2. There are normal responses that would benefit the individual's genes but may be at odds with the individual's self-interest.

3. There are normal responses that may not be useful in a particular case.

4. There are normal responses that may not be useful at present, but would have been useful in a previous time.

5. There are normal responses that are not harmful to the individual, but may be viewed as abnormal by a person's group or culture.

Applying an Evolutionary Perspective to Psychopathology

DEVELOPING FEARS

From an evolutionary perspective, to be fearful in the presence of dangerous situations would be adaptive. One scientific aspect of this is the question of how fixed or plastic these fears are. From research, we know that certain phobias run in families, suggesting a genetic component. However, not everyone has exactly the same fears, suggesting that fear may be a developmental process. One classic study in fear development is that of Susan Mineka and her colleagues (see Öhman & Mineka, 2001 for an overview). It had been observed that primates in the wild show a fear of snakes. Because a similar fear was seen in lab monkeys, it was assumed that the fear was somehow innate. However, Mineka asked whether early experience could influence this. In particular, she wanted to know whether observational learning could play a role. She and her colleagues compared wild-reared rhesus monkeys to those who had been reared in the lab. The wild-reared monkeys who had been brought to the lab some 24 years earlier showed a fear of snakes. This fear existed even though they would have had no experience with snakes during their time in the lab. The lab-reared monkeys, on the other hand, did not show any fear of snakes. If fact, they would reach over the snake to grab food. How did monkeys develop the fear of snakes? What Mineka did next was pair a wild-reared monkey with a young lab-reared one. A snake was then presented and the wild-reared monkey showed fear. The young lab-reared monkey was able to observe this. After this, the lab-reared monkey also showed fear. Clearly, the lab-reared monkey had the ability to quickly acquire the fear, but required an experience in which another monkey showed fear for it to happen. The next question Mineka and her colleagues studied was the importance of the feared object itself. In a very cleaver study, she showed some of the young monkeys a videotape of a wild monkey showing fear toward a snake. As expected, they acquired the fear of snakes. However, with another group of young monkeys, she edited the tape so what the young monkeys saw was the original fear reaction of the older monkey, but this time juxtaposed with a flower. If fear was acquired by a simple associative learning situation in which the stimulus did not matter, then you would expect the young monkeys to acquire a fear of flowers. This was not the case. From this and a variety of other studies, it appears that fear can be learned through observation, but only in relation to evolutionarily important objects. As you remember, this was also the case with the follow-up studies of Watson's work with little Albert described in Chapter 2. At this point I want to describe for you a variety of disorders that have been considered from an evolutionary perspective.

DEPRESSION

Depression is characterized by feeling sad or empty without any sense of pleasure in one's activities. All individuals experience depressed moods for brief periods, which are usually accompanied by feelings of sadness, loss of energy, social withdrawal, and often negative thoughts about oneself. With a depressive disorder, the individual may also experience sleep problems and weight changes. Included in the disorder is a sense of worthlessness and self-blame. Clinical depression is seen when the majority of these symptoms last for a period of time. There is a gender difference in that, over the course of a lifetime, about 1 in 4 females and 1 in 10 males experience a major depressive episode (Rutter, 2006). Genetic studies suggest that depression is equally influenced by genetic and environmental factors (Rutter, 2006). In one set of studies, monkeys with a genetic risk for depression were raised by either highly responsive or less responsive foster mothers (Suomi, 1997). In this situation, the mothers determined the outcome, with the more responsive mothers having less-depressed infants.

Andrews (2007) suggests that there are only a limited number of hypotheses that might explain the existence of depression from an evolutionary perspective. One hypothesis views depression as resulting from a novel reaction of the nervous system to the modern environment. This hypothesis suggests that our environment has changed quickly while our nervous system has not. However, Andrews rejects this hypothesis because depression is seen in a variety of animals, such as rats, cats, and primates, whose environment has not changed drastically in recent times. Another hypothesis views depression as a process that evolved because it was connected to another trait that was extremely adaptive. This connection has yet to be found. A third hypothesis suggests that depression evolved because it had a useful function. Gilbert (2005) asks whether depression might serve as an advantage in situations in which positive affect and drive should be toned down. One simple answer is that a reduction of positive affect could make one more sensitive to threat. Gilbert then takes this question a step further and asks at what point the increase in depressive mood becomes maladaptive. In Chapter 13, we examined situations in which stress resulted in a variety of depression-like symptoms, including reduction of positive affect, activity, and motivational factors, such as hunger. In this chapter, I emphasize theories that examine depression in relation to social factors.

Allen and Badcock (2003) begin with the role of depressed mood in our evolutionary history. They see depressed mood as having evolved in relation to social processes. Like other researchers, they suggest that a depressed state represents a risk management strategy in response to a situation that has a low probability of success and high probability of risk. The emphasis is on social situations in which an individual would be at risk of being excluded, either from groups or a relationship with another individual. Basically they see depressed mood as the result of a computational problem on the part of the individual. That is to say, on some level the individual evaluates the situation. In a situation in which there is high risk of being excluded, this evaluation leads to depressed mood. Intrinsic to this way of thinking is the assumption that a depressed mood was adaptive in our evolutionary history. That is to say, feeling depressed would help the individual solve a problem faced by humans from the earliest times. Overall, there are three questions that need to be approached from an evolutionary perspective in relation to depression (Nesse, 1990, 1998).

1. What are the situations occurring over and over again in our environment of evolutionary adaptiveness that are responsible for depressive states?

2. What are the selection pressures in these situations? What reproductive goals would have been threatened?

3. What are the characteristics of depressed mood that would have enabled the organism to cope with these threats?

These questions have been answered by evolutionary psychologists in terms of three broad models: (1) theories of resource conservation, (2) theories of social competition, and (3) theories of attachment.

Theories of Resource Conservation

Theories of resource conservation suggest that a depressive mood protects the organism by conserving energy. By reducing energy expenditure, the organism can both protect itself in the present situation and conserve energy that can be used in future productive situations. In Chapter 13, considering the work of Jay Weiss and others, we saw how stress, and especially uncontrollable events, can affect the organism and produce a depressed state. According to these theories, clinical depression results when an individual does not move on to the next situation and instead continues in a situation in which there are few positive payoffs.

Theories of Social Competition

In discussing dominance hierarchies across species, it was noted that the most powerful individual has a greater chance of mating and passing on his genes. Typically, two males fight to determine which will be higher in power. It has also been observed that the animal that loses the competition will make submissive gestures. David Buss, in a variety of writings, has extended this type of thinking to humans and suggested that there exists a powerful motivation to acquire rank and status, especially among human males (see Buss, 2006 for an overview). Price (1996) suggested that there is a connection between depressive mood and losing a fight for status and resources. In particular, he suggested that the losing organism adopts a strategy in which he signals a desire to not continue the competition and withdraw. The winner, on the other hand, tends to escalate the competition and increasingly displays threatening behaviors. From this viewpoint, depression is seen as an involuntary deescalating strategy that signals to the other individual that he has won.

Theories of Attachment

As you read in Chapter 5, John Bowlby developed a theoretical understanding of interpersonal relationships based on the interactions of a child with his or her parents. This type of bonding, of course, has great survival value for a human infant who cannot take care of herself. As we also discussed, attachment patterns can be seen in later human interpersonal and sexual relationships. A disruption of the relationship is experienced by the person as a loss. It is this loss that results in the withdrawal and depressed mood. On the infant level, the value of such a depression would be to protect the child by reducing the desire to explore or leave the present environment, which would protect the child from potential danger. A similar process would work on the adult human level, in which a loss of attachment and the resulting depression would protect the individual from further hurt until mental healing could take place.

Social Risk Hypothesis

Allen and Badcock (2003) begin to integrate the three previous broad models of depression with the social risk hypothesis. This hypothesis suggests that when significant interpersonal relationships are disrupted, including by social humiliation or defeat, depressed mood is the outcome. For them, depressed mood is a signal to the individual. It is associated with risk aversion, which has evolved over human history. In this sense, it is a protective mechanism that prevents further critical losses. It is protective in two ways. First, depressed mood reduces the desire of the individual to immediately enter a social relationship in which there could be an adverse outcome. And second, the outward signs of depressed mood, including changes in voice tone, reaction time, eye contact, and facial expression, signal to others signs of submission and helplessness.

OCD

Obsessive compulsive disorder (OCD) is characterized by repetitive thoughts and feelings, usually followed by repetitive behaviors. The thoughts are usually perceived as unpleasant and unwanted. A distinction is made between obsessions and compulsions. *Obsessions* are generally unwelcome thoughts that come into one's head. In persons with OCD, they involve avoiding contamination, aggressive impulses, sexual content, somatic concerns, and the need for order. *Compulsions* are the behaviors that one uses to respond to these thoughts. Some behaviors, like cleaning or placing objects in order, reflect a desire to respond to the obsessions. Other compulsions, such as hand washing, are more avoidant in nature for fear of what one might say, do, or experience in a particular situation. Often individuals with OCD will constantly check to see whether they performed a particular behavior, such as turning off the stove or unplugging an iron. Interestingly, individuals with OCD may be aware that their thoughts and actions may seem bizarre to others, but they cannot dismiss the thoughts or need for action.

There is clearly a parallel between the themes found in OCD and concerns expressed by those without the disorder. Most individuals naturally avoid contamination or express concerns when they experience unusual bodily sensations. On a societal level, there are often rituals concerned with health and success in the world. Tribal cultures perform rituals to banish evil spirits or bring in the good ones. Most modern societies have a variety of rituals, including not walking under a ladder, stepping on sidewalk cracks, or other behaviors, as ways of avoiding bad luck. Sports teams also have rituals for how to prepare for an important game. Not performing these rituals may result in a feeling of anxiety for many individuals.

A variety of studies have suggested that OCD is found throughout the world at similar rates, although it is more frequently found in females than males (see Feygin, Swain, & Leckman, 2006 for an overview). Feygin et al. suggest that OCD results from the exaggeration of normal traits, which can be mapped onto a developmental trajectory. In particular, they discuss four developmental themes as a response to stress. Each of these themes could be tied to a normal developmental stage in which fear or threatening situations were overemphasized:

1. Loss similar to anxious attachment. The obsession is that someone could be lost to the person. There are a wide variety of situations in which this could happen. A friend, lover, or child could be killed in an accident, for example. To prevent this, the compulsion is to check on the person to make sure that he or she is still OK or to create situations in which the person will not be at risk.

2. Physical security in one's own environment. A common manifestation is that the person checks to make sure everything is in its place.

3. Environmental cleanliness. The fear is that objects, or the person herself, are dirty and that this will result in disease or other negative events. The behavior, of course, is to clean obsessively.

4. Fear that the person will be deprived of resources or objects that are important to him. A person who experiences these obsessions will either hoard objects or resources or try to prevent any situation in which he could come in contact with loss.

Another model of OCD draws from animal behavior. In Chapter 1, you learned about fixed action patterns. One of the most familiar of these was Lorenz's ducks that would follow whatever moving object interacted with them during the critical period of 16 to 36 hours after birth. Similar stereotypical behavior is seen in social and sexual displays. For example, some lizards move their heads up and down when they greet another lizard, and the male peacock displays its tail feathers in the presence of a female. The basic idea is that these patterns are triggered by particular stimuli and result in behaviors that are very similar each time they are manifested. Overall, these behaviors help the organism survive and reproduce; thus, they are viewed as adaptive. It also has been observed that these fixed patterns of behavior are repeated frequently under conditions of trauma, stress, or in nonnatural settings such as a zoo (Rauch, Corá-Locatelli, & Greenberg, 2000). Such a frequent manifestation of the same behavior would not be appropriate for the situation. Clearly, you would find it strange if someone kept greeting you over and over again even after you acknowledged his or her presence. Given that the frequent repetition of patterned behaviors is generally associated with highly aroused organisms, one view is that this is the attempt of the organism to reduce stress. In many species, including humans, repetitive patterns, such as rocking movements, grooming, vocalizations, and pacing, are seen during periods of stress. These repetitive processes are seen by some to lie at the basis of OCD and to involve the basal ganglia, which is a more primitive brain area (Rapoport, 1990).

OCD appears to run in families, with first-degree relatives of a person with OCD having an eightfold chance of developing OCD themselves. This would lead one to expect a genetic relationship to exist. However, this has been difficult to demonstrate. Another line of research involves a search for underlying similarities in the brain processing that is associated with OCD. In one study, individuals with OCD, their first-degree relatives without OCD, and a matched control group were given a task that required the individual to reverse what was learned previously (Chamberlain et al., 2008). On each side of a screen, the participant was shown a face superimposed on top of a building. One of the images was considered the target. The faces and building were different, and the person had to guess which image was considered correct. After each guess, feedback was given as to whether the person was correct or not. Thus, after a few trials, the person learned the "correct" image. Once an individual was correct on six trials, either the "correct" image was changed or a new set of images was presented. Either way, new learning was required. Using brain imaging techniques (fMRI), it was shown that individuals with OCD and their unaffected relatives had similar patterns of brain activation as compared to controls. In particular, controls showed greater brain activation in the orbitofrontal cortex than the OCD individuals and their relatives. Other studies have shown this area of the frontal cortex to be related to reversal learning and flexibility.

SCHIZOPHRENIA

Schizophrenia is one of the most debilitating of the mental disorders. It affects one's ability to express oneself clearly, to have close social relationships, and to express and experience positive emotions (see Andreasen, 2000; Walker, Kestler, Bollini, & Hochman, 2004 for reviews). Some individuals with schizophrenia also hear voices, see images not seen by others, or believe that others wish to harm or control them. It affects about 1% of the population. It is seen throughout the world with similar symptoms, regardless of culture or geographical location. Typically, two types of symptoms can be demonstrated in the disorder. One is called negative symptoms because what is important is what is not present. The lack of affect in situations which call for it, poor motivation, and social withdrawal are all examples of negative symptoms. The second is called positive symptoms, and these symptoms relate to what is experienced. Visual or auditory hallucinations, delusions, and bizarre thoughts are all examples of positive symptoms. In general, the onset of schizophrenia occurs in the late teens or early twenties. It affects males more often than females. Because it tends to run in families and is seen throughout the world, it is thought to have a genetic component, but there does not appear to be a simple genetic relationship as seen in Huntington's disease or cystic fibrosis. Twin studies show a higher concordance rate: approximately 40% in monozygotic twins compared to 10% in dizygotic twins. A variety of genetic studies suggest that genetic factors account for about 82% of the variance, suggesting that environmental factors are less critical in the development of schizophrenia (Rutter, 2006). Adopted children from families with schizophrenia show a similar rate to those raised with their natural families, also suggesting rearing factors per se are not related to its development.

It has been noted that highly gifted and creative individuals manifest schizophrenic-like traits, referred to as "schizotypal" traits, without having the disorder. However, it is not uncommon for these individuals to have a first-degree relative with schizophrenia, suggesting a genetic component. Andreasen (2000) suggests there may be a connection between scientific creativity and schizophrenia in one's family. She notes that a number of Nobel Laureates have family members who were thought to have schizophrenia, including Albert Einstein, Bertrand Russell, and John Nash, who had it himself. As you may remember, John Nash's story was described in the film *A Beautiful Mind*. Although a variety of research studies suggest a genetic component, it is clearly not a simple one involving a single gene. An important question for evolutionary psychologists is why schizophrenia hasn't disappeared over time, given that the disorder does not appear to have any reproductive advantage. In fact, the majority of people with schizophrenia do not marry or have children. Thus, one would expect it to disappear within a few generations. One answer to this dilemma is that there might be an advantage to those who carry the gene associated with schizophrenia, but not to its pathological expression (Huxley, Mayr, Osmond, & Hoffer, 1964). However, at this point there is only speculation as to what this advantage might be.

A number of researchers have examined schizophrenia from an evolutionary perspective (see Burns, 2004 for an overview). Tim Crow, as have many researchers, begins with the paradox of how a genetically related disorder can exist without a reproductive advantage (Crow, 2000; Mitchell & Crow, 2005). In order to consider this question, Crow notes that schizophrenia is seen in all cultures, suggesting that its primary determinant is more independent of the environment than other disorders. Multiple sclerosis, for example, occurs at a greater frequency the farther from the equator one grew up, suggesting an important role for environmental conditions in the development of the disorder. The fact that schizophrenia is found throughout the world suggests that the environment plays a less direct role. Further, given that it is found in all groups, Crow suggests that its origin must have occurred before the mass movement from Africa less than 100,000 years ago. What was the event in the entire human population that led to schizophrenia? Crow suggests it was the development of the capacity for language. As discussed in Chapter 4, the anatomical event associated with this was the development of the independence of the two cerebral hemispheres of the human brain. This asymmetry allowed for language to be more specialized in the left hemisphere and for spatial abilities to be more represented in the right hemisphere of the human brain. However, it has been shown that understanding certain emotional aspects of language, as well as understanding humor, sarcasm, and metaphor, may involve the right hemisphere. Crow notes that individuals with schizophrenia display symptoms that represent problems with language. He suggests that schizophrenia is related to problems of development in relation to language, which involve the inability of the person to distinguish his or her thoughts from speech itself, including what others say to the person.

Jonathan Burns (2004, 2006) suggested that schizophrenia is related to the evolution of the social brain in humans. In particular, he sees it as related to the frontal areas and their connections to other parts of the human brain that are involved in our ability to represent our relationships. This includes the ability to know others' intentions or theory of mind, as I discuss previously. The potential for schizophrenia is the result of tradeoffs at two distinct times in our long evolutionary history. The first tradeoff happened between 16 and 2 million years ago. This was the time in which complex cerebral interconnectivity and specialized circuits were being evolved in the brain in relation to the cognitive and intellectual demands of living in social groups. To perform the tasks required for social living, a higher level of cognitive functioning was required. In order for the brain to develop the circuits required, brain maturation was lengthened. That is, given the physical constraints of the developing brain in the human fetus, the period for brain development needed to be lengthened. This tradeoff meant that the developing brain experienced a long period of time in which complex gene interactions or accidents could happen.

According to Burns (2006), the second tradeoff happened more recently, about 100,000 to 150,000 years ago. This date is important. Because schizophrenia is seen in all cultures with similar symptoms, it is assumed that the genes involved in its manifestation would have evolved before humans migrated out of Africa. What happened at this point was that some individuals experienced abnormal connections in the frontal areas of the brain. These connections resulted in some individuals being especially creative and thinking in different ways. These individuals may have been able to make important contributions to culture, much as our present-day artists and creative thinkers do. However, some individuals demonstrated a more severe version of these connections, which resulted in psychopathological experiences. Burns further suggests that this different way of experiencing the world, in either its mild or severe form, did not have any reproductive advantage. However, because the genes that controlled these experiences evolved as a part of the larger cortical networks needed for the cognitive and intellectual demands of social life, these genes continued to be passed on through their connections with adaptive mechanisms. Thus, according to Burns, schizophrenia represents one of the prices paid for evolving complex cognitive and social abilities.

ABNORMAL SOCIAL PSYCHOLOGY

As clinicians have moved from learning theory-directed theories of psychopathology to those derived from the neurosciences, and thus consistent with the evolutionary perspective, a variety of disorders have been reexamined, including autism, Williams syndrome, psychopathy, and social phobia. In the same way that we can speak of affective disorders such as depression or anxiety, we can also speak of social disorders. At this point I want to examine two of these disorders.

Autism

Individuals with autism display problems in three areas (Baron-Cohen & Belmonte, 2005): social functions, communications, and restrictions in behaviors and interests. In particular, individuals with autism look less at other individuals and show a reduced response in the mirror neuron system. The also show difficulty in interpersonal communication and tend to repeat activities in a stereotyped manner. A related disorder—Asperger syndrome—shows social impairments and restricted behaviors but fewer problems in terms of language and communication. One current theory of autism centers on problems related to empathy. In particular, it is suggested that individuals with autism fail to develop a theory of mind. As you remember, *theory of mind* refers to one's ability to infer the mental states of others in relation to their actions or situations. In a variety of studies, individuals with autism were able to describe what was going on in someone else's behavior on the perceptual level, but they showed difficulties when asked to describe the social/emotional processes that would be expected to accompany the behaviors. This appears to be a general lack of ability because they also have problems reflecting on these aspects of their own behavior. Another characteristic of autism is the desire to have a stable set of routines, which results in problems shifting attention. In terms of cortical areas involved, individuals with autism display a variety of differences in those areas previously described as the social brain. Briefly, these are the amygdala, specific areas of the frontal lobes, and areas of the temporal lobe. There is also some suggestion that infants who develop autism show an overgrowth of brain volume followed by deceleration in the first years of life. Amaral, Schumann, and Nordahl (2008) have described the neuroanatomy of autism. Figure 14.1

Figure 14.1 Brain areas involved in social impairment, communication deficits, and repetitive behaviors in autism.

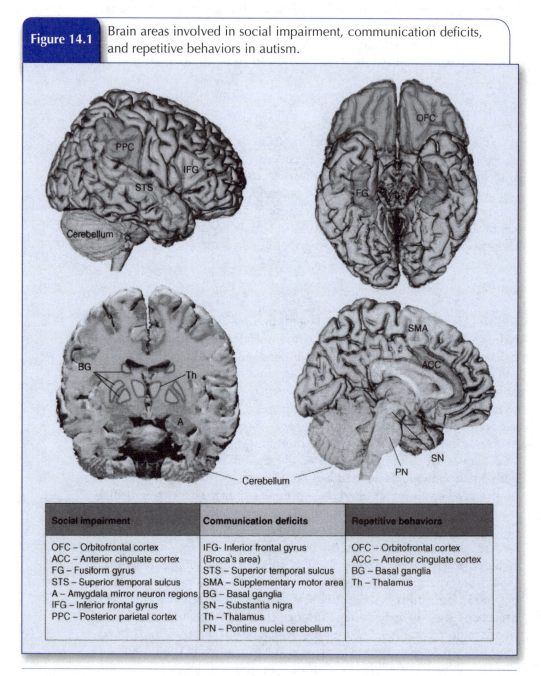

Social impairment	Communication deficits	Repetitive behaviors
OFC – Orbitofrontal cortex	IFG- Inferior frontal gyrus (Broca's area)	OFC – Orbitofrontal cortex
ACC – Anterior cingulate cortex	STS – Superior temporal sulcus	ACC – Anterior cingulate cortex
FG – Fusiform gyrus	SMA – Supplementary motor area	BG – Basal ganglia
STS – Superior temporal sulcus	BG – Basal ganglia	Th – Thalamus
A – Amygdala mirror neuron regions	SN – Substantia nigra	
IFG – Inferior frontal gyrus	Th – Thalamus	
PPC – Posterior parietal cortex	PN – Pontine nuclei cerebellum	

Source: Amaral, Schumann, and Nordahl (2008).

shows areas involved in social impairment, communication deficits, and repetitive behaviors.

Current neuroscience studies show that by the time of full brain development, a person with autism shows deficits in these areas that make up the social brain. For example, whereas individuals without autism tend to scan the eyes when looking at another person, those with autism focus on the mouth. Because various features of the eyes give another person both emotional and social information, those with autism miss out on this information. Coupled with the inability to empathize is the superior ability to systemize. Systemizing is the ability to analyze objects or events in terms of their structure and future behavior. These deficits and abilities make up the empathizing-systemizing theory of autism (Baron-Cohen & Belmonte, 2005). In terms of genetics, twin studies of individuals with these social difficulties show 92% concordance for monozygotic twins versus 10% for dizygotic pairs.

Williams Syndrome

Williams syndrome is a fairly rare genetic condition related to chromosome 7, which leads to a unique pattern of both strengths and weaknesses. Weaknesses include delayed developmental milestones and problems with certain organ systems, such as the heart, and problems with spatial abilities and fine motor coordination. Strengths include good language skills and social behaviors. These individuals are overly social, are especially interested in other people, and are able to recognize the mental states of others. In fact, these individuals are socially fearless and will eagerly engage with strangers. If you were to show individuals with Williams syndrome and those without a series of threatening faces and threatening scenes, you would see that individuals with Williams would show amygdala activation only to threatening scenes, whereas those without Williams would respond to both threatening faces and threatening scenes (Meyer-Lindenberg et al., 2005; Meyer-Lindenberg, Mervis, & Berman, 2006). This is shown in Figure 14.2.

In Figure 14.2, "a" shows the group difference in reactivity to face vs. scene matching, "b" through "e" show the fMRI between the groups and "f" and "g" show the best-fitting model for those without (f) and those with (g) Williams. This research suggests that although those with Williams syndrome display social processes, they lack the ability to read emotional responses in others. Thus, individuals with Williams syndrome show more social responding than those with autism. Given these characteristics, Williams syndrome has become a model syndrome for investigating social engagement (see Tager-Flusberg & Plesa-Skwerer, 2006 for an overview).

Figure 14.2

Brain activation in response to threatening faces and scenes by those with and without Williams syndrome. Graph a shows the group difference in fMRI reactivity to face vs. scene matching. Graphs b-d show fMRI differences in specific areas. Graphs f and g show the best-fitting model for those without (f) and those with (g) Williams.

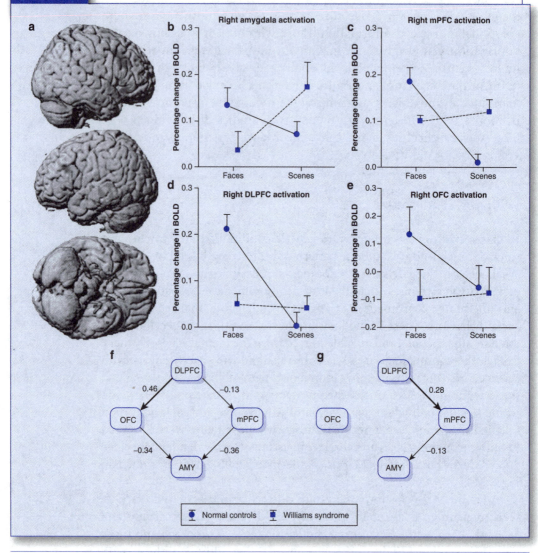

Source: Meyer-Lindenberg et al. (2005).

SUMMARY

Psychopathology is present in all societies. Five ideas have been critical in the definition of psychopathology. First, the processes involved in psychopathology are maladaptive and not in the individual's best interest. Second, the processes cause personal distress. Third, the processes represent a deviance from both cultural and statistical norms. Fourth, the person has difficulty connecting with his or her environment and also with himself or herself. Fifth, there is inability of an individual with a mental disorder to fully consider alternative ways of thinking, feeling, or doing. Schizophrenia is one disorder seen in all cultures with the same frequency. Historically, a variety of researchers have seen psychopathology as related to basic evolutionary mechanisms. Psychopathology may represent situations in which adaptive processes do not function appropriately.

STUDY RESOURCES

Review Questions

1. What are five critical ideas in the definition of psychopathology?

2. How does an evolutionary perspective enhance our understanding of psychopathology?

3. What are the seven potential models presented for characterizing psychopathology? What novel perspectives do they offer for understanding psychopathology?

4. Is psychopathology universal? What evidence would you cite to support your answer?

5. What contribution do Hughlings Jackson's and Paul MacLean's ideas about a hierarchical brain structure make to our understanding of psychopathology?

6. How is Freud's idea of sexual energy as the basis of some types of psychopathology related to Darwin's discussion of instinctual processes?

7. Describe Jung's contributions to the perspective of a universal psychopathology.

8. How does Bowlby's model of attachment help us understand affective disorders?

9. Jaak Panksepp identifies seven basic systems from which emotions develop. What are they, and what psychopathologies develop from them?

10. What are Wakefield's two conditions for a mental disorder to occur?

11. Describe Nesse's five conditions in which normal emotional, cognitive, or behavioral responses should be considered to be psychopathological.

12. Describe the three broad models that have been proposed to explain depression from an evolutionary perspective. How does Allen and Badcock's social risk hypothesis begin to integrate these models?

13. Research studies suggest that genetic factors account for about 82% of the incidence of schizophrenia. How would you explain the paradox of how a genetically related disorder like schizophrenia can persist through human history without a reproductive advantage?

For Further Reading

Brüne, M. (2008). *Textbook of evolutionary psychiatry: The origins of psychopathology.* New York: Oxford University Press.

Gilbert, P., & Bailey, K. (2000). *Genes on the couch: Explorations into evolutionary psychotherapy.* London: Taylor & Francis.

McGuire, M., & Troisi, A. (1998). *Darwinian psychiatry.* New York: Oxford University Press.

Key Terms and Concepts

- Models of psychopathology from an evolutionary perspective
- Universal psychopathology?
- Historical perspective on psychopathology
  - Hughlings Jackson and MacLean
  - Freud
  - Jung
  - Bowlby
  - Jaak Panksepp
- Psychopathology in the context of natural functioning
- Applying an evolutionary perspective to psychopathology
  - Developing fears
  - Depression
    - Theories of resource conservation
    - Theories of social competition
    - Theories of attachment
    - Social risk hypothesis
  - OCD
  - Schizophrenia
  - Abnormal social psychology
    - Autism
    - Williams syndrome

SAGE Study Site

Visit the study site at **www.sagepub.com/ray** for chapter-specific study resources.

Glossary Terms

- Affective disorders
- Darwinian psychiatry

- Evolutionary psychopathology

Culture 15

Culture Develops as We See Ourselves in a Larger Context

This book has emphasized the manner in which all human beings share a common evolutionary history. Some of these processes influence our current ways of being. As we have seen, humans have evolved the ability to process information in terms of broad meta-domains involving self-preservation, sexuality, and social formulations. In this evolutionary process, our brain architecture incorporated evolutionarily older brain structures, giving us access to different ways of processing our environment in terms of sensation, emotion, and cognition, including direct pathways to action. Not only did we increase our abilities to process our world using different channels of information, we also became able to integrate these various sources into a coherent whole. As we developed these greater cognitive abilities, we also gained the ability to reflect on ourselves and others and to make plans for our future. As humans, we have gained the ability to abstract and symbolize these relationships. This has resulted in our development of mathematics and science as a way of describing the universe and ourselves on a variety of levels. We also appear to have a strong need to reflect on our relationship with the universe and our place in it. This is revealed by our interest in the arts as well as our concern with spiritual and religious matters. Seeing ourselves in a larger context has allowed for the development of culture with its many-faceted expression of human totality.

Culture has to do with the manner in which societies place value on various aspects of human existence. We often see these values reflected in the ways in which a society works and what is available to individuals. We often talk about these processes more symbolically in terms of art and architecture, music and dance, religion and spirituality, and education and learning. All of these are symbolic in the sense that they attempt to convey meaning and information of the human experience beyond that of a single individual. In many ways, it is our ability to understand our similarities as humans that helps us to have a culture. Some researchers have even emphasized the development of shared goals and intentions during a human infant's first two years of life as the basic cognitive skills needed for the development of culture (Tomasello, Carpenter, Call, Behne, & Moll, 2005). It is this shared intentionality, which includes the ability to understand another as a person who has goals and seeks to perform self-directed activities, as well as the motivation to share emotions, experiences, and activities, which supports cultural development in humans.

Current views of culture also emphasize the social world in which a person lives (López & Guarnaccia, 2000). In this sense, culture can be viewed as "information capable of affecting individuals' behavior that they acquire from other members of their species through teaching, imitation, and other forms of social transmission" (Richerson & Boyd, 2005, p. 5). From this perspective, culture can be seen as a system of inheritance. Humans learn a variety of things from others in their culture including skills, values, beliefs, and attitudes. Historically, parents and others taught children how to perform particular jobs such as farming, tool making, and hunting. Human culture has also formalized learning in the form of schools and apprenticeships.

Historically, a simplistic view of culture has emphasized how each culture is locally determined, without reference to universal psychological processes. When universal ways of behaving, feeling, or thinking are suggested, this view assumes that this information is acquired by social learning. Although an important aspect of culture, this emphasis will quickly lead one into the outdated nature/nurture debate, which lacks the insights of modern evolutionary perspectives. For example, in Chapter 3 we confronted the question of why foods with milk were found in European diets and not in Asian diets. One answer was cultural preferences. However, a more complete answer includes the fact that Northern Europeans have a gene that allows them to continue digesting milk products after the traditional time of weaning. A person with such a gene would have had an advantage in Northern Europe because dairy products are a high quality food source and, in probably less than 10,000 years, that advantage would have enabled the gene to be passed on to almost all of the European population. Today, 98% of all individuals in Sweden have this gene. Even in America, with its European migration, there is a high percentage of individuals who are lactose tolerant, 88% of white Americans, to be exact. Native Americans, on the other hand, are not lactose tolerant.

The picture becomes even more complicated in terms of psychological process. There is a particular short allele of the 5-HTT gene that is associated with being prone to develop higher levels of anxiety and depression. When its occurrence is examined cross-culturally, studies have shown that 70% to 80% of Japanese individuals carry this gene, whereas only 40% to

45% of Europeans carry it (see Ambady & Bharucha, 2009 for an overview). The large question raised by these studies is whether this genetic variation influences the manner in which cultural structures formalize social interactions. Thus, not only can the environment influence genetics but genetics can influence culture.

A variety of researchers from various fields have begun to study how organisms can modify their environment and how this changes evolutionary selection pressures. This approach has been referred to as the *niche construction perspective* (Odling-Smee, Laland, & Feldman, 2003; Laland, Kendal, & Brown, 2007). Through technology and the construction of cities, humans greatly change their environment. This, in turn, changes the energy requirement and other demands on humans. What this suggests is that humans may be more active in shaping their own evolution than traditionally thought. As you will see, there is a close interaction between evolutionary and environmental factors in relation to culture.

Cultural Differences

Cultural differences have been noted at least since the time of Herodotus in 400 BCE. Not only did Herodotus note these differences, he also remarked that cultural groups see their practices as the best and would choose their approach over those of other cultures. In trying to understand culture, a variety of researchers have begun to study the nature of cultural differences (Gelfand et al., 2011; see Norenzayan, 2011 for an overview).

Gelfand and his colleagues (2011) surveyed 6,823 individuals in 33 nations. They asked individuals from a wide range of occupations to rate the appropriateness of 12 different behaviors (talking, crying, cursing, kissing, arguing, eating, laughing, singing, flirting, listening to music, reading a newspaper, and bargaining) in 15 different situations (bank, doctor's office, job interview, library, funeral, classroom, restaurant, public park, bus, bedroom, city sidewalk, party, elevator, workplace, and movie theater). The survey enabled the researchers to compare the degree to which a culture regulates social behavior and sanctions deviant behavior. Cultures that have strong norms were referred to as "tight cultures" and those with more relaxed norms as "loose" cultures.

What factors may influence whether a culture is tight or loose? What Gelfand and his colleagues (2011) found was that cultures that had present-day or historical threats such as territorial conflicts, resource scarcity, or exposure to high levels of pathogens tended to be tight cultures. That is, they more strictly regulated social behavior and punished deviance. This was true on both a cultural level and an individual level. On a cultural level, there were institutions that regulated social norms. On the personal level, the individuals reported more self-monitoring and less acceptance of those outside the culture. The looser cultures showed the opposite. Overall, this type of research suggests that culture can be seen as involving ecological, historical, institutional, and psychological factors (Norenzayan, 2011).

CULTURAL CHANGE

Is culture different from other types of change? Clearly, change within a culture can move faster than biological evolution. A fad can come and go very quickly. Technological change, such as cell phones, computers, and the Internet, can quickly change the manner in which individuals obtain information and communicate with each other. Reading and writing also reflect changes that are transmitted through culture. It is thought that writing developed as humans made the transition from hunting-gathering to farming. With the development of agriculture, humans remained in one place and had an increased need to keep track of seeds and products related to farming. Initially writing may have developed out of such a system of counting and labeling. Indeed, tokens that were used for counting animals such as sheep and products such as grains have been found dating back at least 9,000 years. Writing was developed some 5,000 years ago by the Sumerians of Mesopotamia. It is assumed to have developed independently in Egypt, China, and Mexico in the following centuries. The point is that writing and reading can be viewed as responses to the requirements of developing an agricultural society. Further, although humans learn language with ease, writing and reading require some form of educational process and thus can be viewed as an aspect of cultural development.

As a system of inheritance, can culture be analyzed using a Darwinian understanding of variation and change? That is to say, can evolutionary approaches help us understand why some cultural changes endure and others are diminished? Can such evolutionary ideas as natural selection, for example, be applied to culture? A number of researchers suggest that culture exhibits key Darwinian evolutionary properties (see Mesoudi, Whiten, & Laland, 2006 for an overview). One key property of Darwinian evolution is variation. Cultural variation is seen in terms of the diversity of cultural beliefs, knowledge, and artifacts. One example of such variation is language, of which there are approximately 6,800 spoken around the world. Cultural selection is seen to occur as the result of humans' limited attention, memory, and expression. Variation and selection lead to specific cultural parameters being passed on. Thus, some social scientists suggest that an approach to culture that models traditional evolutionary thinking offers insights into cultural changes over time that would not be discovered by a purely historical approach. For example, viewing culture as an adaptation allows us to ask different scientific questions than would be the case if we just viewed culture as a random local phenomenon.

If human culture can be viewed through the lens of evolutionary thought, then we might expect to find the basic building blocks of human culture in other species. In the sense of imitation and being influenced by the behavior of others, humans are not the only species that learn and transmit information in this manner (see Boesch & Tomasello, 1998; Boyd & Silk, 2006 for overviews). Some of the earliest work came from Jane Goodall's reports of chimpanzees using long slender twigs to collect termites. The chimpanzees would first strip the leaves from the twig and then place the twig in the termite nest. They could then pull out the twig and eat the termites attached to it. Not only did these chimpanzees demonstrate tool use, but future generations also showed these abilities, suggesting that some type of learning had taken place. Another often-quoted example of imitation is potato washing in a group of Japanese macaque monkeys. One young female in this group began to wash potatoes, which had become sandy. Other members of the group also began to wash their potatoes. In a variety of observations over the years by a variety of researchers, imitation learning has been observed in a variety of organisms. Given that different groups of a specific species may or may not demonstrate a particular ability or show group-specific variations, it has been suggested that imitation learning has taken place. This would be one basic mechanism by which societal techniques could be passed on to the next generation.

What if a chimpanzee and a human infant were raised together? Would the chimp infant copy the behaviors of the human? Such a situation happened in the 1930s when the Kelloggs (1933, 1967) co-reared their 10.5-month-old son Donald with a 7.5-month-old chimp, Gua. Because chimps are known to copy the behaviors of others, the Kelloggs thought this would be the case with Gua. However, it turns out that it was the human infant, Donald, who actually did the most copying of behaviors. This included putting his hands on the ground at times as he walked, chewing on shoes, and using grunts to refer to certain foods (Henrich & McElreath, 2007). The point is that humans in their early years imitate what is around them to an even greater degree than other animals; some researchers have referred to humans as "imitation machines" (Tomasello, 1999).

The hotly-debated topic in relation to nonhuman organisms and culture is the question of what is passed on to the next generation. Is it an understanding of the advantage of a particular tool usage or just an imitation? The question, of course, speaks to an organism's ability to cognitively understand its interaction with the environment, including its social group. Clearly, information can be passed from generation to generation in primates, but it is an open question whether this represents more than just imitation. Further, some researchers have suggested that humans are the only species that actively promotes the transmission of knowledge through both formal and informal mechanisms, such as schools. Other species may learn by observation of elders, but it is unclear whether the elders purposefully create the situation for the goal of teaching information and transmitting culture. From this perspective, one important aspect of the modern human mind is that it is a cultural mind (Boyer, 2000). This cultural mind can be considered in terms of the evolved cognitive capacities that make culture possible.

Flinn (2005) sought to determine the main characteristics of culture. In doing so, he described seven characteristics of culture:

1. Cultural content is transmitted by learning processes (i.e., cognitive information transfer) and not by the transfer of genetic materials. Hence, culture appears to be a separate inheritance system, uncoupled from genetics.

2. Culture (or its effects) is partly extrasomatic. Cultural traits (e.g., stone points, political monuments) exist outside the soma (physical body) of the culture-bearing organism.

3. Human culture, by most definitions, involves mental phenomena, including conscious thought.

4. Human culture involves the use of arbitrary symbols to form mental representations and to communicate information.

5. Culture appears to have emergent properties at the group level, such as shared values and beliefs resulting in political and religious institutions.

6. Culture involves historical processes. History constrains the options (cultural traits) available for individual choice and modification, and culture can change rapidly, apparently outpacing genetic evolution.

7. Complex culture is uniquely human.

In the first characteristic he notes that just as genetics is a system for the transmission of information, so is culture. As such, it can be understood as a separate system of transmission. In the second characteristic, Flinn (2005) notes that unlike genetic transmission, cultural transmission takes place outside the body. This suggests that those physical theories that are able to explain physiological processes may not adequately explain cultural products. The third characteristic is of importance to psychology. It suggests that mental processes are an active mechanism in the distribution and expansion of cultural ideas. Fourth, many symbols of culture are arbitrary. That is to say, much of the meaning ascribed to a cultural symbol is derived from the people involved with that culture. For example, an American flag is given meaning by the people themselves. Styles of clothes or music are likewise given meaning by particular people at particular times. The fifth characteristic is that processes are seen in groups that are not present in every individual. Just like a spontaneous reaction can appear from the fans at a football game, cultural processes can take place on a group level. Sixth, every culture has an historical perspective. However, unlike evolutionary change, any given cultural characteristic can be modified in a short time. The development of computers and cell phones are two examples of this. Seventh, humans have developed the most complex cultures of any species on earth. This includes the ability to modify the environment on a large scale as well as worldwide communication between individuals.

Culture and Technology

Culture is often used to refer to nonbiological means of transferring information across generations. Cultural transmission of information can occur at a much faster rate than evolutionary change. Just considering technological innovation, we can see drastic changes in our world in a very brief time. As I noted in earlier chapters, travel, communication, and connectedness of individuals are very different today than they were at the beginning of the 1900s. Architectural innovations that make possible multistoried high-rises have enabled the development of compact cities within a limited geographical space. Transportation advances enable the cities to be supplied with food and goods from around the world. Communication devices, including cell phones and computers, enable individuals from around the world to be in constant contact with one another. Once an innovation takes place in any location on earth, it can be copied and replicated throughout the world in a very brief period.

Interaction of Culture and Genes

Given that cultural change, especially in terms of technology, can be swift, and that biological change, especially in terms of our bodies, can be very slow, how do we understand the relationship between the two? Culture, by its very nature, produces an environmental influence on a person. In many ways, humans in a relatively short time have moved from living in nature to living in culture. The close interaction between evolutionary and environmental factors suggested by Darwin also applies for cultural factors. In fact, some researchers, such as Tooby and Cosmides (1992), suggest that many aspects of culture are constrained by factors of human nature. Likewise, cultural factors in place will also constrain the manner in which genetic processes are manifested.

These same environmental forces also take place in other primates. In a recent report, Sapolsky and Share (2004) describe a troop of baboons first studied in Kenya in the 1980s. In this troop, which sometimes fed from a garbage dump, there was aggression between males as well as harassment of females. The most aggressive males fought over the food from the dump. This food was not always sanitary and led to the aggressive males developing bovine tuberculosis and dying. This resulted in the doubling of the ratio of females to males. Further, those males that did survive were the less aggressive ones in the original troop. Overall, aggression dropped in the troop. Although new males came into the troop, because males migrate after puberty, these researchers were surprised to find that the troop continued to be less aggressive some 10 years after the initial deaths. This included more social grooming by the males and less aggression against females and lower-ranking males. Although by this time there were none of the original males still with the troop, it appears that new males came to adopt the culture that was found, suggesting an important effect of existing societal conditions on behavior.

Key Concepts in Studying Culture From an Evolutionary Perspective

Based on the work of numerous researchers, Henrich and McElreath (2007) suggest that there are three key concepts that can be used to consider human culture: (1) cultural capacities as adaptations, (2) cultural evolution, and (3) culture-gene coevolution. They can also be thought of as three pathways involved in the transmission of cultural information.

1. **Cultural capacities as adaptations.** The first pathway of cultural learning comes from genetically evolved psychological adaptations. That is to say, how have genetic changes over our evolutionary history allowed for adaptations that support culture? For example, as I discussed in Chapter 11, there are variety of adaptations that support our tendency to imitate those who have resources, fame, and status. These adaptations enable humans to acquire ideas, beliefs, values, practices, mental models, and strategies from other individuals, mainly through observation and inference. In thinking about culture from this standpoint, you would use the logic of natural selection with its emphasis on adaptation and survival. Using this logic, you would then consider how human capacities evolved, which, in turn, could be used in the service of developing and maintaining culture.

2. **Cultural evolution.** The second pathway moves beyond genetics and is seen to operate by a different set of rules. From this standpoint, cultural evolution is understood by first considering what we know about human cognition, social interactions, and cultural learning. For example, we could use social psychology research to describe how humans make individual decisions about other people. We would then move this understanding to the group level and

consider how these psychological mechanisms would result in developing and maintaining culture.

3. **Culture-gene coevolution.** A third system of cultural transmission relates to the close interaction between genes and the environment. In this case, the emphasis is on how culture can change the environment, which, in turn, affects genes. Culture influences not only the social environment, but also the physical environment, as illustrated by our development of cities, communication technologies, and transportation methods. Of course, most of these are recent in evolutionary terms. However, you could consider the preparation of food using fire, which does have a long history. Passing on the ability to cook meat is a cultural process. You can construct a scenario, as we did in Chapter 4, in which eating meat allowed for more developmental energy to be available for other organs, such as the brain, and, in the process, favored certain types of digestive structures and mechanisms. In this way, human physiology could be altered though a cultural change in diet.

Let us now examine some of the ways in which current evolutionary theorists have articulated these three pathways.

JOHN TOOBY AND LEDA COSMIDES: EVOKED VERSUS TRANSMITTED CULTURE

John Tooby and Leda Cosmides (1992) begin their discussion of culture by noting that, in a variety of social science disciplines including anthropology, sociology, and psychology, there has been a mind set commonly called the "Standard Social Science Model." As you read in Chapter 1, this model of human behavior emphasized experience as the major factor in determining our behavior. A variety of theorists during the 20th century saw any approach that did not adopt learning as the only mechanism of development as anti-humanistic and an attempt to reduce humans to only biology and to not see the higher nature of humans. Of course, this was a limited picture of the evolutionary perspective. To suggest that humans have evolved a propensity to cooperate or produce art does not reduce the value of these processes for a society. No one would ignore the important role that learning plays in acquiring culture. However, as I have pointed out throughout this book, the debate is not about whether a process is learned or evolved but how each process plays a role. The evolutionary perspective seeks an interactionist approach that describes the interaction of cultural experience and psychological predispositions. Thus, there is the critical question of what mechanisms direct, focus, and allow for cultural learning to take place.

Tooby and Cosmides (1992) help us not make incorrect conclusions in terms of culture, especially when differences are seen across cultures. They begin by asking what the psychological foundations of culture are. In answering this question, they suggest that it is useful to think of three separate components of culture and the manner in which these aspects are transmitted. Specifically, they describe metaculture, evoked culture, and epidemiological or adopted culture. *Metacultural* components include those aspects, such as language, attachment, kin relations, and so forth, that are universal characteristics of human beings. All cultures have languages, rules of kin relationships, and ways of dealing with basic human experiences. As described and suggested throughout this book, these processes are universal and available to all humans. Another set of processes observed, although universal in their potential, may differ from culture to culture. *Evoked culture* refers to the manner in which environmental conditions bring forth these practices. For example, as we discussed in Chapter 5, some researchers (e.g., Belsky, 2007) suggested that different environmental patterns, such as scarce resources versus supportive environments, may influence which infant attachment patterns are most productive. If we were to see these different attachment patterns in different cultures, we might conclude that they resulted from differences in the cultures. However, an alternative explanation would be that it was the environment itself that evoked a particular pattern. The third aspect of culture has been referred to as *epidemiological, transmitted,* or *adopted culture.* This aspect of culture is the situation in which ideas from an individual or group are passed along to other members in the same, or another, culture. The mechanisms involved in transmitted culture include imitation, modeling, and other forms of learning. Some cultural learning can include fads in clothing, music, and art, as well as the manner in which a culture values ideas and rituals in a more long-term manner.

ROBERT BOYD AND PETER RICHERSON

Robert Boyd and Peter Richerson (Boyd & Richerson, 1985, 2005; Richerson & Boyd, 2005) sought to develop a theory that accounts for the capacity for evolution of culture in humans. In order to understand the evolution of culture, you must consider how information is transmitted or learned by an individual organism. As we have seen throughout this book, learning through experience is one critical mechanism. It is clear that there are a variety of evolutionary mechanisms, such as one-trial learning involving foods that make one sick, which emphasize experience. However, human societies have also utilized social institutions for transmitting information. These social processes range from the parents and kin departing information to more formal religious and educational institutions. The overall idea is that social learning evolved as an adaptation in humans. Mathematically modeling the evolution of social learning, Boyd and Richerson suggest that there is an advantage to social learning compared to individuals completely relying on the results of experience. In a stable environment, social learning increases fitness because it reduces the error rate of individual learning. Further, social learning has evolved in such a manner that we pay more attention to our parents or those held in regard by the community. One basic idea of this approach is that it requires less effort to just do what others around us are doing. However, if everyone just did what others are doing, this would not benefit us because it would detach us from the environment. There is always the need for some individuals to discover what is needed to cope in a new situation. Others then can follow. Thus, one key for understanding human evolution, according to Boyd and Richerson, is to understand the psychological mechanisms that allow for imitation and social learning.

Overall, their theory can be summarized in five propositions.

1. **Culture is information that people acquire from others by teaching, imitation, and other forms of social learning.** Humans, more than any other species, acquire skills, beliefs, and values from those around them. Although other species may acquire information through imitation, human culture shows an accumulation of information not apparent in other species.

2. **Culture change should be modeled as a Darwinian evolutionary process.** By this statement, Boyd and Richerson (2005) suggest that cultural changes can be viewed in the same manner as evolutionary changes. As we know, some biological changes lead to greater survival patterns for the individual and thus are less likely to be lost over evolutionary time. We can examine cultural ideas and values in the same way. That is to say, we can ask why one idea survives in a culture and others do not. Sometimes an idea remains because it fits our psychology and is easier to remember or implement. Other ideas may help increase one's ability to acquire resources or live longer. Such ideas may lead to cultural changes. Overall, the theory should lend itself to empirical research related to how cultural information is stored and transmitted.

3. **Culture is part of human biology.** This suggests that culture is not separate from other human processes. That is to say, those capacities that allow us to acquire culture are part of our biology and psychology. Our minds and bodies, which have been shaped by evolutionary processes, constrain and support culture.

4. **Culture makes human evolution very different from the evolution of other organisms.** The main idea here is that humans are able to make cumulative cultural adaptations. As humans, we learn from others and then we improve on what we have learned. Thus, each generation is

able to modify and improve upon previous ideas. Some ideas, such as air conditioning and heating, have enabled humans to live and be productive in a variety of climates. Compared to evolutionary time, culture is able to evolve quickly. One consequence of this is that individuals may adopt ideas or values that are maladaptive.

5. **Genes and culture coevolve.** The idea here is that culture can produce durable changes in human behavior, which in turn can influence evolutionary changes. Given that culture can influence the environment in which one lives, and given that environments can influence genes, then it follows that culture can influence genetic changes.

One interesting aspect of cultural evolution, according to Richerson and Boyd (2005), is that observations take place largely on the group level. This is easy to note in terms of the norms of different nations and groups. How different groups approach such varied topics as art, politics, and religion highlight these differences. A highly visible culture has the ability to influence other cultures, as is seen with American movies and music. An interesting question not directly addressed by Richerson and Boyd is whether, with greater technological networking (e.g., the Internet), a global culture will develop.

EDWARD O. WILSON AND CHARLES LUMSDEN

We first met Edward Wilson at the end of Chapter 1. Wilson is a biologist interested in the study of ants, but his contribution to evolutionary psychology came from his book *Sociobiology: The New Synthesis*, published in 1975. In a brief chapter on humans, Wilson emphasized our biological uniqueness, which includes the manner in which we represent a single species found throughout the earth. Language, culture, and the ability to create large communities or cities with continuous technological innovations are unique aspects of our species. And our cultural developments occurred in a relatively short period of time. We have also evolved a way of obtaining information through a scientific approach that is not paralleled in other species.

In 1981, Charles Lumsden and E. O. Wilson published a book, *Genes, Mind, and Culture*, examining the manner in which biological evolution and cultural evolution occur. They first note that some philosophers and scientists see the gap between the gene-based approaches of biology and the culture-based approaches of the social sciences to be irreconcilable. However, they suggest it should be viewed as a largely unknown evolutionary process. The relationship between biology and culture is complicated. Specifically, they suggest that culture is generated and shaped by biology, and, simultaneously, biological traits are altered by genetic evolution in response to cultural innovation. One of the hallmarks of their theory is the use of epigenetic rules, which we discussed in Chapter 5. Epigenetic rules relate to the manner in which environmental influences can influence the expression of the genome without directly changing the DNA, even though these patterns of gene expression can be passed on to future generations. The process shows that gene expression is more complicated than a simple "we have traits because of a gene" view would suggest. In the same way that the diet of a mouse before conception can influence the hair color of her infants and even her infants' infants, epigenetic rules can influence cultural processes. Culture, from this perspective, can be seen as the translation of epigenetic rules into mass patterns of mental activity and behavior (Lumsden & Wilson, 1981).

Lumsden and Wilson (1981) define culture in a broad sense to include all mental constructs and behaviors. This would include the making and using of tools and other artifacts. It would also include the transmission of this information through social learning. Taking a larger view, we could ask how information is transmitted in any species. To answer this, Lumsden and Wilson ask us to consider four transmission processes that can vary in terms of a species' ability. The first is simple learning, the second is imitation, the third is teaching, and the fourth is the construction of abstract representations and symbols that stand for a given process. Humans are considered to be the only species that engages in all four types. Intentional instruction is seen in all human societies. Further, socialization of young humans is one important means by which culture is transmitted. The patterns of culture that are transmitted from one person to another are referred to as "culturgens" by Lumsden and Wilson. These culturgens can be specific tools, a set of customs (e.g., for marriage), types of food eaten, and so forth. Like a gene, culturgens can be analyzed in terms of whether they increase the inclusive fitness of those humans that acquire it.

In later writings, Wilson (1998) notes the manner in which the natural sciences, from quantum physics to evolutionary biology, have come together to construct a network of information that allows for an understanding of our world on a variety of levels. What we have not accomplished is a way to extend these understandings into the realm of the humanities and culture. Literary pursuits are very different today than scientific pursuits. Wilson suggests that there may be a way to develop an understanding based on such fields as psychology, biology, and anthropology, which he and Lumsden called "gene-culture coevolution." In essence, what Wilson is saying is that there are parallel tracks, one of genetic evolution and one of cultural evolution. Specifically, he describes it as follows:

> Culture is created by the communal mind, and each mind in turn is the product of the genetically structured human brain. Genes and culture are therefore inseverably linked. But the linkage is flexible, to a degree still mostly unmeasured. The linkage is also tortuous: Genes prescribe epigenetic rules, which are the neural pathways and

regularities in cognitive development by which the individual mind assembles itself. The mind grows from birth to death by absorbing parts of the existing culture available to it, with selections guided through epigenetic rules inherited by the individual brain.

As part of gene-culture coevolution, culture is reconstructed each generation collectively in the minds of individuals. When oral tradition is supplemented by writing and art, culture can grow indefinitely large and it can even skip generations. But the fundamental biasing influence of the epigenetic rules, being genetic and ineradicable, stays constant. (p. 138)

Wilson (1998) further suggests that the quicker the pace of cultural evolution, the looser the connection between genes and culture becomes. Culture offers an advantage in that it allows a rapid adjustment to changes in the environment, which can be transmitted to future generations. In this manner, humans differ from every other species. However, cultural patterns of behavior called culturgens have a physiological relationship to memory and correlated brain activity. Finally, Wilson suggests that his term *culturgen* be replaced with the term *meme.*

Memes

Is there a unit of cultural information? Richard Dawkins (1976) suggested that the answer to this question is yes. Dawkins coined the term *meme* to denote this unit. He derived the terms from the Greek *mimeme,* meaning "that which is imitated." In the same way that genes can be passed on from one generation to another, memes can be the unit of cultural information. A meme can be anything, such as a song, the manner in which a building is built, a style of clothing, or any one of many ideas. Of course, not all ideas, even if true, will be embraced by a particular set of humans and made an important part of their culture. Like genes, memes get copied as they are passed on. Also, like genes, memes do not get copied perfectly, and thus there is the chance that new forms will develop from the old ones. All of the processes associated with genes, such as variation, mutation, competition, and so forth, can be applied to memes as a unit of cultural transmission and evolution. This can be applied to something trivial, such as how a particular song or clothing fad develops, spreads, and dies out, as well as larger cultural movements, such as religions. One important distinction that Susan Blackmore (1999, 2006) and others make is that, from the perspective of memes, culture is not an adaptation. Culture actually consists of memes that have been passed along and reflect interests and choices of human individuals. From this perspective, culture began as a byproduct of the evolved capacity for imitation. From here it took off on its own. In fact, some even see memes more like parasites who are just looking for a host. The host could be humans and their brains. The host could also be computers, the Internet, or other places that aspects of culture can be stored.

Religion

Religion has been part of the human landscape for thousands of years. From the human perspective, we can describe religious attitudes, behaviors, and experiences. Religious attitudes include our beliefs concerning religion. Religious behaviors have to do with the rites and rituals of a religious nature, including those connected with birth, death, marriage, and worship. Religious experiences are one's personal experiences that are seen to be not self-caused. Thus, three key aspects of religion are the acceptance of forces outside ourselves acting in the world, the coming together to perform rites or rituals, and the experience of non-ordinary processes within and outside ourselves. Intertwined with these aspects are the relationship of religion to social processes and the role of individual transcendence. Religious community processes tend to encourage group connectedness, shared values, and an expression of higher-level emotional responses, such as empathy and caring. An advantage of such processes, as discussed previously, is that involvement in these activities is associated with better health outcomes. On an individual level, religious teaching has suggested an ability to move beyond or transcend a need to respond only to one's internal process and to become a part of the larger community and world. Cognitive psychologists (e.g., Kahneman, 2003) have distinguished between one's initial response to a situation, which is fast and often emotionally charged, and a more careful thought-out consideration of a situation with its flexibility in possible outcomes. Many religious practices are designed to slow down quick responses and allow for more contemplative considerations. The more contemplative considerations are often described as virtues. Commonly described virtues include faith, hope, and love. In this manner, religion is one way in which cultures focus on the possibilities of being as well as human potential.

Religions have historically encouraged acts that benefit others, even at a personal cost. All major religions, for example, encourage giving resources to those who are less fortunate. Social scientists have often focused on the manner in which religion is a cultural facilitator of social cohesion and in-group solidarity (see Norenzayan & Shariff, 2008 for an overview). In their discussion of religion and pro-social behavior, Norenzayan and Shariff review three evolutionary theories related to the manner in which religion facilitates pro-social tendencies. The first suggests that particular religious beliefs and behaviors are evolutionary adaptations for group living in large communities that have maximized genetic fitness. The problem with this approach is that it doesn't explain changes in religious beliefs and behaviors over time. A second theory suggests that religious beliefs and actions are cultural byproducts of psychological tendencies evolved for other purposes. One such psychological process would be the ability to infer what another person was experiencing, currently called theory of mind. Knowing one's pro-social reputation in a group would be another psychological process from which religious tendencies may have developed. The religious beliefs and acts would be transmitted by normal social learning mechanisms. These beliefs and acts would help to maintain cooperation in large groups. A third perspective suggests that competition among social groups could favor the spread of fitness-enhancing cultural beliefs and pro-social behavior. This theory is referred to as *cultural group selection.* This is similar to the second theory, but suggests that reputation or theory of mind alone is not sufficient to explain the pro-social behaviors found in religion. Although these theories differ in their particulars, they all focus on the pro-social nature of religious belief and practice as critical.

Is religion special in that it functions differently from other human cognitive and emotional processes? One approach is to suggest that religions are based on the same cognitive and affective processes as non-religious beliefs and practices (Atran & Norenzayan, 2004; Barrett, 2000). These authors claim that there are common psychological roots to the religious experiences found across cultures, and that insights from the neurosciences can help to understand them. Such a perspective leads us to ask whether religion, like language, is a natural part of the human experience. Presently, the focus of this work has emphasized how humans develop, represent, process, and act upon concepts related to non-human powers. Throughout the world, humans assign agency to unexplainable events. When something out of the ordinary happens, there is a tendency to look for a cause or meaning for the event. Often the cause carries with it a nonhuman or divine agent. One specific process is that when humans are confronted with serious existential problems, such as a near-death experience, an innate releasing mechanism produces a nonrational way of thinking and the experience of being connected to higher forces in the universe. There are many examples of individuals in difficult situations reporting that they said to God, "If you will only save me, I will change my life". People also modify their religious concepts depending on the type of cognitive processing required. In one study, individuals in both India and the United States were able to reflect in abstract terms their theological understanding of supreme beings. In particular, such beings were seen as able to exist without a physical or spatial location, know all information at once, and have no need to rely on sensory information. However, when remembering narratives about these same beings, they gave the supreme beings much more human-like characteristics, such as existing at a specific location in space and being unable to attend to multiple events at once

(Barrett & Keil, 1996). Overall, the basic view from an evolutionary perspective is that religious attitudes and experiences can be studied as other cognitive processes have been researched and do not represent a totally different domain of human processing. The historical record suggests that religion developed as culture developed and is not an adaptation in the classical sense of the term.

Culture Determines Which Animals We Love, Which We Hate, and Which We Eat

In Chapter 5, I talked about how all children are fascinated by animals. In fact, some evolutionary scientists suggest that humans are the only species to adopt another species as a pet (Herzog, 2010). Although it true that humans in all cultures have pets, there is a definite cultural manifestation of loving pets that involves which pets we love. For example, whereas Western cultures freely adopt dogs as pets, in Saudi Arabia dogs are generally despised. Japanese kids treat a variety of insects, such as crickets, as pets, whereas American children largely do not. Like other fads in clothing, music, and art, there also appears to be a changing landscape of which species of dog, for example, is popular at any moment in history. For example, there was an increase in Dalmatians as pets after the Walt Disney movie *101 Dalmatians* was released. Although the manner in which we relate to our pets may contain an evolutionary calculus, the particular species that we choose appears to be culturally determined.

Culture also plays a large role in relation to which animals we choose to eat. In Pakistan cattle are eaten, but in India they are not. Of course, some of these differences are related to religious traditions, as is the case with pork in Muslim and Jewish cultures. Other differences are less a prohibition and more a preference. For example, in Germany you see a large selection of pork and little chicken in the grocery stories, whereas in the United States, you tend to see the opposite. Certain cultures in Southeast Asia eat dog meat, but Americans would be upset to see dog on a menu. Horse meat and internal organs are enjoyed or hated depending on the culture in which you live.

Culture and the Brain

As scientists have performed a variety of compelling studies that have reaffirmed Darwin's description of the close connection between an organism and its environment, a new focus has emerged related to culture and the brain. Some refer to this field as **cultural neuroscience** (see Chiao & Ambady, 2007; Ambady & Bharucha, 2009 for overviews). In the field of cultural neuroscience, a number of themes that we have discussed in this book come together. The first, as just noted, is the close connection between an individual and his or her environment. It is clear that the evolution of brain function and culture are interwoven. This idea is connected to a second theme—the plasticity of the brain. Although it was once thought that once cortical pathways were established, they remained fixed for a person's life, today we know that neural networks can be activated in relation to environmental experiences and that these can change across one's lifespan (see Park & Gutchess, 2006 for an overview). Seemingly simple processes such as whether you learned to play a musical instrument early in your life can determine how your brain is organized (Elbert et al., 1995). A third theme, as noted throughout this book, is the manner in which the networks of the brain are ready to establish relationships, such as in the case of infants and their caregivers, and absorb information, such as in our ability to learn language at a young age. This type of absorption sets up a fourth theme, which is the manner in which the brain is involved in social behavior. For example, we quickly experience how we feel about other people as well as look for cues to understand our relationships in a group. In this section, I will describe how these themes have informed cultural neuroscience. To do this, I will utilize the overview of Ambady and Bharucha (2009) and Chiao and Ambady (2007) involving culture mapping and its underlying process of source analysis.

CULTURE MAPPING

The basic research strategy of **culture mapping** focuses on an examination of cognitive and neural differences across cultures. These studies generally take one of two forms. First, studies have examined the manner in which individuals from different cultures process the same information in different ways. For example, in a variety of studies, Nisbett and his colleagues have shown that individuals in East Asia tend to be more holistic when examining information and pay attention to the context, whereas individuals from the West pay more attention to particular objects and their categories independent of the context (Nisbett, 2003; Nisbett & Miyamoto, 2005). What this suggests is that the context in which an event happens is not only important, but not seen as a separate aspect to an East Asian individual. Westerners, on the other hand, are more likely to see individuals and their situations as separate events. Other studies have shown that when individuals are asked to explain an event, Westerners tend to see events as determined by the object or person, whereas Asians are more likely to attribute causality to the situation or context in which the event occurred. Second, studies have examined the manner in which individuals from a single culture process information from different cultures differently. For example, studies have shown that Americans process Western and Indian music differently (Curtis & Bharucha, 2009). Another area of focus is how psychological concepts such as the self are understood in different cultures. For example, whereas Japanese tend to value social harmony and adherence to group norms, Americans tend to emphasize uniqueness and freedom and view the self as independent from others.

SOURCE ANALYSIS

Source analysis is the process of understanding what mechanisms underlie the differences described in cultural mapping. Ambady and Bharucha (2009) describe three possible mechanisms. The first mechanism is similarity and differences in genetic makeup. On a cognitive/emotional level, as discussed previously, infants around the world pick up language without effort, suggesting a set of genetic programs that prepare them for communication. Even deaf children initially babble, which further supports a universal genetic program for language learning. I have discussed a variety of these types of universals in this book. Cultural neuroscience also seeks to articulate differences in genetic processes. For example, Japanese and European populations differ in certain types of genetic makeup. As noted previously, one such difference is related to an allele associated with the development of anxiety and depression (see Ambady & Bharucha, 2009; Chiao and Ambady, 2007 for an overview). The short allele of the serotonin transporter gene (5-HTT) is associated with higher levels of anxiety and depression than in the long allele of the same gene. Individuals with this short allele also show greater activation of the amygdala in emotional tasks as compared to those with the long version of the allele. In a variety of studies, 70% to 80% of a Japanese sample carried this short allele as compared to 40% to 45% in a European sample. One important question based on this type of analysis is the manner in which observable cultural differences are related to underlying genetic variation manifestations in members of that culture.

The second mechanism is cultural learning and the manner in which experiences can influence the structure of the brain. One example suggested by Ambady and Bharucha (2009) is learning a second language. Examining brain activation patterns of individuals who could speak fluently two languages versus one, it was found that bilinguals showed a unique pattern of activation in the left inferior frontal cortex (Kovelman et al., 2009). As would be expected, both bilingual and single-language individuals showed activation in Broca's area. Brain activation differences have also been found when members of different cultures view fear expression in the faces of members of their own culture and those of another culture. Using fear faces of Japanese and Caucasian individuals, Chiao and his colleagues (2008) found participants showed greater amygdala activation when viewing members of their own cultural group. The overall point, in both the bilingual and fear face studies, is that one's cultural experience influences patterns of cortical activation. This is further supported by the fact that Caucasians who had lived in Japan for more than a year also showed brain activation to the Japanese fear faces.

The third mechanism relates to the manner in which scientists see similar patterns and differences in these patterns across cultures. For example, when you examine a variety of brain imaging studies related to reading in different languages, you find both similarities and differences (Bolger, Perfetti, & Schneider, 2005). One similarity seen across languages is in an area in the left mid-fusiform gyrus that is related to word recognition. Differences are found which relate to the nature of the language itself. For example, Chinese is a more visual language than are Western alphabets. As such, imaging studies show more activation in the visual areas of both hemispheres when reading Chinese, as compared to Western languages. It has also been found that language-related disorders, such as dyslexia, are associated with different parts of the brain in different languages.

SUMMARY

Culture can be seen from an evolutionary perspective but also offers a separate means of transmitting information to future generations. Culture both influences genetics and is influenced by genetics. Flinn described seven characteristics of culture: (1) Cultural content is transmitted by learning processes (i.e., cognitive information transfer) and not by the transfer of genetic materials. Hence, culture appears to be a separate inheritance system, uncoupled from genetics. (2) Culture (or its effects) is partly extrasomatic. Cultural traits (e.g., stone points, political monuments) exist outside the soma (physical body) of the culture-bearing organism. (3) Human culture, by most definitions, involves mental phenomena, including conscious thought. (4) Human culture involves the use of arbitrary symbols to form mental representations and to communicate information. (5) Culture appears to have emergent properties at the group level, such as shared values and beliefs resulting in political and religious institutions. (6) Culture involves historical processes. History constrains the options (cultural traits) available for individual choice and modification, and culture can change rapidly, apparently outpacing genetic evolution. (7) Complex culture is uniquely human. Henrich and McElreath suggest that there are three key concepts that can be used to consider human culture: (1) cultural capacities as adaptations, (2) cultural evolution, and (3) culture-gene coevolution. John Tooby and Leda Cosmides describe evoked versus transmitted culture. Richerson and Boyd describe culture in five ways: (1) Culture is information that people acquire from others by teaching, imitation, and other forms of social learning. (2) Culture change should be modeled as a Darwinian evolutionary process. (3) Culture is part of human biology. (4) Culture makes human evolution very different from the evolution of other organisms. (5) Genes and culture coevolve. Lumsden and Wilson define culture in a broad sense to include all mental constructs and behaviors. The term meme was coined by Dawkins to mean a unit of cultural information. Religion has been part of culture since the earliest history of humans. Some human aspects, such as the love of pets, are modified by culture. Culture mapping and source analysis are research strategies for understanding culture.

STUDY RESOURCES

Review Questions

1. As a system of inheritance, can culture be analyzed using a Darwinian understanding of variation and change? Can such evolutionary ideas as natural selection be applied to culture?

2. How is cultural change similar to, and different from, other types of change, e.g., biological change, technological change, environmental change? How does an evolutionary perspective help integrate them?

3. Do other species "have" culture? What evidence supports your answer?

4. Describe Flinn's seven primary characteristics of culture.

5. Henrich and McElreath suggest three key concepts to use in considering human culture. What are they, and how have they been used by other researchers to understand culture from an evolutionary perspective?

6. Tooby and Cosmides present three mechanisms that direct, focus, and allow for cultural learning to take place. How do they differentiate among these concepts: metaculture; evoked culture; and epidemiological, transmitted, or adopted culture?

7. Boyd and Richerson outline five propositions to describe the psychological mechanisms that allow for imitation and social learning. What are they, and how do they help us understand human evolution?

8. What roles do epigenetic rules and memes play in Wilson and Lumsden's perspective on the relationship between biology and culture?

9. How can we understand religion from an evolutionary perspective?

10. What is the scope of cultural neuroscience, and how are culture mapping and its underlying process of source analysis employed in cultural neuroscience research?

For Further Reading

Blackmore, S. (1999). *The meme machine.* New York: Oxford University Press.

Boyd, R., & Richerson, P. (2005). *The origin and evolution of culture.* New York: Oxford University Press.

Nisbett, R. E. (2003). *The geography of thought: Why we think the way we do.* New York: The Free Press.

Richerson, P., & Boyd, R. (2005). *Not by genes alone: How culture transformed human evolution.* Chicago: University of Chicago Press.
Wilson, E. O. (1998). *Consilience: The unity of knowledge.* New York: Alfred A. Knopf.

Key Terms and Concepts

- Culture develops as we see ourselves in a larger context
- Cultural differences
  - Cultural change
- Culture and technology
- Interaction of culture and genes
- Key concepts in studying culture from an evolutionary perspective
  - John Tooby and Leda Cosmides – Evoked versus transmitted culture
  - Robert Boyd and Peter Richerson
  - Edward O. Wilson and Charles Lumsden
- Memes
- Religion
- Culture determines which animals we love, which we hate, and which we eat
- Culture and the brain
  - Culture mapping
  - Source analysis

SAGE Study Site

Visit the study site at **www.sagepub.com/ray** for chapter-specific study resources.

Glossary Terms

- Cultural neuroscience
- Culture mapping

- Source analysis

Glossary

Alternative to the mental module: The alternative approach to the mental module model suggests that increased abilities come with a global increase in neurons and their interconnectedness within the brain that allows for greater information processing. Most neuroscientists today favor this model. See also **Mental module model**.

Adaptation: The evolutionary process by which an organism becomes better able to live in its environment.

Adaptations: Features of an organism that enable it to survive in its environment.

Adaptive problems: The problems that have been with us throughout our history as a species. Most deal with the basics of life—how to provide food and shelter, communicate with others, have pair relationships and produce children, and take care of children.

Affective disorders: Mental disorders that affect mood, thought, behavior, and emotions.

Allele: An alternative form of a gene that occurs by mutation.

Allocortex: The part of the brain that includes the hippocampus, olfactory, and other related areas.

Allometric approach: The study of brain evolution and size that focuses on the entire brain or large subdivisions. See also **Neuroethological approach**.

Allostasis: The body's ability to achieve stability through change. Allostatic systems are thus systems designed to adapt to change.

Altruism: Behaviors that appear not to benefit the individual.

Amygdala: Part of the limbic system, the amygdala is an almond-shaped structure found in the frontal part of the temporal lobe. The amygdala sits between external information brought in through our sensory systems and the necessary attentional, memory, and emotional responses.

Analogous similarity: A situation in which, rather than having a common ancestor, different species independently evolve similar characteristics.

Ancestral characteristic: A particular characteristic present in the ancestors of the group being studied. Also referred to as a *primitive characteristic.*

Anterior: Toward the front of the brain. Also referred to as *rostral.*

Antithesis: Darwin's second principle that suggests that some external movements or habits are carried out merely because they are the opposite of a serviceable habit. These responses may be species-specific. See also **Direct actions of the nervous system; Principle of serviceable associated habits.**

Archetypes: Jung's term for universal patterns available to all humans. They are similar to animal action patterns, although archetypes take place on a psychic level and represent ways our brain organizes particular perceptions and our responses to events.

Archicortex: Part of the allocortex. See also **Allocortex.**

Associationism: Freud's principle that ideas presented together in time will be mentally recalled together. If, as a child, you are in a fearful situation such as an automobile accident, then riding in a car could make you feel fearful or anxious.

Assortative mating: Assortative mating suggests that humans do not randomly choose partners but choose partners like themselves on some selected trait. It is one possible mechanism suggested by researchers to explain what leads to the stability of personality traits across generations.

Authority ranking: A type of relationship in which people are ranked according to some linear hierarchy. Typically, individuals higher in the rankings have more prestige, prerogatives, and privileges than those lower down the hierarchy. One's rank also influences a variety of other processes.

Autosomes: In humans there are 23 separate pairs of chromosomes, making 46 in all. Twenty-two of the pairs are referred to as autosomes. The remaining chromosome pair is called the sex chromosome because it differs in males and females. See also **Chromosome.**

Axons: The part of nerve cells that transfer information throughout the brain. **See also Myelin sheaths; White matter.**

Belief-desire reasoning: Belief-desire reasoning suggests you understand other people by inferring what they desire or believe. By knowing your own motivations, you can understand that you and another may be motivated by different beliefs and desires. See also **Theory of mind.**

Blood typing: There are four major blood types: A, B, AB, and O. Blood type is one of the few characteristics that is passed on genetically and is not influenced by the environment.

Bounded rationality: Herbert Simon's theory that one could learn about human decision making by noting how the environment in which these decisions must be made can allow for simplifications in adaptive decision making. See also **Heuristics.**

Brain stem: The portion of the brain, consisting of the medulla oblongata, pons Varolii, and midbrain, that connects the spinal cord to the forebrain and cerebrum.

Caudal: Toward the back of the brain. Also referred to as *posterior*.

Central nervous system: In vertebrates, the brain and spinal cord.

Centromere: The narrow point of a chromosome where it separates during cell division. See also **Chromosome; Telomeres.**

Cerebellum: The part of the brain at the back of the skull that coordinates and regulates muscle activity.

Chromatids: The two strands of a replicated chromosome that are joined by a single centromere and separate during cell division. See also **Centromere; Mitosis.**

Chromosome: A DNA molecule along with the proteins that are attached to it. See also **DNA.**

Cingulate: Part of the limbic structure and the Paleomammalian brain. Damage to the cingulate results in disrupted maternal behaviors. See also **Paleomammalian brain.**

Codominance: The situation in which non-identical alleles produce two separate phenotypes at the same time, rather than one allele being dominant and one submissive with a single phenotype being expressed, e.g., blood type AB. See also **Allele; Phenotype.**

Codon: The sequence of three letters along a single RNA strand that specifies one particular amino acid. These sequences determine which of 20 amino acids are put together to form a specific protein. See also **Genetic code.**

Collective unconscious: Jung suggested that there were few differences in the psychic structure of humans throughout the world. He referred to this structure as the collective unconscious—how all humans are similar. This collective unconscious is passed on to generations across time.

Communal sharing: A type of relationship in which a community treats material objects as things that belong to all.

Correlation coefficient: A statistical technique developed by Galton for determining the degree of association between two or more variables.

Critical period: The limited temporal period during which imprinting and other similar phenomena work. See also **Imprinting.**

Cultural neuroscience: Cultural neuroscience is represented by close connection between individual and environment; plasticity of the brain;

manner in which networks of the brain are ready to establish relationships; and manner in which the brain is involved in social behavior.

Culture mapping: The basic research strategy of culture mapping focuses
on an examination of cognitive and neural differences across cultures. See
also **Source analysis.**

Darwinian psychiatry: The idea that mental illness is part of the human
condition in its recognition and prevalence. For example, it gives insight
into why certain fears would have more potency than others. Also referred
to as *evolutionary psychopathology.*

Default network: Neural networks that are active during internal processing.

Deferred adaptations: Characteristics that serve later adult development.

Derived characteristic: A characteristic that has evolved in the group
under study. Also referred to as *specialized characteristic.*

Developmental systems approach: A theory describing the close relationship between genes and the environment in relation to development. The
overall approach sees development as interplay between a variety of levels,
including genes, neural activity, behavior, and environment, culture, and
society. See also **Epigenesis.**

Direct actions of the nervous system: Darwin's third principle acknowl-
edges that emotional expression can result from the structure of the nervous
system—there are specific physiological reactions for different emotions,
and the cardiovascular and cortical system mutually interact with one
another. See also **Antithesis; Principle of serviceable associated habits.**

Display rules: Situational and cultural factors that can influence emotional expression.

DNA: Deoxyribonucleic acid; the storehouse of information concerning
heritable traits. DNA is important for its ability to reproduce itself and its
role in producing proteins. See also **Transcription; RNA.**

Encephalization: The principle by which special-purpose control systems
are taken over by a general-purpose control system over evolutionary time.
That is, more recently evolved higher-level centers control the older lower-
level centers.

Encephalization quotient (EQ): Brain weight in relation to an organism's
body weight.

Epigenesis: A key concept of the *developmental systems approach.* Epigenesis
refers to the emergence of new structures and functions during the course
of development. See also **Developmental systems approach.**

Epigenetic inheritance: A form of inheritance in which the processes that
determine which genes turn on and off could themselves be passed on to
the next generation.

Epistasis: The situation in which alleles of one gene mask the expression of another gene's alleles such that an expected phenotype does not appear. See also **Allele; Phenotype**.

Equality matching: Equality matching can be thought of as "tit-for-tat" relationships—you do something for me, and I do something for you. Each person is entitled to an equal amount in the relationship. The structure of equality matching relationships is balance.

Ethology: The study of animals and what they do. The word is derived from the Greek and means *manner, trait,* or *character.* At the heart of ethology is the naturalistic observation of behavior within an organism's natural environment.

Environment of evolutionary adaptedness: The historical environment in which humans experienced difficulties, found food, mated and raised children, formed and lived with others in social groups.

Evolution: The study of the various pathways that led to the current structure and function of a specific organism. It results from the close interaction of organisms with their environment.

Evolutionary perspective: A perspective that helps determine which survival tasks have been critical for humans to solve. There is no single theory of evolution, but a general set of perspectives that determine the scientific questions we ask and the way we perform our research.

Evolutionary psychopathology: See **Darwinian psychiatry**.

Fight-or-flight response: The overall stress reaction has been referred to as the fight-or-flight response. When you are faced with a potential threat, your body prepares you either to fight or to leave the scene. See also **Tend-and-befriend response.**

Fitness: How a specific behavioral pattern contributes to the survival of the offspring.

Fixed action pattern: An action pattern released by a stimulus that always uses the same physiological mechanisms (e.g., muscles) to achieve the same sequence of actions. It requires no learning; it is characteristic of a species; it cannot be unlearned; and once released, it will continue in the absence of the triggering stimulus.

Frontal lobe: The front of each of the brain's hemispheres.

Fundamental life tasks: Universal human predicaments such as losses, frustrations, and achievements.

Gametes: The male's sperm cells and the female's eggs. Also referred to as *Germ cells.*

Gastrulation: The development of three different cell lines from undifferentiated embryonic tissue that occurs about 14 days after conception.

Each of these cell lines is capable of producing cells that will make up different organs in the body.

Gene: A sequence of DNA that carries the instructions that direct the expression of particular traits.

Genetic code: The table of correspondences between codons and amino acids. See also **Codon.**

Genome: The complete set of human genes. This is the biological mechanism by which evolution works.

Genotype: What is inherited through the sperm and the egg at the moment of conception. See also **Phenotype.**

Germ cells: See **Gametes**.

Good gene: A theoretical perspective to explain sexual preferences. The basic idea is that females choose males who possess indicators of underlying genetic fitness. See also **Good provider.**

Good provider: A theoretical perspective to explain sexual preferences. It is not just producing offspring that is key to evolutionary thinking, but also the conditions necessary to nurture these offspring into adulthood so they can also reproduce. See also **Good gene.**

Gray matter: The thin outer shell of the brain consisting of dark-colored cells.

Haploid: A single copy of the genome found in the male's sperm and the female's egg.

Heterozygotes: People who have two different alleles for a particular gene. See also **Allele.**

Heterozygous: Having two different alleles for a particular gene.

Heuristics: A set of rules that help us to understand how people make decisions. See also **Bounded rationality.**

Hierarchical integration: The principle that the various levels of the brain, such as the brain stem, the limbic system, and the neocortex are able to interact with each other. Further, interaction from the higher levels restricts or inhibits the lower levels.

Hippocampus: An area of the cerebral cortex that functions as part of the limbic system and is involved in forming, storing, and processing memory.

Homeostasis: A concept that reflects the manner in which a physiological system tends to center on a set point, like a thermostat that regulates temperature in a building.

Homeotic genes: Specific genes that control the timing of development of body parts. They lay out the basic body plan during development for all species by switching on other genes during development. Also referred to as *Hox genes.*

Hominid: The older term for *Hominin.* See **Hominin.**

Hominin: Any of the modern or extinct bipedal primates, including humans.

Homologous similarity: A situation in which observed similarities are due to a shared evolutionary history (i.e., they were inherited from a common ancestor).

Homozygotes: People who have two copies of the same allele for a particular gene. See also **Allele.**

Homozygous: Having two copies of the same allele for a particular gene.

Hox genes: See **Homeotic genes.**

Imprinting: A built-in pattern in which birds follow an object, usually their mother, which moves in front of them during the first 18 to 36 hours after birth. Imprinting and similar phenomena work like a lock and key. Once in place, it is almost irreversible and cannot be changed.

Impulse: An inborn inclination to produce a particular behavior under specific conditions. One example would be a startle reaction when a loud noise is heard. William James suggested humans have more instincts than animals. See also **Instinct.**

Inclusive fitness: A property that can be measured by considering the reproductive success of the individual plus the effects of an individual's actions on the reproductive success of his or her relatives. Also referred to as *kin selection.*

Incomplete dominance: When one allele is not dominant over the other, and a phenotype is expressed that is in between the two alleles. See also **Allele; Phenotype.**

Innate schema: The inborn tendency to produce a certain behavior. The young geese following a moving object early in life would be one example. See also **Imprinting.**

Innate template: See **Innate schema.**

Instinct: The "faculty of acting in such a way as to produce certain ends, without foresight of the ends, and without previous education in the performance" (James, 1890/1983). See also **Impulse; Instinctual process.**

Instinctual processes: Processes that, once triggered or released by a stimulus, will continue in the absence of that stimulus; an example is a fixed action pattern. See also **Fixed action pattern; Instinct.**

Isolating mechanisms: Conditions, ranging from changes in geography to changes in physiology, in which a part of a species becomes isolated and begins to interbreed. In the process, these organisms become genetically different from the larger population.

Karyotype: A way of representing the chromosomal contents of a cell, including the number of chromosomes followed by a description of the sex chromosomes.

Kin selection: See **Inclusive fitness**.

Lateral fissure: See **Sylvian fissure.**

Lateral structures: Structures farther away from the midline.

Law of independent assortment: The inheritance of the gene of one trait is not affected by the inheritance of the gene for another trait. Also referred to as *Mendel's second law.*

Law of segregation: Mendel suggested that alleles of a specific gene account for variations in inherited characteristics and that an organism receives one allele from each parent. Dominance or recessiveness determines which characteristics are expressed. Also referred to as *Mendel's first law.*

Left hemisphere: The left half of the brain, when looking down on it from the top.

Libido: Freud's principle that the nervous system is capable of retaining and discharging energy. This energy was initially called "Q" but later came to be known as libido or *sexual energy.*

Linkage: When genes violate Mendel's second law, it suggests that they reside close together on the same chromosome. See also **Law of independent assortment.**

Lobes: Curved or rounded divisions of the brain; each hemisphere has four lobes.

Machiavellian intelligence hypothesis: According to Humphrey, social groups lead to both cooperation and competition. Because social intelligence also contributes to survival and reproduction, it becomes a force in the evolution of cognitive processes increasing a species' intelligence. Also referred to as *social intelligence hypothesis.*

Market pricing: A type of relationship that attempts to determine through ratios and rates the value of some aspect of the relationship. The most common examples of market pricing relationships involve money and typically require some detailed analysis of the situation.

Medial structures: Structures closer to the midline dividing the left and right hemispheres of the brain.

Meiosis: A process of cell division in which the new chromosomes are no longer identical to those inherited from the parents. It is this process that eventually leads to variation in the traits of the offspring.

Mendel's first law: See **Law of segregation**.

Mendel's second law: See **Law of independent assortment**.

Mental module model: Describes the nature of the relationship between cognitive abilities and brain areas. The model suggests that the brain, like a Swiss army knife, contains a number of modules devoted to specific tasks. Also referred to as *Swiss army knife model*. See also **Alternative to mental module model.**

Midline: The division between the left and right brain hemispheres.

Mirror cells: Neurons in specific areas of our brain that fire when we watch someone perform a task, as if we were performing the task ourselves. Also referred to as *mirror neurons*.

Mitochondria: Structures within a cell that are involved in the production of energy and have their own DNA (mtDNA).

Mitochondrial inheritance: Generally, mitochondrial DNA is inherited only from the mother. Using mtDNA, it is possible to determine how similar different organisms are to one another. See also **Mitochondria.**

Mitosis: A process of cell division in which the new cell contains the same genetic information as the old.

Monogamy: One male and one female paired more or less exclusively during the mating season.

Morpheme: The smallest meaningful unit of a language.

Mutations: Changes in DNA. Within a given individual, mutations may have positive, negative, or neutral effects. For a mutation to influence evolution, it must be passed on to the next generation.

Myelin sheaths: Myelin is made up of fats and proteins; it wraps around *axons* like insulation around electrical cables and enables increased speed in information transmission. See also **Axons; White matter.**

Natural selection: Darwin's theory that if an individual has a variation that helps it compete successfully for survival, over time the species will have more members with these characteristics and fewer individuals lacking them. For natural selection to work, the particular characteristic must be heritable.

Neocortex: The area of the brain that includes regions devoted to sensory and motor processing and higher cognitive processes. It sends and receives information from different areas within itself and to and from *subcortical* structures. It is considered the most recent structure to evolve.

Neomammalian brain: The third level of the *triune brain*, generally associated with problem solving, executive control, and an orientation toward the external world, with an emphasis on linguistic functions. See also **Triune brain.**

Neuroethological approach: The study of brain evolution and size that examines the relationship between specific behaviors and underlying cortical structures. See also **Allometric approach.**

Nonpyramidal neurons: Neurons that make short-term connections in the cortex. These can be either inhibitory or excitatory.

Occipital lobe: The posterior portion of each brain hemisphere, concerned with the interpretation of visual sensory impulses.

Olfactory cortex: Part of the allocortex that receives and evaluates smells. See also **Allocortex.**

Ontogenetic adaptations: Characteristics that serve only the developmental period.

Ontogeny: The development or evolution of an individual organism. See also **Phylogeny.**

Operant conditioning: Skinner's exemplar experimental procedure. The basic procedure noted that behavior could be elicited or shaped if *reinforcement* followed its occurrence. See also **Reinforcement.**

Paleocortex: The part of the cerebral cortex that is evolutionarily older than the neocortex and contains the olfactory cortex. See also **Olfactory cortex.**

Paleomammalian brain: The second level of the triune brain, which includes the limbic system and its involvement in emotional processing. See also **Triune brain.**

Paradigm: The topics we study and the types of questions we ask.

Parental investment: A crucial idea in bringing together questions of sexual selection and mating behavior. The basic idea is that the sex that invests the most in its offspring will have evolved to be the most discriminating in selecting its mating partner.

Parietal lobe: The area toward the back and at the top of each brain hemisphere that is concerned with bodily sensations.

Parthenogenesis: A type of reproduction in which the eggs produced by the female require no fertilization from sperm, and each offspring is a genetic duplication of the mother. Also referred to as *virgin birth.*

Phenotype: The observed traits of the individual including morphology, physiology, and behavior. The focus of psychology has largely been the study of the phenotype. See also **Genotype.**

Pheromones: Chemicals released into the air that have been shown to signal to other members of a species various aspects of sexuality, including when a female is sexually receptive.

Phoneme: The basic sound of a language. There are approximately 100 different phonemes used in all languages around the world. English uses approximately 40 of these phonemes. A phoneme has no meaning other than the sound we process.

Phonology: The study of the ways phonemes can be combined in a language. See also **Phonemes.**

Phylogeny: The development or evolution of a group of organisms. See also **Ontogeny**.

Plasticity: Conditions in which processes are open to modification.

Pleiotropy: A process in which two or more phenotypes are influenced by a single gene. See also **Gene; Phenotype.**

Polyandry: The practice in animals of a female mating with more than one male during one breeding season.

Polygamy: The general term used to describe the situation in which one member of one sex is paired with more than one member of the opposite sex. These pair bonds can be successive or simultaneous.

Polygyny: The specific term used to describe the situation in which one male mates with multiple females.

Posterior: See **Caudal**.

Predictive adaptive responses (PAR): The idea that current environmental conditions will produce changes in an organism's development that will help the organism match future environmental factors.

Primitive characteristic: See **Ancestral characteristic.**

Principle of serviceable associated habits: Refers to the situation in which ritualized behaviors are performed in response to a particular internal state. Darwin describes a variety of situations that must have been protective to our ancestors and have become part of our human reflexive behaviors. See also **Antithesis; Direct actions of the nervous system.**

Proximate questions: Questions that ask how a phenomenon works. See also **Ultimate questions.**

Pyramidal cells: Triangular neurons in the brain that release an excitatory transmitter substance such as glutamate.

R-complex: The level of the triune brain that processes major life requirements such as breathing, temperature regulation, and sleep-wake cycles. Also involved in this level is olfaction (olfactory bulbs) and instinctive motor processes (basal ganglia). Also referred to as *reptilian brain*. See also **Triune brain.**

Reciprocal altruism: The theory that we help unrelated individuals if we expect them to help us in turn. Our own fitness, in an evolutionary sense, is increased because we have greater chance of surviving and passing on the genes related to these processes. See also **Altruism.**

Recombination: The process of gene swapping during meiosis. After this process, the chromosomes are no longer identical to those inherited from the parents. It is this process that eventually leads to variation in the traits of the offspring. See also **Meiosis.**

Reflex processes: Organisms withdraw when confronted with unpleasant stimuli. Freud extended this idea to cognitive and emotional processes to suggest that, mentally, humans avoid ideas or feelings that are unpleasant to them.

Regression line: A "best-fit" line between two variables whose slope and intercept are determined by regression analysis. See also **Correlation coefficient**.

Reinforcement: To reward an action or response so it is more likely to be performed again. See also **Operant conditioning.**

Repression: The inhibition of lower cortical processes by higher cortical processes.

Reptilian brain: See **R-complex.**

Right hemisphere: The right half of the brain, when looking down on it from the top.

RNA: Ribonucleic acid; the information in RNA determines the sequence of amino acids, which are the building blocks of proteins. See also **DNA; Translation.**

Rostral: See **Anterior**.

Runaway sexual selection: The concept that if a female is more willing to mate with a male with a certain trait, then that trait will be favored and pass on to the next generation. The outcome could eventually be an exaggeration.

Semantics: The study of meaning in language—how we understand what is being said. A critical question has been the way in which humans are able to move between the levels of meaning and syntax. See also **Syntax.**

Senescence: Growing old.

Sensitive period: See **Critical period.**

Sexual energy: See **Libido**.

Sexual monogamy: The situation in which the male and female only mate with each other. See also **Social monogamy.**

Sexual selection: The manner in which males and females choose a mate. See also **Natural selection.**

Sexual strategies theory: An extension of Trivers's parental investment theory as applied to humans. The basic idea is that males and females have evolved a variety of mating strategies, especially in terms of the perceived length of the relationship. See also **Parental investment.**

Sexual swelling: One of the indicators of sexual availability in primate females, often accompanied by a change in color.

Sickness behaviors: A set of typical activities you perform when you feel sick. Researchers suggest sickness behavior should be viewed as a motivational state—a normal response to infection, just as fear is a normal response to a predator.

Social intelligence hypothesis: See **Machiavellian intelligence hypothesis.**

Social monogamy: The situation in which a male and a female of a species live together. See also **Sexual monogamy.**

Social releaser: The stimulus that functions like a key to produce a particular inborn behavior. See also **Imprinting**.

Source analysis: The process of understanding mechanisms underlying the differences described in culture mapping—similarity and differences in genetic makeup; cultural learning and the ways experiences can influence the structure of the brain; the ways scientists see similar patterns and differences in these patterns across cultures. See also **Culture mapping.**

Specialized characteristic: See **Derived characteristic**.

Species: A group of animals or plants that only breeds within itself and does not seek to breed with other groups.

Standard Social Science Model (SSSM): This perspective assumes that organisms come into the world as a blank slate (*tabula rasa* in Latin) written on through experience. From this perspective, humans are completely malleable. It reflects the nurture side of the nature/nurture debate.

Stream of consciousness: The continuous flow of ideas, thoughts, and feelings forming the content of an individual's consciousness.

Strong altruism: Behaviors that appear not to benefit the individual and cost the individual something. See also **Altruism; Weak altruism.**

Subcortical structures: The structures of the brain below the cerebral cortex. The neocortex sends and receives information to and from subcortical structures.

Sulci: Depressions or fissures in the surface of the brain.

Swiss army knife model: See **Mental module model.**

Sylvian fissure: A deep groove that separates the frontal and temporal lobes of the brain.

Syntax: The structure of a sentence and the rules that govern it.

Telomeres: Either end of a chromosome. See also **Chromosome.**

Temporal lobe: A large lobe of each brain hemisphere situated in front of the occipital lobe and associated with sound perception and interpretation and memory recall.

Tend-and-befriend response: Females under stress seek contact with their social group, which is also protective in survival terms. See also **Fight-or-flight response.**

Thalamic structures: Structures near the center of the brain that act as a relay between various subcortical areas and the cerebral cortex. They are considered part of the Neomammalian brain. See also **Neomammalian brain.**

Theory of mind: The theory that humans have the capacity to infer another's mental state from his or her behavior. Mental state can include purpose, intention, knowledge, belief, thinking, doubt, pretending, liking, and so forth. See also **Belief-desire reasoning.**

Thrifty genotype hypothesis: Neel suggested that certain genes may be advantageous in times of famine in that they reduced energy expenditure and thus were thrifty. See also **Genotype; Thrifty phenotype hypothesis.**

Thrifty phenotype hypothesis: An expansion of Baker's thrifty genotype hypothesis, suggesting that the mother's nutrition during early pregnancy could influence both fetal and infant growth—primarily body size and energy-conserving physiological mechanisms. That is, the infant's metabolism is thrifty. See also **Phenotype; Thrifty genotype hypothesis.**

Tit-for-tat: The best strategy for playing the prisoners' dilemma game. Tit-for-tat has only two rules. (1) On your first move, you should cooperate. (2) On every move after that, do what the other person did on the last trial.

Transcription: The DNA synthesis of RNA. See also **DNA; RNA.**

Translation: The step from RNA to protein. See also **RNA.**

Tree branching: Darwin reminds us to consider primitive and specialized characteristics as a tree branching pattern, rather than a direct and single line. Using this metaphor, we realize that different species can have unique histories of evolution.

Triune brain: MacLean suggested that our current brain can be viewed as having the features of three basic evolutionary formations—reptiles, early mammals, and recent mammals. Through rich interconnections, our brains process information in three somewhat independent, although not autonomous, ways. See also **Neomammalian brain; Paleomammalian brain; R-complex.**

Ultimate questions: Questions that ask why a behavior or trait occurs. See also **Proximate questions.**

Universal grammar: Noam Chomsky suggested that all humans have a set of innate principles and parameters underlying the language faculty.

Variation: The manner in which measurements vary within conditions. The statistical measurements of variability are those of standard deviation and variance. Biological variation refers to the manner in which species differ from one another.

Weak altruism: Behaviors that appear not to benefit the individual but cost the individual nothing. See also **Altruism; Strong altruism.**

White matter: The myelin sheaths on axons are light in color and thus these areas are referred to as white matter. See also **Axons; Myelin sheaths.**

Zygote: The single cell that is produced by the joining of the female's egg and the male's sperm.

References

Ader, R. (2002). Psychoneuroimmunology. *Current Directions in Psychological Science, 10*, 94–98.

Ader, R., & Cohen, N. (1993). Psychoneuro-immunology: Condition and stress. *Annual Review of Pharmacology, 44*, 53–85.

Adolphs, R. (2003). Cognitive neuroscience of human social behaviour. *Nature Reviews Neuroscience, 4*, 165–178.

Adolphs, R. (2010). Conceptual challenges and directions for social neuroscience. *Neuron, 65*, 752–767.

Adolphs, R., & Damasio, A. (2000). Neurobiology of emotion at a systems level. In J. Borod (Ed.), *The neuropsychology of emotion* (pp. 194–213). New York: Oxford University Press.

Aiello, L., Bates, N., & Joffe, T. (2001). In defense of the Expensive Tissue Hypothesis. In D. Falk & K. Gibson (Eds.), *Evolutionary anatomy of the primate cerebral cortex* (pp. 57–78). New York: Cambridge University Press.

Ainsworth, M., Blehar, M., Waters, E., & Wall, S. (1978). *Patterns of attachment: A psychological study of the strange situation.* Hillsdale, NJ: Lawrence Erlbaum Associates.

Alcock, J. (2001). *The triumph of sociobiology.* Oxford: Oxford University Press.

Alexander, R. D. (1987). *The biology of moral systems.* New York: Aldine de Gruyter.

Allen, N., & Badcock, P. (2003). The social risk hypothesis of depressed mood: Evolutionary, psychosocial, and neurobiological perspectives. *Psychological Bulletin, 129*, 887–913.

Allman, J. (1999). *Evolving brains.* New York: Scientific American Library.

Amaral, D., Schumann, C., & Nordahl, C. (2008). Neuroanatomy of autism. *Trends in Neurosciences, 31*, 137–145.

Ambady, N., & Bharucha, J. (2009). Culture and the brain. *Current Directions in Psychological Science, 18*, 342–345.

Ambrose, S. (2001). Paleolithic technology and human evolution. *Science, 291*, 1748-1753.

Andersen, B., Cyranowski, J., & Espindle, D. (1999). Men's sexual self-schema. *Journal of Personality and Social Psychology, 76*, 645–661.

Andreasen, N. (2000). Schizophrenia: The fundamental questions. *Brain Research Reviews, 31*, 106–112.

Andrews, P. (2007). Reconstructing the evolution of the mind is depressingly difficult. In S. Gangestad & J. Simpson (Eds.), *The evolution of mind* (pp. 45–52). New York: Guilford Press.

Angell, J. (1909). The influence of Darwin on psychology. *Psychological Review, 16*, 152–169.

Ankney, C. D. (1992). Sex differences in relative brain size: The mismeasure of woman, too? *Intelligence, 16*, 329–336.

Atran, S. (2001). A cheater-detection module? Dubious interpretations of the Wason-selection task and logic. *Evolution and Cognition, 7*, 1–7.

Atran, S., & Norenzayan, A. (2004). Religion's evolutionary landscape: Counterintuition, commitment, compassion, communion. *Behavioral and Brain Sciences, 27*, 713–770.

Axelrod, R. (1984). *The evolution of cooperation.* New York: Basic Books.

Axelrod, R., & Hamilton, W. D. (1981). The evolution of cooperation. *Science, 211*, 1390–1396.

Bach, J. (2002). The effects of infections on susceptibility to autoimmune and allergic diseases. *New England Journal of Medicine, 347,* 911–920.

Bailey, K. (1987). *Human paleopsychology.* Hillsdale, NJ: Lawrence Erlbaum Associates.

Baker, R. R., & Bellis, M. A. (1995). *Human sperm competition: Copulation, masturbation, and infidelity.* London: Chapman and Hall.

Barash, D., & Lipton, J. (2001). *Myth of monogamy: Fidelity and infidelity in animals and people.* New York: W.H. Freeman.

Bard, K. (2005). Emotions in chimpanzee infants: The value of a comparative developmental approach to understand the evolutionary bases of emotion. In J. Nadel & D. Muir (Eds.), *Emotional development* (pp. 31–60). Oxford: Oxford University Press.

Barkow, J., Cosmides, L., & Tooby, J. (Eds.). (1992). *The adaptive mind.* New York: Oxford University Press.

Baron-Cohen, S. (2005). The empathizing system. In B. Ellis & D. Bjorklund, (Eds.), *Origins of the social mind: Evolutionary psychology and child development* (pp. 468–492). New York: Guilford Press.

Baron-Cohen, S., & Belmonte, M. (2005). Autism: A window onto the development of the social and the analytic brain. *Annual Review of Neuroscience, 28,* 109–126.

Barret, H. (2005). Cognitive development and the understanding of animal behavior. In B. Ellis & D. Bjorklund, (Eds.), *Origins of the social mind: Evolutionary psychology and child development* (pp. 438–467). New York: Guilford Press.

Barrett, J. (2000). Exploring the natural foundations of religion. *Trends in Cognitive Sciences, 4,* 29–34.

Barrett, J., & Keil, F. (1996). Anthropomorphism and God concepts: Conceptualizing a non-natural entity. *Cognitive Psycology, 3,* 219–247.

Barrett, L., Mesquita, B., Ochsner, K., & Gross, J. (2007). The experience of emotion. *Annual Review of Psychology, 58,* 373–403.

Bass, A., Gilland, E., & Baker, R. (2008). Evolutionary origins for social vocalization in a vertebrate hindbrain-spinal compartment. *Science, 321,* 417–421.

Baumeister, R. F. (2000). Gender differences in erotic plasticity: The female sex drive as socially flexible and responsive. *Psychological Bulletin, 126,* 347–374.

Bell, J., & Spector, T. (2011). A twin approach to unraveling epigenetics. *Trends in genetics, 27,* 116–125.

Belsky, J. (1997). Attachment, mating, and parenting: An evolutionary interpretation. *Human Nature, 8,* 361–381.

Belsky, J. (1999). Modern evolutionary theory and patterns of attachment. In J. Cassidy & P. Shaver (Eds.), *Handbook of attachment* (pp. 141–161). New York: Guilford Press.

Belsky, J. (2005). Differential susceptibility to rearing influence: An evolutionary hypothesis and some evidence. In B. Ellis & D. Bjorklund (Eds.), *Origins of the social mind: Evolutionary psychology and child development* (pp. 139–163). New York: Guilford Press.

Belsky, J. (2007). Childhood experiences and reproductive strategies. In R. Dunbar & L. Barrett (Eds.), *Oxford handbook of evolutionary psychology* (pp. 237–254). New York: Oxford University Press.

Belsky, J., Steinberg, L., & Draper, P. (1991). Childhood experience, interpersonal development, and reproductive strategy: An evolutionary theory of socialization. *Child Development, 62,* 647–670.

Bennett, M., & Hacker, P. (2005). Emotion and cortical-subcortical function: Conceptual developments. *Progress in Neurobiology, 75,* 29–52.

Bereczkei, T. (2007). Parental impacts on development: How proximate factors mediate adaptive plans. In R. Dunbar & L. Barrett (Eds.), *Oxford handbook of evolutionary psychology* (pp. 255–272). New York: Oxford University Press.

Bernard, C. (1927). *An introduction to the study of experimental medicine, 1865* (Trans.

Henry Copley Greene). New York: Macmillan & Co.

Bernhard, H., Fischbacher, U., & Fehr, E. (2006). Parochial altruism in humans. *Nature, 442,* 912–915.

Berridge, K. (2003). Comparing the emotional brains of humans and other animals. In R. Davidson, K. Scherer, & H. Goldsmith (Eds.), *Handbook of affective sciences* (pp. 25–51). New York: Oxford University Press.

Berwick, R., Okanoya, K., Beckers, G., & Bolhuis, J. (2011). Songs to syntax: The linguistics of birdsong. *Trends in Cognitive Sciences, 15,* 113–121.

Bickerton, D. (1984). The language biopro-gram hypothesis. *The Behavioral and Brain Sciences, 7,* 173–221.

Bickerton, D. (1995). *Language and human behavior.* Seattle: University of Washington Press.

Bickerton, D. (2009). *Adam's tongue: How humans made language, how language made humans.* New York: Hill & Wang.

Bjorklund, D. F. (2003). Evolutionary psychol-ogy from a developmental systems perspec-tive: Comment on Lickliter and Honeycutt (2003). *Psychological Bulletin, 129,* 836–841.

Bjorklund, D., & Blasi, C. (2005). Evolutionary developmental psychology. In D. Buss (Ed.), *The handbook of evolutionary psychology* (pp. 828–850). Hoboken, NJ: John Wiley & Sons.

Bjorklund, D., & Pellegrini, A. (2002). *The origins of human nature: Evolutionary developmental psychology.* Washington, DC: American Psychological Association.

Blackmore, S. (1999). *The meme machine.* New York: Oxford University Press.

Blackmore, S. (2006). Why we need memetics. *Behavioral and Brain Sciences, 29,* 349–350.

Blinkov, S., & Glezer, I. (1968). *The human brain in figures and tables: A quantitative handbook.* New York: Plenum Press.

Boesch, C., & Tomasello, M. (1998). Chimpanzee and human culture. *Current Anthropology, 39,* 591–611.

Bogin, B. (2000). Basic principles of human growth and development. In S. Stinson, B. Bogin, R. Huss-Ashmore, & D. O'Rourke (Eds.), *Human biology: An evolutionary and biocultural perspective* (pp. 163–224). New York: Wiley-Liss.

Bolger, D. J., Perfetti, C. A., & Schneider, W. (2005). Cross-cultural effect on the brain revisited: Universal structures plus writing system variation. *Human Brain Mapping, 25,* 92–104.

Bolhuis, J., Okanoya, K., & Scharff, C. (2010). Twitter evolution: Converging mechanisms in birdsong and human speech. *Nature Neuroscience, 11,* 747–759.

Bornstein, G., & Ben-Yossef, M. (1994). Coope-ration in intergroup and single-group social dilemmas. *Journal of Experimental Social Psychology, 30,* 52–67.

Bouchard, T., Lykken, D., McGue, M., Segal, M., & Tellegen, A. (1990). Sources of human psychological differences: The Minnesota Study of Twins Reared Apart. *Science, 250,* 223–228.

Bourgeois, J. (1997). Synaptogenesis, heter-onomy, and epigenesis in the mamma-lian neocortex. *Acta Paediatrica, 422,* 27–33.

Boveri, T. (1904). *Ergebnisse über die konstitu-tion der chromatischen substanz des zelk-erns.* Jena, Germany: Fisher.

Bowlby, J. (1951). *Maternal care and mental health: A report prepared on behalf of the World Health Organization as a contribu-tion to the United Nations programme for the welfare of homeless children.* Geneva: World Health Organization.

Bowlby, J. (1969). *Attachment and loss, Vol. 1: Attachment.* London: Hogarth.

Bowlby, J. (1982). *Attachment and loss, Vol. 1: Attachment* (2nd ed.). New York: Basic Books.

Bowlby, J. (1988). *A secure base: Parent-child attachment and healthy human develop-ment.* London: Routledge.

Boyd, R. and Richerson, P. (1985) *Culture and the Evolutionary Process,* University of Chicago Press, Chicago, IL.

Boyd, R., & Richerson, P. (2005). *The origin and evolution of culture.* New York: Oxford University Press.

Boyd, R., & Silk, J. (2006). *How humans evolved* (4th ed.). New York: W. W. Norton & Co.

Boyer, P. (2000). Evolution of the modern mind and the origins of culture: Religious concepts as a limiting case. In P. Carruthers & A. Chamberlain (Eds.), *Evolution and the human mind* (pp. 93–112). New York: Cambridge University Press.

Bressan, P., & Stranieri, D. (2008). The best men are (not always) already taken. *Psychological Science, 19,* 145–151.

Britton, J., Phan, K., Taylor, S., Welsh, R., Berridge, K., & Liberzon, I. (2006). Neural correlates of social and nonsocial emotions: An fMRI study. *NeuroImage, 31,* 397–409.

Broca, P. (1878). Anatomie comparee des circonvolutions cerebrales: Le grand lobe limbique et la scissure limbique dans la serie des mammiferes. *Rev. Anthrop., 1,* 385.

Brothers, L. (1990). The social brain: A project for integrating primate behaviour and neurophysiology in a new domain. *Concepts in Neuroscience, 1,* 27–51.

Brüne, M. (2008). *Textbook of evolutionary psychiatry: The origins of psychopathology.* New York: Oxford University Press.

Buckner, R., Andrews-Hanna, J., & Schacter, D. (2008). The brain's default network. *Annals of the New York Academy of Sciences, 1124,* 1–38.

Buller, D. (2005). *Adapting minds.* Cambridge, MA: MIT Press.

Burgess, R., & MacDonald, K. (Eds.). (2005). *Evolutionary perspectives on human development* (2nd ed.). Thousand Oaks, CA: Sage.

Burghardt, G. (2004). Play: How evolution can explain the most mysterious behavior of all. In A. Moya & E. Font (Eds.), *Evolution: From molecules to ecosystems* (pp. 231–246). New York: Oxford University Press.

Burns, J. (2004). An evolutionary theory of schizophrenia: Cortical connectivity, metarepresentation, and the social brain. *Behavioral and Brain Sciences, 27,* 831–885.

Burns, J. (2006). The social brain hypothesis of schizophrenia. *World Psychiatry, 5,* 77–81.

Burnstein, E. (2005). Altruism and genetic relatedness. In D. Buss (Ed.), *The handbook of evolutionary psychology* (pp. 528–551). Hoboken, NJ: John Wiley & Sons.

Buss, D. (1989). Sex differences in human mate preferences: Evolutionary hypotheses tested in 37 cultures. *Behavioral and Brain Sciences, 12,* 1–49.

Buss, D. (2000). The evolution of happiness. *American Psychologist, 55,* 15–23.

Buss, D. (2006). Strategies of human mating. *Psychological Topics, 15,* 239–260.

Buss, D. (2009). How can evolutionary psychology successfully explain personality and individual differences? *Perspectives on Psychological Science, 4,* 359–366.

Buss, D., & Hawley, P. (2011). *The evolution of personality and individual differences.* New York: Oxford University Press.

Buss, D., & Schmitt, D. (1993). Sexual strategies theory: An evolutionary perspective on human mating. *Psychological Review, 100,* 204–232.

Byrne, R. W. (2001). Social and technical forms of primate intelligence. In F. de Waal (Ed.), *Tree of origin* (pp. 147–172). Cambridge, MA: Harvard University Press.

Byrne, R., & Bates, L. (2010). Primate social cognition: Uniquely primate, uniquely social, or just unique? *Neuron, 65,* 815–830.

Byrne, R. W., & Bates, L. A. (2011). Cognition in the wild: Exploring animal minds with observational evidence. *Biological Letters, 7,* 619–622.

Byrne, R. W., & Whiten, A., (Eds.). (1988). *Machiavellian intelligence: Social expertise and the evolution of intellect in monkeys, apes, and humans.* New York: Oxford University Press.

Cacioppo, J., & Berntson, G. (2007). The brain, homeostasis, and health. In H. Friedman & R. Silver (Eds.), *Foundations of health psychology* (pp. 73–91). New York: Oxford University Press.

Call, J., & Tomasello, M. (2008). Does the chimpanzee have a theory of mind? 30 years later. *Trends in Cognitive Sciences, 12,* 187–192.

Callebaut, W., & Rasskin-Gutman, D. (2005). *Modularity: Understanding the development and evolution of natural complex systems.* Cambridge, MA: MIT Press.

Campbell, A. (1999). Staying alive: Evolution, culture, and women's intrasexual aggression. *Behavioral and Brain Sciences, 22,* 203–252.

Campbell, D. (1983). The two distinct routes beyond kin selection to ultrasociality: Implications for the humanities and social sciences. In D. Bridgeman (Ed.), *The nature of prosocial development.* New York: Academic Press.

Campos, J., Bertenthal, B., & Kermoian, R. (1992). Early experience and emotional development: The emergence of wariness of heights. *Psychological Science, 3,* 61–64.

Canessa, N., Gorini, A., Cappa, S., Piattelli-Palmarini, M., Danna, M., Fazio, F., & Perani, D. (2005). The effects of social content on deductive reasoning: An fMRI study. *Human Brain Mapping, 26,* 30–45.

Cannon, W. (1915). *Bodily changes in pain, hunger, fear, and rage.* New York: D. Appleton & Company.

Cannon, W. (1932). *The wisdom of the body.* New York: Norton.

Carey, G. (2003). *Human genetics for the social sciences.* Thousand Oaks, CA: Sage.

Carone, B., Fauquier, L., Habib, N., Shea, J., Hart, C., Li, R., . . . Rando, O. (2010). Paternally induced transgenerational environmental reprogramming of metabolic gene expression in mammals. *Cell, 143,* 1084–1096.

Carroll, L. (1946). *Through the looking glass, special edition.* New York: Random House. (Original work published 1872)

Cartwright, J. (2000). *Evolution and human behavior.* Cambridge, MA: MIT Press.

Cartwright, J. (2001). *Evolutionary explanations of human behavior.* Hove, UK: Routledge.

Caspi, A., McClay, J., Moffitt, T., Mill, J., Martin, J., Craig, I., . . . Poulton, R. (2002). Role of genotype in the cycle of violence in maltreated children. *Science, 297,* 851–854.

Catell, R. (1950). *Personality: A systematic, theoretical, and factual study.* New York: McGraw-Hill.

Caufield, P., Saxena, D., Fitch, D., & Li, Y. (2007). Population structure of plasmid-containing strains of *streptococcus mutans,* a member of the human indigenous biota. *Journal of Bacteriology, 189,* 1238–1243.

Chamberlain, S., Menzies, L., Hampshire, A., Suckling, J., Fineberg, N., del Campo, N., . . . Sahakian, B. (2008). Orbitofrontal dysfunction in patients with obsessive compulsive disorder and their unaffected relatives. *Science, 321,* 421–422.

Changeux, J. (2004). *The physiology of truth: Neuroscience and human knowledge.* Cambridge, MA: Harvard University Press.

Chiao, J., & Ambady, N. (2007). Cultural neuroscience: Parsing universality and diversity across levels of analysis. In S. Kitayama & D. Cohen (Eds.), *Handbook of cultural psychology* (pp. 237–254). New York: Guilford Press.

Chiao, J. Y., Iidaka, T., Gordon, H. L., Nogawa, J., Bar, M., Aminoff, E., et al. (2008). Cultural specificity in amygdala response to fear faces. *Journal of Cognitive Neuroscience, 20,* 2167–2174.

Chomsky, N. (1959). A review of B. F. Skinner's verbal behavior. *Language, 35,* 26–58.

Chomsky, N. (1966). *Topics in the theory of generative grammar.* The Hague, Netherlands: Mouton & Co.

Chomsky, N. (1968). *Language and mind.* New York: Harcourt, Brace, & World.

Christiansen, M., & Kirby, S. (2003). *Language evolution.* New York: Oxford University Press.

Clark, R., & Hatfield, E. (1989). Gender differences in receptivity to sexual offers. *Journal of Psychology & Human Sexuality, 2,* 39–55.

Cohen, S., & Herbert, T. (1996). Health psychology: Psychological factors and physical disease from the perspective of human psychoneuroimmunology. *Annual Review of Psychology, 47*, 113–142.

Coleman, S., Patricelli, G., & Borgia, G. (2004). Variable female preferences drive complex male displays. *Nature, 428*, 742–745.

Cosmides, L. (1989). The logic of social exchange: Has natural selection shaped how humans reason? Studies with the Wason selection task. *Cognition, 31*, 187–276.

Cosmides, L., & Tooby, J. (1989). "Evolutionary Psychology and the Generation of Culture, Part II. Case Study: A Computational Theory of Social Exchange." *Ethology and Sociobiology, 10*, 51–97.

Cosmides, L., & Tooby, J. (1992). Cognitive adaptations for social exchange. In J. Barkow, L. Cosmides, & J. Tooby (Eds.), *The adaptive mind: Evolutionary psychology and the generation of culture* (pp. 163–228). New York: Oxford University Press.

Cosmides, L., & Tooby, J. (1997). *Evolutionary psychology: A primer.* Retrieved from http://www.psych.ucsb.edu/research/cep/primer.html

Crews, D. (2003). *Human senescence: Evolutionary and biocultural perspectives.* Cambridge, UK: Cambridge University Press.

Crick, F. (1988). *What mad pursuit?* New York: Basic Books.

Cropley, J., Suter, C., Beckman, K., & Martin, D. (2006). Germ-line epigenetic modification of the murine A^{vy} allele by nutritional supplementation. *Proceedings of the National Academies of Sciences, 103*, 17308–17312.

Crow, T. (2000). Schizophrenia as the price that Homo sapiens pays for language: A revolution of the central paradox in the origin of the species. *Brain Research Reviews, 31*, 118–129.

Cummings, M. (2009). *Human heredity* (8th ed.). Pacific Grove, CA: Brooks/Cole.

Currie, P. (2004). Muscling in on hominid evolution. *Nature, 428*, 373–374.

Curtis, M. E., & Bharucha, J. J. (2009). Memory and musical expectation for tones in cultural context. *Music Perception, 26*, 365–375.

Dahm, R. (2008). The first discovery of DNA. *American Scientist, 96*, 320–327.

Daly, M. (1988). *Homicide.* New York: Aldine de Druyter.

Daly, M., Salmon, C., & Wilson, M. (1997). Kinship: The conceptual hole in psychological studies of social cognition and close relationships. In J. Simpson & D. Kenrick (Eds.), *Evolutionary social psychology* (pp. 265–296). Hillsdale, NJ: Lawrence Erlbaum Associates.

Daly, M., & Wilson, M. (1983) *Sex, evolution, and behavior* (2nd ed.). Boston: Willard Grant Press.

Daly, M., & Wilson, M. (1985). Child abuse and other risks of not living with both parents. *Ethology and Sociobiology, 6*, 197–210.

Daly, M., & Wilson, M. (1990). Is parent-offspring conflict sex-linked? Freudian and Darwinian models. *Journal of Personality, 58*, 163–189.

Daly, M., & Wilson, M. (1998). The evolutionary social psychology of family violence. In C. Crawford & D. Krebs (Eds.), *Handbook of evolutionary psychology* (pp. 431–456). Mahwah, NJ: Lawrence Erlbaum.

Daly, M., & Wilson, M. (2001). Risk-taking, intrasexual competition, and homicide. *Nebraska Symposium on Motivation, 47*, 1–36.

Dantzer, R., O'Connor, J., Greund, G., Johnson, R., & Kelley, K. (2008). From inflammation to sickness and depression: When the immune system subjugates the brain. *Nature Reviews Neuroscience, 9*, 46–57.

Darwin, C. (1859). *On the origin of species by means of natural selection.* London: J. Murray.

Darwin, C. (1874). *The descent of man and selection in relation to sex.* Chicago: Rand, McNally.

Darwin, C. (1877). A biographical sketch of an infant. *Mind, 2*, 285–294.

Darwin, C. (1998). *The expression of emotions in man and animals* (3rd ed.). New York: Oxford University Press. (Original work published 1872)

Dasser, V. (1988). A social concept in Java monkeys. *Animal Behaviour, 36*, 225–230.

Dawkins, R. (1976). *The selfish gene.* New York: Oxford University Press.

Dawkins, R. (1989). *The selfish gene* (2nd ed.). New York: Oxford University Press.

Dawkins, R. (2009). *The greatest show on earth: The evidence for evolution.* New York: Free Press.

Deacon, T. (1997). *The symbolic species: The coevolution of language and the brain.* New York: Norton.

DeBruine, L. (2002). *Facial resemblance enhances trust. Proceedings of the Royal Society of London B, 269,* 1307–1312.

Delbrück, M. (1949). A physicist looks at biology. *Transactions of The Connecticut Academy of Arts and Sciences, 38,* 173–190.

De Martino, B., Kumaran, D., Seymour, B., & Dolan, R. (2006). Frames, biases, and rational decision-making in the human brain. *Science, 313,* 684–687.

de Waal, F. (1995). Bonobo sex and society. *Scientific American, 272,* 82–88.

de Waal, F. (2002). *Tree of origin: What primate behavior can tell us about human social evolution.* Cambridge, MA: Harvard University Press.

de Waal, F. B. M. (2003). Darwin's legacy and the study of primate visual communication. *Annals of the New York Academy of Sciences, 1000,* 7–31.

de Waal, F., & Lanting, F. (1998). *Bonobo: The forgotten ape.* Berkeley: University of California Press.

DiLalla, L. (Ed.). (2004). *Behavior genetics principles: Perspectives in development, personality, and psychopathology.* Washington, DC: American Psychological Association.

Dimoka, A. (2010). Brain mapping of psychological processes with psychometric scales: An fMRI method for social neuroscience. *Neuroimage, 54,* 5263–5271.

Dixon, A. (2009). *Sexual selection and the origins of human mating systems.* New York: Oxford University Press.

Dixon, A., & Anderson, M. (2002). Sexual selection, seminal coagulation and copulatory plug formation in primates. *Folia Primatologica: International Journal of Primatology, 73,* 63–69.

Dobzhansky, T. (1937). *Genetics and the origin of species.* New York: Columbia University Press.

Dugatkin, L. (2006). *The altruism equation: Seven scientists search for the origins of goodness.* Princeton, NJ: Princeton University Press.

Dunbar, R. (1996). *Grooming, gossip, and the evolution of language.* London: Faber and Faber.

Dunbar, R. (2000). On the origin of the human mind. In P. Carruthers & A. Chamberlain (Eds.), *Evolution and the human mind* (pp. 238–253). New York: Cambridge University Press.

Dunbar, R. (2003). The social brain: Mind, language, and society in evolutionary perspective. *Annual Review of Anthropology, 32,* 161–181.

Dunbar, R. (2004). *The human story: A new history of mankind's evolution.* London: Faber and Faber.

Dunn, J. (2003). Emotional development in early childhood: A social relationship perspective. In R. Davidson, K. Scherer, & H. Goldsmith (Eds.), *Handbook of affective sciences* (pp. 332–346). New York: Oxford University Press.

Eagly, A., & Wood, W. (1999). The origins of sex differences in human behavior. *American Psychologist, 54,* 408–423.

Eberhard, W. G. (1985). *Sexual selection and animal genitalia.* Cambridge, MA: Harvard University Press.

Eibl-Eibesfeldt, I. (1975). *Ethology: The biology of behavior, 2nd Ed.* New York: Holt, Rinehart & Winston.

Eibl-Eibesfeldt, I. (1989). *Human ethology.* New York: Aldine de Gruyter.

Eisenberg, N. (2000). Emotion, regulation, and moral development. *Annual Review of Psychology, 51,* 665–697.

Eisenberger, N., Lieberman, M., & Williams, K. (2003). Does rejection hurt: An fMRI study of social exclusion. *Science, 302,* 290–292.

Eisner, M. (2001). Modernization, self-control, and lethal violence. *British Journal of Criminology, 41,* 618–638.

Ekman, P. (1957). A methodological discussion of nonverbal behavior. *Journal of Psychology, 43,* 141–149.

Ekman, P. (1973). *Darwin and facial expression: A century of research in review.* New York: Academic Press.

Ekman, P. (1999a). Basic emotions. In T. Dalgleish & M. Power (Eds.). *Handbook of cognition and emotion.* Sussex, UK: John Wiley & Sons.

Ekman, P. (1999b). Facial expressions. In T. Dalgleish & M. Power (Eds.), *Handbook of cognition and emotion* (pp. 301–320). Sussex, UK: John Wiley & Sons.

Ekman, P. (2003a). Darwin, deception, and facial expression. *Annals of the New York Academy of Sciences, 1000,* 205–221.

Ekman, P. (2003b). *Emotions revealed.* New York: Times Books.

Ekman, P. (2009). Darwin's contribution to our understanding of emotional expressions. *Philosophical Transactions of the Royal Society B, 364,* 3449–3451.

Ekman, P., & Friesen, W. (1971). Constants across cultures in the face and emotion. *Journal of Personality and Social Psychology, 17,* 124–129.

Elbert, T., Pantev, C., Wienbruch, C., Rockstroh, B., & Taub, E. (1995). Increased cortical representation of the fingers of the left hand in string players. *Science 270,* 305–307.

Elfenbein, H., & Ambady, N. (2002). On the universality and cultural specificity of emotion recognition: A meta-analysis. *Psychological Bulletin, 128,* 203–235.

Ellenberger, H. (1970). *The discovery of the unconscious.* New York: Basic Books.

Ellis, B., & Bjorklund, D. (Eds.). (2005). *Origins of the social mind: Evolutionary psychology and child development.* New York: Guilford Press.

Ellis, B. J., & Garber, J. (2000). Psychosocial antecedents of pubertal maturation in girls: Parental psychopathology, stepfather presence, and family and marital stress. *Child Development, 71,* 485–501.

English, H. (1929). Three cases of the "conditioned fear response." *Journal of abnormal and social psychology, 24,* 221–225.

Evans, R. I. (Director). (1990). *Jung on film* [Video]. London: Public Media Video.

Eysenck, H. (1967). *The biological basis of personality.* Springfield, IL: C.C. Thomas.

Falk, D. (2000). *Primate diversity.* New York: W. W. Norton.

Falk, D. (2001). The evolution of sex differences in primate brains. In D. Falk & K. Gibson (Eds.), *Evolutionary anatomy of the primate cerebral cortex* (pp. 98–112). New York: Cambridge University Press.

Falk, D. (2004). Prelinguistic evolution in early hominins: Whence motherese? *Behavioral and Brain Sciences, 27,* 491–541.

Fehr, E. (2002). The economics of impatience. *Nature, 415,* 269–272.

Fehr, E., & Gächter, S. (2002). Altruistic punishment in humans. *Nature, 415,* 137–140.

Feinstein, J., Adolphs, R., Damasio, A., & Tranel, D. (2010). The human amygdala and the induction and expression of fear. *Current biology, 21,* 1–5.

Felitti, V., Anda, R., Nordenberg, D., Williamson, D., Spitz, A., Edwards, V., . . . Marks, J. (1998). Relationship of childhood abuse and household dysfunction to many of the leading causes of death in adults. *American Journal of Preventive Medicine, 14,* 245–258.

Felson, R. (2002). *Violence & gender reexamined.* Washington, DC: American Psychological Association.

Feygin, D., Swain, J. E., & Leckman J. (2006). The normalcy of neurosis: Evolutionary origins of obsessive-compulsive disorder and related behaviors. *Progress in Neuro-Psychopharmacology and Biological Psychiatry, 30,* 854–864.

Fiddick, L., Cosmides, L., & Tooby, J. (2000). No interpretation without representation: The role of domain-specific representations and inferences in the Wason selection task. *Cognition, 77,* 1–79.

Figueredo, A. J., Sefcek, J. A., Vásquez, G., Brumbach, B. H., King, J. E., & Jacobs, W. J. (2005). Evolutionary personality psychology. In D. M. Buss (Ed.), *Handbook of evolutionary psychology* (pp. 851–877). Hoboken, NJ: Wiley.

Fisher, R. A. (1999). *The genetical theory of natural selection.* Oxford, UK: Oxford University Press. (Original work published 1930)

Fiske, A. (1992). The four elementary forms of sociality: Framework for a unified theory of social relations. *Psychological Review, 99*, 689–723.

Fitch, W. T., Huber, L., & Bugnyar, T. (2010). Social cognition and the evolution of language: Constructing cognitive phylogenies. *Neuron, 65*, 795–814.

Flavell, J. (2000). Development of children's knowledge about the mental world. *International Journal of Behavioral Development, 24*, 15–23.

Flinn, M. (2005). Culture and developmental plasticity: Evolution of the social brain. In R. Burgess & K. MacDonald (Eds.), *Evolutionary perspectives on human development* (2nd ed., pp. 73–98). Thousand Oaks, CA: Sage.

Flinn, M. (2007). Evolution of stress response to social threat. In R. Dunbar & L. Barrett (Eds.), *Oxford handbook of evolutionary psychology* (pp. 273–296). New York: Oxford University Press.

Flinn, M., Quinlan, R., Coe, K., & Ward, C. (2008). Evolution of the human family: Cooperative males, long social childhoods, smart mothers, and extended kin networks. In C. Salmon & T. Shackelford (Eds.), *Family relationships: An evolutionary perspective* (pp. 16–38). New York: Oxford University Press.

Flinn, M., Ward, C., & Noone, R. (2005). Hormones and the human family. In D. Buss (Ed.), *The handbook of evolutionary psychology* (pp. 552–580). Hoboken, NJ: John Wiley & Sons.

Fodor, J. (2000). Why we are so good at catching cheaters. *Cognition, 75*, 29–32.

Folds, J. (2008). Overview of immunity. In M. O'Gorman & A. Donnenberg (Eds.), *Handbook of human immunology* (2nd ed., pp. 1–28). Boca Raton, FL: CRC Press.

Frank, R. (2004). *What price the moral high ground?* Princeton, NJ: Princeton University Press.

Freeman, W. (2000). A neurobiological role for music in social bonding. In N. Wallins, B. Merker, & S. Brown (Eds.), *The origins of music* (pp. 411–424). Cambridge, MA: MIT Press.

Freud, S. (1954). The project for a scientific psychology (Tr. James Strachey). In M. Bonaparte, A. Freud, & E. Kris (Eds.), *The origins of psychoanalysis* (pp. 347–445). London: *Imago*. (Original work published 1895)

Friedman, M. (1996). *Type A behavior: Its diagnosis and treatment.* New York: Plenum Press.

Friedman, M., & Rosenman, R. H. (1959). Association of a specific overt behavior pattern with increases in blood cholesterol, blood clotting time, incidence of arcus senilis and clinical coronary artery diseases. *Journal of the American Medical Association, 2196*, 1286–1296.

Frith, C. D. (1992). *The cognitive neuropsychology of schizophrenia.* London: LEA.

Frith, C., & Frith, U. (2008). Implicit and explicit processes in social cognition. *Neuron, 60*, 503–510.

Galati, D., Scherer, K., & Ricci-Bitti, P. (1997). Voluntary facial expression of emotion: Comparing congenitally blind with normally sighted encoders. *Journal of Personality and Social Psychology, 73*, 1363–1379.

Gallup, G. (1970). Chimpanzees: Self-recognition. *Science, 167*, 86–87.

Galton, F. (1869). *Hereditary genius.* New York: Appleton.

Gangestad, S. W. (2000). Human sexual selection, good genes, and special design. *Annals of the New York Academy of the Sciences, 907*, 50–61.

Gangestad, S., & Simpson, J. (2000). The evolution of mating: Trade-offs and strategic pluralism. *Behavioral and Brain Science, 23*, 675–687.

Gangestad, S., & Thornhill, R. (1998). Menstrual cycle variation in women's preferences for the scent of symmetrical men. *Proceedings of the Royal Society of London B, 265*, 927–933.

Garcia, J., Kimeldorf, D., & Koelling, R. (1955). Conditioned aversion to saccharin resulting from exposure to gamma radiation. *Science, 122,* 157–158.

Gaulin, S. J. C., & FitzGerald, R. W. (1986). Sex differences in spatial ability: An evolutionary hypothesis and test. *American Naturalist, 127,* 74–88.

Gazzaniga, M., & LeDoux, J. (1978). *The integrated mind.* New York: Plenum.

Geary, D. (1995). *The origin of mind: Evolution of brain, cognition, and general intelligence.* Washington, DC: American Psychological Association.

Geary, D. (1998). *Male/female.* Washington, DC: APA Press.

Geary, D. C. (2005a). Evolution of paternal investment. In D. M. Buss (Ed.), *Handbook of evolutionary psychology* (pp. 483–505). Hoboken, NJ: John Wiley & Sons.

Geary, D. (2005b). *The origin of mind: Evolution of brain, cognition, and general intelligence.* Washington, DC: American Psychological Association.

Geary, D. (2008). Evolution of fatherhood. In C. Salmon & T. Shackelford (Eds.), *Family relationships: An evolutionary perspective.* New York: Oxford University Press.

Geary, D., & Bjorklund, D. (2000). Evolutionary developmental psychology. *Child Development, 71,* 57–65.

Geher, G., & Miller, G. (2008). *Mating intelligence: Sex, relationships, and the mind's reproductive system.* New York: Lawrence Erlbaum Associates.

Gelfand, M., Raver, J., Nishii, L., Leslie, L., Lun, J., Lim, B. et al. (2011). Differences between tight and loose cultures: A 33-nation study. *Science, 332,* 1100–1104.

Ghazanfar, A. (2008). Language evolution: Neural differences that make a difference. *Nature Neuroscience, 11,* 382–384.

Ghazanfar, A. A., & Santos, L. R. (2004). Primate brains in the wild: The sensory bases for social interactions. *Nature Review Neuroscience, 5,* 603–616.

Gibbons, A. (2009). A new kind of ancestor: *Ardipithecus* unveiled. *Science, 326,* 36–40.

Gibbons, A. (2010). Close encounters of the prehistoric kind. *Science, 328,* 680–684.

Gibson, K., Rumbaugh, D., & Beran, M. (2001). Bigger is better: Primate brain size in relationship to cognition. In D. Falk & K. Gibson (Eds.), *Evolutionary anatomy of the primate cerebral cortex* (pp. 79–97). New York: Cambridge University Press.

Gilad, Y., Wiebe, V., Przeworski, M., Lancet, D., & Pääbo, S. (2004). Loss of olfactory receptor genes coincides with the acquisition of full trichromatic vision in primates. *PLOS Biology, 2,* 120–125.

Gilbert, P. (2005). Evolution and depression: Issues and implications. *Psychological Medicine, 36,* 287–297.

Gilbert, P., & Bailey, K. (2000). *Genes on the couch: Explorations into evolutionary psychotherapy.* London: Taylor & Francis.

Gluckman, P., & Hanson, M. (2005). *The fetal matrix: Evolution, development, and disease.* Cambridge, UK: Cambridge University Press.

Göncü, A., & Gaskins, S. (Eds.). (2007). *Play and development: Evolutionary, sociocultural, and functional perspectives.* Mahwah, NJ: Lawrence Erlbaum Associates.

Goodall, J. (1990). *Through a window: 30 years observing the Gombe chimpanzees.* Boston: Houghton Mifflin.

Gottesman, I. (1991). *Schizophrenia genesis: The origins of madness.* New York: Freeman.

Gottlieb, G. (1992). *Individual development and evolution.* New York: Oxford University Press.

Gottlieb, G. (1998). Normally occurring environmental and behavioral influences on gene activity: From central dogma to probabilistic epigenesis. *Psychological Review, 105,* 792–802.

Grant, P., & Grant, B. (2006). Evolution of character displacement in Darwin's finches. *Science, 313,* 224–226.

Gruber, H. (1974). *Darwin on man: A psychological study of scientific creativity.* New York: Dutton.

Gur, R., & Sackeim, H. (1979). Self-deception: A concept in search of a phenomenon. *Journal of Personality and Social Psychology, 37,* 147–169.

Gur, R. C., Turetsky, B., Matsui, M., Yan, M., Bilker, W., Hughett, P., & Gur, R. E. (1999). Sex differences in brain gray and white matter in healthy young adults: Correlations with cognitive performance. *Journal of Neuroscience, 19*, 4065–4072.

Haeckel, E. (1905). *Der kampf um den entwicklungs-gedanken.* Berlin: Georg Reimer.

Hales, C., & Barker, D. (2001). The thrifty phenotype hypothesis. *British Medical Bulletin, 60*, 5–20.

Hallgrímsson, B., & Hall, B. (Eds.). (2011). *Epigenetics.* Los Angeles: University of California Press.

Hamann, S., Herman, R., Nolan, C., & Wallen, K. (2004). Men and women differ in amygdala response to visual sexual stimuli. *Nature Neuroscience, 7*, 411–416.

Hamilton, W. D. (1963). The evolution of altruistic behavior. *American Naturalist, 97*, 354–356.

Hamilton, W. (1964). The genetical evolution of social behaviour. *Journal of Theoretical Biology, 7*(1), 1–16.

Hamilton, W. (1967). Extraordinary sex ratios. A sex-ratio theory for sex linkage and inbreeding has new implications in cytogenetics and entomology. *Science, 156*(774), 477–488.

Hamilton, W. D. (1996). *Narrow roads of gene land Vol. 1: Evolution of social behaviour.* Oxford, UK: Oxford University Press.

Hamilton, W. (2002). *Narrow roads of gene land: The evolution of sex.* New York: Oxford University Press.

Harlow, H. (1959). The development of affectional patterns in infant monkeys. In B. M. Foss (Ed.), *Determinants of infant behavior.* London: Methuen.

Harlow, H., McGaugh, J., & Thompson, R. (1971). *Psychology.* San Francisco: Albion.

Harpending, H., & Sobus, J. (1987). Sociopathy as an adaptation. *Ethology and Sociobiology, 8*, 63–72.

Haselton, M., & Funder, D. (2006). The evolution of accuracy and bias in social judgment. In M. Schaller, J. Simpson, & D. Kenrick (Eds.), *Evolution and social psychology* (pp. 15–38). New York: Psychology Press.

Hass, H. (1970). *The human animal.* New York: Pitnam.

Hass, R., Chaudhary, N., Kleyman, E., Nussbaum, A., Pulizzi, A., & Tison, J. (2000). The relationship between the theory of evolution and the social sciences, particularly psychology. *Annals of the New York Academy of Sciences, 907*, 1–20.

Hauser, M., & Fitch, W. (2003). What are the uniquely human components of the language faculty? In M. Christiansen & S. Kirby (Eds.), *Language evolution* (pp. 158–181). New York: Oxford University Press.

Hauser, M., & McDermott, J. (2003). The evolution of the music faculty: A comparative perspective. *Nature Neuroscience, 6*, 663–668.

Hawkes, K. (2003). Grandmothers and the evolution of human longevity. *American Journal of Human Biology, 15*, 380–400.

Hawkes, K., O'Connell, J. F., Blurton Jones, N. G., Charnov, E. L., & Alvarez, H. P. (1998). Grandmothering, menopause, and the evolution of human life histories. *Proceedings of the National Academy of Science USA, 95*, 1336–1339.

Heldon, W. (1942). *The varieties of temperament: A psychology of constitutional differences.* New York: Harper.

Henderson, B., & Baum, A. (2004). Biological mechanisms of health and disease. In S. Sutton, A. Baum, & M. Johnston (Eds.), *The Sage handbook of health psychology* (pp. 89–93). Thousand Oaks, CA: Sage.

Henrich, J. & McElreath, R.(2007) Dual Inheritance Theory: The Evolution of Human Cultural Capacities and Cultural Evolution. In R. Dunbar & L. Barrett (Eds.), *Oxford handbook of evolutionary psychology.* New York: Oxford University Press.

Herzog, H. (2010). *Some we love, some we hate, some we eat.* New York: Harper.

Hill, K. (1993). Life history theory and evolutionary anthropology. *Evolutionary Anthropology, 2*, 78–88.

Hillix, W., & Rumbaugh, D. (2004). *Animal bodies, human minds: Ape, dolphin, and parrot language skills.* New York: Kluwer.

Hirschfeld, L. (1989). Rethinking the acquisition of kinship terms. *International Journal of Behavioral Development, 12*, 541–568.

Hofman, M. (2001). Brain evolution in hominids: Are we at the end of the road? In D. Falk & K. Gibson (Eds.), *Evolutionary* anatomy of the primate cerebral cortex (pp. 113–127). New York: Cambridge University Press.

Hogenson, G. (2001). The Baldwin effect: A neglected influence on C. G. Jung's evolutionary thinking. *Journal of Analytic Psychology, 46*, 591–611.

Holmes, W., & Sherman, P. (1982). The ontogeny of kin recognition in two species of ground squirrels. *American Zoologist, 22*, 491–517.

Hrdy, S. (1979). Infanticide among animals: A review, classification, and examination of the implications for the reproductive strategies of females. *Ethology and Sociobiology, 1*, 13–40.

Hrdy, S. (1999). *Mother nature.* New York: Pantheon Books.

Hrdy, S. (2000). The optimal number of fathers: Evolution, demography, and history in the shaping of female mate preferences. *Annals New York Academy of Sciences* 907:75–96.

Hrdy, S. (2008). Evolutionary context of human development: The cooperative breeding model. In C. Salmon & T. Shackelford (Eds.). (2008). *Family relationships: An evolutionary perspective* (pp. 39–68). New York: Oxford University Press.

Hrdy, S. (2009). *Mothers and others.* Cambridge, MA: Harvard University Press.

Humphrey, N. (1976). The social function of intellect. In P. P. G. Bateson & R. A. Hinde (Eds.), *Growing points in ethology* (pp. 303–317). Cambridge, UK: Cambridge University Press.

Huxley, J. (2010). *Evolution: The modern synthesis.* Cambridge, MA: The MIT Press. (Original work published 1942)

Huxley, J., Mayr, E., Osmond, H., & Hoffer, A. (1964). Schizophrenia as a genetic morphism. *Nature, 204*, 220–221.

Impett, E., & Peplau, L. A. (2003). Sexual compliance: Gender, motivational, and relationship perspectives. *Journal of Sex Research, 40*, 87–100.

Insel, T. R. (2003). Is social attachment an addictive disorder? *Physiology & Behavior, 79*, 351–357.

Insel, T. (2010). The challenge of translation in social neuroscience: a review of oxytocin, vasopressin, and affiliative behavior. *Neuron, 65*, 769–779.

Insel, T. R., & Hulihan, T. J. (1995). A gender-specific mechanism for pair bonding: Oxytocin and partner preference formation in monogamous voles. *Behavioral Neuroscience, 109*, 782–789.

Insel, T. R., & Winslow, J. T. (1999). The neurobiology of social attachment. In D. S. Charney, E. T. Nestler, & B. S. Bunney (Eds.), *Neurobiology of mental illness* (pp. 880–890). New York: Oxford University Press.

Izard, C. (2007). Basic emotions, natural kinds, emotion schemas, and a new paradigm. *Perspectives on Psychological Science, 2*, 260–280.

Jablonka, E., & Lamb, M. (2005). *Evolution in four dimensions.* Cambridge, MA: MIT Press.

Jackendoff, R. (1994). *Patterns in the mind: Language and human nature.* New York: Basic Books.

Jackson, J. (1932). Evolution and dissolution of the nervous system. In J. Taylor (Ed.), *Selected writing of John Hughlings Jackson* (Vol. 2.) London: Hodder & Stroughton.

Jacob, F. (1998). *Of flies, mice, and men.* Cambridge, MA: Harvard University Press.

James, W. (1880). Great men, great thoughts, and the environment. *Atlantic Monthly, 66*, 441–459.

James, W. (1884). What is an emotion? *Mind, 9*, 188–205.

James, W. (1890). *The principles of psychology.* New York: Henry Holt.

James, W. (1983). *The principles of psychology.* Cambridge, MA: Harvard University Press.

Jerison, H. (1973). *Evolution of the brain and intelligence.* New York: Academic Press.

Jobling, M., & Gill, P. (2004). Encoded evidence: DNA in forensic analysis. *Nature Reviews Genetics, 5*, 739–751.

Johnson, M. (2005). Ontogeny of the social brain. In U. Mayr, E. Awh, & S. Keele (Eds.), *Developing individuality in the human brain*. Washington, DC: American Psychological Association.

Johnson, M., & Horn, G. (1988). Development of filial preferences in dark-reared chicks. *Animal Behaviour, 36,* 675–683.

Jones, D. (2003). The generative psychology of kinship: Part 1. Cognitive universals and evolutionary psychology. *Evolution and Human Behavior, 24,* 303–319.

Jones, D. (2008). Killer instincts. *Nature, 451,* 512–515.

Jones, S. (2000). *Darwin's ghost.* New York: Random House.

Jung, C. (1968). *Analytical psychology: Its theory and practice.* New York: Random House.

Kaas, J., & Preuss, T. (2008). Human brain evolution. In L. Squire, D. Berg, F. Bloom, S. du Lac, A. Ghosh, & N. Spitzer (Eds.), *Fundamental neuroscience* (3rd ed. pp. 1019–1103). Nurlington, MA: Academic Press.

Kahneman, D. (2003). A perspective on judgment and choice: Mapping bounded rationality. *American Psychologist, 58,* 697–720.

Kahneman, D., & Tversky, A. (1979). Prospect theory: An analysis of decision under risk. *Econometrica, 47,* 263–291.

Kaplan, H., & Gangestad, S. (2005). Life history theory and evolutionary psychology. In D. Buss (Ed.), *The handbook of evolutionary psychology* (pp. 68–95). Hoboken, NJ: John Wiley & Sons.

Kaplan, J., Adams, M., Clarkson, T., Manuck, S., Shively, C., & Williams, J. (2002). Psychosocial factors, sex differences, and atherosclerosis: Lessons from animal models. In J. Cacioppo, G. Berntson, R. Adolphs, C. Carter, R. Davidson, M. McClintock, . . . S. Taylor (Eds.), *Foundations in social neuroscience* (pp. 1287–1306). Cambridge, MA: MIT Press.

Kaplan, J., Chen, H., & Manuck, S. (2009). The relationship between social status and atherosclerosis in male and female monkeys as revealed by meta-analysis. *American Journal of Primatology, 71,* 732–741.

Kaplan, J., Manuck, S., Clarkson, T., Lusso, F., & Taub, D. (1982). Social status, environment, and atherosclerosis in cynomolgus monkeys. *Arteriosclerosis, 2,* 359–368.

Kaskan, P., & Finlay, B. (2001). Encephalization and its developmental structure: How many ways can a brain get big? In D. Falk & K. Gibson (Eds.), *Evolutionary anatomy of the primate cerebral cortex* (pp. 14–29). New York: Cambridge University Press.

Katsnelson, A. (2010). Epigenome effort makes its mark. *Nature, 467,* 646.

Kellogg, W., & Kellogg, L. (1933, 1967). *The ape and the child.* New York: Hafner.

Keltner, D., & Buswell, B. (1997). Embarrassment: Its distinct form and appeasement functions. *Psychological Bulletin, 122,* 250–270.

Kemeny, M. (2007). Psychoneuroimmunology. In H. Friedman & R. Silver (Eds.), *Foundations of health psychology* (pp. 92–116). New York: Oxford University Press.

Kendler, K., Jaffee, S., & Romer, D. (Eds.). (2011). *The dynamic genome and mental health.* New York: Oxford University Press.

Kendrick, K., Hinton, M., Atkins, K., Haupt, M., & Skinner, J. (1998). Mothers determine sexual preferences. *Nature, 395,* 229–230.

Kenrick, D., & Keefe, R. (1992). Age preferences in mates reflects sex differences in reproductive strategies. *Behavioral and Brain Sciences, 15,* 75–133.

Keverne, E., Fundele, R., Narasimha, M., Barton, S., & Surani, M. (1996a). Genomic imprinting and the differential roles of parental genomes in brain development. *Developmental Brain Research, 92,* 91–100.

Keverne, E., Martel, F., & Nevison, C. (1996b). Primate brain evolution. *Proceedings Biological Sciences, 263,* 689–696.

Kirby, S. (2007). The evolution of language. In R. Dunbar & L. Barrett (Eds.), *Oxford handbook of evolutionary psychology.* New York: Oxford University Press.

Kirschvink, J., Ripperdan, R., & Evans, D. (1997). Evidence of large-scale reorganization of early Cambrian continental masses by inertial interchange true polar wander. *Science, 277,* 541–545.

Kittler, R., Kayser, M., & Stoneking, M. (2003). Molecular evolution of *Pediculus humanus* and the origin of clothing. *Current Biology, 13,* 1414–1417.

Klein, R. (2000). Archeology and the evolution of human behavior. *Evolutionary Anthropology, 9,* 17–36.

Knox, S., & Uvnäs, K. (2002). Social isolation and cardiovascular disease: An atherosclerotic pathway? In J. Cacioppo, G. Berntson, R. Adolphs, C. Carter, R. Davidson, M. McClintock, . . . S. Taylor (Eds.), *Foundations in social neuroscience* (pp. 1241–1254). Cambridge, MA: MIT Press.

Koenigs, M., Young, L., Adolphs, R., Tranel, D., Cushman, F., Hauser, M., & Damasio, A. (2007). Damage to the prefrontal cortex increases utilitarian moral judgements. *Nature, 446,* 908–911.

Kopp, C., & Neufeld, S. (2003). Emotional development during infancy. In R. Davidson, K. Scherer, & H. Goldsmith (Eds.), *Handbook of affective sciences* (pp. 347–374). New York: Oxford University Press.

Kortschak, R. D., Samuel, G., Saint, R., & Miller, D. J. (2003). EST analysis of the cnidarian Acropora millepora reveals extensive gene loss and rapid sequence divergence in the model invertebrates. *Current Biology, 13,* 2190–2195.

Kovelman, I., Shalinsky, M., White, K., Schmitt, S., Berens, M., Paymer, N., & Petitto, L. (2009). Dual language use in sign-speech bimodal bilinguals: fNIRS brain imaging evidence. *Brain & Language, 109,* 112–123.

Krebs, D. L. (2003). Fictions and facts about evolutionary approaches to human behavior: Comment on Lickliter and Honeycutt. *Psychological Bulletin, 129,* 842–847.

Krebs, D. L., & Denton, K. (1997). Social illusions and self-deception: The evolution of biases in person perception. In J. A. Simpson & D. T. Kenrick (Eds.), *Evolutionary social psychology* (pp. 21–47). Hillsdale, NJ: Erlbaum.

Kretschmer, E. (1931). *Physique and character.* London: Routledge.

Kudo, H., & Dunbar, R. (2001). Neocortex size and social network size in primates. *Animal Behavior, 62,* 711–722.

Kuhn, T. (1970). *The structure of scientific revolutions* (2nd ed.). Chicago: University of Chicago Press.

Kurland, J., & Gaulin, S. (2005). Cooperation and conflict among kin. In D. Buss (Ed.), *The handbook of evolutionary psychology*

(pp. 447–482). Hoboken, NJ: John Wiley & Sons.

Kvavadze, E., Bar-Yosef, O., Belfer-Cohen, A., Boaretto, E., Jakeli, N., Matskevich, Z., & Meshveliani, T. (2009). 30,000-year-old wild flax fibers. *Science, 325,* 1359.

Laland, K., Kendal, J., & Brown, G. (2007). The niche construction perspective. *Journal of Evolutionary Psychology, 5,* 51–66.

Lashley, K. (1949). Persistent problems in the evolution of mind. *Quarterly Review of Biology, 24,* 28–42.

Lassek, W., & Gaulin, S. (2008). Waist-hip ratio and cognitive ability: Is gluteofemoral fat a privileged store of neurodevelopmental resources? *Evolution and Human Behavior, 29,* 26–34.

Laughlin, S., & Sejnowski, T. (2003). Communication in neuronal networks. *Science, 301,* 1870–1874.

Le Boeuf, B., & Peterson, R. (1969). Social status and mating activity in elephant seals. *Science, 163,* 91–93.

LeDoux, J. (1996). *The emotional brain.* New York: Simon and Schuster.

Lewis-Williams, D. (2002). *The mind in the cave: Consciousness and the origins of art.* London: Thames & Hudson.

Liberman, A. M. (1985). The motor theory of speech perception revised. *Cognition, 21,* 1–36.

Lieberman, D., Tooby, J., & Cosmides, L. (2003). Does morality have a biological basis? An empirical test of the factors governing moral sentiments relating to incest. *Proceedings of the Royal Society B: Biological Sciences, 270,* 819–826.

Lieberman, D., Tooby, J., & Cosmides, L. (2007). The architecture of human kin detection. *Nature, 445,* 727–731.

Lieberman, P. (2000). *Human language and our reptilian brain: The subcortical bases of speech, syntax, and thought.* Cambridge, MA: Harvard University Press.

Lieberman, P. (2006). *Toward an evolutionary biology of language.* Cambridge, MA.: Harvard University Press.

Linz, B., Balloux, F., Moodley, Y., Manica, A., Liu, H., Roumagnac, P., . . . Achtman, M. (2007). An African origin for the intimate association between humans and *Helicobacter pylori. Nature, 445,* 915–918.

Little, A., Jones, B., Penton-Voak, I., Burt, D., & Perrett, D. (2001). Partnership status and the temporal context of relationships influences human female preferences for sexual dimorphism in male face shape. *Proceedings of the Royal Society of London, 269,* 1095–1100.

Little, A., & Perrett, D. (2011). Facial attractiveness. In R. Adams, N. Ambadym, K. Nakayama, & S. Shimojo (Eds.), *The science of social vision* (pp. 164–185). New York: Oxford University Press.

Locke, J. L. (2010). The development of linguistic systems: Insights from evolution. In J. Guendouzi, F. Loncke, & M. J. Williams (Eds.), *Handbook of psycholinguistic and cognitive processes: Perspectives in communication disorders.* New York: Taylor & Francis.

Locke, J., & Bogin, B. (2006). Language and life history: A new perspective on the development and evolution of human language. *Behavioral and Brain Sciences, 29,* 259–325.

López, S., & Guarnaccia, P. (2000). Cultural psychopathology: Uncovering the social world of mental illness. *Annual Review of Psychology, 51,* 571–598.

Lorenz, K. (1970). *Studies in animal and human behavior, Vol. 1 & 2.* Cambridge, MA: Harvard University Press.

Lorenz, K. (1981). *The foundations of ethology.* New York: Springer-Verlag.

Low, B. S. (2003). Ecological and social complexities in human monogamy. In U. H. Reichard & C. Boesch (Eds.), *Monogamy: Mating strategies and partnerships in birds, humans, and other mammals* (pp. 161–176). Cambridge: Cambridge University Press.

Lumsden, C., & Wilson, E. O. (1981). *Genes, mind, and culture: The coevolutionary process.* Cambridge, MA: Harvard University Press.

Lyell, C. (1830). *Principles of geology.* London: John Murray.

MacDonald, K., & Hershberger, S. (2005). Theoretical issues in the study of evolution and development. In R. Burgess & K. MacDonald (Eds.), *Evolutionary perspectives on human development* (2nd ed., pp. 21–72). Thousand Oaks, CA: Sage.

Mack, K., & Mack, P. (1992). Induction of transcription factors in somatosensory cortex after tactile stimulation. *Brain Research: Molecular Brain Research, 12,* 141–147.

MacLean, P. (1990). *The triune brain in evolution.* New York: Plenum.

MacLean, P. (1993). Perspectives on cingulate cortex in the limbic system. In B. Vogt & M. Gabriel (Eds.), *Neurobiology of cingulate cortex and limbic thalamus: A comprehensive handbook* (pp. 1–15). Boston: Birkhüser.

Maier, S., & Watkins, L. (2002). Cytokines for psychologists: Implications of bidirectional immune-to-brain communication for understanding behavior, mood, and cognition. In J. Cacioppo, G. N. Berntson, R. Adolphs, C. Carter, R. Davidson, M. McClintock, . . . S. Taylor (Eds.), *Foundations in social neuroscience* (pp. 1141–1182). Cambridge, MA: MIT Press.

Malthus, T. (1826). *An essay on the principle of population.* London: John Murray.

Martin, R. D. (1996). Scaling of the mammalian brain: The maternal energy hypothesis. *News in Physiological Sciences, 11,* 149–156.

Masters, W. H., & Johnson, V. E. (1966). *Human sexual response.* London: Churchill.

Mayr, E. (1942). *Systematics and the origin of species.* New York: Columbia University Press.

Mayr, E. (1963). *Animal species and evolution.* Cambridge, MA: Belknap Press.

Mayr, E. (2001). *What evolution is.* New York: Basic Books.

McClintock, M. (1971). Menstrual synchrony and suppression. *Nature, 291,* 244–245.

McCrae, R. (2002). *The five-factor model of personality across cultures.* New York: Kluwer.

McCrae, R. R., & Costa, P. T., Jr. (1987). Validation of the five-factor model of personality across instruments and observers. *Journal of Personality and Social Psychology, 52,* 81–90.

McCrae, R. R., & Costa, P. T., Jr. (1996). Toward a new generation of personality theories: Theoretical contexts for the five-factor model. In J. S. Wiggins (Ed.), *The five-factor model of personality: Theoretical perspectives* (pp. 51–87). New York: Guilford Press.

McCrae, R. R., & Costa, P. T., Jr. (1999). A five-factor theory of personality. In L. A. Pervin & O. P. John (Eds.), *Handbook of personality: Theory and research* (2nd ed., pp. 139–150). New York: Guilford Press.

McCrae, R. R., Costa, P. T., Jr., Del Pilar, G. H., Rolland, J. P., & Parker, W. D. (1998). Cross-cultural assessment of the five-factor model: The revised NEO personality inventory. *Journal of Cross-Cultural Psychology, 29,* 171–188.

McCrae, R. R., Costa, P. T., Jr., Lima, M. P., Simoes, A., Ostendorf, F., Angleitner, A., . . . Piedmont, R. L. (1999). Age differences in personality across the adult lifespan: Parallels in five cultures. *Developmental Psychology, 35,* 466–477.

McCullough, M., Kilpatrick, S., Emmons, R., & Larson, D. (2001). Is gratitude a moral affect? *Psychological Bulletin, 127,* 249–266.

McDougall, W. (1908). *An introduction to social psychology.* London: Methuen & Co.

McEwen, B. (1998). Protective and damaging effects of stress mediators. *New England Journal of Medicine, 338,* 171–179.

McEwen, B. (2002). Protective and damaging effects of stress mediators. In J. Cacioppo, G. N. Berntson, R. Adolphs, C. Carter, R. Davidson, M. McClintock, . . . S. Taylor (Eds.), *Foundations in social neuroscience* (pp. 1127–1140). Cambridge, MA: MIT Press.

McGuire, M., & Troisi, A. (1998). *Darwinian psychiatry.* New York: Oxford University Press.

Medawar, P., & Medawar, J. (1977). *The life science: Current ideas of biology.* New York: Harper & Row.

Mello, C., Vicario, D., & Clayton, D. (1992). Song presentation induces gene expression in the songbird forebrain. *PNAS, 89,* 6818–6822.

Mesoudi, A., Whiten, A., & Laland, K. (2006). Toward a unified science of cultural evolution. *Behavioral and Brain Sciences, 29,* 329–383.

Meyer-Lindenberg, A., Hariri, A., Munoz, K., Mervis, C., Venkata, M., Morris, C., & Faith Berman, K. (2005). Neural correlates of genetically abnormal social cognition in Williams syndrome. *Nature Neuroscience, 8,* 991–993.

Meyer-Lindenberg, A., Mervis, C., & Berman, K. (2006). Neural mechanisms in Williams syndrome: A unique window to genetic influences on cognition and behaviour. *Nature Reviews Neuroscience, 7,* 380–393.

Micklos, D., & Freyer, G. (2003). *DNA science: A first course* (2nd ed.). Cold Springs, NY: Cold Springs Harbor Press.

Miller, D. (2007). From nature to nurture, and back again. *Developmental Psychobiology, 49,* 770–779.

Miller, G. (1998). How mate choice shaped human nature: A review of sexual selection and human evolution. In C. Crawford & D. Krebs (Eds.), *Handbook of evolutionary psychology* (pp. 87–130). Mahwah, NJ: Lawrence Erlbaum.

Miller, G. (2000). *The mating mind: How sexual choice shaped the evolution of human nature.* New York: Random House.

Miller, G. (2008). The roots of morality. *Science, 320,* 734–737.

Miller, S., & Maner, J. (2010). Scent of a woman: Men's testosterone responses to olfactory ovulation cues. *Psychological Science, 21,* 276–283.

Mitchell, R., & Crow, T. (2005). Right hemisphere language functions and schizophrenia: The forgotten hemisphere? *Brain, 128,* 963–978.

Mithen, S. (2006). *The singing Neanderthals: The origins of music, language, mind, and body.* Cambridge, MA: Harvard University Press.

Monod, J. (1972). *Chance and necessity: An essay on the natural philosophy of modern biology.* New York: Vintage Books.

Morgan, E. (1997). *The aquatic ape hypothesis: The most credible theory of human evolution*. London: Souvenir Books.

Murphy, G., & Kovach, J. (1972). *Historical introduction to modern psychology*. New York: Harcourt Brace Jovanovich.

Murphy, J. (1976). Psychiatric labeling in cross-cultural perspective. *Science, 191*, 1019–1028.

Murray, D., & Farahmand, B. (1998). Gestalt theory and evolutionary psychology. In R. Rieber & K. Salzinger (Eds.), *Psychology: Theoretical-historical perspectives* (2nd ed., pp. 254–287). Washington, DC: American Psychological Association.

Neel, J. (1962). Diabetes mellitus: A "thrifty" genotype rendered detrimental by "progress"? *American Journal of Human Genetics, 14*, 353–362.

Nesse, R. (2005). Evolutionary psychology and mental health. In D. Buss (Ed.), *Handbook of evolutionary psychology* (pp. 903–927). Hoboken, NJ: John Wiley & Sons.

Nesse, R., & Williams, G. (1994). *Why we get sick: The new science of Darwinian medicine*. New York: Vintage.

Nelkin, D. (2001). Molecular metaphors: The gene in popular discourse. *Nature Reviews Genetics, 2*, 555–559.

Nelson, K. (2005). Evolution and development of human memory systems. In B. Ellis & D. Bjorklund (Eds.), *Origins of the social mind: Evolutionary psychology and child development* (pp. 354–382). New York: Guilford Press.

Nesse, R. M. (1990). Evolutionary explanations of emotions. *Human Nature, 1*, 261–289.

Nesse, R. (1998). Emotional disorders in evolutionary perspective. *British Journal of Medical Psychology, 71*, 397–415.

Nesse, R. M. (2005). Natural selection and the regulation of defenses: A signal detection analysis of the smoke detector principle. *Evolution and Human Behavior, 26*, 88–105.

Nettle, D. (2006). The evolution of personality variation in humans and other animals. *American Psychologist, 61*, 622–631.

Newell, A., & Simon, H. (1972). *Human problem solving*. Englewood Cliffs, NJ: Prentice-Hall.

Ng, S., Lin, R., Laybutt, D., Barres, R., Owens, J., & Morris, M. (2010). Chronic high-fat diet in fathers programs β-cell dysfunction in female rat offspring. *Nature, 467*, 963–966.

Nisbett, R. E. (2003). *The geography of thought: Why we think the way we do*. New York: The Free Press.

Nisbett, R., & Miyamoto, Y. (2005). The influence of culture: Holistic versus analytic perception. *Trends in Cognitive Sciences, 9*, 467–473.

Norenzayan, A. (2011). Explaining human behavioral diversity. *Science, 332*, 1041–1042.

Norenzayan, A., & Shariff, A. (2008). The origin and evolution of religious prosociality. *Science, 58*, 58–62.

Northcutt, R., & Kaas, J. (1995). The emergence of evolution of mammalian neocortex. *Trends in Neuroscience, 18*, 373–379.

Nowak, M., & Sigmund, K. (2004). Evolutionary dynamics of biological games. *Science, 303*, 793–799.

Nylin, S., & Gotthard, K. (1998). Plasticity in life-history traits. *Annual Review of Entomology, 43*, 63–83.

Odling-Smee, F., Laland, K., & Feldman, W. (2003). *Niche construction: The neglected process in evolution*. Princeton, NJ: Princeton University Press.

Öhman, A. (1999). Distinguishing unconscious from conscious emotional processes: Methodological considerations and theoretical implications. In T. Dalgleish & M. J. Power (Eds.), *Handbook of cognition and emotion* (pp. 321–352). Chichester, UK: Wiley.

Öhman, A., & Mineka, S. (2001). Fear, phobias and preparedness: Toward an evolved module of fear and fear learning. *Psychological Review, 108*, 483–522.

Oliver, M., & Hyde, J. (1993). Gender differences in sexuality: A meta-analysis. *Psychological Bulletin, 114*, 29–51.

Oller, D., & Griebel, U. (2005). Contextual freedom in human infant vocalization and the evolution of language. In R. Burgess & K. MacDonald (Eds.), *Evolutionary perspectives on human development* (2nd ed., pp. 135–166). Thousand Oaks, CA: Sage.

Olson, S. (2002). *Mapping human history*. Boston: Houghton Mifflin.

Orr, H. (2005, May 30). Devolution. *The New Yorker*, p. 52.

Ortony, A., & Turner, T. (1990). What's basic about basic emotions? *Psychological Review, 97*, 315–331.

Os, J., Kenis, G., & Rutter, B. (2010). The environment and schizophrenia. *Nature, 468*, 203–212.

Ostrer, H. (1998). *Non-Mendelian genetics in humans*. New York: Oxford.

Panksepp, J. (1998). *Affective neuroscience: The foundations of human and animal emotions*. New York: Oxford University Press.

Panksepp, J. (2004). *Textbook for biological psychiatry*. Hoboken, NJ: Wiley-Liss.

Panksepp, J. (2006). Emotional endophenotypes in evolutionary psychiatry. *Progress in Neuro-Psychopharmacology and Biological Psychiatry, 30*, 774–784.

Panksepp, J., & Smith-Pasqualini, M. (2005). Development of emotional systems. In J. Nadel & R. Muir (Eds.), *Emotional development* (pp. 5–30). Oxford, UK: Oxford University Press.

Park, D., & Gutchess, A. (2006). The cognitive neuroscience of aging and culture. *Current Directions in Psychological Science, 15*, 105–108.

Pawlowski, B., & Dunbar, R. (1999). Impact of market value on human mate choice decisions. *Proceedings of the Royal Society of London, B, 266*, 281–285.

Peccei, J. (2001). A critique of the grandmother hypotheses: Old and new. *American Journal of Human Biology, 13*, 434–452.

Pembrey, M., Bygren, M., Kaati, G., Edvinsson, S., Northstone, K., Sjöström, M., . . . The ALSPAC Study Team. (2006). Sex-specific, male-line transgenerational responses in humans. *European Journal of Human Genetics, 14*, 159–166.

Pennisi, E. (2008). Evolution: Modernizing the modern synthesis. *Science, 321*, 196–197.

Penton-Voak, I., Perrett, D., Castles, D., Kobayashi, T., Burt, D., Murray, L., & Minamisawa, R. (1999). Menstrual cycle alters face preference. *Nature, 399*, 741–742.

Peplau, L. A. (2003). Human sexuality: How do men and women differ? *Current Directions in Psychological Science, 12*, 37–40.

Perry, G., Dominy, N., Claw, K., Lee, A., Fiegler, H., Redon, R., . . . Stone, A. (2007). Diet and the evolution of human amylase gene copy number variation. *Nature Genetics, 39*, 1256–1260.

Pessoa, L., & Adolphs, R. (2010). Emotion processing and the amygdala: From a "low road" to "many roads" of evaluating biological significance. *Nature Reviews Neuroscience, 11*, 773–782.

Petkov, C., Kayser, C., Studel, T., Whittingstall, K., Augath, M., & Logothetis, N. (2008). A voice region in the monkey brain. *Nature Neuroscience, 11*, 367–374.

Petrie, M. (1994). Improved growth and survival of offspring of peacocks with more elaborate trains. *Nature, 371*, 598–599.

Petrie, M., Doums, C., Møller, A. (1998). The degree of extra-pair paternity increases with genetic variability. *Proceedings of the National Academy of Science, 95*, 930–939.

Phan, K., Wager, T., Taylor, S., & Liberzon, I. (2002). Functional neuroanatomy of emotion: A meta-analysis of emotion activation studies in PET and fMRI. *NeuroImage, 16*, 331–348.

Pinker, S. (1994). *The language instinct*. New York: William Morrow.

Pinker, S. (1997). *How the mind works*. New York: W.W. Norton.

Pinker, S. (2002). *The blank slate*. New York: Viking.

Pinker, S. (2003). Language as an adaptation to the cognitive niche. In M. Christiansen & S. Kirby (Eds.), *Language evolution*. New York: Oxford University Press.

Pinker, S. (2007). *The stuff of thought: Language as a window into human nature*. New York: Viking.

Pinker, S. (2008, January 13). The moral instinct. *The New York Times Magazine*, pp. 32–37.

Pinker, S., & Bloom, P. (1990). Natural language and natural selection. *Behavioral and Brain Sciences, 13,* 707–784.

Pinker, S., & Jackendoff, R. (2005). The faculty of language: What's special about it? *Cognition, 95,* 201–236.

Platek, S., Critton, S., Burch, R., Frederick, D., Myers, T., & Gallup, G. (2003). How much paternal resemblance is enough? Sex differences in hypothetical investment decisions but not in the detection of resemblance. *Evolution and Human Behavior, 24,* 81–87.

Platek, S., Critton, S., Burch, R., Panyavin, I., Wasserman, B., & Gallup, G. (2002). Reactions to children's faces: Resemblance affects males more than females. *Evolution and Human Behavior, 23,* 159–166.

Plomin, R., DeFries, J., & Loehlin, J. (1977). Genotype-environment interaction and correlation in the analysis of human behavior. *Psychological Bulletin, 84,* 309–322.

Plomin, R., DeFries, J., McClearn, G., & McGuffin, P. (2008). *Behavioral genetics* (5th ed.). New York: Worth.

Ploog, D. (1981). Neurobiology of primate audio-vocal behavior. *Brain Research Reviews, 3,* 35–61.

Ploog, D. (2003). The place of the triune brain in psychiatry. *Physiology and Behavior, 79,* 487–493.

Premack, D. (1976). *Intelligence in ape and man.* Hillsdale, NJ: Lawrence Erlbaum.

Premack, D., & Woodruff, G. (1978). Does the chimpanzee have a theory of mind? *Behavior and Brain Sciences, 1,* 515–526.

Preuss, T. (2000). What's human about the human brain? In M. Gazzaniga (Ed.), *The new cognitive neurosciences* (2nd ed., pp. 1219–1234). Cambridge, MA: MIT Press.

Preuss, T. (2001). The discovery of cerebral diversity: An unwelcome scientific revolution. In D. Falk and K. Gibson (Eds.), *Evolutionary anatomy of the primate cerebral cortex* (pp. 138–164). Cambridge: Cambridge University Press.

Preuss, T. M. (2009). The cognitive neuroscience of human uniqueness. In M. S. Gazzaniga (Ed.), *The cognitive neurosciences* (4th ed., pp. 49–64). Cambridge, MA: MIT Press.

Preuss, T., & Kaas, J. (1999). Human brain evolution. In M. Zigmond, F. Bloom, S. Landis, J. Roberts, & L. Squire (Eds.), *Fundamental neuroscience* (pp. 1283–1311). San Diego, CA: Academic Press.

Price, P. (1996). *Biological evolution.* Pacific Grove, CA: Brooks/Cole.

Pusey, A. (2001). Of apes and genes: Chimpanzee social organization and reproduction. In F. de Waal (Ed.), *Tree of origin* (pp. 9–38). Cambridge, MA: Harvard University Press.

Pusey, A., Williams, J., & Goodall, J. (1997). The influence of dominance rank on the reproductive success of female chimpanzees. *Science, 277,* 828–831.

Rakic, P., & Kornack, D. (2001). Neocortical expansion and elaboration during primate evolution: A view from neuroembryology. In D. Falk & K. Gibson (Eds.), *Evolutionary anatomy of the primate cerebral cortex* (pp. 30–56). New York: Cambridge University Press.

Rakison, D. (2005). Developing knowledge of object's motion properties in infancy. *Cognition, 96,* 183–214.

Rampon, C., Jiang, C., Dong, H., Tang, Y., Lickhart, D., Schultz, P., . . . Hu, Y. (2000). Effects of environmental enrichment on gene expression in the brain. *Proceedings of the National Academies of Science, 97,* 12880–12884.

Rapoport, J. (1990). Obsessive compulsive disorder and basal ganglia dysfunction. *Psychological Medicine, 20,* 465–469.

Rauch, L., Corá-Locatelli, G., & Greenberg, B. (2000). Pathogenesis of obsessive compulsive disorders. In D. Stein & E. Hollander (Eds.), *Textbook of anxiety disorders.* Washington, DC: American Psychiatric Press.

Ray, W. J. (2012). *Methods toward a science of behavior and experience* (10th ed.). Belmont, CA: Wadsworth.

Ray, W. J., & Cole, H. W. (1985). EEG alpha reflects attentional demands, beta reflects emotional and cognitive processes. *Science, 228,* 750–752.

Reichard, U., & Boesch, C. (2003). *Monogamy: Mating strategies and partnerships in birds, humans, and other mammals.* Cambridge: Cambridge University Press.

Repetti, R. (1989). Effects of daily workload on subsequent behavior during marital interaction: The roles of social withdrawal and spouse support. *Journal of Personality and Social Psychology, 57,* 651–659.

Ribeiro, S., & Mello, C. (2000). Gene expression and synaptic plasticity in the auditory forebrain of songbirds. *Learning and Memory, 7,* 235–243.

Richerson, P., & Boyd, R. (2005). *Not by genes alone: How culture transformed human evolution.* Chicago: University of Chicago Press.

Ricklefs, R., & Wikelski, M. (2002). The physiology/life history nexus. *Trends in Ecology & Evolution, 17,* 462–468.

Ridley, M. (1993). *The red queen: Sex and the evolution of human nature.* New York: Penguin Books.

Ridley, M. (1996). *The origins of virtue: Human instincts and the evolution of cooperation.* New York: Penguin Books.

Ridley, M. (1999). *Genome.* New York: Perennial.

Ridley, M. (2003a). *The agile gene.* New York: Perennial.

Ridley, M. (2003b). *Nature via nurture.* New York: HarperCollins.

Rilling, J., Glasser, M., Preuss, T., Ma, X., Zhao, T., Hi, X., & Behrens, T. (2008). The evolution of the arcuate fasciculus revealed with comparative DTI. *Nature Neuroscience, 11,* 426–428.

Rilling, J., Kaufman, T., Smith, E., Patel, R., & Worthman, C. (2009). Abdominal depth and waist circumference as influential determinants of human female attractiveness. *Evolution and Human Behavior, 30,* 21–31.

Rizzolatti, G., & Craighero, L. (2004). The mirror-neuron system. *Annual Review of Neuroscience, 27,* 169–192.

Rizzolatti, G., & Fogassi, L. (2007). Mirror neurons and social cognition. In R. Dunbar &

L. Barrett (Eds.), *Oxford handbook of evolutionary psychology* (pp. 179–196). New York: Oxford University Press.

Rockel, A., Hiorns, R., & Powell, T. (1980). The basic uniformity of structure of the neocortex. *Brain, 103,* 221–224.

Romanes, G. (1883). *Animal intelligence.* New York: D. Appleton & Co.

Rosas, A., Martínez-Mazaa, C., Bastir, M., García-Tabernero, A., Lalueza-Fox, C., Huguet, R., . . . Fortea, J. (2010). Paleobiology and comparative morphology of a late Neandertal sample from El Sidrón, Asturias, Spain. *Proceedings of the National Academies of Science, 103,* 19266–19271.

Rosenblum, L., Coplan, J., Friedman, S., Bassoff, T., Gorman, J., & Andrews, M. (1994). Adverse early experiences affect noradrenergic and serotonergic functioning in adult primates. *Biological Psychiatry, 35,* 221–227.

Roth, G., & Dicke, U. (2005). Evolution of the brain and intelligence. *Trends in Cognitive Sciences, 9,* 250–257.

Rushton, J. (1989). Genetic similarity, human altruism, and group selection. *Behavioral and Brain Sciences, 12,* 503–559.

Russell, J. (1980). A circumplex model of affect. *Journal of Personality and Social Psychology, 39,* 1161–1178.

Russell, J. (1994). Is there universal recognition of emotion from facial expression? A review of cross-cultural studies. *Psychological Bulletin, 115,* 102–141.

Russell, J. (1997). Reading emotion from and into faces: Resurrecting a dimensional–contextual perspective. In J. A. Russell & J. M. Fernandez-Dols (Eds.), *The psychology of facial expression* (pp. 295–320). New York: Cambridge University Press.

Russell, J. (2003). Core affect and the psychological construction of emotion. *Psychological Review, 110,* 145–172.

Rutter, M. (2006). *Genes and behavior: Nature/nurture interplay explained.* Malden, MA: Blackwell.

Salisbury, A., Yanni, P., LaGasse, L., & Lester, B. (2004). Maternal-fetal psychobiology: A very early look at emotional development. In J. Nadel & D. Muir (Eds.), *Emotional development: Recent research advances* (pp. 93–124). Oxford, NY: Oxford University Press.

Salmon, C. (2005). Parental investment and parent-offspring conflict. In D. M. Buss (Ed.), *Handbook of evolutionary psychology* (pp. 506–527). Hoboken, NJ: John Wiley & Sons.

Salmon, C., & Shackelford, T. (Eds.). (2008). *Family relationships: An evolutionary perspective.* New York: Oxford University Press.

Sanfey, A., Rilling, J., Aronson, J., Nystrom, L., & Choen, J. (2003). The neural basis of economic decision-making in the ultimatum game. *Science, 300,* 1755–1758.

Sapolsky, R., & Share, L. (2004). A pacific culture among wild baboons: Its emergence and transmission. *PLOS Biology, 2,* 534–541.

Sartorius, N., Jablensky, A., Korten, A., Ernberg, G., Anker, M., Cooper J., & Day, R. (1986). Early manifestations and first-contact incidence of schizophrenia in different cultures. A preliminary report on the initial evaluation phase of the WHO collaborative study on determinants of outcome of severe mental disorders. *Psychological Medicine, 16,* 909–928.

Schaller, M., Simpson, J., & Kenrick, D. (Eds.). (2005). *Evolution and social psychology.* New York: Psychology Press.

Schmitt, D., & 118 members of the International Sexuality Description Project. (2003). Universal sex differences in the desire for sexual variety: Tests from 52 nations, 6 continents, and 13 islands. *Journal of Personality and Social Psychology, 85,* 85–104.

Selye, H. (1956). *The stress of life.* New York: McGraw-Hill.

Serre, D., Langaney, A., Chech, M., Teschler-Nicola, M., Paunovic, M., Mennecier, P., . . . Pääbo, S. (2004). No evidence of Neandertal mtDNA contribution to early modern humans. *PLOS Biology, 2,* 313–317.

Seyfarth, R., & Cheney, D. (2003). Meaning and emotion in animal vocalizations. *Annals of the New York Academy of Sciences, 1000,* 32–55.

Shah, A., & Oppenheimer, D. (2008). Heuristics made easy: An effort-reduction framework. *Psychological Bulletin, 134,* 207–222.

Sheldon, W. (1942). *The varieties of temperament: A psychology of constitutional differences.* New York: Harper.

Silk, J., Alberts, S., & Altmann, J. (2003). Social bonds of female baboons enhance infant survival. *Science, 302,* 1231–1234.

Simon, H. A. (1956). Rational choice and the structure of the environment. *Psychological Review, 63,* 129–138.

Simon, H. (1990a). A mechanism for social selection and successful altruism. *Science, 250,* 1665–1668.

Simon, H. (1990b). Invariants of human behavior. *Annual Review of Psychology, 41,* 1–19.

Singh, D. (1993). Adaptive significance of female physical attractiveness: Role of waist-to-hip ratio. *Journal of Personality and Social Psychology, 65,* 293–307.

Skinner, B. F. (1938). *The behavior of organisms.* New York: Appleton-Century.

Skinner, B. F. (1957). *Verbal behavior.* Acton, MA: Copley.

Skinner, B. F. (1971). *Beyond freedom and dignity.* New York: Knopf.

Skinner, B. F. (1981). Selection by consequences. *Science, 213,* 501–504.

Skinner, B. F. (1986). The evolution of verbal behavior. *Journal of the Experimental Analysis of Behavior, 45,* 115–122.

Skinner, M. (2010). Father's nutritional legacy. *Nature, 467,* 922–923.

Smetana, J., Schlagman, N., & Adams, P. (1993). Preschool children's judgements about hypothetical and actual transgressions. *Child Development, 64,* 202–214.

Smith, J. (1990). The Y of human relationships. *Nature, 344,* 591–592.

Smith, J. (1998). *Shaping life: Genes, embryos, and evolution.* New Haven, CT: Yale University Press.

Smith, P. K. (2005). Play: Types and functions in human development. In B. J. Ellis &

D. F. Bjorklund (Eds.), *Origins of the social mind: Evolutionary psychology and child development* (pp. 271–291). New York: Guilford Press.

Snowdon, C. (2003). Expression of emotion in nonhuman animals. In R. Davidson, K. Scherer, & H. Goldsmith (Eds.), *Handbook of affective sciences* (pp. 457–480). New York: Oxford University Press.

Sperber, D., Cara, F., & Girotto, V. (1995). Relevance theory explains the selection task. *Cognition, 52,* 3–39.

Springer, S., & Deutsch, G. (2001). *Left brain, right brain: Perspectives from cognitive neuroscience* (5th ed.). Boston: Worth.

Starr, C., & Taggart, R. (2006). *Biology: The unity and diversity of life.* Pacific Grove, CA: Brooks/Cole.

Stearns, S. (1977). The evolution of life history traits. *Annual Review of Ecological Systems, 8,* 145–171.

Stedman, H., Kozyak, B., Nelson, A., Thesler, D., Su, L., Low, D., . . . Mitchell, M. (2004). Myosin gene mutation correlates with anatomical changes in human lineage. *Nature, 428,* 415–418.

Stephens, D., McLinn, C., & Stevens, J. (2003). Discounting and reciprocity in an iterated prisoner's dilemma. *Science, 298,* 2216–2218.

Stern, K., & McClintock, M. (1998). Regulation of ovulation by human pheromones. *Nature, 392,* 177–179.

Stevens, S. S. (1946). On the theory of scales of measurement. *Science, 103,* 677–680.

Stevens, S. S. (1951). Mathematics, measurement, and psychophysics. In S. S. Stevens (Ed.), *Handbook of experimental psychology.* New York: Wiley.

Stevens, S. S. (1957). On the psychophysical law. *Psychological Review, 64,* 153–181.

Stiles, J. (2008). *The fundamentals of brain development: Integrating nature and nurture.* Cambridge, MA: Harvard University Press.

Stone, V., Cosmides, L., Tooby, J., Kroll, N., & Knight, R. (2002). Selective impairment of reasoning about social exchange in a patient with bilateral limbic system damage. *Proceedings of the National Academies of Science, 99,* 11531–11536.

Stoneking, M. (2008). Human origins. *EMBO Reports, 9,* S46–S50.

Strasser, T., Thompson, N., Panagopoulou, E., Karkanas, P., Runnels, C., McCoy, F., . . . Wegmann, K. (2010). Stone age seafaring in the Mediterranean. *Hesperia, 79,* 145–190.

Strassmann, B., & Gillespie, B. (2002). Life-history theory, fertility, and reproductive success in humans. *Proceedings of the Royal Society: Series B, 269,* 553–562.

Straus, M., & Gelles, R. (1986). Societal change and change in family violence from 1975 to 1985 as revealed by two national surveys. *Journal of Marriage and the Family, 48,* 465–479.

Streeter, S., & McBurney, D. (2003). Waist-hip ratio and attractiveness: New evidence and a critique of "a critical test." *Evolution and Human Behavior, 24,* 88–98.

Striedter, G. (2005). *Principles of brain evolution.* Sunderland, MA: Sinauer Associates.

Suglyama, L., Tooby, J., & Cosmides, L. (2002). Cross-cultural evidence of cognitive adaptations for social exchange among the Shiwiar of Ecuadorian Amazonia. *Proceedings of the National Academies of Science, 99,* 11537–11542.

Sulloway, F. (1979). *Freud: Biologist of the mind.* New York: Basic Books.

Sulloway, F. (1983). *Freud: Biologist of the mind.* New York: Basic Books.

Suomi, S. (1997). Early determinants of behavior: Evidence from primate studies. *British Medical Bulletin, 53,* 170–184.

Suomi, S. (2002). Attachment in rhesus monkeys. In J. Cacioppo, G. Berntson, R. Adolphs, C. Carter, R. Davidson, M. McClintock, . . . S. Taylor (Eds.), *Foundations in social neuroscience* (pp. 776–795). Cambridge, MA: MIT Press.

Suomi, S. J. (2005). Genetic and environmental factors influencing the expression of impulsive aggression and serotonergic functioning in rhesus monkeys. In R. Tremblay, W. W. Hartup, & J. Archer

(Eds.), *Developmental origins of aggression* (pp. 63–82). New York: Guilford Press.

Susskind, J., Lee, D., Cusi, A., Feiman, R., Grabski, W., & Anderson, A. (2008). Expressing fear enhances sensory acquisition. *Nature Neuroscience, 11,* 843–850.

Sutton, W. (2003). The chromosomes in heredity. *Biological Bulletin, 4,* 231–251.

Swanson, L. (2003). *Brain architecture: Understanding the basic plan.* New York: Oxford University Press.

Szasz, T. (1970). *The manufacture of madness: A comparative study of the inquisition and the mental health movement.* New York: Harper & Row.

Tager-Flusberg, H., & Plesa-Skwerer, D. (2006). Social engagement in Williams syndrome. In P. Marshall & N. Fox (Eds.), *The development of social engagement: Neurobiological perspectives* (pp. 331–354). New York: Oxford University Press.

Tassinary, L. G., & Hansen, K. A. (1998). A critical test of the waist-to-hip ratio hypothesis of female physical attractiveness. *Psychological Science, 9,* 150–155.

Taylor, S. (2002). *The tending instinct: How nurturing is essential to who we are and how we live.* New York: Henry Holt and Co.

Taylor, S. (2007). Social support. In H. Friedman & R. Silver (Eds.), *Foundations of health psychology* (pp. 145–171). New York: Oxford University Press.

Taylor, S., & Gonzaga, G. (2006). Evolution, relationships, and health: The social shaping hypothesis. In M. Schaller, J. Simpson, & D. Kenrick (Eds.), *Evolution and social psychology* (pp. 211–236). New York: Psychology Press.

Taylor, S., Klein, L., Lewis, B., Gruenewald, T., Gurung, R., & Updegraff, J. (2002). Biobehavioral responses to stress in females: Tend-and-befriend, not fight-or-flight. *Psychological Review, 107,* 411–429.

Templeton, C., Greene, E., & Davis, K. (2005). Allometry of alarm calls: Black-capped chickadees encode information about predator size. *Science, 308,* 1934–1937.

Thornhill, R., & Gangestad, S. (2004). The evolutionary psychology of human physical attraction and attractiveness. In A. Moya &

E. Font (Eds.), *Evolution: From molecules to ecosystems* (pp. 247–269). New York: Oxford University Press.

Tinbergen, N. (1963). On aims and methods in ethology. *Zeitschrift für Tierpsychologie, 20,* 410–433.

Tinbergen, N. (1974). *The study of instinct.* New York: Oxford University Press.

Tishkoff, S., Reed, F., Ranciaro, A., Voight, B., Babbitt, C., Silverman, J., . . . Deloukas, P. (2007). Convergent adaptation of human lactase persistence in Africa and Europe. *Nature Genetics, 39,* 31–40.

Todorov, A. (2008). Evaluating faces on trustworthiness. *Annals of the New York Academy of Sciences, 1124,* 181–207.

Tomasello, M. (1999). *The cultural origins of human cognition.* Cambridge, MA: Harvard University Press.

Tomkins, S. (1962). *Affect, imagery, consciousness. Vol. 1, The positive affects.* New York: Springer.

Tomasello, M., Carpenter, M., Call, J., Behne, T., & Moll, H. (2005). Understanding and sharing intentions: The origins of cultural cognition. *Behavioral and Brain Sciences, 28,* 675–735.

Tomkins, S. (1965). *Affect, cognition, and personality: Empirical studies.* New York: Springer.

Tooby, J., & Cosmides, L. (1990). On the universality of human nature and the uniqueness of the individual: The role of genetics and adaptation. *Journal of Personality, 58,* 17–68.

Tooby, J. & Cosmides, L. (1992). The psychological foundations of culture. In J. Barkow, L. Cosmides, & J. Tooby (Eds.), *The adapted mind: Evolutionary psychology and the generation of culture.* New York: Oxford University Press.

Tooby, J., & Cosmides, L. (2005). Conceptual foundations of evolutionary psychology. In D. Buss (Ed.), *The handbook of evolutionary psychology* (pp. 5–67). Hoboken, NJ: John Wiley & Sons.

Tremblay, R., Hartup, W., & Archer, J. (Eds.). (2005). *Developmental origins of aggression.* New York: Guilford Press.

Trivers, R. (1971). The evolution of reciprocal altruism. *The Quarterly Review of Biology, 46,* 35–57.

Trivers, R. (1972). Parental investment and sexual selection. In B. Campbell (Ed.), *Sexual selection and the descent of man*, 1871–1971 (pp. 136–179). Chicago: Aldine.

Trivers, R. (1974). Parent-offspring conflict. *American Zoologist, 14,* 249–264.

Trivers, R. (1985). *Social evolution.* Menlo Park, CA: Benjamin/Cummings.

Trivers, R. (1991). Deceit and self-deception. In M. Robinson & L. Tiger (Eds.), *Man & beast revisited* (pp. 175–191). Washington, DC: Smithsonian Institution Press.

Tucker, D., Derryberry, D., & Luu, P. (2000). Anatomy and physiology of human evolution: Vertical integration of brain stem, limbic, and cortical systems. In J. Borod (Ed.), *The neuropsychology of emotion* (pp. 56–79). New York: Oxford University Press.

Ulrich-Lai, Y., & Herman, J. (2009). Neural regulation of endocrine and autonomic stress response. *Nature Reviews Neuroscience, 10,* 397–409.

van den Boom, D. (1994). The influence of temperament and mothering on attachment and exploration: An experimental manipulation of sensitive responsiveness among lower-class mothers with irritable infants. *Child Development, 65,* 1457–1477.

Van Ijzendoorn, M., & Sagi, A. (1999). Cross-cultural patterns of attachment: Universal and contextual dimensions. In J. Cassidy & P. Shaver (Eds.), *Handbook of attachment* (pp. 713–734). New York: Guilford Press.

Van Valen, L. (1973). A new evolutionary law. *Evolutionary Theory 1,* 1–30.

Vilà, C., Amorim, I. R., Leonard, J. A., Posada, D., Castroviejo, J., Petrucci-Fonseca, F., . . . Wayne, R. K. (1999). Mitochondrial DNA phylogeography and population history of the grey wolf. *Molecular Ecology, 8,* 2089–2103.

von Frisch, K. (1967). *The dance language and orientation of bees.* Cambridge MA: Harvard University Press.

Von Hippel, W., & Trivers, R. (2011). The evolution and psychology of self-deception. *Behavioral and Brain Sciences, 34,* 1–56.

Wade, N. (2006). Lactose tolerance in East Africa points to recent evolution. *New York Times.* Retrieved from http://www.nytimes.com/2006/12/11/science/11evolve.html

Wakefield, J. (1992). The concept of mental disorder: On the boundary between biological facts and social values. *American Psychologist, 47,* 373–388.

Walker, E., Kestler, L., Bollini, A., & Hochman, K. (2004). Schizophrenia: Etiology and course. *Annual Review of Psychology, 55,* 401–430.

Wallen, K. (1990). Desire and ability: Hormones and the regulation of female sexual behavior. *Neuroscience and Biobehavioral Reviews, 1,* 233–241.

Wang, X. (1996). Framing effects: Dynamics and task domains. *Organizational Behavior and Human Decision Processes, 68,* 145–157.

Wang, X. (2002). A kith-and-kin rationality in risky choices: Empirical examinations and theoretical modeling. In F. Salter (Ed.), *Risky transactions: Trust, kinship, and ethnicity* (pp. 47–70). Oxford, UK: Berghahn Books.

Wang, X.T., & Johnston, V. S. (1995). Perceived social context and risk preference: A re-examination of framing effects in a life-death decision problem. *Journal of Behavioral Decision Making, 8,* 279–293.

Ward, C., Kimbel, W., & Johanson, D. (2011). Complete fourth metatarsal and arches in the foot of *Australopithecus afarensis. Science, 331,* 750–753.

Watson, J. (1913). Psychology as the behaviorist views it. *Psychological Review, 20,* 158–177.

Watson, J. (1930). *Behaviorism* (Rev. ed.). Chicago: University of Chicago Press.

Watson, J. (1968). *The double helix.* New York: Atheneum.

Watson, J. (2000). *A passion for DNA.* Cold Spring Harbor, NY: Cold Spring Harbor Laboratory Press.

Watson, J. (2003). *DNA: The secret of life.* New York: Alfred A. Knopf.

Watson, J. (2007). *Avoid boring people: Lessons from a life in science.* New York: Alfred A. Knopf.

Watson, J., & Crick, F. (1953a). Genetical implications of the structure of deoxyribonucleic acid. *Nature, 171,* 964–967.

Watson, J., & Crick, F. (1953b). Molecular structure of nucleic acids. *Nature, 171,* 737–738.

Watson, J., & Rayner, R. (1920). Conditioned emotional reactions. *Journal of Experimental Psychology, 3,* 1–14.

Waynforth, D., & Dunbar, R. (1995). Conditional mate choice strategies in humans: Evidence from "lonely hearts" advertisements. *Behaviour, 132,* 755–779.

Wedekind, C., & Milinski, M. (2000). Cooperation through image scoring in humans. *Science, 288,* 850–852.

Wedekind, C., & Penn, D. (2000). MHC genes, body odours, and odour preferences. *Nephrology Dialysis Transplantation, 15,*1269–1271.

Weiner, J. (1994). *The beak of the finch.* New York: Alfred A. Knopf.

Weiskrantz, L. (1986). *Blindsight: A case study and implications.* New York: Oxford University Press.

Weiss, J., Demetrikopoulos, M., McCurdy, P., West, C., & Bonsall, R. (2000). Depression seen through an animal model. In R. Davidson (Ed.), *Anxiety, depression, and emotion* (pp. 3–35). New York: Oxford University Press.

Wellman, H. M. (1990). *The child's theory of mind.* Cambridge, MA: Bradford.

Westermarck, E. A. (1921). *The history of human marriage* (5th ed.). London: Macmillan.

Wiederman, M. W. (1997). The truth must be in here somewhere: Examining the gender discrepancy in self-reported lifetime number of sex partners. *Journal of Sex Research, 34,* 375–387.

Wiederman, M., & Allgeier, E. (1992). Gender differences in mate selection criteria: Sociobiological or socioeconomic explanations? *Ethology and Sociobiology, 13,* 115–124.

Wigby, S., & Chapman, T. (2004). Sperm competition (Primer). *Current Biology, 14,* R100–R103.

Williams, G. (1966). *Adaptation and natural selection.* Princeton, NJ: Princeton University Press.

Williamson, P., & Allman, J. (2011). *The human illnesses: Neuropsychiatric disorders and the nature of the human brain.* New York: Oxford University Press.

Wilson, E. (2005). *Sociobiology: the new synthesis.* Cambridge, MA: Harvard University Press.

Wilson, E. O. (1998). *Consilience: The unity of knowledge.* New York: Alfred A. Knopf.

Wilson, E. O. (2000). *Sociobiology: The new synthesis, twenty-fifth anniversary edition.* Cambridge, MA: Harvard University Press.

Wilson, M., & Wrangham, R. (2003). Intergroup relations in chimpanzees. *Annual Review of Anthropology, 32,* 363–392.

Wirth, T., Wang, X., Linz, B., Novick, R., Lum, J., Blaser, M., . . . Achtman, M. (2004). Distinguishing human ethnic groups by means of sequences from *Helicobacter pylori:* Lessons from Ladakh. *Proceedings of the National Academy of Sciences, 101,* 4746–4751.

Wolf, M., van Doorn, G., & Weissing, F. (2008). Evolutionary emergence of responsive and unresponsive personalities. *Proceedings of the National Academy of Science, 105,* 15825–15830.

Wundt, W. (1896). *Grundriss der psychologie.* Leipzig: Engelmann.

Wyckoff, G., Wang, W., & Wu, C. (2000). Rapid evolution of male reproductive genes in the descent of man. *Nature, 403,* 304–309.

Yi, X., Liang, Y., Huerta-Sanchez, E., Jin, X., Cuo, Z., Pool, J. E. . . . Wang, J. (2010). Sequencing of 50 human exomes reveals adaptation to high altitude. *Science, 329,* 75–78.

Yik, M. S. M., Russell, J. A., & Barrett, L. F. (1999). Integrating four structures of current mood into a circumplex: Integration and beyond. *Journal of Personality and Social Psychology, 77,* 600–619.

Zak, P. (2004). Neuroeconomics. *Philosophical Transactions of the Royal Society of London B, 359,* 1737–1748.

Zerjal, T., Xue, Y., Bertorelle, G., Wells, R., Bao, W., Zhe, A. et al. (2003). The genetic legacy of the Mongols. *American Journal of Human Genetics, 72,* 717–721.

Zimmer, C. (2001). *Evolution: The triumph of an idea.* New York: HarperCollins.

Credits

CHAPTER 1

Figure 1.1: © Nina Leen Getty Images.

Figure 1.2: Figure 69, "Grey lag goose retrieving egg" from *The Study of Instinct* by Niko Tinbergen (1974). By permission of Oxford University Press.

Figure 1.3: Figure 22, "Models of herring gull heads" from *The Study of Instinct* by Niko Tinbergen (1974). By permission of Oxford University Press.

Figure 1.4: Tinbergen, N. (1974) *The study of instinct.* New York: Oxford University Press.

Figure 1.5: Figure 26, "Bird models used by Lorenz and Tinbergen" from *The Study of Instinct* by Niko Tinbergen (1974). By permission of Oxford University Press.

Figure 1.6: Eibl-Eibesfeldt (1975).

Figure 1.7: © Disney.

CHAPTER 2

Figure 2.1: From Bartlett, J. C., & Searcy, J., Inversion and configuration of faces. *Cognitive Psychology, 25,* 281–316. Copyright © 1993.

Figure 2.2: Ridley (2004) *Evolution 3rd Ed.* Cambridge, MA: Blackwell.

Figure 2.3: N/A.

Figure 2.4: Alcock, J. (2001). *The triumph of sociobiology.* Oxford: Oxford University Press.

Figure 2.5: John Gould. From *The Voyage of the Beagle* (1860).

Figure 2.6: a. Ralph Lee Hopkins/Photo Researchers, Inc.; b. David Hosking/Photo Researchers, Inc.

CHAPTER 3

Figure 3.1: http://upload.wikimedia.org/wikipedia/commons/b/b8/DNA-structure-and-bases.png

Figure 3.2: © Copyright Clinical Tool.

Figure 3.3: N/A.

Figure 3.4: U.S. National Library of Medicine.

Figure 3.5: Huntingon, Willard F. (2003). Genome biology: Tales of the Y chromosome. *Nature, 423,* 810–813.

Figure 3.6: N/A.

Figure 3.7: Wikipedia/Madprime.

Figure 3.10: N/A.

Figure 3.11: N/A.

Figure 3.12: A. E. Mourant et al. (1976). *The Distribution of the Human Blood Groups and Other Polymorphisms.*

Figure 3.13: Omikron/Photo Researchers, Inc.

Figure 3.14: Achilli, A. and Perego, U.A., Sorenson Molecular Genealogy Foundation, 2007.

Figure 3.15: From Zerjal et al. (2003). *American Journal of Human Genetics, 72,* 717–721.

CHAPTER 4

Figure 4.1. N/A.

Figure 4.2: Roth, G., & Dicke, U. (2005). Evolution of the brain and intelligence. *Trends in Cognitive Sciences, 9,* 250–257.

Figure 4.3: MacLean, P. (1990). *The triune brain in evolution.* New York: Plenum. Published with the kind permission from Springer Science+Business Media B.V.

Figure 4.4: N/A.

Figure 4.5: Gazzaniga, M. & LeDoux, J. (1978). *The integrated mind.* New York: Plenum. Published with the kind permission from Springer Science+Business Media B.V.

Figure 4.6: Buckner, R., Andrews-Hanna, J., & Schacter, D. (2008). The brain's default network. *Annals of the New York Academy of Sciences, 1124,* 1–38.

Figure 4.7: Buckner, R., Andrews-Hanna, J., & Schacter, D. (2008). The brain's default network. *Annals of the New York Academy of Sciences, 1124,* 1–38.

Figure 4.8: Allman J. (2000). *Evolving brains.* New York: Scientific American Library.

Figure 4.9: N/A.

Figure 4.10: Striedter, G. (2005). *Principles of brain evolution.* Sunderland, MA: Sinauer Associates.

Figure 4.11: Allman J. (2000). *Evolving brains.* New York: Scientific American Library.

Figure 4.12: N/A.

Figure 4.13: Allman J. (2000). *Evolving brains.* New York: Scientific American Library.

Figure 4.14: N/A.

Figure 4.15: Allman J. (2000). *Evolving brains.* New York: Scientific American Library.

Figure 4.16: Gibbons, A. (2009). *A New Kind of Ancestor: Ardipithecus Unveiled. Science,* October 2nd, 326 (5949), 36–40.

Figure 4.17: Human Origins Program: Smithsonian Institution.

Figure 4.18: Gibbons, A. (2009). *A New Kind of Ancestor: Ardipithecus Unveiled. Science,* October 2nd, 326 (5949), 36–40.

CHAPTER 5

Figure 5.1: Harlow Primate Laboratory, University of Wisconsin-Madison.

Figure 5.2: Harlow Primate Laboratory, University of Wisconsin-Madison.

Figure 5.3: Harlow Primate Laboratory, University of Wisconsin-Madison.

Figure 5.4: Harlow Primate Laboratory, University of Wisconsin-Madison.

Figure 5.5: Hill, K. (1993). Life history theory and evolutionary anthropology. *Evolutionary anthropology, 2*, 78–88.

CHAPTER 6

Figure 6.1: N/A.

Figure 6.2: N/A.

Figure 6.3: Susskind, J., Lee, D., Cusi, A., Feiman, R., Grabski, W., & Anderson, A. (2008). Expressing fear enhances sensory acquisition. *Nature Neuroscience, 11*, 843–850.

Figure 6.4: N/A.

Figure 6.5: Ekman, P. (1973). Darwin and facial expression: A century of research in review. New York: Academic Press.

Figure 6.6: N/A.

Figure 6.7: Russell, J. (1980). A circumplex model of affect. *Journal of Personality and Social Psychology, 39*, 1161–1178.

Figure 6.8: Yik, M. S. M., Russell, J. A., & Barrett, L. F. (1999). Integrating four structures of current mood into a circumplex: Integration and beyond. *Journal of Personality and Social Psychology, 77*, 600–619.

Figure 6.9: Yik, M. S. M., Russell, J. A., & Barrett, L. F. (1999). Integrating four structures of current mood into a circumplex: Integration and beyond. *Journal of Personality and Social Psychology, 77*, 600–619.

Figure 6.10: Yik, M. S. M., Russell, J. A., & Barrett, L. F. (1999). Integrating four structures of current mood into a circumplex: Integration and beyond. *Journal of Personality and Social Psychology, 77*, 600–619.

CHAPTER 7

Figure 7.1: © Great Ape Trust.

Figure 7.2: Hillix and Rambaugh (2004).

Figure 7.3: Hillix and Rambaugh (2004).

Figure 7.4: Reprinted by permission of the publisher from TOWARD AN EVOLUTIONARY BIOLOGY OF LANGUAGE, by Philip Lieberman, p. 81, Cambridge, Mass.: Harvard University Press, Copyright © 1984, 2006 by the President and Fellows of Harvard College.

Figure 7.5: Reprinted by permission of the publisher from UNIQUELY HUMAN: THE EVOLUTION OF SPEECH, THOUGHT AND SELFLESS BEHAVIOR, by Philip Lieberman, p. 55, Cambridge, Mass.: Harvard University Press, Copyright © 1991 by the President and Fellows of Harvard College.

Figure 7.6: N/A.

Figure 7.7: Nature Neuroscience, *11*, 383. (2008).

CHAPTER 8

Figure 8.1: © Dave Blackey/All Canada Photos/Corbis.

Figure 8.2: John Tenniel.

Figure 8.3: ©iStockphoto.com/jgruop.

Figure 8.4: © Michael & Patricia Fogden/CORBIS.

CHAPTER 9

Figure 9.1: Pawlowski, B., & Dunbar, R. (1999). Impact of market value on human mate choice decisions. Proceedings of the Royal Society of London, B, 266, 281–285

Figure 9.2: Singh, D. (1993). Adaptive significance of female physical attractiveness: Role of waist-to-hip ratio. *Journal of Personality and Social Psychology, 65,* 293–307.

Figure 9.3: Streeter, S., & McBurney, D. (2003). Waist-hip ratio and attractiveness: new evidence and a critique of—A critical test. *Evolution and Human Behavior, 24,* 88–98.

CHAPTER 10

Figure 10.1: Platek, S., Critton, S., Burch, R., Panyavin, I., Wasserman, B., & Gallup, G. (2002). Reactions to children's faces:

Resemblance affects males more than females. *Evolution and Human Behavior, 23,* 159–166.

Figure 10.2: Burnstein, E. (2005). Altruism and genetic relatedness. In D. Buss (Ed.), *The Handbook of Evolutionary Psychology.* Hoboken, NJ: John Wiley & Sons.

Figures 10.3, 10.4, 10.5, 10.6, and 10.7: Daly, M. (1988). *Homicide.* New York: Aldine de Druyter.

CHAPTER 11

Figure 11.1: Dunbar, R. (2003). The social brain: Mind, language and society in evolutionary perspective. *Annual Review of Anthropology, 32,* 161–181.

Figure 11.2: Dimoka, A. (2010). Brain mapping of psychological processes with psychometric scales: an fMRI method for social neuroscience. *Neuroimage* (in press).

Figure 11.3: Martin, J. H. *Neuroanatomy: Text & Atlas* 2nd ed. (Appleton and Lange, Stamford, Connecticut, 1996).

Figure 11.4: Fehr, E. (2002) Altruistic punishment in humans. *Nature, 415,* 269–272.

Figure 11.5: Fehr, E. (2002) Altruistic punishment in humans. *Nature, 415,* 269–272.

CHAPTER 12

Figure 12.1: © Peter Hoey, Pacific Coin-Op Studio.

Figure 12.2: © Peter Hoey, Pacific Coin-Op Studio.

CHAPTER 13

Figure 13.1: Bach, J. (2002). The effects of infections on susceptibility to autoimmune and allergic diseases. *New England Journal of Medicine, 347,* 911–920

Figure 13.2: *Nature Reviews Neuroscience, 10,* 397–409. (June, 2009).

Figure 13.3: N/A.

Figure 13.4: McEwen, B. (1998). Protective and damaging effects of stress mediators. *New England Journal of Medicine, 338,* 171–179. © New England Journal of Medicine.

Figure 13.5: Adapted from Kaplan, J., Manuck, S., Clarkson, T., Lusso, F., & Taub, D. (1982). Social status, environment, and atherosclerosis in cynomolgus monkeys. *Arteriosclerosis, 2,* 359–368.

Figure 13.6: http://www.who.int/health-info/statistics/01.whostat2005map_under5mortality.jpg (Accessed 4/12/11).

CHAPTER 14

Figure 14.1: Amaral, D., Schumann, C., & Nordahl, C. (2008). Neuroanatomy of autism. *Trends in neurosciences, 31,* 137–145.

Figure 14.2: Meyer-Lindenberg, A., Hariri, A., Munoz, K., Mervis, C., Venkata, M., Morris, C., & Faith Berman, K. (2005). Neural correlates of genetically abnormal social cognition in Williams syndrome. *Nature Neuroscience, 8* 991–993.

Author Index

Subject Index

$SAGE research methods online

The essential tool for researchers . . .

. . . from the world's leading research methods publisher

Discover SRMO Lists— methods readings suggested by other SRMO users

"I have never really seen anything like this product before, and I think it is really valuable."

John Creswell, University of Nebraska–Lincoln

Find exactly what you are looking for, from basic explanations to advanced discussion

Explore the Methods Map to discover links between methods

Watch video interviews with leading methodologists

Search on a newly designed taxonomy with more than 1,400 qualitative, quantitative, and mixed methods terms

Uncover more than 100,000 pages of book, journal, and reference content to support your learning

find out more at
www.srmo.sagepub.com